Seventh Edition

Strategic Management Theory

An Integrated Approach

Charles W. L. Hill
University of Washington

Gareth R. Jones
Texas A&M University

Houghton Mifflin Company

Boston   New York

For my children, Elizabeth, Charlotte, and Michelle
Charles W. L. Hill

For Nicholas and Julia and Morgan and Nia
Gareth R. Jones

Vice-President and Publisher: George T. Hoffman
Senior Sponsoring Editor: Lise Johnson
Associate Editor: Julia Perez
Editorial Assistant: Amy Galvin
Senior Project Editor: Kerry Falvey
Manufacturing Manager: Karen Fawcett
Executive Marketing Manager: Steven W. Mikels
Marketing Associate: Lisa Boden

Cover image: ©Medioimages/Imagestate

Library of Congress Control Number: 2005935203

ISBNs:
Instructor's Exam Copy:
ISBN-13: 978-0-618-73169-5
ISBN-10: 0-618-73169-5

For orders, use student text ISBNs:
ISBN-13: 978-0-618-64164-2
ISBN-10: 0-618-64164-5

1 2 3 4 5 6 7 8 9—DOW—10 09 08 07 06

Contents

Preface   *xix*

PART 1   Introduction to Strategic Management

1 Strategic Leadership: Managing the Strategy-Making Process for Competitive Advantage   1

Opening Case: Wal-Mart   *1*
Overview   *3*
Strategic Leadership, Competitive Advantage, and Superior Performance   *4*
Superior Performance   *4* ▮ Competitive Advantage and a Company's Business Model   *5* ▮ Industry Differences in Performance   *7* ▮ Performance in Nonprofit Enterprises   *7*
Strategic Managers   *8*
Corporate-Level Managers   *9* ▮ Business-Level Managers   *10* ▮ Functional-Level Managers   *10*
The Strategy-Making Process   *11*
A Model of the Strategic Planning Process   *11* ▮ Mission Statement   *13*
Strategy in Action 1.1: Strategic Planning at Microsoft   *14*
External Analysis   *18* ▮ Internal Analysis   *19* ▮ SWOT Analysis and the Business Model   *19* ▮ Strategy Implementation   *20* ▮ The Feedback Loop   *20*
Strategy as an Emergent Process   *20*
Strategy Making in an Unpredictable World   *21* ▮ Autonomous Action: Strategy Making by Lower-Level Managers   *21*
Strategy in Action 1.2: A Strategic Shift at Microsoft   *22*
Serendipity and Strategy   *22*
Strategy in Action 1.3: The Genesis of Autonomous Action at 3M   *23*
Intended and Emergent Strategies   *24*
Strategic Planning in Practice   *25*
Scenario Planning   *26* ▮ Decentralized Planning   *26* ▮ Strategic Intent   *27*
Strategic Decision Making   *28*
Cognitive Biases and Strategic Decision Making   *28* ▮ Groupthink and Strategic Decisions   *29* ▮ Techniques for Improving Decision Making   *30*
Strategy in Action 1.4: Was Intelligence on Iraq Biased by Groupthink?   *30*
Strategic Leadership   *32*
Vision, Eloquence, and Consistency   *32* ▮ Articulation of the Business Model   *33* ▮ Commitment   *33* ▮ Being Well Informed   *33* ▮ Willingness to Delegate and Empower   *34* ▮ The Astute Use of Power   *34* ▮ Emotional Intelligence   *34*
Summary of Chapter   *35* ▮ Discussion Questions   *36*
Practicing Strategic Management   *36*
Small-Group Exercise: Designing a Planning System ▮ Article File 1 ▮ Strategic Management Project: Module 1 ▮ Exploring the Web: Visiting 3M ▮ General Task
Closing Case: Shattered Dreams: Level 3 Communications   *38*
Appendix to Chapter 1: Enterprise Valuation, ROIC, and Growth   *40*

P.46

2   External Analysis: The Identification of Opportunities and Threats   42

Opening Case: Why Is the Pharmaceutical Industry So Profitable?   *42*
Overview   *43*
Defining an Industry   *44*
   Industry and Sector   *44*   ▌   Industry and Market Segments   *45*   ▌   Changing Industry Boundaries   *46*
Porter's Five Forces Model   *46*
   Risk of Entry by Potential Competitors   *46*   ▌   Economies of Scale   *47*   ▌   Brand Loyalty   *48*   ▌   Absolute Cost Advantages   *48*   ▌   Customer Switching Costs   *48*   ▌   Government Regulation   *48*
Strategy in Action 2.1: Circumventing Entry Barriers into the Soft Drink Industry   *49*
   Rivalry Among Established Companies   *50*   ▌   Industry Competitive Structure   *50*
Strategy in Action 2.2: Price Wars in the Breakfast Cereal Industry   *52*
   Industry Demand   *52*   ▌   Cost Conditions   *53*   ▌   Exit Barriers   *53*   ▌   The Bargaining Power of Buyers   *54*   ▌   The Bargaining Power of Suppliers   *55*
Running Case: Wal-Mart's Bargaining Power over Suppliers   *56*
   Substitute Products   *57*   ▌   A Sixth Force: Complementors   *57*
Summary   *57*
Strategic Groups Within Industries   *57*
   Implications of Strategic Groups   *59*   ▌   The Role of Mobility Barriers   *59*
Industry Life Cycle Analysis   *60*
   Embryonic Industries   *60*   ▌   Growth Industries   *61*   ▌   Industry Shakeout   *61*   ▌   Mature Industries   *62*   ▌   Declining Industries   *63*
Summary   *63*
Limitations of Models for Industry Analysis   *63*
   Life Cycle Issues   *63*   ▌   Innovation and Change   *64*   ▌   Company Differences   *66*
The Macroenvironment   *66*
   Macroeconomic Forces   *66*   ▌   Global Forces   *68*   ▌   Technological Forces   *68*   ▌   Demographic Forces   *69*   ▌   Social Forces   *70*   ▌   Political and Legal Forces   *70*
Summary of Chapter   *71*   ▌   Discussion Questions   *71*
Practicing Strategic Management   *72*
   Small-Group Exercise: Competing with Microsoft   ▌   Article File 2   ▌   Strategic Management Project: Module 2   ▌   Exploring the Web: Visiting Boeing and Airbus   ▌   General Task
Closing Case: Plane Wreck: The Airline Industry in 2001–2004   *73*

该章为
*Industry
Analysis*

PEST 分析

PART 2   The Nature of Competitive Advantage

3   Internal Analysis: Distinctive Competencies, Competitive Advantage, and Profitability   75

Opening Case: Dell's Competitive Advantage   *75*
Overview   *76*
Competencies, Resources, and Competitive Advantage   *77*   ▌   Strategy, Distinctive Competencies, and Competitive Advantage   *77*   ▌   Competitive Advantage, Value Creation, and Profitability   *79*   ▌   Differentiation and Cost Structure   *83*
The Value Chain   *83*
Primary Activities   *83*
Strategy in Action 3.1: Value Creation at Pfizer   *85*
Support Activities   *85*

The Building Blocks of Competitive Advantage   *86*
    Efficiency   *86*
Running Case: Support Activities as a Source of Value Creation at Wal-Mart   *87*
Strategy in Action 3.2: Southwest Airlines' Low-Cost Structure   *89*
    Quality as Excellence and Reliability   *89* ▌ Innovation   *91* ▌ Responsiveness to Customers   *92*
    ▌ Business Models, the Value Chain, and Generic Distinctive Competencies   *92*
Analyzing Competitive Advantage and Profitability   *94*
The Durability of Competitive Advantage   *98*
    Barriers to Imitation   *98* ▌ Capability of Competitors   *100* ▌ Industry Dynamism   *100*
Summary   *101*
Avoiding Failure and Sustaining Competitive Advantage   *101*
    Why Companies Fail   *101* ▌ Steps to Avoid Failure   *103*
Strategy in Action 3.3: The Road to Ruin at DEC   *104*
    The Role of Luck   *105*
Strategy in Action 3.4: Bill Gates's Lucky Break   *105*
Summary of Chapter   *106* ▌ Discussion Questions   *106*
Practicing Strategic Management   *106*
    Small-Group Exercise: Analyzing Competitive Advantage ▌ Article File 3 ▌ Strategic
    Management Project: Module 3 ▌ Exploring the Web: Visiting
    Johnson & Johnson ▌ General Task
Closing Case: Google   *107*

4   Building Competitive Advantage Through Functional-Level Strategy   109

Opening Case: Verizon Wireless   *109*
Overview   *110*
Achieving Superior Efficiency   *111*
    Efficiency and Economies of Scale   *111* ▌ Efficiency and Learning Effects   *113* ▌ Efficiency and the
    Experience Curve   *114*
Strategy in Action 4.1: Too Much Experience at Texas Instruments   *116*
Efficiency, Flexible Manufacturing, and Mass Customization   *117*
Strategy in Action 4.2: Toyota's Lean Production System   *118*
    Marketing and Efficiency   *119* ▌ Materials Management, Just-in-Time, and Efficiency   *121*
Strategy in Action 4.3: Supply-Chain Management at Office Superstores   *122*
    R&D Strategy and Efficiency   *123* ▌ Human Resource Strategy and Efficiency   *123*
Running Case: Human Resource Strategy and Productivity at Wal-Mart   *124*
    Information Systems and Efficiency   *125* ▌ Infrastructure and Efficiency   *126*
Achieving Superior Quality   *127*
    Attaining Superior Reliability   *127* ▌ Implementing Reliability Improvement Methodologies   *128*
Strategy in Action 4.4: General Electric's Six Sigma Quality Improvement Process   *129*
    Improving Quality as Excellence   *133*
Strategy in Action 4.5: Six Sigma at Mount Carmel Health   *133*
Achieving Superior Innovation   *135*
    The High Failure Rate of Innovation   *135* ▌ Building Competencies in Innovation   *137*
Achieving Superior Responsiveness to Customers   *142*
    Focusing on the Customer   *142* ▌ Satisfying Customer Needs   *144*
Summary of Chapter   *145* ▌ Discussion Questions   *146*
Practicing Strategic Management   *146*
    Small-Group Exercise: Identifying Excellence ▌ Article File 4 ▌ Strategic Management
    Project: Module 4 ▌ Exploring the Web: Visiting Applied Materials ▌ General Task
Closing Case: Redesigning the American Car   *147*

Contents

PART 3   **Strategies**

5   Building Competitive Advantage Through Business-Level Strategy   149

Opening Case: Samsung Changes Its Business Model Again and Again   *149*
Overview   *150*
Competitive Positioning and the Business Model   *151*
    Formulating the Business Model: Customer Needs and Product Differentiation   *151* ▍ Formulating the
    Business Model: Customer Groups and Market Segmentation   *153* ▍ Implementing the Business Model:
    Building Distinctive Competencies   *156*
Competitive Positioning and Business-Level Strategy   *158*
Competitive Positioning: Generic Business-Level Strategies   *159*
Cost Leadership   *160*
Strategy in Action 5.1: Ryanair Takes Control over the Sky in Europe   *163*
    Focused Cost Leadership   *164*
Differentiation   *166*
    Focused Differentiation   *169*
Strategy in Action 5.2: L.L. Bean's New Business Model   *170*
Strategy in Action 5.3: Up, Up, and Away in the Restaurant Business   *171*
The Dynamics of Competitive Positioning   *172*
    Competitive Positioning for Superior Performance   *173*
Strategy in Action 5.4: Toyota's Goal? A High-Value Vehicle to Match Every Customer Need   *175*
    Failures in Competitive Positioning   *181*
Strategy in Action 5.5: Holiday Inns on Six Continents   *182*
Summary of Chapter   *183* ▍ Discussion Questions   *184*
Practicing Strategic Management   *185*
    Small-Group Exercise: Finding a Strategy for a Restaurant ▍ Article 5 ▍ Strategic Management
    Project: Module 5 ▍ Exploring the Web: Visiting the Luxury Car Market ▍ General Task
Closing Case: How E*TRADE Uses the Internet to Gain a Low-Cost Advantage   *186*

6   Business-Level Strategy and the Industry Environment   187

Opening Case: Nike's Winning Ways   *187*
Overview   *188*
Strategies in Fragmented Industries   *188*
    Chaining   *189* ▍ Franchising   *190* ▍ Horizontal Merger   *191* ▍ Using Information Technology and the
    Internet   *191*
Strategies in Embryonic and Growth Industries   *191*
Strategy in Action 6.1: Clear Channel Creates a National Chain of Local Radio Stations   *192*
    The Changing Nature of Market Demand   *194* ▍ Strategic Implications: Crossing the Chasm   *195*
Strategy in Action 6.2: How Prodigy Fell into the Chasm   *198*
    Strategic Implications of Market Growth Rates   *198* ▍ Factors Affecting Market Growth Rates   *199*
    ▍ Strategic Implications of Differences in Growth Rates   *200*
Navigating Through the Life Cycle to Maturity   *201*
    Embryonic Strategies   *202* ▍ Growth Strategies   *202* ▍ Shakeout Strategies   *203* ▍ Maturity Strategies
    203
Strategy in Mature Industries   *204*
    Strategies to Deter Entry: Product Proliferation, Price Cutting, and Maintaining Excess Capacity   *205*
    ▍ Strategies to Manage Rivalry   *207*
Strategy in Action 6.3: Toys "R" Us's New Competitors   *208*
    Game Theory   *214*
Strategy in Action 6.4: Coca-Cola and PepsiCo Go Head-to-Head   *221*

Strategies in Declining Industries   *221*
    The Severity of Decline   *222* ❙ Choosing a Strategy   *223*
Strategy in Action 6.5: How to Make Money in the Vacuum Tube Business   *224*
Summary of Chapter   *225* ❙ Discussion Questions   *226*
Practicing Strategic Management   *226*
    Small-Group Exercise: How to Keep the Hot Sauce Hot ❙ Article File 6 ❙ Strategic Management
    Project: Module 6 ❙ Exploring the Web: Visiting Wal-Mart ❙ General Task
Closing Case: Information Technology, the Internet, and Changing Strategies
    in the Fashion World   *227*

7   Strategy in High-Technology Industries   229

Opening Case: The Smart Phone Format War   *229*
Overview   *230*
Technical Standards and Format Wars   *231*
    Examples of Standards   *231* ❙ Benefits of Standards   *232*
Strategy in Action 7.1: Where Is the Standard for DVD Recorders?   *233*
    Establishment of Standards   *234* ❙ Network Effects, Positive Feedback, and Lockout   *235*
Strategy in Action 7.2: How Dolby Became the Standard in Sound Technology   *237*
Strategies for Winning a Format War   *239*
    Ensure a Supply of Complements   *239* ❙ Leverage Killer Applications   *239* ❙ Aggressively Price and Market   *240* ❙ Cooperate with Competitors   *240* ❙ License the Format   *241*
Costs in High-Technology Industries   *241*
    Comparative Cost Economics   *242* ❙ Strategic Significance   *243*
Strategy in Action 7.3: Lowering Costs Through Digitalization   *244*
Managing Intellectual Property Rights   *244*
    Intellectual Property Rights   *245* ❙ Digitalization and Piracy Rates   *245* ❙ Strategies for Managing Digital
    Rights   *246*
Capturing First-Mover Advantages   *247*
    First-Mover Advantages   *248* ❙ First-Mover Disadvantages   *249* ❙ Strategies for Exploiting First-Mover
    Advantages   *250*
Technological Paradigm Shifts   *253*
    Paradigm Shifts and the Decline of Established Companies   *253*
Strategy in Action 7.4: Disruptive Technology in Mechanical Excavators   *257*
    Strategic Implications for Established Companies   *258* ❙ Strategic Implications for New Entrants   *259*
Summary of Chapter   *260* ❙ Discussion Questions   *260*
Practicing Strategic Management   *261*
    Small-Group Exercise: Burning DVDs ❙ Article File 7 ❙ Strategic Management
    Project: Module 7 ❙ Exploring the Web: Visiting Kodak ❙ General Task
Closing Case: Battling Piracy in the Videogame Market   *262*

8   Strategy in the Global Environment   263

Opening Case: The Evolution of Global Strategy at Procter & Gamble   *263*
Overview   *264*
The Global and National Environments   *265*
The Globalization of Production and Markets   *265*
Strategy in Action 8.1: Finland's Nokia   *267*
    National Competitive Advantage   *268*
Increasing Profitability and Profit Growth Through Global Expansion   *270*
    Expanding the Market: Leveraging Products   *271* ❙ Realizing Cost Economies from Global Volume   *271*
Running Case: Wal-Mart's Global Expansion   *272*
    Realizing Location Economies   *273* ❙ Leveraging the Skills of Global Subsidiaries   *275*

Cost Pressures and Pressures for Local Responsiveness   *276*
Pressures for Cost Reductions   *277* ▌ Pressures for Local Responsiveness   *277*
Strategy in Action 8.2: MTV Goes Global, with a Local Accent   *279*
Choosing a Global Strategy   *280*
Global Standardization Strategy   *281* ▌ Localization Strategy   *281* ▌ Transnational Strategy   *282* ▌
International Strategy   *283* ▌ Changes in Strategy over Time   *284*
Basic Entry Decisions   *285*
Which Overseas Markets to Enter   *285*
Strategy in Action 8.3: Merrill Lynch in Japan   *286*
Timing of Entry   *287* ▌ Scale of Entry and Strategic Commitments   *288*
The Choice of Entry Mode   *289*
Exporting   *289* ▌ Licensing   *290* ▌ Franchising   *291* ▌ Joint Ventures   *292* ▌ Wholly Owned
Subsidiaries   *293* ▌ Choosing an Entry Strategy   *294*
Global Strategic Alliances   *296*
Advantages of Strategic Alliances   *296* ▌ Disadvantages of Strategic Alliances   *297*
Making Strategic Alliances Work   *297*
Partner Selection   *297* ▌ Alliance Structure   *298* ▌ Managing the Alliance   *299*
Summary of Chapter   *300* ▌ Discussion Questions   *301*
Practicing Strategic Management   *301*
Small-Group Exercise: Develop a Global Strategy   ▌ Article File 8   ▌ Strategic Management
Project: Module 8   ▌ Exploring the Web: Visiting IBM   ▌ General Task
Closing Case: Planet Starbucks   *302*

9 Corporate-Level Strategy: Horizontal Integration, Vertical Integration, and Strategic Outsourcing

304

Opening Case: Read All About News Corp   *304*
Overview   *305*
Corporate-Level Strategy and the Multibusiness Model   *306*
Horizontal Integration: Single-Industry Strategy   *307*
Benefits of Horizontal Integration   *309*
Strategy in Action 9.1: Beating Dell: Why Hewlett-Packard Wanted to Acquire Compaq   *310*
Running Case: Wal-Mart's New Chain of "Neighborhood Markets"   *312*
Problems with Horizontal Integration   *313*
Strategy in Action 9.2: Horizontal Integration in Health Care   *314*
Vertical Integration: Entering New Industries to Strengthen the "Core" Business Model   *315*
Increasing Profitability Through Vertical Integration   *317*
Strategy in Action 9.3: Specialized Assets and Vertical Integration in the Aluminum Industry   *319*
Problems with Vertical Integration   *320* ▌ The Limits of Vertical Integration   *322*
Alternatives to Vertical Integration: Cooperative Relationships   *322*
Short-Term Contracts and Competitive Bidding   *322* ▌ Strategic Alliances and Long-Term Contracting   *323*
▌ Building Long-Term Cooperative Relationships   *324*
Strategy in Action 9.4: DaimlerChrysler's U.S. *Keiretsu*   *325*
Strategic Outsourcing   *326*
Strategy in Action 9.5: Cisco's $2 Billion Blunder   *328*
Benefits of Outsourcing   *329* ▌ Risks of Outsourcing   *331*
Summary of Chapter   *332* ▌ Discussion Questions   *332*
Practicing Strategic Management   *333*
Small-Group Exercise: Comparing Vertical Integration Strategies   ▌ Article File 9   ▌ Strategic
Management Project: Module 9   ▌ Exploring the Web: Visiting Motorola   ▌ General Task
Closing Case: The Rise of WorldCom   *334*

10 Corporate-Level Strategy: Formulating and Implementing Related and Unrelated Diversification   336

Opening Case: United Technologies Has an "ACE in Its Pocket"   *336*
Overview   *337*
Expanding Beyond a Single Industry   *338*
  A Company as a Portfolio of Distinctive Competencies   *338*
Increasing Profitability Through Diversification   *340*
  Transferring Competencies Across Industries   *341* ❚ Leveraging Competencies   *342* ❚ Sharing Resources: Economies of Scope   *343*
Strategy in Action 10.1: Diversification at 3M: Leveraging Technology   *344*
  Using Product Bundling   *345* ❚ Managing Rivalry: Multipoint Competition   *346* ❚ Utilizing General Organizational Competencies   *346*
Two Types of Diversification   *349*
  Related Diversification   *349* ❚ Unrelated Diversification   *350*
Strategy in Action 10.2: Related Diversification at Intel   *351*
Disadvantages and Limits of Diversification   *352*
  Changing Industry- and Firm-Specific Conditions   *352* ❚ Diversification for the Wrong Reasons   *352* ❚ The Bureaucratic Costs of Diversification   *354*
Choosing a Strategy   *356*
  Related Versus Unrelated Diversification   *356* ❚ The Web of Corporate-Level Strategy   *356*
Entry Strategy: Internal New Ventures   *357*
  The Attractions of Internal New Venturing   *358* ❚ Pitfalls of New Ventures   *358* ❚ Guidelines for Successful Internal New Venturing   *360*
Entry Strategy: Acquisitions   *361*
  The Attractions of Acquisitions   *361* ❚ Acquisition Pitfalls   *362*
Strategy in Action 10.3: Postacquisition Problems at Mellon Bank   *363*
  Guidelines for Successful Acquisition   *365*
Entry Strategy: Joint Ventures   *366*
Restructuring   *367*
  Why Restructure?   *367*
Summary of Chapter   *368* ❚ Discussion Questions   *369*
Practicing Strategic Management   *369*
  Small-Group Exercise: Dun & Bradstreet ❚ Article File 10 ❚ Strategic Management Project: Module 10 ❚ Exploring the Web: Visiting General Electric ❚ General Task
Closing Case: Tyco International   *371*

PART 4 Implementing Strategy

11 Corporate Performance, Governance, and Business Ethics   373

Opening Case: Nike: The Sweatshop Debate   *373*
Overview   *374*
Stakeholders and Corporate Performance   *374*
  Stakeholder Impact Analysis   *375*
Strategy in Action 11.1: Bill Agee at Morrison Knudsen   *376*
  The Unique Role of Stockholders   *377* ❚ Profitability, Profit Growth, and Stakeholder Claims   *378*

Strategy in Action 11.2: Price Fixing at Sotheby's and Christie's   *380*

Agency Theory   *381*

    Principal-Agent Relationships   381   ▮   The Agency Problem   382

Governance Mechanisms   *385*

Strategy in Action 11.3: Did Computer Associates Inflate Revenues to Enrich Managers?   *386*

    The Board of Directors   *387*   ▮   Stock-Based Compensation   *388*   ▮   Financial Statements and Auditors   *390*
    ▮   The Takeover Constraint   *391*   ▮   Governance Mechanisms Inside a Company   *392*

Ethics and Strategy   *394*

    Ethical Issues in Strategy   *395*   ▮   The Roots of Unethical Behavior   *397*

Running Case: Working Conditions at Wal-Mart   *398*

    Philosophical Approaches to Ethics   *399*   ▮   Behaving Ethically   *403*

Summary of Chapter   *406*   ▮   Discussion Questions   *406*

Practicing Strategic Management   *407*

    Small-Group Exercise: Evaluating Stakeholder Claims   ▮   Article File 11   ▮   Strategic Management
    Project: Module 11   ▮   Exploring the Web: Visiting Merck   ▮   General Task

Closing Case: The Collapse of Enron   *408*

12   Implementing Strategy in Companies That Compete in a Single Industry   411

Opening Case: Nokia's New Product Structure   *411*

Overview   *412*

Implementing Strategy Through Organizational Design   *413*

Building Blocks of Organizational Structure   *414*

    Grouping Tasks, Functions, and Divisions   *414*   ▮   Allocating Authority and Responsibility   *415*

Strategy in Action 12.1: Union Pacific Decentralizes to Increase Customer Responsiveness   *418*

    Integration and Integrating Mechanisms   *418*

Strategic Control Systems   *419*

    Levels of Strategic Control   *420*   ▮   Types of Strategic Control Systems   *422*   ▮   Using Information
    Technology   *424*   ▮   Strategic Reward Systems   *424*

Strategy in Action 12.2: Control at Cypress Semiconductor   *425*

Organizational Culture   *425*

    Culture and Strategic Leadership   *426*

Strategy in Action 12.3: How Ray Kroc Established McDonald's Culture   *427*

    Traits of Strong and Adaptive Corporate Cultures   *428*

Building Distinctive Competencies at the Functional Level   *429*

    Functional Structure: Grouping by Function   *429*

Running Case: Sam Walton's Approach to Implementing Wal-Mart's Strategy   *430*

    The Role of Strategic Control   *431*   ▮   Developing Culture at the Functional Level   *431*   ▮   Functional
    Structure and Bureaucratic Costs   *433*   ▮   The Outsourcing Option   *435*

Implementing Strategy in a Single Industry   *435*

    Implementing Cost Leadership   *437*   ▮   Implementing Differentiation   *437*   ▮   Product Structure: Implement-
    ing a Wide Product Line   *438*   ▮   Marketing Structure: Increasing Responsiveness to Customer Groups   *439*
    Geographic Structure: Expanding Nationally   *440*
    Matrix and Product-Team Structures: Competing in Fast-Changing, High-Tech
        Environments   *441*
    Focusing on a Narrow Product Line   *444*

Strategy in Action 12.4: Restructuring at Lexmark   *445*

Restructuring and Reengineering   *446*

Summary of Chapter   *448*   ▮   Discussion Questions   *449*

Practicing Strategic Management   *449*

    Small-Group Exercise: Deciding on an Organizational Structure   ▮   Article File 12   ▮   Strategic
    Management Project: Module 12   ▮   Exploring the Web: Visiting Home Depot   ▮   General Task

Closing Case: Strategy Implementation at Dell Computer   *450*

13 Implementing Strategy in Companies That Compete Across Industries and Countries 452

Opening Case: GM Searches for the Right Global Structure *452*

Overview *453*

Managing Corporate Strategy Through the Multidivisional Structure *453*

Advantages of a Multidivisional Structure *456* ∎ Problems in Implementing a Multidivisional Structure *457*

Strategy in Action 13.1: Amoco, ARCO, and Burmah Castrol Become Part of BP *458*

Structure, Control, Culture, and Corporate-Level Strategy *460* ∎ The Role of Information Technology *464*

Implementing Strategy Across Countries *464*

Strategy in Action 13.2: SAP's ERP Systems *465*

Implementing a Localization Strategy *466* ∎ Implementing an International Strategy *467* ∎ Implementing a Global Standardization Strategy *468* ∎ Implementing a Transnational Strategy *469*

Strategy in Action 13.3: Using IT to Make Nestlé's Global Structure Work *471*

Entry Mode and Implementation *472*

Internal New Venturing *473* ∎ Joint Venturing *475* ∎ Mergers and Acquisitions *476*

Information Technology, the Internet, and Outsourcing *478*

Information Technology and Strategy Implementation *478*

Strategy in Action 13.4: Oracle's New Approach to Control *480*

Strategic Outsourcing and Network Structure *480*

Strategy in Action 13.5: Li & Fung's Global Supply-Chain Management *481*

Summary of Chapter *483* ∎ Discussion Questions *483*

Practicing Strategic Management *484*

Small-Group Exercise: Deciding on an Organizational Structure (Continued)

Article File 13 ∎ Strategic Management Project: Module 13 ∎ Exploring the Web: Visiting Sears ∎ General Task

Closing Case: The New HP Gets Up to Speed *485*

Endnotes *486*

Box Source Notes *501*

Appendix: Analyzing a Case Study and Writing a Case Study Analysis C1

What Is Case Study Analysis? *C1*

Analyzing a Case Study *C2*

Writing a Case Study Analysis *C6*

The Role of Financial Analysis in Case Study Analysis *C8*

Profit Ratios *C8* ∎ Liquidity Ratios *C9* ∎ Activity Ratios *C10* ∎ Leverage Ratios *C10* ∎ Shareholder-Return Ratios *C11* ∎ Cash Flow *C12*

Conclusion *C12*

Index *11*

Preface

The significant revisions we made to the sixth edition of *Strategic Management: An Integrated Approach* have been well received by instructors and students alike. Our book has strengthened its position as the most widely used strategic management textbook on the market. This tells us that we continue to meet the expectations of existing users and attract many new users to our book. It is clear that most strategy instructors share with us a concern for currency in text and examples to ensure that cutting-edge issues and new developments in strategic management are continually addressed.

Just as in the last edition, our objective in rewriting the seventh edition has been to maintain all that was good about prior editions, while refining our approach to discussing established strategic management issues and adding new material to the text to present a more complete, clear, and current account of strategic management in the 2000s. We believe that the result is a book that is more closely aligned with the needs of today's professors and students and the realities of competition in the new global environment.

Comprehensive and Up-to-Date Coverage

Users of our book enjoyed the major chapter additions and changes we made to the sixth edition of *Strategic Management*. In particular, Chapter 7, which discusses strategy in high-technology industries characterized by markets driven by rapid technological change, was well received. Users also liked Chapter 11, which expands coverage of organizational stakeholders, business ethics, and corporate governance in light of the continuing ongoing examples of unethical behavior by corporate managers in organizations such as WorldCom, Adelphia, and Enron, many of whom received long prison sentences in 2005. Finally, our new streamlined approach to strategy implementation in single- and multi-business companies in Chapters 12 and 13 proved easier for students to understand and appreciate—and to use in developing the case studies that many instructors require their students to write.

In this revision we have made no changes to the number or sequencing of our chapters. However, we have made many significant changes inside each chapter and between chapters to refine and update our presentation of strategic management. Continuing real-world changes in strategic management practices such as the increased use of cost reduction strategies, including global outsourcing and lean production, and a renewed emphasis on the "business model" as the driver of differentiation and competitive advantage have led to many changes in our approach. Thus although the overall organization of this edition, depicted in Figure 1.4 on page 12, is similar to the sixth edition, the additional material (in particular our increased use of the concept of the "business model" as a way of framing the issue of competitive advantage) has changed our presentation to reflect current thinking in the field of strategic management.

Major Content Changes Within Chapters

- In Chapter 1 there is a new emphasis on strategic leadership and a new section entitled "Strategic Leadership, Competitive Advantage, and Superior Performance" that highlights the goals of strategic leadership and shows how competitive advantage results in superior performance. Chapter 1 also contains an important new section entitled "Competitive Advantage and a Company's Business Model" that discusses in depth the role of a company's business model in the strategy-making process. A business model is managers' conception of how the set of strategies their company pursues should mesh together into a congruent whole to enable a company to gain a competitive advantage and achieve superior performance. A business model is a mental model or gestalt of how the set of strategies and investments a company makes should fit together if it is to achieve superior performance. The use of the business model concept changes the way we approach the analysis of functional-, business-, and corporate-level strategy and provides us with an additional tool to drive home the message of strategic management to students.

- In Chapter 3 there is a new section explaining the connection between a company's business model, the value chain, and distinctive competencies. We have also revised and expanded the discussion of competitive advantage and profitability. This section explains in detail how an analysis of financial statements can reveal the financial impact of major differences in strategic choices. It also explains how strategic managers must think through the impact of their decisions on the financial position of the company.

■ Chapter 5 presents a whole new approach to examining the issues and tradeoffs in the choice of a generic business-level competitive strategy. Today, the growing ability of companies to pursue both a differentiation and low-cost strategy simultaneously requires that business-level strategy be conceptualized in a new and more sophisticated way. We offer an approach that does this by using the concepts of the business model and value frontier to outline the choices facing companies in pursuing a viable competitive strategy. We believe our new approach offers students additional insights into the competitive issues facing companies today.

■ Chapter 6 continues with this analysis and has been revised to focus on the way in which the nature of competition changes as companies pursue business models based on both differentiation and low-cost strategies, especially as industries pass through different stages of growth.

■ Chapter 7, which focuses on high-tech issues such as the importance of technological standards in industries, the nature of "network economics," and strategies for winning "format wars" has been streamlined and updated given the rapidly changing events in industries such as cell phones, flat-screen TVs, microprocessors, and videogames.

■ Chapter 8 on strategy in the global environment has also been significantly revised and updated to reflect the rapid integration of the global economy, the emergence of new industrial powers such as China and India, and the implication of these developments for strategic management.

■ In Chapter 9, the growing importance of strategic outsourcing as a way of building competitive advantage is reflected in expanded coverage of the issues involved. Also covered is the increase in horizontal integration that has taken place in the last few years as companies seek to offer a wider range of bundled products and to streamline their product offerings to reduce their level of diversification.

■ Chapter 10 has been significantly revised and streamlined to offer new coverage of the advantages and disadvantages of diversification. It also contains a new section called "The Web of Corporate-Level Strategy" that makes it quite clear that a company can potentially pursue each and every strategy if this would strengthen its business model and lead to increased profitability and profit growth. On the other hand, a company should not be afraid to refocus its resources and move back to its core business if changes in the competitive environment make this the most appropriate way to strengthen its business model.

■ Chapter 11, which looks at corporate performance, governance, and business ethics, has been substantially revised to include considerably more material on business ethics and strategy. The chapter explains how poor corporate performance can be caused by a combination of poor corporate governance systems and unethical behavior. The chapter reviews the strategic importance of managing stakeholders, putting strong corporate governance mechanisms in place, and making ethical decisions. Agency theory is used to explain failures of corporate governance and poor managerial ethics. There is an extended look at different approaches to business ethics. The chapter draws heavily on recent examples of corporate fraud at companies such as Enron, WorldCom, and Tyco to illustrate the main points.

■ Finally, Chapters 12 and 13 have been revised to make them compatible with our new treatment of the business model and business- and corporate-level strategy.

Once again, throughout the revision process we have been careful to preserve the *balanced and integrated* nature of our account of strategic management. Moreover, as we have continued to add new material, we have also shortened or deleted coverage of out-of-date or less important models and concepts to help students identify and focus on the core concepts and issues in the field. We have also paid close attention to retaining the book's readability.

Practicing Strategic Management: An Interactive Approach

We have received a lot of positive feedback about the usefulness of the end-of-chapter exercises/assignments in the *Practicing Strategic Management* sections in our book. They offer a wide range of different kinds of hands-on learning experiences for students. Following the Chapter Summary and Discussion Questions, each chapter contains the following assignments/exercises:

■ *Small-Group Exercise*. This short (20-minute) experiential exercise asks students to divide into groups and discuss a scenario concerning some aspect of strategic management. For example, the scenario in Chapter 11 asks students to identify the stakeholders of their educational institution and evaluate how stakeholders' claims are being and should be met.

■ *Exploring the Web*. The Internet exercise requires students to explore a particular website and answer chapter-related questions. For example, the Chapter 8 assignment is to go to the website of IBM and analyze its strategy for competing in the global marketplace. This section also asks students to explore the Web for relevant sites of their own choosing and answer questions.

■ *Article File*. As in the last edition, this exercise requires students to search business magazines to identify a company that is facing a particular strategic management problem. For instance, students are asked to locate and research a company pursuing a low-cost or a differentiation strategy, and to describe this company's strategy, its advantages and disadvantages, and the core competencies required to pursue it. Students' presentations of their findings lead to lively class discussions.

■ *Strategic Management Project*. Students, in small groups, choose a company to study for the whole semester and then analyze the company using the series of questions provided at the end of every chapter. For example, students might select Ford Motor Co. and, using the series of chapter questions, collect information on Ford's top managers, mission, ethical position, domestic and global strategy and structure, and so on. Eventually, students write a case study of their company and present it to the class at the end of the semester. Normally, we also have students present one or more of the cases in the book early in the semester, but in our classes we now treat the students' own projects as the major class assignment and their case presentations as the climax of the semester's learning experience.

■ *Closing Case study*. A short closing case provides an opportunity for a short class discussion of a chapter-related theme.

In creating these exercises it is not our intention to suggest that they should *all* be used for *every* chapter. For example, over a semester an instructor might combine a group Strategic Management Project with five to six Article File assignments and five to six Exploring the Web exercises, while doing eight to ten Small-Group Exercises in class.

We have found that our interactive approach to teaching strategic management appeals to students. It also greatly improves the quality of their learning experience. Our approach is more fully discussed in the *Instructor's Resource Manual*.

Teaching and Learning Aids

Taken together, the teaching and learning features of *Strategic Management* provide a package that is unsurpassed in its coverage and that supports the integrated approach that we have taken throughout the book.

For the Instructor

■ The **Instructor's Resource Manual** has been completely revised. For each chapter we provide a clearly focused synopsis, a list of teaching objectives, a comprehensive lecture outline, suggested answers to discussion questions, and comments on the end-of-chapter activities. Each chapter opening case, Strategy in Action boxed feature, and chapter closing case has a synopsis and a corresponding teaching note to help guide class discussion.

■ The **Test Bank** has been revised and offers a set of comprehensive true/false and multiple-choice questions, and new essay questions for each chapter in the book. The mix of questions has been adjusted to provide fewer fact-based or simple memorization items and to provide more items that rely on synthesis or application. Also, more items now reflect real or hypothetical situations in organizations. Every question is keyed to the teaching objectives in the *Instructor's Resource Manual* and includes an answer and page reference to the textbook.

■ **HM ClassPrep™ with HMTesting CD** provides a variety of teaching resources in electronic format allowing for easy customization to meet specific instructional needs. Included in ClassPrep are electronic *Instructor's Resource Manual* files, Premium and Basic PowerPoint slides, Classroom Response System content, and much more. The computerized version of the Test Bank allows instructors to select, edit, and add questions, or generate randomly selected questions to produce a test master for easy duplication. Online Testing and Gradebook functions allow instructors to administer tests via their local area network or the World Wide Web, set up classes, record grades from tests or assignments, analyze grades, and produce/compile class and individual statistics.

■ The **video program** highlights many issues of interest and can be used to spark class discussion. It offers a compilation of footage from the Videos for Humanities series.

■ An extensive **website** contains many features to aid instructors including downloadable files for the text and case materials from the *Instructor's Resource Manual*, the downloadable Premium and Basic PowerPoint slides, the Video Guide, and sample syllabi. Additional materials on the student website may also be of use to instructors.

■ **Eduspace**®, powered by Blackboard®, is a course management tool that includes downloadable MP3 audio chapter summaries and quizzes, chapter outlines, visual glossaries, all questions from the textbook with suggested answers, Debate Issues, ACE self-test questions, auto-graded quizzes, Premium and Basic PowerPoint slides, Classroom Response System content, links to content on the websites, video activities, and Test Bank content. A Getting Started Guide is also available.

■ **Blackboard**®/**Web CT**® includes course material, downloadable MP3 audio chapter summaries and quizzes, chapter outlines, visual glossaries, all questions from the textbook with suggested answers, Premium and Basic PowerPoint slides, Classroom Response System content, links to content on the websites, video activities, and Test Bank content.

For the Student

■ The **student website** includes downloadable MP3 audio chapter summaries and quizzes, chapter overviews, Internet exercises (repeated from the textbook, with updates as necessary), ACE self-tests, links to the companies highlighted in the chapter opening and closing cases and the Strategy in Action boxed features, glossaries, visual glossaries, flashcards for studying the key terms, and much more.

Acknowledgments

This book is the product of far more than two authors. We are grateful to Lise Johnson, our sponsor, Julia Perez, our editor, and Steve Mikels, our marketing manager, for their help in promoting and developing the book and for providing us with timely feedback and information from professors and reviewers that have allowed us to shape the book to meet the needs of its intended market. We are also grateful to Kerry Falvey, senior project editor, and Sarah Driver, editorial assistant, for their adept handling of production. We are also grateful to the case authors for allowing us to use their materials. We also want to thank the departments of management at the University of Washington and Texas A&M University for providing the setting and atmosphere in which the book could be written, and the students of these universities who reacted to and provided input for many of our ideas. In addition, the following reviewers of this and earlier editions gave us valuable suggestions for improving the manuscript from its original version to its current form:

Ken Armstrong, *Anderson University*
Kunal Banerji, *West Virginia University*
Kevin Banning, *Auburn University–Montgomery*
Glenn Bassett, *University of Bridgeport*
Thomas H. Berliner, *The University of Texas at Dallas*
Richard G. Brandenburg, *University of Vermont*
Steven Braund, *University of Hull*
Philip Bromiley, *University of Minnesota*
Geoffrey Brooks, *Western Oregon State College*
Lowell Busenitz, *University of Houston*

Charles J. Capps III, *Sam Houston State University*
Gene R. Conaster, *Golden State University*
Steven W. Congden, *University of Hartford*
Catherine M. Daily, *Ohio State University*
Robert DeFillippi, *Suffolk University Sawyer School of Management*
Helen Deresky, *SUNY–Plattsburgh*
Gerald E. Evans, *The University of Montana*
John Fahy, *Trinity College, Dublin*
Patricia Feltes, *Southwest Missouri State University*

Mark Fiegener, *Oregon State University*
Isaac Fox, *Washington State University*
Craig Galbraith, *University of North Carolina at Wilmington*
Scott R. Gallagher, *Rutgers University*
Eliezer Geisler, *Northeastern Illinois University*
Gretchen Gemeinhardt, *University of Houston*
Lynn Godkin, *Lamar University*
Robert L. Goldberg, *Northeastern University*
James Grinnell, *Merrimack College*

Todd Hostager, *University of Wisconsin–Eau Claire*

Graham L. Hubbard, *University of Minnesota*

Tammy G. Hunt, *University of North Carolina at Wilmington*

James Gaius Ibe, *Morris College*

W. Grahm Irwin, *Miami University*

Jonathan L. Johnson, *University of Arkansas Walton College of Business Administration*

Marios Katsioloudes, *St. Joseph's University*

Robert Keating, *University of North Carolina at Wilmington*

Geoffrey King, *California State University–Fullerton*

Rico Lam, *University of Oregon*

Robert J. Litschert, *Virginia Polytechnic Institute and State University*

Franz T. Lohrke, *Louisiana State University*

Paul Mallette, *Colorado State University*

Lance A. Masters, *California State University–San Bernardino*

Robert N. McGrath, *Embry-Riddle Aeronautical University*

Charles Mercer, *Drury College*

Van Miller, *University of Dayton*

Tom Morris, *University of San Diego*

Joanna Mulholland, *West Chester University of Pennsylvania*

Francine Newth, *Providence College*

Paul R. Reed, *Sam Houston State University*

Rhonda K. Reger, *Arizona State University*

Malika Richards, *Indiana University*

Stuart Rosenberg, *Dowling College*

Ronald Sanchez, *University of Illinois*

Joseph A. Schenk, *University of Dayton*

Brian Shaffer, *University of Kentucky*

Leonard Sholtis, *Eastern Michigan University*

Pradip K. Shukla, *Chapman University*

Dennis L. Smart, *University of Nebraska at Omaha*

Barbara Spencer, *Clemson University*

Lawrence Steenberg, *University of Evansville*

Kim A. Stewart, *University of Denver*

Ted Takamura, *Warner Pacific College*

Bobby Vaught, *Southwest Missouri State*

Robert P. Vichas, *Florida Atlantic University*

Edward Ward, *St. Cloud State University*

Kenneth Wendeln, *Indiana University*

Daniel L. White, *Drexel University*

Edgar L. Williams, Jr., *Norfolk State University*

Jun Zhao, *Governors State University*

Charles W. L. Hill
Gareth R. Jones

Chapter 1

Strategic Leadership: Managing the Strategy-Making Process for Competitive Advantage

Opening Case

Wal-Mart

Wal-Mart is one of the most extraordinary success stories in business history. Started in 1962 by Sam Walton, Wal-Mart has grown to become the world's largest corporation. In the financial year ending January 31, 2004, the discount retailer whose mantra is "every day low prices" had sales of nearly $256 billion, five thousand stores in ten countries (almost three thousand are in the United States), and 1.3 million employees. Some 8 percent of all retail sales in the United States are made at a Wal-Mart store. Wal-Mart is not only large but also very profitable. In 2003, the company earned a return on invested capital of 14.7 percent, significantly better than rivals Costco and Target, which earned 9.4 percent and 10 percent, respectively (another major rival, Kmart, emerged from bankruptcy protection in 2004). As shown in the accompanying figure, Wal-Mart has been consistently more profitable than its rivals for years.

Wal-Mart's superior profitability reflects a competitive advantage that is based on the successful implementation of a number of strategies. In 1962 Wal-Mart was one of the first companies to apply the self-service supermarket business model developed by grocery chains to general merchandise (two of its rivals, Kmart and Target, were established in the same year). Unlike its rivals, who focused on urban and suburban locations, Sam Walton's Wal-Mart concentrated on small southern towns that were ignored by its rivals. Wal-Mart grew quickly by pricing lower than local mom-and-pop retailers, often putting them out of business. By the time Kmart and Target realized that small towns could support a large discount general merchandise store, Wal-Mart had preempted them. These towns, which were large enough to support one discount retailer, but not two, provided a secure profit base for Wal-Mart.

However, there is far more to the Wal-Mart story than location strategy. The company was also an innovator in information systems, logistics, and human resource practices. Taken together, these strategies resulted in higher productivity and lower costs than rivals, which enabled the company to earn a high profit while charging low prices. Wal-Mart led the way among American retailers in developing and implementing sophisticated product-tracking systems using bar-code technology and checkout scanners. This information technology enabled Wal-Mart to track what was selling and adjust its inventory accordingly so that the products found in a store matched local demand. By avoiding overstocking, Wal-Mart

Profitability in the U.S. Retail Industry, 1994–2003

Data Source: Value Line Investment Survey.

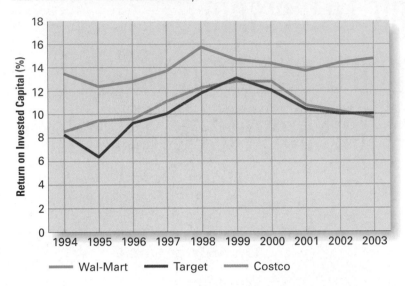

did not have to hold periodic sales to shift unsold inventory. Over time, it linked this information system to a nationwide network of distribution centers where inventory was stored and then shipped to stores within a 300-mile radius on a daily basis. The combination of distribution centers and information centers enabled Wal-Mart to reduce the amount of inventory it held in stores and devote more of that valuable space to selling and reducing the amount of capital it had tied up in inventory.

With regard to human resources, the tone was set by Sam Walton, who believed that employees should be respected and rewarded for helping to improve the profitability of the company. Underpinning this belief, Walton referred to employees as "associates." He established a profit sharing scheme for all employees, and after the company went public in 1970, he initiated a program that allowed employees to purchase Wal-Mart stock at a discount to its market value. Wal-Mart was rewarded for this approach by high employee productivity, which translated into lower operating costs and higher profitability.

As Wal-Mart grew larger, the sheer size and purchasing power of the company enabled it to drive down the prices that it paid suppliers and to pass on those savings to customers in the form of lower prices, which enabled Wal-Mart to gain more market share and hence demand even lower prices. To take the sting out of the persistent demands for lower prices, Wal-Mart shared its sales information with suppliers on a daily basis, enabling them to gain efficiencies by configuring their own production schedules to sales at Wal-Mart.

Already by the 1990s, Wal-Mart was the largest general seller of general merchandise in America. To sustain its growth, Wal-Mart started to diversify into the grocery business, opening 200,000-square-foot supercenter stores that sold groceries and general merchandise under the same roof. Wal-Mart also diversified into the warehouse club business with the establishment of Sam's Club. With its entry into Mexico in 1991, the company began expanding internationally. By pursuing these expansion strategies, Wal-Mart aims to increases sales to over $400 billion by 2010, up from $40 billion today, thereby solidifying its scale-based advantage.

Despite all of its success, Wal-Mart has experienced problems. In some parts of America, such as California and the Northeast, there has been a backlash against Wal-Mart, particularly by small town residents who see Wal-Mart as a threat to local retailers. Increasingly, Wal-Mart has found it difficult to get planning permission to open up new stores in these towns. In addition, despite the long-held belief that employees should be treated well, Wal-Mart has been the target of lawsuits from employees who claim that they were pushed to work long hours without overtime pay, and from female employees claiming that the culture of Wal-Mart discriminates against them. While some observers believe that these complaints have little merit, others argue that they are signs that the company has become too large and may be encountering limits to profitable growth.[1]

Overview

Why do some companies succeed while others fail? Why has Wal-Mart been able to do so well in the fiercely competitive retail industry, while others like Kmart have struggled? In the personal computer industry, what distinguishes Dell from less successful companies such as Gateway? In the airline industry, how is it that Southwest Airlines has managed to keep increasing its revenues and profits through both good times and bad, while rivals such as US Airways and United Airlines have had to seek bankruptcy protection? How did Sony come to dominate the market for videogames with its highly successful PlayStation, while former industry leader Sega saw its market share slump from 60 percent in the early 1990s to less than 10 percent by 2000, and finally pulled out of the market in 2001? What explains the persistent growth and profitability of Nucor Steel, now the largest steel market in America, during a period when many of its once larger rivals disappeared into bankruptcy?

In this book, we argue that the strategies that a company's managers pursue have a major impact on its performance relative to its competitors. A **strategy** is a set of related actions that managers take to increase their company's performance. For most, if not all, companies, achieving superior performance relative to rivals is the ultimate challenge. If a company's strategies result in superior performance, it is said to have a *competitive advantage*. Wal-Mart's strategies produced superior performance from 1994 to 2003; as a result, Wal-Mart has enjoyed a competitive advantage over its rivals. How did Wal-Mart achieve this competitive advantage? As explained in the *Opening Case*, it was due to the successful pursuit of a number of strategies by Wal-Mart's managers, most notably the company's founder, Sam Walton. These strategies enabled the company to lower its cost structure, charge low prices, gain market share, and become more profitable than its rivals. (We will return to the example of Wal-Mart several times throughout this book in a *Running Case* that examines various aspects of Wal-Mart's strategy and performance.)

This book identifies and describes the strategies that managers can pursue to achieve superior performance and provide their company with a competitive advantage. One of its central aims is to give you a thorough understanding of the analytical techniques and skills necessary to identify and implement strategies successfully. The first step toward achieving this objective is to describe in more detail what *superior performance* and *competitive advantage* mean and to explain the pivotal role that managers play in leading the strategy-making process.

Strategic leadership is about how to most effectively manage a company's strategy-making process to create competitive advantage. The **strategy-making process** is the process by which managers select and then implement a set of strategies that aim to achieve a competitive advantage. **Strategy formulation** is the task of selecting strategies, whereas **strategy implementation** is the task of putting strategies into action, which includes designing, delivering, and supporting products; improving the efficiency and effectiveness of operations; and designing a company's organization structure, control systems, and culture. Paraphrasing the well-known saying that "success is 10 percent inspiration and 90 percent perspiration," in the strategic management arena we might say that "success is 10 percent formulation and 90 percent implementation." The task of selecting strategies is relatively easy (but requires good analysis and some inspiration); the hard part is putting those strategies into effect.

By the end of this chapter, you will understand how strategic leaders can manage the strategy-making process by formulating and implementing strategies that enable a company to achieve a competitive advantage and superior performance. Moreover, you will learn how the strategy-making process can go wrong and what managers can do to make this process more effective.

Strategic Leadership, Competitive Advantage, and Superior Performance

Strategic leadership is concerned with managing the strategy-making process to increase the performance of a company, thereby increasing the value of the enterprise to its owners, its shareholders. As shown in Figure 1.1, to increase shareholder value, managers must pursue strategies that increase the profitability of the company *and* ensure that profits grow (for more details, see the Appendix to this chapter). To do this, a company must be able to outperform its rivals; it must have a competitive advantage.

■ Superior Performance

Maximizing shareholder value is the ultimate goal of profit-making companies, for two reasons. First, shareholders provide a company with the risk capital that enables managers to buy the resources needed to produce and sell goods and services. Risk capital is capital that cannot be recovered if a company fails and goes bankrupt. In the case of Wal-Mart, for example, shareholders provided Sam Walton's company with capital to build stores and distribution centers, invest in information systems, purchase inventory to sell to customers, and so on. Had Wal-Mart failed, its shareholders would have lost their money; their shares would have been worthless. Thus, shareholders will not provide risk capital unless they believe that managers are committed to pursuing strategies that give them a good return on their capital investment. Second, shareholders are the legal owners of a corporation, and, their shares therefore represent a claim on the profits generated by a company. Thus, managers have an obligation to invest those profits in ways that maximize shareholder value. Of course (as explained later in this book), managers *must* behave in a legal, ethical, and socially responsible manner while working to maximize shareholder value.

By **shareholder value**, we mean the returns that shareholders earn from purchasing shares in a company. These returns come from two sources: (a) capital appreciation in the value of a company's shares and (b) dividend payments. For example, between January 2 and December 31, 2003, the value of one share in the bank JPMorgan increased from $23.96 to $35.78, which represents a capital appreciation of $11.82. In addition, JPMorgan paid out a dividend of $1.30 a share during 2003. Thus, if an investor had bought one share of JPMorgan on January 2 and held on to it for the entire year, her return would have been $13.12 ($11.82 + $1.30), an impressive 54.8 percent return

FIGURE 1.1

Determinants of Shareholder Value

on her investment. One reason JPMorgan's shareholders did so well during 2003 was that investors came to believe that managers were pursuing strategies that would both increase the long-term profitability of the company and significantly grow its profits in the future.

One way of measuring the **profitability** of a company is by the return that it makes on the capital invested in the enterprise.[2] The return on invested capital (ROIC) that a company earns is defined as its net profit over the capital invested in the firm (profit/capital invested). By *net profit*, we mean net income after tax. By *capital*, we mean the sum of money invested in the company: that is, stockholders' equity plus debt owed to creditors. So defined, profitability is the result of how efficiently and effectively managers use the capital at their disposal to produce goods and services that satisfy customer needs. A company that uses its capital efficiently and effectively makes a positive return on invested capital.

The **profit growth** of a company can be measured by the increase in net profit over time. A company can grow its profits if it sells products in markets that are growing rapidly, gains market share from rivals, increases the amount it sells to existing customers, expands overseas, or diversifies profitably into new lines of business. For example, between 1994 and 2004 Wal-Mart increased its net profit from $2.68 billion to $10.1 billion. It was able to do this because the company (a) took market share from rivals such as Kmart, (b) established stores in nine foreign nations that collectively generated $41 billion in sales by 2004, and (c) entered the grocery business. Because of the increase in net profit, Wal-Mart's earnings per share increased from $0.59 to $2.35; as a result, each share became more valuable.

Together profitability and profit growth are the principal drivers of shareholder value (see the Appendix to this chapter for details). To both boost profitability and to grow profits over time, managers must formulate and implement strategies that give their company a competitive advantage over rivals. Wal-Mart's strategies have done this. As a result, investors who purchased Wal-Mart's stock in January 1994, when the shares were trading at $11 each, would have made a 500 percent return if they had held on to them through until December 2004, when they were trading at $55 each. By pursuing strategies that lead to high and sustained profitability and profit growth, Wal-Mart's managers have thus rewarded shareholders for their decisions to invest in the company.

One of the key challenges managers face is to simultaneously generate high profitability *and* increase the profits of the company. Companies that have high profitability but whose profits are not growing will not be as highly valued by shareholders as a company that has both high profitability and rapid profit growth (see the Appendix for details). At the same time, managers need to be aware that if they grow profits but profitability declines, that too will not be as highly valued by shareholders. What shareholders want to see, and what managers must try to deliver through strategic leadership, is *profitable growth*: that is, high profitability and sustainable profit growth. This is not easy, but some of the most successful enterprises of our era have achieved it—companies such as Dell, Microsoft, Intel, and Wal-Mart.

■ **Competitive Advantage and a Company's Business Model**

Managers do not make strategic decisions in a competitive vacuum. Their company is competing against other companies for customers. Competition is a rough-and-tumble process in which only the most efficient and effective companies win out. It is a race without end. To maximize shareholder value, managers must formulate and implement strategies that enable their company to outperform rivals—that give it a competitive advantage. A company is said to have a **competitive advantage** over its rivals when its profitability is greater than the average profitability of all other companies competing for the same set of customers. The higher its profitability relative to rivals, the greater its competitive advantage will be. A company has a **sustained competitive advantage** when its strategies enable it to maintain above-average profitability for a number of years. As discussed in the *Opening Case*, Wal-Mart had a significant and sustained competitive advantage over rivals such as Target, Costco, and Kmart between 1994 and 2003.

If a company has a sustained competitive advantage, it is likely to gain market share from its rivals, and thus grow its profits more rapidly than those of rivals. Thus, competitive advantage will also lead to higher profit growth than rivals.

The key to understanding competitive advantage is appreciating how the different strategies managers pursue over time can create activities that fit together to make a company unique or different from its rivals and able to persistently outperform them. A **business model** is managers' conception of how the set of strategies their company pursues should mesh together into a congruent whole, enabling the company to gain a competitive advantage and achieve superior profitability and profit growth. In essence, a business model is a kind of mental model, or gestalt, of how the various strategies and capital investments made by a company *should* fit together to generate above-average profitability and profit growth. A business model encompasses the totality of how a company will:

- Select its customers
- Define and differentiate its product offerings
- Create value for its customers
- Acquire and keep customers
- Produce goods or services
- Deliver those goods and services to the market
- Organize activities within the company
- Configure its resources
- Achieve and sustain a high level of profitability
- Grow the business over time

The business model at discount stores such as Wal-Mart, for example, is based on the idea that costs can be lowered by replacing a full-service retail format with a self-service format and providing a wider selection of products that are sold in a large-footprint store that contains minimal fixtures and fittings. These savings can then be passed on to consumers in the form of lower prices, which in turn grow revenues and help the company to achieve further cost reductions from economies of scale. Over time, this business model has proved superior to the business models adopted by smaller full-service mom-and-pop stores and by traditional high-service department stores such as Sears. The business model, known as the self-service supermarket business model, was first developed by grocery retailers in the 1950s and was later refined and improved by general merchandisers such as Wal-Mart. More recently, the same basic business model has been applied to toys (Toys "R" Us), office supplies (Staples, Office Depot), and home improvement supplies (Home Depot and Lowe's).

Wal-Mart outperformed close rivals, like Kmart, who adopted the same basic business model because Wal-Mart's strategies differed in key areas and because it implemented the business model more effectively. As a result, over time Wal-Mart created unique activities that have become the foundation of its competitive advantage. For example, Wal-Mart was one of the first retailers to make strategic investments in distribution centers and information systems, which lowered the costs of managing inventory (see the *Opening Case*). This gave Wal-Mart a competitive advantage over rivals such as Kmart, which suffered from poor inventory controls and thus higher costs. So although Wal-Mart and Kmart pursued a similar business model, key differences in the choice of strategies and the effectiveness of implementation created two unique organizations: one that attained a competitive advantage and one that ended up with a competitive disadvantage.

The business model that managers develop may not only lead to higher profitability and thus competitive advantage at a point in time, but it may also help the firm to grow its profits over time, thereby maximizing shareholder value while maintaining or even increasing profitability. Wal-Mart's business model was so efficient and effective that it enabled the company to take market share from rivals like Kmart and thereby increase its profits over time. In addition, Wal-Mart was able to grow profits further by applying its business model to new international markets and opening stores in nine different countries, as well as by adding groceries to its product mix in large Wal-Mart supercenters.

■ Industry Differences in Performance

It is important to recognize that in addition to its business model and associated strategies, a company's performance is also determined by the characteristics of the industry in which it competes. Different industries are characterized by different competitive conditions. In some, demand is growing rapidly, and in others it is contracting. Some might be beset by excess capacity and persistent price wars, others by excess demand and rising prices. In some, technological change might be revolutionizing competition. Others might be characterized by a lack of technological change. In some industries, high profitability among incumbent companies might induce new companies to enter the industry, and these new entrants might depress prices and profits in the industry. In other industries, new entry might be difficult, and periods of high profitability might persist for a considerable time. Thus, the different competitive conditions prevailing in different industries might lead to differences in profitability and profit growth. For example, average profitability might be higher in some industries and lower in other industries because competitive conditions vary from industry to industry.

Figure 1.2 shows the average profitability, measured by ROIC, among companies in several different industries between 1997 and 2003. The drug industry had a favorable competitive environment: demand for drugs was high and competition was generally not based on price. Just the opposite was the case in the steel and air transport industries: both are extremely price competitive. In addition, the steel industry was characterized by declining demand, excess capacity, and price wars. Exactly how industries differ is discussed in detail in Chapter 2. For now, the important point to remember is that the profitability and profit growth of a company are determined by two main factors: its relative success in its industry and the overall performance of its industry relative to other industries.[3]

■ Performance in Nonprofit Enterprises

A final point concerns the concept of superior performance in the nonprofit sector. By definition, nonprofit enterprises such as government agencies, universities, and charities are not in "business" to make profits. Nevertheless, they are expected to use their resources efficiently and operate effectively, and their managers set goals to

FIGURE 1.2

Return on Invested
Capital in Selected
Industries, 1997–2003

Data Source: Value Line Investment Survey.

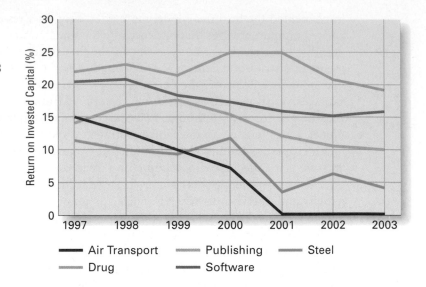

measure their performance. The performance goal for a business school might be to get its programs ranked among the best in the nation. The performance goal for a charity might be to prevent childhood illnesses in poor countries. The performance goal for a government agency might be to improve its services while not exceeding its budget. The managers of nonprofits need to map out strategies to attain these goals. They also need to understand that nonprofits compete with each other for scarce resources, just as businesses do. For example, charities compete for scarce donations, and their managers must plan and develop strategies that lead to high performance and demonstrate a track record of meeting performance goals. A successful strategy gives potential donors a compelling message as to why they should contribute additional donations. Thus, planning and thinking strategically are as important for managers in the nonprofit sector as they are for managers in profit-seeking firms.

Strategic Managers

Managers are the lynchpin in the strategy-making process. It is individual managers who must take responsibility for formulating strategies to attain a competitive advantage and for putting those strategies into effect. They must lead the strategy-making process. The strategies that made Wal-Mart so successful were not chosen by some abstract entity know as the company; they were chosen by the company's founder, Sam Walton, and the managers he hired. Wal-Mart's success, like the success of any company, was based in large part upon how well the company's managers performed their strategic roles. In this section we look at the strategic roles of different managers. Later in the chapter we discuss strategic leadership, which is how managers can effectively lead the strategy-making process.

In most companies, there are two main types of managers: **general managers**, who bear responsibility for the overall performance of the company or for one of its major self-contained subunits or divisions, and **functional managers**, who are re-

FIGURE 1.3

Levels of Strategic
Management

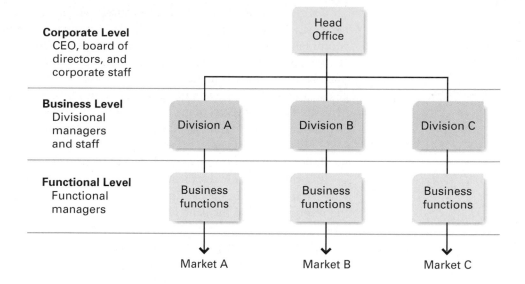

Corporate Level
CEO, board of
directors, and
corporate staff

Business Level
Divisional
managers
and staff

Functional Level
Functional
managers

sponsible for supervising a particular function, that is, a task, activity, or operation, such as accounting, marketing, R&D, information technology, or logistics.

A company is a collection of functions or departments that work together to bring a particular product or service to the market. If a company provides several different kinds of products or services, it often duplicates these functions and creates a series of self-contained divisions (each of which contains its own set of functions) to manage each different product or service. The general managers of these divisions then become responsible for their particular product line. The overriding concern of general managers is for the health of the whole company or division under their direction; they are responsible for deciding how to create a competitive advantage and achieve high profitability with the resources and capital they have at their disposal. Figure 1.3 shows the organization of a **multidivisional company**, that is, a company that competes in several different businesses and has created a separate self-contained division to manage each of these. As you can see, there are three main levels of management: corporate, business, and functional. General managers are found at the first two of these levels, but their strategic roles differ depending on their sphere of responsibility.

■ **Corporate-Level Managers**

The corporate level of management consists of the chief executive officer (CEO), other senior executives, and corporate staff. These individuals occupy the apex of decision making within the organization. The CEO is the principal general manager. In consultation with other senior executives, the role of *corporate-level managers* is to oversee the development of strategies for the whole organization. This role includes defining the goals of the organization, determining what businesses it should be in, allocating resources among the different businesses, formulating and implementing strategies that span individual businesses, and providing leadership for the entire organization.

Consider General Electric as an example. GE is active in a wide range of businesses, including lighting equipment, major appliances, motor and transportation equipment, turbine generators, construction and engineering services, industrial electronics, medical systems, aerospace, aircraft engines, and financial services. The main strategic responsibilities of its CEO, Jeffrey Immelt, are setting overall strategic goals, allocating resources among the different business areas, deciding whether the firm should divest itself of any of its businesses, and determining whether it should acquire any new ones. In other words, it is up to Immelt to develop strategies that span individual businesses; his concern is with building and managing the corporate portfolio of businesses to maximize corporate profitability.

It is *not* his specific responsibility to develop strategies for competing in the individual business areas, such as financial services. The development of such strategies is the responsibility of the general managers in these different businesses, or *business-level managers.* However, it is Immelt's responsibility to probe the strategic thinking of business-level managers to make sure that they are pursuing robust business models and strategies that will contribute toward the maximization of GE's long-run profitability, to coach and motivate those managers, to reward them for attaining or exceeding goals, and to hold them to account for poor performance.

Corporate-level managers also provide a link between the people who oversee the strategic development of a firm and those who own it (the shareholders). Corporate-level managers, and particularly the CEO, can be viewed as the agents of shareholders.[4] It is their responsibility to ensure that the corporate and business strategies that the company pursues are consistent with maximizing profitability and profit growth. If they are not, then ultimately the CEO is likely to be called to account by the shareholders.

■ Business-Level Managers

A **business unit** is a self-contained division (with its own functions—for example, finance, purchasing, production, and marketing departments) that provides a product or service for a particular market. The principal general manager at the business level, or the business-level manager, is the head of the division. The strategic role of these managers is to translate the general statements of direction and intent that come from the corporate level into concrete strategies for individual businesses. Thus, whereas corporate-level general managers are concerned with strategies that span individual businesses, business-level general managers are concerned with strategies that are specific to a particular business. At GE, a major corporate goal is to be first or second in every business in which the corporation competes. Then the general managers in each division work out for their business the details of a business model that is consistent with this objective.

■ Functional-Level Managers

Functional-level managers are responsible for the specific business functions or operations (human resources, purchasing, product development, customer service, and so on) that constitute a company or one of its divisions. Thus, a functional manager's sphere of responsibility is generally confined to *one* organizational activity, whereas general managers oversee the operation of a *whole* company or division. Although they are not responsible for the overall performance of the organization, functional managers nevertheless have a major strategic role: to develop functional strategies in their area that help fulfill the strategic objectives set by business- and corporate-level general managers.

In GE's aerospace business, for instance, manufacturing managers are responsible for developing manufacturing strategies consistent with corporate objectives. Moreover, functional managers provide most of the information that makes it possible for business- and corporate-level general managers to formulate realistic and attainable strategies. Indeed, because they are closer to the customer than the typical general manager is, functional managers themselves may generate important ideas that subsequently may become major strategies for the company. Thus, it is important for general managers to listen closely to the ideas of their functional managers. An equally great responsibility for managers at the operational level is strategy implementation: the execution of corporate- and business-level plans.

The Strategy-Making Process

We can now turn our attention to the process by which managers formulate and implement strategies. Many writers have emphasized that strategy is the outcome of a formal planning process and that top management plays the most important role in this process.[5] Although this view has some basis in reality, it is not the whole story. As we shall see later in the chapter, valuable strategies often emerge from deep within the organization without prior planning. Nevertheless, a consideration of formal, rational planning is a useful starting point for our journey into the world of strategy. Accordingly, we consider what might be described as a typical formal strategic planning model for making strategy.

■ A Model of the Strategic Planning Process

The formal strategic planning process has five main steps:

1. Select the corporate mission and major corporate goals.

2. Analyze the organization's external competitive environment to identify *opportunities* and *threats*.

3. Analyze the organization's internal operating environment to identify the organization's *strengths* and *weaknesses*.

4. Select strategies that build on the organization's strengths and correct its weaknesses in order to take advantage of external opportunities and counter external threats. These strategies should be consistent with the mission and major goals of the organization. They should be congruent and constitute a viable business model.

5. Implement the strategies.

The task of analyzing the organization's external and internal environment and then selecting appropriate strategies constitutes strategy formulation. In contrast, as noted earlier, strategy implementation involves putting the strategies (or plan) into action. This includes taking actions consistent with the selected strategies of the company at the corporate, business, and functional levels, allocating roles and responsibilities among managers (typically through the design of organization structure), allocating resources (including capital and money), setting short-term objectives, and designing the organization's control and reward systems. These steps are illustrated in Figure 1.4 (which can also be viewed as a plan for the rest of this book).

Each step in Figure 1.4 constitutes a *sequential* step in the strategic planning process. At step 1, each round or cycle of the planning process begins with a statement of the corporate mission and major corporate goals. This statement is shaped by the existing business model of the company. The mission statement is followed by the foundation of strategic thinking: external analysis, internal analysis, and strategic choice. The strategy-making process ends with the design of the organizational structure and the culture and control systems necessary to implement the

FIGURE 1.4

Main Components of
the Strategic Planning
Process

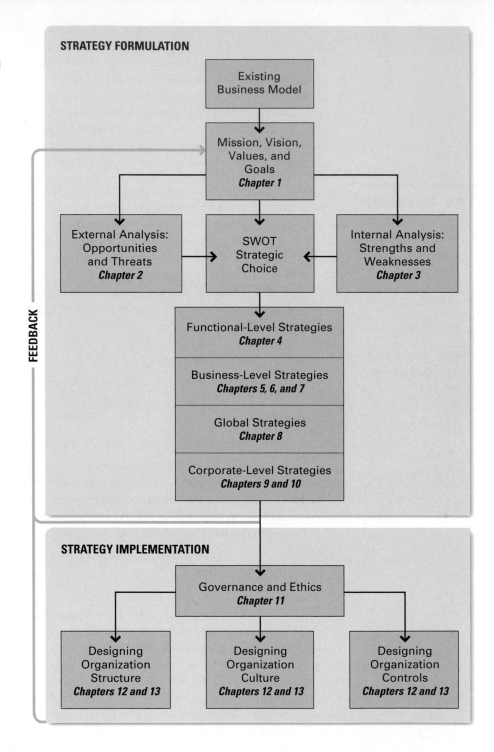

organization's chosen strategy. This chapter discusses how to select a corporate mission and choose major goals. Other parts of strategic planning are reserved for later chapters, as indicated in Figure 1.4.

Some organizations go through a new cycle of the strategic planning process every year. This does not necessarily mean that managers choose a new strategy each year. In many instances, the result is simply to modify and reaffirm a strategy and structure already in place. The strategic plans generated by the planning process generally look out over a period of one to five years, with the plan being updated, or *rolled forward*, every year. In most organizations, the results of the annual strategic planning process are used as input into the budgetary process for the coming year so that strategic planning is used to shape resource allocation within the organization. Strategy in Action 1.1 looks at how Microsoft uses strategic planning to drive its resource allocation decisions.

◼ Mission Statement

The first component of the strategic management process is crafting the organization's mission statement, which provides the framework or context within which strategies are formulated. A mission statement has four main components: a statement of the *raison d'être* of a company or organization—its reason for existence—which is normally referred to as the *mission*; a statement of some desired future state, usually referred to as the *vision*; a statement of the key *values* that the organization is committed to; and a statement of *major goals*.

◼ The Mission
A company's **mission** describes what it is that the company does. For example, the mission of Kodak is to provide "customers with the solutions they need to capture, store, process, output, and communicate images—anywhere, anytime."[6] In other words, Kodak exists to provide imaging solutions to consumers. In its mission statement, Ford Motor Company describes itself as a company that is "passionately committed to providing personal mobility for people around the world…. We anticipate consumer need and deliver outstanding products and services that improve people's lives."[7] In short, Ford is a company that exists to satisfy consumer needs for personal mobility; that is its mission. Both of these missions focus on the customer needs that the company is trying to satisfy rather than on particular products (imaging and personal mobility rather than conventional film or cameras and automobiles). These are customer-oriented rather than product-oriented missions.

An important first step in the process of formulating a mission is to come up with a definition of the organization's business. Essentially, the definition answers these questions: "What is our business? What will it be? What should it be?"[8] The responses guide the formulation of the mission. To answer the question, "What is our business?" a company should define its business in terms of three dimensions: who is being satisfied (what customer groups), what is being satisfied (what customer needs), and how customers' needs are being satisfied (by what skills, knowledge, or distinctive competencies).[9] Figure 1.5 illustrates these dimensions.

This approach stresses the need for a *customer-oriented* rather than a *product-oriented* business definition. A product-oriented business definition focuses on the characteristics of the products sold and the markets served, not on which kinds of customer needs the products are satisfying. Such an approach obscures the company's true mission because a product is only the physical manifestation of applying a particular skill to satisfy a particular need for a particular customer group. In

Strategy in Action

1.1

Strategic Planning at Microsoft

There is a widespread belief that strategic planning does not apply to high-tech industries. "You can't plan for the unpredictable," the argument goes, "and technology markets are characterized by rapid and unpredictable change, so why bother with planning?" Nevertheless, the world's most successful high-tech company, Microsoft, has had a formal strategic planning process in place for many years. The genesis of Microsoft's planning process goes back to 1994 when the rapidly growing company hired Bob Herbold from Procter & Gamble as Microsoft's chief operations officer. Herbold was hired to bring some operating discipline to Microsoft's fluid, freewheeling culture but to do so without undermining the entrepreneurial values and passion for innovation that had made Microsoft so successful. Microsoft's top managers, Bill Gates and Steve Balmer, had been growing increasingly frustrated with the lack of operating efficiency and coherence at Microsoft, and they wanted to do something about it.

One area that Herbold focused on was strategic planning, which was almost nonexistent when he arrived. What did exist was "a rat's nest of incompatible planning approaches used by the different units and divisions.... Bill [Gates] wanted a more formal planning process because, as he said, 'We have no sense of where we will be in two years except for the product guys saying they have great new products coming along.'" At the very least, Gates felt that Microsoft needed some sense of its financial outlook for the next year or two that it could communicate to investors.

Herbold, Gates, and Balmer understood that any assumptions underlying a plan could be made invalid by unforeseen changes in the business environment, and such changes were commonplace in the software industry. At the same time, they acknowledged that Microsoft had some fairly traditional businesses with established revenue streams, such as Microsoft Office and Windows, and the company needed a plan for the future to craft a strategy for these businesses, focus product development efforts, and allocate resources to these businesses. Moreover, the company needed to plan for the future of its newer businesses, such as MSN, the videogame business (Xbox), and its hand-held computer business.

What has emerged at Microsoft is a three-year planning process that compares the subsequent performance of divisions and units against the strategies and goals outlined in the plan to determine future resource allocation. The planning process is built on a standard format that makes it easy to compare the performance data obtained from each of Microsoft's different businesses or divisions. Planning data include projections for market share, revenues, and profits three years into the future, as well as a statement of major strategies and goals. These projections are updated every year in a rolling plan because the industry changes so much.

Unit strategies are hashed out over the year in strategic planning review meetings between top managers (Gates and Balmer) and division managers. Typically, the unit managers develop strategies, and the top managers probe the strategic thinking of unit managers, asking them to justify their assumptions and ultimately approving, amending, or not approving the unit strategy. Unit strategies are also debated at regular strategy conferences, which Gates and Balmer normally attend.

The strategies that result from these processes are the product of an intense dialogue between top management and unit managers. Unit managers are held accountable for any commitments made in the plan. Thus, the plan not only drives resource allocation, it is also used as a control mechanism. Gates and Balmer determine the overall strategy of Microsoft in consultation with the board of directors, although many of the ideas for new businesses, new products, and acquisitions do not come from the top. Instead, they are proposed by employees within the units and approved if they survive scrutiny.

The planning process is formal, decentralized, and flexible. It is formal insofar as it is a regular process that uses standard information to help drive resource allocation for the coming year and holds managers accountable for their performance. It is decentralized insofar as unit managers propose many of the strategies that make up the plan, and those plans are accepted only after scrutiny by the top managers. It is flexible in that top managers do not see the plan as a straitjacket, but as a document that helps to map out where Microsoft may be going over the next few years. All managers recognize that the assumptions contained in the plan may be invalidated by unforeseen events, and they are committed to rapidly changing strategies if the need arises, as it has often in the past.[a]

FIGURE 1.5

Defining the Business

Source: D. F. Abell, *Defining the Business: The Starting Point of Strategic Planning* (Englewood Cliffs, N.J.: Prentice-Hall, 1980), p. 7.

practice, that need may be served in many different ways, and a broad customer-oriented business definition that identifies these ways can safeguard companies from being caught unaware by major shifts in demand.

By helping anticipate demand shifts, a customer-oriented mission statement can also assist companies in capitalizing on changes in their environment. It can help answer the question, "What will our business be?" Kodak's mission statement—to provide "*customers* with the *solutions* they need to capture, store, process, output, and communicate images"—is a customer-oriented statement that focuses on customer needs rather than a particular product (or solution) for satisfying those needs, such as chemical film processing. For this reason, it is helping to drive Kodak's current investments in digital imaging technologies, which are starting to replace its traditional business based on chemical film processing.

The need to take a customer-oriented view of a company's business has often been ignored. History is littered with the wreckage of once-great corporations that did not define their business or defined it incorrectly so that ultimately they declined. In the 1950s and 1960s, many office equipment companies such as Smith Corona and Underwood defined their businesses as being the production of typewriters. This product-oriented definition ignored the fact that they were really in the business of satisfying customers' information-processing needs. Unfortunately for those companies, when a new technology came along that better served customer needs for information processing (computers), demand for typewriters plummeted. The last great typewriter company, Smith Corona, went bankrupt in 1996, a victim of the success of computer-based word-processing technology.

In contrast, IBM correctly foresaw what its business would be. In the 1950s, IBM was a leader in the manufacture of typewriters and mechanical tabulating equipment using punch-card technology. However, unlike many of its competitors, IBM defined its business as *providing a means for information processing and storage*, rather than just supplying mechanical tabulating equipment and typewriters.[10] Given this definition, the company's subsequent moves into computers, software systems, office systems, and printers seem logical.

■ **Vision**   The **vision** of a company lays out some desired future state; it articulates, often in bold terms, what the company would like to achieve. The vision of Ford, for example, is "to become the world's leading consumer company for automotive products and services." This vision is challenging; judged by size, Ford is currently the world's number 3 company behind General Motors and Toyota. Attaining this vision will thus be a stretch for Ford, but that is the point. Good vision statements are meant to challenge a company by articulating some ambitious but attainable future state that will help to motivate employees at all levels and to drive strategies.[11]

Nokia, the world's largest manufacturer of mobile (wireless) phones, operates with a very simple but powerful vision: "If it can go mobile, it will!" This vision implies that not only will voice telephony go mobile (it already has), but so will a host of other services based on data, such as imaging and Internet browsing. This vision has led Nokia to develop multimedia mobile handsets that not only can be used for voice communication but that also take pictures, browse the Internet, play games, and manipulate personal and corporate information.

■ **Values**   The **values** of a company state how managers and employees should conduct themselves, how they should do business, and what kind of organization they should build to help a company achieve its mission. Insofar as they help drive and shape behavior within a company, values are commonly seen as the bedrock of a company's **organizational culture**: the set of values, norms, and standards that control how employees work to achieve an organization's mission and goals. An organization's culture is commonly seen as an important source of its competitive advantage.[12] (We discuss the issue of organization culture in depth in Chapter 12.) For example, Nucor Steel is one of the most productive and profitable steel firms in the world. Its competitive advantage is based in part on the extremely high productivity of its work force, something, the company maintains, that is a direct result of its cultural values, which determine how it treats its employees. These values are as follow:

■ "Management is obligated to manage Nucor in such a way that employees will have the opportunity to earn according to their productivity."

■ "Employees should be able to feel confident that if they do their jobs properly, they will have a job tomorrow."

■ "Employees have the right to be treated fairly and must believe that they will be."

■ "Employees must have an avenue of appeal when they believe they are being treated unfairly."[13]

At Nucor, values emphasizing pay for performance, job security, and fair treatment for employees help to create an atmosphere within the company that leads to high employee productivity. In turn, this has helped to give Nucor one of the lowest cost structures in its industry, which helps to explain the company's profitability in a very price-competitive business.

In one study of organizational values, researchers identified a set of values associated with high-performing organizations that help companies achieve superior financial performance through their impact on employee behavior.[14] These values included respect for the interests of key organizational **stakeholders**: individuals or groups that have an interest, claim, or stake in the company, in what it does, and in how well it performs.[15] They include stockholders, bondholders, employees, customers, the communities in which the company does business, and the general public. The study found that deep respect for the interests of customers, employees, suppliers, and shareholders was associated with high performance. The study also noted that the encouragement of leadership and entrepreneurial behavior by mid- and lower-level managers and a willingness to support change efforts within the organization contributed to high performance. Companies found to emphasize such values consistently throughout their organization include Hewlett-Packard, Wal-Mart, and PepsiCo. The same study identified the values of poorly performing companies—values that, as might be expected, are *not* articulated in company mission statements: (1) arrogance, particularly to ideas from outside the company; (2) a lack of respect for key stakeholders; and (3) a history of resisting change efforts and "punishing" mid- and lower-level managers who showed "too much leadership." General Motors was held up as an example of one such organization. According to the authors, a mid- or lower-level manager who showed too much leadership and initiative there was not promoted!

■ **Major Goals** Having stated the mission, vision, and key values, strategic managers can take the next step in the formulation of a mission statement: establishing major goals. A **goal** is a *precise* and *measurable* desired future state that a company attempts to realize. In this context, the purpose of goals is to specify with precision what must be done if the company is to attain its mission or vision.

Well-constructed goals have four main characteristics:[16]

1. They are *precise and measurable*. Measurable goals give managers a yardstick or standard against which they can judge their performance.

2. They *address crucial issues*. To maintain focus, managers should select a limited number of major goals to assess the performance of the company. The goals that are selected should be crucial or important ones.

3. They are *challenging but realistic*. They give all employees an incentive to look for ways of improving the operations of an organization. If a goal is unrealistic in the challenges it poses, employees may give up; a goal that is too easy may fail to motivate managers and other employees.[17]

4. They *specify a time period* in which they should be achieved when that is appropriate. Time constraints tell employees that success requires a goal to be attained by a given date, not after that date. Deadlines can inject a sense of urgency into goal attainment and act as a motivator. However, not all goals require time constraints.

Well-constructed goals also provide a means by which the performance of managers can be evaluated.

As noted earlier, although most companies operate with a variety of goals, the central goal of most corporations is to maximize shareholder returns, and doing this requires both high profitability and sustained profit growth. Thus, most companies operate with goals for profitability and profit growth. However, it is important that top managers do not make the mistake of overemphasizing current profitability to the detriment of long-term profitability and profit growth.[18] The overzealous pursuit of current profitability to maximize short-term ROIC can encourage such misguided managerial actions as cutting expenditures judged to be nonessential in the short run—for instance, expenditures for research and development, marketing, and new capital investments. Although cutting current expenditure increases current profitability, the resulting underinvestment, lack of innovation, and diminished marketing can jeopardize long-run profitability and profit growth. These expenditures are vital if a company is to pursue its long-term mission and sustain its competitive advantage and profitability over time. Despite these negative consequences, managers may make such decisions because the adverse effects of a short-run orientation may not materialize and become apparent to shareholders for several years or because they are under extreme pressure to hit short-term profitability goals.[19] It is also worth noting that pressures to maximize short-term profitability may drive managers to act unethically. This apparently occurred during the late 1990s at Enron Corporation, Tyco, WorldCom, and Computer Associates, where managers systematically inflated profits by manipulating financial accounts in a manner that misrepresented the true performance of the firm to shareholders. (Chapter 11 provides a detailed discussion of the issues.)

To guard against short-run behavior, managers need to ensure that they adopt goals whose attainment will increase the long-run performance and competitiveness of their enterprise. Long-term goals are related to such issues as product development, customer satisfaction, and efficiency, and they emphasize specific objectives or targets concerning such things as employee and capital productivity, product quality, and innovation. The *Opening Case* mentioned how managers at Wal-Mart used information technology to track sales of individual items at individual stores; this information then enabled them to reduce inventory costs. To achieve long-run performance goals, Wal-Mart had to improve its efficiency, and reducing inventory was one of many steps in that direction. Only by paying constant attention to their processes and operations can companies improve their customer satisfaction, productivity, product quality, and innovation over the long run. Managers' ability to make the right decisions gives their companies a competitive advantage and boosts *long-term* performance. Both analysts and shareholders watch how well a company makes these decisions and attains its goals, and its stock price fluctuates according to the perception of how well it has succeeded. Positive shareholder perceptions boost stock price and help maximize the returns from holding a company's stock.

■ External Analysis

The second component of the strategic management process is an analysis of the organization's external operating environment. The essential purpose of the external analysis is to identify strategic *opportunities* and *threats* in the organization's operating environment that will affect how it pursues its mission. Three interrelated environments should be examined at this stage: the *industry environment* in which the company operates, the country or *national environment,* and the wider socioeconomic or *macroenvironment.*

Analyzing the industry environment requires an assessment of the competitive structure of the company's industry, including the competitive position of the company and its major rivals. It also requires analysis of the nature, stage, dynamics, and history of the industry. Because many markets are now global markets, analyzing the industry environment also means assessing the impact of globalization on competition within an industry. Such an analysis may reveal that a company should move some production facilities to another nation, that it should aggressively expand in emerging markets such as China, or that it should beware of new competition from emerging nations. Analyzing the macroenvironment consists of examining macroeconomic, social, government, legal, international, and technological factors that may affect the company and its industry.

■ Internal Analysis

Internal analysis, the third component of the strategic planning process, serves to pinpoint the *strengths* and *weaknesses* of the organization. Such issues as identifying the quantity and quality of a company's resources and capabilities and ways of building unique skills and company-specific or distinctive competencies are considered here when we probe the sources of competitive advantage. Building and sustaining a competitive advantage requires a company to achieve superior efficiency, quality, innovation, and responsiveness to its customers. Company strengths lead to superior performance in these areas, whereas company weaknesses translate into inferior performance.

■ SWOT Analysis and the Business Model

The next component of strategic thinking requires the generation of a series of strategic alternatives, or choices of future strategies to pursue, given the company's internal strengths and weaknesses and its external opportunities and threats. The comparison of strengths, weaknesses, opportunities, and threats is normally referred to as a **SWOT analysis**.[20] Its central purpose is to identify the strategies that will create a company-specific business model that will best *align, fit,* or *match* a company's resources and capabilities to the demands of the environment in which it operates. Managers compare and contrast the various alternative possible strategies against each other and then identify the set of *strategies* that will create and sustain a competitive advantage:

■ *Functional-level strategy*, directed at improving the effectiveness of operations within a company, such as manufacturing, marketing, materials management, product development, and customer service

■ *Business-level strategy*, which encompasses the business's overall competitive theme, the way it positions itself in the marketplace to gain a competitive advantage, and the different positioning strategies that can be used in different industry settings—for example, *cost leadership, differentiation, focusing on a particular niche or segment of the industry*, or some *combination* of these

■ *Global strategy*, addressing how to expand operations outside the home country to grow and prosper in a world where competitive advantage is determined at a global level

■ *Corporate-level strategy*, which answers the primary questions: What business or businesses should we be in to maximize the long-run profitability and profit growth of the organization, and how should we enter and increase our presence in these businesses to gain a competitive advantage?

The strategies identified through a SWOT analysis should be congruent with each other. Thus, functional-level strategies should be consistent with, or support, the company's business-level strategy and global strategy. Moreover, as we explain later in this book, corporate-level strategies should support business-level strategies. When taken together, the various strategies pursued by a company constitute a viable business model. In essence a SWOT analysis is a methodology for choosing between competing business models and for fine-tuning the business model that managers choose. Thus, at Wal-Mart a SWOT analysis might be used to fine-tune and improve aspects of the self-service supermarket business model. In contrast, when Microsoft entered the videogame market with its Xbox offering, it had to settle on the best business model for competing in this market. Microsoft used a SWOT type of analysis to compare alternatives and settled on a "razor and razor blades" business model in which the Xbox console is priced below cost to build sales (the "razor"), while profits are made from royalties on the sale of games for the Xbox (the "blades").

■ Strategy Implementation

Having chosen a set of congruent strategies to achieve a competitive advantage and increase performance, managers must put those strategies into action: Strategy has to be implemented. Strategy implementation involves taking actions at the functional, business, and corporate levels to execute a strategic plan. Thus implementation can include, for example, putting quality improvement programs into place, changing the way a product is designed, positioning the product differently in the marketplace, segmenting the marketing and offering different versions of the product to different consumer groups, implementing price increases or decreases, expanding through mergers and acquisitions, or downsizing the company by closing down or selling off parts of the company. These and other topics are discussed in detail in Chapters 4 through 10.

Strategy implementation also entails designing the best organization structure and the best culture and control systems to put a chosen strategy into action. In addition, senior managers need to put a governance system in place to make sure that all within the organization act in a manner that is not only consistent with maximizing profitability and profit growth but also legal and ethical. In this book we look at the topic of governance and ethics in Chapter 11, we discuss the organization structure, culture, and controls required to implement business-level strategies in Chapter 12, and the structure, culture, and controls required to implement corporate-level strategies in Chapter 13.

■ The Feedback Loop

The feedback loop in Figure 1.4 indicates that strategic planning is ongoing; it *never* ends. Once a strategy has been implemented, its execution must be monitored to determine the extent to which strategic goals and objectives are actually being achieved and to what degree competitive advantage is being created and sustained. This information and knowledge pass back up to the corporate level through feedback loops and become the input for the next round of strategy formulation and implementation. Top managers can then decide whether to reaffirm the existing business model and the existing strategies and goals or suggest changes for the future. For example, if a strategic goal proves too optimistic, the next time a more conservative goal is set. Or feedback may reveal that the business model is not working, so managers may seek ways to change it.

Strategy as an Emergent Process

The basic planning model suggests that a company's strategies are the result of a plan, that the strategic planning process itself is rational and highly structured, and that the process is orchestrated by top management. Several scholars have criticized the formal planning model for three main reasons: the unpredictability of the real world, the role that lower-level managers can play in the strategic management process, and the fact that many successful strategies are often the result of serendipity, not rational strategizing. They have advocated an alternative view of strategy making.[21]

■ **Strategy Making in an Unpredictable World**

Critics of formal planning systems argue that we live in a world in which uncertainty, complexity, and ambiguity dominate, and in which small chance events can have a large and unpredictable impact on outcomes.[22] In such circumstances, they claim, even the most carefully thought out strategic plans are prone to being rendered useless by rapid and unforeseen change. In an unpredictable world, there is a premium on being able to respond quickly to changing circumstances and to alter the strategies of the organization accordingly.

A dramatic example of this occurred in 1994 and 1995 when Microsoft CEO Bill Gates shifted the company strategy after the unanticipated emergence of the World Wide Web (see Strategy in Action 1.2). According to critics of formal systems, such a flexible approach to strategy making is not possible within the framework of a traditional strategic planning process, with its implicit assumption that an organization's strategies need to be reviewed only during the annual strategic planning exercise.

■ **Autonomous Action: Strategy Making by Lower-Level Managers**

Another criticism leveled at the rational planning model of strategy is that too much importance is attached to the role of top management, particularly the CEO.[23] An alternative view now gaining wide acceptance is that individual managers deep within an organization can and often do exert a profound influence over the strategic direction of the firm.[24] Writing with Robert Burgelman of Stanford University, Andy Grove, the former CEO of Intel, noted that many important strategic decisions at Intel were initiated not by top managers but by the **autonomous action** of lower-level managers deep within Intel who, on their own initiative, formulated new strategies and worked to persuade top-level managers to alter the strategic priorities of the firm.[25] These strategic decisions included the decision to exit an important market (the DRAM memory chip market) and to develop a certain class of microprocessors (RISC-based microprocessors) in direct contrast to the stated strategy of Intel's top managers. Strategy in Action 1.2 details how autonomous action by two young employees drove the evolution of Microsoft's strategy toward the Internet. In addition, the prototype for another Microsoft product, the Xbox videogame system, was developed by four lower-level engineering employees on their own initiative. They then successfully lobbied top managers to dedicate resources toward commercializing their prototype. Another famous example of autonomous action, in this case at 3M, is given in Strategy in Action 1.3.

Autonomous action may be particularly important in helping established companies deal with the uncertainty created by the arrival of a radical new technology that changes the dominant paradigm in an industry.[26] Top managers usually rise to preeminence by successfully executing the established strategy of the firm. Therefore, they may have an emotional commitment to the status quo and are often unable to see things from a different perspective. In this sense, they are a conservative force that promotes inertia. Lower-level managers, however, are less likely to have the same commitment to the status quo and have more to gain from promoting new technologies and strategies. They may be the ones to first recognize new strategic opportunities (as was the case at both Microsoft and 3M) and lobby for strategic change.

Strategy in Action

1.2

A Strategic Shift at Microsoft

The Internet has been around since the 1970s, but prior to the early 1990s, it was a drab place, lacking the color, content, and richness of today's environment. What changed the Internet from a scientific tool to a consumer-driven media environment was the invention of hypertext markup language (HTML) and the related invention of a browser for displaying graphics-rich webpages based on HTML. The combination of HTML and browsers effectively created the World Wide Web (WWW). This was an unforeseen development.

A young programmer at the University of Illinois in 1993, Mark Andreesen, had developed the first browser, known as Mosaic. In 1994, he left Illinois and joined a start-up company, Netscape, which produced an improved browser, the Netscape Navigator, along with software that enabled organizations to create webpages and host them on computer servers. These developments led to a dramatic and unexpected growth in the number of people connecting to the Internet. In 1990, the Internet had 1 million users. By early 1995, the number had exceeded 80 million and was growing exponentially.

Prior to the emergence of the Web, Microsoft did have a strategy for exploiting the Internet, but it was one that emphasized set-top boxes, video on demand, interactive TV, and an online service, MSN, modeled after AOL and based on proprietary standards. In early 1994, Gates received e-mails from two young employees, Jay Allard and Steve Sinofsky, who argued that Microsoft's current strategy was misguided and ignored the rapidly emerging Web. In companies with a more hierarchical culture, such action might have been ignored, but in Microsoft, which operates as a meritocracy in which good ideas trump hierarchical position, it produced a very different response. Gates convened a meeting of senior executives in April 1994 and then wrote a memo to senior executives arguing that the Internet represented a sea change in computing and that Microsoft had to respond.

What ultimately emerged was a 180-degree shift in Microsoft's strategy. Interactive TV was placed on the back burner, and MSN was relaunched as a Web service based on HTML. Microsoft committed to developing its own browser technology and within a few months had issued Internet Explorer to compete with Netscape's Navigator (the underlying technology was gained by an acquisition). Microsoft licensed Java, a computer language designed to run programs on the Web, from a major competitor, Sun Microsystems. Internet protocols were built into Windows 95 and Windows NT, and Gates insisted that henceforth Microsoft's applications, such as the ubiquitous Office, embrace the WWW and have the ability to convert documents into an HTML format. The new strategy was given its final stamp on December 7, 1995, Pearl Harbor Day, when Gates gave a speech arguing that the Internet was now pervasive in everything Microsoft was doing. By then, Microsoft had been pursuing the new strategy for a year. In short, Microsoft quickly went from a proprietary standards approach to one that embraced the public standards on the WWW.[b]

■ **Serendipity and Strategy**

Business history is replete with examples of accidental events that help to push companies in new and profitable directions. What these examples suggest is that many successful strategies are not the result of well-thought-out plans but of serendipity, that is, of stumbling across good things unexpectedly. One such example occurred at 3M during the 1960s. At that time, 3M was producing fluorocarbons for sale as coolant liquid in air-conditioning equipment. One day, a researcher working with fluorocarbons in a 3M lab spilled some of the liquid on her shoes. Later that day when she spilled coffee over her shoes, she watched with interest as the coffee formed into little beads of liquid and then ran off her shoes without leaving a stain. Reflecting on this phenomenon, she realized that a fluorocarbon-based liquid might turn out to be useful for protecting fabrics from liquid stains, and so the idea for Scotch Guard was born. Subsequently, Scotch Guard became one of 3M's most profitable

Strategy in Action   1.3

The Genesis of Autonomous Action at 3M

In the 1920s, the Minnesota Mining and Manufacturing Company (3M) was a small manufacturer of sandpaper. Its best-selling product, wet-and-dry sandpaper, was introduced in 1921 and was sold primarily to automobile companies, which used it to sand auto bodies between paint coats because it produced a smooth finish. A problem with wet and dry, however, was that the grit did not always stay bound to the sandpaper, and bits of grit that had detached from the paper could ruin an otherwise perfect paint job. To deal with this problem in the early 1920s, the CEO, a young William McKnight, hired 3M's first research scientist, Richard Drew. Drew was straight out of college; this was his first job. McKnight charged Drew with developing a stronger adhesive to better bind the grit to the paper backing.

While experimenting with adhesives, Drew developed a weak adhesive that had an interesting quality: if placed on the back of a strip of paper and stuck to a surface, the strip of paper could be peeled off the surface it was adhered to without leaving any adhesive residue on that surface. This serendipitous discovery gave Drew an epiphany. He had been visiting auto body paint shops to see how 3M's sandpaper was used and noticed a problem with paint running. His epiphany was to cover the back of a strip of paper with his weak adhesive and use it as "masking tape" to cover parts of the auto body that were not to be painted. An excited Drew took his idea to McKnight and explained how masking tape might create an entirely new business for 3M. McKnight reminded Drew that he had been hired to fix a specific problem and pointedly suggested that he concentrate on doing that and not on dreaming up other business ideas.

Chastised, Drew went back to his lab but could not get the idea out of his mind, so he continued to work on it at night, long after everyone else had gone home. He succeeded in perfecting the masking tape product and then went to visit several auto body shops to show them his innovation. He quickly received several commitments for orders. Drew then went to McKnight again. He told him that he had continued to work on the masking tape idea on his own time, had perfected the product, and had several customers interested in purchasing it. This time it was McKnight's turn to be chastised. Realizing that he had almost killed a good business idea, McKnight reversed his original position and gave Drew the go-ahead to pursue the idea.

Sticky tape subsequently became a huge business for 3M. Moreover, McKnight went on to become a long-serving CEO and then chairman of 3M's board until 1966. Drew became the chief science officer and also served until the 1960s. Together they helped build 3M and shaped its organization culture. One of the main principles of that culture came out of the original incident between Drew and McKnight: top management should "delegate responsibility and encourage men and women to exercise their initiative." According to McKnight, as business grows, "it becomes increasingly necessary to delegate responsibility and to encourage men and women to exercise their initiative.... Mistakes will be made. But if a person is essentially right, the mistakes he or she makes are not as serious in the long run as the mistakes management will make if it undertakes to tell those in authority exactly how they must do their jobs.... Management that is destructively critical when mistakes are made kills initiative. And it's essential that we have many people with initiative if we are to continue to grow." Based on their own experience, McKnight and Drew established a culture at 3M that encourages autonomous action.[c]

products and took the company into the fabric protection business, an area it had never planned to participate in.[27]

Serendipitous discoveries and events can open up all sorts of profitable avenues for a company. But some companies have missed out on profitable opportunities because serendipitous discoveries or events were inconsistent with their prior (planned) conception of what their strategy should be. In one of the classic examples of such myopia, a century ago the telegraph company Western Union turned down an opportunity to purchase the rights to an invention made by Alexander Graham

Bell. The invention was the telephone, a technology that subsequently made the telegraph obsolete.

■ Intended and Emergent Strategies

Henry Mintzberg's model of strategy development provides a more encompassing view of what strategy actually is. According to this model, illustrated in Figure 1.6, a company's *realized strategy* is the product of whatever planned strategies are actually put into action (the company's deliberate strategies) *and* of any unplanned, or emergent, strategies. In Mintzberg's view, many planned strategies are not implemented because of unpredicted changes in the environment (they are unrealized). **Emergent strategies** are the unplanned responses to unforeseen circumstances. They arise from autonomous action by individual managers deep within the organization, from serendipitous discoveries or events, or from an unplanned strategic shift by top-level managers in response to changed circumstances. They are *not* the product of formal top-down planning mechanisms.

Mintzberg maintains that emergent strategies are often successful and may be more appropriate than intended strategies. Richard Pascale has described how this was the case for the entry of Honda Motor Co. into the U.S. motorcycle market.[28] When a number of Honda executives arrived in Los Angeles from Japan in 1959 to establish a U.S. operation, their original aim (intended strategy) was to focus on selling 250-cc and 350-cc machines to confirmed motorcycle enthusiasts rather than 50-cc Honda Cubs, which were a big hit in Japan. Their instinct told them that the Honda 50s were not suitable for the U.S. market, where everything was bigger and more luxurious than in Japan.

However, sales of the 250-cc and 350-cc bikes were sluggish, and the bikes themselves were plagued by mechanical failure. It looked as if Honda's strategy was going to fail. At the same time, the Japanese executives who were using the Honda 50s to run errands around Los Angeles were attracting a lot of attention. One day they got a

FIGURE 1.6

Emergent and Deliberate Strategies

Data Source: Adapted from H. Mintzberg and A. McGugh, *Administrative Science Quarterly,* Vol. 30. No. 2, June 1985.

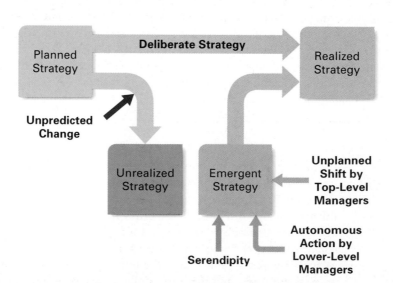

call from a Sears, Roebuck buyer who wanted to sell the 50-cc bikes to a broad market of Americans who were not necessarily motorcycle enthusiasts. The Honda executives were hesitant to sell the small bikes for fear of alienating serious bikers, who might then associate Honda with "wimpy" machines. In the end, however, they were pushed into doing so by the failure of the 250-cc and 350-cc models.

Honda had stumbled onto a previously untouched market segment that was to prove huge: the average American who had never owned a motorbike. Honda had also found an untried channel of distribution: general retailers rather than specialty motorbike stores. By 1964, nearly one out of every two motorcycles sold in the United States was a Honda.

The conventional explanation for Honda's success is that the company redefined the U.S. motorcycle industry with a brilliantly conceived *intended* strategy. The fact was that Honda's intended strategy was a near disaster. The strategy that *emerged* did so not through planning but through unplanned action in response to unforeseen circumstances. Nevertheless, credit should be given to the Japanese management for recognizing the strength of the emergent strategy and for pursuing it with vigor.

The critical point demonstrated by the Honda example is that successful strategies can often emerge within an organization without prior planning in response to unforeseen circumstances. As Mintzberg has noted, strategies can take root virtually wherever people have the capacity to learn and the resources to support that capacity.

In practice, the strategies of most organizations are probably a combination of the intended (planned) and the emergent. The message for management is that it needs to recognize the process of emergence and to intervene when appropriate, killing off bad emergent strategies but nurturing potentially good ones.[29] To make such decisions, managers must be able to judge the worth of emergent strategies. *They must be able to think strategically.* Although emergent strategies arise from within the organization without prior planning—that is, without going through the steps illustrated in Figure 1.4 in a *sequential* fashion—top management still has to evaluate emergent strategies. Such evaluation involves comparing each emergent strategy with the organization's goals, external environmental opportunities and threats, and internal strengths and weaknesses. The objective is to assess whether the emergent strategy fits the company's needs and capabilities. In addition, Mintzberg stresses that an organization's capability to produce emergent strategies is a function of the kind of corporate culture that the organization's structure and control systems foster. In other words, the different components of the strategic management process are just as important from the perspective of emergent strategies as they are from the perspective of intended strategies.

Strategic Planning in Practice

Despite criticisms, research suggests that formal planning systems do help managers make better strategic decisions. A study that analyzed the results of twenty-six previously published studies came to the conclusion that, on average, strategic planning has a positive impact on company performance.[30] Another study of strategic planning in 656 firms found that formal planning methodologies and emergent strategies both form part of a good strategy formulation process, particularly in an unstable environment.[31] For strategic planning to work, it is important that top-level managers plan not just in the context of the *current* competitive environment but also in the context of the *future* competitive environment. To try to forecast what that future will look like, managers can use scenario planning techniques to plan for different possible futures. They can also involve operating managers in the planning process and seek to shape the future competitive environment by emphasizing strategic intent.

■ Scenario Planning

One reason that strategic planning may fail over the long run is that strategic managers, in their initial enthusiasm for planning techniques, may forget that the future is inherently unpredictable. Even the best-laid plans can fall apart if unforeseen contingencies occur, and that happens all the time in the real world. The recognition that uncertainty makes it difficult to forecast the future accurately led planners at Royal Dutch Shell to pioneer the *scenario approach* to planning.

In the scenario approach, managers are given a set of possible future scenarios for the development of competition in their industry. Some scenarios are optimistic and some pessimistic, and then teams of managers are asked to develop specific strategies to cope with each different scenario. A set of industry-specific indicators are chosen and used as signposts to track the development of the industry and to determine the probability that any particular scenario is coming to pass. The idea is to get managers to understand the dynamic and complex nature of their environment, think through problems in a strategic fashion, and generate a range of strategic options that might be pursued under different circumstances.[32]

The scenario approach to planning has spread rapidly among large companies. According to one survey, over 50 percent of the *Fortune 500* companies use some form of scenario planning.[33]

■ Decentralized Planning

A serious mistake that some companies have made in constructing their strategic planning process has been to treat planning as an exclusively top management responsibility. This *ivory tower* approach can result in strategic plans formulated in a vacuum by top managers who have little understanding or appreciation of current operating realities. Consequently, top managers may formulate strategies that do more harm than good. For example, when demographic data indicated that houses and families were shrinking, planners at GE's appliance group concluded that smaller appliances were the wave of the future. Because they had little contact with home builders and retailers, they did not realize that kitchens and bathrooms were the two rooms that were *not* shrinking. Nor did they appreciate that working women wanted big refrigerators to cut down on trips to the supermarket. GE ended up wasting a lot of time designing small appliances with limited demand.

The ivory tower concept of planning can also lead to tensions between corporate-, business-, and functional-level managers. The experience of GE's appliance group is again illuminating. Many of the corporate managers in the planning group were recruited from consulting firms or top-flight business schools. Many of the functional managers took this pattern of recruitment to mean that corporate managers did not think they were smart enough to think through strategic problems for themselves. They felt shut out of the decision-making process, which they believed to be unfairly constituted. Out of this perceived lack of procedural justice grew an us-versus-them mindset that quickly escalated into hostility. As a result, even when the planners were right, operating managers would not listen to them. For example, the planners correctly recognized the importance of the globalization of the appliance market and the emerging Japanese threat. However, operating managers, who then saw Sears Roebuck as the competition, paid them little heed.

Finally, ivory tower planning ignores the important strategic role of autonomous action by lower-level managers and serendipity.

Correcting the ivory tower approach to planning requires recognizing that successful strategic planning encompasses managers at *all* levels of the corporation. Much of the best planning can and should be done by business and functional managers who are closest to the facts; in other words, planning should be decentralized. The role of corporate-level planners should be that of *facilitators* who help business and functional managers do the planning by setting the broad strategic goals of the organization and providing the resources required to identify the strategies that might be required to attain those goals.

It is not enough to involve lower-level managers in the strategic planning process, however; they also need to perceive that the decision-making process is fair, a concept that Chan Kim and Renee Mauborgne refer to as *procedural justice.*[34] If people perceive the decision-making process to be unjust, they are less likely to be committed to any resulting decisions and to cooperate voluntarily in activities designed to implement those decisions. Consequently, the strategy chosen might fail for lack of support among those who must implement it at the operating level.

■ Strategic Intent

The formal strategic planning model has been characterized as the *fit model* of strategy making. This is because it attempts to achieve a fit between the internal resources and capabilities of an organization and external opportunities and threats in the industry environment. Gary Hamel and C. K. Prahalad have criticized the fit model because it can lead to a mindset in which management focuses too much on the degree of fit between the *existing* resources of a company and *current* environmental opportunities, and not enough on building *new* resources and capabilities to create and exploit *future* opportunities.[35] Strategies formulated with only the present in mind, argue Prahalad and Hamel, tend to be more concerned with today's problems than with tomorrow's opportunities. As a result, companies that rely exclusively on the fit approach to strategy formulation are unlikely to be able to build and maintain a competitive advantage. This is particularly true in a dynamic competitive environment, where new competitors are continually arising and new ways of doing business are constantly being invented.

As Prahalad and Hamel note, again and again, companies using the fit approach have been surprised by the ascent of competitors that initially seemed to lack the resources and capabilities needed to make them a real threat. This happened to Xerox, which ignored the rise of Canon and Ricoh in the photocopier market until they had become serious global competitors; to General Motors, which initially overlooked the threat posed by Toyota and Honda in the 1970s; and to Caterpillar, which ignored the danger Komatsu posed to its heavy earthmoving business until it was almost too late to respond.

The secret of the success of companies like Toyota, Canon, and Komatsu, according to Prahalad and Hamel, is that they all had bold ambitions that outstripped their existing resources and capabilities. All wanted to achieve global leadership, and they set out to build the resources and capabilities that would enable them to attain this goal. Consequently, top management created an obsession with winning at all levels of the organization that they sustained over a ten- to twenty-year quest for global leadership. It is this obsession that Prahalad and Hamel refer to as **strategic intent**. They stress that strategic intent is more than simply unfettered ambition. It encompasses an active management process, which includes "focusing the organization's attention on the essence of winning; motivating people by communicating the value of the target; leaving room for individual and team contributions; sustaining enthusiasm by providing new operational definitions as circumstances change; and using intent consistently to guide resource allocations."[36]

Thus, underlying the concept of strategic intent is the notion that strategic planning should be based on setting an ambitious vision and ambitious goals that stretch a company and then finding ways to build the resources and capabilities necessary to attain that vision and those goals. As Prahalad and Hamel note, in practice the two approaches to strategy formulation are not mutually exclusive. All the components of the strategic planning process that we discussed earlier (see Figure 1.4) are important.

In addition, say Prahalad and Hamel, the strategic management process should begin with a challenging vision, such as attaining global leadership, that stretches the organization. Throughout the subsequent process, the emphasis should be on finding ways (strategies) to develop the resources and capabilities necessary to achieve these goals rather than on exploiting *existing* strengths to take advantage of *existing* opportunities. The difference between strategic fit and strategic intent, therefore, may just be one of emphasis. Strategic intent is more internally focused and is concerned with building new resources and capabilities. Strategic fit focuses more on matching existing resources and capabilities to the external environment.

Strategic Decision Making

Even the best-designed strategic planning systems will fail to produce the desired results if managers do not use the information at their disposal effectively. Consequently, it is important that strategic managers learn to make better use of the information they have and understand why they sometimes make poor decisions. One important way in which managers can make better use of their knowledge and information is to understand how common cognitive biases can result in good managers making bad decisions.[37]

■ Cognitive Biases and Strategic Decision Making

The rationality of human decision makers is bounded by our own cognitive capabilities.[38] We are not supercomputers, and it is difficult for us to absorb and process large amounts of information effectively. As a result, when making decisions, we tend to fall back on certain rules of thumb, or heuristics, that help us to make sense out of a complex and uncertain world. However, sometimes these rules lead to severe and systematic errors in the decision-making process.[39] Systematic errors are those that appear time and time again. They seem to arise from a series of **cognitive biases** in the way that human decisionmakers process information and reach decisions. Because of cognitive biases, many managers end up making poor strategic decisions.

A number of biases have been verified repeatedly in laboratory settings, so we can be reasonably sure that they exist and that we are all prone to them.[40] The **prior hypothesis bias** refers to the fact that decisionmakers who have strong prior beliefs about the relationship between two variables tend to make decisions on the basis of these beliefs, even when presented with evidence that their beliefs are wrong. Moreover, they tend to seek and use information that is consistent with their prior beliefs, while ignoring information that contradicts these beliefs. To put this bias in a strategic context, it suggests that a CEO who has a strong prior belief that a certain strategy makes sense might continue to pursue that strategy, despite evidence that it is inappropriate or failing.

Another well-known cognitive bias, **escalating commitment**, occurs when decisionmakers, having already committed significant resources to a project, commit even more resources even if they receive feedback that the project is failing.[41] This may be an irrational response; a more logical response would be to abandon the project and move on (that is, to cut your losses and run), rather than escalate commitment. Feelings of personal responsibility for a project apparently induce decision-makers to stick with a project despite evidence that it is failing.

A third bias, **reasoning by analogy**, involves the use of simple analogies to make sense out of complex problems. The problem with this heuristic is that the analogy may not be valid. A fourth bias, **representativeness**, is rooted in the tendency to generalize from a small sample or even a single vivid anecdote. This bias violates the statistical law of large numbers, which says that it is inappropriate to generalize from a small sample, let alone from a single case. In many respects, the dot-com boom of the late 1990s was based on reasoning by analogy and representativeness. Prospective entrepreneurs saw some of the early dot-com companies such Amazon and Yahoo! achieve rapid success, at least judged by some metrics. Reasoning by analogy from a very small sample, they assumed that any dot-com could achieve similar success. Many investors reached similar conclusions. The result was a massive wave of start-ups that jumped into the Internet space in an attempt to capitalize on the perceived opportunities. That the vast majority of these companies subsequently went bankrupt is testament to the fact that the analogy was wrong and the success of the small sample of early entrants was no guarantee that all dot-coms would succeed.

The final cognitive bias is referred to as the **illusion of control**: the tendency to overestimate one's ability to control events. General or top managers seem to be particularly prone to this bias: having risen to the top of an organization, they tend to be overconfident about their ability to succeed. According to Richard Roll, such overconfidence leads to what he has termed the *hubris hypothesis* of takeovers,[42] Roll argues that top managers are typically overconfident about their ability to create value by acquiring another company. Hence, they end up making poor acquisition decisions, often paying far too much for the companies they acquire. Subsequently, servicing the debt taken on to finance such an acquisition makes it all but impossible to make money from the acquisition.

■ **Groupthink and Strategic Decisions**

Because most strategic decisions are made by groups, the group context within which decisions are made is clearly an important variable in determining whether cognitive biases will operate to adversely affect the strategic decision-making process.

The psychologist Irvin Janis has argued that many groups are characterized by a process known as groupthink and as a result make poor strategic decisions.[43] **Groupthink** occurs when a group of decisionmakers embarks on a course of action without questioning underlying assumptions. Typically, a group coalesces around a person or policy. It ignores or filters out information that can be used to question the policy and develops after-the-fact rationalizations for its decision. Commitment to the mission or goals becomes based on an emotional rather than an objective assessment of the "correct" course of action. The consequences can be poor decisions.

This phenomenon may explain, at least in part, why companies often make poor strategic decisions in spite of sophisticated strategic management. Janis traced many historical fiascoes to defective policymaking by government leaders who received social support from their in-group of advisers. For example, he suggested that President John F. Kennedy's inner circle suffered from groupthink when the members of this group supported the decision to launch the Bay of Pigs invasion of Cuba in 1961, even though available information showed that it would be an unsuccessful venture and would damage U.S. relations with other countries. Janis has observed that groupthink-dominated groups are characterized by strong pressures toward uniformity, which make their members avoid raising controversial issues, questioning weak arguments, or calling a halt to soft-headed thinking. As discussed in Strategy in Action 1.4, the Senate Intelligence Committee believed that groupthink biased CIA and other reports on Iraq's weapons of mass destruction that the Bush Administration subsequently used to justify the 2003 invasion of that nation.

■ Techniques for Improving Decision Making

The existence of cognitive biases and groupthink raises the issue of how to bring critical information to bear on the decision-making mechanism so that a company's strategic decisions are realistic and based on thorough evaluation. Two techniques known to enhance strategic thinking and counteract groupthink and cognitive biases are devil's advocacy and dialectic inquiry (Figure 1.7).[44] **Devil's advocacy** requires the generation of both a plan and a critical analysis of the plan. One member of the decision-making group acts as the devil's advocate, bringing out all the reasons that might make the proposal unacceptable. In this way, decisionmakers can become aware of the possible perils of recommended courses of action.

   Dialectic inquiry is more complex, for it requires the generation of a plan (a thesis) and a counterplan (an antithesis) that reflect *plausible but conflicting* courses of

Strategy in Action   1.4

Was Intelligence on Iraq Biased by Groupthink?

In October 2002 intelligence agencies in the United States issued a National Intelligence Estimate on Iraq's efforts to procure and build weapons of mass destruction (WMDs). The report concluded that there was good evidence that Iraq was actively pursuing a nuclear weapons program and, furthermore, had tried to procure uranium for its bomb-making efforts from the African nation of Niger. In addition, the report claimed that Iraq was stockpiling chemical weapons, including mustard, saran, and nerve gas, and was actively pursuing a research program to produce biological weapons, including anthrax and smallpox viruses. The report was used by the Bush administration to help justify the 2003 invasion of Iraq, which culminated in the removal of Saddam Hussein's regime. The report also helped convince the U.S. Senate that Iraq was violating United Nations conditions imposed after the first Gulf War in 1991. On the basis of this intelligence, seventy-five senators voted to authorize the 2003 war.

   By late 2003, however, it was becoming increasingly apparent that if there were WMDs in Iraq, they were very few in number and extremely well hidden. Had the prewar intelligence been wrong? In mid 2004, the Senate Intelligence Committee published a report evaluating the information contained in the October 2002 National Intelligence Estimate. The findings of the Senate report were endorsed by all seventeen members of the committee, nine Republicans and eight Democrats. In total, they constituted a damning indictment of the prewar intelligence provided by the CIA and others to the Bush administration and Congress.

   The Senate report concluded that a "groupthink" dynamic inside American intelligence agencies generated a "collective presumption that Iraq had an active and growing weapons program." This internal bias, according to the senators, prompted analysts, collectors, and managers in the CIA and other agencies to "interpret ambiguous evidence as being conclusively indicative of a WMD program as well as ignore or minimize evidence that Iraq did not have active or expanding weapons of mass destruction programs." As a consequence, most of the key judgments in the October 2002 National Intelligence Estimate were "either overstated, or were not supported by the underlying intelligence reporting."

One of the most critical parts of the Senate report dealt with the prewar assessment of Iraq's nuclear weapons program. The report stated that the 2002 National Intelligence Estimate represented a sharp break from previous assessments, which had concluded that Iraq had not reconstituted its nuclear weapons program. The Senate report stated that the CIA made a significant shift in its assessment shortly after Vice President Dick Cheney began stating publicly that Iraq had actively reconstituted its nuclear weapons program. The implication was that the CIA gave the administration the information it thought it wanted, rather than accurate information. Moreover, the Senate report claimed that the CIA's leading advocate of the Iraqi nuclear weapons threat withheld evidence from analysts who disagreed with him, misstated the analysis and information produced by others, and distributed misleading information both inside and outside the agency. The committee also concluded that the CIA overstated what it knew about Iraq's attempts to procure uranium from Niger and that it delayed for months examining documents pertaining to those attempts that would later prove to be forgeries.

On the topic of biological weapons, the Senate report concluded that none of the claims about Iraq's biological weapons or capabilities was supported by intelligence and that claims that Iraq had restarted its chemical weapons program were the results of "analytical judgments" and not based on hard evidence. The intelligence on biological weapons came from a single Iraqi defector code-named "Curve Ball" who was apparently an alcoholic and, in the opinion of the one person who had interviewed him, a Pentagon analyst, "utterly useless as a source." When the same analyst saw information provided by Curve Ball included in a speech that Colin Powell made to the United Nations to justify war with Iraq, he contacted the CIA to express his concerns. A CIA official quickly responded in an e-mail: "Let's keep in mind the fact that this war's going to happen regardless of what Curve Ball said or didn't say. The powers that be probably aren't terribly interested in whether Curve Ball knows what he is talking about."

In sum, the Senate report painted a picture of intelligence institutions that selectively interpreted information to support what they thought administration policy was, while ignoring or dismissing contradictory information— sure signs of groupthink. At the same time, the report concluded that there was no evidence of undue political pressure by policymakers in the administration or Congress. Instead, the committee blamed intelligence leaders "who did not encourage analysts to challenge their assumptions, fully consider alternative arguments, accurately characterize the intelligence reporting, or council analysts who lost their objectivity." Be this as it may, an objective observer might also wonder why neither the Senate nor the administration asked hard questions about the quality and source of the intelligence information in the run-up to the war.[d]

action.[45] Strategic managers listen to a debate between advocates of the plan and counterplan and then decide which plan will lead to the higher performance. The purpose of the debate is to reveal the problems with definitions, recommended courses of action, and assumptions of both plans. As a result of this exercise, strategic managers are able to form a new and more encompassing conceptualization of the problem, which then becomes the final plan (a synthesis). Dialectic inquiry can promote strategic thinking.

Another technique for countering cognitive biases is the outside view, which has been championed by Nobel Prize winner Daniel Kahneman and his associates.[46] The **outside view** requires planners to identify a reference class of analogous past strategic initiatives, determine whether those initiatives succeeded or failed, and evaluate the project at hand against those prior initiatives. According to Kahneman, this technique is particularly useful for countering biases such as the illusion of control (hubris), reasoning by analogy, and representativeness. Thus, for example, when considering a potential acquisition, planners should look at the track record of acquisitions made by other enterprises (the reference class), determine if they succeeded or failed, and objectively evaluate the potential acquisition against that reference class.

FIGURE 1.7

Processes for
Improving Decision
Making

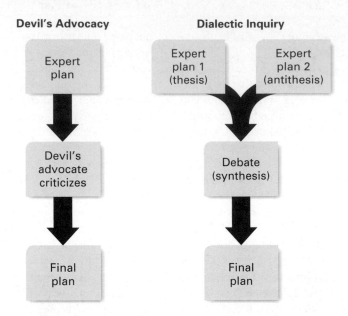

Kahneman argues that such a "reality check" against a large sample of prior events
tends to constrain the inherent optimism of planners and produce more realistic assessments and plans.

Strategic Leadership

One of the key strategic roles of both general and functional managers is to use all
their knowledge, energy, and enthusiasm to provide strategic leadership for their
subordinates and develop a high-performing organization. Several authors have
identified a few key characteristics of good strategic leaders that do lead to high performance: (1) vision, eloquence, and consistency; (2) articulation of a business
model; (3) commitment; (4) being well informed; (5) willingness to delegate and
empower; (6) astute use of power; and (7) emotional intelligence.[47]

■ Vision, Eloquence, and Consistency

One of the key tasks of leadership is to give an organization a sense of direction.
Strong leaders seem to have a clear and compelling vision of where the organization
should go, are eloquent enough to communicate this vision to others within the organization in terms that energize people, and consistently articulate their vision until
it becomes part of the organization's culture.[48]

In the political arena, John F. Kennedy, Winston Churchill, Martin Luther King
Jr., and Margaret Thatcher have all been held up as examples of visionary leaders.
Think of the impact of Kennedy's sentence, "Ask not what your country can do for
you, ask what you can do for your country," of King's "I Have a Dream" speech, and
of Churchill's "we will never surrender." Kennedy and Thatcher were able to use
their political office to push for governmental actions that were consistent with
their vision. Churchill's speech galvanized a nation to defend itself against an aggressor, and King was able to pressure the government from outside to make
changes in society.

Examples of strong business leaders include Microsoft's Bill Gates; Jack Welch,
the former CEO of General Electric; and Sam Walton, Wal-Mart's founder. For years,
Bill Gates's vision of a world in which there would be a Windows-based personal

computer on every desk was a driving force at Microsoft. More recently, the vision has evolved into one of a world in which Windows-based software can be found on any computing device, from PCs and servers to videogame consoles (Xbox), cell phones, and hand-held computers. At GE, Jack Welch was responsible for articulating the simple but powerful vision that GE should be first or second in every business in which it competed, or exit from that business. Similarly, it was Sam Walton who established and articulated the vision that has been central to Wal-Mart's success: passing on cost savings from suppliers and operating efficiencies to customers in the form of everyday low prices.

■ Articulation of the Business Model

Another key characteristic of good strategic leaders is their ability to identify and articulate the business model the company will use to attain its vision. A business model is managers' conception of how the various strategies that the company pursues fit together into a congruent whole. At Wal-Mart, for example, it was Sam Walton who identified and articulated the basic business model of the company: the self-service supermarket business model. The various strategies that Wal-Mart has pursued over the years have refined this basic model, creating one that is now unique in terms of its efficiency and effectiveness. Although individual strategies can take root in many different places in an organization, and although their identification is not the exclusive preserve of top management, only strategic leaders have the perspective required to make sure that the various strategies fit together into a congruent whole and form a valid and compelling business model. If strategic leaders lack a clear conception of what the business model of the company is or should be, it is likely that the strategies the firm pursues will not fit together, and the result will be lack of focus and poor performance.

■ Commitment

Strong leaders demonstrate their commitment to their vision and business model by actions and words, and they often lead by example. Consider Nucor's former CEO, Ken Iverson. Nucor is a very efficient steel maker with perhaps the lowest cost structure in the steel industry. It has turned in thirty years of profitable performance in an industry where most other companies have lost money because of a relentless focus on cost minimization. In his tenure as CEO, Iverson set the example: he answered his own phone, employed only one secretary, drove an old car, flew coach class, and was proud of the fact that his base salary was the lowest of the *Fortune 500* CEOs (Iverson made most of his money from performance-based pay bonuses). This commitment was a powerful signal to employees that Iverson was serious about doing everything possible to minimize costs. It earned him the respect of Nucor employees and made them more willing to work hard. Although Iverson has retired, his legacy lives on in the cost-conscious organization culture that has been built at Nucor, and like all other great leaders, his impact will last beyond his tenure.

■ Being Well Informed

Effective strategic leaders develop a network of formal and informal sources who keep them well informed about what is going on within their company. Herb Kelleher at Southwest Airlines, for example, was able to find out much about the health of his company by dropping in unannounced on aircraft maintenance facilities and helping workers perform their tasks; McDonald's Ray Kroc and Wal-Mart's Sam Walton routinely dropped in unannounced to visit their restaurants and stores. Using informal and unconventional ways to gather information is wise because formal channels can be captured by special interests within the organization or by gatekeepers, managers who may misrepresent the true state of affairs to the leader, such as may have happened at Enron. People like Kelleher who constantly interact with employees at all levels are better able to build informal information networks than leaders who closet themselves and never interact with lower-level employees.

■ Willingness to Delegate and Empower

High-performance leaders are skilled at delegation. They recognize that unless they learn how to delegate effectively, they can quickly become overloaded with responsibilities. They also recognize that empowering subordinates to make decisions is a good motivation tool and often results in decisions being made by those who must implement them. At the same time, astute leaders recognize that they need to maintain control over certain key decisions. Thus, although they will delegate many *important* decisions to lower-level employees, they will not delegate those that they judge to be of *critical importance* to the future success of the organization, such as articulating the company's vision and business model.

■ The Astute Use of Power

In a now classic article on leadership, Edward Wrapp noted that effective leaders tend to be very astute in their use of power.[49] He argued that strategic leaders must often play the power game with skill and attempt to build consensus for their ideas rather than use their authority to force ideas through; they must act as members of a coalition or its democratic leaders rather than as dictators. Jeffery Pfeffer has articulated a similar vision of the politically astute manager who gets things done in organizations through the intelligent use of power.[50] In Pfeffer's view, power comes from control over resources that are important to the organization: budgets, capital, positions, information, and knowledge. Politically astute managers use these resources to acquire another critical resource: critically placed allies who can help them attain their strategic objectives. Pfeffer stresses that one does not need to be a CEO to assemble power in an organization. Sometimes quite junior functional managers can build a surprisingly effective power base and use it to influence organizational outcomes.

■ Emotional Intelligence

Emotional intelligence is a term that Daniel Goldman coined to describe a bundle of psychological attributes that many strong and effective leaders exhibit:[51]

■ Self-awareness—the ability to understand one's own moods, emotions, and drives, as well as their effect on others

■ Self-regulation—the ability to control or redirect disruptive impulses or moods, that is, to think before acting

■ Motivation—a passion for work that goes beyond money or status and a propensity to pursue goals with energy and persistence

■ Empathy—the ability to understand the feelings and viewpoints of subordinates and to take those into account when making decisions

■ Social skills—friendliness with a purpose

According to Goldman, leaders who possess these attributes—who exhibit a high degree of emotional intelligence—tend to be more effective than those who lack these attributes. Their self-awareness and self-regulation help to elicit the trust and confidence of subordinates. In Goldman's view, people respect leaders who, because they are self-aware, recognize their own limitations and, because they are self-regulating, consider decisions carefully. Goldman also argues that self-aware and self-regulating individuals tend to be more self-confident and therefore better able to cope with ambiguity and more open to change. A strong motivation exhibited in a passion for work can also be infectious, helping to persuade others to join together in pursuit of a common goal or organizational mission. Finally, strong empathy and social skills can help leaders earn the loyalty of subordinates. Empathetic and socially adept individuals tend to be skilled at managing disputes between managers, better able to find common ground and purpose among diverse constituencies, and better able to move people in a desired direction than leaders who lack these skills. In short, Goldman argues that the psychological makeup of a leader matters.

Summary of Chapter

1. A strategy is an action that a company takes to attain one or more of its goals.

2. The major goal of companies is to maximize the returns that shareholders get from holding shares in the company. To maximize shareholder value, managers must pursue strategies that result in high and sustained profitability and also in profit growth.

3. The profitability of a company can be measured by the return that it makes on the capital invested in the enterprise. The profit growth of a company can be measured by the growth in earnings per share. Profitability and profit growth are determined by the strategies managers adopt.

4. A company has a competitive advantage over its rivals when it is more profitable than the average for all firms in its industry. It has a sustained competitive advantage when it is able to maintain above-average profitability over a number of years. In general, a company with a competitive advantage will grow its profits more rapidly than rivals.

5. General managers are responsible for the overall performance of the organization or for one of its major self-contained divisions. Their overriding strategic concern is for the health of the total organization under their direction.

6. Functional managers are responsible for a particular business function or operation. Although they lack general management responsibilities, they play a very important strategic role.

7. Formal strategic planning models stress that an organization's strategy is the outcome of a rational planning process.

8. The major components of the strategic management process are defining the mission, vision, and major goals of the organization; analyzing the external and internal environments of the organization; choosing a business model and strategies that align an organization's strengths and weaknesses with external environmental opportunities and threats; and adopting organizational structures and control systems to implement the organization's chosen strategies.

9. Strategy can emerge from deep within an organization in the absence of formal plans as lower-level managers respond to unpredicted situations.

10. Strategic planning often fails because executives do not plan for uncertainty and because ivory tower planners lose touch with operating realities.

11. The fit approach to strategic planning has been criticized for focusing too much on the degree of fit between existing resources and current opportunities, and not enough on building new resources and capabilities to create and exploit future opportunities.

12. Strategic intent refers to an obsession with achieving an objective that stretches the company and requires it to build new resources and capabilities.

13. In spite of systematic planning, companies may adopt poor strategies if their decision-making processes are vulnerable to groupthink and if individual cognitive biases are allowed to intrude into the decision-making process.

14. Devil's advocacy, dialectic inquiry, and the outside view are techniques for enhancing the effectiveness of strategic decision making.

15. Good leaders of the strategy-making process have a number of key attributes: vision, eloquence, and consistency; ability to craft a business model; commitment; being well informed; a willingness to delegate and empower; political astuteness; and emotional intelligence.

Discussion Questions

1. What do we mean by *strategy*? How is a business model different from a strategy?
2. What do you think are the sources of sustained superior profitability?
3. Between 1997 and 2004 Microsoft's ROIC fell from 32 percent to 17.5 percent. Over the same period, Microsoft's profits grew from $3.45 billion to $11.33 billion. How can a company have declining profitability (as measured by ROIC) but growing profits? What do you think explains this situation at Microsoft? For 2004, analysts predicted that Microsoft's ROIC would jump to 35 percent. Why do you think this was the case? Was it due to any change in the company's strategy?
4. What are the strengths of formal strategic planning? What are its weaknesses?
5. Discuss the accuracy of this statement: Formal strategic planning systems are irrelevant for firms competing in high-technology industries where the pace of change is so rapid that plans are routinely made obsolete by unforeseen events.
6. Pick the current or a past president of the United States and evaluate his performance against the leadership characteristics discussed in the text. On the basis of this comparison, do you think that the president was/is a good strategic leader? Why?

Practicing Strategic Management

■ SMALL-GROUP EXERCISE
Designing a Planning System

Break up into groups of three to five people each, and discuss the following scenario. Appoint one group member as a spokesperson for the group, who will communicate your findings to the class when called on to do so by the instructor.

You are a group of senior managers working for a fast-growing computer software company. Your product allows users to play interactive role-playing games over the Internet. In the past three years, your company has gone from being a start-up enterprise with 10 employees and no revenues to a company with 250 employees and revenues of $60 million. It has been growing so rapidly that you have not had time to create a strategic plan, but now your board of directors is telling you that they want to see a plan, and they want it to drive decision making and resource allocation at the company. They want you to design a planning process that will have the following attributes:

1. It will be democratic, involving as many key employees as possible in the process.
2. It will help to build a sense of shared vision within the company about how to continue to grow rapidly.
3. It will lead to the generation of three to five key strategies for the company.
4. It will drive the formulation of detailed action plans, and these plans will be subsequently linked to the company's annual operating budget.

Design a planning process to present to your board of directors. Think carefully about who should be included in this process. Be sure to outline the strengths and weaknesses of the approach you choose, and be prepared to justify why your approach might be superior to alternative approaches.

■ ARTICLE FILE 1

At the end of every chapter in this book is an article file task. The task requires you to search newspapers or magazines in the library for an example of a real company that satisfies the task question or issue.

Your first article file task is to find an example of a company that has recently changed its strategy. Identify whether this change was the outcome of a formal planning process or whether it was an emergent response to unforeseen events occurring in the company's environment.

■ STRATEGIC MANAGEMENT PROJECT
Module 1

To give you practical insight into the strategic management process, we provide a series of strategic modules; one is at the end of every chapter in this book. Each module asks you to collect and analyze information relating to the material discussed in that chapter. By completing these strategic modules, you will gain a clearer idea of the overall strategic management process.

The first step in this project is to pick a company to study. We recommend that you focus on the same company throughout the book. Remember also that we will be asking you for information about the corporate and international strategy of your company, as well as its structure. We strongly recommend that you pick a company for which such information is likely to be available.

There are two approaches that can be used to select a company to study, and your instructor will tell you which one to follow. The first approach is to pick a well-known company that has a lot of information written about it. For example, large publicly held companies such as IBM, Microsoft, and Southwest Airlines are routinely covered in the business and financial press. By going to the library at your university, you should be able to track down a great deal of information on such companies. Many libraries now have comprehensive Web-based electronic data search facilities such as *ABI/ Inform*, the *Wall Street Journal Index*, the *F&S Index*, and the *Nexis-Lexis* databases. These enable you to identify any article that has been written in the business press on the company of your choice within the past few years. A number of nonelectronic data sources are also available and useful. For example, *F&S Predicasts* publishes an annual list of articles relating to major companies that appeared in the national and international business press. *S&P Industry Surveys* is also a great source for basic industry data, and *Value Line Ratings and Reports* contains good summaries of a firm's financial position and future prospects. Collect full financial information on the company that you pick. This can be accessed from Web-based electronic databases such as the Edgar database, which archives all forms that publicly quoted companies have to file with the Securities and Exchange Commission (SEC); for example, 10-K filings can be accessed from the SEC's Edgar database. Most SEC forms for public companies can now be accessed from Internet-based financial sites, such as Yahoo!'s finance site (**www.finance.yahoo.com/**).

A second approach is to pick a smaller company in your city or town to study. Although small companies are not routinely covered in the national business press, they may be covered in the local press. More important, this approach can work well if the management of the company will agree to talk to you at length about the strategy and structure of the company. If you happen to know somebody in such a company or if you have worked there at

some point, this approach can be very worthwhile. However, we *do not* recommend this approach unless you can get a *substantial* amount of guaranteed access to the company of your choice. If in doubt, ask your instructor before making a decision. The key issue is to make sure that you have access to enough interesting information to complete a detailed and comprehensive analysis.

Your assignment for Module 1 is to choose a company to study and to obtain enough information about it to carry out the following instructions and answer the questions:

1. Give a short account of the history of the company, and trace the evolution of its strategy. Try to determine whether the strategic evolution of your company is the product of intended strategies, emergent strategies, or some combination of the two.
2. Identify the mission and major goals of the company.
3. Do a preliminary analysis of the internal strengths and weaknesses of the company and the opportunities and threats that it faces in its environment. On the basis of this analysis, identify the strategies that you think the company should pursue. (You will need to perform a much more detailed analysis later in the book.)
4. Who is the CEO of the company? Evaluate the CEO's leadership capabilities.

■ EXPLORING THE WEB
Visiting 3M

Go to the website of 3M (**www.3m.com**) and visit the section that describes its history (**www.3m.com/profile/looking/index.jhtml**). Using the information contained there, map out the evolution of strategy at 3M from its establishment to the present day. To what degree do you think that this evolution was the result of detailed long-term strategic planning, and to what degree was it the result of unplanned actions taken in response to unpredictable circumstances?

General Task   Search the Web for a company site with sufficient information to map out the evolution of that company's strategy over a significant period of time. What drove this evolution? To what degree was it the result of detailed long-term strategic planning, and to what degree the result of unplanned actions taken in response to unpredictable circumstances?

Closing Case

Shattered Dreams: Level 3 Communications

In 1996 Jim Crowe sold MFS Communications, the local exchange telecommunications company that he had built up from scratch, to WorldCom for $14.3 billion. As part of that sale, WorldCom got MFS's UUNet, which at the time was the owner of the largest fiber-optic network in the nation. The business at UUNet was booming, primarily because of explosive growth in the Internet and a surge in the volume of digital data that was pumped through UUNet's fiber-optic pipes. As for Jim Crowe, at over $150 million his take from the sale of MFS elevated him to the ranks of the superrich. He had no reason to ever work again, but Jim Crowe was not the kind of man to sit back and relax. He wanted back in the game. Like many others at the time, he was convinced that the growth of the Internet was the mother of all business opportunities.

In 1997, Crowe's belief seemed to get validation when UUNet's chief scientist, Michael O'Dell, stated that Internet traffic was doubling every hundred days. This implied a growth rate of over 1,000 percent a year. O'Dell went on to say that there was not enough fiber-optic capacity to go around and that "demand will far outstrip supply for the foreseeable future." Electrified by the potential opportunity, Crowe quickly established a company to build a state-of-the-art fiber-optic network. Called Level 3 Communications, the company was funded by a number of wealthy investors, including Crowe and Walter Scott Jr., an Omaha-based construction billionaire, Crowe's former boss, and a close friend of the legendary investor Warren Buffet. Scott himself had been dazzled by a talk given by Microsoft's Bill Gates in 1995 in which Gates stated that "the Internet was going to radically change the world." Moreover, Scott had funded the establishment of MFS Communications, which started off its life as a subsidiary of Scott's construction company. Not surprisingly, Scott saw Crowe as a strategic visionary.

With Crowe as CEO and Scott as chairman, Level 3 quickly raised $3 billion. In 1998 the company went public and immediately started building its fiber-optic network. By 2001, Level 3 had raised some $13 billion, much of it in the form of debt. Crowe had a very clear strategic plan. The goal was to raise money, rapidly build a high-capacity fiber-optic network that linked major cities in the United States, and then cut prices to attract demand from major users of fiber-optic networks, including corporations, Internet service providers like AOL, and traditional telecommunications companies. Crowe believed that demand for his network would be highly price elastic: a 1 percent cut in price would increase demand significantly more than 1 percent. He argued that if he cut prices, revenues would surge, quickly using the massive capacity that Level 3 was putting in the ground. Crowe was also a big advocate of strategic focus, believing that Level 3 should concentrate exclusively on carrying Internet traffic for service providers and corporations. The business model was straightforward: Since most of the costs of the business were fixed (the costs of building out the network), profitability would be highly leveraged to volume. Once the fixed costs were covered, it would be like printing money.

Level 3 was not alone. Around the same time there was a rush of companies entering the business or expanding their networks, including 360 Networks, Global Crossing, Qwest Communications, WorldCom, Williams Communications Group, Genuity Inc., and XO Communications. In all cases, the strategic plans were remarkably similar: raise the money, build the networks, cut prices, and they will come. Surging demand would soon catch up with capacity, resulting in a profit bonanza for those who had the foresight to build out their networks. It was a gold rush, and the first into the field would stake the best claims.

However, there were dissenting voices. As early as October 1998 an Internet researcher at AT&T Labs named Andrew Odlyzko published a paper that debunked the assertion that demand for Internet traffic was growing at 1,000 percent a year. Odlyzko's careful analysis came to the conclusion that growth was much slower, only 100 percent a year. While still large, that growth rate was not nearly large enough to fill the massive flood of fiber-optic capacity that was entering the market. Moreover, Odlyzko noted that new technologies were increasing the amount of data that could be sent down existing fibers, reducing the need for new fiber. But with investment money flooding into the market, few paid any attention to him. UUNet was still using the 1,000 percent figure as late as September 2000.

As it turned out, Odlyzko was right. Capacity rapidly outstripped demand, and by late 2002 less than 3 percent of the fiber that had been laid in the ground was actually being used. While prices tumbled, the surge in volume that Crowe had bet on did not materialize. Unable to service the debt they had taken on to build out their networks, company after company tumbled into bankruptcy, including WorldCom, 360 Networks, XO Communications, and Global Crossing. Level 3's stock fell by more than 95 percent, but the company avoided bankruptcy because of an infusion of $500 million in cash from a group of investors led by Warren Buffet and some quick-footed work by Jim Crowe.

Crowe's strategic shift involved the purchase of two software distribution companies, Software Spectrum and Corporate Software, that specialized in selling, installing, and maintaining software made by companies such as Microsoft on the PCs and servers of some nine thousand corporate clients. The logic underlying the acquisitions was that Level 3 could ultimately use its fiber-optic network to distribute and maintain the software, as opposed to doing that manually, thereby reducing costs. While neither business was profitable, Crowe was able to use the acquisitions to convince investors that Level 3 still had a viable long-term strategic vision. At the same time, with the balance sheet strengthened by a cash infusion, Level 3 purchased a bankrupt competitor, Genuity, for under $300 million, helping to consolidate the industry and acquiring Genuity's customers. Finally, in early 2004 Level 3 announced that it would use its network to offer Voice over Internet Protocol services to consumers and corporations (voice telephone calls over the Internet, as opposed to over a traditional telecommunications network), thereby taking aim at the market currently dominated by traditional wire line telephone companies.

While none of these strategic moves guarantees the survival of Level 3, the trends are encouraging. Revenues expanded to $4 billion in 2003, up from $1.53 billion in 2002, while losses fell from $4.4 billion in 2002 to $721 million in 2003. Half of 2003 revenues came from the software distribution business. Crowe still believes that ultimately his original vision will be vindicated but that the current industry structure is unsustainable and there are still too many suppliers in the marketplace. Andrew Odlyzko, who debunked the original estimates of Internet growth, believes that the excess capacity situation in the industry will not be resolved until the end of the current decade.[52]

Case Discussion Questions

1. What was the planned strategy of Level 3 Communications in the late 1990s?

2. Why was Level 3 Communications able to raise so much capital?

3. Was that strategy unrealized, or is it still part of the intended strategy of the firm?

4. What have been the emergent strategies of Level 3 over the last few years? How do these emergent strategies fit with Level 3's original plans?

5. Were any cognitive biases at work at Level 3, other communications companies, and the investment community during 1997–2001? What were those biases? What were the effects of those biases? How might an entrepreneur like Jim Crowe have avoided them?

Appendix to Chapter 1

Enterprise Valuation, ROIC, and Growth

The ultimate goal of strategy is to maximize the value of a company to its shareholders (subject to the important constraints that this is done in a legal, ethical, and socially responsible manner). The two main drivers of enterprise valuation are return on invested capital (**ROIC**) and the growth rate of profits, g.[53]

ROIC is defined as net operating profits less adjusted taxes (NOPLAT) over the invested capital of the enterprise (IC), where IC is the sum of the company's equity and debt (the method for calculating adjusted taxes need not concern us here). That is:

$$ROIC = NOPLAT/IC$$

Where

$$\begin{aligned}NOPLAT = \ &revenues - cost\ of\ goods\ sold \\ &- operating\ expenses \\ &- depreciation\ charges \\ &- adjusted\ taxes\end{aligned}$$

$$IC = value\ of\ shareholders'\ equity + value\ of\ debt$$

The growth rate of profits, g, can be defined as the percentage increase in net operating profits (NOPLAT) over a given time period. More precisely:

$$g = [(NOPLAT_{t+1} - NOPLAT_t)/NOPLAT_t] \times 100$$

Note that if NOPLAT is increasing over time, earnings per share will also increase so long as (a) the number of shares stays constant, or (b) the number of shares outstanding increases more slowly than NOPLAT.

The valuation of a company can be calculated using discounted cash flow analysis and applying it to future expected free cash flows (free cash flow in a period is defined as NOPLAT − net investments).

It can be shown that the valuation of a company so calculated is related to the company's weighted average cost of capital (WACC), which is the cost of the equity and debt that the firm uses to finance its business, and the company's ROIC. Specifically:

If ROIC > WACC, the company is earning more than its cost of capital and it is creating value.

If ROIC = WACC, the company is earning its cost of capital and its valuation will be stable.

If ROIC < WACC, the company is earning less than its cost of capital and it is therefore destroying value.

A company that earns more than its cost of capital is even more valuable if it can grow its net operating profits less adjusted taxes (NOPLAT) over time. Conversely, a firm that is not earning its cost of capital destroys value if it grows its NOPLAT. This critical relationship between ROIC, g, and value is shown in Table A1.

In Table A1, the figures in the cells of the matrix represent the discounted present values of future free cash flows for a company that has a starting NOPLAT of $100, invested capital of $1,000, a cost of capital of 10 percent, and a 25-year time horizon after which ROIC = cost of capital.

The important points revealed by this exercise are as follows:

1. A company with an already high ROIC can create more value by increasing its profit growth rate rather than pushing for an even higher ROIC. Thus a company with an ROIC of 15 percent and a 3 percent growth rate can create more value by increasing its profit growth rate from 3 percent to 9 percent than it can by increasing ROIC to 20 percent.

TABLE A1
ROIC, Growth, and Valuation

NOPLAT Growth, g	ROIC 7.5%	ROIC 10.0%	ROIC 12.5%	ROIC 15%	ROIC 20%
3%	887	1,000	1,058	1,113	1,170
6%	708	1,000	1,117	1,295	1,442
9%	410	1,000	1,354	1,591	1,886

2. A company with a low ROIC destroys value if it grows. Thus, if ROIC = 7.5 percent, a 9 percent growth rate for 25 years will produce less value than a 3 percent growth rate. This is because unprofitable growth requires capital investments, the cost of which cannot be covered. Unprofitable growth destroys value.

3. The best of both worlds is high ROIC and high growth.

Very few companies are able to maintain an ROIC > WACC and grow NOPLAT over time, but there are some notable examples, including Dell, Microsoft, and Wal-Mart. Because these companies have generally been able to fund their capital investment needs from internally generated cash flows, they have not had to issue more shares to raise capital. Thus growth in NOPLAT has translated directly into higher earnings per share for these companies, making their shares more attractive to investors and leading to substantial share price appreciation. By successfully pursuing strategies that result in a high ROIC and growing NOPLAT, these firms have maximized shareholder value.

Chapter 2

External Analysis: The Identification of Opportunities and Threats

Opening Case

Why Is the Pharmaceutical Industry So Profitable?

The pharmaceutical industry is highly profitable. Between 2000 and 2003 the average rate of return on invested capital for firms in the industry was 22.6 percent. Put differently, for every dollar of capital invested in the industry, the average pharmaceutical firm generated 22.6 cents of profit. This compares with an average return on invested capital of 15.9 percent for firms in the software industry, 11.9 percent for publishing firms, 11.2 percent for retail firms, 6.6 percent for steel firms, and 1.8 percent for firms in the air transportation industry.

The high profitability of the pharmaceutical industry can be best understood by looking at several aspects of its underlying economic structure. First, demand for pharmaceuticals is strong and has been growing steadily for decades. Between 1990 and 2003 there was a 12.5 percent annual increase in spending on prescription drugs in the United States. This strong growth was driven by favorable demographics. As people grow older, they tend to need and consume more prescription medicines, and the population in most advanced nations has been growing older as the post–World War II babyboom generation ages.

Second, successful new prescription drugs can be extraordinarily profitable. Lipitor, the cholesterol-lowering drug sold by Pfizer, was introduced in 1997, and by 2003 this drug had generated a staggering $9.23 billion in annual sales for Pfizer. The costs of manufacturing, packing, and distributing Lipitor amounted to only about 10 percent of revenues, or under $1 billion. Pfizer spent close to $400 million on promoting Lipitor and perhaps as much again on maintaining a sales force to sell the product. That still left Pfizer with a gross profit of perhaps $7 billion. Since the drug is protected from direct competition by a twenty-year patent, Pfizer has a temporary monopoly and can charge a high price. Once the patent expires, other firms will be able to produce "generic" versions of Lipitor, and the price will fall—typically by 80 percent within a year—but that is some way off.

Competing firms can produce drugs that are similar (but not identical) to a patent-protected drug. Drug firms patent a specific molecule, and competing firms can patent similar, but not identical, molecules that have a similar pharmacological effect. Thus Lipitor does have competitors in the market for cholesterol-lowering drugs, such as Zocor sold by Merck and Crestor sold by AstraZeneca. But these competing drugs are also patent protected. Moreover, the high costs and risks associated with developing a new drug and bringing it to market constitute a formidable barrier to entry, limiting competition. Out of every five thousand compounds tested in the laboratory by a drug company, only five enter clinical trials, and only one of these will ultimately make it to the market. On average, estimates suggest that it costs some $800 million and takes anywhere from ten to fifteen years to bring a new drug to market. Once on the market, only three out of ten drugs ever recoup their R&D and marketing costs and turn a profit. Thus the high profitability of the pharmaceutical industry rests on a handful of blockbuster drugs. To produce a blockbuster, a drug company must spend large amounts of money on research, most of which fails to produce a product. Only very large companies can shoulder the costs and risks of doing this, and it is very difficult for new companies to enter the industry. Pfizer, for example, spent some $7.13 billion on R&D in 2003 alone, equivalent to almost 18 percent of its total revenues. In a testament to just how difficult it is to get into the industry, although a large number of companies have been started in the last twenty years in the hope that they might develop new pharmaceuticals, only one of these companies, Amgen, was ranked among the top twenty in the industry in terms of sales in 2003. Most have failed to bring a product to market.

In addition to R&D spending, the incumbent firms in the pharmaceutical industry spend large amounts of money on advertising and sales promotion. While the $400 million a year that Pfizer spends promoting Lipitor is small relative to the drug's revenues, it is a large amount for a new competitor to match, making market entry very difficult unless the competitor has a significantly better product. Thus promotional spending constitutes another formidable barrier to entry.

In sum, patent protection that grants a temporary monopoly to some firms, high R&D costs, significant risk of failure, and high marketing costs make it very difficult for new firms to enter the pharmaceutical market. The industry tends to be dominated by large established enterprises that have the scale required to bear the considerable costs and risks associated with developing new drugs and can afford to spend large amounts of money to promote those drugs in the marketplace.

Furthermore, there are some big opportunities on the horizon for firms in the industry. New scientific breakthroughs in genomics are holding out the promise that within the next decade pharmaceutical firms might be able to bring new drugs to market that treat some of the most intractable medical conditions, including Alzheimer's, Parkinson's disease, cancer, heart disease, stroke, and AIDS. But there are also some threats to the long-term dominance and profitability of industry giants like Pfizer. Most notably, as spending on health care rises, politicians are looking for ways to limit health care costs, and one possibility is some form of price control on prescription drugs. Price controls are already in effect in most developed nations, and although they have not yet been introduced in the United States, they could be.[1]

Overview   Strategy formulation begins with an analysis of the forces that shape competition in the industry in which a company is based. The goal is to understand the opportunities and threats confronting the firm and to use this understanding to identify strategies that will enable the company to outperform its rivals. **Opportunities** arise when a company can take advantage of conditions in its environment to formulate and implement strategies that enable it to become more profitable. For example, as noted in the *Opening Case*, as scientific understanding of the underlying causes of Alzheimer's advances, pharmaceutical companies have an opportunity to make enormous profits by developing patented medicines that can treat this debilitating condition. **Threats** arise when conditions in the external environment endanger the integrity and profitability of the company's business. One such threat in the pharmaceutical industry is price controls, which, if imposed, will reduce the ability of pharmaceutical firms to charge high prices and earn high profits. Another threat many pharmaceutical firms face is patent expiration and generic competition. When the patent on Eli Lilly's blockbuster antidepressant Prozac expired in 2001, the company was quickly faced by generic competitors and sales of Prozac fell from $2.6 billion in 2000 to $645 million in 2003.

This chapter begins with an analysis of the industry environment. First, it examines concepts and tools for analyzing the competitive structure of an industry and identifying industry opportunities and threats. Second, it analyzes the competitive implications that arise when groups of companies *within* an industry pursue similar and different kinds of competitive strategies. Third, it explores the way an industry evolves over time and the accompanying changes in competitive conditions. Fourth, it looks at the way in which forces in the macroenvironment affect industry structure and influence opportunities and threats. By the end of the chapter, you will understand that to succeed, a company must either fit its strategy to the external environment in which it operates or be able to reshape the environment to its advantage through its chosen strategy.

Defining an Industry

An **industry** can be defined as a group of companies offering products or services that are close substitutes for each other—that is, products or services that satisfy the same basic customer needs. A company's closest **competitors,** its rivals, are those that serve the same basic customer needs. For example, carbonated drinks, fruit punches, and bottled water can be viewed as close substitutes for each other because they serve the same basic customer needs for refreshing and cold nonalcoholic beverages. Thus, we can talk about the soft drink industry, whose major players are Coca-Cola, PepsiCo, and Cadbury Schweppes. Similarly, desktop computers and notebook computers satisfy the same basic need that customers have for computer hardware on which to run personal productivity software, browse the Internet, send e-mail, play games, and store, display, and manipulate digital images. Thus, we can talk about the personal computer industry, whose major players are Dell, Hewlett-Packard, Lenovo (the Chinese company which purchased IBM's personal computer business), Gateway, and Apple Computer.

The starting point of external analysis is to identify the industry that a company competes in. To do this, managers must begin by looking at the basic customer needs their company is serving—that is, they must take a customer-oriented view of their business as opposed to a product-oriented view (see Chapter 1). An industry is the *supply side* of a market, and companies in the industry are the suppliers. Customers are the *demand side* of a market and are the buyers of the industry's products. *The basic customer needs that are served by a market define an industry's boundary.* It is very important for managers to realize this, for if they define industry boundaries incorrectly, they may be caught flat-footed by the rise of competitors that serve the same basic customer needs with different product offerings. For example, Coca-Cola long saw itself as being in the soda industry—meaning carbonated soft drinks—whereas in fact it was in the soft drink industry, which includes noncarbonated soft drinks. In the mid-1990s, Coca-Cola was caught by surprise by the rise of customer demand for bottled water and fruit drinks, which began to cut into the demand for sodas. Coca-Cola moved quickly to respond to these threats, introducing its own brand of water, Dasani, and acquiring orange juice maker Minute Maid. By defining its industry boundaries too narrowly, Coke almost missed the rapid rise of the noncarbonated soft drinks segment of the soft drinks market.

■ Industry and Sector

An important distinction that needs to be made is between an *industry* and a **sector.** A **sector** is a group of closely related industries. For example, as illustrated in Figure 2.1, the computer sector comprises several related industries: the computer component industries (for example, the disk drive industry, the semiconductor industry, and the modem industry), the computer hardware industries (for example, the personal computer industry, the hand-held computer industry, and the mainframe computer industry), and the computer software industry. Industries within a sector may be involved with each other in many different ways. Companies in the computer component industries are the *suppliers* of firms in the computer hardware industries. Companies in the computer software industry provide important *complements* to computer hardware: the software programs that customers purchase to run on their hardware. And companies in the personal, hand-held, and mainframe industries are in indirect *competition* with each other because all provide products that are to a degree *substitutes* for each other.

■ Industry and Market Segments

It is also important to recognize the difference between an *industry* and the *market segments* within that industry. **Market segments** are distinct groups of customers within a market that can be differentiated from each other on the basis of their distinct attributes and specific demands. In the soft drink industry, for example, although all customers demand refreshing and cold nonalcoholic beverages, there is a group within this market who in addition demand (need) sodas that do not contain caffeine. Coca-Cola has recognized the existence of this caffeine-free market segment and sought to satisfy the needs of customers within it by producing and marketing noncaffeinated colas. Similarly, in the personal computer industry, there are different segments where customers desire desktop machines, lightweight portable machines, and servers that sit at the center of a network of personal computers (see Figure 2.1). Personal computer makers recognize the existence of these different segments by producing a range of product offerings that appeal to customers in different segments. Customers in all of these different segments, however, share a common need for PCs on which to run personal software applications.

FIGURE 2.1

The Computer Sector: Industries and Segments

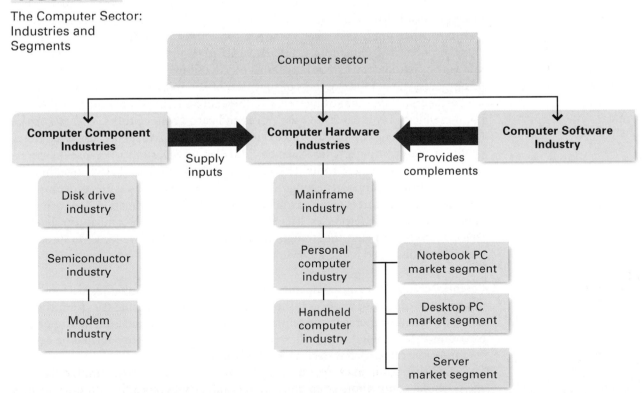

■ **Changing Industry Boundaries**

Industry boundaries may change over time as customer needs evolve or new technologies emerge that enable companies in hitherto unrelated industries to satisfy established customer needs in new ways. We have noted that during the 1990s, as consumers of soft drinks began to develop a taste for bottled water and noncarbonated fruit-based drinks, Coca-Cola found itself in direct competition with the manufacturers of bottled water and fruit-based soft drinks: all were in the same industry.

For an example of how technological change can alter industry boundaries, consider the convergence that is currently taking place between the computer and telecommunications industries. Historically, the telecommunications equipment industry has been considered a distinct entity from the computer hardware industry. However, as telecommunications equipment has moved from traditional analog technology to digital technology, so telecommunications equipment has increasingly come to resemble computers. The result is that the boundaries between these different industries are blurring. A digital wireless phone, for example, is nothing more than a small hand-held computer with a wireless connection, and small hand-held computers often now come with wireless capabilities, transforming them into phones. Thus, Nokia and Motorola, which manufacture wireless phones, are now finding themselves competing directly with Palm, which manufactures hand-held computers.

Industry competitive analysis begins by focusing on the overall industry in which a firm competes before market segments or sector-level issues are considered. Tools that managers can use to perform such industry analysis are discussed in the following sections: Porter's five forces model, strategic group analysis, and industry life cycle analysis.

Porter's Five Forces Model

Once the boundaries of an industry have been identified, the task facing managers is to analyze competitive forces in the industry environment to identify opportunities and threats. Michael E. Porter's well-known framework, known as the five forces model, helps managers with this analysis.[2] His model, shown in Figure 2.2, focuses on five forces that shape competition within an industry: (1) the risk of entry by potential competitors, (2) the intensity of rivalry among established companies within an industry, (3) the bargaining power of buyers, (4) the bargaining power of suppliers, and (5) the closeness of substitutes to an industry's products.

Porter argues that the stronger each of these forces is, the more limited is the ability of established companies to raise prices and earn greater profits. Within Porter's framework, a *strong* competitive force can be regarded as a *threat* because it depresses profits. A *weak* competitive force can be viewed as an *opportunity* because it allows a company to earn greater profits. The strength of the five forces may change through time as industry conditions change. The task facing managers is to recognize how changes in the five forces give rise to new opportunities and threats and to formulate appropriate strategic responses. In addition, it is possible for a company, *through its choice of strategy,* to alter the strength of one or more of the five forces to its advantage. This is discussed in the following chapters.

■ **Risk of Entry by Potential Competitors**

Potential competitors are companies that are not currently competing in an industry but have the capability to do so if they choose. For example, cable television companies have recently emerged as potential competitors to traditional phone companies. New digital technologies have allowed cable companies to offer telephone service over the same cables that transmit television shows.

Established companies already operating in an industry often attempt to discourage potential competitors from entering the industry because the more companies

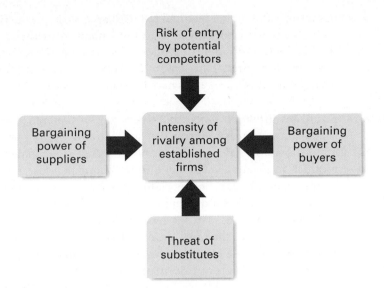

that enter, the more difficult it becomes for established companies to protect their share of the market and generate profits. A high risk of entry by potential competitors represents a threat to the profitability of established companies. But if the risk of new entry is low, established companies can take advantage of this opportunity to raise prices and earn greater returns.

The risk of entry by potential competitors is a function of the height of **barriers to entry,** that is, factors that make it costly for companies to enter an industry. The greater the costs that potential competitors must bear to enter an industry, the greater are the barriers to entry and the *weaker* this competitive force. High entry barriers may keep potential competitors out of an industry even when industry profits are high. Important barriers to entry include economies of scale, brand loyalty, absolute cost advantages, customer switching costs, and government regulation.[3] An important strategy is building barriers to entry (in the case of incumbent firms) or finding ways to circumvent those barriers (in the case of new entrants). We shall discuss this topic in more detail in subsequent chapters.

■ **Economies
of Scale**

Economies of scale arise when unit costs fall as a firm expands its output. Sources of scale economies include (1) cost reductions gained through mass-producing a standardized output, (2) discounts on bulk purchases of raw material inputs and component parts, (3) the advantages gained by spreading fixed production costs over a large production volume, and (4) the cost savings associated with spreading marketing and advertising costs over a large volume of output. If these cost advantages are significant, a new company that enters the industry and produces on a small scale suffers a significant cost disadvantage relative to established companies. If the new company decides to enter on a large scale in an attempt to obtain these economies of scale, it has to raise the capital required to build large-scale production facilities and bear the high risks associated with such an investment. A further risk of large-scale entry is that the increased supply of products will depress prices and result in vigorous retaliation by established companies. For these reasons, the threat of entry is reduced when established companies have economies of scale.

■ Brand Loyalty

Brand loyalty exists when consumers have a preference for the products of established companies. A company can create brand loyalty through continuous advertising of its brand-name products and company name, patent protection of products, product innovation achieved through company research and development programs, an emphasis on high product quality, and good after-sales service. Significant brand loyalty makes it difficult for new entrants to take market share away from established companies. Thus it reduces the threat of entry by potential competitors since they may see the task of breaking down well-established customer preferences as too costly. In the market for colas, for example, consumers have a strong preference for the products of Coca-Cola and PepsiCo, which makes it difficult for other enterprises to enter this market (nevertheless, the Cott Corporation has succeeded in entering the soft drink market: see Strategy in Action 2.1).

■ Absolute Cost Advantages

Sometimes established companies have an **absolute cost advantage** relative to potential entrants, meaning that entrants cannot expect to match the established companies' lower cost structure. Absolute cost advantages arise from three main sources: (1) superior production operations and processes due to accumulated experience, patents, or secret processes; (2) control of particular inputs required for production, such as labor, materials, equipment, or management skills, that are limited in their supply; and (3) access to cheaper funds because existing companies represent lower risks than new entrants. If established companies have an absolute cost advantage, the threat of entry as a competitive force is weaker.

■ Customer Switching Costs

Switching costs arise when it costs a customer time, energy, and money to switch from the products offered by one established company to the products offered by a new entrant. When switching costs are high, customers can be *locked in* to the product offerings of established companies, even if new entrants offer better products.[4] A familiar example of switching costs concerns the costs associated with switching from one computer operating system to another. If a person currently uses Microsoft's Windows operating system and has a library of related software applications (for example, word-processing software, spreadsheet, games) and document files, it is expensive for that person to switch to another computer operating system. To effect the change, this person would have to buy a new set of software applications and convert all existing document files to run with the new system. Faced with such an expense of money and time, most people are unwilling to make the switch *unless* the competing operating system offers a *substantial* leap forward in performance. Thus, the higher the switching costs are, the higher is the barrier to entry for a company attempting to promote a new computer operating system.

■ Government Regulation

Historically, government regulation has constituted a major entry barrier into many industries. For example, until the mid-1990s, U.S. government regulation prohibited providers of long-distance telephone service from competing for local telephone service and vice versa. Other potential providers of telephone service, including cable television service companies such as Time Warner and Comcast (which could in theory

Strategy in Action

2.1

Circumventing Entry Barriers into the Soft Drink Industry

The soft drink industry has long been dominated by two companies, Coca-Cola and PepsiCo. By spending large sums of money on advertising and promotion, both companies have created significant brand loyalty and made it very difficult for new competitors to enter the industry and take market share away from these two giants. When new competitors do try to enter, both companies have responded by cutting prices and thus forcing the new entrant to curtail expansion plans.

However, in the early 1990s the Cott Corporation, then a small Canadian bottling company, worked out a strategy for entering the soft drink market. Cott's strategy was deceptively simple. The company initially focused on the cola segment of the soft drink market. Cott signed a deal with Royal Crown Cola for exclusive global rights to its cola concentrate. RC Cola was a small player in the U.S. cola market. Its products were recognized as having a high quality, but RC Cola had never been able to effectively challenge Coke or Pepsi. Next, Cott signed a deal with a Canadian grocery retailer, Loblaw, to provide the retailer with its own private-label brand of cola. Priced low, the Loblaw private-label brand, known as President's Choice, was very successful and took share from both Coke and Pepsi.

Emboldened by this success, Cott decided to try to convince other retailers to carry private-label cola. To retailers, the value proposition was simple because, unlike its major rivals, Cott spent almost nothing on advertising and promotion. This constituted a major source of cost savings, which Cott passed on to retailers in the form of lower prices. For their part, the retailers found that they could significantly undercut the price of Coke and Pepsi colas and still make better profit margins on private-label brands than on branded colas.

Despite this compelling value proposition, few retailers were willing to sell private-label colas for fear of alienating Coca-Cola and Pepsi, whose products were a major draw of grocery store traffic. Cott's breakthrough came in 1992 when it signed a deal with Wal-Mart to supply the retailing giant with a private-label cola, called "Sam's Choice" (named after Wal-Mart founder Sam Walton). Wal-Mart proved to be the perfect distribution channel for Cott. The retailer was just starting to get into the grocery business, and consumers went to Wal-Mart not to buy branded merchandise but to get low prices.

As Wal-Mart's grocery business grew, so did Cott's sales. Cott soon added other flavors to its offering, such as lemon lime soda, which would compete with Seven Up and Sprite. Moreover, pressured by Wal-Mart, by the late 1990s other U.S. grocers had also started to introduce private-label sodas, often turning to Cott to supply their needs.

By 2003, Cott had grown to become a $1.4 billion company. Its 2003 volume growth in an otherwise stagnant U.S. market for sodas was 12.6 percent. Private-label companies, of which Cott was by far the largest, captured 7.9 percent of the U.S. soda market in 2003, up from almost nothing a decade earlier. The losers in this process were Coca-Cola and PepsiCo, who were now facing the steady erosion of their brand loyalty and market share as consumers increasingly came to recognize the high quality and low price of private-label sodas.[a]

use their cables to carry telephone traffic as well as TV signals), were prohibited from entering the market altogether. These regulatory barriers to entry significantly reduced the level of competition in both the local and long-distance telephone markets, enabling telephone companies to earn higher profits than might otherwise have been the case. All this changed in 1996 when the government deregulated the industry significantly. In the months that followed this announcement, local, long-distance, and cable TV companies all announced their intention to enter each other's markets, and a host of new players entered the market. The five forces model predicts that falling entry barriers due to government deregulation will result in significant new entry, an increase in the intensity of industry competition, and lower industry profit rates, and indeed, that is what occurred.

In summary, if established companies have built brand loyalty for their products, have an absolute cost advantage with respect to potential competitors, have significant scale economies, are the beneficiaries of high switching costs, or enjoy regulatory protection, the risk of entry by potential competitors is greatly diminished; it is a weak competitive force. Consequently, established companies can charge higher prices, and industry profits are higher. Evidence from academic research suggests that the height of barriers to entry is one of the most important determinants of profit rates in an industry.[5] Clearly, it is in the interest of established companies to pursue strategies consistent with raising entry barriers to secure these profits. By the same token, potential new entrants have to find strategies that allow them to circumvent barriers to entry.

Even when entry barriers are very high, new firms may still enter an industry if they perceive that the benefits outweigh the substantial costs of entry. This is what appears to have occurred in the telecommunications industry following deregulation in 1996. Deregulation led to a flood of new entrants such as Level 3 Communications, 360networks, and Global Crossing, who built fiber-optic networks to serve what they perceived as explosive growth in the amount of Internet traffic. These entrants had to undertake billions of dollars in capital expenditure to build out their networks and match the scale advantages of established companies such as World-Com. However, the new entrants were able to raise the capital to do so from investors who shared management's euphoric vision of future demand in the industry (Level 3 alone raised $13 billion). As it turned out, the euphoric vision of demand growth was based on the erroneous assumption that Internet traffic was growing at 1,000 percent a year when in fact it was only growing at 100 percent a year. When the euphoric vision proved to be false, many of the new entrants went bankrupt, but not before their investments had created excess capacity in the industry and sparked intense price competition that depressed the returns for all players, new entrants and established companies alike (see the *Closing Case* to Chapter 1 for further details).

■ Rivalry Among Established Companies

The second of Porter's five competitive forces is the intensity of rivalry among established companies within an industry. **Rivalry** refers to the competitive struggle between companies in an industry to gain market share from each other. The competitive struggle can be fought using price, product design, advertising and promotion spending, direct selling efforts, and after-sales service and support. More intense rivalry implies lower prices or more spending on non-price-competitive weapons, or both. Because intense rivalry lowers prices and raises costs, it squeezes profits out of an industry. Thus, intense rivalry among established companies constitutes a strong threat to profitability. Alternatively, if rivalry is less intense, companies may have the opportunity to raise prices or reduce spending on non-price-competitive weapons, which leads to a higher level of industry profits. The intensity of rivalry among established companies within an industry is largely a function of four factors: (1) industry competitive structure, (2) demand conditions, (3) cost conditions, and (4) the height of exit barriers in the industry.

■ Industry Competitive Structure

The *competitive structure* of an industry refers to the number and size distribution of companies in it, something that strategic managers determine at the beginning of an industry analysis. Industry structures vary, and different structures have different implications for the intensity of rivalry. A **fragmented industry** consists of a large number of small or medium-sized companies, none of which is in a position to determine industry price. A **consolidated industry** is dominated by a small number of large companies (an **oligopoly**) or, in extreme cases, by just one company (a **monopoly**), and companies often are in a position to determine industry prices. Examples of fragmented industries are agriculture, dry cleaning, video rental, health clubs, real estate brokerage, and sun tanning parlors. Consolidated industries include the aerospace, soft drink, automobile, pharmaceutical, and stockbrokerage industries.

Many fragmented industries are characterized by low entry barriers and commodity-type products that are hard to differentiate. The combination of these traits tends to result in boom-and-bust cycles as industry profits rise and fall. Low entry barriers imply that whenever demand is strong and profits are high, new entrants will flood the market, hoping to profit from the boom. The explosion in the number of video stores, health clubs, and sun tanning parlors during the 1980s and 1990s exemplifies this situation.

Often the flood of new entrants into a booming fragmented industry creates excess capacity, so companies start to cut prices in order to use their spare capacity. The difficulty companies face when trying to differentiate their products from those of competitors can exacerbate this tendency. The result is a price war, which depresses industry profits, forces some companies out of business, and deters potential new entrants. For example, after a decade of expansion and booming profits, many health clubs are now finding that they have to offer large discounts in order to hold on to their membership. In general, the more commodity-like an industry's product is, the more vicious will be the price war. This bust part of the cycle continues until overall industry capacity is brought into line with demand (through bankruptcies), at which point prices may stabilize again.

A fragmented industry structure, then, constitutes a threat rather than an opportunity. Most booms are relatively short-lived because of the ease of new entry and will be followed by price wars and bankruptcies. Because it is often difficult to differentiate products in these industries, the best strategy for a company is to try to minimize its costs so it will be profitable in a boom and survive any subsequent bust. Alternatively, companies might try to adopt strategies that change the underlying structure of fragmented industries and lead to a consolidated industry structure in which the level of industry profitability is increased. Exactly how companies can do this is something we shall consider in later chapters.

In consolidated industries, companies are interdependent, because one company's competitive actions or moves (with regard to price, quality, and so on) directly affect the market share of its rivals, and thus their profitability. When one company makes a move, this generally "forces" a response from its rivals, and the consequence of such competitive interdependence can be a dangerous competitive spiral. Rivalry increases as companies attempt to undercut each other's prices or offer customers more value in their products, pushing industry profits down in the process. The fare wars that have periodically created havoc in the airline industry provide a good illustration of this process.

Companies in consolidated industries sometimes seek to reduce this threat by following the prices set by the dominant company in the industry.[6] However, companies must be careful, for explicit face-to-face price-fixing agreements are illegal. (Tacit, indirect agreements, arrived at without direct or intentional communication, are legal.) Instead, companies set prices by watching, interpreting, anticipating, and responding to each other's behavior (something discussed in detail in Chapter 5 when the competitive dynamics of game theory are examined). However, tacit price-leadership agreements often break down under adverse economic conditions, as has occurred in the breakfast cereal industry, profiled in Strategy in Action 2.2.

Strategy in Action   2.2

Price Wars in the Breakfast Cereal Industry

For decades, the breakfast cereal industry was one of the most profitable in the United States. The industry has a consolidated structure dominated by Kellogg, General Mills, and Kraft Foods with its Post brand. Strong brand loyalty, coupled with control over the allocation of supermarket shelf space, helped to limit the potential for new entry. Meanwhile, steady demand growth of around 3 percent per annum kept industry revenues expanding. For years, Kellogg, which accounted for over 40 percent of the market share, acted as the price leader in the industry. Every year Kellogg increased cereal prices, its rivals followed, and industry profits remained high.

This favorable industry structure started to change in the early 1990s when growth in demand slowed and then stagnated as a latte and bagel or muffin replaced cereal as the morning fare for many American adults. Then came the rise of powerful discounters such as Wal-Mart, which entered the grocery industry in the early 1990s and began to promote aggressively its own brand of cereal, priced significantly below the brand-name cereals. As the decade progressed, other grocery chains such as Kroger's started to follow suit, and brand loyalty in the industry began to decline as customers realized that a $2.50 bag of wheat flakes from Wal-Mart tasted about the same as a $3.50 box of Cornflakes from Kellogg. As sales of cheaper store-brand cereals began to take off, supermarkets, no longer as dependent on brand names to bring traffic into their stores, began to demand lower prices from the branded cereal manufacturers.

For several years, the manufacturers of brand cereals tried to hold out against these adverse trends, but in the mid-1990s the dam broke. In 1996, Kraft (then owned by Philip Morris) aggressively cut prices by 20 percent for its Post brand in an attempt to gain market share. Kellogg soon followed with a 19 percent price cut on two-thirds of its brands, and General Mills quickly did the same. The decades of tacit price collusion were officially over.

If the breakfast cereal companies were hoping that the price cuts would stimulate demand, they were wrong. Instead, demand remained flat while revenues and margins followed prices down and Kellogg's operating margins dropped from 18 percent in 1995 to 10.2 percent in 1996, a trend experienced by the other brand cereal manufacturers.

By 2000, conditions had only worsened. Private-label sales continued to make inroads, gaining over 10 percent of the market. Moreover, sales of breakfast cereals started to contract at 1 percent per annum. To cap it off, an aggressive General Mills continued to launch expensive price and promotion campaigns in an attempt to take share away from the market leader. Kellogg saw its market share slip to just over 30 percent in 2001, *behind* the 31 percent now held by General Mills. For the first time since 1906, Kellogg no longer led the market. Moreover, profits at all three major producers remained weak in the face of continued price discounting.

In mid-2001, General Mills finally blinked and raised prices a modest 2 percent in response to its own rising costs. Competitors followed, signaling perhaps that after a decade of costly price warfare, pricing discipline might once more emerge in the industry. Both Kellogg and General Mills tried to move further away from price competition by focusing on brand extensions, such as Special K containing berries and new varieties of Cheerios. Kellogg's efforts with Special K helped the company recapture market leadership from General Mills. More importantly, the renewed emphasis on nonprice competition halted years of damaging price warfare, at least for the time being.[b]

■ **Industry Demand**   The level of industry demand is a second determinant of the intensity of rivalry among established companies. Growing demand from new customers or additional purchases by existing customers tend to moderate competition by providing greater scope for companies to compete for customers. Growing demand tends to reduce rivalry because all companies can sell more without taking market share away from other companies. High industry profits are often the result. Conversely, declining demand results in more rivalry as companies fight to maintain market share and revenues (as in the breakfast cereal industry). Demand declines when customers are leaving the marketplace or each customer is buying less. Now a company can grow only by taking market share away from other companies. Thus, declining demand constitutes a major threat, for it increases the extent of rivalry between established companies.

■ **Cost Conditions**

The cost structure of firms in an industry is a third determinant of rivalry. In industries where fixed costs are high, profitability tends to be highly leveraged to sales volume and the desire to grow volume can spark intense rivalry. **Fixed costs** are the costs that must be borne before the firm makes a single sale. For example, before they can offer service, cable TV companies have to lay cable in the ground; the cost of doing so is a fixed cost. Similarly, to offer air express service, a company like FedEx must invest in planes, package-sorting facilities, and delivery trucks—all fixed costs that require significant capital investments. In industries where the fixed costs of production are high, if sales volume is low firms cannot cover their fixed costs and will not be profitable. They thus have an incentive to cut their prices and/or increase promotion spending to drive up sales volume so that they can cover their fixed costs. In situations where demand is not growing fast enough and too many companies are engaged in the same actions (cutting prices and/or raising promotion spending in an attempt to cover fixed costs), the result can be intense rivalry and lower profits. Research suggests that it is often the weakest firms in an industry that initiate such actions, precisely because they are the ones struggling to cover their fixed costs.[7]

■ **Exit Barriers**

Exit barriers are economic, strategic, and emotional factors that prevent companies from leaving an industry.[8] If exit barriers are high, companies become locked into an unprofitable industry where overall demand is static or declining. The result is often excess productive capacity, which leads to even more intense rivalry and price competition as companies cut prices in the attempt to obtain the customer orders needed to use their idle capacity and cover their fixed costs.[9] Common exit barriers include the following:

■ Investments in assets such as specific machines, equipment, and operating facilities that are of little or no value in alternative uses or cannot be sold off. If the company wishes to leave the industry, it has to write off the book value of these assets.

■ High fixed costs of exit, such as the severance pay, health benefits, and pensions that have to be paid to workers who are being made redundant when a company ceases to operate.

■ Emotional attachments to an industry, as when a company's owners or employees are unwilling to exit from an industry for sentimental reasons or because of pride.

■ Economic dependence on the industry because a company relies on a single industry for its revenue and profit.

■ The need to maintain an expensive collection of assets at or above some minimum level in order to participate effectively in the industry.

■ Bankruptcy regulations, particularly in the United States, where Chapter 11 bankruptcy provisions allow insolvent enterprises to continue operating and reorganize themselves under bankruptcy protection. These regulations can keep unprofitable assets in the industry, result in persistent excess capacity, and lengthen the time required to bring industry supply in line with demand.

As an example of the effect of exit barriers in practice, consider the express mail and parcel delivery industry. The key players in this industry, such as Federal Express and UPS, rely on the delivery business entirely for their revenues and profits. They have to be able to guarantee their customers that they will deliver packages to all major localities in the United States, and much of their investment is specific to this purpose. To meet this guarantee, they need a nationwide network of air routes and ground routes, an asset that is required in order to participate in the industry. If excess capacity develops in this industry, as it does from time to time, Federal Express cannot incrementally reduce or minimize its excess capacity by deciding not to fly to and deliver packages in, say, Miami because that proportion of its network is underused. If it did that, it would no longer be able to guarantee to its customers that it would be able to deliver packages to all major locations in the United States, and its customers would switch to some other carrier. Thus, the need to maintain a nationwide network is an exit barrier that can result in persistent excess capacity in the air express industry during periods of weak demand. Finally, both UPS and Federal Express managers and employees are emotionally tied to this industry because they both were first movers, in the ground and air segments of the industry, respectively, and because their employees are also major owners of their companies' stock and they are dependent financially on the fortunes of the delivery business.

■ **The Bargaining Power of Buyers**

The third of Porter's five competitive forces is the bargaining power of buyers. An industry's buyers may be the individual customers who ultimately consume its products (its end-users) or the companies that distribute an industry's products to end-users, such as retailers and wholesalers. For example, while soap powder made by Procter & Gamble and Unilever is consumed by end-users, the principal buyers of soap powder are supermarket chains and discount stores, which resell the product to end-users. The **bargaining power of buyers** refers to the ability of buyers to bargain down prices charged by companies in the industry or to raise the costs of companies in the industry by demanding better product quality and service. By lowering prices and raising costs, powerful buyers can squeeze profits out of an industry. Thus, powerful buyers should be viewed as a threat. Alternatively, when buyers are in a weak bargaining position, companies in an industry can raise prices and perhaps reduce their costs by lowering product quality and service, thus increasing the level of industry profits. Buyers are most powerful in the following circumstances:

■ When the industry that is supplying a particular product or service is composed of many small companies and the buyers are large and few in number. These circumstances allow the buyers to dominate supplying companies.

■ When the buyers purchase in large quantities. In such circumstances, buyers can use their purchasing power as leverage to bargain for price reductions.

■ When the supply industry depends on the buyers for a large percentage of its total orders.

■ When switching costs are low so that buyers can play off the supplying companies against each other to force down prices.

■ When it is economically feasible for buyers to purchase an input from several companies at once so that buyers can play off one company in the industry against another.

■ When buyers can threaten to enter the industry and produce the product themselves and thus supply their own needs, also a tactic for forcing down industry prices.

The auto component supply industry, whose buyers are large automobile manufacturers such as GM, Ford, and DaimlerChrysler, is a good example of an industry in which buyers have strong bargaining power and thus a strong competitive threat.

Why? The suppliers of auto components are numerous and typically small in scale; their buyers, the auto manufacturers, are large in size and few in number. Daimler-Chrysler, for example, does business with nearly two thousand different component suppliers in the United States and normally contracts with a number of different companies to supply the same part. Additionally, to keep component prices down, both Ford and GM have used the threat of manufacturing a component themselves rather than buying it from auto component suppliers. The automakers have used their powerful position to play off suppliers against each other, forcing down the price they have to pay for component parts and demanding better quality. If a component supplier objects, the automaker uses the threat of switching to another supplier as a bargaining tool.

Another issue is that the relative power of buyers and suppliers tends to change in response to changing industry conditions. For example, because of changes now taking place in the pharmaceutical and health care industries, major buyers of pharmaceuticals (hospitals and health maintenance organizations) are gaining power over the suppliers of pharmaceuticals and have been able to demand lower prices. The *Running Case* discusses how Wal-Mart's buying power has changed over the years as the company has become larger.

■ The Bargaining Power of Suppliers

The fourth of Porter's five competitive forces is the bargaining power of suppliers—the organizations that provide inputs into the industry, such as materials, services, and labor (which may be individuals, organizations such as labor unions, or companies that supply contract labor). The **bargaining power of suppliers** refers to the ability of suppliers to raise input prices, or to raise the costs of the industry in other ways—for example, by providing poor-quality inputs or poor service. Powerful suppliers squeeze profits out of an industry by raising the costs of companies in the industry. Thus, powerful suppliers are a threat. Alternatively, if suppliers are weak, companies in the industry have the opportunity to force down input prices and demand higher-quality inputs (such as more productive labor). As with buyers, the ability of suppliers to make demands on a company depends on their power relative to that of the company. Suppliers are most powerful in these situations:

■ The product that suppliers sell has few substitutes and is vital to the companies in an industry.

■ The profitability of suppliers is not significantly affected by the purchases of companies in a particular industry, in other words, when the industry is not an important customer to the suppliers.

■ Companies in an industry would experience significant switching costs if they moved to the product of a different supplier because a particular supplier's products are unique or different. In such cases, the company depends on a particular supplier and cannot play suppliers off against each other to reduce price.

■ Suppliers can threaten to enter their customers' industry and use their inputs to produce products that would compete directly with those of companies already in the industry.

■ Companies in the industry cannot threaten to enter their suppliers' industry and make their own inputs as a tactic for lowering the price of inputs.

An example of an industry in which companies are dependent on a powerful supplier is the personal computer industry. Personal computer firms are heavily dependent on Intel, the world's largest supplier of microprocessors for PCs. The industry

Running Case

Wal-Mart's Bargaining Power over Suppliers

When Wal-Mart and other discount retailers began in the 1960s, they were small operations with little purchasing power. To generate store traffic, they depended in large part on stocking nationally branded merchandise from well-known companies such as Procter & Gamble and Rubbermaid. Since the discounters did not have high sales volume, the nationally branded companies set the price. This meant that the discounters had to look for other ways to cut costs, which they typically did by emphasizing self-service in stripped-down stores located in the suburbs where land was cheaper (in the 1960s the main competitors for discounters were full-service department stores like Sears that were often located in downtown shopping areas).

Discounters such as Kmart purchased their merchandise through wholesalers, who in turned bought from manufacturers. The wholesaler would come into a store and write an order, and when the merchandise arrived, the wholesaler would come in and stock the shelves, saving the retailer labor costs. However, Wal-Mart was located in Arkansas and placed its stores in small towns. Wholesalers were not particularly interested in serving a company that built its stores in such out-of-the-way places. They would do it only if Wal-Mart paid higher prices.

Wal-Mart's Sam Walton refused to pay higher prices. Instead he took his fledgling company public and used the capital raised to build a distribution center to stock merchandise. The distribution center would serve all stores within a 300-mile radius, with trucks leaving the distribution center daily to restock the stores. Because the distribution center was serving a collection of stores and thus buying in larger volumes, Walton found that he was able to cut the wholesalers out of the equation and order directly from manufacturers. The cost savings generated by not having to pay profits to wholesalers were then passed on to consumers in the form of lower prices, which helped Wal-Mart continue growing. This growth increased its buying power and thus its ability to demand deeper discounts from manufacturers.

Today Wal-Mart has turned its buying process into an art form. Since 8 percent of all retail sales in the United States are made in a Wal-Mart store, the company has enormous bargaining power over its suppliers. Suppliers of nationally branded products, such as Procter & Gamble, are no longer in a position to demand high prices. Instead, Wal-Mart is now so important to Procter & Gamble that it is able to demand deep discounts from them. Moreover, Wal-Mart has itself become a brand that is more powerful than the brands of manufacturers. People don't go to Wal-Mart to buy branded goods; they go to Wal-Mart for the low prices. This simple fact has enabled Wal-Mart to bargain down the prices it pays, always passing on cost savings to consumers in the form of lower prices.

Since 1991 Wal-Mart has provided suppliers with real-time information on store sales through the use of individual Stock Keeping Units (SKUs). These have allowed suppliers to optimize their own production processes, matching output to Wal-Mart's demands and avoiding under- or overproduction and the need to store inventory. The efficiencies that manufacturers gain from such information are passed on to Wal-Mart in the form of lower prices, which then passes on those cost savings to consumers.[c]

standard for personal computers runs on Intel's microprocessor chips. Intel's competitors, such as Advanced Micro Devices (AMD), must develop and supply chips that are compatible with Intel's standard. Although AMD has developed competing chips, Pentium still supplies about 85 percent of the chips used in PCs primarily because only Intel has the manufacturing capacity required to serve a large share of the market. It is beyond the financial resources of Intel's competitors, such as AMD, to match the scale and efficiency of Intel's manufacturing systems. This means that while PC manufacturers can buy some microprocessors from Intel's rivals, most notably AMD, they still have to turn to Intel for the bulk of their supply. Because Intel is in a powerful bargaining position, it can charge higher prices for its microprocessors than would be the case if its competitors were more numerous and stronger (that is, if the microprocessor industry were fragmented).

■ **Substitute Products**

The final force in Porter's model is the threat of **substitute products:** the products of different businesses or industries that can satisfy similar customer needs. For example, companies in the coffee industry compete indirectly with those in the tea and soft drink industries because all three serve customer needs for nonalcoholic drinks. The existence of close substitutes is a strong competitive threat because this limits the price that companies in one industry can charge for their product, and thus industry profitability. If the price of coffee rises too much relative to that of tea or soft drinks, coffee drinkers may switch to those substitutes.

If an industry's products have few close substitutes, so that substitutes are a weak competitive force, then, other things being equal, companies in the industry have the opportunity to raise prices and earn additional profits. Thus, there is no close substitute for microprocessors, which gives companies like Intel and AMD the ability to charge higher prices than would be the case if there were a substitute for microprocessors.

■ **A Sixth Force: Complementors**

Andrew Grove, the former CEO of Intel, has argued that Porter's five forces model ignores a sixth force: the power, vigor, and competence of complementors.[10] **Complementors** are companies that sell products that add value to (complement) the products of companies in an industry because when used *together,* the products better satisfy customer demands. For example, the complementors to the personal computer industry are the companies that make software applications to run on those machines. The greater the supply of high-quality software applications to run on personal computers, the greater is the value of personal computers to customers, the greater the demand for PCs, and the greater the profitability of the personal computer industry.

Grove's argument has a strong foundation in economic theory, which has long argued that *both* substitutes and complements influence demand in an industry.[11] Moreover, recent research has emphasized the importance of complementary products in determining demand and profitability in many high-technology industries, such as the computer industry in which Grove made his mark.[12] The issue, therefore, is that when complements are an important determinant of demand for an industry's products, industry profits depend critically on there being an adequate supply of complementary products. When the number of complementors is increasing and they produce attractive complementary products, this boosts demand and profits in the industry and can open up many new opportunities for creating value. Conversely, if complementors are weak and are not producing attractive complementary products, this can be a threat that slows industry growth and limits profitability.

Summary

The systematic analysis of forces in the industry environment using the Porter framework is a powerful tool that helps managers to think strategically. It is important to recognize that one competitive force often affects the others, so that all forces need to be considered and thought about when performing industry analysis. Indeed, industry analysis leads managers to think systematically about how their strategic choices will be affected by the forces of industry competition and also about how their choices will affect the five forces and change conditions in the industry.

Strategic Groups Within Industries

Companies in an industry often differ significantly from each other with respect to the way they strategically position their products in the market in terms of such factors as the distribution channels they use, the market segments they serve, the quality of their products, technological leadership, customer service, pricing policy, advertising policy, and promotions. As a result of these differences, within most industries, it is

FIGURE 2.3

Strategic Groups in
the Pharmaceutical
Industry

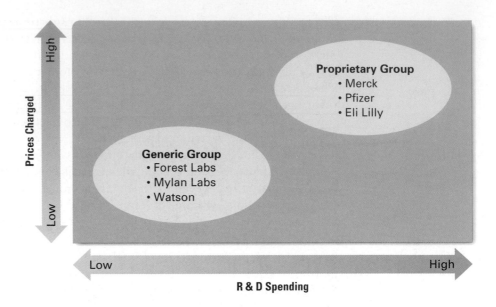

possible to observe groups of companies in which each company follows a business model that is similar to that pursued by other companies in the group, but *different* from the business model followed by companies in other groups. These different groups of companies are known as **strategic groups.**[13]

Normally, the basic differences between the business models that companies in different strategic groups use can be captured by a relatively small number of strategic factors. For example, in the pharmaceutical industry, two main strategic groups stand out (see Figure 2.3).[14] One group, which includes such companies as Merck, Eli Lilly, and Pfizer, is characterized by a business model based on heavy R&D spending and a focus on developing new, proprietary, blockbuster drugs. The companies in this *proprietary* strategic group are pursuing a high-risk, high-return strategy. It is a high-risk strategy because basic drug research is difficult and expensive. As discussed in the *Opening Case*, bringing a new drug to market can cost up to $800 million in R&D money and a decade of research and clinical trials. The risks are high because the failure rate in new drug development is very high: only one out of every five drugs entering clinical trials is ultimately approved by the U.S. Food and Drug Administration. However, the strategy is also a high-return one because a single successful drug can be patented, giving the innovator a twenty-year monopoly on its production and sale. This lets these proprietary companies charge a high price for the patented drug, allowing them to earn millions, if not billions, of dollars over the lifetime of the patent.

The second strategic group might be characterized as the *generic drug* strategic group. This group of companies, which includes Forest Labs, Mylan Labs, and Watson Pharmaceuticals, focuses on the manufacture of generic drugs: low-cost copies of drugs that were developed by companies in the proprietary group whose patents have now expired. Low R&D spending, production efficiency, and an emphasis on low prices characterize the business models of companies in this strategic group. They are pursuing a low-risk, low-return strategy. It is low risk because they are not investing millions of dollars in R&D. It is low return because they cannot charge high prices.

■ Implications of Strategic Groups

The concept of strategic groups has a number of implications for the identification of opportunities and threats within an industry. First, because all the companies in a strategic group are pursuing a similar business model, customers tend to view the products of such enterprises as *direct substitutes* for each other. Thus, a company's *closest* competitors are those in its strategic group, not those in other strategic groups in the industry. The most immediate threat to a company's profitability comes from rivals within its own strategic group. For example, in the retail industry, there is a group of companies that might be characterized as discounters. Included in this group are Wal-Mart, Kmart, Target, and Fred Meyer. These companies compete most vigorously with each other, rather than with other retailers in different groups, such as Nordstrom or The Gap. Kmart, for example, was driven into bankruptcy in late 2001, not because Nordstrom or The Gap took business from it, but because Wal-Mart and Target gained share in the discounting group by virtue of their superior strategic execution of the discounting business model.

A second competitive implication is that different strategic groups can have a different standing with respect to each of the competitive forces; thus, *each strategic group may face a different set of opportunities and threats.* The risk of new entry by potential competitors, the degree of rivalry among companies within a group, the bargaining power of buyers, the bargaining power of suppliers, and the competitive force of substitute and complementary products can each be a relatively strong or weak competitive force depending on the competitive positioning approach adopted by each strategic group in the industry. For example, in the pharmaceutical industry, companies in the proprietary group have historically been in a very powerful position in relation to buyers because their products are patented and there are no substitutes. Also, rivalry based on price competition within this group has been low because competition in the industry revolves around being the first to patent a new drug (so-called patent races), not around drug prices. Thus, companies in this group have been able to charge high prices and earn high profits. In contrast, companies in the generic group have been in a much weaker position because many companies are able to produce different versions of the same generic drug after patents expire. Thus, in this strategic group, products are close substitutes, rivalry has been high, and price competition has led to lower profits for this group as compared to companies in the proprietary group.

■ The Role of Mobility Barriers

It follows from these two issues that some strategic groups are more desirable than others because competitive forces open up greater opportunities and present fewer threats for those groups. Managers, after having analyzed their industry, might identify a strategic group where competitive forces are weaker and higher profits can be made. Sensing an opportunity, they might contemplate changing their business model and move to compete in that strategic group. However, taking advantage of this opportunity may be difficult because of mobility barriers between strategic groups.

Mobility barriers are within-industry factors that inhibit the movement of companies between strategic groups. They include the barriers to entry into a group and the barriers to exit from a company's existing group. For example, Forest Labs would encounter mobility barriers if it attempted to enter the proprietary group in the pharmaceutical industry because it lacks R&D skills, and building these skills would be an expensive proposition. Essentially, over time, companies in different groups develop different cost structures and skills and competencies that give them different pricing options and choices. A company contemplating entry into another strategic group must evaluate whether it has the ability to imitate, and indeed outperform, its potential competitors in that strategic group. Managers must determine if it is cost-effective to overcome mobility barriers before deciding whether the move is worthwhile.

In summary, an important task of industry analysis is to determine the sources of the similarities and differences among companies in an industry and to work out the broad themes that underlie competition in an industry. This analysis often reveals new opportunities to compete in an industry by developing new kinds of products to meet the needs of customers better. It can also reveal emerging threats that can be countered effectively by changing competitive strategy. This issue is taken up in Chapters 5, 6, and 7, which examine crafting competitive strategy in different kinds of markets to build a competitive advantage over rivals and best satisfy customer needs.

Industry Life Cycle Analysis

An important determinant of the strength of the competitive forces in an industry (and thus of the nature of opportunities and threats) is the changes that take place in it over time. The similarities and differences between companies in an industry often become more pronounced over time, and its strategic group structure frequently changes. The strength and nature of each of the competitive forces also change as an industry evolves, particularly the two forces of risk of entry by potential competitors and rivalry among existing firms.[15]

A useful tool for analyzing the effects of industry evolution on competitive forces is the **industry life cycle** model, which identifies five sequential stages in the evolution of an industry that lead to five distinct kinds of industry environment: embryonic, growth, shakeout, mature, and decline (see Figure 2.4). The task facing managers is to *anticipate* how the strength of competitive forces will change as the industry environment evolves and to formulate strategies that take advantage of opportunities as they arise and that counter emerging threats.

■ Embryonic Industries

An *embryonic* industry is just beginning to develop (for example, personal computers and biotechnology in the 1970s, and nanotechnology today). Growth at this stage is slow because of such factors as buyers' unfamiliarity with the industry's product,

FIGURE 2.4

Stages in the Industry Life Cycle

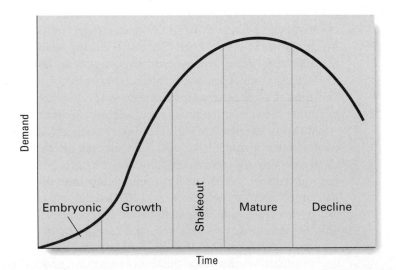

high prices due to the inability of companies to reap any significant scale economies, and poorly developed distribution channels. Barriers to entry tend to be based on access to key technological know-how rather than cost economies or brand loyalty. If the core know-how required to compete in the industry is complex and difficult to grasp, barriers to entry can be quite high, and established companies will be protected from potential competitors. Rivalry in embryonic industries is based not so much on price as on educating customers, opening up distribution channels, and perfecting the design of the product. Such rivalry can be intense, and the company that is the first to solve design problems often has the opportunity to develop a significant market position. An embryonic industry may also be the creation of one company's innovative efforts, as happened with microprocessors (Intel), vacuum cleaners (Hoover), and photocopiers (Xerox). In such circumstances, the company has a major opportunity to capitalize on the lack of rivalry and build a strong hold on the market.

■ **Growth Industries**

Once demand for the industry's product begins to take off, the industry develops the characteristics of a growth industry. In a *growth* industry, first-time demand is expanding rapidly as many new customers enter the market. Typically, an industry grows when customers become familiar with the product, prices fall because experience and scale economies have been attained, and distribution channels develop. The U.S. cellular telephone industry was in the growth stage for most of the 1990s. In 1990, there were only 5 million cellular subscribers in the nation. By 2004, this figure had increased to over 130 million, and overall demand was still growing at a healthy rate.

Normally, the importance of control over technological knowledge as a barrier to entry has diminished by the time an industry enters its growth stage. Because few companies have yet achieved significant scale economies or built brand loyalty, other entry barriers tend to be relatively low as well, particularly early in the growth stage. Thus, the threat from potential competitors generally is highest at this point. Paradoxically, however, high growth usually means that new entrants can be absorbed into an industry without a marked increase in the intensity of rivalry. Thus, rivalry tends to be relatively low. Rapid growth in demand enables companies to expand their revenues and profits without taking market share away from competitors. A strategically aware company takes advantage of the relatively benign environment of the growth stage to prepare itself for the intense competition of the coming industry shakeout.

■ **Industry Shakeout**

Explosive growth cannot be maintained indefinitely. Sooner or later, the rate of growth slows, and the industry enters the shakeout stage. In the *shakeout* stage, demand approaches saturation levels: most of the demand is limited to replacement because there are few potential first-time buyers left.

As an industry enters the shakeout stage, rivalry between companies becomes intense. Typically, companies that have become accustomed to rapid growth continue to add capacity at rates consistent with past growth. However, demand is no longer growing at historic rates, and the consequence is the emergence of excess productive capacity. This condition is illustrated in Figure 2.5, where the solid curve indicates the growth in demand over time and the broken curve indicates the growth in productive capacity over time. As you can see, past point t_1, demand growth becomes slower as the industry becomes mature. However, capacity continues to grow until time t_2. The gap between the solid and broken lines signifies excess capacity. In an attempt to use this capacity, companies often cut prices. The result can be a price war,

FIGURE 2.5

Growth in Demand
and Capacity

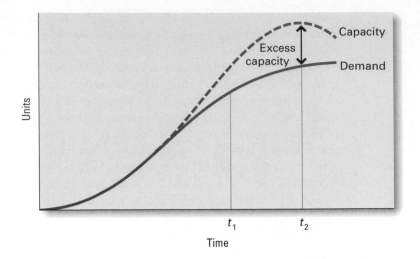

which drives many of the most inefficient companies into bankruptcy, which is enough to deter any new entry.

■ Mature Industries   The shakeout stage ends when the industry enters its *mature* stage: the market is totally saturated, demand is limited to replacement demand, and growth is low or zero. What growth there is comes from population expansion that brings new customers into the market or an increase in replacement demand.

As an industry enters maturity, barriers to entry increase, and the threat of entry from potential competitors decreases. As growth slows during the shakeout, companies can no longer maintain historic growth rates merely by holding on to their market share. Competition for market share develops, driving down prices and often producing a price war, as has happened in the airline and personal computer industry. To survive the shakeout, companies begin to focus on minimizing costs and building brand loyalty. The airlines, for example, tried to cut operating costs by hiring nonunion labor and to build brand loyalty by introducing frequent-flyer programs. Personal computer companies have sought to build brand loyalty by providing excellent after-sales service and working to lower their cost structures. By the time an industry matures, the surviving companies are those that have brand loyalty and efficient low-cost operations. Because both these factors constitute a significant barrier to entry, the threat of entry by potential competitors is greatly diminished. High entry barriers in mature industries give companies the opportunity to increase prices and profits.

As a result of the shakeout, most industries in the maturity stage have consolidated and become oligopolies. In mature industries, companies tend to recognize their interdependence and try to avoid price wars. Stable demand gives them the opportunity to enter into price-leadership agreements. The net effect is to reduce the threat of intense rivalry among established companies, thereby allowing greater profitability. Nevertheless, the stability of a mature industry is always threatened by further price wars. A general slump in economic activity can depress industry demand. As companies fight to maintain their revenues in the face of declining demand, price-leadership agreements break down, rivalry increases, and prices and profits fall. The periodic price wars that occur in the airline industry seem to follow this pattern.

■ **Declining Industries**

Eventually, most industries enter a *decline* stage: growth becomes negative for a variety of reasons, including technological substitution (for example, air travel for rail travel), social changes (greater health consciousness hitting tobacco sales), demographics (the declining birthrate hurting the market for baby and child products), and international competition (low-cost foreign competition pushing the U.S. steel industry into decline). Within a declining industry, the degree of rivalry among established companies usually increases. Depending on the speed of the decline and the height of exit barriers, competitive pressures can become as fierce as in the shakeout stage.[16] The main problem in a declining industry is that falling demand leads to the emergence of excess capacity. In trying to use this capacity, companies begin to cut prices, thus sparking a price war. The U.S. steel industry experienced these problems because steel companies tried to use their excess capacity despite falling demand. The same problem occurred in the airline industry in the 1990–1992 period and again in 2001–2003, as companies cut prices to ensure that they would not be flying with half-empty planes (that is, that they would not be operating with substantial excess capacity). Exit barriers play a part in adjusting excess capacity. The greater the exit barriers, the harder it is for companies to reduce capacity and the greater is the threat of severe price competition.

Summary

In summary, a third task of industry analysis is to identify the opportunities and threats that are characteristic of different kinds of industry environments in order to develop an effective business model and competitive strategy. Strategic managers have to tailor their strategies to changing industry conditions. And they have to learn to recognize the crucial points in an industry's development so that they can forecast when the shakeout stage of an industry might begin or when an industry might be moving into decline. This is also true at the level of strategic groups, for new embryonic groups may emerge because of shifts in customer needs and tastes or some groups may grow rapidly because of changes in technology and others will decline as their customers defect. Thus, for example, companies in the upscale retail group such as Macy's, Dillard's, and Nordstrom are facing declining sales as customers defect to discount retailers like Target and Wal-Mart and online companies like amazon.com and landsend.com.

Limitations of Models for Industry Analysis

The competitive forces, strategic groups, and life cycle models provide useful ways of thinking about and analyzing the nature of competition within an industry to identify opportunities and threats. However, each has its limitations, and managers need to be aware of their shortcomings.

■ **Life Cycle Issues**

It is important to remember that the industry life cycle model is a generalization. In practice, industry life cycles do not always follow the pattern illustrated in Figure 2.4. In some cases, growth is so rapid that the embryonic stage is skipped altogether. In others, industries fail to get past the embryonic stage. Industry growth can be revitalized after long periods of decline through innovation or social change. For example, the health boom brought the bicycle industry back to life after a long period of decline.

The time span of the stages can also vary significantly from industry to industry. Some industries can stay in maturity almost indefinitely if their products become basic necessities of life, as is the case for the car industry. Other industries skip the mature stage and go straight into decline, as in the case of the vacuum tube industry. Transistors replaced vacuum tubes as a major component in electronic products even though the vacuum tube industry was still in its growth stage. Still other industries may go through several shakeouts before they enter full maturity, as appears to be happening in the telecommunications industry.

■ **Innovation and Change**

Over any reasonable length of time, in many industries competition can be viewed as a process driven by innovation.[17] Indeed, innovation is frequently the major factor in industry evolution and causes the movement through the industry life cycle. Innovation is attractive because companies that pioneer new products, processes, or strategies can often earn enormous profits. Consider the explosive growth of Toys "R" Us, Dell Computer, and Wal-Mart. In a variety of different ways, all of these companies were innovators. Toys "R" Us pioneered a new way of selling toys (through large discount warehouse-type stores), Dell pioneered a whole new way of selling personal computers (by mail order), and Wal-Mart pioneered the low-price discount superstore concept.

Successful innovation can transform the nature of industry competition. In recent decades, one frequent consequence of innovation has been to lower the fixed costs of production, thereby reducing barriers to entry and allowing new, and smaller, enterprises to compete with large established organizations. For example, two decades ago, large integrated steel companies such as US Steel, LTV, and Bethlehem Steel dominated the steel industry. The industry was a typical oligopoly, dominated by a small number of large producers, in which tacit price collusion was practiced. Then along came a series of efficient mini-mill producers such as Nucor and Chaparral Steel, which used a new technology: electric arc furnaces. Over the past twenty years, they have revolutionized the structure of the industry. What was once a consolidated industry is now much more fragmented and price competitive. The successor company to US Steel, USX, now has only a 12 percent market share, down from 55 percent in the mid-1960s, and both Bethlehem and LTV went bankrupt. In contrast, the mini-mills as a group now hold over 40 percent of the market, up from 5 percent twenty years ago.[18] Thus, the mini-mill innovation has reshaped the nature of competition in the steel industry.[19] A competitive forces model applied to the industry in 1970 would look very different from a competitive forces model applied in 2004.

Michael Porter, the originator of the competitive forces and strategic group concepts, has explicitly recognized the role of innovation in revolutionizing industry structure. Porter now talks of innovations as "unfreezing" and "reshaping" industry structure. He argues that after a period of turbulence triggered by innovation, the structure of an industry once more settles down into a fairly stable pattern, and the five forces and strategic group concepts can once more be applied.[20] This view of the evolution of industry structure is often referred to as *punctuated equilibrium*.[21] The punctuated equilibrium view holds that long periods of equilibrium, when an industry's structure is stable, are punctuated by periods of rapid change when industry structure is revolutionized by innovation; there is an unfreezing and refreezing process.

Figure 2.6 shows what punctuated equilibrium might look like for one key dimension of industry structure: competitive structure. From time t_0 to t_1, the competitive

FIGURE 2.6

Punctuated
Equilibrium and
Competitive Structure

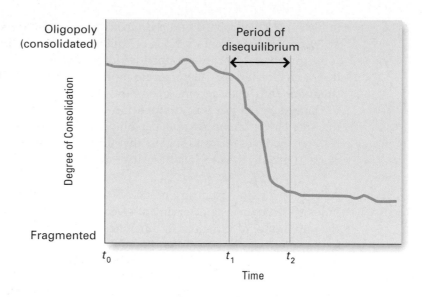

FIGURE 2.6

Punctuated
Equilibrium and
Competitive Structure

structure of the industry is a stable oligopoly, with a few companies sharing the market. At time t_1, a major new innovation is pioneered by either an existing company or a new entrant. The result is a period of turbulence between t_1 and t_2. After a while, the industry settles down into a new state of equilibrium, but now the competitive structure is far more fragmented. Note that the opposite could have happened: the industry could have become more consolidated, although this seems to be less common. In general, innovations seem to lower barriers to entry, allow more companies into the industry, and as a result lead to fragmentation rather than consolidation.

During a period of rapid change when industry structure is being revolutionized by innovation, value typically migrates to business models based on new positioning strategies.[22] In the stockbrokerage industry, value migrated away from the full-service broker model to the online trading model. In the steel industry, the introduction of electric arc technology led to a migration of value away from large, integrated enterprises and toward small mini-mills. In the book-selling industry, value has migrated away from small boutique "bricks and mortar" booksellers toward large bookstore chains like Barnes & Noble and online bookstores such as amazon.com.

Because the competitive forces and strategic group models are static, they cannot adequately capture what occurs during periods of rapid change in the industry environment when value is migrating. Similarly, a simple view of the industry life cycle does not allow for an industry to repeat a stage or even jump stages that technological upheavals can lead to. Nevertheless, they are useful tools for analyzing industry structure during periods of stability.

Some scholars question the validity of the punctuated equilibrium approach. Richard D'Avani has argued that many industries are **hypercompetitive,** meaning that they are characterized by permanent and ongoing innovation and competitive change (the computer industry is often cited as an example of a hypercompetitive industry).[23] The structure of such industries is constantly being revolutionized by innovation, so there are no periods of equilibrium or stability. When this is the case, some might argue that the competitive forces and strategic group models are of limited value because they represent no more than snapshots of a constantly changing situation. Thus, managers must constantly repeat industry analysis and pay attention to changes in the forces of competition. Moreover, D'Avani and others claim that markets have become more hypercompetitive in the modern era, although recent research evidence seems to suggest that this is not the case, and many industries are characterized by long periods of relative stability.[24]

■ **Company Differences**

Another criticism of industry models is that they overemphasize the importance of industry structure as a determinant of company performance and underemphasize the importance of variations or differences among companies within an industry or a strategic group.[25] As we discuss in the next chapter, there can be enormous variance in the profit rates of individual companies within an industry. Research by Richard Rumelt and his associates, for example, suggests that industry structure explains only about 10 percent of the variance in profit rates across companies.[26] The implication is that individual company differences explain much of the remainder. Other studies have put the explained variance closer to 20 percent, which is still not a large figure.[27] Similarly, a growing number of studies have found only weak evidence of a link between strategic group membership and company profit rates, despite the fact that the strategic group model predicts a strong link.[28] Collectively, these studies suggest that the individual resources and capabilities of a company are far more important determinants of its profitability than is the industry or strategic group of which the company is a member. Although these findings do not make the five forces and strategic group models irrelevant, they do mean that the models have limited usefulness. A company will not be profitable just because it is based in an attractive industry or strategic group. As we discuss in Chapters 3 and 4, more is required.

The Macro-environment

Just as the decisions and actions of strategic managers can often change an industry's competitive structure, so too can changing conditions or forces in the wider **macroenvironment**—that is, the broader economic, global, technological, demographic, social, and political context in which companies and industries are embedded (see Figure 2.7). Changes in the forces in the macroenvironment can have a direct impact on any or all of the forces in Porter's model, thereby altering the relative strength of these forces and, with it, the attractiveness of an industry.

■ **Macroeconomic Forces**

Economic forces affect the general health and well-being of a nation or the regional economy of an organization, which in turn affect companies' and industries' ability to earn an adequate rate of return. The four most important factors in the macroenvironment are the growth rate of the economy, interest rates, currency exchange rates, and inflation (or deflation) rates. Economic growth, because it leads to an expansion in customer expenditures, tends to produce a general easing of competitive pressures within an industry. This gives companies the opportunity to expand their operations and earn higher profits. Because economic decline (a recession) leads to a reduction in customer expenditures, it increases competitive pressures. Economic decline frequently causes price wars in mature industries.

The level of interest rates can determine the demand for a company's products. Interest rates are important whenever customers routinely borrow money to finance their

FIGURE 2.7

The Role of the
Macroenvironment

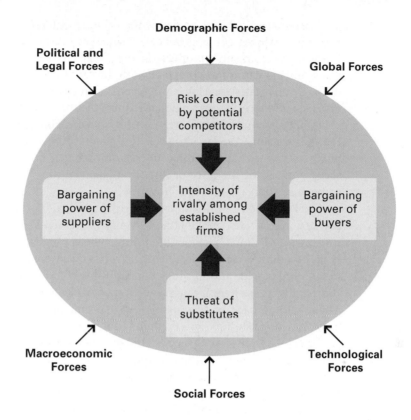

purchase of these products. The most obvious example is the housing market, where mortgage rates directly affect demand. Interest rates also have an impact on the sale of autos, appliances, and capital equipment, to give just a few examples. For companies in such industries, rising interest rates are a threat and falling rates an opportunity.

Interest rates are also important insofar as they influence a company's cost of capital, and therefore its ability to raise funds and invest in new assets. The lower that interest rates are, the lower the cost of capital for companies will be, and the more investment there will be. This is not always a good thing. In the late 1990s, the very low cost of capital allowed dot-com and telecommunications companies with questionable business plans to raise large amounts of money and invest those funds in computers and telecommunications gear (the low cost of capital lowered barriers to entry by enabling start-ups to raise the capital required to circumvent entry barriers). This was initially good for the manufacturers of telecommunications equipment and computers, but the demand signal that was being sent was not sustainable: many of the dot-com and telecommunications start-ups of the 1990s went bankrupt between 2000 and 2002. Secondhand computers and telecommunications equipment from these bankrupt companies flooded the market, depressing first-time demand for that equipment and helping to plunge the computer and telecommunications equipment businesses into a deep slowdown. (For example, in January 2002, Internet auction house eBay listed more than three thousand Cisco products that were being auctioned for much less than their initial prices.)

Currency exchange rates define the value of different national currencies against each other. Movement in currency exchange rates has a direct impact on the competitiveness of a company's products in the global marketplace. For example, when the value of the dollar is low compared with the value of other currencies, products made in the United States are relatively inexpensive and products made overseas are relatively expensive. A low or declining dollar reduces the threat from foreign competitors while creating opportunities for increased sales overseas. For example, the fall in the value of the dollar against the Japanese yen that occurred between 1985 and 1995, when the dollar-to-yen exchange rate declined from 240 yen per dollar to 85 yen per dollar, sharply increased the price of imported Japanese cars, giving U.S. car manufacturers some protection against those imports.

Price inflation can destabilize the economy, producing slower economic growth, higher interest rates, and volatile currency movements. If inflation keeps increasing, investment planning becomes hazardous. The key characteristic of inflation is that it makes the future less predictable. In an inflationary environment, it may be impossible to predict with any accuracy the real value of returns that can be earned from a project five years hence. Such uncertainty makes companies less willing to invest. Their holding back in turn depresses economic activity and ultimately pushes the economy into a slump. Thus, high inflation is a threat to companies.

Price deflation also has a destabilizing effect on economic activity. If prices are deflating, the real price of fixed payments goes up. This is particularly damaging for companies and individuals with a high level of debt who must make regular fixed payments on that debt. In a deflationary environment, the increase in the real value of debt consumes more of household and corporate cash flows, leaving less for other purchases and depressing the overall level of economic activity. Although significant deflation has not been seen since the 1930s, in the 1990s it started to take hold in Japan.

■ **Global Forces**

Over the last half-century there have been enormous changes in the world economic system. We review these changes in some detail in Chapter 8 when we discuss global strategy. For now, the important points to note are that barriers to international trade and investment have tumbled, and more and more countries are enjoying sustained economic growth. Economic growth in places like Brazil, China, and India is creating large new markets for companies' goods and services and is giving companies an opportunity to grow their profits faster by entering these nations. Falling barriers to international trade and investment have made it much easier to enter foreign nations. For example, twenty years ago, it was almost impossible for a Western company to set up operations in China. Today, Western and Japanese companies are investing over $50 billion a year in China. By the same token, however, falling barriers to international trade and investment have made it easier for foreign enterprises to enter the domestic markets of many companies (by lowering barriers to entry), thereby increasing the intensity of competition and lowering profitability. Because of these changes, many formally isolated domestic markets have now become part of a much larger, and more competitive, global marketplace, creating a myriad threats and opportunities for companies. We shall return to this topic and discuss it in more detail in Chapter 8.

■ **Technological Forces**

Since World War II, the pace of technological change has accelerated.[29] This has unleashed a process that has been called a "perennial gale of creative destruction."[30] Technological change can make established products obsolete overnight and simultaneously create a host of new product possibilities. Thus, technological change is both creative and destructive—both an opportunity and a threat.

One of the most important impacts of technological change is that it can affect the height of barriers to entry and therefore radically reshape industry structure. The Internet, because it is so pervasive, has the potential for changing the competitive structure of many industries. It often lowers barriers to entry and reduces customer switching costs, changes that tend to increase the intensity of rivalry in an industry and lower both prices and profits.[31] For example, the Internet has lowered barriers to entry into the news industry. Providers of financial news now have to compete for advertising dollars and customer attention with new Internet-based media organizations that sprang up during the 1990s, such as TheStreet.com, the Motley Fool, and Yahoo!'s financial section. The resulting increase in rivalry has given advertisers more choices, enabling them to bargain down the prices that they must pay to media companies. Similarly, in the automobile industry, the ability of customers to comparison-shop for cars online and purchase cars online from a number of distributors such as Auto Nation has increased the ability of customers to find the best value for money. Customers' increased bargaining power enables them to put downward pressure on car prices and squeeze profits out of the automobile industry.

■ Demographic Forces

Demographic forces are outcomes of changes in the characteristics of a population, such as age, gender, ethnic origin, race, sexual orientation, and social class. Like the other forces in the general environment, demographic forces present managers with opportunities and threats and can have major implications for organizations. Over the past thirty years, for example, women have entered the work force in increasing numbers. Between 1973 and 2002, the percentage of women in the work force increased from 44 to 60 percent in the United States, 48 to 68 percent in Canada, and 51 to 68 percent in Britain.[32] This dramatic increase has brought issues such as equal pay for equal work and sexual harassment at work to the forefront of issues that managers must address if they are to attract and make full use of the talents of female workers.

Changes in the age distribution of a population are another example of a demographic force that affects managers and organizations. Currently, most industrialized nations are experiencing the aging of their populations as a consequence of falling birth and death rates and the aging of the babyboom generation. In Germany, for example, the percentage of the population over age sixty-five is expected to rise from 15.4 percent in 1990 to 20.7 percent in 2010. Comparable figures for Canada are 11.4 and 14.4 percent; for Japan, 11.7 and 19.5 percent; and for the United States, 12.6 and 13.5 percent.[33]

The aging of the population is increasing opportunities for organizations that cater to older people; the home health care and recreation industries, for example, are seeing an upswing in demand for their services. As the babyboom generation from the late 1950s to the early 1960s has aged, it has created a host of opportunities and threats. During the 1980s, many baby boomers were getting married and creating an upsurge in demand for the customer appliances normally bought by couples marrying for the first time. Companies such as Whirlpool Corporation and General Electric capitalized on the resulting upsurge in demand for washing machines, dishwashers, dryers, and the like. In the 1990s, many of these same baby boomers were starting to save for retirement, creating an inflow of money into mutual funds and creating a boom in the mutual fund industry. In the next twenty years, many of these same baby boomers will retire, creating a boom in retirement communities.

■ **Social Forces**

Social forces refer to the way in which changing social mores and values affect an industry. Like the other macroenvironmental forces discussed here, social change creates opportunities and threats. One of the major social movements of recent decades has been the trend toward greater health consciousness. Its impact has been immense, and companies that recognized the opportunities early have often reaped significant gains. Philip Morris, for example, capitalized on the growing health consciousness trend when it acquired Miller Brewing Company and then redefined competition in the beer industry with its introduction of low-calorie beer (Miller Lite). Similarly, PepsiCo was able to gain market share from its rival, Coca-Cola, by being the first to introduce diet colas and fruit-based soft drinks. At the same time, the health trend has created a threat for many industries. The tobacco industry, for example, is in decline as a direct result of greater customer awareness of the health implications of smoking.

■ **Political and Legal Forces**

Political and legal forces are outcomes of changes in laws and regulations. They result from political and legal developments within society and significantly affect managers and companies.

Political processes shape a society's laws, which constrain the operations of organizations and managers and thus create both opportunities and threats.[34] For example, throughout much of the industrialized world, there has been a strong trend toward deregulation of industries previously controlled by the state and privatization of organizations once owned by the state. In the United States, deregulation of the airline industry in 1979 allowed twenty-nine new airlines to enter the industry between 1979 and 1993. The increase in passenger-carrying capacity after deregulation led to excess capacity on many routes, intense competition, and fare wars. To respond to this more competitive task environment, airlines have had to look for ways to reduce operating costs. The development of hub-and-spoke systems, the rise of nonunion airlines, and the introduction of no-frills discount service are all responses to increased competition in the airlines' task environment. Despite these innovations, the airline industry still experiences intense fare wars, which have lowered profits and caused numerous airline company bankruptcies. The global telecommunications service industry is now experiencing the same kind of turmoil following the deregulation of that industry in the United States and elsewhere.

In most countries, the interplay between political and legal forces, on the one hand, and industry competitive structure, on the other, is a two-way process in which the government sets regulations that influence competitive structure, and firms in an industry often seek to influence the regulations that governments enact by a number of means. First, when permitted, they may provide financial support to politicians or political parties that espouse views favorable to the industry and lobby government legislators directly to shape government regulations. For example, during the 1990s and early 2000s, the now-bankrupt energy trading company Enron lobbied government legislators to persuade them to deregulate energy markets in the United States, an action that Enron would benefit from. Second, companies and industries may lobby the government through industry associations. In 2002, the United States Steel Industry Association was a prime mover in persuading President Bush to enact a 30 percent tariff on imports of foreign steel into the United States. The purpose of the tariff was to protect American steel makers from foreign competitors, thereby reducing the intensity of rivalry in the United States steel markets.

Summary of Chapter

1. An industry can be defined as a group of companies offering products or services that are close substitutes for each other. Close substitutes are products or services that satisfy the same basic customer needs.

2. The main technique used to analyze competition in the industry environment is the five forces model. The five forces are (1) the risk of new entry by potential competitors, (2) the extent of rivalry among established firms, (3) the bargaining power of buyers, (4) the bargaining power of suppliers, and (5) the threat of substitute products. The stronger each force is, the more competitive the industry and the lower the rate of return that can be earned.

3. The risk of entry by potential competitors is a function of the height of barriers to entry. The higher the barriers to entry are, the lower is the risk of entry and the greater are the profits that can be earned in the industry.

4. The extent of rivalry among established companies is a function of an industry's competitive structure, demand conditions, cost conditions, and barriers to exit. Strong demand conditions moderate the competition among established companies and create opportunities for expansion. When demand is weak, intensive competition can develop, particularly in consolidated industries with high exit barriers.

5. Buyers are most powerful when a company depends on them for business but they themselves are not dependent on the company. In such circumstances, buyers are a threat.

6. Suppliers are most powerful when a company depends on them for business but they themselves are not dependent on the company. In such circumstances, suppliers are a threat.

7. Substitute products are the products of companies serving customer needs similar to the needs served by the industry being analyzed. The more similar the substitute products are to each other, the lower is the price that companies can charge without losing customers to the substitutes.

8. Some argue for a sixth competitive force of some significance: the power, vigor, and competence of complementors. Powerful and vigorous complementors may have a strong positive impact on demand in an industry.

9. Most industries are composed of strategic groups: groups of companies pursuing the same or a similar strategy. Companies in different strategic groups pursue different strategies.

10. The members of a company's strategic group constitute its immediate competitors. Because different strategic groups are characterized by different opportunities and threats, it may pay a company to switch strategic groups. The feasibility of doing so is a function of the height of mobility barriers.

11. Industries go through a well-defined life cycle: from an embryonic stage, through growth, shakeout, and maturity, and eventually decline. Each stage has different implications for the competitive structure of the industry, and each gives rise to its own set of opportunities and threats.

12. The five forces, strategic group, and industry life cycles models all have limitations. The five forces and strategic group models present a static picture of competition that deemphasizes the role of innovation. Yet innovation can revolutionize industry structure and completely change the strength of different competitive forces. The five forces and strategic group models have been criticized for deemphasizing the importance of individual company differences. A company will not be profitable just because it is based in an attractive industry or strategic group; much more is required. The industry life cycle model is a generalization that is not always followed, particularly when innovations revolutionize an industry.

13. The macroenvironment affects the intensity of rivalry within an industry. Included in the macroenvironment are the macroeconomic environment, the global environment, the technological environment, the demographic and social environment, and the political and legal environment.

Discussion Questions

1. Under what environmental conditions are price wars most likely to occur in an industry? What are the implications of price wars for a company? How should a company try to deal with the threat of a price war?

2. Discuss Porter's five forces model with reference to what you know about the U.S. airline industry. What does the model tell you about the level of competition in this industry?

3. Identify a growth industry, a mature industry, and a declining industry. For each industry, identify the following: (a) the number and size distribution of companies, (b) the nature of barriers to entry, (c) the height of barriers to entry, and (d) the extent of product differentiation. What do these factors tell you about the nature of competition in each industry? What are the implications for the company in terms of opportunities and threats?

4. Assess the impact of macroenvironmental factors on the likely level of enrollment at your university over the next decade. What are the implications of these factors for the job security and salary level of your professors?

Practicing Strategic Management

■ SMALL-GROUP EXERCISE
Competing with Microsoft

Break up into groups of three to five people, and discuss the following scenario. Appoint one group member as a spokesperson who will communicate your findings to the class.

You are a group of managers and software engineers at a small start-up. You have developed a revolutionary new operating system for personal computers that offers distinct advantages over Microsoft's Windows operating system: it takes up less memory space on the hard drive of a personal computer; it takes full advantage of the power of the personal computer's microprocessor, and in theory can run software applications much faster than Windows; it is much easier to install and use than Windows; and it responds to voice instructions with an accuracy of 99.9 percent, in addition to input from a keyboard or mouse. The operating system is the only product offering that your company has produced.

Complete the following exercises:
1. Analyze the competitive structure of the market for personal computer operating systems. On the basis of this analysis, identify what factors might inhibit adoption of your operating system by customers.
2. Can you think of a strategy that your company might pursue, either alone or in conjunction with other enterprises, in order to "beat Microsoft"? What will it take to execute that strategy successfully?

■ ARTICLE FILE 2

Find an example of an industry that has become more competitive in recent years. Identify the reasons for the increase in competitive pressure.

■ STRATEGIC MANAGEMENT PROJECT
Module 2

This module requires you to analyze the industry environment in which your company is based using the information you have already gathered:
1. Apply the five forces model to the industry in which your company is based. What does this model tell you about the nature of competition in the industry?
2. Are any changes taking place in the macroenvironment that might have an impact, positive or negative, on the industry in which your company is based? If

so, what are these changes, and how might they affect the industry?
3. Identify any strategic groups that might exist in the industry. How does the intensity of competition differ across these strategic groups?
4. How dynamic is the industry in which your company is based? Is there any evidence that innovation is reshaping competition or has done so in the recent past?
5. In what stage of its life cycle is the industry in which your company is based? What are the implications of this for the intensity of competition both now and in the future?
6. Is your company based in an industry that is becoming more global? If so, what are the implications of this change for competitive intensity?
7. Analyze the impact of national context as it pertains to the industry in which your company is based. Does national context help or hinder your company in achieving a competitive advantage in the global marketplace?

■ EXPLORING THE WEB
Visiting Boeing and Airbus

Visit the websites of the Boeing Corporation (**www.boeing.com**) and Airbus Industrie (**www.airbus.com**). Go to the news features of both sites, and read through the press releases issued by both companies. Also look at the annual reports and company profile (or history features) contained on both sites. With this material as your guide:
1. Use Porter's five forces model to analyze the nature of competition in the commercial jet aircraft market.
2. Assess the likely outlook for competition over the next ten years in this market. Try to establish whether new entry into this industry is likely, whether demand will grow or shrink, how powerful buyers are likely to become, and what the implications of all this are for the nature of competition ten years out.

General Task   Search the Web for information that allows you to assess the current state of competition in the market for personal computers. Use that information to perform an analysis of the structure of the market in the United States. (Hint: Try visiting the websites of personal computer companies. Also visit *Electronic Business Today* at **www.ebtmag.com**).

Closing Case

Plane Wreck: The Airline Industry in 2001–2004

Between 2001 and 2003, players in the global airline industry lost some $30 billion, more money than the industry had made since its inception. The losses were particularly severe among the big six airlines in the United States (American Airlines, United, Delta, Continental, US Airways, and Northwest). In 2002 these major airlines lost $7.4 billion and another $5.3 billion in 2003. Both US Airways and United were forced to seek Chapter 11 bankruptcy protections. Although forecasts suggest the six major airlines will break even in 2004, a return to the boom years of 1995–2000, when the airlines posted record profits, seems unlikely anytime soon.

The dramatic slump in airline profits began in early 2001 when business travel started to fall off in the wake of the rapidly deflating technology and dot-com bubble of the 1990s. Then, in the aftermath of the terrorist attacks of September 11, demand dropped through the floor. The airlines began cutting prices to try to maintain their passenger loads in the face of declining demand. However, the tactic didn't work. When one airline serving a particular route cut its prices, its competitors, desperate to cover their fixed costs, quickly followed. The result was a downward price spiral. In the fourth quarter of 2001, prices fell by 15 percent as airlines tried to induce people to fly. Despite this effort, passenger traffic fell by 19 percent, and revenue at major airlines fell by over 30 percent.[35]

Even though demand and profits plummeted at the big six airlines, some carriers continued to make profits during 2001–2003, most notably the budget airline Southwest. In addition, other newer budget airlines, including AirTran and JetBlue (which was started in 2000), gained market share during this period. Indeed, between 2000 and 2003 the budget airlines in the United States expanded capacity by 44 percent even as the majors slashed their carrying capacity and parked unused planes in the desert. In 1998 the budget airlines held a 16 percent share of the U.S. market, and by mid 2004 their share had risen to 29 percent.

The key to the success of the budget airlines is their business model, which gives them a 30 to 50 percent cost advantage over traditional airlines. The budget airlines all follow the same basic script: They purchase just one type of aircraft (some standardize on Boeing 737s, others on Airbus 320s). They also hire nonunion labor and cross-train employees to perform multiple jobs (for example, to help meet turnaround times, the pilots might help check

tickets at the gate). As a result of such flexible work rules, Southwest needs only 80 employees to support and fly an aircraft, compared to 115 at the big six airlines. The budget airlines also favor flying "point to point" rather than through hubs, and they often use cheap secondary airports rather than major hubs. They focus on large markets with large traffic volume (such as up and down the East Coast). To cut costs further, they offer no frills on the flights: no in-flight food or complementary drinks. Finally, prices are set low to fill up the seats.

In contrast, the business model of the six major airlines is based on the network or hub-and-spoke system. Under this system, the network airlines route their flights through major hubs. Often a single airline will dominate a hub (thus United dominates Chicago O'Hare airport). This system was developed because it was a way of efficiently using airline capacity when there wasn't enough demand to fill a plane flying point to point. By using a hub-and-spoke system, the major network airlines have been able to serve some 38,000 city pairs, some of which generate fewer than fifty passengers per day. But the budget airlines seem to have found a way around this constraint by focusing on a few hundred city pairs where there is sufficient demand to fill their planes and flying directly between them (point to point). The network carriers also suffer from a higher cost structure because of their legacy of a unionized work force. In addition, their costs are pushed higher by their superior in-flight service. In good times, the network carriers can recoup their costs by charging higher prices than the discount airlines, particularly for business travelers, who pay more to book late and to fly business or first class. In the weak demand environment of the early 2000s, however, this was no longer the case.

To make matters worse for the network airlines, the budget airlines have started to enter the lucrative coast-to-coast markets. The major airlines long dominated these markets and kept fares high. However, by taking advantage of new long-range versions of their favorite aircraft, such as the Boeing 737–800, to fly these routes nonstop, budget airlines have been able to directly compete with the network airlines. JetBlue, for example, has over 50 percent of its capacity on coast-to-cost routes. To protect their turf, the network airlines have responded by adding more flights in an attempt to squeeze the budget carriers out. As a result, between June 2003 and June 2004, capacity on coast-to-coast routes increased anywhere from 14 to 100 percent. With all these extra seats to fill, airlines have had to slash fares, which have fallen by as much as 60 to 70 percent on some routes.

The major network airlines have also moved to cut their operating costs. Between 2001 and 2004, they cut their operating costs by $13.4 billion and reduced payrolls by 100,000. Yet it has not been enough to check the expansion of the budget airlines or to close the cost advantage the discounters enjoy. To make matters worse, in 2004 prices for jet fuel soared as oil peaked at over $40 a barrel. Some of the major airlines responded by trying to raise prices, only to give up within days. Some observers have also commented that the industry's problems are exacerbated by bankruptcy laws that keep troubled airlines such as United in the industry by allowing them time to reorganize under Chapter 11 bankruptcy protection rules.[36]

Case Discussion Questions

1. Use the competitive forces model to analyze the structure of the airline industry during 2001–2004. How well does this analysis explain the low profitability of the industry?

2. Are the budget airlines in a different strategic group than the major network airlines?

3. Compare and contrast the business models of the network and budget airlines. What are the strengths and weaknesses of each model?

4. What is required for the industry to return to profitability?

5. What must the major network airlines do to respond to the competitive threat posed by the budget airlines? Have they taken steps in this direction? Have they done enough?

Chapter 3

Internal Analysis: Distinctive Competencies, Competitive Advantage, and Profitability

Opening Case

Dell's Competitive Advantage

Dell Computer has a sustained history of very high profitability. Between 1998 and 2003 its average return on invested capital (ROIC) was a staggering 39 percent, far ahead of the profitability of competing manufacturers of personal computers. For comparison, Apple Computer earned an average ROIC of 7 percent over the same period, Gateway 10 percent, and Hewlett-Packard 13 percent. Moreover, Dell managed to maintain a very high ROIC even in the tough selling environment for personal computers that existed in 2001–2003, while the profitability of its competitors fell sharply during this same period (see the figure on page 76). Clearly, Dell has a sustained competitive advantage over its rivals. Where does this competitive advantage come from?

The answer can be found in Dell's business model: selling directly to customers. Michael Dell reasoned that by cutting out wholesalers and retailers he could obtain the profits they would otherwise receive and give part of those profits to customers in the form of lower prices. Initially, Dell sold directly through mailings and telephone contacts, but since the mid 1990s most of its sales have been made through its web site. By 2001, 85 percent of Dell's sales were made through the Internet. Dell's sophisticated interactive web site allows customers to mix and match product features such as microprocessors, memory, monitors, internal hard drives, CD and DVD drives, keyboard and mouse format, and so on to customize their own computer system. The ability to customize orders keeps customers coming back to Dell. This strong customer loyalty helped to drive sales up to a record $41.5 billion in fiscal 2004.

Another major reason for Dell's high performance is that Dell minimizes the cost structure of its supply chain, in particular, the costs of holding inventory, yet it can still build a computer to individual customer specifications within three days. Dell has about two hundred suppliers, over half of them located outside the United States. It uses the Internet to feed real-time information about order flow to its suppliers so they have up-to-the-minute information about demand trends for the components they produce, along with volume expectations for the upcoming four to twelve weeks. Dell's suppliers use this information to adjust their own production schedules, manufacturing just enough components for Dell's needs and shipping them by the

Profitability in the U.S. Personal Computer Industry, 1998–2003

Data Source: Value Line Investment Survey.

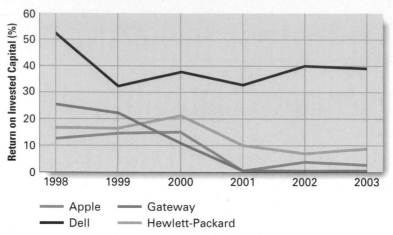

Apple — Gateway
Dell — Hewlett-Packard

most appropriate mode so that they arrive just in time for production. This tight coordination is pushed back even further down the supply chain because Dell shares this information with its suppliers' biggest suppliers. For example, Selectron Technologies builds motherboards for Dell that incorporate digital signal processing chips from Texas Instruments. To coordinate the supply chain, Dell passes information to both Texas Instruments and Selectron. Texas Instruments then adjusts its schedules to Selectron's needs, and Selectron adjusts its schedule to fit the order data it receives from Dell. All of this coordination results in lower costs along the supply chain.

Dell's ultimate goal is to drive all inventories out of the supply chain apart from those actually in transit between suppliers and Dell, effectively replacing inventory with information. Although it has not yet achieved this goal, it has succeeded in driving down inventory to the lowest level in the industry. Dell has about three days of inventory on hand, compared to twenty to thirty at com-

petitors such as Hewlett-Packard and Gateway. This is a major source of competitive advantage in the computer industry, where component costs account for 75 percent of revenues and typically fall by 1 percent per week due to rapid obsolescence.

In sum, Dell's competitive advantage is based on a direct selling business model that eliminates wholesalers and retailers and allows the company to lower prices. This, combined with strong customer loyalty and efficient internal operations, particularly in supply-chain management, has given Dell the lowest cost structure in the industry. When demand for personal computers fell in 2001, Dell was able to take advantage of its cost-leadership position to cut prices aggressively and gain market share while still maintaining high profitability through economies of scale and other efficiencies. By early 2004 Dell had 16.5 percent of the global market for PCs, up from 14.6 percent a year earlier. Hewlett-Packard, which held second place, had a 14 percent share in early 2004.[1]

Overview

Why, within a particular industry or market, do some companies outperform others? What is the basis of their (sustained) competitive advantage? The *Opening Case* provides some clues. The competitive advantage of Dell Computer comes from its direct selling business model, which lowers costs and enables the company to respond to customer demands, and also from its focus on efficient supply-chain management. As you will see in this chapter, efficiency and customer responsiveness are two of the four main building blocks of competitive advantage. The other two are *innovation* and the *quality of product or service offering*.

This chapter focuses on internal analysis, which is concerned with identifying the *strengths* and *weaknesses* of the company. Together with an analysis of the company's external environment, internal analysis gives managers the information they need to choose the business model and strategies that will enable their company to attain a sustained competitive advantage. Internal analysis is a three-step process. First, managers must understand the process by which companies create value for customers and profit for themselves, and they need to understand the role of *resources, capabilities,* and *distinctive competencies* in this process. Second, they need to understand how important superior *efficiency, innovation, quality*, and *responsiveness to customers* are in creating value and generating high profitability. Third, they must be able to analyze the sources of their company's competitive advantage to identify what is driving the profitability of their enterprise and where opportunities for improvement might lie. In other words, they must be able to identify how the *strengths* of the enterprise boost its profitability and how any *weaknesses* lead to lower profitability.

Three more critical issues in internal analysis are addressed in this chapter. First, what factors influence the *durability* of competitive advantage? Second, why do successful companies often lose their competitive advantage? Third, how can companies avoid competitive failure and sustain their competitive advantage over time?

After reading this chapter, you will understand the nature of competitive advantage and why managers need to perform internal analysis, just as they must conduct industry analysis, to achieve superior performance and profitability.

Competencies, Resources, and Competitive Advantage

A company has a *competitive advantage* over its rivals when its profitability is greater than the average profitability of all companies in its industry. It has a *sustained competitive advantage* when it is able to maintain above-average profitability over a number of years (as Dell has done in the personal computer industry). What are the sources of competitive advantage and superior profitability, and what is the link between strategy, competitive advantage, and profitability?

■ Strategy, Distinctive Competencies, and Competitive Advantage

The primary objective of strategy is to achieve a sustained competitive advantage, which in turn will result in superior profitability and profit growth. All the levels of strategy identified in Chapter 1—functional, business, global, and corporate—are involved in creating a competitive advantage, and they are discussed in detail in the next chapters. No matter what the level, however, to use strategy to achieve a competitive advantage, a company must create distinctive competencies.

Distinctive competencies are firm-specific strengths that allow a company to *differentiate* its products and/or achieve substantially *lower costs* than its rivals and thus gain a competitive advantage. It can be argued, for example, that Toyota has distinctive competencies in the development and operation of manufacturing processes. Toyota pioneered a whole range of manufacturing techniques, such as just-in-time inventory systems, self-managing teams, and reduced setup times for complex equipment. These competencies, collectively known as the Toyota *lean production* system, helped it attain superior efficiency and product quality, which are the basis of its competitive advantage in the global automobile industry.[2] Distinctive competencies arise from two complementary sources: *resources* and *capabilities*.[3]

■ Resources

Resources are financial, physical, social or human, technological, and organizational factors that allow a company to create value for its customers. Company resources can be divided into two types: tangible and intangible resources. **Tangible resources** are physical entities, such as land, buildings, plant, equipment, inventory, and money. **Intangible resources** are nonphysical entities that are created by managers and other employees, such as brand names, the reputation of the company, the knowledge that employees have gained through experience, and the intellectual property of the company, including that protected through patents, copyrights, and trademarks.

The more *firm specific* and *difficult to imitate* is a resource, the more likely a company is to have a distinctive competency. For example, Polaroid's distinctive competency in instant photography was based on a firm-specific and valuable intangible resource: technological know-how in instant film processing that was protected from imitation by a thicket of patents. Once a process can be imitated, as when patents expire, or a superior technology, such as digital photography, comes along, the distinctive competency disappears, as has happened to Polaroid. Another important quality of a resource that leads to a distinctive competency is that it is *valuable*: in some way, it helps to create strong *demand* for the company's products. Thus, Polaroid's technological know-how was valuable while it created strong demand for its photographic products; it became far less valuable when superior digital technology came along.

■ **Capabilities** **Capabilities** refer to a company's skills at coordinating its resources and putting them to productive use. These skills reside in an organization's rules, routines, and procedures, that is, the style or manner through which it makes decisions and manages its internal processes to achieve organizational objectives. More generally, a company's capabilities are the product of its organizational structure, processes, and control systems. They specify how and where decisions are made within a company, the kind of behaviors the company rewards, and the company's cultural norms and values. (We discuss how organizational structure and control systems help a company obtain capabilities in Chapters 12 and 13.) Capabilities are intangible. They reside not so much in individuals as in the way individuals interact, cooperate, and make decisions within the context of an organization.[4]

■ **A Critical Distinction** The distinction between resources and capabilities is critical to understanding what generates a distinctive competency. A company may have firm-specific and valuable resources, but unless it has the capability to use those resources effectively, it may not be able to create a distinctive competency. It is also important to recognize that a company may not need firm-specific and valuable resources to establish a distinctive competency so long as it *does have* capabilities that no competitor possesses. For example, the steel mini-mill operator Nucor is widely acknowledged to be the most cost-efficient steel maker in the United States. Its distinctive competency in low-cost steel making does not come from any firm-specific and valuable resources. Nucor has the same resources (plant, equipment, skilled employees, know-how) as many other mini-mill operators. What distinguishes Nucor is its unique capability to manage its resources in a highly productive way. Specifically, Nucor's structure, control systems, and culture promote efficiency at all levels within the company.

In sum, for a company to have a distinctive competency it must at a minimum have either (1) a firm-specific and valuable resource and the capabilities (skills) necessary to take advantage of that resource (as illustrated by Polaroid) or (2) a firm-specific capability to manage resources (as exemplified by Nucor). A company's distinctive competency is strongest when it possesses *both* firm-specific and valuable resources and firm-specific capabilities to manage those resources.

Figure 3.1 illustrates the relationship of a company's strategies, distinctive competencies, and competitive advantage. Distinctive competencies shape the strategies that the company pursues, which lead to competitive advantage and superior profitability. However, it is also very important to realize that the strategies a company adopts can build new resources and capabilities or strengthen the existing resources and capabilities of the company, thereby enhancing the distinctive competencies of the enterprise. Thus, the relationship between distinctive competencies and strategies is not a linear one; rather, it is a reciprocal one in which distinctive competencies shape strategies, and strategies help to build and create distinctive competencies.[5]

FIGURE 3.1

Strategy, Resources,
Capabilities, and
Competencies

The history of The Walt Disney Company since the 1980s illustrates the way this process works. In the early 1980s, Disney suffered a string of poor financial years that culminated in a 1984 management shakeup when Michael Eisner was appointed CEO. Four years later, Disney's sales had increased from $1.66 billion to $3.75 billion, its net profits from $98 million to $570 million, and its stock market valuation from $1.8 billion to $10.3 billion. What brought about this transformation was the company's deliberate attempt to use its resources and capabilities more aggressively: Disney's enormous film library, its brand name, and its filmmaking skills, particularly in animation. Under Eisner, many old Disney classics were re-released, first in movie theaters and then on video, earning the company millions in the process. Then Eisner reintroduced the product that had originally made Disney famous: the full-length animated feature. Putting together its brand name and in-house animation capabilities, Disney produced a stream of major box office hits, including *The Little Mermaid, Beauty and the Beast, Aladdin, Pocahontas*, and *The Lion King*. Disney also started a cable television channel, the Disney Channel, to use this library and capitalize on the company's brand name. In other words, Disney's existing resources and capabilities shaped its strategies.

Through his choice of strategies, Eisner also developed new competencies in different parts of the business. In the filmmaking arm of Disney, for example, Eisner created a new low-cost film division under the Touchstone label, and the company had a string of low-budget box office hits. It entered into a long-term agreement with the computer animation company Pixar to develop a competency in computer-generated animated films. This strategic collaboration has produced several hits, including *Toy Story* and *Monsters Incorporated*. In sum, Disney's transformation was based not only on strategies that took advantage of the company's existing resources and capabilities, but also on strategies that built new resources and capabilities, such as those that underlie the company's competency in computer-generated animated films.

■ **Competitive Advantage, Value Creation, and Profitability**

Competitive advantage leads to superior profitability. At the most basic level, how profitable a company becomes depends on three factors: (1) the *value* customers place on the company's products, (2) the *price* that a company charges for its products, and (3) the *costs* of creating those products. The value customers place on a product reflects the *utility* they get from a product, the happiness or satisfaction gained from consuming or owning the product. *Utility* must be distinguished from *price*. Utility is something that customers get from a product. It is a function of the attributes of the product, such as its performance, design, quality, and point-of-sale and after-sale service. For example, most customers would place a much higher utility value on a top-end Lexus car from Toyota than on a low-end basic economy car from General Motors (they would value it more), precisely because they perceive the Lexus to have better performance and superior design, quality, and service. A company that strengthens the utility (or value) of its products in the eyes of customers has more *pricing options:* it can raise prices to reflect that utility (value) or hold prices lower to induce more customers to purchase its products, thereby expanding unit sales volume.

Whatever pricing option a company chooses, however, the price a company charges for a good or service is typically less than the utility value placed on that good or service by the customer. This is so because the customer captures some of that utility in the form of what economists call a *consumer surplus.*[6] The customer is able to do this because the company is competing with other companies for the customer's business, so the company must charge a lower price than it could were it a monopoly supplier. Moreover, it is normally impossible to segment the market to such a degree that the company can charge each customer a price that reflects that individual's unique assessment of the utility of a product—what economists refer to as a customer's *reservation price.* For these reasons, the price that gets charged tends to be less than the utility value placed on the product by many customers. Nevertheless, remember the basic principle here: *the more utility that consumers get from a company's products or services, the more pricing options it has.*

These concepts are illustrated in Figure 3.2: U is the average utility value per unit of a product to a customer, P is the average price per unit that the company decides to charge for that product, and C is the average unit cost of producing that product (including actual production costs and the cost of capital investments in production systems). The company's average profit per unit is equal to $P - C$, and the consumer surplus is equal to $U - P$. In other words, $U - P$ is a measure of the value the consumer captures, and $P - C$ is a measure of the value the company captures. The company makes a profit so long as P is more than C, and its profitability will be greater the lower C is *relative* to P. Bear in mind that the difference between U and P is in part determined by the intensity of competitive pressure in the marketplace; the lower the intensity of competitive pressure is, the higher the price that can be charged relative to U, but the difference between U and P is also determined by the company's pricing

FIGURE 3.2

Value Creation
per Unit

U = **Utility** to consumer
P = **Price**
C = **Costs** of production

U – P = Consumer surplus
P – C = **Profit** margin
U – C = **Value** created

Includes **cost** of capital
per unit

FIGURE 3.3

Value Creation and
Pricing Options

choice.[7] As we shall see, a company may choose to keep prices low relative to volume because lower prices enable the company to sell more products, attain scale economies, and boost its profit margin by lowering C relative to P.

Note also that the *value created* by a company is measured by the difference between the utility a consumer gets from the product (U) and the costs of production (C), that is, $U - C$. A company creates value by converting factors of production that cost C into a product from which customers gets a utility of U. A company can create more value for its customers by lowering C or making the product more attractive through superior design, performance, quality, service, and the like. When customers assign a greater utility to the product (U increases), they are willing to pay a higher price (P increases). This discussion suggests that a company has a competitive advantage and high profitability when it creates more value for its customers than do rivals.[8]

The company's pricing options are captured in Figure 3.3. Suppose a company's current pricing option is the one pictured in the middle column of Figure 3.3. Imagine that the company decides to pursue strategies to increase the utility of its product offering from U to U^* in order to boost its profitability. Increasing utility initially raises production costs because the company has to spend money to increase product performance, quality, service, and other factors. Now there are two different pricing options that the company can pursue. Option 1 is to raise prices to reflect the higher utility: the company raises prices more than its costs increase, and profit per unit ($P - C$) increases. Option 2 involves a very different set of choices: the company *lowers* prices in order to expand unit volume. Basically, what is happening here is that customers recognize that they are getting a great bargain because price is now much lower than utility (the *consumer surplus* has increased), so they rush out to buy more (*demand* has increased). As unit volume expands due to increased demand, the company is able to realize scale economies and reduce its average unit costs. Although creating the extra utility initially cost more and prices are now lowered, profit margins widen because the average unit costs of production fall as volume increases and scale economies are attained.

Managers need to understand the dynamic relationships among *utility, pricing, demand,* and *costs* and make decisions on the basis of that understanding to maximize competitive advantage and profitability. Option 2 in Figure 3.3, for example, might not be a viable strategy if demand did not increase rapidly with lower prices or if there are few economies of scale to be had by increasing volume. Managers must understand how value creation and pricing decisions affect demand and also how unit costs change with increases in volume. In other words, they must have a good grasp of the demand for the company's product and its cost structure at different levels of output if they are to make decisions that maximize profitability.

Consider the automobile industry. According to a 2004 study by Harbour & Associates, in 2003 Toyota made $2,402 in profit on every vehicle it manufactured in North America. General Motors, in contrast, made only $178 profit per vehicle.[9] What accounts for the difference? First, Toyota has the best reputation for quality in the industry. According to annual surveys issued by J.D. Power and Associates, Toyota consistently tops the list in terms of quality, while GM cars are at best in the middle of the pack. The higher quality translates into a higher utility and allows Toyota to charge 5 to 10 percent higher prices than General Motors for equivalent cars. Second, Toyota has a lower cost per vehicle than General Motors, in part because of its superior labor productivity. For example, in Toyota's North American plants, it took an average of 31.06 employee hours to build a car, compared to 40.52 at GM plants in North America. That 9.5-hour productivity advantage translates into much lower labor costs for Toyota and, hence, a lower overall cost structure. Therefore, as summarized in Figure 3.4, Toyota's advantage over GM derives from greater utility (U), which has allowed the company to charge a higher price (P) for its cars, and from a lower cost structure (C), which taken together implies significantly greater profitability per vehicle ($P - C$).

Toyota's decisions with regard to pricing are guided by its managers' understanding of the relationship of utility, prices, demand, and costs. Given its ability to build more utility into its products, Toyota could have charged even higher prices than illustrated in Figure 3.4, but that might have led to lower sales volume, fewer scale economies, higher unit costs, and lower profit margins. Toyota's managers have sought to find the pricing option that enables the company to maximize its profits given their assessment of demand for its products and its cost function. Thus, to create superior value a company does not have to have the lowest cost structure in an industry or create the product with the highest utility in the eyes of customers. All that is necessary is that the gap between perceived utility (U) and costs of production (C) is greater than the gap attained by competitors.

FIGURE 3.4

Comparing Toyota and General Motors

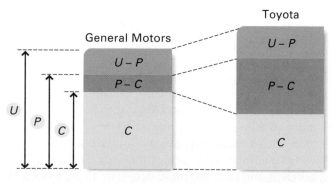

■ **Differentiation and Cost Structure**

Note that Toyota has *differentiated* itself from General Motors by its superior quality, which allows it to charge higher prices, and its superior productivity translates into a *lower cost structure*. Thus, its competitive advantage over General Motors is the result of strategies that have led to distinctive competencies, resulting in greater *differentiation* and a *lower cost structure*.

Indeed, at the heart of any company's business model is the combination of congruent strategies aimed at creating distinctive competencies that (1) *differentiate* its products in some way so that its consumers derive more utility from them, which gives the company more pricing options, and (2) result in a *lower cost structure*, which also gives it a broader range of pricing choices.[10] Achieving a sustained competitive advantage and superior profitability requires the right choices with regard to utility through differentiation and pricing given the demand conditions in the company's market and the company's cost structure at different levels of output. This issue is addressed in detail in the following chapters.

The Value Chain

All of the functions of a company—such as production, marketing, R&D, service, information systems, materials management, and human resources—have a role in lowering the cost structure and increasing the perceived utility (value) of the products through differentiation. As the first step in examining this concept, consider the value chain, which is illustrated in Figure 3.5.[11] The term **value chain** refers to the idea that a company is a chain of activities for transforming inputs into outputs that customers value. The transformation process involves a number of primary activities and support activities that add value to the product.

■ **Primary Activities**

Primary activities have to do with the design, creation, and delivery of the product, its marketing, and its support and after-sales service. In the value chain illustrated in Figure 3.5, the primary activities are broken down into four functions: research and development, production, marketing and sales, and customer service.

■ **Research and Development** **Research and development** (R&D) is concerned with the design of products and production processes. Although we think of R&D as being associated with the design of physical products and production processes in manufacturing enterprises, many service companies also undertake R&D. For example, banks compete with each other by developing new financial products and new ways of delivering those products to customers. Online banking and smart

FIGURE 3.5

The Value Chain

Primary Activities

INPUT → Research and development → Production → Marketing and sales → Customer service → OUTPUT

Company infrastructure | Information systems | Materials management | Human resources

Support Activities

debit cards are two recent examples of the fruits of new-product development in the banking industry. Earlier examples of innovation in the banking industry were ATM machines, credit cards, and debit cards.

By creating superior product design, R&D can increase the functionality of products, which makes them more attractive to customers, thereby adding value. Alternatively, the work of R&D may result in more efficient production processes, thereby lowering production costs. Either way, the R&D function can help to lower costs or raise the utility of a product and permit a company to charge higher prices. At Intel, for example, R&D creates value by developing ever more powerful microprocessors and helping to pioneer ever more efficient manufacturing processes (in conjunction with equipment suppliers).

■ **Production** Production is concerned with the creation of a good or service. For physical products, when we talk about production, we generally mean manufacturing. For services such as banking or retail operations, "production" typically takes place when the service is delivered to the customer, as when a bank makes a loan to a customer. By performing its activities efficiently, the production function of a company helps to lower its cost structure. For example, the efficient production operations of Honda and Toyota help those automobile companies achieve higher profitability relative to competitors such as General Motors. The production function can also perform its activities in a way that is consistent with high product quality, which leads to differentiation (and higher value) and lower costs.

■ **Marketing and Sales** There are several ways in which the **marketing and sales** functions of a company can help to create value. Through brand positioning and advertising, the marketing function can increase the value that customers perceive to be contained in a company's product (and thus the utility they attribute to the product). Insofar as these help to create a favorable impression of the company's product in the minds of customers, they increase utility. For example, in the 1980s, the French company Perrier persuaded U.S. customers that slightly carbonated bottled water was worth $1.50 per bottle rather than a price closer to the $0.50 that it cost to collect, bottle, and distribute the water. Perrier's marketing function essentially increased the perception of utility that customers ascribed to the product.

Marketing and sales can also create value by discovering customer needs and communicating them back to the R&D function of the company, which can then design products that better match those needs. For another example of value creation by the marketing function of an enterprise, see Strategy in Action 3.1, which looks at how Pfizer's sales force increased the perception of the utility associated with one of its main pharmaceuticals, Zoloft.

■ **Customer Service** The role of the **service** function of an enterprise is to provide after-sales service and support. This function can create superior utility by solving customer problems and supporting customers after they have purchased the product. For example, Caterpillar, the U.S.-based manufacturer of heavy earth-moving equipment, can get spare parts to any point in the world within twenty-four hours, thereby minimizing the amount of downtime its customers have to face if their Caterpillar equipment malfunctions. This is an extremely valuable support capability in an industry where downtime is very expensive. It has helped to increase the utility that customers associate with Caterpillar products, and thus the price that Caterpillar can charge for its products.

Strategy in Action   3.1

Value Creation at Pfizer

The antidepressant drug Prozac, introduced by Eli Lilly & Company in 1988, was one of the most lucrative mental health drugs in history. In 1995, U.S. customers alone filled almost 19 million prescriptions for Prozac, which was used to mitigate the effects of a wide range of mental disorders, including chronic depression, bulimia, and obsessive disorders. Worldwide sales of the drug topped $2 billion in 1995, making it a gold mine for Lilly.

During the 1990s, Prozac's market position came under attack from an aggressive marketing and sales campaign by rival pharmaceutical company Pfizer. In 1992, Pfizer introduced its own antidepressant, Zoloft. According to medical experts, the differences between Prozac and Zoloft are slight at best. Both drugs function in the same basic manner, by boosting serotonin, a brain chemical believed to be in short supply in many depressed people. Both drugs also have a similar list of possible side effects. Prozac's label cites nausea, nervousness, anxiety, insomnia, and drowsiness as possible side effects. Zoloft's label lists nausea and other stomach problems, diarrhea, sexual dysfunction, and sleepiness. As one expert noted, "These drugs are so similar that you have to be kidding yourself if you think one drug is going to be consistently superior to the other in treating patients."

Despite the similarity between the two products, Pfizer gained share from Lilly in the antidepressant market. By 1998, Zoloft accounted for 40 percent of the market, up from little more than zero in 1992. The main reason for this success seems to have been Pfizer's aggressive marketing and sales campaign, which created an impression in the eyes of physicians that Zoloft is a safer drug. Pfizer sales representatives bill their product as just as effective as Prozac but without its occasional downside, anxiety. The

reference to anxiety seems carefully designed to remind doctors of a spate of failed lawsuits alleging that Prozac caused suicides and other violent acts. Pfizer's sales force also logged more "face time" with physicians than Lilly's. According to Scott-Levin and Associates, in 1995 Zoloft sales representatives made 660,000 sales visits to doctors, 70,000 more than the Prozac sales force logged. About three-quarters of these were not to psychiatrists but to basic primary care physicians, who increasingly prescribe antidepressants but presumably are less familiar with their more subtle properties than psychiatrists are. Doctors also claim that Pfizer salespeople play up Prozac's clinical reputation for being more agitating than Zoloft. They also emphasize that unlike Zoloft, Prozac remains in the bloodstream for weeks after a patient stops taking it, raising the possibility of adverse drug interaction if a patient switches to other medications.

The important point here is that Pfizer's marketing and sales force altered physicians' perceptions of the relative utility of Prozac and Zoloft. For Pfizer, the payoff came in terms of rapidly increasing revenues and market share and, of course, a greater return on the company's investment in developing Zoloft. Just how successful Pfizer had been was demonstrated in August 2001 when Prozac came off patent, allowing generic competitors to enter the market. Sales of Prozac fell by 80 percent within months as low-priced generic versions of Prozac grabbed market share. However, despite the fact that Zoloft is chemically very similar to Prozac, sales of Zoloft remained robust and hit a record $3.12 billion in 2003, up from $2.74 billion in the prior year. The Zoloft brand was strong enough to ward off competition from low-priced generic versions of Prozac.[a]

■ **Support Activities**   The **support activities** of the value chain provide inputs that allow the primary activities to take place. These activities are broken down into four functions: materials management (or logistics), human resources, information systems, and company infrastructure (see Figure 3.5).

■ **Materials Management (Logistics)**   The **materials-management** (or logistics) function controls the transmission of physical materials through the value chain, from procurement through production and into distribution. The efficiency with which this is carried out can significantly lower cost, thereby creating more value. As noted in the *Running Case*, Wal-Mart has the most efficient materials-management setup in the retail industry. By tightly controlling the flow of goods from its suppliers through its stores and into the hands of customers, Wal-Mart has eliminated the need to hold large inventories of goods. Lower inventories mean lower costs, and hence greater value creation.

■ **Human Resources** There are a number of ways in which the **human resource** function can help an enterprise to create more value. This function ensures that the company has the right mix of skilled people to perform its value creation activities effectively. It is also the job of the human resource function to ensure that people are adequately trained, motivated, and compensated to perform their value creation tasks. If the human resources are functioning well, employee productivity rises (which lowers costs) and customer service improves (which raises utility), thereby enabling the company to create more value.

■ **Information Systems** **Information systems** are the largely electronic systems for managing inventory, tracking sales, pricing products, selling products, dealing with customer service inquiries, and so on. Information systems, when coupled with the communications features of the Internet, are holding out the promise of being able to improve the efficiency and effectiveness with which a company manages its other value creation activities. As noted in the *Running Case,* Wal-Mart uses information systems to alter the way it does business. By tracking the sale of individual items very closely, its materials-management function has enabled it to optimize its product mix and pricing strategy. Wal-Mart is rarely left with unwanted merchandise on its hands, which saves on costs, and the company is able to provide the right mix of goods to customers, which increases the utility that customers associate with Wal-Mart.

■ **Company Infrastructure** **Company infrastructure** is the companywide context within which all the other value creation activities take place: the organizational structure, control systems, and company culture. Because top management can exert considerable influence in shaping these aspects of a company, top management should also be viewed as part of the infrastructure of a company. Indeed, through strong leadership, top management can shape the infrastructure of a company and, through that, the performance of all other value creation activities that take place within it.

The Building Blocks of Competitive Advantage

The four factors that build and sustain competitive advantage—superior efficiency, quality, innovation, and customer responsiveness—are the product of the company's distinctive competencies. Indeed, in a very real sense they are "generic" distinctive competencies. These generic competencies allow a company to (1) differentiate its product offering, and hence offer more utility to its customers, and (2) lower its cost structure (see Figure 3.6). These factors can be considered *generic* distinctive competencies because any company, regardless of its industry or the products or services it produces, can pursue them. Although they are discussed sequentially below, they are highly interrelated, and the important ways they affect each other should be noted. For example, superior quality can lead to superior efficiency, and innovation can enhance efficiency, quality, and responsiveness to customers.

■ **Efficiency**

In one sense, a business is simply a device for transforming inputs into outputs. Inputs are basic factors of production such as labor, land, capital, management, and technological know-how. Outputs are the goods and services that the business produces. The simplest measure of efficiency is the quantity of inputs that it takes to

Running Case

Support Activities as a Source of Value Creation at Wal-Mart

One of the foundations of Wal-Mart's competitive advantage is the way it uses information systems and logistics to manage its massive supply chain and closely match what customers want with what its suppliers are producing. Wal-Mart's goal is to have goods from a manufacturer arrive at a store and be placed on shelves just before consumers walk into the store to purchase them. This would eliminate the need to hold extensive inventory either in the store or at distribution centers. Moreover, by anticipating what customers want and supplying just enough goods to each store, Wal-Mart is striving to eliminate the twin evils of the retail business: understocking and overstocking. Understocking implies that a sale is not made because the product a customer wants is not in stock. Overstocking requires the retailers to cut prices to shift unsold or slow-moving merchandise.

As measured by inventory turnover, Wal-Mart is probably closer to attaining this goal than any other major retailer. In 2003 Wal-Mart turned over its inventory 7.72 times. Target, another discount retailer, turned over its inventory 6.29 times, and Kmart just 5.51 times. Sears, the department store, turns over its inventory 5.02 times a year. Because Wal-Mart turns its inventory over more rapidly, it has less capital tied up in inventory. This reduces the capital Wal-Mart needs to generate sales and boosts the company's profitability as measured by return on invested capital. How does Wal-Mart do this?

Wal-Mart's high inventory turnover rests on the twin foundations of leading-edge information systems and efficient logistics. Wal-Mart stores its inventory in massive distribution centers, of which there are over one hundred in the United States alone. Each distribution center serves two hundred to three hundred stores within a 300-mile radius. Manufacturers deliver their products to the distribution centers, where they are sorted, stored, and then shipped out to Wal-Mart stores on a fleet of company-owned trucks.

The key to this process is Wal-Mart's information systems. Wal-Mart was one of the first retailers to introduce bar-coding scanners at its checkouts and also one of the first to require manufacturers to place bar codes on their products. The scanning system enables Wal-Mart to track what is selling in a particular store, right down to individual items. This information is then uploaded from the stores to Wal-Mart's central headquarters, where it is communicated on a real-time basis to distribution centers. There merchandise is loaded onto a Wal-Mart truck and shipped out to the store on a daily basis. Because stores are clustered closely together, each truck may serve several stores. Moreover, since many of Wal-Mart's suppliers have manufacturing plants located close to a Wal-Mart store, a truck will often stop at a plant on the way back to a distribution center to pick up merchandise. As a result, by the time the truck arrives at the distribution center, it is 60 to 70 percent full. Thus, not only does Wal-Mart replenish store inventory on a daily basis, but it also uses its trucking capacity efficiently.

To gain further supply-chain efficiencies, Wal-Mart also transmits sales information to manufacturers on a real-time basis. This allows the manufacturers to optimize their own production schedules and deliver products to a Wal-Mart distribution center just when they are needed. Over the years, Wal-Mart has refined this process by introducing a process known as *cross-docking*. With cross-docking, the merchandise from the supplier's truck is unloaded and then immediately transferred to Wal-Mart trucks that are ready to head out to stores. Cross-docking reduces the need to sort and store inventory at a distribution center. This technique boosts profitability in two ways: it reduces labor costs, and it also allows Wal-Mart to operate with smaller distribution centers, thereby lowering capital requirements.

Wal-Mart continues to look for ways to improve the efficiency of its logistics and information systems. In July 2003, it announced that, starting January 1, 2005, it would require its one hundred top suppliers to affix radio frequency identification tags (RFID tags) on all cases and pallets delivered to a distribution center. Radio tags eliminate the need to manually scan inventory with a bar-code scanner, reducing labor costs. Moreover, with radio tags inventory can be automatically scanned at multiple points in a supply chain. This gives Wal-Mart more information and thus more ability to optimize its inventory position. Many observers believe that it is only a matter of time before Wal-Mart requires RFID tags on individual items. When this is achieved, products can be scanned automatically as a customer walks up to a checkout, reducing checkout time and thus labor costs.[b]

FIGURE 3.6

Building Blocks of
Competitive
Advantage

produce a given output—that is, efficiency = outputs/inputs. The more efficient a
company is, the fewer the inputs required to produce a given output. For example, if
it takes General Motors thirty hours of employee time to assemble a car and it takes
Ford twenty-five hours, we can say that Ford is more efficient than GM. And as long
as other things are equal, such as wage rates, we can assume from this information
that Ford will have a lower cost structure than GM. Thus, efficiency helps a company
attain a competitive advantage through a lower cost structure. Similarly, an analysis
of financial statements suggests that in 2003 Wal-Mart generated $4.02 of sales for
every dollar of capital it invested in its business, whereas its competitor Target generated $2.26 of sales for every dollar of capital it invested in its business (capital is used
to build stores, purchase equipment, buy inventory, and so forth). Clearly Wal-Mart
is more efficient in its use of capital: it needs less capital (the input) to generate a dollar of sales (the output) than Target.

As these examples suggest, two of the most important components of efficiency
for many companies are employee productivity and capital productivity. *Employee
productivity* is usually measured by output per employee and *capital productivity* by
output per unit of invested capital (this is discussed in depth in the next section).
Holding all else constant, the company with the highest labor and capital productivity in an industry will typically have the lowest cost structure and therefore a cost-
based competitive advantage. The concept of productivity is not limited to employee
and capital productivity. Pharmaceutical companies, for example, often talk about
the productivity of their R&D spending, by which they mean how many new drugs
they develop from their investment in R&D. Other companies talk about their sales
force productivity, which means how many sales they generate from every sales call,
and so on. The important point to remember is that high productivity leads to
greater efficiency and lower costs.

Strategy in Action 3.2 looks at how Southwest Airlines has attained its low-cost
position in the U.S. airline industry. As you will see, its competitive advantage derives
from its superior labor productivity.

Strategy in Action   3.2

Southwest Airlines' Low Cost Structure

Southwest Airlines has long been one of the standout performers in the U.S. airline industry. It is famous for its low fares, which are generally some 30 percent below those of its major rivals, and these are balanced by an even lower cost structure, which has enabled it to record superior profitability even in bad years such as 2003, when the industry faced slumping demand. Southwest was the only airline among the top eight in the United States to show a profit for the quarter immediately following the September 11 terrorist attacks on the World Trade Center and the Pentagon.

A major source of Southwest's low cost structure seems to be its very high employee productivity. One way the airlines measure employee productivity is by the ratio of employees to passengers carried. According to figures from company 10-K statements, in 2003 Southwest had an employee-to-passenger ratio of 1 to 1,999, one of the best in the industry. By comparison, the ratio at one of the better major airlines, Continental, was 1 to 1,420. These figures suggest that, holding size constant, Southwest runs its operation with far fewer people than competitors. How does it do this?

First, Southwest devotes enormous attention to the people it hires. On average, the company hires only 3 percent of those interviewed in a year. When hiring, it emphasizes teamwork and a positive attitude. Southwest rationalizes that skills can be taught but a positive attitude and a willingness to pitch in cannot. Southwest also creates incentives for its employees to work hard. All employees are covered by a profit-sharing plan, and at least 25 percent of an employee's share of the profit-sharing plan has to be invested in Southwest Airlines stock. This gives rise to a simple formula: the harder employees work, the more profitable Southwest becomes, and the richer the employees get. The results are clear. At other airlines, one would never see a pilot helping to check passengers onto the plane. At Southwest, pilots and flight attendants have been known to help clean the aircraft and check in passengers at the gate. They do this to turn around an aircraft as quickly as possible and get it into the air again, because an aircraft doesn't make money when it is sitting on the ground.

Southwest also reduces its costs by striving to keep its operations as simple as possible. By operating only one type of plane, the Boeing 737, it reduces training costs, maintenance costs, and inventory costs while increasing efficiency in crew and flight scheduling. The operation is nearly ticketless, which reduces cost and back-office accounting functions. Because there is no seat assignment, costs are again reduced. There are no meals or movies in flight, and the airline will not transfer baggage to other airlines, reducing the need for baggage handlers. Another major difference between Southwest and most other airlines is that Southwest flies point to point rather than operating from congested airport hubs. As a result, its costs are lower because there is no need for dozens of gates and thousands of employees to handle banks of flights that come in and then disperse within a two-hour window, leaving the hub empty until the next flights a few hours later.

However, success can bring its own problems, and this is starting to occur at Southwest. While other airlines have been able to get significant pay concessions from their employees in recent years, employees at Southwest have successfully lobbied for higher pay. After two years of sometimes bitter disputes, which have damaged the once harmonious culture at Southwest, in mid 2004 the company's airlines attendants won a 31 percent pay increase spread out over five years. With mechanics and pilots set to enter negotiations next, some observers are now worrying that Southwest's cost structure will rise, eroding the airline's cost-based competitive advantage.[c]

■ Quality as Excellence and Reliability   A product can be thought of as a bundle of attributes.[12] The attributes of many physical products include their form, features, performance, durability, reliability, style, and design.[13] A product is said to have *superior quality* when customers perceive that its attributes provide them with higher utility than the attributes of products sold by rivals. For example, a Rolex watch has attributes—such as design, styling, performance, and reliability—that customers perceive as being superior to the same attributes in many other watches. Thus, we can refer to a Rolex as a high-quality product: Rolex has *differentiated* its watches by these attributes.

When customers evaluate the quality of a product, they commonly measure it against two kinds of attributes: those related to *quality as excellence* and those related to *quality as reliability*. From a quality-as-excellence perspective, the important attributes are things such as a product's design and styling, its aesthetic appeal, its features and functions, the level of service associated with the delivery of the product, and so on. For example, customers can purchase a pair of imitation leather boots for $20 from Wal-Mart, or they can buy a handmade pair of butter-soft leather boots from Nordstrom for $500. The boots from Nordstrom will have far superior styling, feel more comfortable, and look much better than those from Wal-Mart. The utility consumers will get from the Nordstrom boots will in all probability be much greater than the utility derived from the Wal-Mart boots, but of course, they will have to pay far more for them. That is the point: when excellence is built into a product offering, consumers have to pay more to own or consume it.

With regard to *quality as reliability*, a product can be said to be *reliable* when it consistently does the job it was designed for, does it well, and rarely, if ever, breaks down. As with excellence, reliability increases the utility a consumer gets from a product, and thus the price the company can charge for that product. Toyota's cars, for example, have the highest reliability ratings in the automobile industry, and therefore consumers are prepared to pay more for them than for cars that are very similar in other attributes. As we shall see, increasing product reliability has been the central goal of an influential management philosophy that came out of Japan in the 1980s and is commonly referred to as **total quality management.**

The position of a product against two dimensions, *reliability* and *other attributes,* can be plotted on a map similar to Figure 3.7. For example, a Lexus has attributes—such as design, styling, performance, and safety features—that customers perceive as demonstrating excellence in quality and that are viewed as being superior to those of most other cars. Lexus is also a very reliable car. Thus, the overall level of quality of the Lexus is very high, which means that the car offers consumers significant utility, and that gives Toyota the option of charging a premium price for the Lexus. Toyota also produces another very reliable vehicle, the Toyota Corolla, but this is aimed at less wealthy

FIGURE 3.7

A Quality Map for Automobiles

customers and it lacks many of the superior attributes of the Lexus. Thus, although this is also a high-quality car in the sense of being reliable, it is not as high quality as a Lexus in the sense of being an excellent product. At the other end of the spectrum, we can find poor-quality products that have both low reliability and inferior attributes, such as poor design, performance, and styling. An example is the Proton, which is built by the Malaysian car firm of the same name. The design of the car is over a decade old and has a dismal reputation for styling and safety. Moreover, Proton's reliability record is one of the worst of any car, according J.D. Power.[14]

The concept of quality applies whether we are talking about Toyota automobiles, clothes designed and sold by the Gap, the customer service department of Citibank, or the ability of airlines to arrive on time. Quality is just as relevant to services as it is to goods.[15] The impact of high product quality on competitive advantage is twofold.[16] First, providing high-quality products increases the utility those products provide to customers, which gives the company the option of charging a higher price for them. In the automobile industry, for example, Toyota can charge a higher price for its cars because of the higher quality of its products. Thus, compared with General Motors, Toyota has had both lower costs and the ability to charge higher prices. As a result, historically it has been more profitable than GM.

The second impact of high quality on competitive advantage comes from the greater efficiency and the lower unit costs associated with *reliable* products. When products are reliable, less employee time is wasted making defective products or providing substandard services and less time has to be spent fixing mistakes, which translates into higher employee productivity and lower unit costs. Thus, high product quality not only enables a company to differentiate its product from that of rivals, but if the product is reliable, it also lowers costs.

The importance of reliability in building competitive advantage has increased dramatically over the past decade. Indeed, so crucial is the emphasis placed on reliability by many companies that achieving high product reliability can no longer be viewed as just one way of gaining a competitive advantage. In many industries, it has become an absolute imperative for survival.

■ Innovation

Innovation refers to the act of creating new products or processes. There are two main types of innovation: product innovation and process innovation. **Product innovation** is the development of products that are new to the world or have superior attributes to existing products. Examples are Intel's invention of the microprocessor in the early 1970s, Cisco's development of the router for routing data over the Internet in the mid 1980s, and Palm's development of the PalmPilot, the first commercially successful hand-held computer, in the mid 1990s. **Process innovation** is the development of a new process for producing products and delivering them to customers. Examples include Toyota, which developed a range of new techniques collectively known as the Toyota *lean production system* for making automobiles: just-in-time inventory systems, self-managing teams, and reduced setup times for complex equipment. Wal-Mart pioneered efforts to use information systems to manage its logistics and inventory (see the *Running Case*), and Staples applied the supermarket business model to the retail office supplies business.

Product innovation creates value by creating new products, or enhanced versions of existing products, that customers perceive as having more utility, thus increasing the company's pricing options. Process innovation often allows a company to create more value by lowering production costs. Toyota's lean production system, for example, helped to boost employee productivity, thus giving Toyota a cost-based competitive advantage.[17] Similarly, Staples' application of the supermarket business model to retail office supplies dramatically lowered the cost of selling office supplies. Staples passed on some of this cost saving to customers in the form of lower prices, which enabled the company to increase its market share rapidly.

In the long run, innovation of products and processes is perhaps the most important building block of competitive advantage.[18] Competition can be viewed as a process driven by innovations. Although not all innovations succeed, those that do can be a major source of competitive advantage because, by definition, they give a company something **unique**—something its competitors lack (at least until they imitate the innovation). Uniqueness can allow a company to differentiate itself from its rivals and charge a premium price for its product or, in the case of many process innovations, reduce its unit costs far below those of competitors.

■ Responsiveness to Customers

To achieve superior responsiveness to customers, a company must be able to do a better job than competitors of identifying and satisfying its customers' needs. Customers will then attribute more utility to its products, creating a differentiation based on competitive advantage. Improving the quality of a company's product offering is consistent with achieving responsiveness, as is developing new products with features that existing products lack. In other words, achieving superior quality and innovation is integral to achieving superior responsiveness to customers.

Another factor that stands out in any discussion of responsiveness to customers is the need to customize goods and services to the unique demands of individual customers or customer groups. For example, the proliferation of soft drinks and beers can be viewed partly as a response to this trend. Automobile companies have become more adept at customizing cars to the demands of individual customers. For instance, following the lead of Toyota, the Saturn division of General Motors builds cars to order for individual customers, letting them choose from a wide range of colors and options.

An aspect of responsiveness to customers that has drawn increasing attention is **customer response time**: the time that it takes for a good to be delivered or a service to be performed.[19] For a manufacturer of machinery, response time is the time it takes to fill customer orders. For a bank, it is the time it takes to process a loan or that a customer must stand in line to wait for a free teller. For a supermarket, it is the time that customers must stand in checkout lines. Customer survey after customer survey has shown slow response time to be a major source of customer dissatisfaction.[20]

Other sources of enhanced responsiveness to customers are superior design, superior service, and superior after-sales service and support. All of these factors enhance responsiveness to customers and allow a company to differentiate itself from its less responsive competitors. In turn, differentiation enables a company to build brand loyalty and charge a premium price for its products. Consider how much more people are prepared to pay for next-day delivery of Express Mail, as opposed to delivery in three to four days. In 2004, a two-page letter sent by overnight Express Mail within the United States cost about $14, compared with 37 cents for regular mail. Thus, the price premium for express delivery (reduced response time) was $13.63, or a premium of 3,684 percent over the regular price.

■ Business Models, the Value Chain, and Generic Distinctive Competencies

As noted in Chapter 1, a business model is managers' conception, or gestalt, of how the various strategies that a firm pursues fit together into a congruent whole, enabling the firm to achieve a competitive advantage. More precisely, a business model represents the way in which managers configure the value chain of the firm through strategy, as well as the investments they make to support that configuration, so that they can build the distinctive competencies necessary to attain the efficiency, quality,

FIGURE 3.8

Competitive Advantage and the Value Creation Cycle

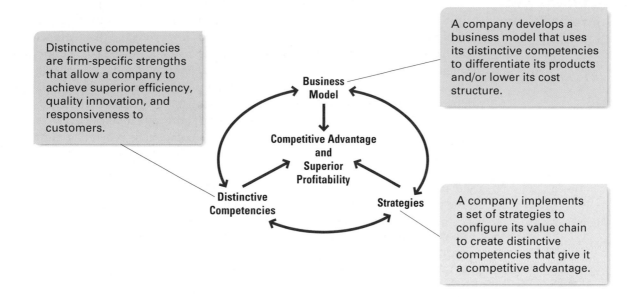

innovation, and customer responsiveness required to support the firm's low-cost or differentiated position, thereby achieving a competitive advantage and generating superior profitability (see Figure 3.8).

For example, the main strategic goal of Wal-Mart is to be the lowest-cost operator offering a wide display of general merchandise in the retail industry. Wal-Mart's business model involves offering general merchandise in a self-service supermarket type of setting. As discussed in the *Running Case*, Wal-Mart's strategies flesh out this business model and help the company to attain its strategic goal. For example, to reduce costs, Wal-Mart limits investments in the fittings and fixtures of its stores. One of the keys to generating sales and lowering costs in this setting is rapid inventory turnover, which is achieved through strategic investments in logistics and information systems. Wal-Mart in fact makes major investments in process innovation to improve the effectiveness of its information and logistics systems, which enables the company to respond to customer demands for low-priced goods when they walk in the door and to do so in a very efficient manner.

Wal-Mart's business model is very different from that found at a retailer such as Nordstrom. Nordstrom's business model is to offer high quality, and high-priced apparel, in a full-service and sophisticated setting. This implies differences in the way the value chain is configured. Nordstrom devotes far more attention to in-store customer service than Wal-Mart does, which implies significant investments in its salespeople. Moreover, Nordstrom invests far more in the furnishings and fittings for its stores, as opposed to Wal-Mart, whose stores have a basic warehouse feel to them. Nordstrom recaptures the costs of this investment by charging higher prices for higher-quality merchandise. Thus, even though Wal-Mart and Nordstrom both sell apparel (Wal-Mart is in fact the biggest seller of apparel in the United States), their business models imply a very different positioning in the marketplace, and a very different configuration of value chain activities and investments.

Analyzing Competitive Advantage and Profitability

If a company's managers are to perform a good internal analysis, they need to be able to analyze the financial performance of their company, identifying how its strategies contribute (or not) to profitability. To identify strengths and weaknesses effectively, they need to be able to compare, or *benchmark,* the performance of their company against that of competitors and the historic performance of the company itself. This will help them determine whether they are more or less profitable than competitors and whether the performance of the company has been improving or deteriorating through time; whether their company strategies are maximizing the value being created; whether their cost structure is out of line with those of competitors; and whether they are using the resources of the company to the greatest effect.

As we noted in Chapter 1, the key measure of a company's financial performance is its profitability, which captures the return that a company is generating on its investments. Although several different measures of profitability exist, such as return on assets and return on equity, many authorities on the measurement of profitability argue that return on invested capital (ROIC) is the best measure because "it focuses on the true operating performance of the company."[21] (However, return on assets is very similar in formulation to return on invested capital.)

ROIC is defined as net profit over invested capital, or ROIC = net profit/invested capital. Net profit is calculated by subtracting the total costs of operating the company away from its total revenues (total revenues–total costs). *Net profit* is what is left over after the government takes its share in taxes. *Invested capital* is the amount that is invested in the operations of a company: property, plant, equipment, inventories, and other assets. Invested capital comes from two main sources: interest-bearing debt and shareholders' equity. Interest-bearing debt is money the company borrows from banks and those who purchase its bonds. Shareholders' equity is the money raised from selling shares to the public, *plus* earnings that the company has retained in prior years and are available to fund current investments. ROIC measures the effectiveness with which a company is using the capital funds that it has available for investment. As such, it is recognized to be an excellent measure of the value a company is creating.[22]

A company's ROIC can be algebraically decomposed into two major components: *return on sales* and *capital turnover.*[23] Specifically:

$$\text{ROIC} = \text{net profits/invested capital}$$
$$= \text{net profits/revenues} \times \text{revenues/invested capital}$$

where net profits/revenues is the return on sales, and revenues/invested capital is capital turnover. Return on sales measures how effectively the company converts revenues into profits. Capital turnover measures how effectively the company employs its invested capital to generate revenues. These two ratios can be further decomposed into some basic accounting ratios, as shown in Figure 3.9 (these ratios are defined in Table 3.1).[24]

The decomposition of ROIC shown in Figure 3.9 was first developed by managers at the DuPont Company in the early 1900s as a methodology for identifying the drivers of profitability, and the decomposition formula is sometimes referred to as "the DuPont Formula." Figure 3.9 says that a company's managers can increase ROIC by pursuing strategies that increase the company's return on sales. To increase the company's return on sales, they can pursue strategies that reduce the cost of goods sold (COGS) for a given level of sales revenues (COGS/sales); reduce the level of spending on sales force, marketing, general, and administrative expenses (SG&A) for a given level of sales revenues (SG&A/sales); and reduce R&D spending for a given level of sales revenues (R&D/sales). Alternatively, they can increase return on sales by pursuing strategies that increase sales revenues more than they increase the costs of the

FIGURE 3.9

FIGURE 3.9

Drivers of Profitability
(ROIC)

business, as measured by COGS, SG&A, and R&D expenses. That is, they can increase the return on sales by pursuing strategies that *lower costs* or increase value through *differentiation,* and thus allow the company to increase its prices more than its costs.

Figure 3.9 also tells us that a company's managers can boost the profitability of their company by getting greater sales revenues from their invested capital, thereby increasing capital turnover. They do this by pursuing strategies that reduce the

TABLE 3.1

Definitions of Basic Accounting Terms

Term	Definition	Source
Cost of goods sold (COGS)	Total costs of manufacturing products	Income statement
Sales, general, and administrative expenses (SG&A)	Costs associated with selling products and administering the company	Income statement
R&D expenses (R&D)	Research and development expenditure	Income statement
Working capital	The amount of money the company has to work with in the short term: current assets minus current liabilities	Balance sheet
Property, plant, and equipment (PPE)	The value of investments in the property, plant, and equipment that the company uses to manufacture and sell its products; also known as *fixed capital*	Balance sheet
Return on sales (ROS)	Net profit expressed as a percentage of sales; measures how effectively the company converts revenues into profits	Ratio
Capital turnover	Revenues divided by invested capital; measures how effectively the company uses its capital to generate revenues	Ratio
Return on invested capital (ROIC)	Net profit after tax divided by invested capital	Ratio
Net profit	Total revenues minus total costs after tax	Income statement
Invested capital	Interest-bearing debt plus shareholders' equity	Balance sheet

amount of *working capital,* such as the amount of capital invested in inventories, needed to generate a given level of sales (working capital/sales) and then pursuing strategies that reduce the amount of *fixed capital* that they have to invest in plant, property, and equipment (PPE) to generate a given level of sales (PPE/sales). That is, they pursue strategies that reduce the amount of capital that they need to generate every dollar of sales, and thus their cost of capital. Now recall that cost of capital is part of the cost structure of a company (see Figure 3.2), so strategies designed to increase capital turnover also *lower the cost structure.*

To see how these basic drivers of profitability help us to understand what is going on in a company and to identify its strengths and weaknesses, let us compare the financial performance of Wal-Mart against one of its closest and more efficient competitors, Target. For the financial year ending January 2004, Wal-Mart earned an ROIC of 14.21 percent, while Target earned a respectable 8.65 percent. Wal-Mart's superior profitability can be understood in terms of the impact of its strategies on the various ratios identified in Figure 3.9. These are summarized in Figure 3.10.

First, note that Wal-Mart has a *lower* return on sales than Target. The main reason for this is that Wal-Mart's cost of goods sold (COGS) as a percentage of sales is higher than Target's (76.8 percent against 66 percent). For a retailer, the COGS reflects the price that Wal-Mart pays to its suppliers for merchandise. The lower COGS/sales ratio implies that Wal-Mart does not mark up prices as much as Target: its profit margin on each item sold is lower. Consistent with its long-time strategic goal, Wal-Mart passes on the low prices it gets from suppliers to customers. Wal-Mart's higher COGS/sales ratio reflects its strategy of being the lowest-price retailer.

On the other hand, Wal-Mart spends significantly less on sales, general, and administrative expenses (SG&A) as a percentage of sales than Target (17.36 percent against 23.95 percent). There are three reasons for this difference. First, Wal-Mart's early strategy

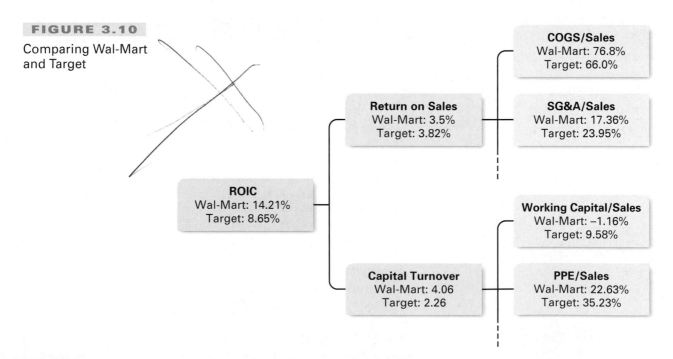

FIGURE 3.10

Comparing Wal-Mart and Target

was to focus on small towns that could only support one discounter. In small towns, the company does not have to advertise heavily because it is not competing against other discounters. Second, Wal-Mart has become such a powerful brand that the company does not need to advertise as heavily as its competitors, even when its stores are located close to them in suburban areas. Third, because Wal-Mart sticks to its low-price philosophy, and because the company manages its inventory so well, it does not usually have an overstocking problem. Thus, the company does not have to hold periodic sales, nor does it have to bear the costs of promoting those sales (such as by sending out advertisements and coupons in local newspapers). These factors reduce Wal-Mart's SG&A/sales ratio.

In addition, Wal-Mart operates with a flat organization structure that has very few layers of management between the head office and store managers (the company has no regional headquarters). This reduces administrative expenses (which are a component of SG&A) and hence the SG&A/sales ratio. Wal-Mart can operate with this flat structure because its information systems allow the company's top managers to monitor and control individual stores directly, rather than rely on intervening layers of subordinates to do that for them.

It is when we consider the capital turnover side of the ROIC equation, however, that the financial impact of Wal-Mart's competitive advantage in information systems and logistics becomes apparent. Wal-Mart generates $4.06 for every dollar of capital invested in the business, whereas Target generates only $2.26 for every dollar of capital invested. Wal-Mart is much more efficient in its use of capital than Target. Why?

One crucial reason is that Wal-Mart has a much lower working capital/sales ratio than Target. In fact, Wal-Mart has a *negative* ratio (−1.16 percent), while Target has a positive ratio (9.58 percent). The negative working capital ratio implies that Wal-Mart does not need any capital to finance its day-to-day operations. In fact, it is using its suppliers' capital to finance these operations, a rare accomplishment. Wal-Mart is able to do this for two reasons. First, Wal-Mart is so powerful that it can demand and get very favorable payment terms from its suppliers. It does not have to pay for merchandise for sixty days after it is delivered. Second, Wal-Mart turns over its inventory so rapidly—7.72 times a year, or every 47 days—that it typically sells merchandise *before* it has to pay its suppliers. Thus, suppliers finance Wal-Mart's inventory and the company's short-term capital needs. As you will recall from the *Running Case*, Wal-Mart's high inventory turnover is the result of strategic investments in information systems and logistics. It is these value chain activities more than any other that explain Wal-Mart's competitive advantage.

Finally, Wal-Mart has a significantly lower PPE/sales ratio than Target: 22.63 percent versus 35.23 percent. There are several explanations for this lower ratio. First, many of Wal-Mart's stores are still located in small towns where land is cheap, whereas most of Target's stores are located in more expensive suburban mall locations. Thus, on average, Wal-Mart needs to spend less on a store than Target. Again, strategy has a clear impact on financial performance. Second, because Wal-Mart turns its inventory over so rapidly, it does not need to devote as much in-store space to storing inventory. This means that more floor space can be devoted to selling merchandise. Other things being equal, this will result in a higher PPE/sales ratio. By the same token, efficient inventory management means that less space is needed at a distribution center to support a store, which again reduces total capital spending on property, plant, and equipment. Third, the higher PPE/sales ratio may also reflect the fact that Wal-Mart's brand is so powerful, and its commitment to low pricing so strong, that store traffic is higher than at comparable discounters such as Target. The stores are simply busier. Hence the PPE/sales ratio is higher.

In sum, Wal-Mart's high profitability is a function of its strategy and the distinctive competencies that strategic investments have built over the years, particularly in information systems and logistics. As in the Wal-Mart example, the methodology described in this section can be a very useful tool for analyzing why and how well a company is achieving and sustaining a competitive advantage. It highlights a company's strengths and weaknesses, showing where there is room for improvement and where a company is excelling. As such, it can drive strategy formulation. Moreover, the same methodology can be used to analyze the performance of competitors and gain a greater understanding of their strengths and weakness. This understanding can then inform strategy.

The Durability of Competitive Advantage

The next question we must address is how long a competitive advantage will last once it has been created. In other words, what is the *durability* of competitive advantage given that other companies are also seeking to develop distinctive competencies that will give them a competitive advantage? The answer depends on three factors: barriers to imitation, the capability of competitors, and the general dynamism of the industry environment.

■ Barriers to Imitation

A company with a competitive advantage will earn higher-than-average profits. These profits send a signal to rivals that the company has some valuable distinctive competency that allows it to create superior value. Naturally, its competitors will try to identify and imitate that competency, and insofar as they are successful, ultimately their increased success may whittle away the company's superior profits.[25]

How quickly rivals will imitate a company's distinctive competencies is an important issue, because the speed of imitation has a bearing on the durability of a company's competitive advantage. Other things being equal, the more rapidly competitors imitate a company's distinctive competencies, the less durable its competitive advantage will be, and the more important it is that the company endeavor to improve its competencies to stay one step ahead of the imitators. It is important to stress at the outset that ultimately almost any distinctive competency can be imitated by a competitor. The critical issue is *time:* the longer it takes competitors to imitate a distinctive competency, the greater the opportunity the company has to build a strong market position and reputation with customers, which are then more difficult for competitors to attack. Moreover, the longer it takes to achieve an imitation, the greater is the opportunity for the imitated company to improve on its competency or build other competencies, thereby staying one step ahead of the competition.

Barriers to imitation are a primary determinant of the speed of imitation. **Barriers to imitation** are factors that make it difficult for a competitor to copy a company's distinctive competencies; the greater the barriers to imitation, the more sustainable is a company's competitive advantage.[26] Barriers to imitation differ depending on whether a competitor is trying to imitate resources or capabilities.

■ **Imitating Resources** In general, the easiest distinctive competencies for prospective rivals to imitate tend to be those based on possession of firm-specific and valuable tangible resources, such as buildings, plant, and equipment. Such resources are visible to competitors and can often be purchased on the open market. For example, if a company's competitive advantage is based on sole possession of efficient-scale manufacturing facilities, competitors may move fairly quickly to establish similar facilities. Although Ford gained a competitive advantage over General Motors in the 1920s by being the first to adopt an assembly line manufacturing technology to produce automobiles, General Motors quickly imitated that innovation, competing away Ford's distinctive competency in the process. A similar process is occurring in the auto industry now, as companies try to imitate Toyota's famous production system.

Intangible resources can be more difficult to imitate. This is particularly true of brand names, which are important because they symbolize a company's reputation. In the heavy earthmoving equipment industry, for example, the Caterpillar brand name is synonymous with high quality and superior after-sales service and support. Similarly, the St. Michael's brand name used by Marks & Spencer, Britain's largest retailer, symbolizes high-quality but reasonably priced clothing. Customers often display a preference for the products of such companies because the brand name is an important guarantee of high quality. Although competitors might like to imitate well-established brand names, the law prohibits them from doing so.

Marketing and technological know-how are also important intangible resources and can be relatively easy to imitate. The movement of skilled marketing personnel between companies may facilitate the general dissemination of marketing know-how. For example, in the 1970s, Ford was acknowledged as the best marketer among the big three U.S. auto companies. In 1979, it lost a lot of its marketing know-how to Chrysler when its most successful marketer, Lee Iacocca, joined Chrysler and subsequently hired many of Ford's top marketing people to work with him at Chrysler. More generally, successful marketing strategies are relatively easy to imitate because they are so visible to competitors. Thus, Coca-Cola quickly imitated PepsiCo's Diet Pepsi brand with the introduction of its own brand, Diet Coke.

With regard to technological know-how, the patent system in theory should make technological know-how relatively immune to imitation. Patents give the inventor of a new product a twenty-year exclusive production agreement. For example, the biotechnology company Immunex discovered and patented Enbrel, which is capable of halting the disease-causing mechanism that leads to rheumatoid arthritis. All prior treatments simply provided patients with some relief from the symptoms of rheumatoid arthritis. Approved by the Food and Drug Administration in 1998, Enbrel racked up sales of over $400 million in its first year on the market and may ultimately generate annual revenues of $4 billion. (In 2002, Immunex was acquired by Amgen.) Despite the large market, Immunex's patent stops potential competitors from introducing their own version of Enbrel. However, whereas it is relatively easy to use the patent system to protect a biological product from imitation, this is not true of many other inventions. In electrical and computer engineering, for example, it is often possible to invent around patents: that is, produce a product that is functionally equivalent but does not rely on the patented technology. One study found that 60 percent of patented innovations were successfully invented around in four years.[27] This suggests that, in general, distinctive competencies based on technological know-how can be relatively short-lived.

■ **Imitating Capabilities** Imitating a company's capabilities tends to be more difficult than imitating its tangible and intangible resources, chiefly because capabilities are based on the way in which decisions are made and processes managed deep within a company. It is hard for outsiders to discern them.

On its own, the invisible nature of capabilities would not be enough to halt imitation; competitors could still gain insights into how a company operates by hiring people away from that company. However, a company's capabilities rarely reside in a single individual. Rather, they are the product of how numerous individuals interact within a unique organizational setting.[28] It is possible that no one individual within a company may be familiar with the totality of a company's internal operating routines and procedures. In such cases, hiring people away from a successful company in order to imitate its key capabilities may not be helpful.

■ Capability of Competitors

According to work by Pankaj Ghemawat, a major determinant of the capability of competitors to imitate a company's competitive advantage rapidly is the nature of the competitors' prior strategic commitments.[29] By **strategic commitment**, Ghemawat means a company's commitment to a particular way of doing business—that is, to developing a particular set of resources and capabilities. Ghemawat's point is that once a company has made a strategic commitment, it will have difficulty responding to new competition if doing so requires a break with this commitment. Therefore, when competitors have long-established commitments to a particular way of doing business, they may be slow to imitate an innovating company's competitive advantage. Its competitive advantage will thus be relatively durable.

The U.S. automobile industry again offers an example. From 1945 to 1975, the industry was dominated by the stable oligopoly of General Motors, Ford, and Chrysler, all of which geared their operations to the production of large cars, which American customers demanded at the time. When the market shifted from large cars to small, fuel-efficient ones during the late 1970s, U.S. companies lacked the resources and capabilities required to produce these cars. Their prior commitments had built the wrong kind of skills for this new environment. As a result, foreign producers, and particularly the Japanese, stepped into the market breach by providing compact, fuel-efficient, high-quality, and low-cost cars. The failure of U.S. auto manufacturers to react quickly to the distinctive competency of Japanese auto companies gave the latter time to build a strong market position and brand loyalty, which subsequently have proved difficult to attack.

Another determinant of the ability of competitors to respond to a company's competitive advantage is the absorptive capacity of competitors.[30] **Absorptive capacity** refers to the ability of an enterprise to identify, value, assimilate, and use new knowledge. For example, in the 1960s and 1970s, Toyota developed a competitive advantage based on its innovation of lean production systems. Competitors such as General Motors were slow to imitate this innovation, primarily because they lacked the necessary absorptive capacity. General Motors was such a bureaucratic and inward-looking organization that it was very difficult for the company to identify, value, assimilate, and use the knowledge that underlay lean production systems. Indeed, long after General Motors had identified and understood the importance of lean production systems, it was still struggling to assimilate and use that new knowledge. Put differently, internal inertia forces can make it difficult for established competitors to respond to a rival whose competitive advantage is based on new products or internal processes—that is, on innovation.

Taken together, factors such as existing strategic commitments and low absorptive capacity limit the ability of established competitors to imitate the competitive advantage of a rival, particularly when that competitive advantage is based on innovative products or processes. This is why when innovations reshape the rules of competition in an industry, value often migrates away from established competitors and toward new enterprises that are operating with new business models.

■ Industry Dynamism

A dynamic industry environment is one that is changing rapidly. We examined the factors that determine the dynamism and intensity of competition in an industry in Chapter 2 when we discussed the external environment. The most dynamic industries tend to be those with a very high rate of product innovation—for instance, the customer electronics industry and the personal computer industry. In dynamic industries, the rapid rate of innovation means that product life cycles are shortening and that competitive advantage can be fleeting. A company that has a competitive advantage today may find its market position outflanked tomorrow by a rival's innovation.

In the personal computer industry, the rapid increase in computing power during the past two decades has contributed to a high degree of innovation and a turbulent environment. Reflecting the persistence of innovation, Apple Computer in the late 1970s and early 1980s had an industrywide competitive advantage due to its innovation. In 1981, IBM seized the advantage by introducing its first personal computer. By the mid 1980s, IBM had lost its competitive advantage to high-power "clone" manufacturers such as Compaq that had beaten IBM in the race to introduce a computer based on Intel's 386 chip. In turn, in the 1990s, Compaq subsequently lost its competitive advantage to Dell, which pioneered new low-cost ways of delivering computers to customers using the Internet as a direct selling device.

Summary

The durability of a company's competitive advantage depends on the height of barriers to imitation, the capability of competitors to imitate its innovation, and the general level of dynamism in the industry environment. When barriers to imitation are low, capable competitors abound, and the environment is dynamic, with innovations being developed all the time, then competitive advantage is likely to be transitory. But even within such industries, companies can build a more enduring competitive advantage if they are able to make investments that build barriers to imitation.

During the 1980s, Apple Computer built a competitive advantage based on the combination of a proprietary disk operating system and an intangible product image. The resulting brand loyalty enabled Apple to carve out a fairly secure niche in an industry where competitive advantage has otherwise proven to be very fleeting. However, by the mid 1990s its strategy had been imitated, primarily because of the introduction of Microsoft's Windows operating system, which imitated most of the features that had enabled Apple to build brand loyalty. By 1996, Apple was in financial trouble, providing yet another example that no competitive advantage lasts forever. Ultimately, anything can be imitated. However, Apple has shown remarkable resilience; in the late 1990s, it clawed its way back from the brink of bankruptcy to establish a viable position within its niche once again, a position it still held on to by the mid 2000s.

Avoiding Failure and Sustaining Competitive Advantage

How can a company avoid failure and escape the traps that have snared so many once successful companies? How can managers build a sustainable competitive advantage? Much of the remainder of this book deals with these issues. Here, we make a number of key points that set the scene for the coming discussion.

■ Why Companies Fail

When a company loses its competitive advantage, its profitability falls. The company does not necessarily fail; it may just have average or below-average profitability and can remain in this mode for a considerable time, although its resource and capital base is shrinking. Failure implies something more drastic. A failing company is one whose profitability is now substantially lower than the average profitability of its competitors; it has lost the ability to attract and generate resources so that its profit margins and invested capital are shrinking rapidly.

Why does a company lose its competitive advantage and fail? The question is particularly pertinent because some of the most successful companies of the twentieth century have seen their competitive position deteriorate at one time or another. IBM, General Motors, American Express, Digital Equipment, and Sears, among many others, which all at one time were held up as examples of managerial excellence, have gone through periods where their financial performance was poor and they clearly lacked any competitive advantage. We explore three related reasons for failure: inertia, prior strategic commitments, and the Icarus paradox.

■ **Inertia** The inertia argument says that companies find it difficult to change their strategies and structures in order to adapt to changing competitive conditions.[31] IBM is a classic example of this problem. For thirty years, it was viewed as the world's most successful computer company. Then in the space of a few years, its success turned into a disaster: it lost $5 billion in 1992, leading to layoffs of more than 100,000 employees. IBM's troubles were caused by a dramatic decline in the cost of computing power as a result of innovations in microprocessors. With the advent of powerful low-cost microprocessors, the locus of the computer market shifted from mainframes to small, low-priced personal computers, leaving IBM's huge mainframe operations with a diminished market. Although IBM had, and still has, a significant presence in the personal computer market, it had failed to shift the focus of its efforts away from mainframes and toward personal computers. This failure meant deep trouble for one of the most successful companies of the twentieth century (although IBM has now executed a successful turnaround with a repositioning as a provider of e-commerce infrastructure and solutions).

One reason that companies find it so difficult to adapt to new environmental conditions seems to be the role of capabilities in causing inertia. Organizational capabilities— the way a company makes decisions and manages its processes—can be a source of competitive advantage, but they are difficult to change. IBM always emphasized close coordination among operating units and favored decision processes that stressed consensus among interdependent operating units as a prerequisite for a decision to go forward.[32] This capability was a source of advantage for IBM during the 1970s, when coordination among its worldwide operating units was necessary to develop, manufacture, and sell complex mainframes. But the slow-moving bureaucracy that it had spawned was a source of failure in the 1990s, when organizations had to adapt readily to rapid environmental change.

Capabilities are difficult to change because a certain distribution of power and influence is embedded within the established decision-making and management processes of an organization. Those who play key roles in a decision-making process clearly have more power. It follows that changing the established capabilities of an organization means changing its existing distribution of power and influence, and those whose power and influence would diminish resist such change. Proposals for change trigger turf battles. This power struggle and the political resistance associated with trying to alter the way in which an organization makes decisions and manages its process—that is, trying to change its capabilities—bring on inertia. This is not to say that companies cannot change. However, because change is so often resisted by those who feel threatened by it, change in most cases has to be induced by a crisis. By then, the company may already be failing, as happened at IBM.

■ **Prior Strategic Commitments** Ghemawat has argued that a company's prior strategic commitments not only limit its ability to imitate rivals but may also cause competitive disadvantage.[33] IBM, for instance, had major investments in the mainframe computer business, so when the market shifted, it was stuck with significant resources specialized to that particular business: its manufacturing facilities were geared to the production of mainframes, its research organization was similarly specialized, and so was its sales force. Because these resources were not well suited to the newly emerging personal computer business, IBM's difficulties in the early 1990s were in a sense inevitable. Its prior strategic commitments locked it into a business that was shrinking. Shedding these resources was bound to cause hardship for all organization stakeholders.

■ **The Icarus Paradox** Danny Miller has postulated that the roots of competitive failure can be found in what he termed the *Icarus paradox*.[34] Icarus is a figure in Greek mythology who used a pair of wings, made for him by his father, to escape from an island where he was being held prisoner. He flew so well that he went higher and higher, ever closer to the sun, until the heat of the sun melted the wax that held his wings together and he plunged to his death in the Aegean Sea. The paradox is that his greatest asset, his ability to fly, caused his demise. Miller argues that the same paradox applies to many once successful companies. According to Miller, many companies become so dazzled by their early success that they believe more of the same type of effort is the way to future success. As a result, they can become so specialized and inner directed that they lose sight of market realities and the fundamental requirements for achieving a competitive advantage. Sooner or later, this leads to failure.

Miller identifies four major categories among the rising and falling companies, which he labels "craftsmen," "builders," "pioneers," and "salesmen." The "craftsmen," such as Texas Instruments and Digital Equipment Corporation (DEC), achieved early success through engineering excellence. But then they became so obsessed with engineering details that they lost sight of market realities. (The story of DEC's demise is summarized in Strategy in Action 3.3.) Among the "builders" are Gulf & Western and ITT. Having built successful, moderately diversified companies, they then became so enchanted with diversification for its own sake that they continued to diversify far beyond the point at which it was profitable to do so. Miller's third group are the "pioneers" like Wang Labs. Enamored of their own originally brilliant innovations, managers here continued to search for additional brilliant innovations and ended up producing novel but completely useless products. The final category comprises the "salesmen," exemplified by Procter & Gamble and Chrysler. They became so convinced of their ability to sell anything that they paid scant attention to product development and manufacturing excellence and as a result spawned a proliferation of bland, inferior products.

■ Steps to Avoid Failure

Given that so many traps wait for companies, the question arises as to how strategic managers can use internal analysis to find them and escape them. We now look at several tactics that managers can use.

■ Focus on the Building Blocks of Competitive Advantage

Maintaining a competitive advantage requires a company to continue focusing on all four generic building blocks of competitive advantage—efficiency, quality, innovation, and responsiveness to customers—and to develop distinctive competencies that contribute to superior performance in these areas. One of the messages of Miller's Icarus paradox is that many successful companies become unbalanced in their pursuit of distinctive competencies. DEC, for example, focused on engineering quality at the expense of almost everything else, including, most importantly, responsiveness to customers. Other companies forget to focus on any distinctive competency at all.

■ Institute Continuous Improvement and Learning

The only constant in the world is change. Today's source of competitive advantage may soon be rapidly imitated by capable competitors or made obsolete by the innovations of a rival. In such a dynamic and fast-paced environment, the only way that a company can maintain a competitive advantage over time is to continually improve its efficiency, quality, innovation, and responsiveness to customers. The way to do this is to recognize the importance of learning within the organization.[35] The most successful companies are not those that stand still, resting on their laurels. They are those that are always seeking out ways of improving their operations and in the process are constantly upgrading the value of their distinctive competencies or creating new competencies. Companies such as General Electric and Toyota have a reputation for being learning

Strategy in Action   3.3

The Road to Ruin at DEC

Digital Equipment Corporation (DEC) was one of the premier computer companies of the 1970s and 1980s. DEC's original success was founded on the minicomputer, a cheaper, more flexible version of its mainframe cousins that Ken Olson and his brilliant team of engineers invented in the 1960s. They then improved on their original minicomputers until they could not be beat for quality and reliability. In the 1970s, their VAX series of minicomputers was widely regarded as the most reliable series of computers ever produced, and DEC was rewarded by high profit rates and rapid growth. By 1990, it was number 27 on the *Fortune 500* list of the largest corporations in America.

Buoyed by its success, DEC turned into an engineering monoculture: its engineers became idols; its marketing and accounting staff, however, were barely tolerated. Component specs and design standards were all that senior managers understood. Technological fine-tuning became such an obsession that the needs of customers for smaller, more economical, user-friendly computers were ignored. DEC's personal computers, for example, bombed because they were out of touch with the needs of customers, and the company failed to respond to the threat to its core market presented by the rise of computer workstations and client-server architecture. Indeed, Ken Olson was known for dismissing such new products. He once said, "We always say that customers are right, but they are not always right." Perhaps. But DEC, blinded by its early success, failed to remain responsive to its customers and changing market conditions.

By the early 1990s, DEC was in deep trouble. Olson was forced out in July 1992, and the company lost billions of dollars between 1992 and 1995. It returned to profitability in 1996, primarily because of the success of a turnaround strategy aimed at reorienting the company to serve precisely those areas that Olson had dismissed. In 1998, the company was acquired by Compaq Computer Corporation and disappeared from the business landscape as an independent entity.[d]

organizations. This means that they are continually analyzing the processes that underlie their efficiency, quality, innovation, and responsiveness to customers. Their objective is to learn from prior mistakes and to seek out ways to improve their processes over time. This has enabled Toyota, for example, to continually upgrade its employee productivity and product quality, and thus stay ahead of imitators.

■ **Track Best Industrial Practice and Use Benchmarking** One of the best ways to develop distinctive competencies that contribute to superior efficiency, quality, innovation, and responsiveness to customers is to identify and adopt best industrial practice. Only in this way will a company be able to build and maintain the resources and capabilities that underpin excellence in efficiency, quality, innovation, and responsiveness to customers. (We discuss what constitutes best industrial practice in some depth in Chapter 4.) It requires tracking the practice of other companies, and perhaps the best way to do so is through **benchmarking**: measuring the company against the products, practices, and services of some of its most efficient global competitors. For example, when Xerox was in trouble in the early 1980s, it decided to institute a policy of benchmarking to identify ways to improve the efficiency of its operations. Xerox benchmarked L. L. Bean for distribution procedures, Deere & Company for central computer operations, Procter & Gamble for marketing, and Florida Power & Light for total quality management processes. By the early 1990s, Xerox was benchmarking 240 functions against comparable areas in other companies. This process has been credited with helping it dramatically improve the efficiency of its operations.[36]

■ **Overcome Inertia** Overcoming the internal forces that are a barrier to change within an organization is one of the key requirements for maintaining a competitive advantage, and an entire chapter, Chapter 14, is spent discussing this issue. Suffice it to say here that identifying barriers to change is an important first step. Once this step has been taken, implementing change requires good leadership, the judicious use of power, and appropriate changes in organizational structure and control systems.

■ **The Role of Luck**

A number of scholars have argued that luck plays a critical role in determining competitive success and failure.[37] In its most extreme version, the luck argument devalues the importance of strategy altogether. Instead, it states that, in the face of uncertainty, some companies just happen to pick the correct strategy.

Although luck may be the reason for a company's success in particular cases, it is an unconvincing explanation for the persistent success of a company. Recall our argument that the generic building blocks of competitive advantage are superior efficiency, quality, innovation, and responsiveness to customers. Keep in mind also that competition is a process in which companies are continually trying to outdo each other in their ability to achieve high efficiency, superior quality, outstanding innovation, and quick responsiveness to customers. It is possible to imagine a company getting lucky and coming into possession of resources that allow it to achieve excellence on one or more of these dimensions. However, it is difficult to imagine how *sustained* excellence on any of these four dimensions could be produced by anything other than conscious effort, that is, by strategy. Luck may indeed play a role in success, and managers must always exploit a lucky break (Strategy in Action 3.4 discusses the role of luck in the early history of Microsoft and how Bill Gates exploited that luck). However, to argue that success is entirely a matter of luck is to strain credibility. As the great banker of the early twentieth century, J. P. Morgan, once said, "The harder I work, the luckier I seem to get." Managers who strive to formulate and implement strategies that lead to a competitive advantage are more likely to be lucky.

Strategy in Action 3.4

Bill Gates's Lucky Break

The product that launched Microsoft into its leadership position in the software industry was MS-DOS, the operating system for IBM and IBM-compatible PCs. The original DOS program, however, was developed not by Microsoft but by Seattle Computer, where it was known as Q-DOS (which stood for "quick and dirty operating system"). When IBM was looking for an operating system to run its original PC, it talked to a number of software companies, including Microsoft, asking whether they could develop such a system. Seattle Computer was not one of those companies. Bill Gates, already a player in the emerging Seattle computer community, knew that Seattle Computer had developed a disk operating system and took action: he borrowed $50,000 from his father, a senior partner in a prominent Seattle law firm, and then went to see the CEO of Seattle Computer and offered to purchase the rights to the company's Q-DOS system. He did not, of course, reveal that IBM was looking for a disk operat-

ing system. Seattle Computer, short of cash, quickly agreed. Gates then renamed the system MS-DOS, upgraded it somewhat, and licensed it to IBM. The rest, as they say, is history.

So was Gates lucky? Of course he was. It was lucky that Seattle Computer had not heard about IBM's request. It was lucky that IBM approached Microsoft. It was lucky that Gates knew about Seattle Computer's operating system. And it was lucky that Gates had a father wealthy enough to lend him $50,000 on short notice. Nevertheless, to attribute all of Microsoft's subsequent success to luck would be wrong. Although MS-DOS gave Microsoft a tremendous head start in the industry, it did not guarantee that Microsoft would continue to enjoy the kind of worldwide success that it has. To do that, Microsoft had to build the appropriate set of resources and capabilities required to produce a continual stream of innovative software, which is precisely what the company did with the cash generated from MS-DOS.[e]

Summary of Chapter

1. Distinctive competencies are the firm-specific strengths of a company. Valuable distinctive competencies enable a company to earn a profit rate that is above the industry average.

2. The distinctive competencies of an organization arise from its resources (its financial, physical, human, technological, and organizational assets) and capabilities (its skills at coordinating resources and putting them to productive use).

3. In order to achieve a competitive advantage, a company needs to pursue strategies that build on its existing resources and capabilities and formulate strategies that build additional resources and capabilities (develop new competencies).

4. The source of a competitive advantage is superior value creation.

5. To create superior value, a company must lower its costs or differentiate its product so that it creates more value and can charge a higher price, or do both simultaneously.

6. Managers must understand how value creation and pricing decisions affect demand and how costs change with increases in volume. They must have a good grasp of the demand conditions in the company's market and the cost structure of the company at different levels of output if they are to make decisions that maximize the profitability of their enterprise.

7. The four building blocks of competitive advantage are efficiency, quality, innovation, and responsiveness to customers. These are generic distinctive competencies. Superior efficiency enables a company to lower its costs; superior quality allows it to charge a higher price and lower its costs; and superior customer service lets it charge a higher price. Superior innovation can lead to higher prices, particularly in the case of product innovations, or lower unit costs, particularly in the case of process innovations.

8. If a company's managers are to perform a good internal analysis, they need to be able to analyze the financial performance of their company, identifying how the strategies of the company relate to its profitability, as measured by the return on invested capital.

9. The durability of a company's competitive advantage depends on the height of barriers to imitation, the capability of competitors, and environmental dynamism.

10. Failing companies typically earn low or negative profits. Three factors seem to contribute to failure: organizational inertia in the face of environmental change, the nature of a company's prior strategic commitments, and the Icarus paradox.

11. Avoiding failure requires a constant focus on the basic building blocks of competitive advantage, continuous improvement, identification and adoption of best industrial practice, and victory over inertia.

Discussion Questions

1. What are the main implications of the material discussed in this chapter for strategy formulation?

2. When is a company's competitive advantage most likely to endure over time?

3. It is possible for a company to be the lowest-cost producer in its industry and simultaneously have an output that is the most valued by customers. Discuss this statement.

4. Why is it important to understand the drivers of profitability, as measured by the return on invested capital?

5. Which is more important in explaining the success and failure of companies: strategizing or luck?

Practicing Strategic Management

■ SMALL-GROUP EXERCISE
Analyzing Competitive Advantage

Break up into groups of three to five people. Drawing on the concepts introduced in this chapter, analyze the competitive position of your business school in the market for business education. Then answer the following questions:

1. Does your business school have a competitive advantage?

2. If so, on what is this advantage based, and is this advantage sustainable?

3. If your school does not have a competitive advantage in the market for business education, identify the inhibiting factors that are holding it back.

4. How might the Internet change the way in which business education is delivered?

5. Does the Internet pose a threat to the competitive position of your school in the market for business education, or is it an opportunity for your school to enhance its competitive position? (Note that it can be both.)

■ ARTICLE FILE 3

Find a company that has sustained its competitive advantage for more than ten years. Identify the source of the competitive advantage, and explain why it has lasted so long.

■ STRATEGIC MANAGEMENT PROJECT

Module 3

This module deals with the competitive position of your company. With the information you have at your disposal, perform the tasks and answer the questions listed:

1. Identify whether your company has a competitive advantage or disadvantage in its primary industry. (Its primary industry is the one in which it has the most sales.)

2. Evaluate your company against the four generic building blocks of competitive advantage: efficiency, quality, innovation, and responsiveness to customers. How does this exercise help you understand the performance of your company relative to its competitors?

3. What are the distinctive competencies of your company?

4. What role have prior strategies played in shaping the distinctive competencies of your company? What has been the role of luck?

5. Do the strategies your company is pursuing now build on its distinctive competencies? Are they an attempt to build new competencies?

6. What are the barriers to imitating the distinctive competencies of your company?

7. Is there any evidence that your company finds it difficult to adapt to changing industry conditions? If so, why do you think this is the case?

■ EXPLORING THE WEB

Visiting Johnson & Johnson

Visit the website of Johnson & Johnson (**www.jnj.com**). Read through the material contained on the site, paying particular attention to the features on company history, Johnson & Johnson's credo, innovations, and company news. On the basis of the information contained here, answer the following questions:

1. Do you think that Johnson & Johnson has a distinctive competence?

2. What is the nature of this competence? How does it help the company to attain a competitive advantage?

3. What are the resources and capabilities that underlie this competence? Where do these resources and capabilities come from?

4. How imitable is Johnson & Johnson's distinctive competence?

General Task   Search the Web for a company site that goes into depth about the history, products, and competitive position of that company. On the basis of the information you collect, answer the following questions:

1. Does the company have a distinctive competence?

2. What is the nature of this competence? How does it help the company to attain a competitive advantage?

3. What are the resources and capabilities that underlie this competence? Where do these resources and capabilities come from?

4. How imitable is the company's distinctive competence?

Closing Case

Google

In 1996 two computer science PhD students at Stanford University, Sergey Brin and Larry Page, were wondering how they could sort through the massive amount of information that was starting to appear on the Web in order to find specific and useful information on a topic. While there were several different technologies, or search engines, available to search the Web for information,

none of them seemed particularly useful to Brin and Page. The basic problem was that existing search engines did a poor job of distinguishing between useful and trivial websites. Brin and Page decided to build a search engine that would not only examine the words on webpages and then index them as other search engines did, but would also look at how and where these words were being used, and also at the number of other websites linked to a page. The goal was to have the search engine return a list of webpages, with the most useful appearing at the top.

The first iteration of their search engine, which relied on a proprietary algorithm developed by Brin and Page, was known as BackRub. BackRub soon created a buzz among other computer science students at Stanford, but it was the encouragement of another former Stanford student, David Filo, one of the founders of yahoo.com, that persuaded Brin and Page to start their own company.

By July 1998 Brin and Page had put their PhD studies on hold and were actively raising money from family, friends, and angel investors. Initially they found it very difficult to raise money, but in mid 1998 they had a chance encounter with another former Stanford student, Andy Bechtolsheim, who had been one of the founders of Sun Microsystems. Impressed by a demonstration of BackRub, Bechtolsheim wrote Brin and Page a check for $100,000 on the spot. By September 1998 they had raised $1 million, enough to capitalize their company, which they called Google.

By December 1998 the beta version of Google's search engine had been up and running on the Web for months and was answering over 10,000 search queries a day. From that point on, growth was exponential. By December 2000, Google's index included more than 1.3 billion webpages, and the company was answering some 60 million search inquiries a day. By 2004 the number of webpages indexed by Google exceeded 4 billion and the search engine was handling more than 300 million inquiries a day. Google's technology quickly became pervasive. Soon most major Web portals were using Google's search engine technology, including Yahoo! and AOL Time Warner. Estimates suggested that in 2003 some 75 percent of Internet searches were made using Google.

What was most impressive about Google, however, was that, unlike many other dot-com businesses of the 1990s, Google found a way to make money. In 2003 the company made $967 million in revenues and $105 million in net profit. In the first six months of 2004 alone, revenues surged to $1.35 billion and net income to $143 million. The basic business model is simple. Google sells to advertisers the words that people enter when they search for something on the Web. This means that whoever bids the most for a particular term, say, *digital cameras*, gets their link put at the top of a Google-generated list. Google distinguishes between independent search results and those that are paid for by listing "sponsored links" on the right side of its page. However, a sponsor does not pay Google unless a user clicks through to it from a Google-generated link.

To determine the price to charge advertisers for a term, Google uses an automated bidding process known as a Vickery second price auction. Under this bidding methodology, winning bidders pay only 1 cent more than the bidder below them. Thus if there are three bids for the term *digital cameras*—say, $1 a click, $0.50 a click, and $0.25 click—the winner will pay $0.51 a click to Google.

In August 2004, Google went public and raised over $1.5 billion. With no debt and flush with cash, the company looks set to build on its lead in the search engine business. However, competitors have not been sitting on the sidelines. In 2003 Yahoo! purchased a rival search engine company, Overture Services, for some $1.6 billion. Then in February 2004 Yahoo! replaced Google as the search engine on its site with a proprietary search engine based on Overture's technology. Microsoft, too, seems to have its sights set on Google. Microsoft is reportedly working on its own search engine technology, which it plans to integrate with its technology, including Microsoft Office and Longhorn, the next version of the Windows operating system that is due for release in 2006. [38]

Case Discussion Questions

1. What is the value that Google creates for (a) customers and (b) advertisers? How does this value translate into higher revenues and profits?

2. What are the sources of Google's competitive advantage? How secure are these advantages from imitation by competitors? What must Google do to keep the competitors at bay?

3. Do competitors such as Yahoo! and Microsoft potentially have assets and capabilities that give them an advantage over Google in the search engine business?

Chapter 4

Building Competitive Advantage Through Functional-Level Strategy

Opening Case

Verizon Wireless

In the wireless telecommunications industry one metric above all others determines a company's profitability: customer churn, or the number of subscribers who leave a service within a given time period. Churn is important because it costs between $300 and $400 to acquire a customer. With monthly bills in the United States averaging $50, it can take six to eight months just to recoup the fixed costs of a customer acquisition. If churn rates are higher, profitability is eaten up by the costs of acquiring customers who do not stay long enough to provide a profit to the service provider.

The risk of churn increased significantly in the United States after November 2003 when the Federal Communications Commission allowed wireless subscribers to take their numbers with them when they switched to a new service provider. Over the next six months, a clear winner emerged in the battle to limit customer defections: Verizon Wireless. Between November 2003 and May 2004 the churn rate at Verizon Wireless averaged 1.6 percent a month, implying that 20 percent of the company's customers were leaving the service each year. While this might sound high, it was considerably lower than the churn rate at AT&T Wireless, whose monthly churn rate of 3.7 percent was the highest among the big six wireless service providers in the United States, or T-Mobile, which had a 3.2 percent monthly churn rate.

Verizon's low churn rate has enabled the company to grow its subscriber base faster than rivals, which allows the company to better achieve economies of scale by spreading the fixed costs of building a wireless network over a larger customer base. In the quarter ending June 30, 2004, Verizon added 1.5 million customers, bringing its total up to 40.4 million. These customer additions easily outpaced those of its rivals. Sprint, for example, added 505,000 subscribers in the quarter, Cingular 428,000, and AT&T Wireless just 15,000.

There are several reasons for Verizon's success. First, in its early years the company invested heavily in building a high-quality nationwide wireless network. It has the largest coverage area of any wireless provider and has successfully differentiated itself on the quality of its service. Customers report clearer connections and fewer dropped calls on the Verizon network than on any other network.

A technological choice has also played into this advantage. Verizon is one of two U.S. wireless companies that took a chance and bet on a new wireless technology know as CDMA (the other was Sprint). CDMA is less costly to install than a competing wireless technology, known as GSM, and is well suited to providing broadband services, such as wireless connections to the Internet. When Verizon chose to build a nationwide CDMA network, the technology was unproven and critics questioned its reliability and cost. But the critics were wrong, and Verizon now has an advantage over most of its competitors, who opted for the more established GSM technology. Utilizing the broadband capabilities of its CDMA network, in 2005 Verizon was the first wireless provider to offer a nationwide "broadband" service that will allow subscribers to connect to the Internet in major metropolitan areas via a laptop or cell phone. This may well prove to be another source of differential advantage.

Verizon has communicated its coverage and quality advantage to customers with its "Test Man" advertisements. In these ads, a Verizon Test Man wearing horn-rimmed glasses and a Verizon uniform wanders around remote spots in the nation asking on his Verizon cell phone, "Can you hear me now?" Verizon says that the Test Man is actually the personification of a crew of fifty Verizon employees who each drive some 100,000 miles annually in specially outfitted vehicles to test the reliability of Verizon's network.

To further reduce customer churn, Verizon has invested heavily in its customer care function. Almost as soon as new customers receive their first monthly bill, Verizon Wireless representatives are on the phone, asking how they like the service. In that same call, a Verizon representative will ask what parts of the service a customer isn't using. If someone isn't yet using voice mail, for example, the representative will offer to set it up and get it working.

In addition, Verizon's automated software programs analyze the call habits of individual customers. Using that information, Verizon representatives will contact customers and suggest alternative calling plans that might better suit their needs. For example, Verizon might contact a customer and say, "We see that because of your heavy use on weekends, an alternative calling plan might make more sense for you and help reduce your monthly bills." The goal is to anticipate customer needs and proactively satisfy them, rather than have the customer take the initiative and possibly switch to another service provider.[1]

Overview

In this chapter, we take a close look at **functional-level strategies**: those aimed at improving the effectiveness of a company's operations and thus its ability to attain superior efficiency, quality, innovation, and customer responsiveness.

It is important to keep in mind the relationships among functional strategies, distinctive competencies, differentiation, low cost, value creation, and profitability (see Figure 4.1). Note that distinctive competencies shape the functional-level strategies that a company can pursue and that managers, through their choices with regard to functional-level strategies, can build resources and capabilities that enhance a company's distinctive competencies. Note also that the ability of a company to attain superior efficiency, quality, innovation, and customer responsiveness will determine if its product offering is *differentiated* from that of rivals and if it has a *low cost structure*. Recall that companies that increase the utility consumers get from their products through differentiation, while simultaneously lowering their cost structure, create more value than their rivals, and this leads to a competitive advantage and superior profitability and profit growth.

The *Opening Case* illustrates some of these relationships. Verizon Wireless has differentiated itself from its competitors through the reliability and coverage of its wireless network (a tangible resource) and through its superior after-sales service and support, or customer care (a capability). Verizon's network advantages have been communicated to customers through the "Can you hear me now?" advertisement campaign. Its successful differentiation, which is based on quality and customer responsiveness and is achieved through actions taken at the functional level, has reduced customer churn rates to the lowest level in the industry, boosting profitability and enabling Verizon to capture more market share, which implies greater profit growth. Consistent with the Verizon case, much of this chapter is devoted to looking

FIGURE 4.1

The Roots of Competitive Advantage

at the basic strategies that can be adopted at the operating level to improve competitive position. By the end of this chapter, you will understand how functional-level strategies can be used to build a sustainable competitive advantage.

Achieving Superior Efficiency

A company is a device for transforming inputs (labor, land, capital, management, and technological know-how) into outputs (the goods and services produced). The simplest measure of efficiency is the quantity of inputs that it takes to produce a given output; that is, efficiency = outputs/inputs. The more efficient a company is, the fewer the inputs required to produce a given output and therefore the lower its cost structure will be. Put another way, an efficient company has higher productivity, and therefore lower costs, than its rivals. Here we review the steps that companies can take at the functional level to increase their efficiency and thereby lower their cost structure.

■ Efficiency and Economies of Scale

Economies of scale are unit cost reductions associated with a large scale of output. You will recall from the last chapter that it is very important for managers to understand how the cost structure of their enterprise varies with output because this understanding should help to drive strategy. For example, if unit costs fall significantly as output is expanded—that is, if there are significant economies of scale—a company may benefit by keeping prices down and increasing volume.

One source of economies of scale is the ability to spread fixed costs over a large production volume. *Fixed costs* are costs that must be incurred to produce a product whatever the level of output; examples are the costs of purchasing machinery, setting up machinery for individual production runs, building facilities, and advertising and R&D. For example, Microsoft spent approximately $1 billion to develop the latest version of its Windows operating system, Windows XP. It can realize substantial scale economies by spreading the fixed costs associated with developing the new operating system over the enormous unit sales volume it expects for this system (95 percent of the world's personal computers use a Microsoft operating system). These scale economies are significant because of the trivial incremental (or marginal) cost of producing additional copies of Windows XP: once the master copy has been produced, additional CDs containing the operating system can be produced for a few cents. The key to Microsoft's efficiency and profitability (and that of other companies with high fixed costs and trivial incremental or marginal costs) is to increase sales rapidly enough that fixed costs can be spread out over a large unit volume and substantial scale economies can be realized.

Another source of scale economies is the ability of companies producing in large volumes to achieve a greater division of labor and specialization. Specialization is said to have a favorable impact on productivity, mainly because it enables employees to become very skilled at performing a particular task. The classic example of such economies is Ford's Model T car. The world's first mass-produced car, the Model T Ford was introduced in 1923. Until then, Ford had made cars using an expensive hand-built craft production method. By introducing mass-production techniques, the company achieved greater division of labor (it split assembly into small, repeatable tasks) and specialization, which boosted employee productivity. Ford was also able to spread the fixed costs of developing a car and setting up production machinery over a large volume of output. As a result of these economies, the cost of manufacturing a car at Ford fell from $3,000 to less than $900 (in 1958 dollars).

These examples illustrate that economies of scale can boost profitability, as measured by return on invested capital (ROIC), in a number of ways. Economies of scale exist in production, sales and marketing, and R&D, and the overall effect of realizing scale economies is to reduce spending as a percentage of revenues on cost of goods sold (COGS); sales, general, and administrative expenses (SG&A); and R&D expenses, thereby boosting return on sales and, by extension, ROIC (see Figure 3.9). Moreover, by making more intensive use of existing capacity, a company can increase the amount of sales generated from its property, plant, and equipment (PPE), thereby reducing the amount of capital it needs to generate a dollar of sales, and thus increasing its capital turnover and its ROIC.

The concept of scale economies is illustrated in Figure 4.2, which shows that as a company increases its output, unit costs fall. This process comes to an end at an output of Q_1, where all scale economies are exhausted. Indeed, at outputs of greater than Q_1, the company may encounter **diseconomies of scale**, which are the unit cost increases associated with a large scale of output. Diseconomies of scale occur primarily because of the increasing bureaucracy associated with large-scale enterprises and the managerial inefficiencies that can result.[2] Larger enterprises have a tendency to develop extensive managerial hierarchies in which dysfunctional political behavior is commonplace, information about operating matters is accidentally and deliberately distorted by the number of managerial layers through which it has to travel to reach top decisionmakers, and poor decisions are the result. As a result, past some point (such as Q_1 in Figure 4.2), the inefficiencies that result from such developments outweigh any additional gains from economies of scale, and unit costs start to rise as output expands.

Managers must know not only the extent of economies of scale, but also where diseconomies of scale begin to occur. At Nucor Steel, for example, the realization that diseconomies of scale exist has led to a decision not to build plants that employ more

FIGURE 4.2

Economies and
Diseconomies of
Scale

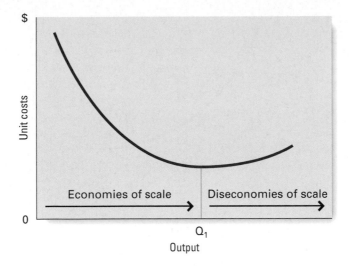

than 300 individuals. The belief is that it is more efficient to build two plants, each employing 300 people, than one plant employing 600 people. Although the larger plant might theoretically be able to reap greater scale economies, Nucor's management believes that these would be swamped by the diseconomies of scale that come with larger organizational units.

■ **Efficiency and Learning Effects**

Learning effects are cost savings that come from learning by doing. Labor, for example, learns by repetition how best to carry out a task. Therefore, labor productivity increases over time, and unit costs fall as individuals learn the most efficient way to perform a particular task. Equally important, management in new manufacturing facilities typically learns over time how best to run the new operation. Hence, production costs decline because of increasing labor productivity and management efficiency. Japanese companies like Toyota are noted for making learning a central part of their operating philosophy.

Learning effects tend to be more significant when a technologically complex task is repeated because there is more to learn. Thus, learning effects will be more significant in an assembly process that has 1,000 complex steps than in one with 100 simple steps. Although learning effects are normally associated with the manufacturing process, there is every reason to believe that they are just as important in service industries. For example, one famous study of learning in the context of the health care industry found that more experienced medical providers posted significantly lower mortality rates for a number of common surgical procedures, suggesting that learning effects are at work in surgery.[3] The authors of this study used the evidence to argue for establishing regional referral centers for the provision of highly specialized medical care. These centers would perform many specific surgical procedures (such as heart surgery), replacing local facilities with lower volumes and presumably higher mortality rates. Another recent study found strong evidence of learning effects in a financial institution. The study looked at a newly established document-processing unit with one hundred staff members and found that, over time, documents were processed much more rapidly as the staff learned the process. Overall, the study

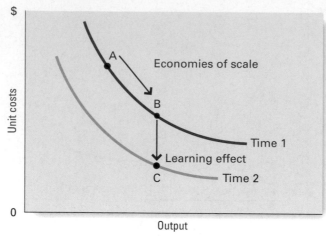

concluded that unit costs fell every time the cumulative number of documents processed doubled.[4]

In terms of the unit cost curve of a company, although economies of scale imply a movement along the curve (say, from A to B in Figure 4.3), the realization of learning effects implies a downward shift of the *entire* curve (B to C in Figure 4.3) as both labor and management become more efficient over time at performing their tasks at every level of output. In accounting terms, learning effects in a production setting will reduce the cost of goods sold as a percentage of revenues, enabling the company to earn a higher return on sales and return on invested capital.

No matter how complex the task is, however, learning effects typically die out after a limited period of time. Indeed, it has been suggested that they are really important only during the start-up period of a new process and cease after two or three years.[5] When changes occur to a company's production system—as a result of merger or the use of new information technology, for example—the learning process has to begin again.

■ Efficiency and the Experience Curve

The experience curve refers to the systematic lowering of the cost structure, and consequent unit cost reductions, that have been observed to occur over the life of a product.[6] According to the experience-curve concept, unit manufacturing costs for a product typically decline by some characteristic amount each time *accumulated* output of the product is doubled (accumulated output is the total output of a product since its introduction). This relationship was first observed in the aircraft industry, where it was found that each time accumulated output of airframes was doubled, unit costs declined to 80 percent of their previous level.[7] Thus, the fourth airframe typically costs only 80 percent of the second airframe to produce, the eighth airframe only 80 percent of the fourth, the sixteenth only 80 percent of the eighth, and so on. The outcome of this process is a relationship between unit manufacturing costs and accumulated output similar to that illustrated in Figure 4.4. Economies of scale and learning effects underlie the experience-curve phenomenon. Put simply, as a company increases the accumulated volume of its output over time, it is able to realize both economies of scale (as volume increases) and learning effects. Consequently, unit costs and cost structure fall with increases in accumulated output.

FIGURE 4.4

The Experience Curve

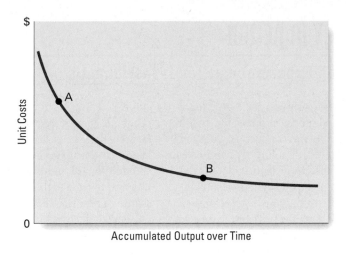

The strategic significance of the experience curve is clear: increasing a company's product volume and market share will lower its cost structure relative to its rivals. Thus, company B in Figure 4.4, because it is farther down the experience curve, has a cost advantage over company A because of its lower cost structure. The concept is perhaps most important in industries that mass-produce a standardized output (for example, the manufacture of semiconductor chips). A company that wishes to become more efficient and lower its cost structure must try to ride down the experience curve as quickly as possible. This means constructing efficient scale manufacturing facilities even before it has generated demand for the product and aggressively pursuing cost reductions from learning effects. It might also need to adopt an aggressive marketing strategy, cutting prices to the bone and stressing heavy sales promotions and extensive advertising in order to build up demand, and hence accumulated volume, as quickly as possible. The need to be aware of the relationship of demand, price options, and costs noted in Chapter 3 is clear.

Once down the experience curve because of its superior efficiency, the company is likely to have a significant cost advantage over its competitors. For example, it has been argued that Intel uses such tactics to ride down the experience curve and gain a competitive advantage over its rivals in the market for microprocessors. Similarly, one reason Matsushita came to dominate the global market for VHS videotape recorders is that it based its strategy on the experience curve.[8] The early success of Texas Instruments was also based on exploiting the experience curve, as Strategy in Action 4.1 details.

The company farthest down the experience curve cannot become complacent about its cost advantage. Strategy in Action 4.1 explains how obsession with the experience curve at Texas Instruments harmed the company. More generally, there are three reasons that managers should not become complacent about their efficiency-based cost advantages derived from experience effects. First, since neither learning effects nor economies of scale go on forever, the experience curve is likely to bottom out at some point; indeed, it must do so by definition. When this occurs, further unit cost reductions from learning effects and economies of scale will be hard to come by. Thus, in time, other companies can lower their cost structures and match

Strategy in Action 4.1

Too Much Experience at Texas Instruments

Texas Instruments (TI) was an early user of the experience-curve concept. TI was a technological innovator, first in silicon transistors and then in semiconductors. The company discovered that with every doubling of accumulated production volume of a transistor or semiconductor, unit costs declined to 73 percent of their previous level. Building on this insight, when TI first produced a new transistor or semiconductor, it would slash the price of the product to stimulate demand. The goal was to drive up the accumulated volume of production and so drive down costs through the realization of experience-curve economies. As a result, during the 1960s and 1970s, TI hammered its competitors in transistors and moved on to prevail in semiconductors and, ultimately, in hand-held calculators and digital watches. Until 1982, TI enjoyed rapid growth, with sales quadrupling between 1977 and 1981 alone.

After 1982, things began to go wrong for TI. The company's single-minded focus on cost reductions, an outgrowth of its strategic reliance on the experience curve, left it with a poor understanding of customer needs and market trends. Competitors such as Casio and Hewlett-Packard began to make major inroads into TI's hand-held calculator business by focusing on features in addition to cost and price that customers demanded. TI was slow to react to this trend and lost substantial market share as a result. In the late 1970s, it also decided to focus on semiconductors for watches and calculators, where it had gained substantial experience-curve-based cost economies, rather than developing metal oxide semiconductors for computer memories and advanced semiconductors. As it turned out, with the growth in minicomputers and personal computers in the early 1980s, the market shifted toward high-power metal oxide semiconductors. Consequently, TI found itself outflanked by Intel and Motorola. In sum, TI's focus on realizing experience-curve economies initially benefited the company, but then it seems to have contributed toward a myopia that cost the company dearly.[a]

the cost leader. Once this happens, a number of low-cost companies can have cost parity with each other. In such circumstances, a sustainable competitive advantage must rely on strategic factors besides the minimization of production costs by using existing technologies—factors such as better responsiveness to customers, product quality, or innovation.

Second, as noted in Chapter 2, changes that are always taking place in the external environment disrupt a company's business model, so cost advantages gained from experience effects can be made obsolete by the development of new technologies. The price of television picture tubes followed the experience-curve pattern from the introduction of television in the late 1940s until 1963. The average unit price dropped from $34 to $8 (in 1958 dollars) in that time. However, the advent of color TV interrupted the experience curve. To make picture tubes for color TVs, a new manufacturing technology was required, and the price of color TV tubes shot up to $51 by 1966. Then the experience curve reasserted itself. The price dropped to $48 in 1968, $37 in 1970, and $36 in 1972.[9] In short, technological change can alter the rules of the game, requiring that former low-cost companies take steps to reestablish their competitive edge.

A further reason for avoiding complacency is that producing a high volume of output does not necessarily give a company a lower cost structure. Different technologies have different cost structures. For example, the steel industry has two alternative manufacturing technologies: an integrated technology, which relies on the basic oxygen furnace, and a mini-mill technology, which depends on the electric arc furnace. Whereas the basic oxygen furnace requires high volumes to attain maximum efficiency, mini-mills are cost efficient at relative low volumes. Moreover, even when both technologies are producing at their most efficient output levels, steel companies with basic oxygen furnaces do not have a cost advantage over mini-mills. Consequently, the pursuit of experience economies by an integrated company using basic oxygen technology may not bring the kind of cost advantages that a naive reading of the experience-curve phenomenon would lead the company to expect. Indeed, there have been significant periods of time when integrated companies have not been able to get enough orders to run at optimum capacity. Hence, their production costs have been considerably higher than those of mini-mills.[10] As we discuss next, in many industries new flexible manufacturing technologies hold out the promise of allowing small manufacturers to produce at unit costs comparable to those of large assembly-line operations.

Efficiency, Flexible Manufacturing, and Mass Customization

Central to the concept of economies of scale is the idea that the best way to achieve high efficiency and a lower cost structure is through the mass production of a standardized output. The tradeoff implicit in this idea is between unit costs and product variety. Producing greater product variety from a factory implies shorter production runs, which implies an inability to realize economies of scale and higher costs. That is, a wide product variety makes it difficult for a company to increase its production efficiency and thus reduce its unit costs. According to this logic, the way to increase efficiency and achieve a lower cost structure is to limit product variety and produce a standardized product in large volumes (see Figure 4.5a).

This view of production efficiency has been challenged by the rise of flexible manufacturing technologies. The term **flexible manufacturing technology**—or **lean production**, as it is sometimes called—covers a range of manufacturing technologies designed to reduce setup times for complex equipment, increase the use of individual

FIGURE 4.5

Tradeoff Between Costs and Product Variety

machines through better scheduling, and improve quality control at all stages of the manufacturing process.[11] Flexible manufacturing technologies allow the company to produce a wider variety of end products at a unit cost that at one time could be achieved only through the mass production of a standardized output (see Figure 4.5b). Indeed, research suggests that the adoption of flexible manufacturing technologies may increase efficiency and lower unit costs relative to what can be achieved by the mass production of a standardized output, while at the same time enabling the company to customize its product offering to a much greater extent than was once thought possible. The term **mass customization** has been coined to describe the ability of companies to use flexible manufacturing technology to reconcile two goals that were once thought to be incompatible: *low cost* and *differentiation through product customization*.[12]

Flexible manufacturing technologies vary in their sophistication and complexity. One of the most famous examples, Toyota's production system, is relatively unsophisticated, but it has been credited with making Toyota the most efficient auto company in the global industry. Toyota's flexible manufacturing system is profiled in Strategy in Action 4.2. **Flexible machine cells** are another common flexible manufacturing technology. A flexible machine cell is a grouping of various types of machinery, a common materials handler, and a centralized cell controller (a computer). Each cell normally contains four to six machines capable of performing a variety of operations but dedicated to producing a family of parts or products. The settings on the machines are computer controlled, which allows each cell to switch quickly between the production of different parts or products.

Strategy in Action   4.2

Toyota's Lean Production System

Toyota's flexible manufacturing system was developed by one of the company's engineers, Ohno Taiichi. After working at Toyota for five years and visiting Ford's U.S. plants, Ohno became convinced that the mass-production philosophy for making cars was flawed. He saw numerous problems, including three major drawbacks. First, long production runs created massive inventories, which had to be stored in large warehouses. This was expensive because of the cost of warehousing and because inventories tied up capital in unproductive uses. Second, if the initial machine settings were wrong, long production runs resulted in the production of a large number of defects (that is, waste). And third, the mass-production system was unable to accommodate consumer preferences for product diversity.

In looking for ways to make shorter production runs economical, Ohno developed a number of techniques designed to reduce setup times for production equipment, a major source of fixed costs. By using a system of levers and pulleys, he was able to reduce the time required to change dies on stamping equipment from a full day in 1950 to three minutes by 1971. This advance made small production runs economical, which allowed Toyota to respond better to consumer demands for product diversity. Small production runs also eliminated the need to hold large inventories, thereby reducing warehousing costs. Furthermore, small production runs and the lack of inventory meant that defective parts were produced only in small numbers and entered the assembly process immediately. This reduced waste and made it easier to trace defects to their source and fix the problem. In sum, Ohno's innovations enabled Toyota to produce a more diverse product range at a lower unit cost than was possible with conventional mass production.[b]

Improved capacity utilization and reductions in work-in-progress (that is, stockpiles of partly finished products) and waste are major efficiency benefits of flexible machine cells. Improved capacity utilization arises from the reduction in setup times and from the computer-controlled coordination of production flow between machines, which eliminates bottlenecks. The tight coordination between machines also reduces work-in-progress. Reductions in waste are due to the ability of computer-controlled machinery to identify ways to transform inputs into outputs while producing a minimum of unusable waste material. Freestanding machines might be in use 50 percent of the time; the same machines when grouped into a cell can be used more than 80 percent of the time and produce the same end product with half the waste, thereby increasing efficiency and resulting in lower costs.

The effects of installing flexible manufacturing technology on a company's cost structure can be dramatic. Ford Motor Company is currently introducing flexible manufacturing technologies into its automotive plants around the world. These new technologies should allow Ford to produce multiple models from the same line and to switch production from one model to another much more quickly than in the past. In total, Ford hopes to take $2 billion out of its cost structure by 2010.[13]

More generally, in terms of the profitability framework developed in Chapter 3, flexible manufacturing technology should boost profitability (measured by ROIC) by reducing the cost of goods sold as a percentage of revenues, reducing the working capital needed to finance work-in-progress (because there is less of it), and reducing the amount of capital that needs to be invested in property, plant, and equipment to generate a dollar of sales (because less space is needed to store inventory).

Marketing and Efficiency

The marketing strategy that a company adopts can have a major impact on efficiency and cost structure. **Marketing strategy** refers to the position that a company takes with regard to pricing, promotion, advertising, product design, and distribution. Some of the steps leading to greater efficiency are fairly obvious. For example, riding down the experience curve to achieve a lower cost structure can be facilitated by aggressive pricing, promotions, and advertising, all of which are the task of the marketing function. Other aspects of marketing strategy have a less obvious but no less important impact on efficiency. One important aspect is the relationship of customer defection rates, cost structure, and unit costs, which was touched on in the *Opening Case* on Verizon.[14]

Customer defection rates (churn rates) are the percentage of a company's customers who defect every year to competitors. Defection rates are determined by customer loyalty, which in turn is a function of the ability of a company to satisfy its customers. Because acquiring a new customer entails certain one-time fixed costs for advertising, promotions, and the like, there is a direct relationship between defection rates and costs. The longer a company holds on to a customer, the greater is the volume of customer-generated unit sales that can be set against these fixed costs and the lower the average unit cost of each sale. Thus, lowering customer defection rates allows a company to achieve a lower cost structure.

One consequence of the defection-cost relationship depicted is illustrated in Figure 4.6. Because of the relatively high fixed costs of acquiring new customers, serving customers who stay with the company only for a short time before switching to competitors often leads to a loss on the investment made to acquire those customers. The longer a customer stays with the company, the more the fixed costs of acquiring that customer can be spread out over repeat purchases, boosting

FIGURE 4.6

The Relationship
Between Customer
Loyalty and Profit
per Customer

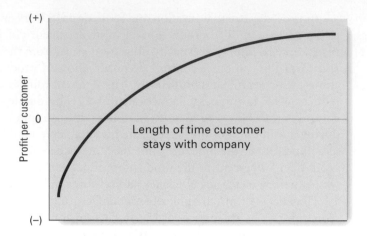

FIGURE 4.6

The Relationship
Between Customer
Loyalty and Profit
per Customer

the profit per customer. Thus, there is a positive relationship between the length of time that a customer stays with a company and profit per customer. If a company can reduce customer defection rates, it can make a much better return on its investment in acquiring customers and thereby boost its profitability. In terms of the profitability framework developed in Chapter 3, reduced customer defection rates mean that the company needs to spend less on sales, general, and administrative expenses to generate a dollar of sales revenue, which increases both return on sales and return on invested capital.

We discussed one example of the importance of customer defection rates in the *Opening Case*, when we looked at customer churn in the wireless industry. For another example, consider the credit card business.[15] Most credit card companies spend an average of $50 to recruit a customer and set up a new account. These costs come from the advertising required to attract new customers, the credit checks required for each customer, and the mechanics of setting up an account and issuing a card. These one-time fixed costs can be recouped only if a customer stays with the company for at least two years. Moreover, when customers stay a second year, they tend to increase their use of the credit card, which raises the volume of revenues generated by each customer over time. As a result, although the credit card business loses $50 per customer in year 1, it makes a profit of $44 in year 3 and $55 in year 6.

Another economic benefit of long-time customer loyalty is the free advertising that customers provide for a company. Loyal customers can dramatically increase the volume of business through referrals. A striking example is Britain's largest retailer, the clothing and food company Marks & Spencer, whose success is built on a well-earned reputation for providing its customers with high-quality goods at reasonable prices. The company has generated such customer loyalty that it does not need to advertise in Britain, a major source of cost saving.

The key message, then, is that reducing customer defection rates and building customer loyalty can be major sources of a lower cost structure. One study has estimated that a 5 percent reduction in customer defection rates leads to the following increases in profits per customer over average customer life: 75 percent in the credit card business, 50 percent in the insurance brokerage industry, 45 percent in the industrial laundry business, and 35 percent in the computer software industry.[16]

A central component of developing a strategy to reduce defection rates is to identify customers who have defected, find out why they defected, and act on that information so that other customers do not defect for similar reasons in the future. To take these measures, the marketing function must have information systems capable of tracking customer defections.

■ **Materials Management, Just-in-Time, and Efficiency**

The contribution of materials management (logistics) to boosting the efficiency of a company can be just as dramatic as the contribution of production and marketing. **Materials management** encompasses the activities necessary to get inputs and components to a production facility (including the costs of purchasing inputs), through the production process, and out through a distribution system to the end-user.[17] Because there are so many sources of cost in this process, the potential for reducing costs through more efficient materials-management strategies is enormous. For a typical manufacturing company, materials and transportation costs account for 50 to 70 percent of its revenues, so even a small reduction in these costs can have a substantial impact on profitability. According to one estimate, for a company with revenues of $1 million, a return on invested capital of 5 percent, and materials-management costs that amount to 50 percent of sales revenues (including purchasing costs), increasing total profits by $15,000 would require either a 30 percent increase in sales revenues or a 3 percent reduction in materials costs.[18] In a typical competitive market, reducing materials costs by 3 percent is usually much easier than increasing sales revenues by 30 percent.

Improving the efficiency of the materials-management function typically requires the adoption of a just-in-time (JIT) inventory system, designed to economize on inventory holding costs by having components arrive at a manufacturing plant just in time to enter the production process or to have goods arrive at a retail store only when stock is almost depleted. The major cost saving comes from increasing inventory turnover, which reduces inventory holding costs, such as warehousing and storage costs, and the company's need for working capital. For example, through efficient logistics Wal-Mart can replenish the stock in its stores at least twice a week; many stores receive daily deliveries if they are needed. The typical competitor replenishes its stock every two weeks, so it has to carry a much higher inventory and needs more working capital per dollar of sales. Compared to its competitors, Wal-Mart can maintain the same service levels with a lower investment in inventory, a major source of its lower cost structure. Thus, faster inventory turnover has helped Wal-Mart achieve an efficiency-based competitive advantage in the retailing industry.[19] More generally, in terms of the profitability model developed in Chapter 3, JIT inventory systems reduce the need for working capital (since there is less inventory to finance) and the need for fixed capital to finance storage space (since there is less to store), which reduces capital needs, increases capital turnover, and, by extension, boosts the return on invested capital.

The drawback of JIT systems is that they leave a company without a buffer stock of inventory. Although buffer stocks are expensive to store, they can help tide a company over shortages on inputs brought about by disruption among suppliers (for instance, a labor dispute at a key supplier) and can help a company respond quickly to increases in demand. However, there are ways around these limitations. For example, to reduce the risks linked to dependence on just one supplier for an important input, a company might decide to source inputs from multiple suppliers.

Recently, the efficient management of materials and inventory has been recast in terms of **supply-chain management**: the task of managing the flow of inputs and components from suppliers into the company's production processes to minimize inventory holding and maximize inventory turnover. One of the exemplary companies in terms of supply-chain management is Dell, whose goal is to streamline its supply chain to such an extent that it "replaces inventory with information." Strategy in Action 4.3 looks at how the three major office superstores—Office Depot, Staples, and Office Max—are competing against each other by trying to manage their supply chains more efficiently.

Strategy in Action 4.3

Supply-Chain Management at Office Superstores

Over the past decade, Office Depot, Staples, and Office Max have been engaged in an intense race to dominate the office superstore business. Office superstores have adopted a supermarket approach to selling office supplies and equipment, which includes everything from paper and printer ink to computers and office furniture. Like all other supermarket-type retailers, their margins are razor thin. So to boost their profitability, all three have been looking at ways of managing their supply chains more efficiently. The goal is to coordinate the flow of materials from vendors to such a degree that inventory turns over more rapidly and so less store space needs to be devoted to storing inventory, which allows for smaller, less expensive stores. To the extent that they are successful, this strategy should produce higher sales per square foot, require less investment in store real estate, and tie up less working capital in inventory. All of this will boost profitability as measured by the return on invested capital.

Using inventory turnover as a metric, Office Depot is the clear leader, with a 7.1 inventory turn rate; its inventory turns over (is replaced) 7.1 times per year. Staples is next, with 4.2 inventory turns, followed by Office Max, with 3.2 inventory turns. Office Depot attributes its high inventory turnover to an early investment in information systems, which allow it to track the sales of individual items closely and link them to an optimal reordering cycle. In addition, these systems have helped it to identify slow-moving, low-margin items. Over the past few years, Office Depot has scaled back the number of products it keeps in stock—its stock keeping units (SKUs)—by about 20 percent by removing slow-moving, low-margin items from its stores. As a result, it can operate with slightly smaller stores and still generate comparable sales levels; its new stores are 25,000 square feet, compared to 30,000 square feet in older stores. As it has grown larger, Office

Depot has also been able to use its buying power to persuade vendors to drop-ship supplies at Office Depot warehouses on a just-in-time basis, thereby removing the need to hold expensive inventory.

For its part, Staples announced in 2001 that more efficient supply-chain management was one of its top priorities. Staples has put some thirty initiatives in place in recent years in an attempt to manage its inventory better. Among them is working closely with its top thirty suppliers to develop joint processes for streamlining the supply process. Regular meetings with Hewlett-Packard, for example, have prompted the retailer to move ink cartridges, one of its major categories, to the front of the store to yield faster inventory turns. Staples credits this action with a $6 million to $8 million reduction in inventory. More generally, Staples maintains that between 1998, when it started work on these initiatives, and 2001, the average inventory per store has fallen by some 30 percent. One of the most dramatic steps Staples has taken has been to eliminate the in-store stock of personal computers from some two hundred stores and to replace the product displays and on-floor inventory with a web-based display that allows Staples customers to enter a customized order for a PC, which a Staples vendor then builds.

Office Max too is investing aggressively in supply-chain management initiatives in an attempt to take inventory out of its system. Like its competitors, it has invested in information systems to track the sale of individual items and to link that information to reordering cycles. It is in the process of reducing its SKUs, removing slow-selling, low-margin items from stores, and downscaling the size of its stores while planning to boost sales per square foot. As a result, the average size of a new Office Max store has fallen by 15 percent over the last few years.[c]

■ **R&D Strategy and Efficiency**

The role of superior research and development (R&D) in helping a company achieve a greater efficiency and a lower cost structure is twofold. First, the R&D function can boost efficiency by designing products that are easy to manufacture. By cutting down on the number of parts that make up a product, R&D can dramatically decrease the required assembly time, which translates into higher employee productivity, lower costs, and higher profitability. For example, after Texas Instruments redesigned an infrared sighting mechanism that it supplies to the Pentagon, it found that it had reduced the number of parts from 47 to 12, the number of assembly steps from 56 to 13, the time spent fabricating metal from 757 minutes per unit to 219 minutes per unit, and unit assembly time from 129 minutes to 20 minutes. The result was a substantial decline in production costs. Design for manufacturing requires close coordination between the production and R&D functions of the company, of course. Cross-functional teams that contain production and R&D personnel who work jointly on the problem best achieve this.

The second way in which the R&D function can help a company achieve a lower cost structure is by pioneering process innovations. A *process innovation* is an innovation in the way production processes operate that improves their efficiency. Process innovations have often been a major source of competitive advantage. Toyota's competitive advantage is based partly on the company's invention of new flexible manufacturing processes that dramatically reduced setup times. This process innovation enabled it to obtain efficiency gains associated with flexible manufacturing systems years ahead of its competitors.

■ **Human Resource Strategy and Efficiency**

Employee productivity is one of the key determinants of an enterprise's efficiency, cost structure, and profitability.[20] Productive manufacturing employees can lower the cost of goods sold as a percentage of revenues, a productive sales force can increase sales revenues for a given level of expenses, and productive employees in the company's R&D function can boost the percentage of revenues generated from new products for a given level of R&D expenses. Thus, productive employees lower the costs of generating revenues, increase the return on sales, and by extension boost the company's return on invested capital. The challenge for a company's human resource function is to devise ways to increase employee productivity. Among the choices it has are using certain hiring strategies, training employees, organizing the work force into self-managing teams, and linking pay to performance. The *Running Case* looks at the steps Wal-Mart has taken to boost employee productivity.

■ **Hiring Strategy** Many companies that are well known for their productive employees devote considerable attention to hiring. Southwest Airlines hires people who have a positive attitude and work well in teams because it believes that people who have a positive attitude will work hard and interact well with customers, therefore helping to create customer loyalty. Nucor hires people who are self-reliant and goal oriented, because its employees work in self-managing teams where they have to be self-reliant and goal oriented to perform well. As these examples suggest, it is important to make sure that the hiring strategy of the company is consistent with its own internal organization, culture, and strategic priorities. The people a company hires should have attributes that match the strategic objectives of the company.

Running Case

Human Resource Strategy and Productivity at Wal-Mart

Wal-Mart has one of the most productive work forces in the retail industry. In 2002, for example, it generated $175,000 in sales for every employee, compared to $144,000 at Target and $141,000 at Sears. The roots of Wal-Mart's high productivity go back to the company's early days and the business philosophy of the company's founder, Sam Walton.

Sam Walton began his career in 1940 as a management trainee at J.C. Penney. There he noticed that all employees were called associates, and moreover, that treating them with respect seemed to reap dividends in the form of high employee productivity. Twenty-two years later, when he founded Wal-Mart, Walton decided to call all employees "associates" to symbolize their importance to the company. He reinforced this policy by emphasizing that, at Wal-Mart, "our people make the difference." Unlike many managers who have stated this mantra, Walton believed it and put it into action. He believed that if you treat people well, they will return the favor by working hard, and that if you empower them, then ordinary people can work together to achieve extraordinary things. These beliefs formed the basis for a decentralized organization that operated with an open door policy and open books, allowing associates to see how their store and the company were doing.

Consistent with the open door policy, Walton continually emphasized that management needed to listen to associates and their ideas. As he noted in his 1992 book, "The folks on the front lines—the ones who actually talk to the customer—are the only ones who really know what's going on out there. You'd better find out what they know. This really is what total quality is all about. To push responsibility down in your organization, and to force good ideas to bubble up within it, you must listen to what your associates are trying to tell you."

Despite his belief in empowerment, however, Walton was notoriously tight on salaries. Walton opposed unionization, fearing that it would lead to higher pay and restrictive work rules that would sap productivity. The culture of Wal-Mart also encouraged people to work hard. One of Walton's favorite homilies was the "sundown rule," which stated that one should never leave until tomorrow what can be done today. The sundown rule was enforced by senior managers, including Walton, who would drop in unannounced at a store and pepper store managers and employees with questions, at the same time praising them for a job well done and celebrating the "heroes" who took the sundown rule to heart.

The key to getting extraordinary effort out of employees while paying them meager salaries was to reward them with profit sharing plans and stock ownership schemes. Long before it became fashionable in American business, Walton was placing a chunk of Wal-Mart's profits into a profit sharing plan for associates and the company was putting matching funds into employee stock ownership programs. The idea was simple: reward associates by giving them a stake in the company, and they will work hard for low pay because they know they will make it up in profit sharing and stock price appreciation.

For years this formula worked extraordinarily well, but there are now signs that Wal-Mart's very success is creating problems. In 2004 the company, with a staggering 1.4 million associates, was the largest private employer in the world. As the company has grown, it has become increasingly difficult to hire the kinds of people that Wal-Mart has traditionally relied on: those willing to work long hours for low pay based on the promise of advancement and reward through profit sharing and stock ownership. The company has come under attack for paying its associates low wages and pressuring them to work long hours without overtime pay. Labor unions have made a concerted but so far unsuccessful attempt to unionize stores, and the company is the target of lawsuits from employees alleging sexual discrimination. Wal-Mart claims that the negative publicity is based on faulty data, and perhaps that is right, but if the company has indeed become too big to put Walton's principles into practice, the glory days may be over.[d]

■ **Employee Training** Employees are a major input into the production process. Those who are highly skilled can perform tasks faster and more accurately and are more likely to learn the complex tasks associated with many modern production methods than individuals with lesser skills. Training upgrades employee skill levels, bringing the company productivity-related efficiency gains from learning and experimentation.[21]

■ **Self-Managing Teams**   The use of **self-managing teams**, whose members coordinate their own activities and make their own hiring, training, work, and reward decisions, has been spreading rapidly. The typical team comprises five to fifteen employees who produce an entire product or undertake an entire task. Team members learn all team tasks and rotate from job to job. Because a more flexible work force is one result, team members can fill in for absent coworkers and take over managerial duties such as scheduling work and vacation, ordering materials, and hiring new members. The greater responsibility thrust on team members and the empowerment it implies are seen as motivators. (Empowerment is the process of giving lower-level employees decision-making power.) People often respond well to being given greater autonomy and responsibility. Performance bonuses linked to team production and quality targets work as an additional motivator.

The effect of introducing self-managing teams is reportedly an increase in productivity of 30 percent or more and a substantial increase in product quality. Further cost savings arise from eliminating supervisors and creating a flatter organizational hierarchy, which also lowers the cost structure of the company. In manufacturing companies, perhaps the most potent way to lower the cost structure is to combine self-managing teams with flexible manufacturing cells. For example, after the introduction of flexible manufacturing technology and work practices based on self-managing teams, a General Electric plant in Salisbury, North Carolina, increased productivity by 250 percent compared with GE plants that produced the same products four years earlier.[22]

Still, teams are no panacea; in manufacturing companies, self-managing teams may fail to live up to their potential unless they are integrated with flexible manufacturing technology. Also, teams put a lot of management responsibilities on team members, and helping team members to cope with these responsibilities often requires substantial training—a fact that many companies often forget in their rush to drive down costs, with the result that the teams don't work out as well as planned.[23]

■ **Pay for Performance**   It is hardly surprising that linking pay to performance can help increase employee productivity, but the issue is not quite so simple as just introducing incentive pay systems. It is also important to define what kind of job performance is to be rewarded and how. Some of the most efficient companies in the world, mindful that cooperation among employees is necessary to realize productivity gains, link pay to group or team (rather than individual) performance. Nucor divides its work force into teams of thirty or so, with bonus pay, which can amount to 30 percent of base pay, linked to the ability of the team to meet productivity and quality goals. This link creates a strong incentive for individuals to cooperate with each other in pursuit of team goals; that is, it facilitates teamwork.

■ **Information Systems and Efficiency**   With the rapid spread of computers, the explosive growth of the Internet and corporate intranets (internal corporate computer networks based on Internet standards), and the spread of high-bandwidth fiber optics and digital wireless technology, the information systems function is moving to center stage in the quest for operating efficiencies and a lower cost structure.[24] The impact of information systems on productivity is wide ranging and potentially affects all other activities of a company. For example, Cisco Systems has been able to realize significant cost savings by moving its ordering and customer service functions online. The company has just 300 service agents handling all of its customer accounts, compared to the 900 it would need if sales were not handled online. The difference represents an annual saving of $20 million a year. Moreover, without automated customer service functions, Cisco calculates that it would need at least 1,000 additional service engineers, which would cost around $75 million.[25]

Like Cisco, many companies are using web-based information systems to reduce the costs of coordination between the company and its customers and the company and its suppliers. By using web-based programs to automate customer and supplier interactions, they can substantially reduce the number of people required to manage these interfaces, thereby reducing costs. This trend extends beyond high-tech companies. Banks and financial service companies are finding that they can substantially reduce costs by moving customer accounts and support functions online. Such a move reduces the need for customer service representatives, bank tellers, stockbrokers, insurance agents, and others. For example, it costs an average of about $1.07 to execute a transaction at a bank, such as shifting money from one account to another; executing the same transaction over the Internet costs $0.01.[26]

Similarly, the theory behind Internet-based retailers such as amazon.com is that by replacing physical stores and their supporting personnel with an online virtual store and automated ordering and checkout processes, a company can take significant costs out of the retailing system. Cost savings can also be realized by using web-based information systems to automate many internal company activities, from managing expense reimbursements to benefits planning and hiring processes, thereby reducing the need for internal support personnel.

■ Infrastructure and Efficiency

A company's infrastructure—that is, its structure, culture, style of strategic leadership, and control system—determines the context within which all other value creation activities take place. It follows that improving infrastructure can help a company increase efficiency and lower its cost structure. Above all, an appropriate infrastructure can help foster a companywide commitment to efficiency and promote cooperation among different functions in pursuit of efficiency goals. These issues are addressed at length in later chapters.

For now, it is important to note that strategic leadership is especially important in building a companywide commitment to efficiency. The leadership task is to articulate a vision that recognizes the need for *all* functions of a company to focus on improving efficiency. It is not enough to improve the efficiency of production, or of marketing, or of R&D in a piecemeal fashion. Achieving superior efficiency requires a companywide commitment to this goal that must be articulated by general and functional managers. A further leadership task is to facilitate the cross-functional cooperation needed to achieve superior efficiency. For example, designing products that are easy to manufacture requires that production and R&D personnel communicate; integrating JIT systems with production scheduling requires close communication between materials management and production; designing self-managing teams to perform production tasks requires close cooperation between human resources and production; and so on.

Table 4.1 summarizes the primary roles that various functions must take to achieve superior efficiency. Bear in mind that achieving superior efficiency is not something that can be tackled on a function-by-function basis. It requires an organization-wide commitment and an ability to ensure close cooperation among functions. Top management, by exercising leadership and influencing the infrastructure, plays a major role in this process.

TABLE 4.1

Primary Roles of Value Creation Functions in Achieving Superior Efficiency

Value Creation Function	Primary Roles
Infrastructure (leadership)	1. Provide companywide commitment to efficiency. 2. Facilitate cooperation among functions.
Production	1. Where appropriate, pursue economies of scale and learning economics. 2. Implement flexible manufacturing systems.
Marketing	1. Where appropriate, adopt aggressive marketing to ride down the experience curve. 2. Limit customer defection rates by building brand loyalty.
Materials management	1. Implement JIT systems. 2. Implement supply-chain coordination.
R&D	1. Design products for ease of manufacture. 2. Seek process innovations.
Information systems	1. Use information systems to automate processes. 2. Use information systems to reduce costs of coordination.
Human resources	1. Institute training programs to build skills. 2. Implement self-managing teams. 3. Implement pay for performance.

Achieving Superior Quality

In Chapter 3, we noted that quality can be thought of in terms of two dimensions: *quality as reliability* and *quality as excellence*. High-quality products are reliable, in the sense that they do the job they were designed for and do it well, and are also perceived by consumers to have superior attributes. We also noted that superior quality gives a company two advantages. First, a strong reputation for quality allows a company to *differentiate* its products from those offered by rivals, thereby creating more utility in the eyes of customers, which gives the company the option of charging a premium price for its products. Second, eliminating defects or errors from the production process reduces waste, increases efficiency, and lowers the cost structure of the company and increases its profitability. For example, reducing the number of defects in a company's manufacturing process will lower the cost of goods sold as a percentage of revenues, thereby raising the company's return on sales and return on invested capital. In this section, we look in more depth at what managers can do to enhance the reliability and other attributes of the company's product offering.

Attaining Superior Reliability

The principal tool that most managers now use to increase the reliability of their product offering is the Six Sigma quality improvement methodology. The Six Sigma methodology is a direct descendant of the total quality management (TQM) philosophy that was widely adopted, first by Japanese companies and then by American companies, during the 1980s and early 1990s.[27] The TQM concept was developed by a number of American management consultants, including W. Edwards Deming, Joseph Juran, and A. V. Feigenbaum.[28] Originally, these consultants won few converts in the United States. However, managers in Japan embraced their ideas enthusiastically and even named their premier annual prize for manufacturing excellence after Deming. The philosophy underlying TQM, as articulated by Deming, is based on the following five-step chain reaction:

1. Improved quality means that costs decrease because of less rework, fewer mistakes, fewer delays, and better use of time and materials.

2. As a result, productivity improves.

3. Better quality leads to higher market share and allows the company to raise prices.

4. This increases the company's profitability and allows it to stay in business.

5. Thus the company creates more jobs.[29]

Deming identified a number of steps that should be part of any quality improvement program:

■ A company should have a clear business model to specify where it is going and how it is going to get there.

■ Management should embrace the philosophy that mistakes, defects, and poor-quality materials are not acceptable and should be eliminated.

■ Quality of supervision should be improved by allowing more time for supervisors to work with employees and giving them appropriate skills for the job.

■ Management should create an environment in which employees will not fear reporting problems or recommending improvements.

■ Work standards should not only be defined as numbers or quotas but should also include some notion of quality to promote the production of defect-free output.

■ Management is responsible for training employees in new skills to keep pace with changes in the workplace.

■ Achieving better quality requires the commitment of everyone in the company.

It took the rise of Japan to the top rank of economic powers in the 1980s to alert Western business to the importance of the TQM concept. Since then, quality improvement programs have spread rapidly throughout Western industry. Strategy in Action 4.4 describes one of the most successful implementations of a quality improvement process, General Electric's Six Sigma program.

Despite such instances of spectacular success, quality improvement practices are not universally accepted. A study by the American Quality Foundation found that only 20 percent of U.S. companies regularly review the consequences of quality performance, compared with 70 percent of Japanese companies.[30] Another study, this one by Arthur D. Little, of five hundred American companies using TQM found that only 36 percent believed that TQM was increasing their competitiveness.[31] A prime reason for this, according to the study, was that many companies had not fully understood or embraced the TQM concept. They were looking for a quick fix, whereas implementing a quality improvement program is a long-term commitment.

■ Implementing Reliability Improvement Methodologies

Among companies that have successfully adopted quality improvement methodologies, certain imperatives stand out. These are discussed below in the order in which they are usually tackled in companies implementing quality improvement programs. What needs to be stressed first, however, is that improvement in product reliability is a cross-functional process. Its implementation requires close cooperation among all

Strategy in Action   4.4

General Electric's Six Sigma Quality Improvement Process

Six Sigma, a quality and efficiency program adopted by several major corporations, including Motorola, General Electric, and Allied Signal, aims to reduce defects, boost productivity, eliminate waste, and cut costs throughout a company. "Sigma" comes from the Greek letter that statisticians use to represent a standard deviation from a mean: the higher the number of sigmas, the smaller the number of errors. At 6 sigma, a production process would be 99.99966 percent accurate, creating just 3.4 defects per million units. Although it is almost impossible for a company to achieve such perfection, several companies strive toward that goal.

General Electric is perhaps the most fervent adopter of Six Sigma programs. Under the direction of long-serving CEO Jack Welch, GE spent nearly $1 billion between 1994 and 1998 to convert all of its divisions to the Six Sigma faith. Welch credits the program with raising GE's operating profit margins to 16.6 percent in 1998, up from 14.4 percent three years earlier.

One of the first products designed from start to finish using Six Sigma processes was a $1.25 million diagnostic computer tomography (CT) scanner, the Lightspeed, which produces rapid three-dimensional images of the human body. The new scanner captures multiple images simultaneously, requiring only twenty seconds to do full-body scans that once took three minutes—important because patients must remain perfectly still during the scan. GE spent $50 million to run 250 separate Six Sigma analyses designed to improve the reliability and lower the manufacturing cost of the new scanner. Its efforts were rewarded when the Lightspeed's first customers soon noticed that it ran without downtime from the start, a testament to the reliability of the product.

Achieving that reliability took a lot of work. GE's engineers deconstructed the scanner into its basic components and tried to improve the reliability of each component through a detailed step-by-step analysis. For example, the most important part of CT scanners is vacuum tubes that focus x-ray waves. The tubes that GE used in previous scanners, which cost $60,000 each, suffered from low reliability. Hospitals and clinics wanted the tubes to operate for twelve hours a day for at least six months, but typically they lasted only half that long. Moreover, GE was scrapping some $20 million in tubes each year because they failed preshipping performance tests, and a disturbing number of faulty tubes were slipping past inspection, only to be pronounced dead on arrival.

To try to solve the reliability problem, the Six Sigma team took the tubes apart. They knew that one problem was a petroleum-based oil used in the tube to prevent short circuits by isolating the anode, which has a positive charge, from the negatively charged cathode. The oil often deteriorated after a few months, leading to short circuits, but the team did not know why. By using statistical "what-if" scenarios on all parts of the tube, the researchers learned that the lead-based paint on the inside of the tube was adulterating the oil. Acting on this information, the team developed a paint that would preserve the tube and protect the oil.

By pursuing this and other improvements, the Six Sigma team was able to extend the average life of a vacuum tube in the CT scanner from three months to over a year. Although the improvements increased the cost of the tube from $60,000 to $85,000, the increased cost was outweighed by the reduction in replacement costs, making it an attractive proposition for customers.[e]

functions in the pursuit of the common goal of improving quality; it is a process that cuts across functions. The roles played by the different functions in implementing reliability improvement methodologies are summarized in Table 4.2.

■ **Build Organizational Commitment to Quality** There is evidence that quality improvement programs will do little to improve the performance of a company unless everyone in the organization embraces it.[32] When Xerox launched its quality program, its first step was to educate the entire work force, from top management down, in the importance and operation of the program. It did so by forming

TABLE 4.2

Roles Played by Different Functions in Implementing Reliability Improvement Methodologies

Value Creation Function	Primary Roles
Infrastructure (leadership)	1. Provide leadership and commitment to quality. 2. Find ways to measure quality. 3. Set goals, and create incentives. 4. Solicit input from employees. 5. Encourage cooperation among functions.
Production	1. Shorten production runs. 2. Trace defects back to source.
Marketing	1. Focus on the customer. 2. Provide customers' feedback on quality.
Materials management	1. Rationalize suppliers. 2. Help suppliers implement quality improvement methodologies. 3. Trace defects back to suppliers.
R&D	1. Design products that are easy to manufacture.
Information systems	1. Use information systems to monitor defect rates.
Human resources	1. Institute quality improvement training programs. 2. Identify and train "black belts." 3. Organize employees into quality teams.

groups, beginning with a group at the top of the organization that included the CEO. The top group was the first to receive basic TQM training. Each member of this group was then given the task of training a group at the next level in the hierarchy, and so on down throughout the organization until all 100,000 employees had received basic TQM training. Both top management and the human resource function of the company can play a major role in this process. Top management has the responsibility of exercising the leadership required to make a commitment to quality an organization-wide goal. The human resource function must take on responsibility for companywide training in TQM techniques.

■ **Create Quality Leaders** If a quality improvement program is to be successful, individuals must be identified to lead the program. Under the Six Sigma methodology, exceptional employees are identified and put through a "black belt" training course on the Six Sigma methodology. The black belts are taken out of their normal job roles and assigned to work solely on Six Sigma projects for the next two years. In effect, they become internal consultants and project leaders. Because they are dedicated to Six Sigma programs, they are not distracted from the task at hand by day-to-day operating responsibilities. To make a black belt assignment attractive, many companies now use it as a step in a career path. Successful black belts may not return to their prior job after two years, but instead are promoted and given more responsibility.

■ **Focus on the Customer** Quality improvement practitioners see a focus on the customer as the starting point, and indeed, the raison d'être, of the whole quality philosophy.[33] The marketing function, because it provides the primary point of contact with the customer, should play a major role here. It needs to identify what customers want from the good or service that the company provides, what the company actually provides to customers, and the gap between what customers want and what they get, which could be called the quality gap. Then, together with the other functions of the company, it needs to formulate a plan for closing the quality gap.

■ **Identify Processes and the Source of Defects** One of the hallmarks of the Six Sigma quality improvement methodology is identifying discrete repetitive processes that can be improved. This is normally done by using flow chart methodology to break an operation into its constituent parts. Thus, as noted in Strategy in Action 4.4, to improve its Lightspeed CT scanner, GE's engineers deconstructed the scanner into its basic components and tried to improve the reliability of each component through a detailed step-by-step analysis.

Quality improvement methodologies preach the need to identify defects that arise from processes, trace them to their source, find out what caused them, and make corrections so that they do not recur. Production and materials management typically have primary responsibility for this task.

To uncover defects, Deming advocated the use of statistical procedures to pinpoint variations in the quality of goods or services. Deming viewed variation as the enemy of quality.[34] The Six Sigma methodology also relies heavily on statistical analysis of variation. Once variations have been identified, they must be traced to their source and eliminated. One technique that helps greatly in tracing defects to their source is reducing lot sizes for manufactured products. With short production runs, defects show up immediately. Consequently, they can be quickly traced to the source, and the problem can be addressed. Reducing lot sizes also means that, when defective products are produced, their number will not be large, thus decreasing waste. Flexible manufacturing techniques, discussed earlier, can be used to reduce lot sizes without raising costs. Consequently, adopting flexible manufacturing techniques is an important aspect of a TQM program.

JIT inventory systems also play a part. Under a JIT system, defective parts enter the manufacturing process immediately; they are not warehoused for several months before use. Hence, defective inputs can be quickly spotted. The problem can then be traced to the supply source and corrected before more defective parts are produced. Under a more traditional system, the practice of warehousing parts for months before they are used may mean that many defects are produced by a supplier before they enter the production process.

■ **Find Ways to Measure Quality** Another imperative of any quality improvement program is to create a metric that can be used to measure quality. This is relatively easy in manufacturing companies, where quality can be measured by criteria such as defects per million parts. It tends to be more difficult in service companies, but with a little creativity, suitable metrics can be devised. For example, one of the metrics Florida Power & Light uses to measure quality is meter-reading errors per month. Another is the frequency and duration of power outages. L. L. Bean, the Freeport, Maine, mail-order retailer of outdoor gear, uses the percentage of orders that are correctly filled as one of its quality measures. For some banks, the key measures are the number of customer defections per year and the number of statement errors per thousand customers. The common theme that runs through all these examples is identifying what quality means from a customer's perspective and devising a method to gauge this.

■ **Set Goals and Create Incentives**   Once a metric has been devised, the next step is to set a challenging quality goal and create incentives for reaching it. Xerox again provides an example. When it introduced its TQM program, its initial goal was to reduce defective parts from 25,000 per million to 1,000 per million. Under Six Sigma programs the goal is 3.4 defects per million units. One way of creating incentives to attain such a goal is to link rewards, like bonus pay and promotional opportunities, to the goal. Thus, within many companies that have adopted self-managing teams, the bonus pay of team members is determined in part by their ability to attain quality goals. Setting goals and creating incentives are key tasks of top management.

■ **Solicit Input from Employees**   Employees can be a vital source of information regarding the sources of poor quality. Therefore, a framework must be established for soliciting employee suggestions for improvements. Quality circles, which are meetings of groups of employees, have often been used to achieve this goal. Other companies have used self-managing teams as forums for discussing quality improvement ideas. Whatever forum is used, soliciting input from employees requires that management be open to receiving, and acting on, bad news and criticism from employees. According to Deming, one problem with U.S. management is that it has grown used to "killing the bearer of bad tidings." But, he argues, managers who are committed to the quality concept must recognize that bad news is a gold mine of information.[35]

■ **Build Long-Term Relationships with Suppliers**   A major source of poor-quality finished goods is poor-quality component parts. To decrease product defects, a company has to work with its suppliers to improve the quality of the parts they supply. The primary responsibility in this area falls on the materials-management function, which interacts with suppliers.

To implement JIT systems with suppliers and to get suppliers to adopt their own quality improvement programs, two steps are necessary. First, the number of suppliers has to be reduced to manageable proportions. Second, the company must commit to building a cooperative long-term relationship with the suppliers that remain. Asking suppliers to invest in JIT and quality improvement programs is asking them to make major investments that tie them to the company. For example, in order to implement a JIT system fully, the company may ask a supplier to relocate its manufacturing plant so that it is next-door to the company's assembly plant. Suppliers are likely to be hesitant about making such investments unless they feel that the company is committed to an enduring, long-term relationship with them.

■ **Design for Ease of Manufacture**   The more assembly steps a product requires, the more opportunities there are for making mistakes. Designing products with fewer parts should make assembly easier and result in fewer defects. Both R&D and manufacturing need to be involved in designing products that are easy to manufacture.

■ **Break Down Barriers Among Functions**   Implementing quality improvement methodologies requires organization-wide commitment and substantial cooperation among functions. R&D has to cooperate with production to design products that are easy to manufacture, marketing has to cooperate with production and R&D so that customer problems identified by marketing can be acted on, human resource management has to cooperate with all the other functions of the company in order to devise suitable quality-training programs, and so on. The issue of achieving cooperation among subunits within a company is explored in Chapter 12. What needs stressing at this point is that ultimately it is the responsibility of top management to ensure that such cooperation occurs. Strategy in Action 4.5 describes the efforts of a service company to put quality improvement programs into practice and the benefits it has gained as a result.

■ **Improving Quality as Excellence**

As we stated in Chapter 3, a product is a bundle of different attributes, and reliability is just one of them, albeit an important one. Products can also be *differentiated* by attributes that collectively define product excellence. These attributes include the form, features, performance, durability, and styling of a product. In addition, a company can create quality as excellence by emphasizing attributes of the service associated with the product, such as ordering ease, prompt delivery, easy installation, the availability of customer training and consulting, and maintenance services. Dell Computer, for example, differentiates itself on ease of ordering (via the Web), prompt delivery, easy installation, and the ready availability of customer support and maintenance services. Differentiation can also be based on the attributes of the people in the company whom customers interact with when making a product purchase, such as their

Strategy in Action   4.5

Six Sigma at Mount Carmel Health

Following the lead of General Electric, a number of health care organizations have adopted the Six Sigma approach or similar quality improvement tools as a way of trying to improve the quality of their service offerings. One of them is Mount Carmel Health, a health care provider in Ohio. Mount Carmel Health implemented a Six Sigma program after suffering from poor financial performance in 2000. It was initiated in late 2000, and by early 2001 forty-four employees had been trained in Six Sigma principles. These "black belts" were pulled out of their original positions and were not replaced. By the second half of 2001 they were leading some sixty projects in different phases of implementation.

One of the first projects focused on a simple and common problem among health care providers: timely and accurate reimbursement of costs. Mount Carmel discovered that it was writing off large amounts of potential revenues from the government-run Medicare programs as uncollectible because the charges were denied by Medicare administrators. Mount Carmel had low expectations for this business anyway so had never analyzed why the write-offs were so high. After conducting a careful analysis as part of a Six Sigma project, it discovered that a significant portion of the denials were due to the incorrect coding of reports submitted to Medicare. If the reports were coded correctly—that is, if fewer errors were made in the "production" of forms—the Six Sigma team estimated that annual income would be some $300,000 higher, so they devised improved processes for coding the forms to reduce the error rate. The result was that net income rose by over $800,000. It appeared that improving the coding process for this one parameter improved the reporting of many other parameters and led to a reimbursement rate much higher than anticipated.

Mount Carmel now estimates that Six Sigma projects saved the organization some $1 million in 2001, $6.5 million in 2002, and $9 million in 2003.[f]

TABLE 4.3

Attributes Associated with a Product Offering

Product Attributes	Service Attributes	Associated Personnel Attributes
Form	Ordering ease	Competence
Features	Delivery	Courtesy
Performance	Installation	Credibility
Durability	Customer training	Reliability
Reliability	Customer consulting	Responsiveness
Style	Maintenance and repair	Communication

competence, courtesy, credibility, responsiveness, and communication. Singapore Airlines, for example, enjoys an excellent reputation for quality service, largely because passengers perceive their flight attendants as competent, courteous, and responsive to their needs. Thus, we can talk about the product attributes, service attributes, and personnel attributes associated with a company's product offering (see Table 4.3).

For a product to be regarded as high in the excellence dimension, a company's product offering must be seen as superior to that of rivals. Achieving a perception of high quality on any of these attributes requires specific actions by managers. First, it is important for managers to collect marketing intelligence indicating which of these attributes are most important to customers. For example, consumers of personal computers may place a low weight on durability because they expect their PC to be made obsolete by technological advances within three years, but they may place a high weight on features and performance. Similarly, ease of ordering and timely delivery may be very important attributes for customers of online booksellers (as they indeed are for customers of amazon.com), whereas customer training and consulting may be very important attributes for customers who purchase complex business-to-business software to manage their relationships with suppliers.

Second, once the company has identified the attributes that are important to customers, it needs to design its products, and the associated services, so that those attributes are embodied in the product, and it needs to make sure that personnel in the company are appropriately trained so that the correct attributes are emphasized. This requires close coordination between marketing and product development (the topic of the next section) and the involvement of the human resource management function in employee selection and training.

Third, the company must decide which of the significant attributes to promote and how best to position them in the minds of consumers, that is, how to tailor the marketing message so that it creates a consistent image in the minds of customers.[36] At this point, it is important to recognize that although a product might be differentiated on the basis of six attributes, covering all of those attributes in the company's communication messages may lead to an unfocused message. Many marketing experts advocate promoting only one or two central attributes to customers. For example, Volvo consistently emphasizes the safety and durability of its vehicles in all marketing messages, creating the perception in the minds of consumers (backed by product design) that Volvo cars are safe and durable. Volvo cars are also very reliable and have high performance, but the company does not emphasize these attributes in its marketing messages. In contrast, Porsche emphasizes performance and styling in all of its marketing messages; thus, a Porsche is positioned differently in the minds of consumers than a Volvo is. Both are regarded as high-quality products because both have superior attributes, but the attributes that the two companies have chosen to emphasize are very different. They are differentiated from the average car in different ways.

Finally, it must be recognized that competition does not stand still, but instead produces continual improvement in product attributes and often the development of new-product attributes. This is obvious in fast-moving high-tech industries where product features that were considered leading edge just a few years ago are now obsolete, but the same process is also at work in more stable industries. For example, the rapid diffusion of microwave ovens during the 1980s required food companies to build new attributes into their frozen food products: they had to maintain their texture and consistency while being microwaved. A product could not be considered high quality unless it could do that. This speaks to the importance of having a strong R&D function in the company that can work with marketing and manufacturing to continually upgrade the quality of the attributes that are designed into the company's product offerings. Exactly how to achieve this is covered in the next section.

Achieving Superior Innovation

In many ways, building distinctive competencies that result in innovation is the most important source of competitive advantage. This is because innovation can result in new products that better satisfy customer needs, can improve the quality (attributes) of existing products, or can reduce the costs of making products that customers want. Thus, the ability to develop innovative new products or processes gives a company a major competitive advantage that allows it to (1) *differentiate* its products and charge a premium price and/or (2) *lower its cost structure* below that of its rivals. Competitors, however, attempt to imitate successful innovations and often succeed. Therefore, maintaining a competitive advantage requires a continuing commitment to innovation.

Robert Cooper found that successful new-product launches are major drivers of superior profitability. Cooper looked at more than two hundred new-product introductions and found that of those classified as successes, some 50 percent achieve a return on investment in excess of 33 percent, half have a payback period of two years or less, and half achieve a market share in excess of 35 percent.[37] Many companies have established a track record for successful innovation. Among them are DuPont, which has produced a steady stream of successful innovations, such as cellophane, Nylon, Freon, and Teflon; Sony, whose successes include the Walkman, the Compact Disc, and the PlayStation; Nokia, which has been a leader in the development of wireless phones; Pfizer, a drug company that during the 1990s and early 2000s produced eight blockbuster new drugs; 3M, which has applied its core competency in tapes and adhesives to developing a wide range of new products; Intel, which has consistently managed to lead in the development of innovative new microprocessors to run personal computers; and Cisco Systems, whose innovations helped to pave the way for the rapid growth of the Internet.

■ The High Failure Rate of Innovation

Although promoting innovation can be a source of competitive advantage, the failure rate of innovative new products is high. One study of product development in the chemical, drug, petroleum, and electronics industries suggested that only about 20 percent of major R&D projects ultimately result in a commercially successful product or process.[38] An in-depth case study of product development in three companies (one in chemicals and two in drugs) reported that about 60 percent of R&D projects reached technical completion, 30 percent were commercialized, and only 12 percent earned a profit that exceeded the company's cost of capital.[39] Along the same lines, another study concluded that one in nine major R&D projects, or about 11 percent, produced commercially successful products.[40] In sum, the evidence suggests that only 10 to 20 percent of major R&D projects give rise to a commercially successful product. Well-publicized product failures include Apple Computer's Newton, a personal digital assistant; Sony's Betamax format in the video player and recorder market; and Sega's Dreamcast videogame console. While many reasons have been advanced to explain why so many new products fail to generate an economic return, five explanations for failure appear on most lists: uncertainty, poor commercialization, poor positioning strategy, technological myopia, and being slow to market.[41]

■ **Uncertainty** New-product development is an inherently risky process. It requires testing a hypothesis whose answer is impossible to know prior to market introduction: Have we tapped an unmet customer need? Is there sufficient market demand for this new technology? Although good market research can reduce the uncertainty about likely future demand for a new technology, uncertainty cannot be eradicated, so a certain failure rate is to be expected.

The failure rate is higher for quantum product innovations than for incremental innovations. A **quantum innovation** represents a radical departure from existing technology—the introduction of something that is new to the world. The development of the World Wide Web can be considered a quantum innovation in communications technology. Other quantum innovations include the development of the first photocopier by Xerox, the first contact lenses by Bausch and Lomb, and the first microprocessor by Intel in 1971. **Incremental innovation** refers to an extension of existing technology. For example, Intel's Pentium Pro microprocessor is an incremental product innovation because it builds on the existing microprocessor architecture of Intel's X86 series. The uncertainty of future demand for a new product is much greater if that product represents a quantum innovation that is new to the world than if it is an incremental innovation designed to replace an established product whose demand profile is already well known. Consequently, the failure rate tends to be higher for quantum innovations.

■ **Poor Commercialization** A second reason frequently cited to explain the high failure rate of new-product introductions is **poor commercialization**—something that occurs when there is definite customer demand for a new product, but the product is not well adapted to customer needs because of factors such as poor design and poor quality. For instance, many of the early personal computers failed to sell because customers needed to understand computer programming to use them. Steve Jobs at Apple Computer understood that if the technology could be made user friendly (if it could be *commercialized*), there would be an enormous market for it. Hence, the original personal computers that Apple marketed incorporated little in the way of radically new technology, but they made existing technology accessible to the average person. Paradoxically, the failure of Apple Computer to establish a market for the Newton, the hand-held personal digital system that Apple introduced in the summer of 1993, can be traced to poor commercialization of a potentially attractive technology. Apple predicted a $1 billion market for the Newton, but sales failed to materialize when it became clear that the Newton's handwriting software, an attribute that Apple chose to emphasize in its marketing promotions, could not adequately recognize messages written on the Newton's message pad.

■ **Poor Positioning Strategy** Poor positioning strategy arises when a company introduces a potentially attractive new product, but sales fail to materialize because it is poorly positioned in the marketplace. **Positioning strategy** is the specific set of options a company adopts for a product on four main dimensions of marketing: price, distribution, promotion and advertising, and product features. Apart from poor product quality, another reason for the failure of the Apple Newton was poor positioning strategy. The Newton was introduced at such a high initial price (close to $1,000) that there would probably have been few buyers even if the technology had been adequately commercialized.

■ **Technological Myopia** Another reason that many new-product introductions fail is that companies often make the mistake of marketing a technology for which there is not enough customer demand. **Technological myopia** occurs when a company gets blinded by the wizardry of a new technology and fails to examine whether there is customer demand for the product. This problem may have been a factor in the failure of the desktop computer introduced by NeXT in the late 1980s (NeXT was founded by Steve Jobs, the founder of Apple Computer). Technologically, the NeXT machines were clearly ahead of their time with advanced software and hardware features that would not be incorporated into most PCs for another decade. However, customer acceptance was very slow, primarily because of the complete lack of applications software such as spreadsheet and word processing programs to run on the machines. Management at NeXT was so enthused by the technology incorporated in their new computer that they ignored this basic market reality. After several years of slow sales, NeXT eventually withdrew the machines from the marketplace.

■ **Being Slow to Market** Finally, companies fail when they are slow to get their products to market. The more time that elapses between initial development and final marketing—that is, the slower the "cycle time"—the more likely it is that someone else will beat the company to market and gain a first-mover advantage.[42] By and large, slow innovators update their products less frequently than fast innovators do. Consequently, they can be perceived as technical laggards relative to the fast innovators. In the car industry, General Motors has suffered from being a slow innovator. Its product development cycle has been about five years, compared with two to three years at Honda, Toyota, and Mazda and three to four years at Ford. Because they are based on five-year-old technology and design concepts, GM cars are already out of date when they reach the market.

■ **Building Competencies in Innovation**

Companies can take a number of steps to build a competency in innovation and avoid failure. Five of the most important steps seem to be (1) building skills in basic and applied scientific research, (2) developing a good process for project selection and project management, (3) achieving cross-functional integration, (4) using product development teams, and (5) using partly parallel development processes.[43]

■ **Skills in Basic and Applied Research** Building skills in basic and applied research requires the employment of research scientists and engineers and the establishment of a work environment that fosters creativity. A number of top companies try to achieve this by setting up university-style research facilities, where scientists and engineers are given time to work on their own research projects, in addition to projects that are linked directly to ongoing company research. At Hewlett-Packard, for example, company labs are open to engineers around the clock. Hewlett-Packard even encourages its corporate researchers to devote 10 percent of company time to exploring their own ideas and does not penalize them if they fail. 3M allows researchers to spend 15 percent of the workweek researching any topic that intrigues them, as long as there is the potential of a payoff for the company. The most famous outcome of this policy is the ubiquitous Post-its. The idea for them evolved from a researcher's desire to find a way to keep the bookmark from falling out of his hymnal. Post-its are now a major 3M business, with annual revenues of around $300 million.

■ **Project Selection and Management** Project management is the overall management of the innovation process, from generation of the original concept, through development, and into final production and shipping. Project management requires three important skills: the ability to generate as many good ideas as possible, the ability to select among competing projects at an early stage of development so that the most promising receive funding and potential costly failures are killed off, and the ability to minimize time to market. The concept of the development funnel, divided into three phases, summarizes what is required to build these skills (see Figure 4.7).[44]

The objective in phase I is to widen the mouth of the tunnel to encourage as much idea generation as possible. To this end, a company should solicit input from all its functions, as well as from customers, competitors, and suppliers. At gate 1, the funnel narrows. Here ideas are reviewed by a cross-functional team of managers who did not participate in the original concept development. Concepts that are ready to proceed then move to phase II, where the details of the project proposal are worked out. Note that gate 1 is not a go/no-go evaluation point. At this screen, ideas may be sent back for further concept development and then resubmitted for evaluation.

During phase II, which typically lasts only one or two months, the data and information from phase I are put into a form that will enable senior management to

The Development Funnel

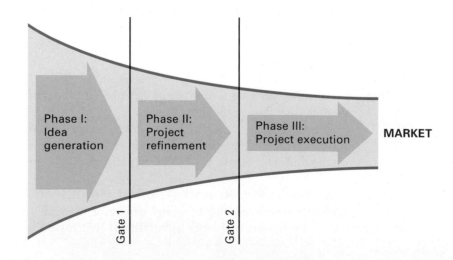

Phase I: Idea generation

Phase II: Project refinement

Phase III: Project execution

MARKET

Gate 1

Gate 2

evaluate proposed projects against competing projects. Normally, this requires the development of a careful project plan, complete with details of the proposed target market, attainable market share, likely revenues, development costs, production costs, key milestones, and the like. The next big selection point, gate 2, is a go/no-go evaluation point. Senior managers review the projects under consideration and select those that seem likely winners and make most sense from a strategic perspective given the long-term goals of the company. The overriding objective is to select projects whose successful completion will help to maintain or build a competitive advantage for the company. A related objective is to ensure that the company does not spread its scarce capital and human resources too thinly over too many projects and instead concentrates resources on projects where the probability of success and potential returns is most attractive. Any project selected to go forward at this stage will be funded and staffed, the expectation being that it will be carried through to market introduction. In phase III, the project development proposal is executed by a cross-functional product development team.

■ **Cross-Functional Integration** Tight cross-functional integration between R&D, production, and marketing can help a company to ensure that:

1. Product development projects are driven by customer needs.

2. New products are designed for ease of manufacture.

3. Development costs are kept in check.

4. Time to market is minimized.

5. Close integration between R&D and marketing is achieved to ensure that product development projects are driven by the needs of customers.

A company's customers can be one of its primary sources of new product ideas. The identification of customer needs, and particularly unmet needs, can set the context within which successful product innovation takes place. As the point of contact with customers, the marketing function can provide valuable information. Moreover, integrating R&D and marketing is crucial if a new product is to be properly commercialized. Otherwise, a company runs the risk of developing products for which there is little or no demand.

The case of Techsonic Industries illustrates the benefits of integrating R&D and marketing. This company manufactures depth finders—electronic devices that fishermen use to measure the depth of water beneath a boat and to track their prey. Techsonic had weathered nine new-product failures in a row when the company decided to interview sportspeople across the country to identify what it was they needed. They discovered an unmet need for a depth finder with a gauge that could be read in bright sunlight, so that is what Techsonic developed. In the year after the $250 depth finder hit the market, Techsonic's sales tripled to $80 million, and its market share surged to 40 percent.[45]

Integration between R&D and production can help a company to ensure that products are designed with manufacturing requirements in mind. Design for manufacturing lowers manufacturing costs and leaves less room for mistakes and thus can lower costs and increase product quality. Integrating R&D and production can help lower development costs and speed products to market. If a new product is not designed with manufacturing capabilities in mind, it may prove too difficult to build, given existing manufacturing technology. In that case, the product will have to be redesigned, and both overall development costs and time to market may increase significantly. For example, making design changes during product planning could increase overall development costs by 50 percent and add 25 percent to the time it takes to bring the product to market.[46] Moreover, many quantum product innovations require new processes to manufacture them, which makes it all the more important to achieve close integration between R&D and production, since minimizing time to market and development costs may require the simultaneous development of new products and new processes.[47]

■ **Product Development Teams**   One of the best ways to achieve cross-functional integration is to establish cross-functional product development teams, composed of representatives from R&D, marketing, and production. The objective of a team should be to take a product development project from the initial concept development to market introduction. A number of attributes seem to be important in order for a product development team to function effectively and meet all its development milestones.[48]

First, a heavyweight project manager—one who has high status within the organization and the power and authority required to get the financial and human resources that the team needs to succeed—should lead the team and be dedicated primarily, if not entirely, to the project. The leader should believe in the project (a champion) and be skilled at integrating the perspectives of different functions and helping personnel from different functions work together for a common goal. The leader should also be able to act as an advocate of the team to senior management.

Second, the team should be composed of at least one member from each key function. The team members should have a number of attributes, including an ability to contribute functional expertise, high standing within their function, a willingness to share responsibility for team results, and an ability to put functional advocacy aside. It is generally preferable if core team members are 100 percent dedicated to the project for its duration. This ensures that their focus is on the project, not on the ongoing work of their function.

Third, the team members should be physically co-located to create a sense of camaraderie and facilitate communication. Fourth, the team should have a clear plan and clear goals, particularly with regard to critical development milestones and development budgets. The team should have incentives to attain those goals, such as pay bonuses when major development milestones are hit. Fifth, each team needs to develop its own processes for communication and conflict resolution. For example, one product development team at Quantum Corporation, a California-based manufacturer of disk drives for personal computers, instituted a rule that all major decisions would be made and conflicts resolved at meetings that were held every Monday afternoon. This simple rule helped the team to meet its development goals.[49]

■ **Partly Parallel Development Processes**   One way in which a product development team can compress the time it takes to develop a product and bring it to market is to use a partly parallel development process. Traditionally, product development processes have been organized on a sequential basis, as illustrated in Figure 4.8a. A problem with this kind of process is that product development proceeds without manufacturing issues in mind. Most significant, because the basic design of a product is completed prior to the design of a manufacturing process and full-scale commercial production, there is no early warning system to indicate manufacturability.

FIGURE 4.8

Sequential and Partly
Parallel Development
Processes

FIGURE 4.8

Sequential and Partly Parallel Development Processes

(a) A Sequential Process

Opportunity identification → Concept development → Product design → Process design → Commercial production

(b) A Partly Parallel Process

Opportunity identification → Concept development → Product design → Process design → Commercial production

As a consequence, the company may find that it cannot cost-efficiently manufacture the product and may have to send it back to the design stage for redesign. The cycle time lengthens as the product bounces back and forth between stages.

To solve this problem, companies typically use a process similar to that illustrated in Figure 4.8b. In the partly parallel development process, development stages overlap so that, for example, work starts on the development of the production process before the product design is finalized. By reducing the need for expensive and time-consuming product redesigns, such a process can significantly reduce the time it takes to develop a new product and bring it to market.

For an example, consider what occurred after Intel Corporation introduced its 386 microprocessor in 1986. A number of companies, including IBM and Compaq, were racing to be the first to introduce a 386-based personal computer. Compaq beat IBM by six months and gained a major share of the high-power market mainly because it used a cross-functional team and a partly parallel process to develop the product. The team included engineers (R&D) and marketing, production, and finance people. Each function worked in parallel rather than sequentially. While engineers were designing the product, production people were setting up the manufacturing facilities, marketing people were working on distribution and planning marketing campaigns, and finance people were working on project funding.

The primary role that the various functions play in achieving superior innovation is summarized in Table 4.4. The table makes two matters clear. First, top management must bear primary responsibility for overseeing the whole development process. This entails both managing the development funnel and facilitating cooperation among the functions. Second, the effectiveness of R&D in developing new products and processes depends on its ability to cooperate with marketing and production.

TABLE 4.4

Functional Roles for Achieving Superior Innovation

Value Creation Function	Primary Roles
Infrastructure (leadership)	1. Manage overall project (i.e., manage the development function).
	2. Facilitate cross-functional cooperation.
Production	1. Cooperate with R&D on designing products that are easy to manufacture.
	2. Work with R&D to develop process innovations.
Marketing	1. Provide market information to R&D.
	2. Work with R&D to develop new products.
Materials management	1. No primary responsibility.
R&D	1. Develop new products and processes.
	2. Cooperate with other functions, particularly marketing and manufacturing, in the development process.
Information systems	1. Use information systems to coordinate cross-functional and cross-company product development work.
Human resources	1. Hire talented scientists and engineers.

Achieving Superior Responsiveness to Customers

To achieve superior responsiveness to customers, a company must give customers what they want, when they want it, and at a price they are willing to pay—so long as the company's long-term profitability is not compromised in the process. Customer responsiveness is an important *differentiating* attribute that can help to build brand loyalty. Strong product differentiation and brand loyalty give a company more pricing options; it can charge a premium price for its products or keep prices low to sell more goods and services to customers. Either way, the company that is more responsive to its customers' needs than rivals will have a competitive advantage, all else being equal.

Achieving superior responsiveness to customers means giving customers value for money, and steps taken to improve the efficiency of a company's production process and the quality of its products should be consistent with this aim. In addition, giving customers what they want may require the development of new products with new features. *In other words, achieving superior efficiency, quality, and innovation are all part of achieving superior responsiveness to customers.* There are two other prerequisites for attaining this goal. First, a company has to develop a competency in listening to and focusing on its customers and in investigating and identifying their needs. Second, it constantly needs to seek better ways to satisfy those needs.

■ Focusing on the Customer

A company cannot be responsive to its customers' needs unless it knows what those needs are. Thus, the first step to building superior responsiveness to customers is to motivate the whole company to focus on the customer. The means to this end are demonstrating leadership, shaping employee attitudes, and using mechanisms for bringing customers into the company.

■ Demonstrating Leadership Customer focus must start at the top of the organization. A commitment to superior responsiveness to customers brings attitudinal changes throughout a company that ultimately can be built only through strong leadership. A mission statement that puts customers first is one way to send a clear message to employees about the desired focus. Another avenue is top management's own actions. For example, Tom Monaghan, the founder of Domino's Pizza, stayed close to the customer by visiting as many stores as possible every week, running some deliveries himself, insisting that other top managers do the same, and eating Domino's pizza regularly.[50]

■ **Shaping Employee Attitudes** Leadership alone is not enough to attain a superior customer focus. All employees must see the customer as the focus of their activity and be trained to focus on the customer, whether their function is marketing, manufacturing, R&D, or accounting. The objective should be to make employees think of themselves as customers—to put themselves in customers' shoes. At that point, employees will be better able to identify ways to improve the quality of a customer's experience with the company.

To reinforce this mindset, incentive systems within the company should reward employees for satisfying customers. For example, senior managers at the Four Seasons hotel chain, who pride themselves on their customer focus, like to tell the story of Roy Dyment, a doorman in Toronto who neglected to load a departing guest's briefcase into his taxi. The doorman called the guest, a lawyer, in Washington, D.C., and found that he desperately needed the briefcase for a morning meeting. Dyment hopped on a plane to Washington and returned it—without first securing approval from his boss. Far from punishing Dyment for making a mistake and for not checking with management before going to Washington, the Four Seasons responded by naming Dyment Employee of the Year.[51] This action sent a powerful message to Four Seasons employees about the importance of satisfying customer needs.

■ **Bringing Customers into the Company** "Know thy customer" is one of the keys to achieving superior responsiveness to customers. Knowing the customer not only requires that employees think like customers themselves; it also demands that they listen to what their customers have to say and, as much as possible, bring them into the company. Although this may not involve physically bringing customers into the company, it does mean bringing in customers' opinions by soliciting feedback from customers on the company's goods and services and by building information systems that communicate the feedback to the relevant people.

For an example, consider direct selling clothing retailer Lands' End. Through its catalog, the Internet, and customer service telephone operators, Lands' End actively solicits comments from its customers about the quality of its clothing and the kind of merchandise they want it to supply. Indeed, it was customers' insistence that initially prompted the company to move into the clothing segment. Lands' End used to supply equipment for sailboats through mail-order catalogs. However, it received so many requests from customers to include outdoor clothing in its offering that it responded by expanding the catalog to fill this need. Soon clothing became the main business, and Lands' End dropped the sailboat equipment. Today, the company still pays close attention to customer requests. Every month, a computer printout of customer requests and comments is given to managers. This feedback helps the company to fine-tune the merchandise it sells. Indeed, frequently new lines of merchandise are introduced in response to customer requests.[52]

■ Satisfying Customer Needs

Once a focus on the customer is an integral part of the company, the next requirement is to satisfy the customer needs that have been identified. As already noted, efficiency, quality, and innovation are crucial competencies that help a company satisfy customer needs. Beyond that, companies can provide a higher level of satisfaction if they differentiate their products by (1) customizing them, where possible, to the requirements of individual customers and (2) reducing the time it takes to respond to or satisfy customer needs.

■ Customization

Customization is varying the features of a good or service to tailor it to the unique needs or tastes of groups of customers or, in the extreme case, individual customers. Although extensive customization can raise costs, the development of flexible manufacturing technologies has made it possible to customize products to a much greater extent than was feasible ten to fifteen years ago without experiencing a prohibitive rise in cost structure (particularly when flexible manufacturing technologies are linked with web-based information systems). For example, online retailers such as amazon.com have used web-based technologies to develop a homepage customized for each individual user. When a customer accesses amazon.com, he or she is offered a list of recommendations for books or music to purchase based on an analysis of prior buying history, a powerful competency that gives amazon.com a competitive advantage.

The trend toward customization has fragmented many markets, particularly customer markets, into ever smaller niches. An example of this fragmentation occurred in Japan in the early 1980s when Honda dominated the motorcycle market there. Second-place Yamaha decided to go after Honda's lead. It announced the opening of a new factory that, when operating at full capacity, would make Yamaha the world's largest manufacturer of motorcycles. Honda responded by proliferating its product line and stepping up its rate of new-product introduction. At the start of what became known as the "motorcycle wars," Honda had 60 motorcycles in its product line. Over the next eighteen months, it rapidly increased its range to 113 models, customizing them to ever smaller niches. Honda was able to accomplish this without bearing a prohibitive cost penalty because it has a competency in flexible manufacturing. The flood of Honda's customized models pushed Yamaha out of much of the market, effectively stalling its bid to overtake Honda.[53]

■ Response Time

Giving customers what they want when they want it requires speed of response to customer demands. To gain a competitive advantage, a company must often respond to customer demands very quickly, whether the transaction is a furniture manufacturer's delivery of a product once it has been ordered, a bank's processing of a loan application, an automobile manufacturer's delivery of a spare part for a car that broke down, or the wait in a supermarket checkout line. We live in a fast-paced society, where time is a valuable commodity. Companies that can satisfy customer demands for rapid response build brand loyalty, differentiate their products, and can charge higher prices for them.

Increased speed often lets a company choose a premium pricing option, as the mail delivery industry illustrates. The air express niche of the mail delivery industry is based on the notion that customers are often willing to pay considerably more for overnight Express Mail as opposed to regular mail. Another example of the value of rapid response is Caterpillar, the manufacturer of heavy earthmoving equipment, which can get a spare part to any point in the world within twenty-four hours.

TABLE 4.5

Primary Roles of Different Functions in Achieving Superior Responsiveness to Customers

Value Creation Function	Primary Roles
Infrastructure (leadership)	1. Through leadership by example, build a companywide commitment to responsiveness to customers.
Production	1. Achieve customization through implementation of flexible manufacturing. 2. Achieve rapid response through flexible manufacturing.
Marketing	1. Know the customer. 2. Communicate customer feedback to appropriate functions.
Materials management	1. Develop logistics systems capable of responding quickly to unanticipated customer demands (JIT).
R&D	1. Bring customers into the product development process.
Information systems	1. Use web-based information systems to increase responsiveness to customers.
Human resources	1. Develop training programs that get employees to think like customers themselves.

Downtime for heavy construction equipment is very costly, so Caterpillar's ability to respond quickly in the event of equipment malfunction is of prime importance to its customers. As a result, many of them have remained loyal to Caterpillar despite the aggressive low-price competition from Komatsu of Japan.

In general, reducing response time requires (1) a marketing function that can quickly communicate customer requests to production, (2) production and materials-management functions that can quickly adjust production schedules in response to unanticipated customer demands, and (3) information systems that can help production and marketing in this process.

Table 4.5 summarizes the steps different functions must take if a company is to achieve superior responsiveness to customers. Although marketing plays the critical role in helping a company attain this goal, primarily because it represents the point of contact with the customer, Table 4.5 shows that the other functions also have major roles. Moreover, like achieving superior efficiency, quality, and innovation, achieving superior responsiveness to customers requires top management to lead in building a customer orientation within the company.

Summary of Chapter

1. A company can increase efficiency through a number of steps: exploiting economies of scale and learning effects, adopting flexible manufacturing technologies, reducing customer defection rates, implementing just-in-time systems, getting the R&D function to design products that are easy to manufacture, upgrading the skills of employees through training, introducing self-managing teams, linking pay to performance, building a companywide commitment to efficiency through strong leadership, and designing structures that facilitate cooperation among different functions in pursuit of efficiency goals.

2. Superior quality can help a company lower its costs, differentiate its product, and charge a premium price.

3. Achieving superior quality demands an organization-wide commitment to quality and a clear focus on the customer. It also requires metrics to measure quality

goals and incentives that emphasize quality, input from employees regarding ways in which quality can be improved, a methodology for tracing defects to their source and correcting the problems that produce them, a rationalization of the company's supply base, cooperation with the suppliers that remain to implement total quality management programs, products that are designed for ease of manufacturing, and substantial cooperation among functions.

4. The failure rate of new-product introductions is high because of factors such as uncertainty, poor commercialization, poor positioning strategy, slow cycle time, and technological myopia.

5. To achieve superior innovation, a company must build skills in basic and applied research; design good processes for managing development projects; and achieve close integration between the different functions of the company, primarily through the adoption of cross-functional product development teams and partly parallel development processes.

6. To achieve superior responsiveness to customers often requires that the company achieve superior efficiency, quality, and innovation.

7. To achieve superior responsiveness to customers, a company needs to give customers what they want when they want it. It must ensure a strong customer focus, which can be attained by emphasizing customer focus through leadership; training employees to think like customers; bringing customers into the company through superior market research; customizing products to the unique needs of individual customers or customer groups; and responding quickly to customer demands.

Discussion Questions

1. How are the four generic building blocks of competitive advantage related to each other?

2. What role can top management play in helping a company achieve superior efficiency, quality, innovation, and responsiveness to customers?

3. In the long run, will adoption of Six Sigma quality improvement processes give a company a competitive advantage, or will it be required just to achieve parity with competitors?

4. In what sense might innovation be called the single most important building block of competitive advantage?

Practicing Strategic Management

■ SMALL-GROUP EXERCISE
Identifying Excellence

Break up into groups of three to five people, and appoint one group member as a spokesperson who will communicate your findings to the class.

You are the management team of a start-up company that will produce disk drives for the personal computer industry. You will sell your product to manufacturers of personal computers (original equipment manufacturers). The disk drive market is characterized by rapid technological change, product life cycles of only six to nine months, intense price competition, high fixed costs for manufacturing equipment, and substantial manufacturing economies of scale. Your customers, the original equipment manufacturers, issue very demanding technological specifications that your product has to comply with. They also pressure you to deliver

your product on time so that it fits in with their own product introduction schedule.

1. In this industry, what functional competencies are the most important for you to build?

2. How will you design your internal processes to ensure that those competencies are built within the company?

■ ARTICLE FILE 4

Choose a company that is widely regarded as excellent. Identify the source of its excellence, and relate it to the material discussed in this chapter. Pay particular attention to the role played by the various functions in building excellence.

■ STRATEGIC MANAGEMENT PROJECT
Module 4

This module deals with the ability of your company to achieve superior efficiency, quality, innovation, and responsiveness to customers. With the information you have at your disposal, answer the questions and perform the tasks listed:

1. Is your company pursuing any of the efficiency-enhancing practices discussed in this chapter?

2. Is your company pursuing any of the quality-enhancing practices discussed in this chapter?

3. Is your company pursuing any of the practices designed to enhance innovation discussed in this chapter?

4. Is your company pursuing any of the practices designed to increase responsiveness to customers discussed in this chapter?

5. Evaluate the competitive position of your company in the light of your answers to questions 1–4. Explain what, if anything, the company needs to do to improve its competitive position.

■ EXPLORING THE WEB

Visiting Applied Materials

Visit the website of Applied Materials, the world's largest manufacturer of semiconductor fabrication equipment (**www.appliedmaterials.com**). Go to the section titled "About" Applied Materials, and read the company's mission statement. What does this mission statement tell you about the kind of competitive advantage that Applied Materials is trying to build? How important are efficiency, quality, innovation, and responsiveness to customers to this company?

Now go to the sections of Applied's website that detail the company's financial results, products, and press releases. Read through these sections and try to establish how successful Applied has been at meeting the objectives set down in its mission statement. What do you think the company has done at the functional level to increase its efficiency, responsiveness to customers, innovative ability, and product quality?

General Task Search the Web for a company whose homepage describes in some detail its approach to achieving one of the following: superior productivity, product quality, customer service, or innovation. Using this information, document the company's functional-level strategy and assess whether the strategy makes sense given what you have learned so far in this book.

Closing Case

Redesigning the American Car

In 2003 Detroit's big three carmakers, GM, Ford, and DaimlerChrysler, accounted for only 60.2 percent of the vehicles sold in the United States, the lowest number ever. The market share loss has been greatest in the U.S. passenger car market, where foreign producers walked away with 55 percent of the market in 2003, up from 34 percent in 1993. For most of the last decade, strong sales of sports utility vehicles, where Detroit dominates, have held overall market share losses in check, but now foreign producers such as Toyota, Honda, and Kia are going after that segment too, creating huge potential problems for Detroit.

The American automobile makers have responded by trying to reinvigorate their passenger car business and coming out with a host of new designs. Just as importantly, they are trying to cut the costs of developing and producing those cars. The old rule of thumb was that it took four years and cost $1 billion to design a new car and tool a factory to produce it. To recoup these costs, Detroit would typically sell a car for seven years before developing a new design. Unfortunately for the American producers, the Japanese shortened the life cycle of a typical vehicle to five years, and by lowering development and tooling costs, they have been able to make good money on their car models.

Now the American producers are trying to strike back. Typical is Ford, which has reduced its product development time by a quarter since the late 1990s and continues to reduce it by 10 percent per year. Ford now designs almost one-third of its models in less than thirty months. One reason for this progress has been the increased communication among designers. Ford designers used to work in different teams and did not share enough knowledge about parts and platform design. Now teams get together to see how they can share the design work.

Moreover, design teams are trying to use the same parts in a wider variety of car models and, where appropriate, use parts from old models in new cars. Detroit auto designers used to boast that new models were completely redesigned from the floor up with all new parts. Now that is seen as costly and time consuming. At General Motors, for example, the goal is now to reuse 40 to 60 percent of parts from one car generation to the next, thereby reducing design time and tooling costs. At Ford, the number of parts has been slashed. For example, Ford engineers now choose from just four steering wheels, instead of contemplating fourteen different designs.

Another important trend has been to reduce the number of platforms used for car models, as Japanese producers have long been doing. Honda, for example, builds its Odyssey minivan and its Pilot and Acura MDX sports utility vehicles on the same platform, and it has added a pickup truck to the mix. Currently Chrysler bases its vehicle fleet on thirteen distinct platforms. The company is trying to bring this down to just four platforms, reducing the product development budget from $42 billion to $30 billion in the process. Ford and General Motors have similar aims. The platform for GM's new small car offering, the Pontiac Solstice, will also be used for its new Saturn coupe and perhaps one more GM car. As GM develops its next generation of Chevy Silverado and GMC Sierra pickups, it plans to reuse much of the existing platform, cutting development costs in half to nearly $3 billion. Over the next eight years, Ford plans to use its Mazda 6 sedan platform (Ford owns Mazda) as the basis for ten new vehicles. The idea, according to Ford's head of operations, is to engineer it once and use it often.

Hand in hand with changes in design philosophy, the Detroit companies are retooling their factories to reduce costs and make them capable of producing several car models from the same line. By doing so, they hope to be able to reduce the breakeven point for a new car model. GM's Solstice, for example, is forecast to sell around 25,000 units a year—too few to recoup fixed costs under the old design-and-build philosophy. But GM has cut design costs by using a common platform and common parts, and it has cut tooling costs by investing in flexible manufacturing technologies that can be used to produce multiple designs based on the Solstice platform from the same basic line. GM has also worked hard to get unions to agree to changes in inflexible work rules. Assembly line workers now perform several different jobs, which reduces waste and boosts productivity. Similarly, Ford hopes to have 75 percent of its production built on flexible assembly lines by 2010, and, if successful, its investments in flexible factories could reduce annual costs by some $2 billion a year.

Critics say that the new vision coming out of Detroit is not that new. Although the techniques being discussed will reduce development time and tooling costs, Japanese automakers have been pursuing the same techniques for years. The critics fear that Detroit automakers are chasing a moving target and that when they arrive in the promised land, it will be too late, since their global competitors will have already taken competition to the next level.[54]

Case Discussion Questions

1. How have lower development and tooling costs given Japanese auto manufacturers an advantage in the marketplace?

2. What steps are the Detroit automobile makers taking to reduce product development time and tooling costs? If they are successful, what are the implications of these initiatives for (a) the number of car models they can sell and (b) breakeven volumes for an individual model? Will these initiatives benefit Detroit's customers? How?

3. The Japanese producers have been pursuing for years many of the methodologies now being introduced in Detroit. Why do you think it has taken the Detroit automakers so long to respond to their foreign competitors?

4. If the Detroit companies successfully implement their new operating strategies, do you think they will gain a competitive advantage in the marketplace?

Chapter 5

Building Competitive Advantage Through Business-Level Strategy

Samsung Changes Its Business Model Again and Again

In the last five years Samsung, based in Seoul, Korea, has risen to become the most profitable consumer electronics company in the world. Since 1999 its revenues have doubled, and in 2004 it made a record $12 billion profit, thus becoming the second most profitable global technology company after Microsoft.[1] The story of how Samsung's business model has changed over time explains how the company has reached its enviable position.

In the 1980s, Samsung watched as Japanese companies like Sony and Matsushita (the maker of Panasonic and JVC products) turned out thousands of innovative new consumer electronics such as the Walkman, home video recorders, high-quality televisions, and compact disk players. Samsung's strategy was to see which of these products and which of their specific features, such as a TV with a hard disk that can store movies, customers liked the best. Then Samsung's engineers would find ways to imitate this technology, just as Japanese companies had imitated U.S. electronics companies in the 1950s when they were the world's leading electronics makers. Samsung would make a low-cost copy of these products and sell them at lower prices than Japanese companies. However, while this strategy was profitable, Samsung was not in the league of Japanese companies like Sony, which could charge premium prices for their electronics and then continually plow their enormous profits back into research to make ever more advanced state-of-the-art electronics—and thus increase their profitability.

Samsung continued to pursue its low-cost strategy until the mid 1990s, when its chairman, Lee Kun Hee, made a major decision. Sensing the emerging threat posed by China and other Asian countries whose cheap labor would rob Samsung of its low-cost advantage, Lee realized that Samsung needed to find a way to enter the big league and compete directly against the Japanese giants. The question was how to do this, given that companies like Sony, Panasonic, and Hitachi were leaders in electronics research and development.

Lee began his new strategy by closing down thirty-two unprofitable product divisions and laying off 40 percent of Samsung's work force. Having lowered its cost structure, Samsung could now invest much more of its capital in research and development activities. Lee decided to concentrate Samsung's research budget on new-product opportunities in areas like microprocessors, LCD screens, and other new kinds of digital components that he sensed would be in demand in the coming digital revolution. Today, Samsung is a major supplier of chips and LCD screens to all global electronics makers, and it can produce these components at a much lower cost than they can because it is farther down the experience curve.[2]

The focus of Lee's new strategy, however, was on developing research and engineering skills that would allow the company to quickly capitalize on the technology being innovated by Sony, Matsushita, Phillips, and Nokia. His engineers would take this technology and rapidly develop and improve it to create new and improved products that were more advanced than those offered by Japanese competitors. Samsung would produce a wider variety of products than competitors but only in relatively small quantities. Then, as its new products were sold in stores, newer electronic models that were still more advanced would replace them. One advantage of speeding products to market is that inventory does not sit in Samsung's warehouses or stores, nor does Samsung need to stock large quantities of components because it needs only enough to make its budgeted output of a particular product. So, by making speed the center of its differentiation strategy, Samsung was able to make more efficient use of its capital even as it introduced large numbers of new products to the market.

At the same time, Samsung's ability to innovate a large number of advanced products attracts customers and has allowed it to build its market share. Today, for example, while Nokia can claim to be a leading cell phone innovator, Samsung was the first to realize that customers wanted a color screen for their phone to allow them to play games and a built-in camera that would allow them to send photographs to their friends. Both these incremental advances have allowed Samsung to dramatically increase its share of the cell phone market, while Nokia's has fallen just as dramatically. To compete with Samsung, Nokia has had to learn how to innovate new models of cell phones rapidly. In 2004, while Nokia introduced only a score of new phones, Samsung brought out ninety new models; however, Nokia announced that it would be introducing over fifty new phones in 2005 to meet Samsung's challenge.[3]

By making speed of new-product development the center of its business model, Samsung also was able to move ahead of its other major competitors like Sony. Sony, because of its focus on developing new technology and because of the slow speed of decision making typical in Japanese companies, was hard hit by Samsung's success, and its profitability and stock price declined sharply in the 2000s. Moreover, today Samsung is not just imitating Sony's leading-edge technology but is also developing its own, as shown by the fact that in 2004 Sony and Samsung announced a major agreement to share the costs of basic research into improving LCDs, which run into billions of dollars.

Today, Samsung is in the first tier of electronics makers and is regarded by many as one of the most innovative companies in the world. Almost a quarter of Samsung's 80,000 employees work in one of its four research divisions—semiconductors, telecommunications, digital media, and flat-screen panels. Because many of its products require components developed by all four divisions, it brings researchers, designers, engineers, and marketers from all its divisions together in teams at its research facility outside of Seoul to spur the innovation that is the major source of its success. At the same time, it can still make many electronic components at a lower cost than its competitors, which has further contributed to its high profitability. Given the rapid technological advances in China, however, it appears that Chinese companies may soon be able to make some of their components at a lower cost than Samsung, thus doing to Samsung what Samsung did to companies like Sony. Samsung is relying on the speed of its research and engineering to fight off their challenge, but all global electronics makers are now in a race to speed their products to market.

Overview

As the *Opening Case* suggests, this chapter examines how a company selects and pursues a business model that will allow it to compete effectively in an industry and grow its profits and profitability. A successful business model results from business-level strategies that create a competitive advantage over rivals and achieve superior performance in an industry.

In Chapter 2 we examined how the competitive forces at work inside an industry affect its profitability. As industry forces change, so they change the profitability of an industry, and thus the profitability of any particular business model. Industry analysis is vital in formulating a successful business model because it determines (1) how existing companies will decide to change their business-level strategies to improve the performance of their business model over time, (2) whether or not established companies outside an industry may decide to create a business model to enter it, and (3) whether entrepreneurs can devise a business model that will allow them to compete successfully against existing companies in an industry.

In Chapter 3, we examined how competitive advantage depends on a company developing a business model that allows it to achieve superior efficiency, quality, innovation, and customer responsiveness, the building blocks of competitive advantage. And in Chapter 4, we discussed how every function must develop the distinctive competencies that allow a company to implement a business model that will lead to superior performance and competitive advantage in an industry.

In this chapter we examine the competitive decisions involved in creating a business model that will attract and retain customers, and continue to do so over time so that a company enjoys growing profits and profitability. To create a successful business model, strategic managers must (1) formulate business-level strategies that will allow a company to attract customers away from other companies in the industry (its competitors), and (2) implement those business-level strategies, which also involves the use of functional-level strategies to increase responsiveness to customers, efficiency, innovation, and quality.

By the end of this chapter, you will be able to distinguish between the principal generic business models and business-level strategies that a company uses to obtain a competitive advantage over its rivals. You will also understand why, and under what circumstances, strategic leaders like Samsung's Lee Kun Hee change their company's strategies over time to pursue different kinds of business models.

Competitive Positioning and the Business Model

To create a successful business model, managers must choose a set of business-level strategies that work together to give a company a competitive advantage over its rivals; that is, they must optimize **competitive positioning**. As we noted in Chapter 1, to craft a successful business model a company must first define its business, which entails decisions about (1) customers' needs, or what is to be satisfied, (2) customer groups, or who is to be satisfied, and (3) distinctive competencies, or how customer needs are to be satisfied.[4] The decisions managers make about these three issues determine which set of strategies they formulate and implement to put a company's business model into action and create value for customers. Consequently, we need to examine the principal choices facing managers as they make these three decisions.

■ Formulating the Business Model: Customer Needs and Product Differentiation

Customer needs are desires, wants, or cravings that can be satisfied by means of the attributes or characteristics of a product—a good or service. For example, a person's craving for something sweet can be satisfied by a box of Godiva chocolates, a carton of Ben & Jerry's ice cream, a Snickers bar, or a spoonful of sugar. Two factors determine which product a customer chooses to satisfy these needs: (1) the way a product is differentiated from other products of its type so that it appeals to customers, and (2) the price of the product. All companies must differentiate their products to a certain degree to attract customers. Some companies, however, decide to offer customers a low-priced product and do not engage in much product differentiation. Companies that seek to create something unique about their product differentiate their products to a much greater degree than others so that they satisfy customers' needs in ways other products cannot.

Product differentiation is the process of designing products to satisfy customers' needs. A company obtains a competitive advantage when it creates, makes, and sells a product in a way that better satisfies customer needs than its rivals do. It is here that the four building blocks of competitive advantage come into play, for a company's decision to pursue one or more of these building blocks determines its approach to product differentiation. If managers devise strategies to differentiate a product by innovation, excellent quality, or responsiveness to customers, they are choosing a business model based on offering customers differentiated products. On the other hand, if managers base their business model on finding ways to increase efficiency and reliability to reduce costs, they are choosing a business model based on offering customers low-priced products.

Creating unique or distinctive products can be achieved in countless different ways, which explains why there are usually many different companies competing in an industry. Distinctiveness obtained from the physical characteristics of a product commonly results from pursuing innovation or quality, such as when a company focuses on developing state-of-the-art car safety systems or on engineering an SUV to give it sports-car-like handling. Similarly, companies might try to design their cars with features such as butter-soft hand-sewn leather interiors, fine wood fittings, and sleek, exciting body styling to appeal to customers' psychological needs, such as a personal need for prestige, status, or to declare a particular "lifestyle."[5]

Differentiation has another important aspect. Companies that invest their resources to create something distinct or different about their products can often charge a *higher,* or *premium, price* for their product. For example, superb design or technical sophistication allows companies to charge more for their products because customers are willing to pay these higher prices. Mercedes-Benz buyers pay a high premium price to enjoy their sophisticated vehicles, as do customers of Godiva chocolates, which retail for about $26 a pound—much more than, say, a box of Whitman's candies or a Hershey bar.

Consider the high-price segment of the car market, where customers are willing to pay more than $35,000 to satisfy their needs for a "personal luxury vehicle." In this segment, Cadillac, Mercedes-Benz, Infiniti, BMW, Jaguar, Lexus, Lincoln, Audi, Volvo, Acura, and others are engaged in a continuing battle to design the "perfect" luxury vehicle—the one that best meets the needs of those who want such a vehicle. Over time, the companies that attract the most luxury car buyers—because they have designed the cars that possess the innovative features or excellent quality and reliability these customers desire the most—are the ones that achieve a sustained competitive advantage over rivals. For example, some customers value a sporty ride and performance handling; Mercedes-Benz and BMW, because of their cutting-edge technical design, can offer this driving experience better than any other maker. Toyota's Lexus division is well known for the smoothness and quietness of its cars and their exceptional reliability. Lexus cars consistently outrank all other cars in published reliability rankings, and this excellence appeals to a large group of customers who appreciate these qualities. Volvo has a reputation for producing safe cars, and Rolls-Royce has a reputation for prestige cars. Other luxury carmakers have not fared so well. Cadillac, Lincoln, Audi, Acura, and Infiniti have found it more difficult to differentiate their cars, which sometimes compare unfavorably to their rivals in terms of ride, comfort, safety, or reliability. Although these less successful companies still sell many cars, customers often find their needs better satisfied by the attributes and qualities of their rivals' cars.

Even in the luxury car segment, however, carmakers must be concerned with efficiency, because price affects a buying decision even for highly differentiated products. Luxury carmakers compete to offer customers the car with the ride, performance, and features that provide them with the most value (satisfy their needs) given the price of the car. Thus, Lexus cars are always several thousand dollars less than comparable cars, and Toyota can price these cars lower because of its low cost structure. For example, the Lexus ES300, introduced in 2003 at around $35,000, is about $10,000 less than the BMW 5 Series and Mercedes E Class, its nearest rivals. Most customers are discriminating and match price to differentiation even in the luxury car segment of the market, so BMW and Mercedes have to offer customers something that justifies their vehicles' higher prices.

At every price range in the car market—under $15,000, from $15,000 to $25,000, $25,000 to $35,000, and the luxury segment above $35,000—many models of cars compete to attract customers. For each price range a carmaker has to decide how best to differentiate a particular car model to suit the needs of customers in that price range. Typically, the more differentiated a product is, the more it will cost to design and produce, and so differentiation leads to a higher cost structure. Thus, if a carmaker is to stay within the $15,000 to $25,000 price range and yet design and produce a differentiated car that will give it a competitive advantage and allow it to outperform its rivals in the same price range, its strategic managers have to make crucial and difficult decisions. They have to forecast what features customers will most value; for example, they may decide to trade off styling, safety, and performance so that the car will not cost too much to produce, enabling them to make a profit and to still sell the car for less than $25,000.

In sum, in devising a business model, strategic managers are always constrained by the need to differentiate their products against the need to keep their cost structure under control so that they can offer the product at a competitive price—a price that offers customers as much or more value than the products of its rivals. Companies that have built a competitive advantage through innovation, quality, and reliability can differentiate their products more successfully than their rivals. In turn, because customers perceive there is more value in their products, these companies can charge a premium price.

Formulating the Business Model: Customer Groups and Market Segmentation

The second main choice involved in formulating a successful business model is to decide which kind of product(s) to offer to which customer group(s). Customer groups are the sets of people who share a similar need for a particular product. Because a particular product usually satisfies several different kinds of desires and needs, many different customer groups normally exist in a market. In the car market, for example, some customers want basic transportation, some want top-of-the-line luxury, and others want the thrill of driving a sports car: these are three of the customer groups in the car market.

In the athletic shoe market, the two main customer groups are those people who use them for sporting purposes and those who like to wear them because they are casual and comfortable. Within each customer group there are often subgroups composed of people who have an even more specific need for a product. Inside the group of people who buy athletic shoes for sporting purposes, for example, are subgroups of people who buy shoes suited to a specific kind of activity, such as running, aerobics, walking, and tennis (see Figure 5.1).

A company searching for a successful business model has to group customers according to the similarities or differences in their needs to discover what kinds of

Identifying Customer Groups and Market Segments

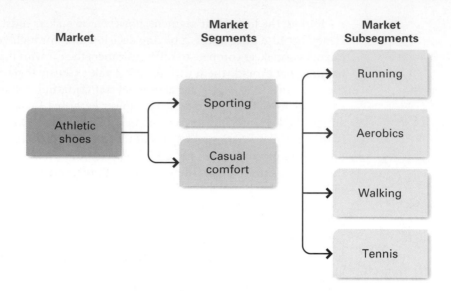

products to develop for different kinds of customers. The marketing function performs research to discover a group of customers' primary need for a product, how they will use it, and their income or buying power (to determine the balance between differentiation and price). Other important attributes of a customer group are then identified that more narrowly target their specific needs. Once a group of customers who share a similar or specific need for a product has been identified, this group is treated as a market segment. Companies then decide whether to make and sell a product designed to satisfy the specific needs of this customer segment.

■ **Three Approaches to Market Segmentation** Market segmentation is the way a company decides to group customers, based on important differences in their needs or preferences, in order to gain a competitive advantage.[6] First, the company must segment the market according to how much customers are able and willing to pay for a particular product—such as the different price ranges for cars mentioned above. Once price has been taken into consideration, customers can be segmented according to the specific needs that are being satisfied by a particular product, such as the economy, luxury, or speed of cars mentioned above.

In crafting a business model, managers have to think strategically about which segments they are going to compete in and how they will differentiate their products for each segment. In other words, once market segments have been identified, a company has to decide how *responsive it should be to the needs of customers in the different segments*. This decision determines a particular company's product range. There are three main approaches toward market segmentation in devising a business model (Figure 5.2):

■ First, a company might choose not to recognize that different market segments exist and make a product targeted at the average or typical customer. In this case customer responsiveness is at a *minimum*, and the focus is on price, not differentiation.

■ Second, a company can choose to recognize the differences between customer groups and make a product targeted toward most or all of the different market

FIGURE 5.2

Three Approaches to
Market Segmentation

**No Market
Segmentation**
A product is targeted at
the "average customer."

**High Market
Segmentation**
A different product is offered
to each market segment.

**Focused Market
Segmentation**
A product is offered to one
or a few market segments.

segments. In this case customer responsiveness is *high* and products are being *customized* to meet the specific needs of customers in each group, so the emphasis is on differentiation, not price.

■ Third, a company might choose to target just *one or two market segments* and devote its resources to developing products for customers in just these segments. In this case, it may be highly responsive to the needs of customers in only these segments, or it may offer a bare-bones product to undercut the prices charged by companies who do focus on differentiation.

Since a company's cost structure and operating costs increase when it makes a different product for each market segment rather than just one product for the whole market, why would a company devise a business model based on serving customers in multiple market segments? The answer is that although operating costs increase, the decision to produce a range of products that are closely aligned with the needs of customers in different market segments attracts many more customers (because responsiveness to customers increases), and therefore sales revenues and profits increase. Recall from the *Opening Case* that Samsung's revenues have increased because of its ability to offer customers a continual supply of new and improved cell phones that it can sell at a premium price. As long as a company's revenues increase faster than its operating costs as its product range expands, profitability increases.

This does not mean that all companies should decide to produce a wide range of products aimed at each market segment to increase their profitability. It depends on how much customer needs for a product differ in a particular market or industry. In some industries, like cars, customer needs differ widely. There are considerable differences in buyers' primary needs for a car, income levels, lifestyles, ages, and so on. For this reason, major global carmakers broaden their product range and make vehicles to serve most market segments. A company that produces just one car model, compared to a company that produces twenty-five models, may find itself at a serious competitive disadvantage.

On the other hand, in some markets customers have similar needs for a product and so the relative price of competing products drives their buying choices. In this situation, a company that chooses to use its resources to make and sell a single product as inexpensively as possible might gain a major competitive advantage. The average customer buys the product because it's "OK" and good "value for the money." This is the business model followed by companies that specialize in making a low-cost product, such as BIC, which makes low-cost razors and ballpoint pens, and Arm & Hammer, which makes baking soda. These are products that most people use in the same way. This is also the business model followed by companies like Wal-Mart, with its mission to buy products from suppliers as cheaply as possible and then sell them to customers at the lowest possible prices. BIC and Wal-Mart do not segment the market; they decide to serve the needs of customers who want to buy products as inexpensively as possible. Wal-Mart promises everyday low prices and price rollbacks; BIC promises the lowest-priced razor blades that work acceptably.

The third approach to market segmentation is to target a product just at one or two market segments. To pursue this approach a company must develop something very special or distinctive about its product to attract a large share of customers in those particular market segments. In the car market, for example, Rolls-Royce and Porsche target their products at specific market segments. Porsche, for example, targets its well-known sports cars at buyers in the high-priced sports car segment. In a similar way, specialty retailers compete for customers in a particular market segment, such as the segment composed of affluent people who can afford to buy expensive hand-made clothing, or people who enjoy wearing "trendy" shoes such as Nike's Converse brand. A retailer might also specialize in a particular style of clothing, such as western wear, beachwear, or accessories. In many markets these are enormous opportunities for small companies to specialize in satisfying the needs of a specific market segment. Often, these companies can better satisfy their customers' needs because they are so close to them and understand how their needs are changing over time.

Market segmentation is an evolving, ongoing process that presents considerable opportunities for strategic managers to improve their company's business model. For example, in the car industry, savvy strategists often identify a "new" customer group whose specific needs have not been met and who have had to "satisfice" and buy a model that does not meet their needs exactly but is a reasonable compromise. Now a car company can decide to treat this group as a market segment and create a product designed to meet their specific needs; if it makes the right choice, it has a blockbuster product. This was the origin of the minivan, sports utility vehicle, and all the recently introduced "hybrid" vehicles like the Honda Pilot, Toyota Scion, or Dodge Magnum. In the case of SUVs, many car buyers wanted a more rugged and powerful vehicle capable of holding many people or towing heavy loads. They liked the comfort of a car but also the qualities of a pickup; by combining these two, carmakers created the SUV market segment. If managers make mistakes, however, and design a product for a market segment that is much smaller than they expected, the opposite can occur. In 2004, for example, Ford announced that it was ending production of its expensive luxury Lincoln truck and Excursion SUV because sales had been only in the hundreds a year, not the thousands a year it had projected.

■ **Implementing the Business Model: Building Distinctive Competencies**

To develop a successful business model, strategic managers have to devise a set of strategies that determine (1) how to differentiate and price their product and (2) how much to segment a market and how wide a range of products to develop. Whether these strategies will result in a profitable business model now depends on strategic managers' ability to implement their business model, that is, to choose strategies that will create products that provide customers with the most value, while keeping their cost structure viable (because of the need to be price competitive).

In practice, this involves deciding how to invest a company's capital to build and shape distinctive competencies that result in a competitive advantage based on superior efficiency, quality, innovation, and/or responsiveness to customers. Hence, implementing a company's business model sets in motion *the specific set of functional-level strategies needed to create a successful differentiation and low cost business strategy.* We discussed how functional strategies can build competitive advantage in Chapter 4. The better the fit between a company's business strategy and its functional-level strategies, the more value and profit a company creates.

Figure 5.3 illustrates Wal-Mart's business model. As we discuss in previous chapters, Sam Walton, the company's founder, devised a business model based on the strategy of keeping operating costs to a minimum so that he could offer customers everyday low prices and continuous price rollbacks. To this end, Walton chose business-level strategies to increase efficiency, such as having low product differentiation (Wal-Mart chooses minimal advertising and low responsiveness to customers) and targeting the mass market. His discount retail business model was based on the idea that lower costs mean lower prices.

Having devised a way to compete for customers, Walton's task was now to implement the business model in ways that would create a low-cost structure to allow

FIGURE 5.3

Wal-Mart's Business Model

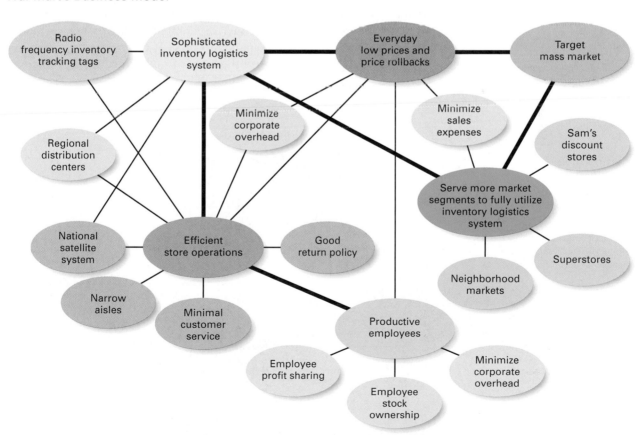

him to charge lower prices. One business-level strategy he implemented was to locate his stores outside large cities in small towns where there were no low-cost competitors; a second was to find ways to manage the value chain to reduce the costs of getting products from manufacturers to customers; and a third was to design and staff store operations to increase efficiency. The task of all functional managers in logistics, materials management, sales and customer service, store management, and so on was to implement specific functional-level strategies that supported the low-cost/low-price business model. Figure 5.3 illustrates some of the thousands of specific choices that Wal-Mart has made to allow it to implement its business model successfully.

Competitive Positioning and Business-Level Strategy

Figure 5.4 presents a way of thinking about the competitive positioning decisions that strategic managers make to create a successful business model.[7] The decision to differentiate a product increases its perceived value to the customer so that market demand for the product increases. However, differentiation is expensive; for example, additional expenditures on resources are needed to improve product quality or support a higher level of service. Therefore, the decision to increase product differentiation also raises a company's cost structure and results in a higher unit cost. (In some cases, however, if increased demand for the product allows a company to make large volumes of the product and achieve economies of scale, these economies can offset some of these extra costs; this effect is showed by the dotted line in Figure 5.4.)[8]

To maximize profitability, managers must choose a premium pricing option that compensates for the extra costs of product differentiation but is not so high it chokes off the increase in expected demand (to prevent customers from deciding that the extra differentiation is not worth the higher price). Once again, to increase

FIGURE 5.4

Competitive Positioning at the Business Level

Source: Copyright © C. W. L. Hill and G. R. Jones, "The Dynamics of Business-Level Strategy" (unpublished manuscript, 2005).

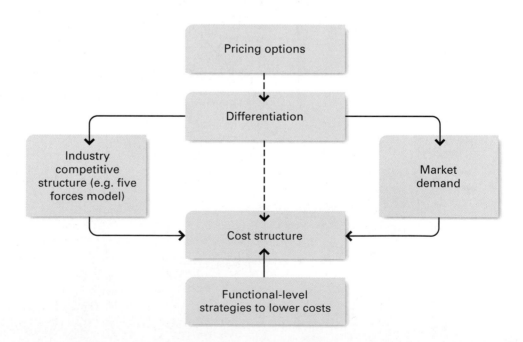

profitability, managers must also search for other ways to reduce the cost structure, but not in ways that will harm the differentiated appeal of its products. There are many specific functional strategies a company can adopt to achieve this. For example, Nordstrom, the luxury department store retailer, differentiates itself in the retail clothing industry by providing a high-quality shopping experience with elegant store operations and a high level of customer service, all of which raise Nordstrom's cost structure. However, Nordstrom can still lower its cost structure by, for example, managing its inventories efficiently and increasing inventory turnover. Also, its strategy of being highly responsive to customers results in more customers and higher demand, which means that sales per square foot increase, and this revenue enables it to make more intensive use of its facilities and salespeople, which leads to scale economies and lower costs. Thus, no matter what the level of differentiation is that a company chooses to pursue in its business model, it always has to recognize the way its cost structure will vary as a result of its choice of differentiation and the other specific strategies it adopts to lower its cost structure; in other words, *differentiation and cost structure decisions affect one another.*

The last main dynamic shown in Figure 5.4 concerns the impact of the industry's competitive structure on a company's differentiation, cost structure, and pricing choices. Recall that strategic decision making takes place in an environment where watchful and agile competitors exist; therefore, one company's choice of competitive positioning is always made *with reference to those of its competitors.* If, for example, competitors start to offer products with new or improved features, a company may be forced to increase its level of differentiation to remain competitive, even if this reduces its profitability. Similarly, if competitors decide to develop products for new market segments, the company will have to follow suit or become uncompetitive. Thus, because differentiation increases costs, increasing industry competition can drive up a company's cost structure. When that happens, a company's ability to charge a premium price to cover these high costs depends on whether its profitability increases or decreases.

In sum, maximizing the profitability of a company's business model is about making the right choices with regard to value creation through differentiation, costs, and pricing given both the demand conditions in the company's market and the competitive conditions in the company's industry. Because *all the different variables in Figure 5.4 change as the others change,* managers can never accurately predict the outcome of their decisions. This is why devising and managing a successful business model is such a difficult thing to do.

Competitive Positioning: Generic Business-Level Strategies

As we discuss above, a successful business model is the result of the way a company formulates and implements a set of business-level strategies to achieve a fit between its differentiation, cost, and pricing options. While no diagram can ever model all the complexities involved in business-level strategy decisions, Figure 5.5 represents a way to bring together the three issues involved in developing a successful business model. In the figure, the vertical and horizontal axes represent the decisions of strategic managers to position a company's products with respect to the tradeoff between differentiating products (higher costs/higher prices) and achieving the lowest cost structure or cost leadership (lower costs/lower prices). In Figure 5.5 the curve connecting the axes represents the "value creation frontier," meaning the maximum amount of value that the products of different companies in an industry can provide at any one time with different business models. In other words, companies on

FIGURE 5.5

Competitive
Positioning and the
Value Creation
Frontier

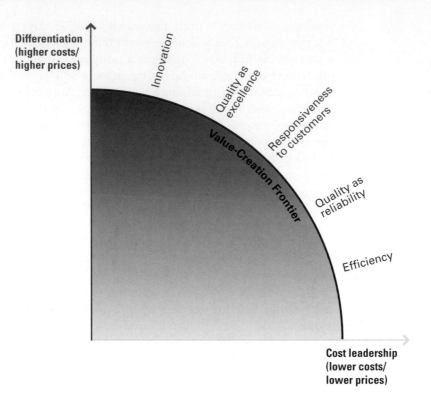

the value frontier are those that have the most successful business models in a particular industry.

As Figure 5.5 illustrates, the value creation frontier is reached by pursuing one or more of the four building blocks of competitive advantage (quality has been split into two), which have been listed from top to bottom according to how much they can contribute to the creation of a differentiation or cost-leadership advantage. Thus innovation, a costly process that results in unique products, is nearest the differentiation axis, followed by quality as excellence, customer responsiveness, and quality as reliability; efficiency is closest to the cost-leadership axis.

To reach the value creation frontier and so achieve above-average profitability, a company must formulate and implement a business model using a consistent set of business-level strategies that give it a *specific competitive position vis-à-vis its rivals*. A **generic competitive strategy** is a specific business-level strategy that gives a company a competitive advantage, and four principal ones can be identified: cost leadership, focused cost leadership, differentiation, and focused differentiation.[9] *Generic* means that all companies can potentially pursue these strategies regardless of whether they are manufacturing, service, or nonprofit enterprises; they are also generic because they can be pursued across different kinds of industries.

■ Cost Leadership

A company's business model in pursuing a cost-leadership strategy is based on doing everything it can to lower its cost structure so it can make and sell goods or services at a lower cost than its competitors. In essence, a company seeks to achieve a competitive advantage and above-average profitability by developing a cost-leadership business model that positions it on the value creation frontier as close as possible to the lower costs/lower prices axis.

Two advantages accrue from a cost-leadership strategy. First, if a company's closest rivals, such as those that compete in the same price range or for the same customer group, charge similar prices for their products, the cost leader will be more profitable than its competitors because of its lower costs. Second, and more commonly, the cost leader gains a competitive advantage by being able to charge a lower price than its competitors because of its lower cost structure. As discussed earlier, offering customers the same kind of value from a product but at a lower price attracts many more customers, so that even though the company has chosen a lower price option, the increased volume of sales will cause profits to surge. If its competitors try to get lost customers back by reducing their prices and all companies start to compete on price, the cost leader will still be able to withstand competition better than the other companies because of its lower costs. It is likely to win any competitive struggle. For these reasons, cost leaders are likely to earn above-average profits. A company becomes a cost leader when its strategic managers develop a business model that is based on the following business-level strategic choices.

■ **Strategic Choices** The cost leader chooses a low to moderate level of product differentiation relative to its competitors. Differentiation is expensive; the more a company expends resources to make its products distinct, the more its costs rise.[10] The cost leader aims for a level of differentiation obtainable at low cost.[11] Wal-Mart, for example, does not spend hundreds of millions of dollars on store design to create an attractive shopping experience as chains like Macy's, Dillard's, or Saks Fifth Avenue have done. As Wal-Mart explains in its mission statement, "We think of ourselves as buyers for our customers and we apply our considerable strengths to get the best value for you," and such value is not obtained by building lavish stores.[12] Cost leaders often wait until customers want a feature or service before providing it, as Samsung did in the *Opening Case.* For example, a cost leader is never the first to offer theater-quality sound in a DVD player; instead, it adds such sound quality only when it is obvious that customers demand it.

The cost leader also ignores the many different market segments in an industry and positions its products to appeal to the "average" customer to reduce the costs of developing and selling many different products tailored to the needs of different market segments. In targeting the average customer, strategic managers try to produce or provide the least or smallest number of products that will be desired by the highest number of customers, something at the heart of Wal-Mart's approach to stocking its stores. Thus, although customers may not get exactly the products they want, they are attracted by the lower prices.

To implement cost leadership, the overriding goal of the cost leader must be to choose strategies to increase its efficiency and lower its cost structure compared with its rivals. The development of distinctive competencies in manufacturing, materials management, and information technology is central to achieving this goal. For example, manufacturing companies pursuing a cost-leadership strategy concentrate on doing all they can to continually ride down the experience curve so that their cost structure keeps getting lower and lower. Achieving a cost-leadership position requires that a company develop skills in flexible manufacturing, adopt efficient materials-management techniques, and do all it can to increase inventory turnover and reduce the cost of goods sold. (Table 4.1 outlined the ways in which a company's functions can be used to increase efficiency.)

Consequently, for companies that make products, the manufacturing and materials-management functions are the center of attention, and the other functions shape their distinctive competencies to meet the needs of manufacturing and materials management.[13] The sales function, for example, may develop the competency of capturing large, stable sets of customers' orders. In turn, this allows manufacturing to make longer production runs and so achieve economies of scale and reduce costs. At Dell, for example, online customers are provided with a limited set of choices so that Dell can customize PCs to a customer's needs at low cost. Finding ways to customize products at low cost is an important task for managers pursuing a cost-leadership strategy. The human resource function may focus on instituting training programs and compensation systems that lower costs by improving employees' productivity, and the research and development function may specialize in process improvements to lower the manufacturing costs.

By contrast, companies supplying services, such as retail stores like Wal-Mart, must develop distinctive competencies in whatever functions contribute most to their cost structure. In Wal-Mart this is the cost of purchasing products, so the logistics or materials-management function becomes of central importance. Wal-Mart has taken advantage of advances in information technology to lower the costs associated with getting goods from manufacturers to customers, just as Dell, the cost leader in the PC industry, uses the Internet to lower the cost of selling its computers. Another major source of cost savings in pursuing cost leadership is to choose an organizational structure and culture to implement this strategy in the most cost-efficient way. Thus, a low-cost strategy implies minimizing the number of managers in the hierarchy and the rigorous use of budgets to control production and selling costs. An interesting example of the way a company can craft a business model to become the cost leader in an industry is Ryanair, discussed in Strategy in Action 5.1.

■ **Advantages and Disadvantages** Porter's five forces model, introduced in Chapter 2, explains why each of the business models allows a company to reach the value creation frontier shown in Figure 5.5.[14] The five forces are threats from competitors, powerful suppliers, powerful buyers, substitute products, and new entrants. The cost leader is protected from industry competitors by its cost advantage. Its lower costs also mean that it will be less affected than its competitors by increases in the price of inputs if there are powerful suppliers, and less affected by a fall in the prices it can charge if there are powerful buyers. Moreover, since cost leadership usually requires a large market share, the cost leader purchases in relatively large quantities, increasing its bargaining power over suppliers. If substitute products begin to come onto the market, the cost leader can reduce its price to compete with them and retain its market share. Finally, the leader's cost advantage constitutes a barrier to entry because other companies are unable to enter the industry and match the leader's costs or prices. The cost leader is therefore relatively safe as long as it can maintain its low-cost advantage.

The principal dangers of the cost-leadership approach lurk in competitors' ability to find ways to lower their cost structures and beat the cost leader at its own game. For instance, if technological change makes experience-curve economies obsolete, new companies may apply lower-cost technologies that give them a cost advantage. The steel mini-mills discussed in Chapter 4 gained this advantage. Competitors may also draw a cost advantage from labor-cost savings. Global competitors located in countries overseas often have very low labor costs; wage costs in the United States are

Strategy in Action   5.1

Ryanair Takes Control over the Sky in Europe

Ryanair, based in Dublin, Ireland, imitated and improved on the cost-leadership business model pioneered by Southwest Airlines in the United States and used it to become a leading player in the European air travel market. Ryanair's CEO, the flamboyant Michael O'Leary, saw the specific strategies Southwest had developed to cut costs and used the same strategies to position Ryanair as the lowest-cost, lowest-priced European airline. Today, the average cost of a Ryanair ticket within Europe is $48, compared to $330 on British Airways and $277 on Lufthansa, which have long dominated the European air travel market. The result is that Ryanair now flies more passengers inside Britain than British Airways, and its share of the European market is growing as fast as it can gain access to new landing spots and buy the new planes needed to service its expanding route structure.

O'Leary has managed to improve on Southwest's low-cost business model. Ryanair imitated the main elements of Southwest's model, such as only using one plane, the 737, to reduce maintenance costs, selling tickets directly to customers, and eliminating seat assignments and free in-flight meals. It also avoids high-cost airports like Heathrow and chooses smaller ones outside big cities, such as Luton, its London hub, just as Wal-Mart chose to move into smaller towns. However, to reduce clean-up costs, O'Leary also eliminated the seat back pockets that often contain trash left by previous passengers, as well as blankets, pillows, free sodas or snacks, and even "sick" bags—anything at all a passenger might expect to receive on a more differentiated airline. "You get what you pay for" is Ryanair's philosophy. To implement his cost-leadership strategy, O'Leary and all employees are expected to find ways to wipe out or reduce the small, incremental expenses that arise in performing the tens of thousands of specific operations needed to run an airline. His goal is to eliminate all the differentiated qualities of an airline that can raise costs. Through all these tactics

Ryanair has lowered its cost structure so far that no other European airline can come close to offering its low-cost fares and break even, let alone make a profit.

The other side of Ryanair's business model is to add to its revenues by getting its customers to spend as much as possible while they are on its flights. To this end, Ryanair offers snacks, meals, and a variety of drinks to encourage customers to open their wallets. In addition, to cut costs his planes have no back-seat LCD screens for viewing movies and playing games. In 2004 Ryanair introduced a new digital hand-held device that passengers can rent for $6 a flight to watch movies and sitcoms or play games or music. Fourteen percent of its revenues come from these sources, and they are so important that in 2003 the airline gave away over 1 million of its unsold seats free to customers so that it could at least get some revenue from passengers sitting in what otherwise would be empty seats.

How have competitors reacted to Ryanair's cost-leadership strategy? Some airlines have started a low-price subsidiary, just as United's Song division was created to compete with Southwest in the United States. However, this often results in cannibalization as their passengers move from the high-price to the low-price service. Some airlines that pursue the differentiation strategy, like British Airways, are not suffering because they are solidly profitable in the business segment of the market. However, other airlines, such as Italy's flagship airline, Alitalia, are close to bankruptcy, and the Irish carrier Aer Lingus has had to cut its costs by 50 percent in the last few years just to survive. O'Leary sees brutal price wars ahead: new low-cost entrants like easyJet have entered the market, and more will do so. The lower-cost, lower-fare business model will fare well if price wars develop, and if the large national airlines are going to prosper they will have to offer customers something that makes them willing to pay higher prices.[a]

roughly 600 percent more than they are in Malaysia, China, or Mexico. Most U.S. companies now assemble their products abroad as part of their low-cost strategy; many are forced to do so simply to compete and stay in business.

Competitors' ability to imitate the cost leader's methods easily is another threat to the cost-leadership strategy. For example, companies in Hong Kong and China routinely take apart the electronic products of Japanese companies like Sony and Panasonic to see how they are designed and assembled. Then, using Chinese-made components and a huge pool of inexpensive domestic labor, they manufacture clones of these products and flood the U.S. market with inexpensive tape players, radios, phones, and DVD players. This was part of Samsung's early strategy.

Finally, the cost-leadership strategy carries a risk that strategic managers in their single-minded desire to reduce costs might make decisions that decrease costs but then drastically affect demand for the product. This happened to Gateway in the early 2000s when, to reduce the costs of customer service, customer support people were instructed not to help customers who were experiencing problems with their new Gateway computers if they had installed their own new software on the machines. New buyers, most of whom install their own software, began to complain vociferously, and Gateway's sales began to fall as word spread. Within six months, managers had reversed their decision, and once again Gateway began offering full customer support.

■ Focused Cost Leadership

A cost leader is not always a large, national company that targets the average customer. Sometimes a company can target one or a few market segments and successfully pursue cost leadership by developing the right strategies to serve those segments. These companies pursue a business model based on **focused cost leadership**. They compete for customers in a narrow market segment, which can be defined geographically, by type of customer, or by segment of the product line.[15] In Figure 5.6, focus cost leaders are represented by the smaller circles next to the cost leader's circle. For example, since a geographic niche can be defined by region or even by locality, a cement-making company, a carpet-cleaning business, or a pizza chain could pursue a cost-leadership

FIGURE 5.6

Generic Business Models and the Value Creation Frontier

FIGURE 5.7

Why Focus Strategies
Are Different

strategy in one or more cities in a region. Figure 5.7 compares a focused cost-leadership business model with a pure cost-leadership model.

If a company uses a focused cost-leadership approach, it competes against the cost leader in the market segments where it can operate at no cost disadvantage. For example, in local lumber, cement, bookkeeping, or pizza delivery markets, the focuser may have lower materials or transportation costs than the national cost leader. The focuser may also have a cost advantage because it is producing complex or custom-built products that do not lend themselves easily to economies of scale in production and therefore offer few cost-saving possibilities. Pursuing a focus strategy, a cost leader concentrates on small-volume custom products, for which it has a cost advantage, and leaves the large-volume standardized market to the national cost leader—for example, low-priced Mexican food specials versus Big Macs.

Because it has no cost disadvantage in its market segments, a focused cost leader also operates on the value creation frontier and so earns above average profits. Such a company has great opportunity to develop its own niche and compete against companies pursuing cost-leadership or differentiated strategies. Ryanair, for example, began as a focus company because at first it only operated flights between Dublin and London. Since there was no cost leader in the European market, it was able to quickly expand its operations, and today it is the cost leader. Similarly, Southwest began as a focused cost leader within the Texas market but is now a national air carrier and competes against new companies that pursue focused cost leadership, such as Jet Blue and Song.[16]

Because a focused company only makes and sells a relatively small quantity of a product, its cost structure will often be higher than that of the cost leader. In some industries, like cars, this can make it very difficult or impossible to compete with the cost leader. However, sometimes, by targeting some new market segment or by implementing a business model in a superior way—such as by adopting a more advanced technology—focused companies can be a threat to large cost leaders. For example, flexible manufacturing systems have opened up many new opportunities for focused companies because small production runs become possible at a lower cost. Increasingly, small, specialized companies are competing with large companies in specific market segments in which they have no cost disadvantage. The steel mini-mills discussed in Chapter 4 provide another good example of how a focused company, in this case Nucor, by specializing in one market can grow so efficient that it becomes the cost leader. Similarly, the growth of the Internet has opened up many new opportunities for focused companies to develop business models based on being the cost leader compared to bricks-and-mortar companies. Amazon.com shows how effectively a company can craft a business model to become the cost leader.

■ **Implications and Conclusions** To pursue a cost-leadership strategy, strategic managers need to devote enormous efforts to incorporate all the latest information, materials management, and manufacturing technology into their operations to find new ways to reduce costs. Often, as we saw in Chapter 4, using new technology will also raise quality and increase responsiveness to customers. A low-cost approach requires ongoing strategic thinking to make sure the business model is aligned with changing environmental opportunities and threats.

Strategic managers in companies throughout the industry are watching the cost leader and will move quickly to imitate its innovations because they also want to reduce their costs. Today, a differentiator cannot let a cost leader get too great a cost advantage because the leader might then be able to use its high profits to invest more in product differentiation and beat the differentiator at its own competitive game. For example, Toyota and Honda began as cost leaders, manufacturing simple low-priced cars. Their cars sold well, and they then invested their profits to design and make new models of cars that became increasingly differentiated in features and quality. Today, Toyota and Honda, with cars in every market segment, pursue a differentiation strategy, although Toyota also has the lowest cost structure of any global car company.

A cost leader must also respond to the strategic moves of its differentiated competitors and increase the quality and features of its products if it is to prosper in the long run. Even low-priced products, such as Timex watches and BIC razors, cannot be too inferior to the more expensive Seiko watches or Gillette razors if the lower-costs/lower-prices policy is to succeed. All business-level strategies play out with rivals closely watching each other's strategic moves. If Seiko brings out a novel kind of LCD watch dial or Gillette a three- or four-bladed razor, managers at Timex and BIC will respond within months by incorporating these innovations in their low-priced products if required. This situation is also very common in the high-priced women's fashion industry. As soon as the famous designers like Gucci and Dior have shown their spring and fall collections, their designs are copied and the plans transmitted to factories in Malaysia, where workers are ready to manufacture low-priced imitations that within months will reach low-price clothing retail stores around the world.

A business model like cost leadership should be thought of as a specific set of strategies that helps strategic managers stay focused on how to compete most effectively over time. It is all too easy for strategic managers, flush with the success of their cost-leadership strategy, to become less vigilant and lose sight of changes in the five forces of competition and in the macroenvironment that change the rules of the competitive game. McDonald's, long the cost leader in the fast-food industry, was surprised when rivals like Taco Bell began to offer 99-cent daily specials. McDonald's had to learn how to make fast food more cheaply to compete, and its managers have adopted new cooking techniques and food management practices that have ratcheted it down the experience curve, so that today 99-cent meals are a permanent fixture on McDonald's menu.

■ **Differentiation** A **differentiation** business model is based on pursuing a set of generic strategies that allows a company to achieve a competitive advantage by creating a product that customers perceive as different or distinct in some important way. A differentiator (that is, a differentiated company) has the ability to satisfy customers' needs in a way that its competitors cannot. This means that it can charge a premium price (one higher than that charged by its closest rivals). The ability to increase revenues by charging premium prices (rather than by reducing costs, as the cost leader does) allows the differentiator to reach the value frontier, outperform its competitors, and achieve superior profitability, as shown in Figure 5.6. As noted earlier, customers pay a premium price when they believe the product's differentiated qualities are worth the extra money. Consequently, differentiated products are often priced on the basis of what the market will bear.[17]

Mercedes-Benz cars are more expensive than the cars of its closest rivals because customers believe they offer more features and confer more status on their owners. Similarly, a BMW is not much more expensive to produce than a Honda, but its high price is determined by customers who want its distinctive sporty ride and the prestige of owning a BMW. (In fact, in Japan, BMW prices its entry cars quite modestly to attract young, well-heeled Japanese customers from Honda.) Similarly, Rolex watches do not cost much to produce, their design has not changed very much for years, and their gold content represents only a small fraction of the price. Customers, however, buy a Rolex because of the distinct qualities they perceive in it: its beautiful design, its intrinsic value, and its ability to confer status on its wearer.

■ **Strategic Choices** A differentiator invests its resources to gain a competitive advantage from superior innovation, excellent quality, and responsiveness to customer needs—the three principal routes to high product differentiation. For example, Procter & Gamble claims that its product quality is high and that Ivory soap is 99.44 percent pure. Maytag stresses reliability and the best repair record of any other washer on the market. IBM promotes the quality service provided by its well-trained sales force. Innovation is commonly the source of differentiation for technologically complex products, and many people pay a premium price for new and innovative products, such as a state-of-the-art computer, DVD player, or car.

When differentiation is based on responsiveness to customers, a company offers comprehensive after-sales service and product repair. This is an especially important consideration for complex products such as cars and domestic appliances, which are likely to break down periodically. Maytag, Dell Computer, and BMW all excel in responsiveness to customers. In service organizations, quality-of-service attributes are also very important. Neiman Marcus, Nordstrom, and FedEx can charge premium prices because they offer an exceptionally high level of service. Firms of lawyers, accountants, and consultants stress the service aspects of their operations to clients: their knowledge, professionalism, and reputation.

Finally, a product's appeal to customers' psychological desires is a source of differentiation. The appeal can be prestige or status, as it is with BMWs and Rolex watches; safety of home and family, as with Aetna or Prudential Insurance; or simply providing a superior shopping experience, as with Target and Macy's. Differentiation can also be tailored to age groups and socioeconomic groups. Indeed, the bases of differentiation are endless.

A company pursuing a business model based on differentiation frequently strives to differentiate itself along as many dimensions as possible. The less it resembles its rivals, the more it is protected from competition and the wider is its market appeal. Thus, BMWs offer more than prestige; they also offer technological sophistication, luxury, reliability, and good, although very expensive, repair service. All these bases of differentiation help increase sales.

Generally, a differentiator chooses to segment its market into many segments and niches, just as Samsung does. Strategic managers recognize the revenue-enhancing ability of being able to attract more customers willing to pay a premium price in each market segment. Some companies base their business models on offering a product designed for most market segments, but a company might choose to serve just the handful of segments in which it has a specific differentiation advantage. For example, Sony produces twenty-four models of television sets, filling all the niches from mid-priced to high-priced sets. However, its lowest-priced model is always priced about $60 above that of its competitors, bringing into play the premium-price factor. Consumers have to pay extra for a Sony. Similarly, although Mercedes-Benz has filled niches below its high-priced models with its S and C series, recently it has produced a car for the low-priced market segment. It sells this car only in Europe because it fears that introducing it in the United States would dilute its exclusive image and affect its differentiated appeal.

Finally, in choosing how to implement its business model, a differentiated company concentrates on developing distinctive competencies in the functions that provide the source of its competitive advantage. Differentiation on the basis of innovation and technological competency depends on the R&D function, as discussed in Chapter 4. Efforts to improve service to customers depend on the quality of the sales and customer service function.

Because developing a differentiation advantage is expensive, a differentiator has a higher cost structure than the cost leader does. However, building new competencies in the functions that sustain a company's differentiated appeal does not mean neglecting the cost structure. As noted earlier, the differentiator studies how the cost leader operates and attempts to copy cost-saving innovations that will reduce its costs while preserving the source of its competitive advantage. The differentiator must control all costs that do not contribute to its differentiation advantage so that the price of the product does not exceed what customers are willing to pay, as noted in Nordstrom's case. Otherwise, it risks letting the cost leader go upmarket and steal its customers. Also, since superior profitability is the result of controlling costs as well as maximizing value and revenues, it pays to watch costs closely. The key is not to minimize them to the point of losing the source of differentiation.[18] The owners of the famous Savoy Hotel in London, England, face just this problem. The Savoy's reputation has always been based on the incredibly high level of service it offers its customers. Three hotel employees serve the needs of each guest, and in every room, a guest can summon a waiter, maid, or valet by pressing a button at bedside. The cost of offering this level of service has been so high that the hotel makes less than 1 percent net profit every year.[19] Its owners try to find ways to reduce costs to increase profits, but if they reduce the number of hotel staff (the main source of the Savoy's high costs), they may destroy the main source of its differentiated appeal.

■ **Advantages and Disadvantages** The advantages of the differentiation strategy can also be discussed in the context of the five forces model. Differentiation safeguards a company against competitors to the degree that customers develop brand loyalty for its products, a valuable asset that protects the company on all fronts. Powerful suppliers are rarely a problem because the differentiated company's strategy is geared more toward the price it can charge than toward costs. Also, differentiators can often pass on price increases to customers because they are willing to pay the premium price. Thus, a differentiator can tolerate moderate increases in input prices better than the cost leader can. Differentiators are unlikely to experience problems with powerful buyers because they offer a distinct product. Only they can supply the product, and it commands brand loyalty. Differentiation and brand loyalty also create a barrier to entry for other companies seeking to enter the indus-

try. New companies are forced to develop their own distinctive competency to be able to compete, an expensive undertaking.

Finally, the threat of substitute products depends on the ability of competitors' products to meet the same customers' needs as the differentiator's products and to break customers' brand loyalty. This can happen; phone companies are suffering as alternative ways of making phone calls through digital fiber-optic cable, satellite, and the Internet are becoming increasingly available. The issue is how much of a premium price a company can charge for distinctness before customers switch products. In the phone industry, the answer is "not much"; the large carriers were forced to reduce prices drastically so that 2.5 cents a minute is a common rate, down from 37 cents just a decade ago.

The main problems with a differentiation strategy center on strategic managers' long-term ability to maintain a product's perceived difference or distinctness in customers' eyes. What has become increasingly apparent is how quickly agile competitors move to imitate and copy successful differentiators. This has happened across many industries, such as retailing, computers, autos, home electronics, telecommunications, and pharmaceuticals. Patents and first-mover advantages (the advantages of being the first to market a product or service) last only so long, and as the overall quality of products produced by all companies goes up, brand loyalty declines. The problems L.L. Bean has had in maintaining its competitive advantage, described in Strategy in Action 5.2, highlight many of the threats that face a differentiator.

■ **Implications and Conclusions** A business model based on differentiation requires a company to formulate and implement business-level strategies that reinforce each other and together increase the value of a good or service in the eyes of customers. When a product has distinctness in customers' eyes, differentiators can charge a premium price. The disadvantages of a differentiation strategy are the ease with which competitors can imitate a differentiator's product and the difficulty of maintaining a premium price. When differentiation stems from the design or physical features of the product, differentiators are at great risk because imitation is easy. The risk is that, over time, products such as DVD players or televisions become commodity-like products, for which the importance of differentiation diminishes as customers become more price sensitive. However, when differentiation stems from functional-level strategies that lead to superior service or reliability, or from any intangible source, such as FedEx's guarantee or the prestige of a Rolex, a company is much more secure. It is difficult to imitate intangibles, and the differentiator can reap the benefits of this strategy for a long time. Nevertheless, all differentiators must watch out for imitators and be careful that they do not charge a price higher than the market will bear.

■ **Focused Differentiation** As in the case of the focused cost leader, a company that pursues a business model based on **focused differentiation** chooses to specialize in serving the needs of one or two market segments or niches. Once it has chosen its market segment, a focused company positions itself using differentiation. If a company uses a focused differentiation approach, then all the means of differentiation that are open to the differentiator are available to the focused company. The point is that the focused company develops a business model that allows it to successfully position itself to compete with the differentiator in just one or a few segments. For example, Porsche, a focused company, competes against GM in the sports car and luxury SUV segments of the car market.

Strategy in Action   5.2

L.L. Bean's New Business Model

In 1911, Leon Leonwood Bean, a hunter who grew weary of walking miles with wet feet in search of game, decided he would invent a waterproof boot with leather uppers attached to a large rounded rubber base and sole. Soon he began selling his shoes through mail order, and as word spread about their reliability, backed by his policy of being responsive to customers who complained (often replacing their boots years after a sale), his company's reputation spread. As the years went by, L.L. Bean expanded its now well-known product line to include products such as its canvas tote bags and, of course, its flannel dog bed. By 2000 the company's mail order revenues exceeded $1 billion a year, and L.L. Bean became known for offering one of the broadest and highest-quality product lines of sporting clothes and accessories.

To display its product line, the company built a 160,000-square-foot signature store in Freeport, Maine, that stocks hundreds of versions of its backpacks, fleece vests, shirts, moccasins, tents, and other items, and over 3 million visitors a year shop its store. L.L. Bean established this store partly to give customers hands-on access to its products so that they would have a better understanding of the high quality they were being offered. Of course, L.L. Bean expects to command a premium price for offering such a wide variety of high-quality products, and historically it has enjoyed high profit margins. Customers buy its products for their personal use but also as gifts for friends and relatives.

Bean's business model began to suffer in the mid 1990s, however, when there was an explosion in the number of companies touting high-quality, high-priced products to customers, and Bean's catalogue lost its unique appeal. Furthermore, the growth of the Internet through the 1990s gave customers access to many more companies that offered quality products, often at much lower prices, such as Lands' End, which also began to feature fleece vests, dog baskets, and so on in its product lineup. The problem facing any differentiator is how to protect or defend the uniqueness of its products from imitators, who will always be seeking to steal away its customers by offering them similar kinds of products at reduced prices.

Finding ways to protect Bean's business model has proved to be a major challenge. Its catalogue sales have been stagnant for several years because customers have switched loyalty to lower-priced companies, just as Ryanair stole away business from its well-known but much higher-cost competitors, the national airlines. Bean's current CEO, Chris McCormick, is trying to craft some new strategies to help the company build its competitive advantage. One of these is to build a chain of L.L. Bean stores in major urban locations to show more customers the quality of its products and so attract them to either buy them there or to use its website; it hopes to have ten stores open by 2010. This has not proved easy to date, however, because physical retail stores have a high cost structure, and Bean has had to search for the right way to implement its strategy. It has also had to lower the price of its sporting clothes and accessories in these stores; it can longer charge premium prices. Another strategy has been to launch an aggressive advertising campaign aimed at younger customers who may not know the Bean story. Then, with physical stores, the Internet, and its catalogues it may have a better chance of getting their business.

The jury is out, however. Not only are other differentiated sporting goods chains expanding, such as Dick's Sporting Goods and Gander Mountain, but sites like amazon.com and landsend.com, now owned by Sears, are offering lower-priced products. Whether McCormick will be able to successfully change L.L. Bean's business model to allow it to reach the value creation frontier remains to be seen.[b]

For the focused differentiator, selecting a niche often means focusing on one type of customer, such as serving only the very rich, the very young, or the very adventurous; or focusing on only a segment of the product line, such as only on vegetarian foods or very fast automobiles, designer clothes, or sunglasses. Focused differentiators are able to reach the value frontier because they are frequently able to develop a differentiated product that better meets the needs of customers in a particular segment than a differentiator (Figure 5.6). For example, a focused differentiator may gain better knowledge of the needs of a small customer set (such as sports car buyers), knowledge of a region, or expertise in a particular field (such as corporate law, management consulting, or website management for retail customers or restaurants). Alternatively, it might develop superior skills in responsiveness to customers, based on its ability to serve the particular needs of regional or industry customers in ways that a national differentiator would find very expensive. Similarly, concentration on a narrow range of products sometimes allows a focuser to develop innovations more quickly than a large differentiator can.

The focuser does not attempt to serve all market segments because that would bring it into direct competition with the differentiator. Instead, it concentrates on building market share in one market segment; if it is successful, it may begin to serve more and more market segments and chip away at the differentiator's competitive advantage. However, if it is too successful at what it does, or if it does try to compete with the differentiator, it may run into trouble because the differentiator has the resources to imitate the focused company's business model. For example, when Ben & Jerry's innovated a luxury ice cream, their huge success led other companies like Haagen-Dazs and Godiva to bring out their own competing products. A good example of another luxury product made by a focused differentiator is profiled in Strategy in Action 5.3.

Strategy in Action   5.3

Up, Up, and Away in the Restaurant Business

The restaurant business is crowded with thousands of companies, ranging from giant fast-food chains like McDonald's and Taco Bell, through more upscale chains like The Outback and Chili's, all the way up to expensive gourmet restaurants, which typically are found in major cities. Some of these expensive restaurants also have several branches in different cities, such as Brennan's or Ruth's Chris Steak House, but many are just single-establishment operations, run by a well-trained and sometimes well-known chef, that attract customers because of the quality of their food or the ingenuity of their cuisine.

In this top echelon of restaurants, which compete by the quality of their food and the impeccable way in which their waiters anticipate, not just respond to, customer needs, the drive to excel and beat the competition is ever present. The world-famous chef Alaine Ducasse opened a restaurant called the Essex House in New York in 2000. He deliberately set out to design a prix fixe menu (one that offers a number of different courses at a fixed price) that was the most expensive one in the world. He charged $160 a person for his meals, and his restaurant has been packed every day by rich people wishing to taste his mouth-watering cuisine.

In adopting this focused approach, however, Ducasse simply seemed to be opening the door to a new wave of specialized competitors in this most expensive of all market niches. In 2003, Japanese chef Masayoshi Takayama decided to offer his exquisite sushi at a prix fixe price that starts at $300. Not to be outdone, Chef Ducasse then appointed another world-famous chef, Christian Delouvrier, to take over at the Essex House, and he has now designed a menu that starts with a prix fixe of $225 a person but can go up to $400, serving such dishes as baby sea scallops topped with caviar, pâté de foie gras (a luxurious duck paté), and the freshest possible exotic seafood cooked to perfection.

How can these restaurants attract customers when they ask such exorbitant prices? The answer is that they limit the number of seats in their restaurants, often serving just a hundred or fewer people a night, and customers often book months in advance. By limiting the supply of seats, they create a scarcity for their products that drives up the prices they can charge and allows them to make high profits in this tiny market segment.

As in the case of cost leadership, many companies that started with a focus differentiation strategy have grown to become the leading differentiators in their industry. Sometimes they have achieved this through internal growth and by issuing stocks and building debt to raise the capital they needed to expand their businesses—as amazon.com and Google have done. At other times, a focus company may expand quickly by taking over other focused companies and combining their resources. For example, Cisco Systems, the largest Internet router maker, grew to be the leading differentiator in its industry by buying over fifty small specialist software and hardware companies. Its managers believed these companies possessed the products and knowledge that would allow it to become the leader, and despite the downturn in e-commerce, Cisco remains the dominant industry competitor.

In summary, a focused differentiator can protect its competitive advantage and niche to the extent that it can provide a product or service that its rivals cannot, for example, by being close to its customers and responding to their changing needs. However, if the focuser's niche disappears over time because of technological change or changes in customers' tastes, it cannot move easily to new niches, and this can be a major danger. For example, clothing store chain Brooks Brothers, whose focus was on providing formal business attire, ran into great difficulty in the 1990s when business casual became the clothing norm at most companies. It found it hard to adapt to the changing market and was bought out in 2001. Similarly, corner diners have become almost a thing of the past because they are unable to compete with the low prices and speed of fast-food chains like McDonald's and the upscale atmosphere of Starbuck's. The disappearance of niches is one reason that so many small companies fail.

The Dynamics of Competitive Positioning

So far we have discussed the differences between the kinds of generic strategies companies use to formulate and implement a particular business model. Each of the four models just discussed can be thought of as an "ideal" type of competitive positioning that results in competitive advantage and above-average profitability. The companies that are able to use these models to position themselves at the frontier are the most successful in their industry. In most industries, however, while some companies are able to pursue business-level strategies that allow them to reach the value creation frontier and obtain superior performance, other companies are unable to reach this frontier and have average or below-average profitability. As Figure 5.8 shows, companies in the retail industry such as Neiman Marcus, Foley's, Target, Wal-Mart, and Costco reach this frontier, but others like Nordstrom, Dillard's, Sears, and Kmart do not. The question is, why are some companies in an industry able to reach this frontier while others fail—even when they seem to be using the same business model, such as Wal-Mart and Kmart? Moreover, companies that can continually outperform their rivals, such as Dell and Wal-Mart, are rare. Many successful companies lose their position on the frontier at some point in their history, and to turn around their declining performance they need to change their business models.

To understand why some companies perform better than others and why the performance of one company can change over time, it is necessary to understand the dynamics involved in positioning a company's business model so it can successfully compete in the long term. In this section we first explore why some companies are able to sustain superior performance. Then we examine why differences in performance among companies in an industry are to be expected and why some companies run into major problems that can affect their survival.

FIGURE 5.8

FIGURE 5.8

The Dynamics
of Competitive
Positioning

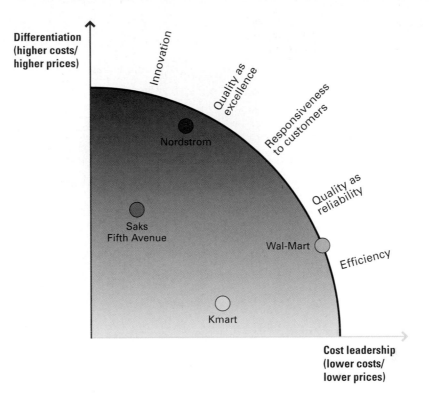

**Competitive
Positioning
for Superior
Performance**

Both differentiation and cost leadership are business models that can result in superior performance; many of the most successful companies in an industry are well known because they offer luxurious, excellent products or products that can be bought at a rock-bottom price. However, as we have emphasized throughout this chapter, no company can afford to ignore its cost structure. Managers must always try to find ways to reduce costs in this era of intense global competition in which new (focused) companies might appear with some kind of differentiation or cost advantage and use it to become a dominant competitor, as Toyota and Wal-Mart have done. At the same time, companies need to increase their market share to grow their profits over time, and this requires differentiation—finding new ways to increase product differentiation and market segmentation.

For these reasons, in the middle of the value creation frontier is an area occupied by companies whose intent is to develop business-level strategies to improve their differentiation and cost structure simultaneously. These **broad differentiators** also operate on the value frontier because they have chosen a level of differentiation that gives them a competitive advantage in the market segments they have targeted but have also pursued this strategy *in a way that has allowed them to lower their cost structure over time* (see Figure 5.9). Thus, although they may have higher costs than cost leaders, and offer a less differentiated product than differentiators, they have found a competitive position that offers their customers as much value as their industry rivals, and sometimes more. Broad differentiators continually use their distinctive competencies to increase the range of their products, and they are constantly seeking to enter new market segments to increase their market share to grow their profits.

FIGURE 5.9

The Broad
Differentiation
Business Model

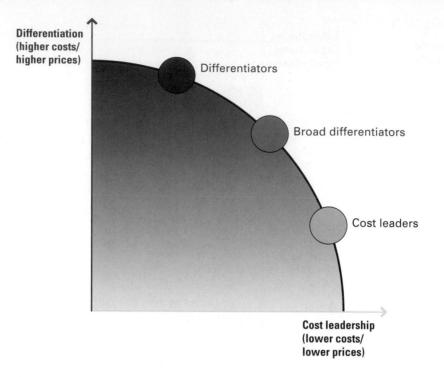

At the same time they also work continuously to find ways to lower their cost structure and increase their ROIC.

Importantly, the companies that have formulated and implemented the business-level strategies that enable them to get to this middle, or broadly differentiated, position may pose serious threats to both differentiators and cost leaders over time. These companies make a differentiated product that allows them to charge a premium price for their product compared to a cost leader. However, because of their low cost structure, they can choose to price their product with just *some "small" premium* over the price charged by cost leaders—and of course a much lower price than a differentiator has to charge to cover its higher cost structure. As a result, customers may now perceive the value offered by the broad differentiator's products to be well worth the premium price and so are attracted away from the cost leader's product. At the same time, those customers who are reluctant to pay the high premium price differentiators command may decide that the qualities of the broad differentiator's product (and its price) more than make up for the loss of the "extra" differentiated features of the luxury premium-priced products—such as a Mazda RX7 versus a Mercedes sports coupe or a regular pint of ice cream on sale versus a pint of Godiva.

Essentially, when they pursue their business model successfully, broad differentiators may steadily increase their market share over time; thus they grow their profits and gain increasing capital to reinvest in their business and continually improve their business model. And, in a dynamic, changing, competitive environment, this leads to a second problem for their rivals. Over time, their growing profits allow broad differentiators to invest in new technology that may both increase their differentiation advantage and lower their cost structure. As they build their competitive advantage, they become able to offer customers more and more value for money, which means that they push the value creation frontier to the right.

As broad differentiators constantly improve their business-level strategy to formulate and implement their broad differentiation business model, industry differentiators and cost leaders may find over time that they have lost the distinctive competencies that led to their superior performance. Toyota, profiled in Strategy in Action 5.4, provides a good example of a company that used a broad differentiation business model to put its rivals at a competitive disadvantage, with the result that today it is the second largest global carmaker by sales after GM, but many times as profitable as GM and most other global carmakers.

Strategy in Action   5.4

Toyota's Goal? A High-Value Vehicle to Match Every Customer Need

The car industry has always been one of the most competitive in the world because of the huge revenues and profits that are at stake: in 2004, annual global car sales were over $300 billion. It is small wonder, then, that industry rivalry has been increasing as carmakers have been fighting to develop new car models that better satisfy the needs of particular groups of buyers. One company at the forefront of these endeavors is Toyota.

Toyota, which pioneered lean production, produced its first car thirty years ago, an ugly, boxy affair that was, however, inexpensive. As the quality of its car became apparent, sales increased, and Toyota, which was then a focused cost leader, plowed back its profits into improving the styling of its vehicles and into efforts to continually reduce production costs. Over time, it used its low cost structure, including its efficient design processes, to produce an ever increasing range of reasonably priced vehicles tailored to different segments of the car market. By the 1980s its ability to go from the initial design stage to the production stage in two to three years allowed it to bring out new models faster than its competitors and to capitalize on the development of new market segments. Low costs and fast time to market have also allowed it to correct mistakes quickly if it designs a car that proves to have little market appeal—and Toyota has made mistakes.

In 1999, for example, Toyota brought out the Echo, a subcompact car that featured state-of-the-art engineering to deliver exceptional fuel economy: around fifty to sixty miles per gallon. The Echo was designed to be inexpensive to run and buy, and Toyota targeted this vehicle at buyers in their twenties, expecting them to appreciate these qualities. Its designers were disappointed when this age group displayed little enthusiasm for the car; its styling did not appeal to them even if its performance did fit their budget. The Echo's buyers turned out to be individuals in their forties who appreciated its economy and found it a useful second car to get around in.

Recognizing that they failed to position their product to hit the important market segment of young adults, the main car buyers of the future, Toyota's designers went back to the drawing board. Analyzing changing market trends and demographics, they sought to find the styling and features that would offer a car that was good-looking and fun to drive for this market segment and that could be sold for $16,000 to $18,000. Toyota (and several other carmakers) realized that perhaps the time was ripe for the return to the hatchback, but an updated version of it. Hatchbacks had been very popular in the early 1980s; however, the cars then were small and often had an ungainly appearance. Sales of hatchbacks had dropped off quickly when carmakers began to offer new sports utility vehicles and updated small sedans; by 1995, relatively few were available.

Drawing on its design and manufacturing competencies, Toyota's engineers updated and shaped the hatchback to suit the needs of the young adults in their twenties: the result was the Toyota Matrix, introduced in 2002 at a price starting at $17,000. The Matrix features revolutionary body styling reflective of much more expensive, sporty cars. It is spacious inside and geared to the needs of its intended young buyers; for example, seats fold back to allow for carrying a large cargo volume, and many storage bins and two-prong plugs for power outlets allow for the use of VCRs, MP3 players, and other devices. The message is that the Matrix is designed to be functional, fun, and a sporty ride. Then in 2003 Toyota introduced a new car, the Scion, once again a hybrid car designed to appeal to young people.

Toyota has also been a leader in positioning its whole range of vehicles to take advantage of emerging market segments. In the sports utility segment, its first offering was the expensive Toyota Land Cruiser, priced at over $35,000. Realizing the need for sports utility vehicles in other price ranges, it next introduced the 4Runner, priced at $20,000 and designed for the average sports utility customer; the RAV4, a small sports utility vehicle in the low $20,000 range, followed; then came the Sequoia, a bigger, more powerful version of the 4Runner in the upper $20,000 range. Finally, taking the technology from its Lexus R3000 vehicle, it introduced the luxury Highlander sports utility vehicle in the low $30,000 range. It now offers six models of sports utility vehicles, each offering a particular combination of price, size, performance, styling, and luxury to appeal to a particular customer group within the sports utility segment of the car market. Toyota also positions its sedans to appeal to different sets of buyers. For example, the

Camry, one of the best-selling cars in the United States, is targeted toward the middle of the market, to customers who can afford to pay about $25,000 and want a balance of luxury, performance, safety, and reliability. The Camry also has a small premium price relative to similar cars of its U.S. competitors, such as the Ford Taurus and the GM Impala.

Toyota's broad differentiation business model is based, on the demand side, at making a range of vehicles that optimizes the amount of value it can create for different groups of customers. On the supply side, the number of models it makes is constrained by the need to maintain a low cost structure and to choose the car-pricing options that will generate maximum sales revenues and profits. The decision about how many kinds of vehicles to produce is also affected by the strategies of its rivals, for they are also trying to determine the optimum range of cars to produce. Toyota was not alone in its decision to produce a hatchback in 2002; other noticeable competitors included BMW, which introduced the redesigned Mini Cooper; Honda's new Civic hatchbacks; the already well-received PT Cruiser from DaimlerChrysler; and Ford's Focus. In fact, the number of hatchback models doubled between 2000 and 2002, as did the expected number of sales (to 650,000 vehicles). Competition in this market segment is now intense. Each car company needs to anticipate the actions of its rivals, and each hopes, like Toyota, that it has made the right choices to obtain a large share of customers in this important market segment.[c]

Why has Toyota been so successful in pursuing a business model based on broad differentiation? Toyota is a leader in continuously improving manufacturing techniques to lower its cost structure. Recall that changes in technology, such as the constantly improving flexible manufacturing technologies we discussed in Chapter 4, as well as new digital, electronic, and information technologies (which we examine in detail in Chapter 7), have made it possible for all companies to reduce their cost structure if they can implement it in the right way. New technologies also provide many opportunities to increase product differentiation while maintaining a low cost structure. Technological developments often provide many ways for a company that has traditionally pursued a pure differentiation strategy to do so at a significantly lower cost so that it can choose a lower pricing option and build demand.

Companies like Toyota are continuously experimenting with new ways to reduce costs and segment their markets. The use of robots and flexible manufacturing cells reduces the costs of retooling the production line, and the costs associated with small production runs make it much easier to produce a wide variety of vehicle models and maintain an efficient cost structure. Today, flexible manufacturing enables a company pursuing differentiation to manufacture a range of products at a cost comparable to that of the cost leader. BMW, for example, has taken advantage of flexible manufacturing technologies to reduce its costs, and it has also chosen to charge only a modest premium price to boost its sales revenues. This new strategy has worked: its market share and profitability have increased in recent years.

Indeed, the ability of flexible manufacturing to substantially reduce the costs of differentiating products has promoted the trend toward market fragmentation and niche marketing in many consumer goods industries, such as mobile phones, computers, and appliances. Another way that a differentiated producer may be able to realize significant economies of scale is by standardizing many of the component parts used in its end products. Toyota's various models of sports utility vehicles are built on only three different car platforms. As a result, Toyota is able to realize significant economies of scale in the manufacture and bulk purchase of standardized component parts, despite its high level of market segmentation.

The way in which a business model based on broad differentiation can disrupt industry competition and change the rules of the competitive game is illustrated in Figure 5.10, which contrasts the car industry as it was in the days of mass production with the industry in the days of lean production. The value frontier (V_0) represents the most value that could be produced using mass-production technology, and at this time GM was the broad differentiator, with its five divisions producing cars that gave it an 80 percent share of the U.S. car market. Toyota is shown as the focused cost leader on the value creation frontier because it was learning the skills involved in lean production. On the other hand, Porsche and Jaguar are shown as

FIGURE 5.10

Using a Business Model to Push Out the Value Creation Frontier

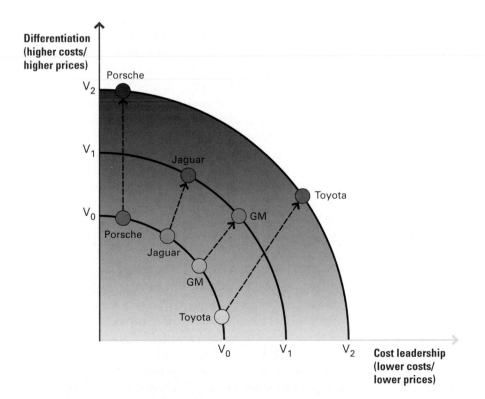

the differentiators on the value frontier: their pricey cars sold because of their innovative features, exceptional styling, and European origin.

On the V_0 frontier GM was the dominant company, but as Toyota grew, its continuous ability to make high-quality cars in an efficient way and then to expand into more and more market segments changed the rules of the competitive game. Today, in an era of lean production, Toyota is the successful broad differentiator and has pushed out the value frontier to V_2, meaning that customers now receive substantially more performance, safety, and luxury from their cars than they did ten or twenty years ago; in essence, they get more "value for their money." Where is GM today? To survive, GM has had to develop skills in lean manufacturing, and these have allowed it to move up to the V_1 frontier. However, GM cannot match Toyota's low cost structure, and it has also had to dramatically cut the number of models it offers customers because it cannot sell its cars at profitable prices. By 2004 its market share had fallen to 26 percent, and today it is creating far less value than Toyota, something reflected in its ROIC and stock price.

Jaguar, now owned by Ford, is also in a desperate position. Ford has tried to reduce Jaguar's cost structure and strengthen its styling and image, which has always been the key to its cars' differentiated appeal. By 2004, it was clear its strategies had not worked: demand for Jaguars has been falling while demand for BMWs, Mercedes, and Lexus's has been soaring. As for Porsche, it also had to learn lean production skills; however, its task is a little easier because it only produces a few sports car models. In addition, its engineers have kept their performance and handling at the leading edge of technological developments, so that today Porsche enjoys record sales and profits. Toyota and Porsche are on the value frontier at V_2; although GM and Jaguar have moved forward to V_1, their enormous losses in the last twenty years because of their failure to reach the value creation frontier have led to major falls in their market share and profits. Intense competition from ever advancing technology and from countries like China that have low-cost labor has been transforming competition in many industries, including the car industry. Increasingly carmakers have been trying to find ways to compete with Toyota and reach the new value frontier—however, Toyota is continually pushing the frontier out to the right.

One set of business-level strategies a broad differentiator commonly uses to maintain a low cost structure is to make a vehicle targeted at one segment of the global market and then allow only limited customization of that vehicle. Increasingly, for example, carmakers throughout the world are offering customers a mid-priced sedan with an economy, luxury, or sports package to appeal to this principal market segment. Package offerings substantially lower manufacturing costs because long production runs of the various packages are possible. Once again, the company is getting gains from differentiation and from low cost at the same time. Just-in-time inventory systems can also help reduce costs and improve the quality and reliability of a company's products. Toyota's cost of goods sold is the lowest of any carmaker, and although Ford and Chrysler have spent billions to lower their costs, Toyota continues to push the value frontier out to the right, as already mentioned. In 2004, for example, its hybrid car, the Prius, which is powered by both a gasoline engine and a battery, became popular because of rising gas prices. Toyota has licensed the rights to use its hybrid technology to Ford and GM, and more and more companies are planning to bring out a range of hybrid vehicles.

Finally, many companies, such as Dell and amazon.com, have been using the Internet and e-commerce as a way of becoming a broad differentiator. Both of these companies have been rapidly expanding the range of products they offer customers and taking advantage of their highly efficient materials-management systems to drive down costs compared to bricks-and mortar retailers. The Internet is a highly cost-effective way to inform millions of potential customers about the nature and quality of a company's products. Also, when customers do their own work on the Internet, such as by managing their own finances, stock trades, bill paying, travel booking, and purchasing, a company has shifted these costs to the customer and is no longer bearing them. Direct selling to the customer also avoids the need to use wholesalers and other intermediaries, which results in great cost savings. It has been estimated that 40 percent of the profit in a new car goes to the dealership that sells the car and for costs such as those associated with marketing the car.

■ **Competitive Positioning and Strategic Groups** As the preceding discussion suggests, competition in an industry is dynamic. New developments such as (1) technological innovations that permit increased product differentiation, (2) the identification of new customer groups and market segments, and (3) the continual discovery of better ways to implement a business model to lower the cost structure continually change the competitive forces at work in an industry. In such a dynamic situation, the competitive position of companies can change rapidly. Some companies are able to gain from positioning themselves competitively to pursue broad differentiation. On the other hand, companies that are slow to recognize how their competitive position is changing because of the actions of their rivals may find their competitive advantage and ability to make above-average profits disappearing. Strategic-group analysis, which we discuss in Chapter 2, is a useful tool to help companies in an industry better understand the dynamics of competitive positioning so they can position themselves to achieve superior performance.

A company's business model determines how it will compete for customers in a particular market segment, market, or industry, and typically several companies are competing for the same set of customers. This means that the business-level strategies pursued by one company affect the strategies pursued by the others, and over time companies competing for the same customers become rivals locked in a competitive struggle. The goal is to be the company that reaches or pushes out the value frontier to obtain a competitive advantage and achieve above-average profitability.

Within most industries, strategic groups emerge, with all companies within each group pursuing a similar business model.[20] All companies in an industry competing to be the cost leader form one strategic group, all those seeking some form of differentiation advantage form another, and companies that have developed a broad differentiation strategy constitute another strategic group. Companies pursuing focused differentiation or focused cost leadership form yet other strategic groups.

The concept of strategic groups has a number of implications for competitive positioning. First, strategic managers must map their competitors according to their choice of business model. They can then identify the sets of strategies their rivals have decided to pursue, such as what customers' needs to satisfy, which customer groups to serve, and which distinctive competencies to develop. They can then use this knowledge to position themselves closer to customers and differentiate themselves from their competitors. In other words, careful strategic-group analysis allows managers to uncover the most important bases of competition in an industry and to identify products and market segments where they can compete most successfully for customers. Such analysis also helps to reveal what competencies are likely to be most valuable in the future so that companies can make the right investment decision. For example, the need to develop new models of cars that can be sold across the world and are assembled reliably by low-cost labor has dominated competitive positioning in the global car industry. U.S. car companies have bought or formed alliances with almost every foreign car manufacturer to obtain marketing, design, or manufacturing knowledge.

Second, once a company has mapped its competitors, it can better understand how changes taking place in the industry are affecting its relative standing vis-à-vis differentiation and cost structure, as well as identify opportunities and threats. Often a company's nearest competitors are those companies in its strategic group that are pursuing a similar business model. Customers tend to view the products of such companies as direct substitutes for each other. Thus, a major threat to a company's profitability can arise from within its own strategic group when one or more companies find ways to either improve product differentiation and get closer to customers or lower their cost structure. This is why today companies benchmark their closest competitors on major performance dimensions to determine if they are falling behind in some important respect. For example, UPS and FedEx are constantly examining each other's performance.

Because strategic-group analysis also forces managers to focus on the activities of companies in other strategic groups, it helps them to identify emerging threats from companies outside their strategic group, such as when a focused company has devised a business model that will bring sweeping changes to the industry. It also helps them understand opportunities that might be arising because of changes in the environment; in response to these changes, they might purchase a focused company and implement its business model across the entire company to absorb the threat.

Recall from Chapter 2 that different strategic groups can have a different standing with respect to each of Porter's five competitive forces because these forces affect companies in different ways. In other words, the risk of new entry by potential competitors, the degree of rivalry among companies within a group, the bargaining power of buyers, the bargaining power of suppliers, and the competitive force of substitute products can all vary in intensity among different strategic groups within the same industry. In the global car industry, for example, the smaller focused differentiators and cost leaders ran into trouble in the 1990s. Their input costs were rising, and they could not afford billions of dollars to design new models and build the new flexible manufacturing plants needed to produce them. Indeed, some European, Korean, and even Japanese companies started to lose billions of dollars. Large U.S. and European carmakers, which were also suffering from the emergence of Toyota and Honda as broad differentiators, realized that they had to reduce their cost structure to survive. The need to compete with Toyota and Honda led to a huge wave of global merger activity that has left just a handful of global giants to compete in the 2000s. For example, Daimler Benz took over Chrysler Suzuki, GM took control of Isuzu and Saab, Ford merged with Mazda and took over Jaguar and Volvo, and Renault took a controlling stake in Nissan to learn lean production techniques. Thus, the strategic group map in the global car industry changed dramatically. Today, only a handful of focused companies like BMW and Porsche remain, and even they have forged alliances with other carmakers. If they make a mistake in managing their business models, they will also become a target for one of the large global companies seeking to increase product differentiation.

In sum, strategic-group analysis involves identifying and charting the business models and business-level strategies that industry rivals are pursuing. Managers can then determine which strategies are successful and unsuccessful and why a certain business model is working or not. Importantly, they can also analyze how the relative competitive position of industry rivals, both those pursuing the same business model and those pursuing different business models, is changing over time. This knowledge allows them to either fine-tune or radically alter their business models and strategies to improve their competitive position.

■ **Failures in Competitive Positioning**

Successful competitive positioning requires that a company achieve a fit between its strategies and its business model. Thus, a cost leader cannot strive for a high level of market segmentation, as a differentiator does, and provide a wide range of products because those choices would raise its cost structure too much and the company would lose its low-cost advantage. Similarly, a differentiator with a competency in innovation that tries to reduce its expenditures on research and development, or one with a competency in after-sales service that seeks to economize on its sales force to decrease costs, is asking for trouble because it has implemented its business model in the wrong way.

To pursue a successful business model, managers must be careful to ensure that the set of business-level strategies they have formulated and implemented are working in harmony to support each other and do not result in conflicts that ruin the competitive position a company is aiming for through its choice of business model. Many companies, through neglect, ignorance, or error—perhaps because of the Icarus paradox discussed in Chapter 1—do not work to continually improve their business model, do not perform strategic-group analysis, and often fail to identify and respond to changing opportunities and threats in the industry environment. As a result, the company's business model starts to fail because its business-level strategies do not work together and its profitability starts to decline. Sometimes its performance can decline so quickly that the company is taken over by other companies or goes bankrupt.

These companies have lost their position on the value frontier, either because they have lost the source of their competitive advantage or because their rivals have found ways to push out the value creation frontier and leave them behind. Sometimes these companies initially pursued a successful cost-leadership or differentiation business model but then gradually began to pursue business-level strategies that worked against them. Unfortunately, it seems that most companies lose control of their business models over time, often because they become large, complex companies that are difficult to manage or because the environment is changing faster than they can change their business model—such as by adjusting product and market choices to suit changing industry conditions. This is why it is so important that managers *think strategically*.

In Chapter 1, we defined *strategic intent* as the way managers think about where they want their organization to be in the future and what kinds of resources and capabilities they will need to achieve this vision. Strategic intent provides a company with a sense of direction and stretches managers at all levels to be more inventive or innovative and to think how to make better use of resources. Moreover, it "implies a competitive distinct point of view about the future; it holds out to employees the promise of exploring new competitive territory."[21] The experience of Holiday Inns described in Strategy in Action 5.5 shows how a company can lose control of its business model, but also how managers can change it to suit the changing competitive landscape.

There are many factors that can cause a company to make competitive positioning errors. While some focused companies may succeed spectacularly for a time, a focuser can also make a major error when, in its rush to implement its business

Strategy in Action   5.5

Holiday Inns on Six Continents

The history of the Holiday Inns motel chain is one of the great success stories in U.S. business. Its founder, Kemmons Wilson, vacationing in the early 1950s, found motels to be small, expensive, and of unpredictable quality. This discovery, along with the prospect of unprecedented highway travel that would come with the new interstate highway program, triggered a realization: there was an unmet customer need—a gap in the market for quality accommodations. Holiday Inns was founded to meet that need. From the beginning, Holiday Inns set the standard for offering motel features such as air conditioning and icemakers while keeping room rates reasonable. These amenities enhanced the motels' popularity, and motel franchising, Wilson's invention, made rapid expansion possible. By 1960, Holiday Inns could be found in virtually every city and on every major highway. Before the 1960s ended, more than one thousand of them were in full operation, and occupancy rates averaged 80 percent. The concept of mass accommodation had arrived.

The service Holiday Inns offered appealed to the average traveler, who wanted a standardized product (a room) at an average price—the middle of the hotel room market. But by the 1970s, travelers were beginning to make different demands on hotels and motels. Some wanted luxury and were willing to pay higher prices for better accommodations and service. Others sought low prices and accepted rock-bottom quality and service in exchange. As the market fragmented into different groups of customers with different needs, Holiday Inns was still offering an undifferentiated, average-cost, average-quality product.

Although Holiday Inns missed the change in the market and thus failed to respond appropriately to it, the competition did not. Companies such as Hyatt siphoned off the top end of the market, where quality and service sold rooms. Chains such as Motel 6 and Days Inns captured the basic-quality, low-price end of the market. In between were many specialty chains that appealed to business travelers, families, or self-caterers (people who

want to be able to cook in their hotel rooms). Holiday Inns' position was attacked from all sides. As occupancy rates dropped drastically with increasing competition, profitability declined.

Wounded but not dead, Holiday Inns began a counterattack. The original chain was upgraded to suit quality-oriented travelers. Then to meet the needs of different kinds of travelers, Holiday Inns created new hotel and motel chains: the luxury Crowne Plazas; the Hampton Inns serving the low-priced end of the market; and the all-suite Embassy Suites. Thus Holiday Inns attempted to meet the demands of the many niches, or segments, of the hotel market that have emerged as customers' needs have changed over time. These moves were successful in the early 1990s, and Holiday Inns grew to become one of the largest suppliers of hotel rooms in the industry. However, by the late 1990s, falling revenues made it clear that with intense competition in the industry from other chains such as Marriott, Holiday Inns was once again losing its differentiated appeal.

In the fast-changing hotel and lodging market, positioning each hotel brand or chain to maximize customer demand is a continuing endeavor. In 2000, the pressure on all hotel chains to adapt to the challenges of global competition and become globally differentiated brands led to the takeover of Holiday Inns and its incorporation into the international Six Continents Hotels chain. Today, around the globe, more than 3,200 hotels flying the flags of Holiday Inn, Holiday Inn Express, Crowne Plaza, Staybridge Suites by Holiday Inn, and luxury Inter-Continental Hotels and Resorts are positioning themselves to offer the services, amenities, and lodging experiences that will cater to virtually every travel occasion and guest need. In the 2000s, the company has undertaken a massive modernization campaign in the United States to take existing full-service Holiday Inns to their next evolution. Holiday Inns plans to have a room to meet the need of every segment of the lodging market anywhere in the world.[d]

model, it overexpands and so loses control of its business model. Take People Express, a U.S. airline that was the first cost leader to emerge after deregulation of the U.S. airline industry. It started out as a specialized air carrier serving a narrow market niche: low-priced travel on the eastern seaboard. In pursuing focused cost leadership, it was very successful, but in its rush to expand to other geographic regions it decided to take over other airlines. These airlines were differentiators that had never pursued cost leadership, and the move raised the company's cost structure and it lost its competitive advantage against the other national carriers. In the end, People Express was swallowed up by Texas Air and incorporated into Continental Airlines. Herb Kelleher, the founder of Southwest Airlines, watched how People Express had failed, and he stuck to the cost-leadership business model. He took *twenty* years to build his national airline, but he never deviated from the strategies necessary to pursue cost leadership.

Interestingly, in 2004 Southwest announced it might do away with its strategy of no seat reservations and might make other changes to deal with its expanding route structure. This means that its top managers need to be vigilant in managing its cost structure. Another focus differentiator that ran into problems in 2004 was Krispy Kreme Doughnuts, which began to expand the number of its stores rapidly in the 2000s as demand for its tasty product soared. By 2004, its cost structure was out of control, and its failure to implement its business model, combined with the fall in the demand for doughnuts because of the Atkins diet craze, resulted in its first loss. By the end of 2004 the value of its stock had declined by 80 percent. The question is, can it recover?

Differentiators can also fail in the market and end up stuck in the middle if focused competitors attack their markets with more specialized or low-cost products that blunt their competitive edge. This happened to IBM in the large-frame computer market as PCs became more powerful and able to do the job of the much more expensive mainframes. Of course, the increasing movement toward flexible manufacturing has aggravated the problems facing both cost leaders and differentiators. No company is safe in the jungle of competition, and each must be constantly on the lookout to take advantage of competitive advantages as they arise.

In sum, strategic managers must employ the tools discussed in this book to continually monitor how well the business-level strategies that formulate and implement their company's business model are working. There is no more important task than ensuring that their company is optimally positioned against its rivals to compete for customers. And, as we have discussed, the constant changes occurring in the external environment, as well as through the actions of competitors who work to push out the value frontier, make competitive positioning a complex, demanding task that requires the highest degree of strategic thinking. This is why companies pay tens of millions of dollars a year to CEOs and other top managers who have demonstrated their ability to create and sustain successful business models.

Summary of Chapter

1. To create a successful business model, managers must choose business-level strategies that give a company a competitive advantage over its rivals; that is, they must optimize competitive positioning. They must first decide on (1) customer needs, or what is to be satisfied, (2) customer groups, or who is to be satisfied, and (3) distinctive competencies, or how customer needs are to be satisfied. These decisions determine which strategies they formulate and implement to put a company's business model into action.

2. Customer needs are desires, wants, or cravings that can be satisfied through the attributes or characteristics of a product. Customers choose a product based on (1) the way a product is differentiated from other products of its type and (2) the price of the product. Product differentiation is the process of designing products to satisfy customers' needs in ways that competing

products cannot. Companies that create something distinct or different can often charge a higher, or premium, price for their product.

3. If managers devise strategies to differentiate a product by innovation, excellent quality, or responsiveness to customers, they are choosing a business model based on offering customers differentiated products. If managers base their business model on finding ways to reduce costs, they are choosing a business model based on offering customers low-priced products.

4. The second main choice in formulating a successful business model is to decide which kind of product(s) to offer to which customer group(s). Market segmentation is the way a company decides to group customers, based on important differences in their needs or preferences, in order to gain a competitive advantage.

5. There are three main approaches toward market segmentation. First, a company might choose to ignore differences and make a product targeted at the average or typical customer. Second, a company can choose to recognize the differences between customer groups and make a product targeted toward most or all of the different market segments. Third, a company might choose to target just one or two market segments.

6. To develop a successful business model, strategic managers have to devise a set of strategies that determine (1) how to differentiate and price their product, and (2) how much to segment a market and how wide a range of products to develop. Whether these strategies will result in a profitable business model now depends on strategic managers' ability to provide customers with the most value while keeping their cost structure viable.

7. The value creation frontier represents the maximum amount of value that the products of different companies inside an industry can give customers at any one time by using different business models. Companies on the value frontier are those that have the most successful business models in a particular industry.

8. The value creation frontier can be reached by choosing among four *generic competitive strategies:* cost leadership, focused cost leadership, differentiation, and focused differentiation.

9. A cost-leadership business model is based on lowering the company's cost structure so it can make and sell goods or services at a lower cost than its rivals. A cost leader is often a large, national company that targets the average customer. Focused cost leadership is developing the right strategies to serve just one or two market segments.

10. A differentiation business model is based on creating a product that customers perceive as different or distinct in some important way. Focused differentiation is providing a differentiated product for just one or two market segments.

11. The middle of the value creation frontier is occupied by broad differentiators, which have pursued their differentiation strategy in a way that has also allowed them to lower their cost structure over time.

12. Strategic-group analysis helps companies in an industry better understand the dynamics of competitive positioning. In strategic-group analysis, managers identify and chart the business models and business-level strategies their industry rivals are pursuing. Then they can determine which strategies are successful and unsuccessful and why a certain business model is working or not. In turn, this allows them to either fine-tune or radically alter their business models and strategies to improve their competitive position.

13. Many companies, through neglect, ignorance, or error, do not work to continually improve their business model, do not perform strategic-group analysis, and often fail to identify and respond to changing opportunities and threats. As a result, their business-level strategies do not work together, their business model starts to fail, and their profitability starts to decline. There is no more important task than ensuring that one's company is optimally positioned against its rivals to compete for customers.

Discussion Questions

1. Why does each generic business model require a different set of business-level strategies? Give examples of pairs of companies in (a) the computer industry, (b) the electronics industry, and (c) the fast-food industry that pursue different types of business models?

2. How do changes in the environment affect the success of a company's business model?

3. What is the value creation frontier? How does each of the four generic business models allow a company to reach this frontier?

4. How can companies pursuing cost leadership and differentiation lose their place on the value frontier? In what ways can they regain their competitive advantage?

5. How can a focused company push the value frontier to the right? How does this affect other industry competitors? On the other hand, how can changes in the value frontier threaten focused companies?

6. Why is strategic-group analysis important for superior competitive positioning?

7. What are some of the reasons companies lose control over their business models, and thus their competitive advantage, over time?

Practicing Strategic Management

■ SMALL-GROUP EXERCISE
Finding a Strategy for a Restaurant

Break up into groups of three to five people, and discuss the following scenario. You are a group of partners contemplating opening a new restaurant in your city. You are trying to decide how to position your restaurant to give it the best competitive advantage.

1. Create a strategic-group map of the restaurants in your city by analyzing their generic business models and strategies. What are the similarities or differences between these groups?
2. Identify which restaurants you think are the most profitable and why.
3. On the basis of this analysis, decide what kind of restaurant you want to open and why.

■ ARTICLE FILE 5

Find an example (or several examples) of a company pursuing one of the generic business models. What set of business-level strategies does the company use to formulate and implement its business model? How successful has the company been?

■ STRATEGIC MANAGEMENT PROJECT
Module 5

This part of the project focuses on the nature of your company's business model and business-level strategies. If your company operates in more than one business, concentrate on either its core, or most central, business or on its most important businesses. Using all the information you have collected on your company so far, answer the following questions:

1. How differentiated are the products or services of your company? What is the basis of their differentiated appeal?
2. What is your company's strategy toward market segmentation? If it segments its market, on what basis does it do so?
3. What distinctive competencies does your company have? (Use the information on functional-level strategy in the last chapter to answer this question.) Is efficiency, quality, innovation, responsiveness to customers, or a combination of these factors the main driving force in your company?
4. What generic business model is your company pursuing? How has it formulated and implemented a set of business-level strategies to pursue this business model?
5. What are the advantages and disadvantages associated with your company's choice of business model and strategies?
6. Is your company a member of a strategic group in an industry? If so, which one?
7. How could you improve your company's business model and strategies to strengthen its competitive advantage?

■ EXPLORING THE WEB
Visiting the Luxury Car Market

Enter the websites of three luxury carmakers, such as Lexus (**www.lexususa.com**), BMW (**www.bmw.com**), and Cadillac (**www.cadillac.com, www.gm.com**), all of which compete in the same strategic group. Scan the sites to determine the key features of each company's business model and strategies. In what ways are their business models and strategies similar and different? Which of these companies do you think has a competitive advantage over the others?

General Task Search the Web for a company that is a differentiator, cost leader, or broad differentiator. What specific set of strategies does the company use to pursue its business model? How successful has it been in its industry? Has it reached the value frontier?

Closing Case

How E*TRADE Uses the Internet to Gain a Low-Cost Advantage

In many industries, new entrants have taken advantage of the opportunities opened up by the Internet to overcome barriers to entry and compete successfully against market leaders. Consider the situation of E*TRADE, the online brokerage company. For many years, large, established brokerages like Merrill Lynch had dominated the industry and used their protected positions to charge high brokerage fees. E*TRADE's managers bought and developed software and hardware that allowed their customers to make their own trades and to do so at a price as low as $19.95.

The low-cost competition story in the brokerage industry did not stop there. By 1999, E*TRADE itself had come under pressure from a new generation of online brokerage houses such as Suretrade, Ameritrade, and DLJ, which began offering customers trades for only $9.95 and even $7.95, undercutting E*TRADE's prices by 100 percent. How could E*TRADE, which had made its reputation by being the low-cost leader in the industry, compete against companies boasting that they were the new cost leaders?

The answer for E*TRADE was to enhance its differentiated appeal to its customers by offering a higher quality of service and a broader product line. E*TRADE introduced a new software package that made it even easier for customers to use the Internet to trade shares. Very importantly, the new software was more reliable in that customers were able to make their trades when they wanted. Previously, E*TRADE, like other brokerage companies, had experienced many problems when too many customers made trades at once; often the overloaded system simply crashed, and customers were unable to buy or sell shares. In addition, E*TRADE's new package offered customers more financial research tools and gave them access to more information about specific companies to aid in their investment decisions. E*TRADE also offered customers increased access to real-time stock quotes so that they could take advantage of second-to-second changes in stock prices. Finally, it offered customers the opportunity to invest in initial public offerings of shares from new companies, where both potential risks and returns are high.

In 1999, E*TRADE decided to merge with an online bank, TeleBank, so that it could offer its customers a broad range of online banking services, such as bill paying online, and thus become a one-stop online shopping site for all of a customer's financial needs. It also took over a variety of other insurance and financial service companies to offer its customers a broad financial service product line.

The realization that it could not just be a low-cost company but also had to create a differentiation advantage in the quickly evolving online financial services industry has paid off for E*TRADE. Its customers did not switch to the new low-cost leaders because they perceived that they were receiving extra value in terms of service and reliability for the $19.95 price. E*TRADE's customer accounts have increased steadily, and its stock price has risen as investors perceive that the company's competitive advantage is sustainable and that it is likely to remain a dominant player in the changed industry environment. Indeed, E*TRADE has shown the other companies in the industry that, to remain viable, they must all pursue a differentiation strategy to attract customers, even as they do all they can to control their cost structure.[22]

Case Discussion Questions

1. How have E*TRADE's business model and business-level strategies changed over time?

2. What is happening in the stockbrokerage industry today? How has E*TRADE been altering its business model and strategies to compete?

Chapter 6

Business-Level Strategy and the Industry Environment

Opening Case

Nike's Winning Ways

Nike, headquartered in Beaverton, Oregon, was founded over thirty years ago by Bill Bowerman, a former University of Oregon track coach, and Phil Knight, an entrepreneur in search of a profitable business opportunity. Bowerman's goal was to dream up a new kind of sneaker tread that would enhance a runner's traction and speed, and he came up with the idea for Nike's "waffle tread" after studying the waffle iron in his home. Bowerman and Knight made their shoe and began by selling it out of the trunks of their car at track meets. From this small beginning Nike has grown into a company that sold over $12 billion worth of shoes in the $35 billion athletic footwear and apparel industries in 2004.[1]

Nike's amazing growth came from its business model, which has always been based on two original functional strategies: to innovate state-of-the-art athletic shoes and then to publicize the qualities of its shoes through dramatic "guerrilla" marketing. Nike's marketing is designed to persuade customers that its shoes are not only superior but also a high fashion statement and a necessary part of a lifestyle based on sporting or athletic interests. A turning point came in 1987 when Nike increased its marketing budget from $8 million to $48 million to persuade customers its shoes were the best. A large part of this advertising budget soon went to pay celebrities like Michael Jordan millions of dollars to wear and champion its products. The company has consistently pursued this strategy: in 2003 it signed basketball star LeBron James to a $90 million endorsement contract, and many other sporting stars, such as Tiger Woods and Serena Williams, are already part of its charmed circle.

Nike's strategy to emphasize the uniqueness of its product has obviously paid off; its market share soared and its revenues hit $9.6 billion in 1998. However, 1998 was also a turning point, for in that year sales began to fall. Nike's $200 Air Jordans no longer sold like they used to, and inventory built up in stores and warehouses. Suddenly it seemed much harder to design new shoes that customers perceived to be significantly better. Nike's stunning growth in sales was actually reducing its profitability; somehow it had lost control of its business model. Phil Knight, who had resigned his management position, was forced to resume the helm and lead the company out of its troubles. He recruited a team of talented top managers from leading consumer products companies to help him improve Nike's business model. As a result, Nike has changed its business model in some fundamental ways.

In the past, Nike shunned sports like golf, soccer, rollerblading, and so on and focused most of its efforts on making shoes for the track and basketball market to build its market share in this area. However, when its sales started to fall, it realized that using marketing to increase sales in a particular market segment can only grow sales and profits so far; it needed to start to sell more types of shoes to more segments of the athletic shoe market. So Nike took its design and marketing competencies and began to craft new lines of shoes for new market segments. For example, it launched a line of soccer shoes and perfected their design over time, and by 2004 it had won the biggest share of the soccer market from its archrival Adidas.[2] In addition, in 2004 it launched its Total 90 III shoes, which are aimed at the millions of casual soccer players throughout the world who want a shoe they can just "play" in. Once more, Nike's dramatic marketing campaigns aim to make their shoes part of the "soccer lifestyle," to persuade customers that traditional sneakers do not work because soccer shoes are sleeker and fit the foot more snugly.

To take advantage of its competencies in design and marketing, Nike then decided to enter new market segments by purchasing other footwear companies that offered shoes that extended or complemented its product lines.[3] For example, it bought Converse, the maker of retro-style sneakers; Hurley International, which makes skateboards and Bauer in-line and hockey skates; and Official Starter, a licensor of athletic shoes and apparel whose brands include the low-priced Shaq brand. Allowing Converse to take advantage of Nike's in-house competencies has resulted in dramatic increases in the sales of its sneakers, and Converse has made an important contribution to Nike's profitability.[4]

Nike had also entered another market segment when it bought Cole Haan, the dress shoemaker, in the 1980s. Now it is searching for other possible acquisitions. It decided to enter the athletic apparel market to use its skills there, and by 2004 sales were over $1 billion. In making all these changes to its business model, Nike was finding ways to invest its capital in new products where it could increase its market share and profitability. Its new focus on developing new and improved products for new market segments is working. Nike's ROIC has soared from 14 percent in 2000 to 21 percent in 2004, and in 2004 it made over $1 billion in profits.

Overview

As Nike's success story suggests, a company's business model cannot just be created and left to take care of itself. If strategic managers do create a successful business model, they still face another challenge: the need to continually formulate and implement business-level strategies to sustain their competitive advantage over time in different kinds of industry environments. Different industry environments present particular kinds of opportunities and threats for companies, and a company's business model and strategies have to adapt and change to meet the changing environment.

This chapter first examines how companies in fragmented industries can develop new kinds of business-level strategies to strengthen their business models. It then considers the challenges of developing and sustaining a competitive advantage in embryonic, growth, mature, and declining industries. By the end of this chapter, you will understand how forces in the changing industry environment require managers to pursue new kinds of business-level strategies to strengthen their company's business model and keep it at the value creation frontier.

Strategies in Fragmented Industries

A *fragmented industry* is one composed of a large number of small and medium-sized companies—for example, the dry cleaning, restaurant, health club, and legal services industries. There are several reasons that an industry may consist of many small companies rather than a few large ones.[5]

First, fragmented industries are characterized by low barriers to entry because of the lack of economies of scale. Many homebuyers, for example, prefer dealing with local real estate agents, whom they perceive as having better local knowledge than national chains. Second, in some industries, there may even be diseconomies of scale. In the restaurant business, for example, customers often prefer the unique food and style of a popular local restaurant rather than the standardized offerings of some national chain. Third, low entry barriers that permit constant entry by new companies also serve to keep an industry fragmented. The restaurant industry exemplifies this situation. The costs of opening a restaurant are moderate and can be borne by a single entrepreneur. High transportation costs, too, can keep an industry fragmented, and local or regional production may be the only efficient way to satisfy customers' needs, as in the cement business. Finally, an industry may be fragmented because customers' needs are so specialized that only small job lots of products are required, and thus there is no room for a large mass-production operation to satisfy the market.

For some fragmented industries, these factors dictate that the focus business model will be the most profitable to pursue. Companies may specialize by customer group, customer need, or geographic region, so that many small specialty companies operate in local or regional markets. All kinds of custom-made products—furniture, clothing, hats, boots, and so on—fall into this category, as do all small service operations that cater to particular customers' needs, such as laundries, restaurants, health clubs, and furniture rental stores. Indeed, service companies make up a large proportion of the enterprises in fragmented industries because they provide personalized service to clients and therefore need to be responsive to their needs.

However, strategic managers are eager to gain the cost advantages of pursuing cost leadership or the sales-revenue-enhancing advantages of differentiation by circumventing the competitive conditions that have allowed focus companies to dominate an industry. Essentially, companies have searched for new business-level strategies that will allow them to consolidate a fragmented industry in order to enjoy the much higher potential returns possible in a consolidated industry. These companies include large retailers such as Wal-Mart and Target, fast-food chains such as McDonald's and Burger King, video rental chains such as Blockbuster Video and Hollywood Video (which announced a plan to merge in 2004), chains of health clubs such as Bally's and President and First Lady, repair shops like Midas Muffler, and even lawyers, consultants, and tax preparers.

To grow, consolidate their industries, and become the industry leaders, these companies have developed strategies such as chaining, franchising, creating a horizontal merger, and also using the Internet and information technology (IT) in order to realize the advantages of a cost-leadership or differentiation business model. In doing so, these companies have pushed out the value creation frontier to the right, with the result that many focus companies have lost their competitive advantage and have disappeared.

Many of the new leaders pioneered a new business model in an industry that lowers costs or confers a differentiation advantage (or both). They do this by competing in a very different way from established rivals. Managers in a fragmented industry must seek out cost or differentiation advantages that others have not recognized.

■ **Chaining**   Companies such as Wal-Mart and Midas International pursue a **chaining** strategy to obtain the advantages of cost leadership. They establish networks of linked merchandising outlets that are so interconnected by advanced IT that they function as one large business entity. The consolidated buying power that these companies possess through their nationwide store chains allows them to negotiate large price reductions with their suppliers, which promotes their competitive advantage. They overcome the barrier of high transportation costs by establishing sophisticated regional distribution centers, which can economize on inventory costs and maximize responsiveness to the needs of stores and customers. They also realize economies of scale from sharing managerial skills across the chain and from using nationwide, rather than local, advertising.

The U.S. food retail business during the 1950s, when supermarkets revolutionized the business model behind the selling of food products, is a good example of the advantages of chaining. Prior to the development of supermarkets, the food retail industry was fragmented, with many small mom-and-pop retailers selling a limited range of products and providing full service to customers, including home delivery. The first supermarkets were usually regionally based, with fewer than a hundred stores, and they differentiated themselves by offering a much larger selection of items in a big store layout. At the same time, they lowered their costs by moving from a full-service to a self-service strategy (they needed far fewer employees to run a store), and they passed on those cost savings to customers in the form of lower prices. In other words, the supermarkets competed in a very different way from established food retailers: they adopted a new business model.

As the supermarkets started to grow, opening hundreds of more stores, they were able to capture scale economies that were not available to smaller retailers. For example, by clustering their stores around central distribution warehouses in different cities and eventually regions, they were able to gain distribution efficiencies and reduce the amount of inventory they had to hold in a store. Also, by buying from vendors in large quantities, they were able to demand deep price discounts that they passed on to customers in the form of lower prices, enabling them to gain even more market share from smaller retailers. In the 1970s and 1980s, the supermarkets were also the first to introduce information systems based on point-of-sale terminals that tracked the sale of individual items. The information provided enabled the supermarkets to optimize their stocking of items, quickly cutting back on items that were not selling and devoting more shelf space to items that were selling faster. Reducing the need to hold inventory took even more costs out of the systems and ensured a good match between customer demands and items in the supermarket, which further differentiated the supermarkets from smaller retailers. Although these information systems were expensive to implement, the supermarkets could spread the costs over a large volume of sales. The small mom-and-pop retailers could not afford such systems because their sales base was too small. As a consequence of these developments, the food retail industry was becoming consolidated by the 1980s, a trend that is accelerating today. The small mom-and-pop food retailer is now almost extinct.

The new supermarket business model that provided cost and differentiation advantages over the old established mom-and-pop model has been applied to a wide range of retail industries, consolidating one after the other. Barnes & Noble and Borders applied the supermarket business model to book retailing, Staples applied it to office supplies, Best Buy to electronic retailing, Home Depot to building supplies, and so on. In each case, the companies that pursued a business model based on cost leadership or differentiation changed the competitive structure of the industry to its advantage, consolidating the industry and weakening the five forces of competition in the process.

■ **Franchising**   Like chaining, franchising is a business-level strategy that allows companies, particularly service companies such as McDonald's or Century 21 Real Estate, to enjoy the competitive advantages that result from cost leadership or differentiation. In franchising, the franchisor (parent) grants to its franchisees the right to use the parent's name, reputation, and business model in a particular location or area in return for a sizable franchise fee and often a percentage of the profits.[6]

One particular advantage of this strategy is that because franchisees essentially own their businesses, they are strongly motivated to make the companywide business model work effectively and make sure that quality and standards are consistently high so that customers' needs are always satisfied. Such motivation is particularly critical for a differentiator that must continually work to maintain its unique or distinctive appeal. In addition, franchising lessens the financial burden of swift expansion and so permits rapid growth of the company. Finally, a nationwide franchised company can reap the advantages of large-scale advertising, as well as economies in purchasing, management, and distribution, as McDonald's does very efficiently in pursuing its cost-leadership model.

■ Horizontal Merger

Companies such as Anheuser-Busch, Dillard's, and Blockbuster have been choosing a strategy of *horizontal merger* to consolidate their respective industries. For example, Dillard's arranged the merger of regional store chains in order to form a national company. By pursuing horizontal merger, companies are able to obtain economies of scale or secure a national market for their product. As a result, they are able to pursue a cost-leadership or a differentiation business model (although, as we noted in Chapter 5, Dillard's has not been pursuing its differentiation model effectively). The many important strategic implications of horizontal merger are discussed in detail in Chapter 9.

■ Using Information Technology and the Internet

The arrival of new technology often gives a company the opportunity to develop new business strategies to consolidate a fragmented industry. eBay and amazon.com, for example, used the Internet, and the associated strategies e-commerce makes possible, to pursue a cost-leadership model and consolidate the fragmented auction and bookselling industries. Before eBay, the auction business was extremely fragmented, with local auctions in cities being the principal way in which people could dispose of their antiques and collectibles. By harnessing the Internet, eBay can now assure sellers that they are getting wide visibility for their collectibles and are likely to receive a higher price for their product. Similarly, amazon.com's success in the book market has accelerated the consolidation of the book retail industry, and many small bookstores have closed because they cannot compete by price or selection. Clear Channel Communications, profiled in Strategy in Action 6.1, has used many of the strategies discussed above to become the biggest radio broadcaster in the United States.

The challenge in a fragmented industry is to figure out the best set of strategies to overcome a fragmented market so that the competitive advantages associated with pursuing one of the different business models can be realized. It is difficult to think of any major service activities—from consulting and accounting firms to businesses satisfying the smallest customer need, such as beauty parlors and car repair shops—that have not been consolidated by companies seeking to pursue a more profitable business model.

Strategies in Embryonic and Growth Industries

As Chapter 2 discusses, an embryonic industry is one that is just beginning to develop, and a growth industry is one in which first-time demand is expanding rapidly as many new customers enter the market. In choosing the strategies needed to pursue a business model, embryonic and growth industries pose special challenges because the *attributes of customers change* as market demand expands and *new groups of customers* who have different and evolving needs emerge. Also, other factors affect the rate at which a market grows and expands. Strategic managers have to be aware of the way competitive forces in embryonic and growth industries change over time because they

Strategy in Action   6.1

Clear Channel Creates a National Chain of Local Radio Stations

In 2004, Clear Channel Communications, Inc., based in San Antonio, Texas, operated over 1,200 U.S. radio stations, far more than its largest competitors: Viacom with 220 and Citadel with 205. The company started out with only one station in San Antonio in 1995, following a pattern that used to be typical of the radio broadcasting industry. Historically, the industry was fragmented because a federal law prevented any company from owning more than 40 stations nationwide; as a result, a large proportion of the local radio stations were independently owned and operated.

Clear Channel took advantage of the repeal of this law in 1996 to start to buy up radio stations and, most importantly, to develop a business model (which today is one of *broad differentiation*) that would allow it to obtain the gains from consolidating this fragmented industry. Its strategic managers recognized from the beginning that the major way to increase the profitability of city and small town radio stations was to obtain economies of scale from operating and marketing on a national level. The issue was to find ways to raise the quality of its programming to increase its value to listeners, increase the number of listeners, and thus increase advertising revenues (because advertising rates are based on the number of listeners). At the same time, it needed to find ways to reduce each station's high operating costs, that is, lower its cost structure. How to do both simultaneously was the challenge.

On the value side of the equation, an important issue was how to achieve economies of scale from having a national reach while maintaining local ties to the community. Many listeners like to feel they are listening to a local station that understands who they are and what their needs are. Yet if all programming and service are handled on a local level, how can economies of scale from a national base be achieved? Most cost savings come from standardizing service across stations, from broadcasting uniform content. In addition, local listeners often become used to the glitzy, slick productions put on by national cable television broadcasting companies such as MTV and the main TV networks. Because they are national, these companies can afford to pay large sums to stars and celebrities and invest heavily in developing quality products. Such large expenditures are beyond most radio stations' budgets and simply increase the cost of goods sold too much. Moreover, advertising rates had to be kept at a level that both large national companies and small local ones would find acceptable; they could not simply be raised to cover higher costs.

Clear Channel's managers began to experiment with information technology and the Internet and took advantage of emerging digital technology that allowed for the easy and rapid manipulation and transfer of large volumes of data. By the late 1990s, music and programming could easily be recorded, stored in digital format, and edited. Its managers hit on a strategy called "voice tracking." To obtain economies of scale, Clear Channel employed popular regional or national DJs to record its daily programs, and these same DJs customized their productions to suit the needs of local markets. For example, one technology allows DJs to isolate and listen to the end of one track and the beginning of the next; then they can insert whatever talk, news, or information is appropriate between tracks as and when they like. The local stations supply this local information; after they have customized their program, the DJs send it over the Internet, where the local operators handle it. This practice has enormous advantages. On the cost side, the programming costs of a limited number of popular DJs are much lower than the cost of employing an army of local DJs. On the differentiation side, the quality of programming is much higher because Clear Channel can invest more in its programming and because the appeal of some DJs is much higher than others. Over time, higher-quality programming increases the number of listeners, and this attracts more national advertisers, whose digital advertisements can be easily inserted in the programming by local operators.

In addition, Clear Channel is developing its own proprietary brand name, KISS, across its radio stations so that when people travel, they will be attracted to its local stations wherever they are. It also hopes this move will stimulate word-of-mouth advertising. As its brand becomes national, this widened scope will attract larger advertisers and boost its sales revenues. To speed this process, Clear Channel is also linking its different businesses—for example, it is the largest billboard and concert operator in the United States—to its KISS label. It hopes that the resulting increased customer demand will drive up advertising revenues, which will allow it to start or buy more radio stations and expand its reach, thereby lowering its cost structure and increasing its future profitability.[a]

commonly have to build and develop new kinds of competencies and refine their business models to compete effectively in the long term.

Most embryonic industries emerge when a technological innovation creates new product or market opportunities. For example, a century ago, the car industry was born following the development of a new technology, the internal combustion engine, which gave rise to many new products, including the motorcar and motorbus. In 1975, the PC industry was born after new microprocessor technology was developed to build the world's first commercially available PC, the Altair 8800, sold by MITS. Shortly afterward, the PC software industry was born when a Harvard dropout, Bill Gates, and his old school friend, Paul Allen, wrote a version of a popular computer language, BASIC, that would run on the Altair 8800.[7] In 1986, the Internet protocol (IP) network equipment industry was born following the development of the router, an IP switch, by an obscure California start-up, Cisco Systems.

Customer demand for the products of an embryonic industry is frequently limited at first, for a variety of reasons. Moreover, strategic managers who understand how markets develop are in a much better position to pursue a business model and strategies that will lead to a sustained competitive advantage. Reasons for slow growth in market demand include (1) the limited performance and poor quality of the first products, (2) customer unfamiliarity with what the new product can do for them, (3) poorly developed distribution channels to get the product to customers, (4) a lack of complementary products to increase the value of the product for customers, and (5) high production costs because of small volumes of production.

Customer demand for the first cars, for example, was limited by their poor performance (they were no faster than a horse, far noisier, and frequently broke down), a lack of important complementary products such as a network of paved roads and gas stations, and high production costs, which made them a luxury item. Similarly, demand for the first PCs was limited because buyers had to be able to program a computer to use it, and there were no software application programs that could be purchased to run on the PCs. Because of such problems, early demand for the products of embryonic industries comes from a small set of technologically sophisticated customers who are willing to put up with, and may even enjoy, imperfections in the product. Computer hobbyists, who got great joy out of tinkering with their imperfect machines and finding ways to make them work, bought the first PCs.

An industry moves from an embryonic to a growth stage when a *mass market* starts to develop for the industry's product (a mass market is one in which large numbers of customers enter the market). Mass markets typically start to develop when three things occur: (1) ongoing technological progress makes a product easier to use and increases the value of the product to the average customer, (2) key complementary products are developed that do the same, and (3) companies in the industry strive to find ways to reduce production costs so they can lower their cost structure and choose a low price option, and this stimulates high demand.[8] For example, a mass market for cars emerged when (1) technological progress increased the performance of cars, (2) a network of paved roads and gas stations was established (which meant a car could go more places and thus had more value), and (3) Henry Ford began to mass-produce cars, which dramatically lowered production costs and allowed him to reduce prices, causing the demand for cars to surge. Similarly, the mass market for PCs started to emerge when technological advances made them easier to use, a supply of complementary software such as spreadsheets and word processing programs was developed that increased the value of owning a PC, and companies in the industry started to use mass production to build PCs at low cost.

FIGURE 6.1

Market Development
and Customer Groups

FIGURE 6.1

Market Development
and Customer Groups

Strategic managers who understand how the demand for a product is affected by changing customer needs and groups can focus their energies on developing new strategies to protect and strengthen their business models, such as building competencies in low-cost manufacturing or speedy product development. One strategy, for example, would be to share information about new products under development with the companies that supply complementary products so that customers will be convinced the new product is worth buying. Another strategy would be to involve customers in the product development process to gain their input and their acceptance of a new product.

The Changing Nature of Market Demand

The development of most markets follows an **S**-shaped growth curve similar to that illustrated in Figure 6.1. As the stage of market development moves from embryonic to mature, customer demand first accelerates and then decelerates as a market approaches saturation. As we note in Chapter 2, in a saturated market, most customers have already bought the product, and demand is limited to replacement demand; the market is mature. Figure 6.1 shows that different groups of customers who have different needs enter the market over time—and this has major implications for a company's product differentiation and market segmentation decisions.

The first group of customers to enter the market are referred to as the *innovators*. Innovators are "technocrats" who get great delight from being the first to purchase and experiment with products based on a new technology, even though that technology is imperfect and expensive. They often have an engineering mindset and want to own the technology for its own sake. In the PC industry, the first customers were software engineers and computer hobbyists who wanted to write computer code at home.[9]

The *early adopters* are the second group of customers to enter the market. Early adopters understand that the technology might have important future applications and are willing to experiment with it to see if they can pioneer uses for it, often by finding new ways to satisfy customer needs. Early adopters are often visionaries who appreciate how the technology may be used in the future and try to be the first to profit from its use. Jeff Bezos, the founder of amazon.com, was an early adopter of the Internet and web-based technology, who saw in 1994 that the Internet could be used in innovative ways to sell books. He saw this possibility before anyone else and was one of the first dot-com pioneers to purchase web servers and related software and use it to sell products over the Internet. Amazon was thus an early adopter.

Both innovators and early adopters enter the market while the industry is in its embryonic stage. The next group of customers, the *early majority*, represents the leading wave or edge of the mass market; their entry signifies the beginning of the growth stage. Customers in the early majority are comfortable with the new technology and products. However, they are pragmatists: they weigh the benefits of adopting new products against their costs and wait to enter the market until they are confident that products will offer them tangible benefits. Once they start to enter the market, however, they do so in large numbers. This is what happened in the PC market after IBM's introduction of the PC in 1981. For the early majority, IBM's entry into the market legitimized the technology and signaled that the benefits of adoption would be worth the costs of purchasing and learning to use the product. The growth of the PC market was then given further impetus by the development of important applications that added value to it, such as new spreadsheet and word processing programs. These applications transformed the PC from a hobbyist's toy into a business productivity tool.

Once the mass market attains a critical mass, with something like 30 percent of the potential market penetrated, the next wave of customers enters the market. This wave is characterized as the *late majority*: the customers who purchase a new technology or product only when it is clear it will be around for a long time. A typical late majority customer group is the customers who started to enter the PC market in the mid 1990s who were older and somewhat intimidated by computers. However, watching others similar to themselves buying PCs to send e-mail and browse the Web, they overcame their hesitancy and started to purchase PCs. By 2002, some 65 percent of homes in the United States had at least one PC, suggesting that the product was well into the late majority group and thus the market was approaching saturation. Indeed, the entry of the late majority signals the end of the growth stage.

Laggards, the last group of customers to enter the market, are inherently conservative and technophobic. They often refuse to adopt a new technology even if its benefits are obvious or unless they are forced by circumstances—to reply to a colleague's e-mail, for example—to do so. People who stick to using typewriters rather than computers to write letters and books could be considered laggards today.

Figure 6.2 looks at the differences among these groups of consumers in a somewhat different way. The bell-shaped curve represents the total market, and the divisions in the curve show the percentage of customers who on average fall into each customer group. The early adopters are a very small percentage of the total customers who will ultimately buy the product. Thus, the figure illustrates a vital competitive fact: *Most market demand and industry profits arise when the early and late majority enter the market.* And research has found that although many of the early pioneering companies do well in attracting innovators and early adopters, many of these companies often *fail* to attract a significant share of early and late majority customers and ultimately go out of business.

■ **Strategic Implications: Crossing the Chasm**

Why are pioneering companies often unable to create a business model that allows them to be successful over time and remain the market leaders? *Innovators and early adopters have very different customer needs from the early majority.* In an influential book, Geoffrey Moore argues that because of the differences in customer needs

FIGURE 6.2

Market Share of
Different Customer
Segments

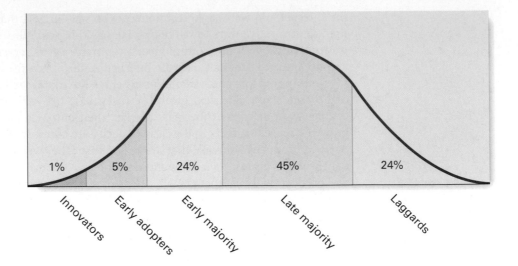

| 1% | 5% | 24% | 45% | 24% |

Innovators   Early adopters   Early majority   Late majority   Laggards

between these groups, the business-level strategies required for companies to succeed in the emerging mass market are quite different from those required to succeed in the embryonic market.[10] Pioneering companies that do not change the strategies they use to pursue their business model will therefore lose their competitive advantage to those companies that implement new strategies that push the value creation frontier out to the right. Different strategies are often required to support and strengthen a company's business model as a market develops over time, for the following reasons:

■ Innovators and early adopters are technologically sophisticated individuals who are willing to tolerate engineering imperfections in the product. The early majority, however, value ease of use and reliability. Companies competing in an embryonic market typically pay more attention to increasing the performance of a product than to its ease of use and reliability. Those competing in a mass market need to make sure that the product is reliable and easy to use. Thus, the product development strategies required for success are different as a market develops over time.

■ Innovators and early adopters are typically reached through specialized distribution channels, and products are often sold by word of mouth. Reaching the early majority requires mass-market distribution channels and mass media advertising campaigns that require a different set of marketing and sales strategies.

■ Because innovators and the early majority are relatively few in number and are not particularly price sensitive, companies serving them typically pursue a focus model and produce small quantities of a product. To serve the rapidly growing mass market, a cost-leadership model based on large-scale mass production may be critical to ensure that a high-quality product can be produced reliably at a low price point.

In sum, the business model and strategies required to compete in an embryonic market populated by early adopters and innovators are very different from those required to compete in a high-growth mass market populated by the early majority.

FIGURE 6.3

The Chasm: AOL and
Prodigy

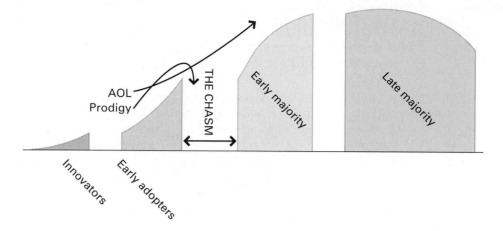

As a consequence, the transition between the embryonic market and the mass market is not a smooth, seamless one. Rather, it represents a *competitive chasm,* or gulf, that companies must cross. According to Moore, many companies do not or cannot develop the right business model; they fall into the chasm and go out of business. This insight is consistent with the observation that although embryonic markets are frequently populated by large numbers of small companies, once the mass market begins to develop, the number of companies in the marketplace drops off sharply.[11]

Figure 6.3, which compares the strategies of AOL Time Warner and Prodigy, illustrates Moore's thesis by showing that a wide chasm exists between innovators and the early majority, that is, between the embryonic market and the rapidly growing mass market. Note also that other smaller chasms exist between other sets of customers, and that these too represent important, although less dramatic, breaks in the nature of the market that require changes in business-level strategy (for example, a different approach to market segmentation). The implication of Moore's thesis is that a company must often formulate and implement new strategies, and build new competencies, if it is to create a business model that can successfully cross the chasm. Strategy in Action 6.2 describes how the early leader in online services, Prodigy, fell into the chasm, while AOL successfully built a business model to cross it.

To cross this chasm successfully, managers must correctly identify the customer needs of the first wave of early majority users—the leading edge of the mass market. Once companies have identified these customers needs, they must alter their business model by developing new strategies to redesign products and create distribution channels and marketing campaigns to reach the early majority. In this way, they will have ready a suitable product, at a reasonable price, that they can sell to the early majority as they start to enter the market in large numbers. In sum, industry pioneers must abandon their old focused business model that was directed solely on the needs of their early or initial customers, because this focus may lead them to ignore the needs of the early majority and the need to pursue a differentiation or cost-leadership model to become the dominant competitor in the future.

Strategy in Action 6.2

How Prodigy Fell into the Chasm

Before America Online (AOL) became a household name, Prodigy Communications was a market leader. Founded in 1984, Prodigy was a joint venture between Sears, IBM, and CBS. CBS soon dropped out, but IBM and Sears stuck with it, investing $500 million in developing the network and finally launching it in 1990. Prodigy's business model was differentiation, and the goal was to build the largest proprietary online shopping network: the system would give its customers the ability to buy anything, even plane tickets, online. IBM knew about computers, and Sears knew about retail. It seemed like the perfect marriage.

Launched in the fall of 1990, the service quickly accumulated half a million users. There was little sense of competition at the time. The largest competitor, CompuServe, was conservatively managed, and it pursued a focused business model based on servicing the needs of technical users and financial services (CompuServe was owned by H&R Block, America's largest tax return service). There was another small competitor, AOL, but in the words of one Prodigy executive, "It was just a little thing off to the side." Ten years later, the little thing had become the largest online service in the world, with 33 million members, and Prodigy had exited the online business altogether after IBM and Sears had invested, and lost, some $1.2 billion on the venture.

Why did Prodigy fail? The company appeared to be focusing on the mass market. Its target customers were not computer-oriented early adopters but typical middle-class Americans. And its business model to sell products online seemed correct; surely this ultimately had to become a major application of the Internet. The problem was that Prodigy's managers did not choose the right set of strategies to formulate the business model; in particular, they did not understand the full range of needs customers were trying to satisfy by using the Internet.

One of the surprise early drivers of customer demand for online services, and a major factor in creating the mass market, was e-mail. AOL's strategy was to offer its members unlimited e-mail, but Prodigy charged members a fee for sending more than thirty e-mails per month—a big difference in business models. Another important application of online service was chatrooms, a service that customers were increasingly embracing. AOL saw chatrooms as one of the unique possibilities of online service for satisfying customer needs, and its strategy was to quickly implement the software that would soon make chatrooms one of its most popular features.

The lawyers at Prodigy's corporate headquarters, however, feared that Prodigy might be held legally liable for comments made in chatrooms or events that arose from them, and they discouraged Prodigy from offering this service. This censorship, lack of chatrooms, and charges for e-mail rankled members, who soon started to switch in droves to AOL.

The nature of the software interface used to allow customers to connect to an online service also became a critical competitive issue as the market developed. When it was introduced, Prodigy's primitive graphical user interface was acceptable by the PC standards of the time, which were based on Microsoft's MS-DOS operating system. When Microsoft introduced its much more user-friendly Windows 3.0 systems in 1990, AOL moved quickly to redesign its software interface to be compatible with Windows, and this made AOL much easier to use. Prodigy, however, was part owned by IBM, which at that time was trying to promote its own new PC operating system, the ill-fated OS/2. So Prodigy dragged its feet. It waited to implement a Windows version of its own interface until December 1993, by which time it had lost the majority of Windows users to AOL.

By 1996, the battle was effectively over: AOL was growing by leaps and bounds and Prodigy was losing customers at a rapid pace because its strategies had pushed out the value frontier. AOL, by correctly sensing the way customer needs were changing and then providing a differentiated product that met those needs, crossed the chasm with ease.[b]

■ **Strategic Implications of Market Growth Rates**

A final important issue that strategic managers must understand in embryonic and growth industries is that different markets develop at different rates. The speed at which a market develops can be measured by its growth rate, that is, the rate at which the industry's product is bought by customers in that market. Figure 6.4 charts the growth rates of a number of important products in the United States

FIGURE 6.4

Differences in Diffusion Rates

Source: Peter Brimelow, "The Silent Boom," *Forbes,* July 7, 1997, pp. 170–171. Reprinted by permission of Forbes Magazine © 2002 Forbes, Inc.

Automobile (1886)
Cell phone (1983)
Electricity (1873)
Microwave (1953)
PC (1975)
Radio (1905)
Telephone (1876)
Television (1926)
VCR (1952)

from their initial introduction to the present time. Although many of these products display the classic S-shaped growth curve, their markets have grown at different rates. For example, demand for TVs has grown more rapidly than demand for cars. The market growth rates for new kinds of products seem to have accelerated over time, probably because the increasing use of the mass media and low-cost mass production help to accelerate the demand for new products. However, there are also differences in the growth rate for new products introduced at around the same time. For example, the cell phone was introduced somewhat later than the PC, and yet market demand has grown more rapidly.

■ **Factors
Affecting
Market Growth
Rates**

A number of factors explain the variation in market growth rates for different products and thus the speed with which a particular industry develops. It is important for strategic managers to understand the source of these differences, for by their choice of business model and strategies, they can accelerate or retard the rate at which a particular market grows.[12] *In other words, business-level strategy is a major determinant of industry profitability.*

The first factor that accelerates customer demand is a new product's *relative advantage,* that is, the degree to which a new product is perceived as better at satisfying customer needs than the product it supersedes. For example, the early growth in demand for cell phones was partly driven by their economic benefits. Studies showed that because business customers could always be reached by cell phone, they made better use of their time—for example, by not showing up at a meeting that had been cancelled at the last minute—and saved two hours per week in time that would otherwise have been wasted. For busy executives, the early adopters, the productivity benefits of owning a cell phone outweighed the costs. Cell phones also diffused rapidly for social reasons, in particular, because they conferred glamour or prestige on their users (something that also drives demand for advanced kinds of hand-held computers and smart phones).

Another factor driving growth in demand is *compatibility*, the degree to which a new product is perceived as being consistent with the current needs or existing values of potential adopters. Demand for cell phones grew rapidly because their operation was compatible with the prior experience of potential adopters who used traditional wire-line phones.

Complexity is a third factor. Complexity is the degree to which a new product is perceived as difficult to understand and use. Early PCs with their clunky operating system interfaces were complex to use and so were slow to be adopted. The first cell phones were simple to use and were adopted quickly.

A fourth factor is *trialability*, which is the degree to which a new product can be experimented with on a hands-on trial basis. Many people first used cell phones by borrowing one from a colleague to make a call, and this positive experience helped accelerate growth rates. In contrast, early PCs were more difficult to experiment with because they were rare and expensive and because some training was needed in how to use them. These complications led to slower growth rates.

A last factor is *observability*, the degree to which the results of using and enjoying a new product can be seen and appreciated by other people. The PalmPilot diffused rapidly because it was easy to observe how easily its users could schedule meetings, enter addresses, record expenses, and so on. The convenience of the device was clear, and the same was true of the cell phone, so they were rapidly adopted.

Young companies must be sure to use devise strategies that address these issues if they are to grow their market share. Nike, for example, worked hard to show how its new sneakers offered customers major advantages in sports performance and how its new shoes were compatible with the sporting lifestyle that was sweeping the United States. Obviously, trialability was easy and complexity was low, for its shoes were conveniently displayed and could be tried on in stores. Nike also used its guerrilla marketing to increase the observability of its products, and as people watched others wearing Nike shoes, a kind of contagion effect took over as people just had to have a pair of its shoes. Thus Nike was highly successful in using these strategies to pursue its differentiation business model.

■ Strategic Implications of Differences in Growth Rates

From a strategic perspective, companies can increase the demand for a new product if they develop business-level strategies to clearly show its relative advantage, make it as compatible as possible with customers' prior needs and experiences, reduce its complexity, and make it possible for customers to try out or observe others using the product. These considerations must drive the product development process that takes a product from the design stage and puts it into customers' hands. Companies that develop the distinctive competencies needed to do this gain a competitive advantage and thus increased market share.

Apple Computer succeeded at first because the less complex design of its Apple II PC made it easier to use than competing designs, and also because some key complements (particularly VisiCalc, the first business spreadsheet) soon became available for the machine. Similarly, the first Sony PlayStation was very popular because Sony pioneered the marketing strategy of setting up displays in retail stores where potential customers could try a PlayStation and others could observe them enjoying it.

Another important strategic issue at the growth stage is that the popularity of a new product often increases or spreads in a way that is analogous to a *viral model of infection*. Lead adopters (the first customers who buy a product) in a market become "infected" or enthused with the product. Subsequently, they infect other people by telling them about its advantages, and after having observed the benefits of the product, these people also adopt it. A good example of this model of diffusion occurred with Hotmail, when its developers decided to add a tag line on the bottom of an e-mail that read "get your free e-mail at Hotmail.com." This tag line proved to be remarkably effective in recruiting new members. Someone would sign on at one institution, say, the University of Washington, and send e-mail via Hotmail to friends. Some of the recipients would also sign on. Within a few days, there would be ten members at the University of Washington, then one hundred, and within a month a thousand—all "infected" from the original user.

Companies promoting new products can take advantage of this viral diffusion phenomenon by identifying and aggressively courting potential opinion leaders in a community—customers whose views command respect. For example, when the manufacturers of new high-tech medical equipment, such as an MRI scanner, start to sell a new product, they first try to get well-known doctors at major research and teaching hospitals to use the product. They may give these opinion leaders free machines for their research purposes and work closely with them in developing the technology. Once these opinion leaders commit to the product and give it their stamp of approval, doctors at many other hospitals often follow.

In sum, understanding competitive dynamics in embryonic and growth industries is an important strategic issue. The ways in which different kinds of customer groups emerge and customer needs change are important determinants of the strategies that need to be pursued to make a business model successful over time. Similarly, understanding the factors that affect a market's growth rate allows managers to tailor their business model to a changing industry environment. (Much more is said about competition in dynamic, changing, high-tech industries in the next chapter.)

Navigating Through the Life Cycle to Maturity

Another crucial decision that faces strategic managers at each stage of the industry life cycle is which investment strategy to pursue. An investment strategy determines the amount and type of resources and capital—human, functional, and financial—that must be spent to configure a company's value chain so that it can pursue a business model successfully over time.[13] In deciding on an investment strategy, managers must evaluate the potential return (on invested capital) from investing in a generic business model against the cost. In this way, they can determine whether pursuing a certain business model strategy is likely to be profitable and how the profitability of a particular business model will change as competition within the industry changes.

Two factors are crucial in choosing an investment strategy: the competitive advantage a company's business model gives it in an industry relative to its competitors, and the stage of the industry's life cycle in which the company is competing.[14] In determining the strength of a company's relative competitive position, market share and distinctive competencies become important. A large market share signals greater potential returns from future investment because it suggests a company has brand loyalty and is in a strong position to grow its profits in the future. Similarly, the more difficult it is to imitate a company's distinctive competencies, such as those in R&D or manufacturing and marketing, the more sustainable is the competitive advantage supplied by its business model and the greater the likelihood that investment in it will lead to a higher ROIC. These two attributes also reinforce one another; for example, a large market share may help a company to create and develop distinctive competencies that strengthen its business model over time because high demand allows it to ride down the experience curve and lower its cost structure. Also, a large market share can create a large cash flow, which may allow for more investment to develop competencies in R&D or elsewhere. In general, companies with the largest market share and the strongest distinctive competencies are in the best position to build and sustain their competitive advantage. Companies with a small market share and little potential for developing a distinctive competency are in a much weaker competitive position.[15]

Because different kinds of opportunities and threats are found in each life cycle stage, the stage of the industry life cycle also influences a company's choice of how much to invest in its business model. Each stage therefore has different implications for the investment of resources needed to obtain a competitive advantage. Competition is strongest in the shakeout stage of the life cycle and least important in the embryonic stage, for example. The *risks* associated with pursuing a certain business model therefore change over time. The difference in risk explains why the potential returns from investing in a particular business model depend on the life cycle stage.

■ Embryonic Strategies

In the embryonic stage, all companies, weak and strong, emphasize the development of a distinctive competency and an associated business model. During this stage, investment needs are great because a company has to establish a competitive advantage. Many fledgling companies in the industry are seeking resources to develop a distinctive competency. Thus, the appropriate business-level investment strategy is a **share-building strategy**. The aim is to build market share by developing a stable and distinct competitive advantage to attract customers who have no knowledge of the company's products.

Companies require large amounts of capital to develop R&D or sales and service competencies. They cannot generate much of this capital internally. Thus, a company's success depends on its ability to demonstrate a distinctive competency to attract outside investors, or venture capitalists. If a company gains the resources to develop a distinctive competency, it will be in a relatively stronger competitive position. If it fails, its only option may be to exit the industry. In fact, companies in weak competitive positions at all stages in the life cycle may choose to exit the industry to cut their losses.

■ Growth Strategies

At the growth stage, the task facing a company is to strengthen its business model to provide the base it needs to survive the coming shakeout. Thus, the appropriate investment strategy is the **growth strategy**. The goal is to maintain its relative competitive position in a rapidly expanding market and, if possible, to increase it—in other words, to grow with the expanding market. However, other companies are entering the market and catching up with the industry's innovators. As a result, the companies first into the market with a particular kind of product often require successive waves of capital infusion to maintain the momentum generated by their success in the embryonic stage. For example, differentiators need to engage in extensive research and development to maintain their technological lead, and cost leaders need to invest in state-of-the-art machinery and computers to obtain new experience-curve economies. All this investment to strengthen their business model is very expensive. And, as we discuss above, many companies fail to recognize the changing needs of customers in the market and invest their capital in ways that do not lead to the distinctive competencies required for long-term success.

The growth stage is also the time when companies attempt to secure their grip over customers in existing market segments and enter new segments so that they can increase their market share. Increasing the level of market segmentation to become a broad differentiator is expensive as well. A company has to invest resources to develop a new sales and marketing competency, for example. Consequently, at the growth stage, companies must make investment decisions about the relative advantages of differentiation, cost-leadership, or focus business models given their financial needs and relative competitive position. If one or a few companies have emerged as the clear cost leaders, for example, other companies might realize that it is futile to compete head-to-head with these companies and instead decide to pursue a growth strategy using a differentiation or focus approach and invest resources in developing other competencies. As a result, strategic groups start to develop in an industry as each company seeks the best way to invest its scarce resources to maximize its competitive advantage.

Companies must spend a lot of money just to keep up with growth in the market, and finding additional resources to develop new skills and competencies is a difficult task for strategic managers. Consequently, companies in a weak competitive position at this stage engage in a **market concentration** strategy to find a viable competitive position. They seek to specialize in some way and adopt a focus business model to reduce their investment needs. If they are very weak, they may also choose to exit the industry and sell out to a stronger competitor.

■ **Shakeout Strategies**

By the shakeout stage, demand is increasing slowly, and competition by price or product characteristics becomes intense. Companies in strong competitive positions need resources to invest in a **share-increasing strategy** to attract customers from weak companies exiting the market. In other words, companies attempt to maintain and increase market share despite fierce competition. The way companies invest their resources depends on their business model.

For cost leaders, because of the price wars that can occur, investment in cost control is crucial if they are to survive the shakeout stage; they must do all they can to reduce costs. Differentiators in a strong competitive position choose to forge ahead and increase their market share by investing in marketing, and they are likely to develop a sophisticated after-sales service network. Differentiators in a weak position reduce their investment burden by withdrawing to a focused model, the market concentration strategy, to specialize in a particular market segment. A market concentration strategy generally indicates that a company is trying to turn around its business so that it can survive in the long run.

Weak companies exiting the industry engage in a harvest strategy. A company using a **harvest strategy** must limit or decrease its investment in a business and extract, or milk, the investment as much as it can. For example, a company reduces to a minimum the assets it employs in the business and forgoes investment to reduce its cost structure.[16] Then the company "harvests" all the sales revenues it can profitably obtain before it liquidates all its assets and exits the industry. Companies that have lost their cost-leadership position to more efficient companies are more likely to pursue a harvest strategy because a smaller market share means higher costs and they are unable to move to a focus strategy. Differentiators, in contrast, have a competitive advantage in this stage if they can move to a focus model.

■ **Maturity Strategies**

By the maturity stage, companies want to reap the rewards of their previous investments in developing the business models that have made them dominant industry competitors. Until now, profits have been reinvested in the business, and dividends have been small. Investors in leading companies have obtained their rewards through the appreciation of the value of their stock, because the company has reinvested most of its capital to maintain and increase market share. As market growth slows in the maturity stage, a company's investment strategy depends on the level of competition in the industry and the source of the company's competitive advantage.

In environments in which competition is high because of technological change or low barriers to entry, companies need to defend their competitive position. Strategic managers need to continue to invest heavily in maintaining the company's competitive advantage. Both cost leaders and differentiators adopt a **hold-and-maintain strategy** to defend their business models and to ward off threats from focused companies who might be appearing. They expend resources to develop their distinctive competency so as to remain the market leaders. For example, differentiated companies may invest in improved after-sales service, and low-cost companies may invest in the latest production technologies.

It is at this point too that many companies realize the benefits that can be obtained by investing resources to become broad differentiators to protect themselves from aggressive competitors (both at home and abroad) that are watching for any opportunity or perceived weakness to take the lead in the industry. Differentiators enter new market segments to increase their market share; they also take advantage of their growing profits to develop flexible manufacturing systems to reduce their production costs. Cost leaders also begin to enter more market segments and increase product differentiation to expand their market share. For example, Gallo moved from the bulk wine segment and began marketing premium wines and wine coolers to take advantage of its low production costs. Soon Gallo's new premium brands, like Falling Leaf chardonnay, became the best-selling wines in the United States. As time goes on, the competitive positions of the leading differentiators and cost leaders become closer, and the pattern of industry competition changes yet again, as we discuss in the next section.

Strategy in Mature Industries

As a result of fierce competition in the shakeout stage, an industry becomes consolidated, and so a mature industry is often dominated by a small number of large companies. Although it may also contain many medium-sized companies and a host of small, specialized ones, the large companies determine the nature of competition in the industry because they can influence the five competitive forces. Indeed, these large companies owe their leading positions to the fact that they have developed the most successful business models and strategies in the industry.

By the end of the shakeout stage, companies have learned how important it is to analyze each other's business model and strategies. They also know that if they change their strategies, their actions are likely to stimulate a competitive response from industry rivals. For example, a differentiator that starts to lower its prices because it has adopted a more cost-efficient technology not only threatens other differentiators but may also threaten cost leaders that see their competitive advantage being eroded. Hence, by the mature stage of the life cycle companies have learned the meaning of competitive independence.

As a result, in mature industries, business-level strategy revolves around understanding how established companies *collectively* try to reduce the strength of industry competition to preserve both company and industry profitability. Interdependent companies can help protect their competitive advantage and profitability by adopting

FIGURE 6.5

Strategies for
Deterring Entry
of Rivals

FIGURE 6.5

Strategies for
Deterring Entry
of Rivals

strategies and tactics, first, to deter entry into an industry, and second, to reduce the level of rivalry within an industry.

■ **Strategies to Deter Entry: Product Proliferation, Price Cutting, and Maintaining Excess Capacity**

Companies can use three main methods to deter entry by potential rivals and hence maintain and increase industry profitability: product proliferation, price cutting, and maintaining excess capacity (see Figure 6.5). Of course, *potential entrants* will try to circumvent such entry-deterring strategies by incumbent companies. Competition is rarely a one-way street.

■ **Product Proliferation** As we note above, in the maturity stage most companies move to increase their market share by producing a wide range of products targeted at different market segments. Sometimes, however, to reduce the threat of entry, existing companies ensure that they are offering a product targeted at every segment in the market. This creates a barrier to entry because potential competitors find it hard to break into an industry and establish a "beachhead" when there is no obvious group of customers whose needs are not being met by existing companies.[17] This strategy of "filling the niches," or catering to the needs of customers in all market segments to deter entry, is known as **product proliferation**.

Because the large U.S. carmakers were so slow to fill the small-car niches (they did *not* pursue a product proliferation strategy), they were vulnerable to the entry of the Japanese into these market segments in the United States in the 1980s. Ford and GM really had no excuse for this situation, for in their European operations, they had a long history of small-car manufacturing. Managers should have seen the opening and filled it ten years earlier, but the (mistaken) view was that "small cars mean small profits." Better small profits than no profits! In the soap and detergent industry, on the other hand, competition is based on the production of new kinds of soaps and detergents to satisfy or create new desires by customers. Thus, the number of soaps and detergents, and especially the way they are packaged (powder, liquid, or tablets), proliferates, making it very difficult for prospective entrants to attack a new market segment.

Figure 6.6 indicates how product proliferation can deter entry. It depicts product space in the restaurant industry along two dimensions: atmosphere, which ranges from fast food to candlelight dining, and quality of food, which ranges from average to gourmet. The circles represent product spaces filled by restaurants located along the

FIGURE 6.6

Product Proliferation
in the Restaurant
Industry

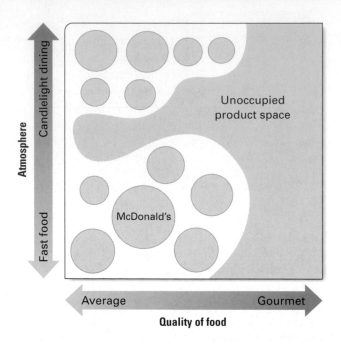

two dimensions. Thus, McDonald's is situated in the average quality/fast food area. A gap in the product space gives a potential entrant or an existing rival an opportunity to enter the market and make inroads. The shaded unoccupied product space represents areas where new restaurants can enter the market. When all the product spaces are filled, this barrier to entry makes it much more difficult for a new company to gain a foothold in the market and differentiate itself.

■ **Price Cutting** In some situations, pricing strategies can be used to deter entry by other companies, thus protecting the profit margins of companies already in an industry. One entry-deterring strategy is to cut prices every time a new company enters the industry or, even better, every time a potential entrant is *contemplating* entry, and then raise prices once the new or potential entrant has withdrawn. The goal here is to send a signal to potential entrants that new entry will be met with price cuts. If incumbent companies in an industry consistently pursue such a strategy, potential entrants will come to understand that their entry will spark off a price war, the threat of new entry will be reduced, average prices will be higher, and industry profitability will increase.

However, a price-cutting strategy will not keep out an entrant that plans to adopt a new technology that will give it a cost advantage over established companies or that has pioneered a new business model that its managers expect will also give it a competitive advantage. In fact, many of the most successful entrants into mature industries are companies that have done just this. For example, the Japanese car companies were able to enter the U.S. market because they had pioneered new lean manufacturing technologies that gave them a cost and quality advantage over established U.S. companies. Today, Japanese car companies' share of the U.S. market is limited only by an informal trade agreement; it could easily double if they were allowed to import all the cars they wished and sell them at lower prices, which might drive one or more U.S. car companies out of the market.

A second price-cutting strategy is to charge a high price initially for a product and seize short-term profits but then to cut prices aggressively in order to build market share *and* deter potential entrants simultaneously.[18] The incumbent companies thus signal to potential entrants that if they enter the industry, the incumbents will use their competitive advantage to drive down prices to a level at which new companies will be unable to cover their costs. This pricing strategy also allows a company to ride down the experience curve and obtain substantial economies of scale. Since costs fall with prices, profit margins could still be maintained.

Still, this strategy is unlikely to deter a strong potential competitor—an established company that is trying to find profitable investment opportunities in other industries. It is difficult, for example, to imagine 3M's being afraid to enter an industry because companies there threaten to drive down prices. A company such as 3M has the resources to withstand any short-term losses. Dell also had few worries about entering the highly competitive electronics industry and starting to sell televisions, digital cameras, and so on because of its powerful set of distinctive competencies. Hence, when faced with such a scenario, it may be in the interests of incumbent companies to accept new entry gracefully, giving up market share gradually to the new entrants to prevent price wars from developing and thus saving their profits, if this is feasible. As Strategy in Action 6.3 details, Toys "R" Us has been forced to give up market share in the toy market, and it has lost much of its prominence as a result.

■ **Maintaining Excess Capacity** A third competitive technique that allows companies to deter entry involves maintaining excess capacity, that is, maintaining the physical capability to produce more of a product than customers currently demand. Existing industry companies may deliberately develop some limited amount of excess capacity to warn potential entrants that if they enter the industry, existing firms can retaliate by increasing output and forcing down prices until entry would become unprofitable. However, the threat to increase output has to be *credible*; that is, companies in an industry must collectively be able to raise the level of production quickly if entry appears likely.

■ **Strategies to Manage Rivalry** Beyond seeking to deter entry, companies also wish to develop strategies to manage their competitive interdependence and decrease price rivalry. Unrestricted competition over prices reduces both company and industry profitability. Several strategies are available to companies to manage industry rivalry. The most important are price signaling, price leadership, nonprice competition, and capacity control (Figure 6.7).

■ **Price Signaling** A company's ability to choose the price option that leads to superior performance is a function of several factors, including the strength of demand for a product and the intensity of competition between rivals. Price signaling is a first means by which companies attempt to control rivalry among competitors so as to allow the *industry* to choose the most favorable pricing option.[19] **Price signaling** is the process by which companies increase or decrease product prices to convey their intentions to other companies and so influence the way they price their products.[20] Companies use price signaling to improve industry profitability.

Companies may use price signaling to announce that they will respond vigorously to hostile competitive moves that threaten them. For example, they may signal that if one company starts to cut prices aggressively, they will respond in kind. A **tit-for-tat strategy** is a well-known price signaling strategy in which a company does

Strategy in Action   6.3

Toys "R" Us's New Competitors

Toys "R" Us, based in Paramus, New Jersey, grew at an astonishing 25 percent annual rate to become the market leader in the retail toy market in 1990 with a 20 percent share. To reach its dominant position, the company consolidated the fragmented toy market by developing a nationwide chain of retail outlets so that it could pursue a cost-leadership strategy. To lower its cost structure, Toys "R" Us developed efficient materials-management techniques for ordering and distributing toys to its stores, and it provided a low level of customer service compared to traditional small toy shops. This business model allowed it to achieve a low expense-to-sales ratio of 17 percent, and it then used this favorable cost structure to promote a philosophy of everyday low pricing. The company deliberately set out to undercut the prices of its rivals, and it succeeded: two of its largest competitors, Child World and Lionel, went bankrupt.

With its dominant position in the industry established, Toys "R" Us continued to build its chain of toy stores, and it began stocking an ever larger and more complex array of products. This would raise its costs; nevertheless, its managers reasoned that they could afford to do so since they were in the driver's seat, and customers would find more value in a wider toy selection. Moreover, raising prices to customers could offset any cost increases, or perhaps the company could negotiate higher price discounts from toy makers like Mattel or Parker Bros.

The company received a shock in 1995 when its commanding position was threatened by the entry of a new set of rivals. Recognizing the high profits that Toys "R" Us was earning, rapidly expanding companies such as Wal-Mart, Kmart, and Target began to make toy selling a major part of their business model. What could Toys "R" Us do to stop them? Not much. Because of its failure to control costs, Toys "R" Us could not stop their entry into its business by reducing its prices; in other words, by failing to pursue its cost-leadership strategy faithfully, it had lost its ability to

play pricing games as it had done with its earlier rivals. The entry of these other companies also reduced its power over its suppliers, the toy makers, because they now had important new customers. Finally, some of the new entrants, Wal-Mart in particular, were now the cost leaders in the retail industry, and their size gave them the resources to withstand any problems if Toys "R" Us attempted to start a price war. In fact, Wal-Mart simply imitated the Toys "R" Us earlier approach and began selling toys at prices that were below those of Toys "R" Us! Indeed, Toys "R" Us's sales fell from 25 percent in 1990 to 17 percent by 1999, when Wal-Mart became the market leader with 18 percent.

To survive, Toys "R" Us has tried to lower its cost structure in its core toy business. It installed new IT to increase the efficiency of its purchasing and distribution operations. It reduced the number of items its stores carry by over 30 percent to slash its cost structure. At the same time, recognizing that it will never be able to match Wal-Mart's low costs, it changed its business model to try to create customer value by developing other kinds of stores for related market segments, such as Kids "R" Us and Babies "R" Us. It also went online and attempted to develop a major Web presence. However, faced with the high costs of online selling today, it partnered with amazon.com; toys bought in its shop on amazon's website can be picked up at any Toys "R" Us store.

By 2004, it was clear that these moves had not halted the decline in the company's market share and profitability. In fact, in 2004 it made the surprise announcement that it was thinking of getting out of the toy business and would henceforth focus on its specialty Kids "R" Us and Babies "R" Us stores, which are making money. However, in November 2004 it still had not found a buyer for its toy stores, and it was not clear if its managers felt that liquidating its toy store assets was a better solution than staying in the toy business and hoping for a turnaround.[c]

exactly what its rivals do: if its rivals cut prices, the company follows; if its rivals raise prices, the company follows. By pursuing this strategy consistently over time, a company sends a clear signal to its rivals that it will match any pricing moves they make, the idea being that, sooner or later, rivals will learn that the company will always pursue a tit-for-tat strategy. Because rivals now know that the company will match any

FIGURE 6.7

Strategies for
Managing Industry
Rivalry

price reductions and cutting prices will only reduce profits, price cutting becomes less common in the industry. Moreover, a tit-for-tat strategy also signals to rivals that price increases will be immitated, increasing the probability that rivals will initiate price increases to raise profits. Thus, a tit-for-tat strategy can be a useful way of shaping pricing behavior in an industry.[21]

The airline industry is a good example of the power of price signaling when prices typically rise and fall depending on the current state of customer demand. If one carrier signals the intention to lower prices, a price war frequently ensues as other carriers copy each other's signals. If one carrier feels demand is strong, it tests the waters by signaling an intention to increase prices, and price signaling becomes a strategy to obtain uniform price increases. Nonrefundable tickets, another strategy adopted to obtain a more favorable pricing option, originated as a market signal by one company that was quickly copied by all other companies in the industry. Carriers recognized that they could stabilize their revenues and earn interest on customers' money if they collectively acted to force customers to assume the risk of buying airline tickets in advance. In essence, price signaling allows companies to give one another information that enables them to understand each other's competitive product or market strategy and make coordinated, price-competitive moves.

■ **Price Leadership** Price leadership—in which one company assumes the responsibility for choosing the most favorable industry pricing option—is a second tactic used to reduce price rivalry and thus enhance the profitability of companies in a mature industry.[22] Formal price leadership, or price setting by companies jointly, is illegal under antitrust laws, so the process of price leadership is often very subtle. In the car industry, for example, prices are set by imitation. The price set by the weakest company—that is, the one with the highest cost structure—is often used as the basis for competitors' pricing. Thus, U.S. carmakers set their prices, and Japanese carmakers then set theirs with reference to the U.S. prices. The Japanese are happy to do this because they have lower costs than U.S. companies, so they make higher profits than U.S. carmakers without competing with them by price. Pricing is done by market segment. The prices of different auto models in the model range indicate the customer segments that the companies are aiming for and the price range they believe the market segment can tolerate. Each manufacturer prices a model in the segment with reference to the prices charged by its competitors, not by reference to competitors' costs. Price leadership also allows differentiators to charge a premium price.

Although price leadership can stabilize industry relationships by preventing head-to-head competition and thus raise the level of profitability within an industry, it has its dangers. It helps companies with high cost structures, allowing them to survive without having to implement strategies to become more productive and efficient. In the long term, such behavior makes them vulnerable to new entrants that have lower costs because they have developed new low-cost production techniques. That is what happened in the U.S. car industry after the Japanese entered the market. After years of tacit price fixing, with GM as the price leader, the carmakers were subjected to growing low-cost Japanese competition, to which they were unable to respond. Indeed, most U.S. carmakers survived only because the Japanese carmakers were foreign firms. Had the foreign firms been new U.S. entrants, the government would probably not have taken steps to protect Chrysler, Ford, or GM.

■ **Nonprice Competition** A third very important aspect of product and market strategy in mature industries is the use of **nonprice competition** to manage rivalry within an industry. The use of strategies to try to prevent costly price cutting and price wars does not preclude competition by product differentiation. Indeed, in many industries, product differentiation strategies are the principal tool companies use to deter potential entrants and manage rivalry within their industry. Nike, the broad differentiator profiled in the *Opening Case*, offers an excellent example of such a company.

Product differentiation allows industry rivals to compete for market share by offering products with different or superior features or by applying different marketing techniques. In Figure 6.8, product and market segment dimensions are used to identify four nonprice competitive strategies based on product differentiation: market penetration, product development, market development, and product proliferation. (Notice that this model applies to new market segments, not new markets.)[23]

■ **Market Penetration** When a company concentrates on expanding market share in its existing product markets, it is engaging in a strategy of **market penetration**.[24] Market penetration involves heavy advertising to promote and build product differentiation, which Nike has actively pursued through its guerrilla marketing, for example. In a mature industry, advertising aims to influence customers' brand choice and create a brand-name reputation for the company and its products; hence

FIGURE 6.8

Four Nonprice
Competitive Strategies

Nike's use of famous sportspeople. In this way, a company can increase its market share by attracting the customers of its rivals. Because brand-name products often command premium prices, building market share in this situation is very profitable.

In some mature industries—for example, soap and detergent, disposable diapers, and brewing—a market-penetration strategy becomes a way of life.[25] In these industries, all companies engage in intensive advertising and battle for market share. Each company fears that, by not advertising, it will lose market share to rivals. Consequently, in the soap and detergent industry, Proctor & Gamble spends more than 20 percent of sales revenues on advertising, with the aim of maintaining and perhaps building market share. These huge advertising outlays constitute a barrier to entry for prospective entrants.

■ **Product Development** **Product development** is the creation of new or improved products to replace existing ones.[26] The wet-shaving industry depends on product replacement to create successive waves of customer demand, which then create new sources of revenue for companies in the industry. Gillette, for example, periodically comes out with a new and improved razor, such as its new vibrating razor that competes with Schick's four-bladed razor, to try to boost its market share. Similarly, in the car industry, each major car company replaces its models every three to five years to encourage customers to trade in their old models and buy the new one.

Product development is crucial for maintaining product differentiation and building market share. For instance, the laundry detergent Tide has gone through more than fifty changes in formulation during the past forty years to improve its performance. The product is always advertised as Tide, but it is a different product each year. Refining and improving products is a crucial strategy companies use to fine-tune and improve their business models in a mature industry, but this kind of competition can be as vicious as a price war because it is very expensive and can dramatically increase a company's cost structure. One of Nike's central strategies is product development, and in the early 2000s its cost structure started to soar because its managers had not realized how much the attempt to develop literally thousands of new models of shoes a year was affecting its bottom line.

■ **Market Development** **Market development** finds new market segments for a company's products. A company pursuing this strategy wants to capitalize on the brand name it has developed in one market segment by locating new market segments in which to compete—just as Nike has done in many segments of the shoe market. In this way, it can exploit the product differentiation advantages of its brand name. The Japanese auto manufacturers provide an interesting example of the use of market development. When they entered the market, each Japanese manufacturer offered a car such as the Toyota Corolla and the Honda Accord aimed at the economy segment of the auto market. Then they upgraded each car over time, and now each is directed at a more expensive market segment. The Accord is a leading contender in the midsize car segment, and the Corolla fills the small-car segment that used to be occupied by the Celica, which is now aimed at a sportier market segment. By redefining their product offerings, Japanese manufacturers have profitably developed their market segments and successfully attacked their industry rivals, wresting market share from these companies. Although the Japanese used to compete primarily as cost leaders, market development has allowed them to become differentiators as well. In fact, as we noted in the last chapter, Toyota has used market development to be-

FIGURE 6.9

Toyota's Product
Lineup

Price	Sports Utility Vehicles	Passenger/ Sports Sedans	Passenger Vans	Personal Luxury Vehicles	Sporty Cars	Pickup Trucks
$11–20K	RAV4, Scion xB	Echo, Matrix, Corolla, Prism, Scion xA			Celica GT	Tacoma
$21–30K	4-Runner, Highlander	Camry, Avalon	Sienna	Avalon	MR2, Spyder	Tundra
$31–45K	Sequoia, RX330	GS 300, IS 300		ES 330	Camry, Solara	Tundra Double Cab
$46–75K	Land Cruiser, GX, LX	GS 430		LS 430	SC 430	

come a broad differentiator. Figure 6.9 illustrates how, over time, Toyota has used market development to develop a vehicle for almost every main segment of the car market.[27]

■ **Product Proliferaton** **Product proliferation** can be used to manage rivalry within an industry and to deter entry. The strategy of product proliferation generally means that large companies in an industry all have a product in each market segment or niche and compete head-to-head for customers. If a new niche develops, such as sports utility vehicles, designer sunglasses, or Internet websites, then the leader gets a first-mover advantage, but soon all the other companies catch up. Once again, competition is stabilized, and rivalry within the industry is reduced. Product proliferation thus allows the development of stable industry competition based on product differentiation, not price—that is, nonprice competition based on the development of new products. The battle is over a product's perceived quality and uniqueness, not over its price. Once again, this is the strategy adopted by Nike in its battle with Adidas. Today Nike offers shoes to most of the major subsegments of the athletic shoe segment and uses the power of advertising to promote the Nike "lifestyle" across all these segments.

■ **Capacity Control** Although nonprice competition helps mature industries avoid the cutthroat price cutting that reduces company and industry levels of profitability, price competition does periodically break out when excess capacity exists in an industry. Excess capacity arises when companies collectively produce too much output and, to dispose of it, they cut prices. When one company cuts prices, the others quickly follow (a game theory prediction; see the discussion in a later section of this chapter) because they fear that the price cutter will be able to sell its entire inventory while they will be left with unwanted goods. The result is that a price war develops.

Excess capacity may be caused by a shortfall in demand, as when a recession lowers the demand for cars and causes car companies to give customers price incentives to purchase a new car. In this situation, companies can do nothing except wait for better times. By and large, however, excess capacity results from companies within an industry simultaneously responding to favorable conditions: they all invest in new plants to be able to take advantage of the predicted upsurge in demand. Paradoxically, each individual company's effort to outperform the others means that, collectively, the companies create industry overcapacity, which hurts them all. Although demand is rising, the consequence of each company's decision to increase capacity is a surge in industry capacity, which drives down prices. To prevent the accumulation of costly excess capacity, companies must devise strategies that let them control—or at least benefit from—capacity expansion programs. Before we examine these strategies, however, we need to consider in greater detail the factors that cause excess capacity.[28]

■ **Factors Causing Excess Capacity** The problem of excess capacity often derives from technological developments. Sometimes new low-cost technology is the culprit because all companies invest in it simultaneously to prevent being left behind. Excess capacity occurs because the new technology can produce more than the old. In addition, new technology is often introduced in large increments, which generate overcapacity. For instance, an airline that needs more seats on a route must add another plane, thereby adding hundreds of seats even if only fifty are needed. To take another example, a new chemical process may operate efficiently only at the rate of a 1,000 gallons a day, whereas the previous process was efficient at 500 gallons a day. If all companies within an industry change technologies, industry capacity may double and enormous problems can result.

Overcapacity may also be caused by competitive factors within an industry. Entry into an industry is one such a factor. The entry of South Korean companies into the global semiconductor industry in the 1990s caused massive overcapacity and price declines. Similarly, the entry of steel producers from the former Soviet Union countries into the global steel market produced excess capacity and plunging prices in the world steel market in the late 1990s and early 2000s. Sometimes the age of a company's plant is the source of the problem. For example, in the hotel industry, given the rapidity with which the quality of hotel furnishings declines, customers are always attracted to new hotels. When new hotel chains are built alongside the old chains, excess capacity can result. Often companies are simply making simultaneous competitive moves based on industry trends, but those moves eventually lead to head-to-head competition. Most fast-food chains, for instance, establish new outlets whenever demographic data show population increases. However, the companies seem to forget that all other chains use the same data (they are not fully anticipating their rivals' actions). Thus, a locality that has no fast-food outlets may suddenly see several being built at the same time. Whether they can all survive depends on the growth rate of demand relative to the growth rate of the chains.

■ **Choosing a Capacity-Control Strategy** Given the various ways in which capacity can expand, companies clearly need to find some means of controlling it. If they are always plagued by price cutting and price wars, they will be unable to recoup the investments in their generic strategies. Low profitability within an industry caused by overcapacity forces not just the weakest companies but also sometimes the major players to exit the industry. In general, companies have two strategic choices: either (1) each company individually must try to preempt its rivals and seize the initiative, or (2) the companies collectively must find indirect means of coordinating with each other so that they are all aware of the mutual effects of their actions.

To *preempt* rivals, a company must forecast a large increase in demand in the product market and then move rapidly to establish large-scale operations that will be able to satisfy the predicted demand. By achieving a first-mover advantage, the company may deter other firms from entering the market since the preemptor will usually be able to move down the experience curve, reduce its costs and therefore its prices as well, and threaten a price war if necessary.

This strategy, however, is extremely risky, for it involves investing resources before the extent and profitability of the future market are clear. Wal-Mart, with its strategy of locating in small rural towns to tap an underexploited market for discount goods, preempted Sears and Kmart. Wal-Mart has been able to engage in market penetration and market expansion because of the secure base it established in its rural strongholds.

A preemptive strategy is also risky if it does not deter competitors and they decide to enter the market. If the competitors have a stronger generic strategy or more resources, such as Microsoft or Intel, they can make the preemptor suffer. Thus, for the strategy to succeed, the preemptor must generally be a credible company with enough resources to withstand a possible price war.

To *coordinate* with rivals as a capacity-control strategy, caution must be exercised since collusion on the timing of new investments is illegal under antitrust law. However, tacit coordination is practiced in many industries as companies attempt to understand and forecast one another's competitive moves. Generally, companies use market signaling to secure coordination. They make announcements about their future investment decisions in trade journals and newspapers. In addition, they share information about their production levels and their forecasts of demand within an industry to bring supply and demand into equilibrium. Thus, a coordination strategy reduces the risks associated with investment in the industry. This is very common in the chemical refining and oil business, where new capacity investments frequently cost hundreds of millions of dollars.

■ Game Theory

As we have discussed, companies are in a constant competitive struggle with rivals in their industry to gain more business from customers. A useful way of viewing this struggle is as a competitive game between companies, in which companies are continually using competitive moves and tactics to compete effectively in an industry. Companies that understand the nature of the competitive game they are playing can often improve their competitive positioning and increase the profitability of their business models. For example, managers can implement better strategies to pursue cost leadership or differentiation.

A branch of work in the social sciences known as *game theory* can be used to model competition between a company and its rivals and help managers improve their business models and strategies.[29] From a game theory perspective, companies in an industry can be viewed as players that are all simultaneously making choices about which business models and strategies to pursue to maximize their profitability. The problem strategic managers face is that the potential profitability of each business model is not some fixed amount; it varies depending on the strategies one company selects and also the strategies that its rivals select. There are two basic types of game: sequential move games and simultaneous move games. In a *sequential move game*, such as chess, players move in turn, and one player can select a strategy to pursue after considering its rival's choice of strategies. In a *simultaneous move game*, the players act at the same time, in ignorance of their rival's current actions. The classic game of rock-paper-scissors is a simultaneous move game.

In the business world, both sequential and simultaneous move games are commonplace as strategic managers jockey for competitive position in the industry. Indeed, game theory is particularly useful in analyzing situations in which a company is competing against a limited number of rivals and there is a considerable level of interdependence in the industry, as occurs in a mature industry. Several of the basic principles that underlie game theory are examined below; these principles can be useful in determining which business model and strategies managers should pursue.

■ **Look Forward and Reason Back** One of the most basic messages of game theory is that managers need to think strategically in two related ways: (1) look forward, think ahead, and anticipate how rivals will respond to whatever strategic moves they make, and (2) reason backward to determine which strategic moves to pursue today given their assessment of how the company's rivals will respond to various future strategic moves. Managers who do both of these things should be able to discover the specific competitive strategy that will lead to the greatest potential returns. This cardinal principle of game theory is known as *look forward and reason back*. To understand its importance, consider this scenario.

Two large companies, UPS and FedEx, which specialize in next-day delivery of packages, dominate the U.S. air express industry. They have a very high fixed cost structure because they need to invest in a capital-intensive nationwide network of aircraft, trucks, and package-sorting facilities. The key to their profitability is to increase volume sufficiently so that these fixed costs can be spread out over a large number of packages, reducing the unit cost of transporting each package.

Imagine that a bright young manager at UPS calculates that if UPS cuts prices for next-day delivery service by 15 percent, the volume of packages the company ships will grow by over 30 percent, and so will UPS's total revenues and profitability. Is this a smart move? The answer depends on whether the bright young manager has remembered to look forward and reason back and think through how FedEx would respond to UPS's price cuts.

Because UPS and FedEx are competing directly against each other, their strategies are interdependent. If UPS cuts prices, FedEx will lose market share, its volume of shipments will decline, and its profitability will suffer. Because FedEx is unlikely to accept this result, if UPS cuts prices by 15 percent, FedEx is likely to follow and cut its prices by 15 percent to hold on to market share. The net result is that the average level of prices in the industry will fall by 15 percent, as will revenues, and both players will see their profitability decline—a lose-lose situation. By looking forward and reasoning back, the new manager discovers that the strategy of cutting prices is not a good one.

Decision trees can be used to help in the process of looking forward and reasoning back. Figure 6.10 maps out the decision tree for the simple game analyzed above from the perspective of UPS. (Note that this is a sequential move game.) UPS moves first, and then FedEx must decide how to respond. Here, you see that UPS has to

FIGURE 6.10

A Decision Tree for
UPS's Pricing Strategy

choose between two strategies: cutting prices by 15 percent or leaving them unchanged. If it leaves prices unchanged, it will continue to earn its current level of profitability, which is $100 million. If it cuts prices by 15 percent, one of two things can happen: FedEx matches the price cut, or FedEx leaves its prices unchanged. If FedEx matches UPS's price cut (FedEx decides to fight a price war), profits are competed away and UPS's profit will be $0. If FedEx does not respond and leaves its prices unaltered, UPS will gain market share and its profits will rise to $180 million. So the best pricing strategy for UPS to pursue depends on its assessment of FedEx's likely response.

Figure 6.10 assigns probabilities to the different responses from FedEx: specifically, there is a 70 percent chance that FedEx will match UPS's price cut and a 30 percent chance that it will do nothing. These probabilities come from an assessment of how UPS's price cut will affect FedEx's sales volume and profitability. The bigger the negative impact of UPS's price cut is on FedEx's sales volume and profitability, the more likely it is that FedEx will match UPS's price cuts. This is another example of the principle of looking forward and reasoning backward. Assigning a 70 percent probability to the top branch in Figure 6.10 assumes that the price cut from UPS will have a significant negative impact on FedEx's business and will force the company to respond with a price cut of its own. The probabilities can also come from looking at the history of FedEx's responses to UPS's price moves. If FedEx has a long history of matching UPS's price cuts, the probability that it will do so this time is high. If FedEx does not have a history of matching UPS's price cuts, the probability will be lower.

Now let us revisit the question of what strategy UPS should pursue. If UPS does not cut prices, its profits are $100 million. If it cuts prices, its expected profits are $(.70) \times \$0 + (.30) \times \$180 = \$60$ million. Since $60 million is less than $100 million, UPS should not pursue the price-cutting strategy. If it did, FedEx would probably respond, and the net effect would be to depress UPS's profitability. Another way of looking at this scenario is to ask under what assumptions about the probability of FedEx's responding it would be worthwhile for UPS to cut prices by 15 percent. For UPS to move forward with its price cuts, the expected profits from doing so must be greater than $100 million, which is the profit from doing nothing. The way to work this out is to find the probability for which UPS is indifferent between leaving prices unaltered or changing them. Signifying probability by p, $100 m = $p \times$ $180 m, and solving for p, $p = $100 m/$180 m = 0.556$. In other words, for UPS to go ahead with the proposed price cut, the probability that FedEx will do nothing must be greater than 55.6 percent.

■ **Know Thy Rival** At this juncture, the question of whether this example is rather contrived might arise. After all, could UPS managers *really* anticipate how FedEx's profits could be affected if UPS cut its prices by 15 percent? And could UPS really assign a probability to FedEx's likely response? The answer is that although UPS's managers cannot calculate exactly what the profit impact and probabilities would be, they can make an informed decision by collecting competitive information and thinking strategically. For example, they could estimate FedEx's cost structure by looking at FedEx's published financial accounts. And because they are in the same business as FedEx, they can assess the effect of falling demand on FedEx's cost structure and bottom line. Moreover, by looking at the history of FedEx's competitive behavior, they can assess how FedEx will respond to a price cut.

This illustrates a second basic principle of game theory: know thy rivals. In other words, in thinking strategically, managers put themselves in the position of a rival to answer the question of how that rival is likely to act in a particular situation. If a company's managers are to be effective at looking forward and reasoning back, they must have a good understanding of what their rival is likely to do under different scenarios, and they need to be able to extrapolate their rival's future behavior based on this understanding.

■ **Find the Dominant Strategy** A **dominant strategy** is one that makes you better off than you would be if you played any other strategy, *no matter what strategy your opponent uses.* To grasp this concept, consider a simultaneous move game based on a situation that developed in the U.S. car industry in the early 1990s (so far we have been considering a sequential move game). Two car companies, Ford and GM, both differentiators, have to decide whether to introduce cash-back rebate programs in November to move unsold inventory that is building up on the lots of car dealers nationwide. Each company can make one of two moves: offer rebates or do not offer rebates. Because the advanced planning associated with launching such a strategy is fairly extensive, both companies must make a decision about what to do by mid-October, which is before they have had a chance to see what their rival is doing.

In each of the previous four years, both companies have introduced just such programs on November 1 and kept them in place until December 31. Customers have become conditioned to expect these programs and increasingly have held back their new car purchases in anticipation of the cash rebate programs beginning in November. This learned behavior by customers has increased the strategic importance of the rebate programs and made the rebate programs themselves increasingly expensive for the automobile companies. Figure 6.11 lays out a payoff matrix associated with each strategy.

The four cells in this matrix represent the four possible outcomes of pursuing or not pursuing a cash rebate strategy. The numbers in parentheses in the center of each cell represent the profit that General Motors and Ford, respectively, will get in each case (in millions of dollars). If both General Motors and Ford decide not to introduce cash rebates (cell 1), each will get $800 million in profit for the November 1–December 31 period. If GM introduces a cash rebate program but Ford doesn't, GM will gain market share at Ford's expense, and GM will get $1,000 million in profit, while Ford gets just $200 million (cell 2). The converse holds if Ford introduces a rebate program but GM doesn't (cell 3). If both companies introduce rebate programs, both get $400 million (remember, the rebates are expensive and essentially represent deep price discounting to move unsold inventory)(cell 4). Finally, the figures in parentheses in the lower-right-hand corner of each cell represent the joint profit associated with each outcome.

If you look at this payoff matrix, you will see that GM's dominant strategy is to offer cash rebates, because whatever strategy Ford pursues, GM does better if it offers cash rebates than if it doesn't. If Ford's strategy is to offer no cash rebates, GM's best strategy is to offer rebates and capture a profit of $1,000 million. If Ford's strategy is to offer cash rebates, GM's best strategy is again to offer cash rebates and get a profit of $400 million. So whatever Ford does, GM's best strategy is to offer cash rebates.

An interesting aspect of this game is that Ford also goes through the same reasoning process. Indeed, the payoff matrix shows that Ford's dominant strategy is also to offer cash rebates. The net result is that while both players get $400 million profit, the combined payoff of $800 million is the lowest of any combination! Clearly, both automakers could have done better if they had cooperated and jointly decided not to offer cash rebates. Why didn't they do this? There are two reasons. First, cooperation to set prices is illegal under U.S. antitrust law. Second, even though neither party will gain from offering rebates, *it cannot trust the other party not to offer a cash rebate since then it would be even worse off.* As the payoff matrix shows, if Ford does not offer cash rebates, GM has a very big incentive to do so, and vice versa. So both companies assume that the other will offer rebates, both end up doing so, and customers receive the value and are the winners!

The payoff structure in this game is very famous. It is known as the *prisoner's dilemma game* because it was first explained using an example of two suspects, or "prisoners," who are being interrogated for possible involvement in a crime. In the original exposition, the prisoners could confess to the crime and also implicate their partner in the crime to get a reduced sentence, or not confess or implicate the other. If the other prisoner also either doesn't confess or implicate the other, they both end up going free. The problem is that neither prisoner can trust the other not to implicate the other in order to get a reduced sentence. So to reduce their losses (length of jail time), both end up confessing and implicate the other, and both go to jail.

The prisoner's dilemma is thought to capture the essence of many situations where two or more companies are competing against each other and their dominant strategy is to fight a price war, even if they would collectively be better off by *not* doing so. In other words, the prisoner's dilemma can be used to explain the mutually destructive price competition that breaks out in many industries from time to time. It also raises the question of whether companies can do anything to extricate themselves from such a situation. This brings us to the final principle of game theory explored here.

■ **Strategy Shapes the Payoff Structure of the Game** An important lesson of game theory is that through its choice of strategy, a company can alter the payoff structure of the competitive game being played in the industry. To understand this, consider once more the cash rebate game played by Ford and GM in which both companies are compelled to choose a dominant strategy that depresses total payoffs. How can they extricate themselves from this predicament? They can do it by changing the behavior of customers.

Recall that rebates were necessary only because customers had come to expect them and held off purchasing a car until the rebates were introduced. In a self-fulfilling prophecy, this depresses demand and forces the companies to introduce rebates to move unsold inventory on the lots of car dealers. If these expectations could be changed, customers would not hold off their purchases in anticipation of the rebates being introduced in November of each year, and companies would no longer have to introduce rebates to move unsold inventory on the lots of car dealers. A company can change customer behavior through its choice of strategy.

This is what GM actually did. After several years of rebate wars, GM decided to issue a new credit card that allowed cardholders to apply 5 percent of their charges toward buying or leasing a new GM car, up to $500 a year with a maximum of $3,500. The credit card launch was one of the most successful in history: within two years, there were 9 million GM credit card holders, and the card had replaced the other incentives that GM offered, principally the end-of-year cash rebates. Because of the card, price-sensitive customers who typically waited for the rebates could purchase a reduced price car any time of the year. Moreover, once they had the card, they were much more likely to buy from GM than Ford. This strategy changed customer behavior. Customers no longer waited for rebates at the end of the year before buying, an inventory of unsold cars did not build up on the lots of dealers, and GM was not forced into fighting a rebate war to clear inventory.

If this strategy was so successful, what was to stop Ford from imitating it? Nothing! Ford began to offer its own credit card soon after GM. In this case, however, imitation of the strategy led to increased profitability because both GM and Ford had found a clever way to differentiate themselves from each other: by issuing credit cards that created stronger brand loyalty. With the new cards, a GM cardholder was more likely to buy a GM car and a Ford cardholder was more likely to buy a Ford car. By reducing the tendency of customers to play GM and Ford dealers off against each other, the card also had the effect of enabling both GM and Ford to raise their prices. Figure 6.12 illustrates how strategy can change the payoff matrix.

FIGURE 6.12

Altered Payoff Matrix
for GM and Ford

By issuing credit cards and strengthening the differentiation component of their strategy, both Ford and GM reduced the value of cash rebates and made it less likely that customers would switch to the company that offers rebates. The payoff structure of the game changed, and so did the dominant strategy. Now that GM's dominant strategy is to not offer cash rebates, for whatever Ford does, GM is better off by not offering rebates. The same is true for Ford. In other words, by their choice of strategy, General Motors and Ford have changed their dominant strategy in a way that boosts their profitability.

More generally, this example suggests that the way out of mutually destructive price competition associated with a prisoner's dilemma type of game is for the players to change their business models and differentiate their product offerings in the minds of customers, thereby reducing their sensitivity to price competition. In other words, by their choice of strategy and business model (one principally based on differentiation), companies can alter the payoff structure associated with the game, alter their dominant strategy, and move it away from a prisoner's dilemma type of game structure.

This insight also points to the need for companies to think through how their choice of business strategy might change the structure of the competitive game they are playing. Although we have looked at how strategy can transform the payoff structure of the game in a way that is more favorable, the opposite can and does occur. Companies often unintentionally change their business models and pursue strategies that change the payoff structure of the game in a way that is much less favorable to them and comes to resemble a prisoner's dilemma, as the competitive dynamics between Coca-Cola and PepsiCo in the soft drink industry suggests in Strategy in Action 6.4.

In retrospect, what happened was that the Pepsi challenge changed the long-established competitive rules in the industry. As the basis of competition shifted from differentiation by abstract lifestyle advertising to direct product comparisons, and then to price competition, the payoff structure associated with their game changed and became more of a prisoner's dilemma type of structure. Had Pepsi's managers looked ahead and reasoned back, they might have realized that price competition would be the outcome of its new aggressive strategy and might not have launched the Pepsi challenge, especially because the company was gaining market share from Coke, albeit slowly. However, because Pepsi's strategy changed the nature of differentiation in the industry, it led to a lose-lose situation.

Strategy in Action   6.4

Coca-Cola and PepsiCo Go Head-to-Head

For thirty years, until the late 1970s, the cola segment of the soft drink industry went through a golden age in which the main players, Coca-Cola and PepsiCo, were very profitable. These two companies competed against each other on the basis of advertising their products, Coke and Pepsi, based on abstract lifestyle product attributes. PepsiCo would introduce advertisements showing that it was cool to drink Pepsi, and Coca-Cola would produce advertisements with catchy jingles such as "things go better with Coke." Neither company competed on price. Coke led the market throughout the period, although by the mid-1970s, Pepsi was closing in.

It was at this juncture that Pepsi launched a new and innovative strategy: the Pepsi challenge. The Pepsi challenge was a taste test in which customers were blindfolded and asked which drink they preferred, Pepsi or Coke. In the test, about 55 percent of customers consistently said they preferred Pepsi, a significant result given that Pepsi trailed Coke in market share. Pepsi test-marketed the Pepsi challenge in Dallas, and it was so successful that in the late 1970s Pepsi rolled out the challenge nationally, a situation that presented a real dilemma for Coke. It could

not respond with its own blind taste test, because in the tests, the majority of people preferred Pepsi. Moreover, the Pepsi challenge had changed the nature of competition in the industry. After thirty years of competition through product differentiation based on lifestyle product attributes with no direct (and aggressive) product comparisons, Pepsi had shifted to a direct product comparison based on a real attribute of the product: taste.

PepsiCo had altered its business model and changed how it chose to differentiate its product from Coke. As Pepsi was now gaining market share, Coca-Cola's managers decided to make an aggressive response: deep price discounts for Coke in local markets where they controlled the Coke bottler and the local Pepsi bottler was weak. This was a successful move; in markets where price discounting was used, Coke started to gain its share back. PepsiCo then decided to respond in kind and cut prices too. Before long, price discounting was widespread in the industry. Customers were coming to expect price discounting, brand loyalty had been eroded, and the value associated with differentiation had been reduced. Both Coke and Pepsi experienced declining profitability.[d]

So how did the soft drink manufacturers try to extricate themselves from this situation? Over the course of a few years, they once more shifted the way in which they differentiated their products. They introduced new products, such as Diet Coke and Cherry Coke, to rebuild brand loyalty, and they reemphasized abstract advertising by using celebrities to help create a brand image for their soda, thus differentiating it from their competitors' offerings and reducing customer price sensitivity. They are still doing this today—advertising Pepsi, for example, using the gyrations and music of Britney Spears as a device for building a brand image that differentiates its offering from Coke. However, it took several years for Pepsi and Coke to do this, and in the interim they had to grapple with a payoff structure that reduced profitability in the industry; moreover, price discounting is still common today.

Strategies in Declining Industries

Sooner or later, many industries enter into a decline stage, in which the size of the total market starts to shrink. Examples are the railroad industry, the tobacco industry, and the steel industry. Industries start declining for a number of reasons, including technological change, social trends, and demographic shifts. The railroad and steel industries began to decline when technological changes brought viable substitutes for their

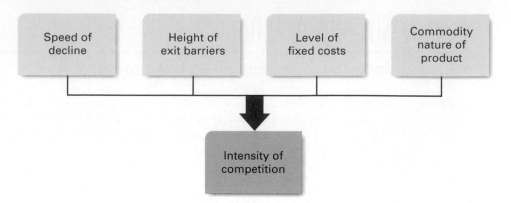

Factors that Determine the Intensity of Competition in Declining Industries

products. The advent of the internal combustion engine drove the railroad industry into decline, and the steel industry fell into decline with the rise of plastics and composite materials. As for the tobacco industry, changing social attitudes toward smoking, which are themselves a product of growing concerns about the health effects of smoking, have caused decline.

■ The Severity of Decline

When the size of the total market is shrinking, competition tends to intensify in a declining industry and profit rates tend to fall. The intensity of competition in a declining industry depends on four critical factors, which are indicated in Figure 6.13. First, the intensity of competition is greater in industries in which decline is rapid as opposed to industries, such as tobacco, in which decline is slow and gradual.

Second, the intensity of competition is greater in declining industries in which exit barriers are high. As you recall from Chapter 2, high exit barriers keep companies locked into an industry even when demand is falling. The result is the emergence of excess productive capacity and, hence, an increased probability of fierce price competition.

Third, and related to the previous point, the intensity of competition is greater in declining industries in which fixed costs are high (as in the steel industry). The reason is that the need to cover fixed costs, such as the costs of maintaining productive capacity, can make companies try to use any excess capacity they have by slashing prices, which can trigger a price war.

Finally, the intensity of competition is greater in declining industries in which the product is perceived as a commodity (as it is in the steel industry) in contrast to industries in which differentiation gives rise to significant brand loyalty, as was true until very recently of the declining tobacco industry.

Not all segments of an industry typically decline at the same rate. In some segments, demand may remain reasonably strong despite decline elsewhere. The steel industry illustrates this situation. Although bulk steel products, such as sheet steel, have suffered a general decline, demand has actually risen for specialty steels, such as those used in high-speed machine tools. Vacuum tubes provide another example. Although demand for them collapsed when transistors replaced them as a key component in many electronics products, vacuum tubes still had some limited applications in radar equipment for years afterward. Consequently, demand in this vacuum tube segment remained strong despite the general decline in the demand for vacuum tubes. The point, then, is that there may be pockets of demand in an industry in which demand is declining more slowly than in the industry as a whole or not declining at all. Price competition thus may be far less intense among the companies serving such pockets of demand than within the industry as a whole.

■ **Choosing a Strategy**   There are four main strategies that companies can adopt to deal with decline: (1) a **leadership strategy**, by which a company seeks to become the dominant player in a declining industry; (2) a **niche strategy**, which focuses on pockets of demand that are declining more slowly than the industry as a whole; (3) a **harvest strategy**, which optimizes cash flow; and (4) a **divestment strategy**, by which a company sells off the business to others. Figure 6.14 provides a simple framework for guiding strategic choice. Note that the intensity of competition in the declining industry is measured on the vertical axis and that a company's strengths relative to remaining pockets of demand are measured on the horizontal axis.

■ **Leadership Strategy**   A leadership strategy aims at growing in a declining industry by picking up the market share of companies that are leaving the industry. A leadership strategy makes most sense (1) when the company has distinctive strengths that allow it to capture market share in a declining industry and (2) the speed of decline and the intensity of competition in the declining industry are moderate. Philip Morris has pursued such a strategy in the tobacco industry. Through aggressive marketing, Philip Morris has increased its market share in a declining industry and earned enormous profits in the process.

The tactical steps companies might use to achieve a leadership position include using aggressive pricing and marketing to build market share, acquiring established

FIGURE 6.14

Strategy Selection in a Declining Industry

Strategy in Action 6.5

How to Make Money in the Vacuum Tube Business

At its peak in the early 1950s, the vacuum tube business was a major industry in which companies such as Westinghouse, General Electric, RCA, and Western Electric had a large stake. Then along came the transistor, making most vacuum tubes obsolete, and one by one all the big companies exited the industry. One company, however, Richardson Electronics, not only stayed in the business but also demonstrated that high returns are possible in a declining industry. Primarily a distributor (although it does have some manufacturing capabilities), Richardson bought the remains of a dozen companies in the United States and Europe as they exited the vacuum tube industry, and it now has a warehouse that stocks more than 10,000 different types of vacuum tubes. The company is the world's only supplier of many of them, which helps explain why its gross margin is in the 35 to 40 percent range.

Richardson survives and prospers because vacuum tubes are vital parts of some older electronic equipment that would be costly to replace with solid-state equipment. In addition, vacuum tubes still outperform semiconductors in some limited applications, including radar and welding machines. The U.S. government and General Motors are big customers of Richardson.

Speed is the essence of Richardson's business. The company's Illinois warehouse offers overnight delivery to some 40,000 customers, and it processes 650 orders a day at an average price of $550. Customers such as GM do not really care whether a vacuum tube costs $250 or $350; what they care about is the $40,000 to $50,000 downtime loss that they face when a key piece of welding equipment isn't working. By responding quickly to the demands of such customers and being the only major supplier of many types of vacuum tubes, Richardson has placed itself in a position that many companies in growing industries would envy: a monopoly position. However, a new company, Westrex, was formed to take advantage of the growing popularity of vacuum tubes in high-end stereo systems, and today it is competing head-to-head with Richardson in some market segments. Clearly, competition can be found even in a declining industry.[e]

competitors to consolidate the industry, and raising the stakes for other competitors—for example, by making new investments in productive capacity. Such competitive tactics signal to other competitors that the company is willing and able to stay and compete in the declining industry. These signals may persuade other companies to exit the industry, which would further enhance the competitive position of the industry leader. Strategy in Action 6.5 offers an example of a company, Richardson Electronics, that has prospered by taking a leadership position in a declining industry. It is one of the last companies in the vacuum tube business.

■ **Niche Strategy** A niche strategy focuses on pockets of demand in the industry in which demand is stable or declining less rapidly than the industry as a whole. The strategy makes sense when the company has some unique strengths relative to those niches where demand remains relatively strong. As an example, consider Naval, a company that manufactures whaling harpoons and small guns to fire them and makes money doing so. This might be considered rather odd, since the world community has outlawed whaling. However, Naval survived the terminal decline of the harpoon industry by focusing on the one group of people who are still allowed to hunt whales, although only in very limited numbers: North American Eskimos. Eskimos are permitted to hunt bowhead whales, provided that they do so only for food and not for commercial purposes. Naval is the sole supplier of small harpoon whaling guns to

Eskimo communities, and its monopoly position allows it to earn a healthy return in this small market.

■ **Harvest Strategy**   As we noted earlier, a harvest strategy is the best choice when a company wishes to get out of a declining industry and optimize cash flow in the process. This strategy makes the most sense when the company foresees a steep decline and intense future competition or lacks strengths relative to remaining pockets of demand in the industry. A harvest strategy requires the company to cut all new investments in capital equipment, advertising, R&D, and the like. The inevitable result is that it will lose market share, but because it is no longer investing in this business, initially its positive cash flow will increase. Essentially, the company is taking cash flow in exchange for market share. Ultimately, cash flows will start to decline, and at this stage it makes sense for the company to liquidate the business. Although this strategy is very appealing in theory, it can be somewhat difficult to put into practice. Employee morale in a business that is being run down may suffer. Furthermore, if customers catch on to what the company is doing, they may defect rapidly. Then market share may decline much faster than the company expected.

■ **Divestment Strategy**   A divestment strategy rests on the idea that a company can recover the most of its investment in an underperforming business by selling it early, before the industry has entered into a steep decline. This strategy is appropriate when the company has few strengths relative to whatever pockets of demand are likely to remain in the industry and when the competition in the declining industry is likely to be intense. The best option may be to sell out to a company that is pursuing a leadership strategy in the industry. The drawback of the divestment strategy is that it depends for its success on the ability of the company to spot its industry's decline before it becomes serious and to sell out while the company's assets are still valued by others.

Summary of Chapter

1. In fragmented industries composed of a large number of small and medium-sized companies, the principal forms of competitive strategy are chaining, franchising, and horizontal merger, as well as using the Internet.

2. In embryonic and growth industries, strategy is determined partly by market demand. The innovators and early adopters have different needs from the early and the late majority, and a company must be prepared to cross the chasm between the two. Similarly, managers must understand the factors that affect a market's growth rate so they can tailor their business model to a changing industry environment.

3. Companies need to navigate the difficult road from growth to maturity by choosing an investment strategy that supports their business model. In choosing this strategy, managers must consider the company's competitive position in the industry and the stage of the industry's life cycle. Some main types of investment strategy are share building, growth, market concentration, share increasing, harvest, and hold-and-maintain.

4. Mature industries are composed of a few large companies whose actions are so highly interdependent that the success of one company's strategy depends on the responses of its rivals.

5. The principal strategies used by companies in mature industries to deter entry are product proliferation, price cutting, and maintaining excess capacity.

6. The principal strategies used by companies in mature industries to manage rivalry are price signaling,

price leadership, nonprice competition, and capacity control.

7. Game theory suggests several management principles: look forward and reason back, know thy rival, pursue your dominant strategy, remember that strategy can alter the payoff structure of the game, and use strategy to change the payoff structure in a way that increases the profitability of your dominant strategy.

8. In declining industries, in which market demand has leveled off or is falling, companies must tailor their price and nonprice strategies to the new competitive environment. They also need to manage industry capacity to prevent the emergence of capacity expansion problems.

9. There are four main strategies a company can pursue when demand is falling: leadership, niche, harvest, and divestment. The choice is determined by the severity of industry decline and the company's strengths relative to the remaining pockets of demand.

Discussion Questions

1. Why are industries fragmented? What are the main ways in which companies can turn a fragmented industry into a consolidated one?

2. What are the key problems in maintaining a competitive advantage in embryonic and growth industry environments? What are the dangers associated with being the leader?

3. In managing their growth through the life cycle, what investment strategies should be made by (a) differentiators in a strong competitive position and (b) differentiators in a weak competitive position?

4. Discuss how companies can use (a) product differentiation and (b) capacity control to manage rivalry and increase an industry's profitability.

5. What insights would game theory offer (a) a small pizza place operating in a crowded college market and (b) a detergent manufacturer seeking to bring out new products in established markets?

Practicing Strategic Management

■ SMALL-GROUP EXERCISE
How to Keep the Hot Sauce Hot

Break up into groups of three to five people, and discuss the following scenario. Appoint one group member as a spokesperson who will communicate your findings to the class. You are the managers of a company that has pioneered a new kind of hot sauce for chicken that has taken the market by storm. The hot sauce's differentiated appeal has been based on a unique combination of spices and packaging that has allowed you to charge a premium price. Over the past three years, your hot sauce has achieved a national reputation, and now major food companies such as Kraft and Nabisco, seeing the potential of this market segment, are beginning to introduce hot sauces of their own, imitating your product.

1. Describe your business model and the strategies you are pursuing.
2. Describe the industry's environment in which you are competing.

3. What kinds of competitive strategies could you adopt to strengthen your business model in this kind of environment?

■ ARTICLE FILE 6

Choose a company or group of companies in a particular industry environment, and explain how it has adopted a competitive strategy to protect or enhance its business-level strategy.

■ STRATEGIC MANAGEMENT PROJECT
Module 6

This part of the project considers how conditions in the industry environment affect the success of your company's business model and strategies. With the information you have at your disposal, perform the tasks and answer the questions listed:

1. In what kind of industry environment (for example, embryonic, mature) does your company operate? Use the information from Strategic Management Project: Module 2 to answer this question.

2. Discuss how your company has attempted to develop strategies to protect and strengthen its business model. For example, if your company is operating in an embryonic industry, how has it attempted to increase its competitive advantage over time? If it operates in a mature industry, discuss how it has tried to manage industry competition.

3. What new strategies would you advise your company to pursue to increase its competitive advantage? For example, how should it attempt to differentiate its products in the future or lower its cost structure?

4. On the basis of this analysis, do you think your company will be able to maintain its competitive advantage in the future? Why or why not?

EXPLORING THE WEB
Visiting Wal-Mart

Enter the website of retailer Wal-Mart (**www.walmartstores.com**). Click on "About Wal-Mart," and then click on "Timeline." Study the events in Wal-Mart's timeline, and then outline the development of Wal-Mart's business model and strategies in the retailing industry over time.

General Task Search the Web for a company that has recently changed its business model and strategy in some way. What precipitated the change? What changes did the company make?

Closing Case

Information Technology, the Internet, and Changing Strategies in the Fashion World

Well-known fashion houses like Chanel, Dior, Gucci, and Armani charge thousands of dollars for the fashionable suits and dresses that they introduce twice yearly in the fall and spring. Since only the very rich can afford such differentiated and expensive clothing, to expand demand for its luxury products most luxury designers produce less expensive lines of clothing and accessories that are sold in upscale fashion retailers such as Neiman Marcus, Nordstrom, and Saks Fifth Avenue.

Both fashion clothes designers and retailers have experienced enormous problems in the past decade. New kinds of competitors have taken advantage of the opportunities opened by the Internet and advances in information technology (IT) to enter the high fashion market segment and compete head-to-head with them by offering high-quality clothes at significantly lower prices. Essentially, all of these new competitors have developed capabilities in using IT that allow them to pursue a focused differentiation strategy but at a much lower cost than the luxury fashion houses. This has allowed them to circumvent barriers to entry into the high fashion segment and develop well-received brand names.

First, upscale department stores and retail chains like Dillard's and Macy's, which target the middle of the fashion clothing market, have developed their own store-specific prestigious clothing labels. These well-made clothes are often sold at a significant price discount from luxury brands and thus attract customers away. Second, many small, agile fashion designers such as England's Jaeger and Laura Ashley and Spain's Zara now produce fashionable clothes at lower prices and sell them in their own chains of clothing stores. Zara, in particular, has achieved significant success, and its sales have soared. It has managed to position itself as the low-price cost leader in the fashion segment of the clothing market because it has created innovative information systems that lower costs and speed time to market.

Zara uses IT to manage the interface between its design and manufacturing operations efficiently. Major fashion houses like Dior and Gucci can take six or more months to design their collections and then three to six more before their moderately priced lines become available in upscale retailers. Zara's designers closely watch the trends in the high fashion industry and the kinds of innovations that the major houses are introducing. Then, using their information systems, which are linked to their suppliers and the low-cost manufacturers the company uses abroad, they can create a new collection in only five weeks, and these clothes can then be made in a week and delivered to stores soon after.

This short time to market gives Zara great flexibility and has allowed it to compete effectively in the rapidly changing fashion market, where customer tastes evolve quickly.

IT also gives Zara instant feedback on which of its clothes are selling well and in which countries. This information enables Zara to engage in continual product development and remain at the cutting edge of fashion, a major source of differentiation advantage. For example, Zara can manufacture more of a particular kind of dress or suit to meet high customer demand, and it can keep up with fashion by constantly changing its mix of clothes in its rapidly expanding network of global stores. Moreover, since it is following a focused strategy, it can do this at relatively small output levels.

Indeed, IT has allowed Zara to minimize the inventory it has to carry, which is the major cost of goods sold for a clothing maker/retailer. For this reason, IT is a major driver of profitability. Because of the quick manufacturing-to-sales cycle and just-in-time fashion, Zara has been able to offer its collections at comparatively low prices and still make profits that are the envy of the fashion clothing industry. In fact, pricing has become the major competitive tool for managing competition in the fashion industry. When Zara offered its shares to the public for the first time in 2001, they soared in price because of the company's high return on invested capital. Investors believe that there will soon be a chain of Zara stores in most major cities around the world as its name becomes as common as those of well-known designers.

Many of the other clothing design and retail companies have awakened to the threat posed by companies like Zara and have pioneered their own proprietary lines of clothes (Dillard's Daniel Cremieux line is one), using a similar strategy to Zara's. Clothing designers like Ralph Lauren and Tommy Hilfiger have been forced to adopt similar approaches, bringing out new clothes collections several times a year and instituting price markdowns to sell inventory quickly. Even the major fashion houses have taken note of what is happening. Gucci, for example, which began to experience problems in the 1990s, brought in Thomas Ford, an American, as its chief designer and invested its resources to produce a new Ford-designed clothes line for both men and women to attract back Gucci's customers. Using IT, Gucci has also been able to design, manufacture, and distribute its clothing at a faster rate.

Increasingly, these companies are realizing that a competitive advantage and superior profitability cannot be maintained by brand image alone; all clothing companies must learn to use new strategies to defend their differentiated appeal, something that can be quickly lost in today's fast-changing global marketplace.[30]

Case Discussion Questions

1. What business model and strategies is Zara pursuing?

2. How has Zara's business model changed the nature of industry competition?

3. What new strategies have emerged in the fashion industry as a result?

Chapter 7

Strategy in High-Technology Industries

Opening Case

The Smart Phone Format War

At the present time the cell phone business is witnessing a format war. Symbian, a consortium led by Finnish cell phone maker Nokia, is engaged in a winner-takes-all struggle with Microsoft and PalmSource to establish its software as the operating system that will run applications on smart phones. Smart phones are hand-held devices that combine traditional cell phone functions with functions once only found on hand-held computers or PCs. Leading-edge smart phones are in effect powerful hand-held computers and communicators that come with a full range of personal information and management applications such as addresses and date books; the ability to browse the Internet; the ability to send and receive e-mail and digital photos; and the ability to run a growing number of other software programs ranging from pocket-sized versions of Microsoft Office to videogames.

Although the global market for such software is still relatively small—valued at $250 million a year in 2004—sales of smart phones are growing rapidly and may exceed 30 million units worldwide in 2005, up from a mere 5 million in 2003. Ultimately, many analysts believe that the development of the market for smart phone operating systems will mirror the development of the market for personal computer operating systems, where Microsoft dominates with a share of over 90 percent. They argue that independent software developers will write programs for whichever operating system is found on the largest number of smart phones. Thus if Symbian is outselling its rivals 2 to 1, developers will write applications for Symbian first. This will make Symbian smart phones more attractive to customers, and thus demand for smart phones with a Symbian operating system will increase. As demand grows, even more applications will become available for smart phones with a Symbian operating system, and Symbian's lead over its rivals will increase until its rivals are marginalized in the industry. Symbian could in effect become the Microsoft of the smart phone business.

Symbian has some big advantages on its side. In addition to Nokia, with about 48 percent of Symbian's equity, members of the consortium include some of the world's largest cell phone manufacturers, most notably Ericsson, Sony, Matsushita, and Siemens. These manufacturers clearly have an incentive to push smart phones that use the Symbian operating system. Perhaps for this reason, as of mid 2004 Symbian held a 41 percent share of the market for smart phone operating systems, up from 37 percent a year earlier. Symbian is followed by PalmSource and Microsoft, each with a 23 percent share. However, Symbian's influence is constrained by the fact that ultimately it is smart phone service providers, such as Verizon, that place orders for smart phones on behalf of their customers, and the service providers may request a Microsoft or Palm operating system. PalmSource's operating system is based in the software originally developed for the Palm series of personal digital assistants, while Microsoft uses its Pocket PC software, which is derived from and compatible with Microsoft Windows. Both PalmSource and Microsoft have an advantage in that there are already a wide range of applications written to run on their operating systems. Moreover, many people are already familiar with the Palm and Microsoft user interfaces (for example, the interface on a Microsoft smart phone is similar to that on a Microsoft Windows PC). Still, these advantages have not been sufficient to halt the rise of Symbian. While Microsoft's market share held steady between 2003 and 2004, PalmSource saw its share fall to 23 percent from 31 percent a year earlier. Neither company is ready to concede defeat to Symbian just yet, however. Microsoft claims that a range of new phones based on its operating system will hit the market in 2005, while PalmSource has just introduced a more powerful version of its operating system, which it hopes will halt its declines in market share.[1]

Overview

In this chapter, we look at the nature of competition and strategy in high-technology industries. **Technology** refers to the body of scientific knowledge used in the production of goods or services. **High-technology (high-tech) industries** are those in which the underlying scientific knowledge that companies in the industry use is advancing rapidly, and by implication so are the attributes of the products and services that result from its application. The computer industry is often thought of as the quintessential example of a high-technology industry. Other industries often considered high tech are telecommunications, where new technologies based on wireless and the Internet have proliferated in recent years; consumer electronics, where the digital technology underlying products from DVD players to videogame terminals and digital cameras is advancing rapidly; pharmaceuticals, where new technologies based on cell biology, recombinant DNA, and genomics are revolutionizing the process of drug discovery; power generation, where new technologies based on fuel cells and cogeneration may change the economics of the industry; and aerospace, where the combination of new composite materials, electronics, and more efficient jet engines may give birth to a new era of near-supersonic commercial aircraft.

This chapter focuses on high-technology industries for a number of reasons. First, technology is accounting for an ever larger share of economic activity. Estimates suggest that 12 to 15 percent of total economic activity in the United States is accounted for by information technology industries.[2] This figure actually underestimates the true impact of technology on the economy, because it ignores the other high-technology areas we just mentioned. Moreover, as technology advances, many low-technology industries are becoming more high tech. For example, the development of biotechnology and genetic engineering transformed the production of seed corn, long considered a low-technology business, into a high-technology business. Moreover, high-technology products are making their way into a wide range of businesses; today a Ford Taurus contains more computing power than the multimillion-dollar mainframe computers used in the Apollo space program, and the competitive advantage of physical stores, such as Wal-Mart, is based on their use of information technology.[3] The circle of high-technology industries is both large and expanding, and even in industries not thought of as high tech, technology is revolutionizing aspects of the product or production system.

Although high-tech industries may produce very different products, when it comes to developing a business model and strategies that will lead to a competitive advantage and superior profitability and profit growth, they often face a similar situation. This chapter examines the competitive features found in many high-tech industries and the kinds of strategies that companies must adopt to build business models that will allow them to achieve superior profitability and profit growth.

By the time you have completed this chapter, you will have an understanding of the nature of competition in high-tech industries and the strategies that companies can pursue to succeed in those industries.

Technical Standards and Format Wars

Especially in high-tech industries, ownership of **technical standards**—a set of technical specifications that producers adhere to when making the product or a component of it—can be an important source of competitive advantage.[4] *Indeed, the source of product differentiation is based on the technical standard.* Often, only one standard will come to dominate a market, so many battles in high-tech industries revolve around companies competing to be the one that sets the standard.

Battles to set and control technical standards in a market are referred to as **format wars**; they are essentially battles to control the source of differentiation and thus the value that such differentiation can create for the customer. Because differentiated products often command premium prices and are often expensive to develop, the competitive stakes are enormous. The profitability and very survival of a company may depend on the outcome of the battle. For example, the outcome of the battle now being waged over the establishment and ownership of the operating system used by smart phones will help determine which companies will be leaders for decades to come in that marketplace (see the *Opening Case*).

■ Examples of Standards

A familiar example of a standard is the layout of a computer keyboard. No matter what keyboard you buy, the letters are all in the same pattern.[5] The reason is quite obvious. Imagine if each computer maker changed the ways the keys were laid out—if some started with QWERTY on the top row of letters (which is indeed the format used and is known as the QWERTY format), some with YUHGFD, and some with ACFRDS. If you learned to type on one layout, it would be irritating and time-consuming to have to relearn on a YUHGFD layout. The standard format (QWERTY) makes it easy for people to move from computer to computer because the input medium, the keyboard, is set out in a standard way.

Another example of a technical standard concerns the dimensions of containers used to ship goods on trucks, railcars, and ships: all have the same basic dimensions—the same height, length, and width—and all make use of the same locking mechanisms to hold them onto a surface or to bolt against each other. Having a standard ensures that containers can easily be moved from one mode of transportation to another—from trucks, to railcars, to ships, and back to railcars. If containers lacked standard dimensions and locking mechanisms, it would suddenly become much more difficult to ship containers around the world. Shippers would have to make sure that they had the right kind of container to go on the ships and trucks and railcars scheduled to carry a particular container around the world—very complicated indeed.

Consider, finally, the personal computer. Most share a common set of features: an Intel or Intel-compatible microprocessor, random access memory (RAM), a Microsoft operating system, an internal hard drive, a floppy disk drive, a CD drive, a keyboard, a monitor, a mouse, a modem, and so on. We call this set of features the dominant design for personal computers (a **dominant design** refers to a common set of features or design characteristics). Embedded in this design are several technical standards (see Figure 7.1). For example, there is the Wintel technical standard based on an Intel microprocessor

FIGURE 7.1

Technical Standards
for Personal
Computers

and a Microsoft operating system. Microsoft and Intel own that standard, which is central to the personal computer. Developers of software applications, component parts, and peripherals such as printers adhere to this standard when developing their own products because this guarantees that their products will work well with a personal computer based on the Wintel standard. Another technical standard for connecting peripherals to the PC is the Universal Serial Bus (or USB), established by an industry standards-setting board. No one owns it; the standard is in the public domain. A third technical standard is for communication between a PC and the Internet via a modem. Known as TCP/IP, this standard was also set by an industry association and is in the public domain. Thus, as with many other products, the PC is actually based on several technical standards. It is also important to note that when a company owns a standard, as Microsoft and Intel do with the Wintel standard, it may be a source of competitive advantage and high profitability.

■ **Benefits of Standards**

Standards emerge because there are economic benefits associated with them. First, having a technical standard helps to guarantee *compatibility* between products and their complements—other products used with them. For example, containers are used with railcars, trucks, and ships, and PCs are used with software applications. Compatibility has the tangible economic benefit of reducing the costs associated with making sure that products work well with each other.

Second, having a standard can help to *reduce confusion* in the minds of consumers. A few years ago, several consumer electronics companies were vying with each other to produce and market the first DVD players, and they were championing different variants of the basic DVD technology—different standards—that were incompatible with each other; a DVD disk designed to run on a DVD player made by Toshiba would not run on a player made by Sony, and vice versa. The companies feared that selling these incompatible versions of the same technology would produce confusion in the minds of consumers, who would not know which version to purchase and might decide to wait and see which technology ultimately dominated the marketplace. With lack of demand, the technology might fail to gain traction in the marketplace and would not be successful. To avoid this possibility, the developers of DVD equipment established a standard-setting body for the industry, the DVD Forum, which established a common technical standard for DVD players and disks that all companies adhered to. The result was that when DVDs were introduced, there was a common standard and no confusion in consumers' minds. This helped to boost demand for DVD players, making this one of the fastest-selling technologies of the late 1990s and early 2000s. First introduced in 1997, by 2001 some 13 million DVD players were sold in the United States, and they are now in one in four homes in the country.[6] However, so far the DVD Forum has not been able to agree on a common standard for the next version of DVDs, DVD recorders, which is slowing diffusion and adoption of the technology (see Strategy in Action 7.1).

Third, the emergence of a standard can help to *reduce production costs*. Once a standard emerges, products based on that standard design can be mass-produced, enabling the manufacturers to realize substantial economies of scale and lower their cost structures. The fact that there is a central standard for PCs (the Wintel

Strategy in Action   7.1

Where Is the Standard for DVD Recorders?

A few years ago, the 200-member DVD Forum achieved something of a coup when it managed to broker an agreement among some of its most important members on a common set of standards for DVD players. This common standard reduced consumer confusion and helped to propel DVD players into a mass-market phenomenon, replacing VHS video players in living rooms. Nevertheless, the DVD players found in most homes currently lack one attribute of VHS technology: they cannot record. It's not that a technology for making DVD recorders does not exist; in fact, several do, and therein lies the problem. The DVD Forum has been unable to get some of its most powerful members to agree on a common technical standard for DVD recorders, primarily because different companies want to see their variant of the technology become the industry standard.

There are at least three versions of DVD recorders now on offer: Hewlett-Packard is pushing one format, Sony and Philips are sponsoring another, and Matsushita yet another. And most important, DVD disks recorded using one format may not play on widely used DVD players or on computers that use another recording format.

First introduced in 1999, by 2003 some 1 million DVD recorders had been sold in the United States, many of them incorporated into new personal computers. But

industry observers feel that sales could have been much higher had there been harmonization of standards. By way of comparison, some 40 million CD recorders were sold in 2001, making CD recording technology solidly mainstream (DVDs can hold ten times as many data as CDs and are thus better suited to recording video). One reason for the slow takeup of DVD recorders has been the confusion over standards, and it's not just consumers who are confused. Many retailers are hesitant about stocking the technology until the battle over standards is resolved.

Another reason for the slow market growth has been the high price of DVD recorders. As of early 2004, a stand-alone DVD recorder still cost around $500. Although down from $1,500, the price tag for a DVD recorder is still substantially above that of a DVD player, which often can be purchased for under $100. For the price to fall lower, producers need to be able to manufacture in high volume and realize significant scale economies. But here lies the catch: to generate significant demand to support mass production and bring prices down, it may first be necessary to harmonize standards and reduce consumer confusion— and that is something that the producers currently seem unwilling to do. For the time being, the different companies are continuing to push their own proprietary standard in the hope that they establish it as the leading standard in the industry and reap the associated gains.[a]

standard) means that the component parts for a PC can be mass-produced. A manufacturer of internal hard drives, for example, can mass-produce drives for Wintel PCs, and so can realize substantial scale economies. If there were several competing and incompatible standards, each of which required a unique type of hard drive, production runs for hard drives would be shorter, unit costs would be higher, and the cost of PCs would go up.

Fourth, the emergence of standards can help to reduce the *risks associated with supplying complementary products* and thus increase the supply for those complements. Consider the risks associated with writing software applications to run on personal computers. This is a risky proposition, requiring the investment of considerable sums of money for developing the software before a single unit is sold. Imagine what would occur if there were ten different operating systems in use for PCs, each with only 10 percent of the market, rather than the current situation, where 95 percent of the world's PCs adhere to the Wintel standard. Software developers would be faced with the need to write ten different versions of the same software application, each for a much smaller market segment. This would change the economics of software development, increase its risks, and reduce potential profitability. Moreover, because of their higher cost structure and fewer economies of scale, the price of software programs would increase.

Thus, although many people complain about the consequences of Microsoft's near monopoly of PC operating systems, that monopoly does have at least one good effect: it substantially reduces the risks facing the makers of complementary products and the costs of those products. In fact, standards lead to both low-cost and differentiation advantages for individual companies and can help raise the level of industry profitability.

■ Establishment of Standards

Standards emerge in an industry in three main ways. First, recognizing the benefits of establishing a standard, companies in an industry might lobby the government to mandate an industry standard. In the United States, for example, the Federal Communications Commission (FCC), after detailed discussions with broadcasters and consumer electronics companies, has mandated a single technical standard for digital television broadcasts (DTV) and is requiring broadcasters to have capabilities in place for broadcasting digital signals based on this standard by 2006. The FCC took this step because it believed that without government action to set the standard, the rollout of DTV would be very slow. With a standard set by the government, consumer electronics companies can have greater confidence that a market will emerge, and this should encourage them to develop DTV products.

Second, technical standards are often set by cooperation among businesses, without government help, often through the medium of an industry forum, such as the DVD Forum. Companies cooperate in this way when they decide that competition among them to create a standard might be harmful because of the uncertainty that it would create in the minds of consumers.

When standards are set by the government or an industry association, they fall into the **public domain**, meaning that any company can freely incorporate the knowledge and technology on which the standard is based into its products. For example, no one owns the QWERTY format, and therefore no one company can profit from it directly. Similarly, the language that underlies the presentation of text and graphics on the Web, hypertext markup language (HTML), is in the public domain; it is free for all to use. The same is true for TCP/IP, the communications standard used for transmitting data on the Internet.

Often, however, the industry standard is selected competitively by the purchasing patterns of customers in the marketplace—that is, by *market demand*. In this case, the strategy and business model a company has developed for promoting its technological standard are of critical importance because ownership of an industry standard that is protected from imitation by patents and copyrights is a valuable asset—a source of sustained competitive advantage and superior profitability. Microsoft and Intel, for example, both owe their competitive advantage to their ownership of format wars, which exist between two or more companies competing against each other to get their designs adopted as the industry standard. Format wars are common in high-tech industries because of the high stakes. The Wintel standard became the dominant standard for PCs only after Microsoft and Intel won format wars against Apple Computer's proprietary system and later against IBM's OS/2 operating system. Microsoft and Real Networks are currently competing head-to-head in a format war to establish rival technologies—Windows Media Player and RealPlayer—as the standard for streaming video and audio technology on the Web. The *Opening Case* tells how Symbian, Microsoft, and PalmSource are engaged in a format war in the wireless business as they try to get their respective operating systems established as the standard for smart phones.

■ **Network Effects, Positive Feedback, and Lockout**

There has been a growing realization that when standards are set by competition between companies promoting different formats, network effects are a primary determinant of how standards are established.[7] **Network effects** arise in industries where the size of the "network" of *complementary* products is a primary determinant of demand for an industry's product. For example, the demand for automobiles early in the twentieth century was an increasing function of the *network* of paved roads and gas stations. Similarly, the demand for telephones is an increasing function of the number of other numbers that can be called with that phone; that is, of the size of the telephone network (the telephone network is the complementary product). When the first telephone service was introduced in New York City, only a hundred numbers could be called. The network was very small because of the limited number of wires and telephone switches, which made the telephone a relatively useless piece of equipment. As more and more people got telephones and as the network of wires and switches expanded, the value of a telephone connection increased. This led to an increase in demand for telephone lines, which further increased the value of owning a telephone, setting up a positive feedback loop. The same type of positive feedback loop is now at work in the Internet.

To understand why network effects are important in the establishment of standards, consider the classic example of a format war: the battle between Sony and Matsushita to establish their respective technology for videocassette recorders (VCRs) as the standard in the marketplace. Sony was first to market with its Betamax technology, followed by Matsushita with its VHS technology. Both companies sold VCR recorder-players, and movie studios issued films prerecorded on VCR tapes for rental to consumers. Initially, all tapes were issued in Betamax format to play on Sony's machine. Sony *did not* license its Betamax technology, preferring to make all of the player-recorders itself. When Matsushita entered the market, it realized that to make its VHS format players valuable to consumers, it would have to encourage movie studios to issue movies for rental on VHS tapes. The only way to do that, Matsushita's managers reasoned, was to increase the installed base of VHS players as rapidly as possible. They believed that the greater the installed base of VHS players, the greater the incentive would be for movie studios to issue movies for

FIGURE 7.2

Positive Feedback in
the Market for VCRs

FIGURE 7.2

Positive Feedback in the Market for VCRs

rental on VHS format tapes. The more prerecorded VHS tapes were available for rental, the greater the value of a VHS player became to consumers, and therefore, the greater the demand would be for VHS players (see Figure 7.2). Matsushita wanted to exploit a positive feedback loop.

To do this, Matsushita chose a licensing strategy under which any consumer electronics company was allowed to manufacture VHS format players under license. The strategy worked. A large number of companies signed on to manufacture VHS players, and soon far more VHS players were available for purchase in stores than Betamax players. As sales of VHS players started to grow, movie studios issued more films for rental in VHS format, and this stoked demand. Before long, it was clear to anyone who walked into a video rental store that there were more and more VHS tapes available for rent and fewer and fewer Betamax tapes. This served to reinforce the positive feedback loop, and ultimately Sony's Betamax technology was shut out of the market. The pivotal difference between the two companies was strategy: Matsushita chose a licensing strategy, and Sony did not. As a result, Matsushita's VHS technology became the de facto standard for VCRs, while Sony's Betamax technology was locked out.

The general principle that emerges from this example is that when two or more companies are competing with each other to get their technology adopted as a standard in an industry, and when network effects and positive feedback loops are important, the company that wins the format war will be the one whose strategy best exploits positive feedback loops. It turns out that this is a very important strategic principle in many high-technology industries, particularly computer hardware, software, telecommunications, and consumer electronics. Microsoft is where it is today because it exploited a positive feedback loop. So did Dolby (see Strategy in Action 7.2).

An important implication of the positive feedback process is that as the market settles on a standard, companies promoting alternative standards can become **locked out** of the market when consumers are unwilling to bear the switching costs required for them to abandon the established standard and adopt the new standard. In this context, **switching costs** are the costs that consumers must bear to switch from a product based on one technological standard to a product based on another.

Strategy in Action 7.2

How Dolby Became the Standard in Sound Technology

Inventor Ray Dolby's name has become synonymous with superior sound in homes, movie theaters, and recording studios. The technology produced by his company, Dolby Laboratories, is part of nearly every music cassette and cassette recorder, prerecorded videotape, and, most recently, DVD movie disk and player. Since 1976, close to 1.5 billion audio products that use Dolby's technology have been sold worldwide. More than 44,000 movie theaters now show films in Dolby Digital Surround Sound, and some 40 million Dolby Digital home theater receivers have been sold since 1999. Dolby technology has become the industry standard for high-quality sound in the music and film industry. Any company that wants to promote its products as having superior technology licenses sound technology from Dolby. How did Dolby build this technology franchise?

The story goes back to 1965 when Dolby Laboratories was founded in London by Ray Dolby (the company's headquarters moved to San Francisco in 1976). Dolby, who had a PhD in physics from Cambridge University in England, had invented a technology for reducing the background hiss in professional tape recording without compromising the quality of the material being recorded. Dolby manufactured the sound systems incorporating his technology, but sales to professional recording studios were initially slow. Then in 1968 Dolby had a big break. He met Henry Kloss, whose company, KLH, was a highly regarded American producer of audio equipment (record players and tape decks) for the consumer market. Dolby reached an agreement to license his noise-reduction technology to KLH, and soon other manufacturers of consumer equipment started to approach Dolby to license the technology. Dolby briefly considered manufacturing record players and tape decks for the consumer market, but as he later commented, "I knew that if we entered that market and tried to make something like a cassette deck, we would be in competition with any licensee that we took on. . . . So we had to stay out of manufacturing in that area in order to license in that area."

Dolby adopted a licensing business model and then had to determine what licensing fee to charge. He knew his technology was valuable, but he also understood that charging a high licensing fee would encourage manufacturers to invest in developing their own noise-reduction technology. He decided to charge a modest fee to reduce the incentive that manufacturers would have to develop their own technology. Then there was the question of which companies to license to. Dolby wanted the Dolby name associated with superior sound, so he needed to make sure that licensees adhered to quality standards. Therefore, the company set up a formal quality control program for its licensees' products. Licensees have to agree to have their products tested by Dolby, and the licensing agreement states that they cannot sell products that do not pass Dolby's quality tests. By preventing products with substandard performance from reaching the market, Dolby has maintained the quality image of products featuring Dolby technology and trademarks. Today, Dolby Laboratories tests samples of hundreds of licensed products every year under this program. By making sure that the Dolby name is associated with superior sound quality, Dolby's quality assurance strategy has increased the power of the Dolby brand, making it very valuable to license.

Another key aspect of Dolby's strategy was born in 1970 when Dolby began to promote the idea of releasing prerecorded cassettes encoded with Dolby noise-reduction technology so that they would have low noise when played on players equipped with Dolby noise-reduction technology. Dolby decided to license the technology on prerecorded tapes for free, instead collecting licensing fees just from the sales of tape players that used Dolby technology. This strategy was hugely successful and set up a positive feedback loop that helped to make Dolby technology ubiquitous. Growing sales of prerecorded tapes encoded with Dolby technology created a demand for players that contained Dolby technology, and as the installed base of players with Dolby technology grew, the proportion of prerecorded tapes that were encoded with Dolby technology surged, further boosting demand for players incorporating Dolby technology. By the mid 1970s, virtually all prerecorded tapes were encoded with Dolby noise-reduction technology. This strategy remains in effect today for all media recorded with Dolby technology and encompasses not only videocassettes but also videogames and DVD releases encoded with Dolby Surround or Dolby Digital.

As a result of its licensing and quality assurance strategies, Dolby has become the standard for high-quality sound in the music and film industries. Although the company is small—its revenues were around $250 million in 2004—its influence is large. It continues to push the boundaries of sound-reduction technology (it has been a leader in digital sound since the mid 1980s) and has successfully extended its noise-reduction franchise, first into films, then into DVD and videogame technology, and finally onto the Web, where it has licensed its digital technology to a wide range of media companies for digital music delivery and digital audio players, such as those built into personal computers and hand-held music players.[b]

For illustration, imagine that a company developed an operating system for personal computers that was both faster and more stable (crashed less) than the current standard in the marketplace, Microsoft Windows. Would this company be able to gain significant market share from Microsoft? Only with great difficulty. Consumers buy personal computers not for their operating system but for the applications that run on that system. A new operating system would initially have a very small installed base, so few developers would be willing to take the risks in writing word processing programs, spreadsheets, games, and other applications for that operating system. Because there would be very few applications available, consumers who did make the switch would have to bear the switching costs associated with giving up some of their applications—something that they might be unwilling to do. Moreover, even if applications were available for the new operating system, consumers would have to bear the costs of purchasing those applications, another source of switching costs. In addition, they would have to bear the costs associated with learning to use the new operating system, yet another source of switching costs. Thus, many consumers would be unwilling to switch even if the new operating system performed better than Windows, and the company promoting the new operating system would be locked out of the market.

Consumers *will* bear switching costs if the benefits of adopting the new technology outweigh the costs of switching. For example, in the late 1980s and early 1990s, millions of people switched from analog record players to digital CD players even though the switching costs were significant: they had to purchase the new player technology, and many people purchased duplicate copies of their favorite music recordings. They nevertheless made the switch because for many people, the perceived benefit—the incredibly better sound quality associated with CDs—outweighed the costs of switching.

As this process started to get under way, a positive feedback started to develop, with the growing installed base of CD players leading to an increase in the number of music recordings issued on CDs, as opposed to or in addition to vinyl records. Past some point, the installed base of CD players got so big that music companies started to issue recordings only on CDs. Once this happened, even those who did not want to switch to the new technology were required to if they wished to purchase new music recordings. The industry standard had shifted: the new technology had locked in as the standard, and the old technology was locked out. It follows that despite its dominance, the Wintel standard for personal computers could one day be superseded if a competitor finds a way of providing sufficient benefits that enough consumers are willing to bear the switching costs associated with moving to a new operating system.

Strategies for Winning a Format War

From the perspective of a company pioneering a new technological standard in a marketplace where network effects and positive feedback loops operate, the key question becomes, "What strategy should we pursue to establish our format as the dominant one?"

The various strategies that companies should adopt to win format wars revolve around *finding ways to make network effects work in their favor and against their competitors*. Winning a format war requires a company to build the installed base for its standard as rapidly as possible, thereby leveraging the positive feedback loop, inducing consumers to bear switching costs, and ultimately locking the market into its technology. It requires the company to jump-start and then accelerate demand for its technological standard or format such that it becomes established as quickly as possible as the industry standard, thereby locking out competing formats. There are a number of key strategies and tactics that can be adopted to try to achieve this.[8]

■ Ensure a Supply of Complements

It is important for the company to make sure that, in addition to the product itself, there is an adequate supply of complements. For example, no one will buy the Sony PlayStation 2 unless there is an adequate supply of games to run on that machine. And no one will purchase a Palm hand-held computer unless there are enough software applications to run on it. Companies normally take two steps to ensure an adequate supply of complements.

First, they may diversify into the production of complements and seed the market with sufficient supply to help jump-start demand for their format. Before Sony produced the original PlayStation in the early 1990s, it established its own in-house unit to produce videogames for the PlayStation. When it launched the PlayStation, Sony also simultaneously issued sixteen games to run on the machine, giving consumers a reason to purchase the format. Second, companies may create incentives or make it easy for independent companies to produce complements. Sony also licensed the right to produce games to a number of independent game developers, charged the developers a lower royalty rate than they had to pay to competitors such as Nintendo and Sega, and provided them with software tools that made it easier for them to develop the games. Thus, the launch of the Sony PlayStation was accompanied by the simultaneous launch of thirty or so games, which quickly helped to stimulate demand for the machine.

■ Leverage Killer Applications

Killer applications are applications or uses of a new technology or product that are so compelling that they persuade customers to adopt the new format or technology in droves, thereby "killing" demand for competing formats. Killer applications often help to jump-start demand for the new standard. For example, in the late 1990s, hand-held computers based on the Palm operating system became the dominant format in the market for personal digital assistants (PDAs). The killer applications that drove adoption of the Palm format were the personal information management functions and a pen-based input medium (based on **Graffiti**) that Palm bundled with its original PalmPilot, which it introduced in 1996. There had been PDAs before the PalmPilot, including Apple Computer's ill-fated Newton, but it was the applications and ease of use of the PalmPilot that persuaded many consumers to enter this market. Within eighteen months of its initial launch, more than 1 million PalmPilots had been launched, making for a faster demand ramp-up than the first cell phones and pagers. Similarly, the killer applications that induced consumers to sign up to online services such as AOL were e-mail, chatroom, and the ability to browse the Web.

Ideally, the company promoting a technological standard will want to develop the killer applications itself—that is, develop the appropriate complementary products—as Palm did with the PalmPilot. However, it may also be able to leverage the applications that others develop. For example, the early sales of the IBM PC following its 1981 introduction were driven primarily by IBM's decision to license two important software programs for the PC, VisiCalc (a spreadsheet program) and Easy Writer (a word processing program), both developed by independent companies. IBM saw that they were driving rapid adoption of rival personal computers, such as the Apple II, so it quickly licensed them, produced versions that would run on the IBM PC, and sold them as complements to the IBM PC, a strategy that was to prove very successful.

■ Aggressively Price and Market

A common tactic to jump-start demand is to adopt a **razor-and-razor-blades strategy:** pricing the product (razor) low in order to stimulate demand and increase the installed base, and then trying to make high profits on the sale of complements (razor blades), which are priced relatively high. This strategy owes its name to the fact that it was pioneered by Gillette to sell its razors and razor blades. Many other companies have followed this strategy—for example, Hewlett-Packard typically sells its printers at cost but makes significant profits on the subsequent sale of its replacement cartridges. In this case, the printer is the "razor," and it is priced low to stimulate demand and induce consumers to switch from their existing printer, while the cartridges are the "blades," which are priced high to make profits. The inkjet printer represents a proprietary technological format because only Hewlett-Packard cartridges can be used with the printers, and not cartridges designed for competing inkjet printers, such as those sold by Canon. A similar strategy is used in the videogame industry: manufacturers price videogame consoles at cost to induce consumers to adopt their technology, while making profits on the royalties they receive from the sales of games that run on their system.

Aggressive marketing is also a key factor in jump-starting demand to get an early lead in an installed base. Substantial upfront marketing and point-of-sales promotion techniques are often used to try to get potential early adopters to bear the switching costs associated with adopting the format. If these efforts are successful, they can be the start of a positive feedback loop. Again, the Sony PlayStation provides a good example. Sony colinked the introduction of the PlayStation with nationwide television advertising aimed at its primary demographic (eighteen- to thirty-four-year-olds) and in-store displays that allowed potential buyers to play games on the machine before making a purchase. More recently, Microsoft earmarked $500 million for marketing its new Xbox in 2002. Successful marketing can set the ball rolling and create a positive feedback loop.

■ Cooperate with Competitors

Companies have been close to simultaneously introducing competing and incompatible technological standards a number of times. A good example is the compact disk. Initially four companies—Sony, Philips, JVC, and Telefunken—were developing CD players using different variations of the underlying laser technology. If this situation had persisted, they might have ultimately introduced incompatible technologies into the marketplace, so a CD made for a Philips CD player would not play on a Sony CD player. Understanding that the nearly simultaneous introduction of such incompatible technologies can create significant confusion among consumers and often leads them to delay their purchases, Sony and Philips decided to join forces with each other and cooperate on developing the technology. Sony contributed its error correction technology, and Philips contributed its laser technology. The result of this cooperation was that momentum among other players in the industry shifted toward the Sony-Philips alliances; JVC and Telefunken were left with little support. Most important, recording labels announced that they would support the Sony-Philips format but not the Telefunken or JVC format. Telefunken and JVC subsequently decided to abandon their efforts to develop CD technology. The cooperation between Sony and Philips was important because it reduced confusion in the industry and allowed a single format to rise to the fore, which speeded up adoption of the technology. The cooperation was a win-win situation for both Philips and Sony, eliminating their competitors and allowing them to share in the success of the format.

■ **License the Format**

Another strategy often adopted is to license the format to other enterprises so that they can produce products based on it. The company that pioneered the format gains from the licensing fees that flow back to it and from the enlarged supply of the product, which can stimulate demand and help accelerate market adoption. This was the strategy that Matsushita adopted with its VHS format for the videocassette recorder. In addition to producing VCRs at its own factory in Osaka, Matsushita let a number of other companies produce VHS format players under license (Sony decided not to license its competing Betamax format and produced all Betamax format players itself), and so VHS players were more widely available. More people purchased VHS players, which created an incentive for film companies to issue more films on VHS tapes (as opposed to Betamax tapes), which further increased demand for VHS players, and hence helped Matsushita to lock in VHS as the dominant format in the marketplace. Sony, ironically the first to market, saw its position marginalized by the reduced supply of the critical complement, prerecorded films, and ultimately withdrew Betamax players from the consumer marketplace.

Dolby, we saw in Strategy in Action 7.2, adopted a similar licensing strategy to get its noise-reduction technology adopted as the technological standard in the music and film industries. By charging a modest licensing fee for use of the technology in recording equipment and forgoing licensing fees on media recorded using Dolby technology, Dolby deliberately sought to reduce the financial incentive that potential competitors might have to develop their own, possibly superior, technology. Dolby calculated that its long-run profitability would be maximized by adopting a licensing strategy that limited the incentive of competitors to enter the market.

The correct strategy to pursue in a particular scenario requires that the company consider all of these different strategies and tactics and pursue those that seem most appropriate given the competitive circumstances prevailing in the industry and the likely strategy of rivals. Although there is no one best mix of strategies and tactics, the company must keep the goal of rapidly increasing the installed base of products based on its standard at the front of its mind. By helping to jump-start demand for its format, a company can induce consumers to bear the switching costs associated with adopting its technology and leverage any positive feedback process that might exist. Also important is not pursuing strategies that have the opposite effect. For example, pricing high to capture profits from early adopters, who tend not to be as price sensitive as later adopters, can have the unfortunate effect of slowing demand growth and letting a more aggressive competitor pick up share and establish its format as the industry standard.

Costs in High-Technology Industries

In many high-tech industries, the fixed costs of developing the product are very high, but the costs of producing one extra unit of the product are very low. This is most obvious in the case of software. For example, it reportedly cost Microsoft $1 billion to develop Windows XP, the latest version of its Windows operating system, but the cost of producing one more copy of Windows XP is virtually zero. Once Windows XP was completed, Microsoft produced master disks that it sent out to PC manufacturers, such as Dell Computer, which then loaded a copy of Windows XP onto every PC it sold. The cost to Microsoft was effectively zero, and yet it receives a significant licensing fee for each copy of Windows XP installed on a PC.[9] For Microsoft, the *marginal cost* of making one more copy of Windows XP is close to zero, although the *fixed costs* of developing the product are $1 billion.

Many other high-technology products have similar cost economics: very high fixed costs and very low marginal costs. Most software products share these features, although if the software is sold through stores, the costs of packaging and distribution will raise the marginal costs, and if it is sold by a sales force direct to end-users, this too will raise the marginal costs. Many consumer electronics products have the same basic economics. The fixed costs of developing a DVD player or a videogame console can be very expensive, but the costs of producing an incremental unit are very low. The costs of developing a new drug, such as Viagra, can run to over $500 million, but the marginal cost of producing each additional pill is at most a few cents.

■ Comparative Cost Economics

To grasp why this cost structure is strategically important, it must be understood that, in many industries, marginal costs *rise* as a company tries to expand output (economists call this the *law of diminishing returns*). To produce more of a good, a company has to hire more labor and invest in more plant and machinery. At *the margin*, the additional resources used are not as productive, so this leads to increasing marginal costs. However, the law of diminishing returns often does not apply in many high-tech settings, such as the production of software or sending one more bit of data down a digital telecommunications network.

Consider two companies, α and β (see Figure 7.3). Company α is a conventional producer and faces diminishing returns, so as it tries to expand output, its marginal

FIGURE 7.3

Cost Structures in High-Technology Industries

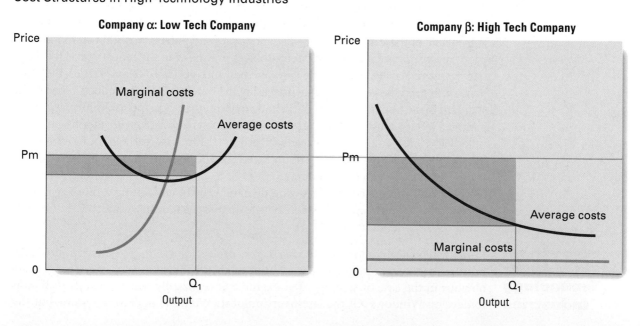

costs rise. Company β is a high-tech producer, and its marginal costs do not rise at all as output is increased. Note that in Figure 7.3, company β's marginal cost curve is drawn as a straight line near to the horizontal axis, implying that marginal costs are close to zero and do not vary with output, whereas company α's marginal costs rise as output is expanded, illustrating diminishing returns. Company β's flat and low marginal cost curve means that its average cost curve will fall continuously over all ranges of output as it spreads its fixed costs out over greater volume. In contrast, the rising marginal costs encountered by company α mean that its average cost curve is the U-shaped curve familiar from basic economics texts. For simplicity, assume that both companies sell their product at the same price, P_m, and both sell exactly the same quantity of output, $0 - Q_1$. You will see from Figure 7.3 that at an output of Q_1, company β has much lower average costs than company α and as a consequence is making far more profit (profit is the blue shaded area in Figure 7.3).

■ **Strategic Significance**

If a company can shift from a cost structure where it encounters increasing marginal costs to one where fixed costs may be high but marginal costs are much lower, its profitability may increase. In the consumer electronics industry, such a shift has been playing out for two decades. Music recordings used to be based on analog technology where marginal costs rose as output expanded due to diminishing returns (as in the case of company α in Figure 7.3). Since the 1980s, digital systems such as CD players have replaced analog systems. Digital systems are software based, and this implies much lower marginal costs of producing one more copy of a recording. As a result, the music labels have been able to lower prices, expand demand, and see their profitability increase (their production system has more in common with company β in Figure 7.3).

This process is still unfolding. The latest technology for making copies of music recordings is based on distribution over the Internet (for example, by downloading onto an MP3 player). Here, the marginal costs of making one more copy of a recording are lower still. In fact, they are close to zero and do not increase with output. The only problem is that the low costs of copying and distributing music recordings have created a major copyright problem that the major music labels have yet to solve (we discuss this in more detail shortly when we consider intellectual property rights). The same shift is now beginning to affect other industries. Some companies are building their strategies around trying to exploit and profit from this shift. For an example, Strategy in Action 7.3 looks at SonoSite.

Another implication of its cost structure is that when a high-tech company faces high fixed costs and low marginal costs, its strategy should emphasize the low-cost option: deliberately drive prices down to drive volume up. Look again at Figure 7.3 and you will see that *the high-tech company's average costs fall rapidly as output expands.* This implies that prices can be reduced to stimulate demand, and so long as prices fall less rapidly than average costs, per unit profit margins will expand as prices fall. This is a consequence of the fact that the firm's marginal costs are low and do not rise with output. This strategy of pricing low to drive volume and reap wider profit margins is central to the business model of some very successful high-technology companies, including Microsoft. When Microsoft founder Bill Gates was called into a U.S. Senate hearing during the Microsoft antitrust investigation in 2000, he explained to the bemused senators that Microsoft did not behave like a classic monopolist, raising prices and restricting output to maximize profits. Rather, he said, Microsoft cut prices to stimulate sales and thus increase its profit margins. Gates claimed that the strategy was good for consumers—they got cheaper software—and good for Microsoft's

Strategy in Action   7.3

Lowering Costs Through Digitalization

The ultrasound unit has been an important piece of diagnostic equipment in hospitals for some time. Ultrasound units use the physics of sound to produce images of soft tissues in the human body. They can produce detailed three-dimensional color images of organs and, by using contrast agents, track the flow of fluids through an organ. A cardiologist, for example, can use an ultrasound in combination with contrast agents injected into the bloodstream to track the flow of blood through a beating heart. In additional to the visual diagnosis, ultrasound also produces an array of quantitative diagnostic information of great value to physicians.

Modern ultrasound units are sophisticated instruments that cost around $250,000 to $300,000 each for a top-line model. They are fairly bulky instruments, weighing some three hundred pounds, and are wheeled around hospitals on carts.

A few years back, a group of researchers at ATL, one of the leading ultrasound companies, came up with an idea for reducing the size and cost of a basic unit. They theorized that it might be possible to replace up to 80 percent of the solid circuits in an ultrasound unit with software, in the process significantly shrinking the size and reducing the weight of machines and thereby producing portable ultrasound units. Moreover, by digitalizing much of the ultrasound, replacing hardware with software, they could considerably drive down the marginal costs of making additional units, and would thus be able to make a good profit at much lower price points.

The researchers reasoned that a portable and inexpensive ultrasound unit would find market opportunities in totally new niches. For example, a small, inexpensive ultrasound unit could be placed in an ambulance or carried into battle by an army medic, or purchased by family physicians for use in their offices. Although they realized that it would be some time, perhaps decades, before such small, inexpensive machines could attain the image quality and diagnostic sophistication of top-of-the-line machines, they saw the opportunity in terms of creating market niches that previously could not be served by ultrasound companies because of the high costs and bulk of the product.

The researchers ultimately became a project team within ATL and were then spun out of ATL as an entirely new company, SonoSite. In late 1999, they introduced their first portable product, weighing just six pounds and costing around $25,000. SonoSite targeted niches that full-sized ultrasound products could not reach: ambulatory care and foreign markets that could not afford the more expensive equipment. In 2003, the company sold $85 million worth of its product. In the long run, SonoSite plans to build more features and greater image quality into the small hand-held machines, primarily by improving the software. This could allow the units to penetrate U.S. hospital markets that currently purchase the established technology, much as client-server systems based on PC technology came to replace mainframes for some functions in business corporations.[c]

---

profit margins. It was clear from the questioning that the senators had trouble believing this explanation, but for Gates and his company, it has been a central aspect of their strategy since the early 1980s.

Managing Intellectual Property Rights

Ownership of a technology can be a source of sustained competitive advantage and superior profitability, particularly when the company owns a technology that is the standard in an industry, such as Microsoft and Intel's Wintel standard for personal computers and Dolby's ownership of the standard for noise-reduction technology in the music and film recording industries. Even if a technology is not standard but is valued by a sufficient number of consumers, ownership of that technology can still be very profitable. Apple's current personal computer technology is by no means the standard in the marketplace, much as Apple would like it to be. In fact, the company's iMac technology accounts for less than 10 percent of the personal computers sold every year. But that small slice of a very large market is still a valuable niche for Apple.

■ Intellectual Property Rights

Because new technology is the product of intellectual and creative effort, we call it intellectual property. The term **intellectual property** refers to the product of any intellectual and creative effort and includes not only new technology but also a wide range of intellectual creations, including music, films, books, and graphic art. As a society, we value the products of intellectual and creative activity. Intellectual property is seen as a very important driver of economic progress and social wealth.[10] But it is also often expensive, risky, and time-consuming to create intellectual property.

For example, a new drug to treat a dangerous medical condition such as cancer can take twelve to sixteen years to develop and cost as much as $800 million. Moreover, only 20 percent of new drugs that are tested in humans actually make it to the market.[11] The remainder fail because they are found to be unsafe or ineffective. Given the costs, risks, and time involved in this activity, few companies would be willing to embark on the road required to develop a new drug and bring it to market unless they could be reasonably sure that if they were successful in developing the drug, their investment would be profitable. If the minute they introduced a successful cancer drug, their competitors produced imitations of that drug, no company would even consider making the initial investment.

To make sure that this does not happen, we grant the creators of intellectual property certain rights over their creation. These rights, which stop competitors from copying or imitating the creation for a number of years, take the legal forms of patents, copyrights, and trademarks, which all serve the same basic objective: to give individuals and companies an incentive to engage in the expensive and risky business of creating new intellectual property.

The creation of intellectual property is a central endeavor in high-technology industries, and the management of intellectual property rights has moved to center stage in many of these companies. Developing strategies to protect and enforce intellectual property rights can be an important aspect of competitive advantage. For many companies, this amounts to making sure that their patents and copyrights are respected. It is not uncommon, therefore, to see high-technology companies bringing lawsuits against their competitors for patent infringement. In general, companies often use such lawsuits not only to sanction those they suspect of violating the company's intellectual property rights, but also to signal to potential violators that the company will aggressively defend its property. Legal action alone suffices to protect intellectual property in many industries, but in others, such as software, the low costs of illegally copying and distributing intellectual property call for more creative strategies to manage intellectual property rights.

■ Digitalization and Piracy Rates

Protecting intellectual property has become more complicated in the past few decades because of **digitalization,** that is, the rendering of creative output in digital form. This can be done for music recordings, films, books, newspapers, magazines, and computer software. Digitalization has dramatically lowered the cost of copying and distributing digitalized intellectual property or digital media. As we have seen, the marginal cost of making one more copy of a software program is very low, and the same is true for any other intellectual property rendered in digital form. Moreover, digital media can be distributed at a very low cost (again, almost zero), for example, by distributing over the Internet. Reflecting on this, one commentator has described the

Internet as a "giant out-of-control copying machine."[12] The low marginal costs of copying and distributing digital media have made it very easy to sell illegal copies of such property. In turn, this has helped to produce a high level of piracy (in this context, **piracy** refers to the theft of intellectual property).

The International Federation of the Phonographic Industry claims that around one-third of all CDs and cassettes around the globe were illegally produced and sold in 2002, suggesting that piracy cost the industry over $4.6 billion per annum.[13] The computer software industry also suffers from lax enforcement of intellectual property rights. Estimates suggest that violations of intellectual property rights cost computer software firms revenues equal to $13.08 billion in 2002.[14] According to the Business Software Alliance, a software industry association, in 2002 some 39 percent of all software applications used in the world were pirated. The worst region was Eastern Europe, where the piracy rate was 71 percent. One of the worst countries was China, where the piracy rate in 2002 ran 92 percent and cost the industry over $2.4 billion in lost sales, up from $444 million in 1995. Although the piracy rate was much lower in the United States, the value of sales lost was more significant because of the size of the market, reaching an estimated $2.0 billion in 2002.[15]

The scale of this problem is so large that simply resorting to legal tactics to enforce intellectual property rights has amounted to nothing more than a partial solution to the piracy problem. Many companies now build sophisticated encryption software into their digital products, which can make it more difficult for pirates to copy digital media and thereby can raise the costs of stealing. But the pirates too are sophisticated and often seem to be able to find their way around encryption software. This raises the question of whether there are additional strategies that can be adopted to manage digital rights, and thereby limit piracy.

■ Strategies for Managing Digital Rights

One strategy is simply to recognize that while the low costs of copying and distributing digital media make some piracy inevitable, the same attributes can be used to the company's advantage. The basic strategy here represents yet another variation of the basic razor-and-razor-blades principle: give something away for free to boost the sales of a complementary product. A familiar example concerns Adobe Acrobat Reader, the software program for reading documents formatted by Adobe Acrobat (that is, PDF formatted documents). Adobe developed Adobe Acrobat to allow people to format documents in a manner that resembled a high-quality printed page and to display and distribute these documents over the Web. Moreover, Adobe documents are formatted in a read-only format, meaning that they cannot be altered by individuals, nor can parts of those documents be copied and pasted to other documents. Its strategy has been to give away Adobe Acrobat Reader for free and then make money by selling its Acrobat software for formatting documents. The strategy has worked extremely well. Anyone can download a copy of Acrobat Reader from Adobe's website. Because the marginal costs of copying and distributing this software over the Web are extremely low, the process is almost costless for both Adobe and its customers. The result is that the Acrobat Reader has diffused very rapidly and is now the dominant format for viewing high-quality documents distributed and downloaded over the Web. As the installed base of Acrobat Readers has grown, sales of Adobe Acrobat software have soared as more and more organizations and individuals realize that formatting their digital documents in Acrobat format makes sense.

Another strategy is to take advantage of the low costs of copying and distributing digital media to drive down the costs of purchasing those media, thereby reducing the incentive that consumers have to steal. When coupled with encryption software that makes piracy more difficult and vigorous legal actions to enforce intellectual property regulations, this can slow the piracy rate and generate incremental revenues that cost little to produce.

Several music companies are now experimenting with variants of this strategy. Roxio, a manufacturer of software for copying, or "burning," music onto CDs, has begun to partner with several music labels to develop just such a strategy.[16] In 2001, Roxio's Easy CD Creator and Toast software accounted for 70 percent of the CD burning software sold. The software is now preloaded onto most new personal computers. However, Roxio's sales growth has been hampered by opposition from music labels, which argue that Roxio's software is promoting music piracy and hurting CD sales. In response, Roxio persuaded several music companies to start experimenting with a service that allows users to burn music onto CDs. In January 2002, Pressplay, a service backed by Sony, Universal Music, and EMI, began to allow users to download songs digitally and burn them onto CDs. Users pay $25 a month to burn twenty songs, although they can burn only two tracks from a single artist each month. This business model allows subscribers to customize a CD, which is what many do anyway when pirating CDs by burning them. However, in theory, the service saves customers money because they do not have to purchase the original CDs. Pressplay and Roxio hope that the strategy will reduce piracy rates, while generating incremental revenues that cost very little to produce because of the extremely low marginal costs of copying and distributing music in this manner (in 2003 Pressplay was sold to Roxio).

Capturing First-Mover Advantages

In high-technology industries, companies often compete by striving to be the first to develop revolutionary new products, that is, to be a **first mover**. By definition, the first mover with regard to a revolutionary product is in a monopoly position. If the new product satisfies unmet consumer needs and demand is high, the first mover can capture significant revenues and profits. Such revenues and profits signal to potential rivals that there is money to be made by imitating the first mover. As illustrated in Figure 7.4, in the absence of strong barriers to imitation, this implies that imitators will rush into the market created by the first mover, competing away the first mover's monopoly profits and leaving all participants in the market with a much lower level of returns.

FIGURE 7.4

The Impact of Imitation on Profits of a First Mover

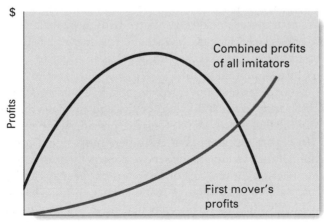

Despite imitation, some first movers have the ability to capitalize on and reap substantial **first-mover advantages**—the advantages of pioneering new technologies and products that lead to an enduring competitive advantage. Intel introduced the world's first microprocessor in 1971 and today still dominates the microprocessor segment of the semiconductor industry. Xerox introduced the world's first photocopier and for a long time enjoyed a leading position in the industry. Cisco introduced the first Internet protocol network router in 1986 and still dominates the market for that equipment today. Some first movers can reap substantial advantages from their pioneering activities that lead to an enduring competitive advantage. They can, in other words, limit or slow the rate of imitation.

But there are plenty of counterexamples suggesting that first-mover advantages might not be easy to capture and, in fact, that there might be **first-mover disadvantages**—the competitive *disadvantages* associated with being first. For example, Apple Computer was the first company to introduce a hand-held computer, the Apple Newton, but the product failed; a second mover, Palm, succeeded where Apple had failed. In the market for commercial jet aircraft, DeHavilland was first to market with the Comet, but it was the second mover, Boeing, with its 707 jetliner, that went on to dominate the market.

Clearly being a first mover does not by itself guarantee success. As we shall see, the difference between innovating companies that capture first-mover advantages and those that fall victim to first-mover disadvantages in part turns on the strategy that the first mover pursues. Before considering the strategy issue, however, we need to take a closer look at the nature of first-mover advantages and disadvantages.[17]

■ First-Mover Advantages

There are five main sources of first-mover advantages.[18] First, the first mover has an opportunity to *exploit network effects* and positive feedback loops, locking consumers into its technology. In the VCR industry, Sony could have exploited network effects by licensing its technology, but instead the company ceded its first-mover advantage to the second mover, Matsushita.

Second, the first mover may be able to establish significant *brand loyalty*, which is expensive for later entrants to break down. Indeed, if the company is successful in this endeavor, its name may become closely associated with the entire class of products, including those produced by rivals. People still talk of "Xeroxing" when they are going to make a photocopy or "FedExing" when they are going to send a package by overnight mail.

Third, the first mover may be able to ramp up sales volume ahead of rivals and thus reap cost advantages associated with the realization of *scale economies and learning effects* (see Chapter 4). Once the first mover has these cost advantages, it can respond to new entrants by cutting prices in order to hold on to its market share and still earn significant profits.

Fourth, the first mover may be able to create *switching costs* for its customers that subsequently make it difficult for rivals to enter the market and take customers away from the first mover. Wireless service providers, for example, will give new customers a "free" wireless phone, but customers must sign a contract agreeing to pay for the phone if they terminate the service contract within a specified time period, such as a year. Because the real cost of a wireless phone may run from $100 to $200, this represents a significant switching cost that later entrants have to overcome.

Finally, the first mover may be able to *accumulate valuable knowledge* related to customer needs, distribution channels, product technology, process technology, and so on. This accumulated knowledge gives it a knowledge advantage that later entrants might find difficult or expensive to match. Sharp, for example, was the first mover in the commercial manufacture of active matrix liquid crystal displays used in laptop computers. The process for manufacturing these displays is very difficult, with a high reject rate for flawed displays. Sharp has accumulated such an advantage with regard to production processes that it has been very difficult for later entrants to match it on product quality, and thus costs.

■ **First-Mover Disadvantages**

Balanced against these first-mover advantages are a number of disadvantages.[19] First, the first mover has to bear significant *pioneering costs* that later entrants do not. The first mover has to pioneer the technology, develop distribution channels, and educate customers about the nature of the product. All of this can be expensive and time-consuming. Later entrants, by way of contrast, might be able to *free-ride* on the first mover's investments in pioneering the market and customer education.

Related to this, first movers are more prone to *make mistakes* because there are so many uncertainties in a new market. Later entrants may be able to learn from the mistakes made by first movers, improve on the product or the way in which it is sold, and come to market with a superior offering that captures significant market share from the first mover. For example, one of the reasons that the Apple Newton failed was that the handwriting software in the hand-held computer failed to recognize human handwriting. The second mover in this market, Palm, learned from Apple's error. When it introduced the PalmPilot, it used software that recognized letters written in a particular way, Graffiti, and then persuaded customers to learn this method of inputting data into the hand-held computer.

Third, first movers run the risk of *building the wrong resources and capabilities* because they are focusing on a customer set that is not going to be characteristic of the mass market. This is the *crossing the chasm* problem that we discussed in the previous chapter. You will recall that the customers in the early market—those we categorized as innovators and early adopters—have different characteristics from the first wave of the mass market, the early majority. The first mover runs the risk of gearing its resources and capabilities to the needs of innovators and early adopters and not being able to switch when the early majority enters the market. As a result, first movers run a greater risk of plunging into the chasm that separates the early market from the mass market.

Finally, the first mover may invest in *inferior or obsolete technology*. This can happen when its product innovation is based on underlying technology that is advancing rapidly. By basing its product on an early version of the technology, it may lock itself into something that rapidly becomes obsolete. In contrast, later entrants may be able to leapfrog the first mover and introduce products that are based on later versions of the underlying technology. This happened in France during the 1980s when, at the urging of the government, France Telecom introduced the world's first consumer online service, Minitel. France Telecom distributed crude terminals to consumers for free, which they could hook up to their phone line and use to browse phone directories. Other simple services were soon added, and before long the French could carry out online shopping, banking, travel, weather, and news—all years before the Web was invented. The problem was that by the standards of the Web, Minitel was very crude and inflexible, and France Telecom, as the first mover, suffered. The French were very slow to adopt personal computers and then the Internet primarily because Minitel had such a presence. As late as 1998, only a fifth of French households had a computer, compared with two-fifths in the United States, and only 2 percent of households were connected to the Internet, compared to over 30 percent in the United States. As the result of a government decision, France Telecom, and indeed an entire nation, was slow to adopt a revolutionary new online medium, the Web, because they were the first to invest in a more primitive version of the technology.[20]

■ Strategies for Exploiting First-Mover Advantages

The task facing a first mover is how to exploit its lead to capitalize on first-mover advantages and build a sustainable long-term competitive advantage while simultaneously reducing the risks associated with first-mover disadvantages. There are three basic strategies available: (1) develop and market the innovation itself, (2) develop and market the innovation jointly with other companies through a strategic alliance or joint venture, and (3) license the innovation to others and let them develop the market.

The optimal choice of strategy depends on the answers to three questions:

1. Does the innovating company have the *complementary assets* to exploit its innovation and capture first-mover advantages?

2. How difficult is it for imitators to copy the company's innovation? In other words, what is the *height of barriers to imitation?*

3. Are there *capable competitors* that could rapidly imitate the innovation?

■ Complementary Assets

Complementary assets are the assets required to exploit a new innovation and gain a competitive advantage.[21] Among the most important complementary assets are competitive manufacturing facilities capable of handling rapid growth in customer demand while maintaining high product quality. State-of-the-art manufacturing facilities enable the first mover to move quickly down the experience curve without encountering production bottlenecks or problems with the quality of the product. The inability to satisfy demand because of these problems, however, creates the opportunity for imitators to enter the marketplace. For example, in 1998, Immunex was the first company to introduce a revolutionary new biological treatment for rheumatoid arthritis. Sales for this product, Enbrel, ramped up very rapidly, hitting $750 million in 2001. However, Immunex had not invested in sufficient manufacturing capacity. In mid-2000, it announced that it lacked the capacity to satisfy demand and that bringing additional capacity on line would take at least two years. This manufacturing bottleneck gave the second mover in the market, Johnson & Johnson, the opportunity to expand demand for its product rapidly, which by early 2002 was outselling Enbrel. Immunex's first-mover advantage had been partly eroded because it lacked an important complementary asset, the manufacturing capability required to satisfy demand.

Complementary assets also include marketing know-how, an adequate sales force, access to distribution systems, and an after-sales service and support network. All of these assets can help an innovator build brand loyalty and achieve market penetration more rapidly.[22] In turn, the resulting increases in volume facilitate more rapid movement down the experience curve and the attainment of a sustainable cost-based advantage due to scale economies and learning effects. One of the reasons that EMI, the first mover in the market for CT scanners, ultimately lost out to established medical equipment companies, such as GE Medical Systems, was that it lacked the marketing know-how, sales force, and distribution systems required to compete effectively in the world's largest market for medical equipment, the United States.

Developing complementary assets can be very expensive, and companies often need large infusions of capital for this purpose. That is why first movers often lose out to late movers that are large, successful companies in other industries with the resources to develop a presence in the new industry quickly. Microsoft and 3M exemplify companies that can move quickly to capitalize on the opportunities when other companies open up new product markets, such as compact disks or floppy disks. For example, although Netscape pioneered the market for Internet browsers with Netscape Navigator, Microsoft's Internet Explorer ultimately dominated the market for Internet browsers.

■ **Height of Barriers to Imitation** Recall from Chapter 3 that **barriers to imitation** are factors that prevent rivals from imitating a company's distinctive competencies and innovations. Although ultimately any innovation can be copied, the higher the barriers are, the longer it takes for rivals to imitate, and the more time the first mover has to build an enduring competitive advantage.

Barriers to imitation give an innovator time to establish a competitive advantage and build more enduring barriers to entry in the newly created market. Patents, for example, are among the most widely used barriers to imitation. By protecting its photocopier technology with a thicket of patents, Xerox was able to delay any significant imitation of its product for seventeen years. However, patents are often easy to "invent around." For example, one study found that this happened to 60 percent of patented innovations within four years.[23] If patent protection is weak, a company might try to slow imitation by developing new products and processes in secret. The most famous example of this approach is Coca-Cola, which has kept the formula for Coke a secret for generations. But Coca-Cola's success in this regard is an exception. A study of one hundred companies has estimated that proprietary information about a company's decision to develop a major new product or process is known to its rivals within about twelve to eighteen months of the original development decision.[24]

■ **Capable Competitors** **Capable competitors** are companies that can move quickly to imitate the pioneering company. Competitors' capability to imitate a pioneer's innovation depends primarily on two factors: (1) R&D skills and (2) access to complementary assets. In general, the greater the number of capable competitors with access to the R&D skills and complementary assets needed to imitate an innovation, the more rapid imitation is likely to be.

In this context, R&D skills refer to the ability of rivals to reverse-engineer an innovation in order to find out how it works and quickly develop a comparable product. As an example, consider the CT scanner. GE bought one of the first CT scanners produced by EMI, and its technical experts reverse-engineered it. Despite the product's technological complexity, GE developed its own version, which allowed it to imitate EMI quickly and ultimately to replace EMI as the major supplier of CT scanners.

With regard to complementary assets, the access that rivals have to marketing, sales know-how, or manufacturing capabilities is one of the key determinants of the rate of imitation. If would-be imitators lack critical complementary assets, not only do they have to imitate the innovation, but they may also have to imitate the innovator's complementary assets. This is expensive, as AT&T discovered when it tried to enter the personal computer business in 1984. AT&T lacked the marketing assets (sales force and distribution systems) necessary to support personal computer products. The lack of these assets and the time it takes to build them partly explain why, four years after it entered the market, AT&T had lost $2.5 billion and still had not emerged as a viable contender. It subsequently pulled out of this business.

TABLE 7.1

Strategies for Profiting from Innovation

Strategy	Does the Innovator Have the Required Complementary Assets?	Likely Height of Barriers to Imitation	Number of Capable Competitors
Going it alone	Yes	High	Very few
Entering into an alliance	No	High	Moderate number
Licensing the innovation	No	Low	Many

■ **Three Innovation Strategies** The way in which these three factors—complementary assets, height of barriers to imitation, and the capability of competitors—influence the choice of innovation strategy is summarized in Table 7.1. The competitive strategy of *developing and marketing the innovation alone* makes most sense when (1) the innovator has the complementary assets necessary to develop the innovation, (2) the barriers to imitating a new innovation are high, and (3) the number of capable competitors is limited. Complementary assets allow rapid development and promotion of the innovation. High barriers to imitation buy the innovator time to establish a competitive advantage and build enduring barriers to entry through brand loyalty or experience-based cost advantages. The fewer the capable competitors there are, the less likely it is that any one of them will succeed in circumventing barriers to imitation and quickly imitating the innovation.

The competitive strategy of *developing and marketing the innovation jointly with other companies through a strategic alliance or joint venture* makes most sense when (1) the innovator lacks complementary assets, (2) barriers to imitation are high, and (3) there are several capable competitors. In such circumstances, it makes sense to enter into an alliance with a company that already has the complementary assets—in other words, with a capable competitor. Theoretically, such an alliance should prove to be mutually beneficial, and each partner can share in high profits that neither could earn on its own. Moreover, such a strategy has the benefit of co-opting a potential rival. For example, had EMI teamed up with a capable competitor to develop the market for CT scanners, such as GE Medical Systems, instead of going it alone, the company might not only have been able to build a more enduring competitive advantage, but it would also have co-opted a potentially powerful rival into its camp.

The third strategy, *licensing*, makes most sense when (1) the innovating company lacks the complementary assets, (2) barriers to imitation are low, and (3) there are many capable competitors. The combination of low barriers to imitation and many capable competitors makes rapid imitation almost certain. The innovator's lack of complementary assets further suggests that an imitator will soon capture the innovator's competitive advantage. Given these factors, because rapid diffusion of the innovator's technology through imitation is inevitable, the innovator can at least share in some of the benefits of this diffusion by licensing out its technology.[25] Moreover, by setting a relatively modest licensing fee, the innovator may be able to reduce the incentive that potential rivals have to develop their own competing, and possibly superior, technology. This seems to have been the strategy Dolby adopted to get its technology established as the standard for noise reduction in the music and film businesses (see Strategy in Action 7.2).

Technological Paradigm Shifts

Technological paradigm shifts occur when new technologies come along that revolutionize the structure of the industry, dramatically alter the nature of competition, and require companies to adopt new strategies in order to survive. A good example of a paradigm shift that is currently unfolding is the shift from chemical to digital photography (another example of *digitalization*). For over half a century, the large incumbent enterprises in the photographic industry such as Kodak and Fuji film have generated most of their revenues from selling and processing film using traditional silver halide technology. The rise of digital photography is a huge threat to their business models. Digital cameras do not use film, the mainstay of Kodak's and Fuji's business. Moreover, these cameras are more like specialized computers than conventional cameras and are thus based on scientific knowledge that Kodak and Fuji have little knowledge of. Although both Kodak and Fuji are investing heavily in the development of digital cameras, they are facing intense competition from companies such as Sony, Canon, and Hewlett-Packard, which have developed their own digital cameras; from software developers such as Adobe and Microsoft, which make the software for manipulating digital images; and from printer companies such as Hewlett-Packard and Canon, which are making the printers that consumers can use to print out their own high-quality pictures at home. As digital substitution gathers speed in the photography industry, it is not clear that the traditional incumbents will be able to survive this shift; the new competitors might well rise to dominance in the new market.

If Kodak and Fuji do decline, they will not be the first large incumbents to be felled by a technological paradigm shift in their industry. In the early 1980s, the computer industry was revolutionized by the arrival of personal computer technology, which gave rise to client-server networks that replaced traditional mainframe and minicomputers for many business uses. Many incumbent companies in the mainframe era, such as Wang, Control Data, and DEC, ultimately did not survive, and even IBM went through a decade of wrenching changes and large losses before it reinvented itself as a provider of e-business solutions. In their place, new entrants such as Microsoft, Intel, Dell, and Compaq rose to dominance in this new computer industry.

Examples such as these raise four questions:

1. When do paradigm shifts occur, and how do they unfold?

2. Why do so many incumbents go into decline following a paradigm shift?

3. What strategies can incumbents adopt to increase the probability that they will survive a paradigm shift and emerge on the other side of the market abyss created by the arrival of new technology as a profitable enterprise?

4. What strategies can new entrants into a market adopt to profit from a paradigm shift?

We shall answer each of these questions in the remainder of this chapter.

■ Paradigm Shifts and the Decline of Established Companies

Paradigm shifts appear to be more likely to occur in an industry when one, or both, of the following conditions are in place.[26] First, the established technology in the industry is mature and approaching or at its "natural limit," and second, a new "disruptive technology" has entered the marketplace and is taking root in niches that are poorly served by incumbent companies using the established technology.

■ The Natural Limits to Technology   Richard Foster has formalized the relationship between the performance of a technology and time in terms of what he

FIGURE 7.5

The Technology
S-Curve

calls the technology S-curve (see Figure 7.5).[27] This curve shows the relationship over time of *cumulative* investments in R&D and the performance (or functionality) of a given technology. Early in its evolution, R&D investments in a new technology tend to yield rapid improvements in performance as basic engineering problems are solved. After a time, diminishing returns to cumulative R&D begin to set in, the rate of improvement in performance slows, and the technology starts to approach its natural limit, where further advances are not possible. For example, one can argue that there was more improvement in the first fifty years of the commercial aerospace business following the pioneering flight by the Wright Brothers than there has been in the second fifty years. Indeed, the world's largest commercial jet aircraft, the Boeing 747, is based on a 1960s design, as is the world's fastest commercial jet aircraft, the Concorde. In commercial aerospace, therefore, we are now in the region of diminishing returns and may be approaching the natural limit to improvements in the technology of commercial aerospace.

Similarly, it can be argued that we are approaching the natural limit to technology in the performance of silicon-based semiconductor chips. Over the past two decades, the performance of semiconductor chips has been increased dramatically by packing ever more transistors onto a single small silicon chip. This process has helped to increase the power of computers, lower their cost, and shrink their size. But we are starting to approach limits to the ability to shrink the width of lines on a chip and therefore pack ever more transistors onto a single chip. The limit is imposed by the natural laws of physics. Light waves are used to help etch lines onto a chip, and one cannot etch a line that is smaller than the wavelength of light being used. Semiconductor companies are already using light with very small wavelengths, such as extreme ultraviolet, to etch lines onto a chip, but there are limits to how far this technology can be pushed, and many believe that we will reach those limits within the decade. Does this mean that our ability to make smaller, faster, cheaper computers is coming to an end? Probably not. It is more likely that we will find another technology to replace silicon-based computing and enable us to continue building smaller, faster, cheaper computers. In fact, several exotic competing technologies are already being developed that may replace silicon-based computing. These include self-organizing molecular computers, three-dimensional microprocessor technology, quantum computing technology, and using DNA to perform computations.[28]

FIGURE 7.6

Established and
Successor
Technologies

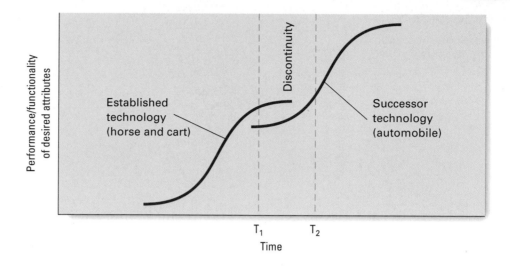

What does all of this have to do with paradigm shifts? According to Foster, when a technology approaches its natural limit, research attention turns to possible alternative technologies, and sooner or later one of those alternatives might be commercialized and replace the established technology. That is, the probability that a paradigm shift will occur increases. Thus, sometime in the next decade or two, another paradigm shift might shake the very foundations of the computer industry as exotic computing technology replaces silicon-based computing. If history is any guide, if and when this happens, many of the incumbents in today's computer industry will go into decline, and new enterprises will rise to dominance.

Foster pushes this point a little further, noting that, initially, the contenders for the replacement technology are not as effective as the established technology in producing the attributes and features that consumers demand in a product. For example, in the early years of the twentieth century, automobiles were just starting to be produced. They were valued for their ability to move people from place to place, but so was the horse and cart (the established technology). When automobiles originally appeared, the horse and cart was still quite a bit better than the automobile at doing this (see Figure 7.6). After all, the first cars were slow, noisy, and prone to breakdown. Moreover, they needed a network of paved roads and gas stations to be really useful, and that network didn't exist, so for most applications, the horse and cart was still the preferred mode of transportation—to say nothing of the fact that it was cheaper.

However, this comparison ignored the fact that in the early twentieth century, automobile technology was at the very start of its S-curve and was about to experience dramatic improvements in performance as major engineering problems were solved (and those paved roads and gas stations were built). In contrast, after 3,000 years of continuous improvement and refinement, the horse and cart was almost definitely at the end of its technological S-curve. The result was that the rapidly improving automobile soon replaced the horse and cart as the preferred mode of transportation. At time T_1 in Figure 7.6, the horse and cart was still superior to the automobile. By time T_2, the automobile had surpassed the horse and cart.

FIGURE 7.7

Swarm of Successor
Technologies

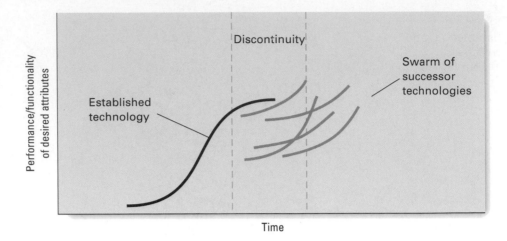

Foster notes that because the successor technology is initially less efficient than the established technology, established companies and their customers often make the mistake of dismissing it, only to be taken off-guard by its rapid performance improvement. A final point here is that often there is not one potential successor technology but a swarm of potential successor technologies, only one of which might ultimately rise to the fore (see Figure 7.7). When this is the case, established companies are put at a disadvantage. Even if they recognize that a paradigm shift is imminent, they may not have the resources to invest in all the potential replacement technologies. If they invest in the wrong one, something that is easy to do given the uncertainty that surrounds the entire process, they may be locked out of subsequent development.

■ **Disruptive Technology**   Clayton Christensen has built on Foster's insights and his own research to develop a theory of disruptive technology that has become very influential in high-technology circles.[29] Christensen uses the term **disruptive technology** to refer to a new technology that gets its start away from the mainstream of a market and then, as its functionality improves over time, invades the main market. Such technologies are disruptive because they revolutionize industry structure and competition, often causing the decline of established companies. They cause a technological paradigm shift.

Christensen's greatest insight is that established companies are often aware of the new technology but do not invest in it because they listen to their customers, and their customers do not want it. Of course, this arises because the new technology is early in its development, and thus only at the beginning of the S-curve for that technology. Once the performance of the new technology improves, customers *do* want it, but by this time it is new entrants, as opposed to established companies, that have accumulated the knowledge required to bring the new technology into the mass market. Christensen supports his view by several detailed historical case studies, one of which is summarized in Strategy in Action 7.4.

In addition to listening too closely to their customers, Christensen also identifies a number of other factors that make it very difficult for established companies to adopt a

Strategy in Action

Disruptive Technology in Mechanical Excavators

7.4

Excavators are used to dig out foundations for large buildings, trenches to lay large pipes for sewers and the like, and foundations and trenches for residential construction and farm work. Prior to the 1940s, the dominant technology used to manipulate the bucket on a mechanical excavator was based on a system of cables and pulleys. Although these mechanical systems could lift large buckets of earth, the excavators themselves were quite large, cumbersome, and expensive. Thus, they were rarely used to dig small trenches for house foundations, irrigation ditches for farmers, and the like. In most cases, these small trenches were dug by hand.

In the 1940s, a new technology made its appearance: hydraulics. In theory, hydraulic systems had certain advantages over the established cable and pulley systems. Most important, their energy efficiency was higher: for a given bucket size, a smaller engine would be required using a hydraulic system. However, the initial hydraulic systems also had drawbacks. The seals on hydraulic cylinders were prone to leak under high pressure, effectively limiting the size of bucket that could be lifted using hydraulics. Notwithstanding this drawback, when hydraulics first appeared, many of the incumbent firms in the mechanical excavation industry took the technology seriously enough to ask their primary customers whether they would be interested in products based on hydraulics. Since the primary customers of incumbents needed excavators

with large buckets to dig out the foundations for buildings and large trenches, their reply was negative. For this customer set, the hydraulic systems of the 1940s were not reliable or powerful enough. Consequently, after consulting with their customers, these established companies in the industry made the strategic decision not to invest in hydraulics. Instead, they continued to produce excavation equipment based on the dominant cable and pulley technology.

It was left to a number of new entrants, which included J. I. Case, John Deere, J. C. Bamford, and Caterpillar, to pioneer hydraulic excavation equipment. Because of the limits on bucket size imposed by the seal problem, these companies initially focused on a poorly served niche in the market that could make use of small buckets: residential contractors and farmers. Over time, these new entrants were able to solve the engineering problems associated with weak hydraulic seals, and as they did this, they manufactured excavators with larger buckets. Ultimately, they invaded the market niches served by the old-line companies: general contractors that dug the foundations for large buildings, sewers, and so on. At this point, Case, Deere, Caterpillar, and their kin rose to dominance in the industry, while the majority of established companies from the prior era lost share. Of the thirty or so manufacturers of cable-actuated equipment in the United States in the late 1930s, only four survived to the 1950s.[d]

---

new disruptive technology. He notes that many established companies declined to invest in new disruptive technologies because initially they served such small market niches that it seemed unlikely that they would have an impact on the company's revenues and profits. As the new technology started to improve in functionality and invade the main market, their investment was often hindered by the fact that exploiting the new technology required a new business model totally different from the company's established model, and thus very difficult to implement.

Both of these points can be illustrated by reference to one more example: the rise of online discount stockbrokers during the 1990s such as Ameritrade and E*TRADE, which made use of a new technology, the Internet, to allow individual investors to trade stocks for a very low commission fee, whereas full-service stockbrokers, such as Merrill Lynch, where orders had to be placed through a stockbroker who earned a commission for performing the transaction, did not.

Christensen also notes that a new network of suppliers and distributors typically grows up around the new entrants. Not only do established companies initially ignore disruptive technology, but so do their suppliers and distributors. This creates an opportunity for new suppliers and distributors to enter the market to serve the new entrants. As the new entrants grow, so does the associated network. Ultimately, Christensen suggests, the new entrants and their network may replace not only established enterprises, but also the entire network of suppliers and distributors associated with established companies. Taken to its logical extreme, this view suggests that disruptive technologies may result in the demise of the entire network of enterprises associated with established companies in an industry.

The established companies in an industry that is being rocked by a technological paradigm shift often have to cope with internal inertia forces that limit their ability to adapt, but the new entrants do not and thereby have an advantage. They do not have to deal with an established and conservative customer set and an obsolete business model. Instead, they can focus on optimizing the new technology, improving its performance, and riding the wave of disruptive technology into new market segments until they invade the main market and challenge the established companies, by which time they may be well equipped to beat them.

■ Strategic Implications for Established Companies

Although Christensen has uncovered an important tendency, it is by no means written in stone that all established companies are doomed to fail when faced with disruptive technologies, as we have seen with IBM and Merrill Lynch. Established companies must meet the challenges created by the emergence of disruptive technologies.[30]

First, having access to the knowledge about how disruptive technologies can revolutionize markets is itself a valuable strategic asset. Many of the established companies that Christensen examined failed because they took a myopic view of the new technology and asked their customers the wrong question. Instead of asking, "Are you interested in this new technology?" they should have recognized that the new technology was likely to improve rapidly over time and instead have asked, "Would you be interested in this new technology if it improves its functionality over time?" If they had done this, they may have made very different strategic decisions.

Second, it is clearly important for established enterprises to invest in newly emerging technologies that may ultimately become disruptive technologies. Companies have to hedge their bets about new technology. As we have noted, at any time, there may be a swarm of emerging technologies, any one of which might ultimately become a disruptive technology. Large, established companies that are generating significant cash flows can and often should establish and fund central R&D operations to invest in and develop such technologies. In addition, they may wish to acquire newly emerging companies that are pioneering potentially disruptive technologies or enter into alliances with them to develop the technology jointly. The strategy of acquiring companies that are developing potentially disruptive technology is one that Cisco Systems, a dominant provider of Internet network equipment, is famous for pursuing. At the heart of this strategy must be a recognition on the part of the incumbent enterprise that it is better for the company to develop disruptive technology and then cannibalize its established sales base than to have that sales base taken away by new entrants.

However, Christensen makes the very important point that even when established companies do undertake R&D investments in potentially disruptive technologies, they often fail to commercialize those technologies because of internal forces that suppress change. For example, managers in the parts of the business that are currently generating the most cash may claim that they need the greatest R&D investment to maintain their market position and may lobby top management to delay investment in a new technology. Early on in the S-curve, when it is very unclear what the long-term prospects of a new technology may be, this can be a powerful argument. The consequence, however, may be that the company fails to build a competence in the new technology and will suffer accordingly.

In addition, Christensen argues that the commercialization of new disruptive technology often requires a radically different value chain with a completely different cost structure—a new business model. For example, it may require a different manufacturing system, a different distribution system, and different pricing options and involve very different gross margins and operating margins. Christensen argues that it is almost impossible for two distinct business models to coexist within the same organization. When they try to do that, almost inevitably the established business model will suffocate the business model associated with the disruptive technology.

The solution to this problem is to separate out the disruptive technology and place it in its own autonomous operating division. For example, during the early 1980s Hewlett-Packard (HP) built a very successful laser jet printer business. Then along came ink jet technology. Some in the company believed that ink jet printers would cannibalize sales of laser jets and consequently argued that HP should not produce ink jets. Fortunately for HP, senior management at the time saw ink jet technology for what it was: a potential disruptive technology. Far from not investing in it, they allocated significant R&D funds toward its commercialization. Furthermore, when the technology was ready for market introduction, they established an autonomous ink jet division at a different geographic location with its own manufacturing, marketing, and distribution activities. They accepted that the ink jet division might take sales away from the laser jet division and decided that it was better to have an HP division cannibalize the sales of another HP division than have those sales cannibalized by another company. Happily for HP, it turns out that ink jets cannibalize sales of laser jets only on the margin and that both have profitable market niches. This felicitous outcome, however, does not detract from the message of the story: if your company is developing a potentially disruptive technology, the chances of success will be enhanced if it is placed in a stand-alone product division and given its own mandate.

■ Strategic Implications for New Entrants

This work just discussed also holds implications for new entrants. The new entrants, or attackers, have several advantages over established enterprises. Pressures to continue the existing out-of-date business model do not hamstring new entrants, which do not have to worry about product cannibalization issues. They do not have to worry about their established customer base or relationships with established suppliers and distributors. Instead, they can focus all their energies on the opportunities offered by the new disruptive technology, ride the S-curve of technology improvement, and grow rapidly with the market for that technology. This does not mean that the new entrants have no problems to solve. They may be constrained by a lack of capital or have to manage the organizational problems associated with rapid growth; most important, they may need to find a way to take their technology from a small out-of-the-way niche into the mass market.

Perhaps one of the most important issues facing new entrants is the choice of whether to partner with an established company or go it alone in their attempt to develop and profit from a new disruptive technology. Although a new entrant may enjoy all of the advantages of the attacker, it may lack the resources required to exploit them fully. In such a case, it might want to consider forming a strategic alliance with a larger, established company to gain access to those resources. The main issues here are the same as those that we discussed earlier when examining the three strategies that a company can pursue to capture first-mover advantages: go it alone, enter into a strategic alliance, or license its technology.

Summary of Chapter

1. Technical standards are important in many high-tech industries: they guarantee compatibility, reduce confusion in the minds of customers, allow for mass production and lower costs, and reduce the risks associated with supplying complementary products.

2. Network effects and positive feedback loops often determine which standard comes to dominate a market.

3. Owning a standard can be a source of sustained competitive advantage.

4. Establishing a proprietary standard as the industry standard may require the company to win a format war against a competing and incompatible standard. Strategies for doing this include producing complementary products, leveraging killer applications, using aggressive pricing and marketing, licensing the technology, and cooperating with competitors.

5. Many high-tech products are characterized by high fixed costs of development but very low or zero marginal costs of producing one extra unit of output. These cost economics create a presumption in favor of strategies that emphasize aggressive pricing to increase volume and drive down average total costs.

6. Many digital products suffer from very high piracy rates because of the low marginal costs of copying and distributing such products. Piracy can be reduced by the appropriate combination of strategy, encryption software, and vigorous defense of intellectual property rights.

7. It is very important for a first mover to develop a strategy to capitalize on first-mover advantages. A company can choose from three strategies: develop and market the technology itself, do so jointly with another company, or license the technology to existing companies. The choice depends on the complementary assets required to capture a first-mover advantage, the height of barriers to imitation, and the capability of competitors.

8. Technological paradigm shifts occur when new technologies come along that revolutionize the structure of the industry, dramatically alter the nature of competition, and require companies to adopt new strategies in order to survive.

9. Technological paradigm shifts are more likely to occur when progress in improving the established technology is slowing because it is giving diminishing returns and a new disruptive technology is taking root in a market niche.

10. Established companies can deal with paradigm shifts by hedging their bets with regard to technology or setting up a stand-alone division to exploit the technology.

Discussion Questions

1. What is different about high-tech industries? Were all industries once high tech?

2. Why are standards so important in many high-tech industries? What are the competitive implications of this?

3. You work for a small company that has the leading position in an embryonic market. Your boss believes that the company's future is ensured because it has a 60 percent share of the market, the lowest cost structure in the industry, and the most reliable and highest-valued product. Write a memo to him outlining why his assumptions might be incorrect.

4. You are working for a small company that has developed an operating system for PCs that is faster and more stable than Microsoft's Windows operating system. What strategies might the company pursue to unseat Windows and establish its new operating system as the dominant technical standard in the industry?

5. You are a manager for a major music record label. Last year, music sales declined by 10 percent, primarily because of very high piracy rates for CDs. Your boss has asked you to develop a strategy for reducing piracy rates. What would you suggest that the company do?

Practicing Strategic Management

■ SMALL-GROUP EXERCISE
Burning DVDs

Break up into groups of three to five people, and discuss the following scenario. Appoint one group member as a spokesperson who will communicate your findings to the class.

You are a group of managers and software engineers at a small start-up that has developed software that enables customers with PCs to copy films from one DVD to another (that is, to "burn" DVDs).

1. How do you think the market for this software is likely to develop? What factors might inhibit adoption of this software?

2. Can you think of a strategy that your company might pursue in combination with film studios that will enable your company to increase revenues and the film companies to reduce piracy rates?

■ ARTICLE FILE 7

Find an example of an industry that has undergone a technological paradigm shift in recent years. What happened to the established companies as that paradigm shift unfolded?

■ STRATEGIC MANAGEMENT PROJECT
Module 7

This module requires you to analyze the industry environment in which your company is based and determine if it is vulnerable to a technological paradigm shift. With the information you have at your disposal, answer the following questions:

1. What is the dominant product technology used in the industry in which your company is based?

2. Are technical standards important in your industry? If so, what are they?

3. What are the attributes of the majority of customers purchasing the product of your company (for example, early adopters, early majority, late majority)? What does this tell you about the strategic issues that the company is likely to face in the future?

4. Did the dominant technology in your industry diffuse rapidly or slowly? What drove the speed of diffusion?

5. Where is the dominant technology in your industry on its S-curve? Are alternative competing technologies

being developed that might give rise to a paradigm shift in your industry?

6. Are intellectual property rights important to your company? If so, what strategies is it adopting to protect those rights? Is it doing enough?

■ EXPLORING THE WEB
Visiting Kodak

Visit the website of Kodak (**www.kodak.com**), and search it to find out what Kodak is doing in the area of digital photography. Use this information to answer the following questions:

1. How important do you think digital photography is in Kodak's total revenues?

2. How is this likely to change over the next decade?

3. Where is digital photography on the S-curve? Where is traditional photography? What are the implications of this comparison for Kodak?

4. Identify Kodak's competitors in (a) its traditional film business and (b) the digital photography business. What are the implications of the change in the set of competitors confronting Kodak?

5. How does the switch from traditional to digital photography change the economics of the photography business?

6. Do you think that Kodak is pursuing the correct strategies to deal with digital substitution? What do you think is the long-term outlook for Kodak's business if it continues pursuing its current strategies? Do you think the company should make some changes? If so, what?

General Task Search the Web for information that allows you to assess the current state of competition in the market for hand-held computers such as those produced by Palm, Handspring, and Compaq. Use that information to perform an analysis of the market in the United States. Answer the following questions:

1. What is the leading standard for operating systems in this market?

2. How did this standard emerge to become the market leader?

3. How secure is this standard? Could it be supplanted by another standard over the next few years?

Closing Case

Battling Piracy in the Videogame Market

Over the last decade the videogame industry has grown into a global colossus worth more than $22 billion a year in revenues. For the three biggest players in the industry—Sony with its PlayStation 2, Microsoft with Xbox, and Nintendo—this potentially represents a huge growth engine. But the engine is threatened by a rise in piracy, which in 2004 cost the industry close to $4 billion.

The piracy problem is particularly serious in East Asia (excluding Japan), where videogame consoles are routinely "chipped"—sold with modified chips, called "mod chips," that override the console's security system, allowing it to play illegally copied games and CDs. Importers or resellers, who charge a small markup for making the modification, illegally install the mod chips. In some regions, such as Hong Kong, it is almost impossible to find a console that hasn't been modified.

Because they allow users to play illegally copied games, consoles with mod chips installed offer a gaping gateway for software pirates, and they directly threaten the profitability of console and game makers. The big three in the industry all follow a razor-and-razor-blades business model, where the console (razor) is sold at a loss and profit is made on the sale of the games (razor blades). In the case of Microsoft's Xbox, estimates suggest that the company loses as much as $200 on each Xbox it sells. To make profits, Microsoft collects royalties on the sale of games developed under license, in addition to producing and selling some games itself. Each game typically retails for around $50, and Microsoft must sell six to twelve games to each Xbox user to recoup the $200 loss on the initial sale and start making a profit. If those users are purchasing pirated games and playing them on "chipped" Xbox consoles, Microsoft collects nothing in royalties and may never reach the breakeven point. Sony and Nintendo face similar problems. In East Asia, some 70 percent of game software sold in the region may be pirated thanks to the popularity of "chipped" consoles and the low price of pirated games, which may sell for one-third the price of a legal game.

Historically, all of the big videogame companies tried to deal with the piracy problem in East Asia by ignoring the market. Sony launched its PlayStation 2 in East Asia two years after its Japanese launch, and Microsoft delayed its East Asian launch for a year after it launched it elsewhere in the world. But this tactic is increasingly questionable in a region where there may soon be more gamers than in the United States. Industry estimates suggest that

Asian gamers will spend some $7.6 billion on videogame software in 2004, much of it on low-priced pirated games, compared to $7.4 billion in the United States.

Another tactic that both Sony and Microsoft are now using is to regularly alter the hardware specifications of its consoles, rendering the existing mod chips useless. But the companies have found that this is just a temporary solution, for within a few weeks the new system is cracked and mod chips are available on the market that are tailor-made to override the new specifications.

A third tactic is to push the local authorities to legally enforce existing intellectual property rights law, which in theory outlaws the mod chip practice. In late 2002, Microsoft, Sony, and Nintendo joined forces to sue a Hong Kong company called Lik-Sang, which sold mod chips through its website and which is one of the world's largest distributors of the chips. Some observers question the value of this move, however, for they argue that if Lik-Sang is shut down, there are many others in Hong Kong that may be willing to take its place. What is needed, they argue, is concerted government action to stop the pirates, and so far East Asian governments have not been quick to act.[31]

Case Discussion Questions

1. Why do the console manufacturers in the videogame industry all adopt a "razor-and-razor-blades" strategy?

2. Why is piracy rampant in the videogame industry? What are the implications of high piracy rates for (a) the profitability of the console manufacturers and (b) the supply of new videogames?

3. What impact do you think the spread of peer-to-peer file-sharing networks, such as Kazaa, might have on the rate of software piracy in the videogame industry?

4. What strategies and tactics are Microsoft, Sony, and Nintendo adopting to reduce the rate of piracy? What are the limitations of these strategies and tactics? Do you think they will be successful at limiting piracy?

5. Can you think of any other steps that Microsoft, Sony, and Nintendo might take to limit piracy? Could they change their business model in some way so that piracy would be less of a problem?

6. How might a shift to online gaming change the piracy rate?

Chapter 8

Strategy in the Global Environment

Opening Case

The Evolution of Global Strategy at Procter & Gamble

Founded in 1837, Cincinnati-based Procter & Gamble has long been one of the world's most international of companies. Today P&G is a global colossus in the consumer products business with annual sales in excess of $50 billion, some 54 percent of which are generated outside of the United States. P&G sells over three hundred brands—including Ivory Soap, Tide, Pampers, IAM pet food, Crisco, and Folgers—to consumers in 160 countries. It has operations in 80 countries and employs close to 100,000 people globally. P&G established its first foreign factory in 1915 when it opened a plant in Canada to produce Ivory Soap and Crisco. This was followed in 1930 by the establishment of the company's first foreign subsidiary in Britain. The pace of international expansion quickened in the 1950s and 1960s as P&G expanded rapidly in Western Europe, and then again in the 1970s when the company entered Japan and other Asian nations. Sometimes P&G entered a nation by acquiring an established competitor and its brands, as occurred in Britain and Japan, but more typically the company set up operations from the ground floor.

By the late 1970s the business model at P&G was well established. The company developed new products in Cincinnati and then relied on semiautonomous foreign subsidiaries to manufacture, market, and distribute those products in different nations. In many cases, foreign subsidiaries had their own production facilities and tailored the packaging, brand name, and marketing message to local tastes and preferences. For years this business model delivered a steady stream of new products and reliable growth in sales and profits. By the 1990s, however, profit growth at P&G was slowing down.

The essence of the problem was simple: P&G's costs were too high primarily because of extensive duplication of manufacturing, marketing, and administrative facilities in different national subsidiaries. The duplication of assets made sense in the world of the 1960s, when national markets were segmented from each other by barriers to cross-border trade. Products produced in Britain, for example, could not be sold economically in Germany because of the high tariff duties levied on imports into Germany. By the 1980s, however, barriers to cross-border trade were falling rapidly worldwide and fragmented national markets were merging into larger regional or global markets. Moreover, the retailers through which P&G distributed its products were themselves growing larger and more global, such as Wal-Mart from the United States, Tesco from the United Kingdom, and Carrefour from France. These emerging global retailers were demanding price discounts from P&G.

In 1993 P&G embarked on a major reorganization in an attempt to control its cost structure and recognize the new reality of emerging global markets. The company shut down some thirty manufacturing plants around the globe, laid off 13,000 employees, and concentrated production in fewer plants that could better realize economies of scale and serve regional markets. These actions cut some $600 million a year out of P&G's cost structure. It wasn't enough: profit growth remained sluggish.

In 1998 P&G launched its second reorganization of the decade. Named "Organization 2005," the goal was to transform P&G into a truly global company. The company tore up its old organization, which was based on countries and regions, and replaced it with one based on seven self-contained global business units, ranging from baby care to food products. Each business unit was given complete responsibility for generating profits from its products, as well as for manufacturing, marketing, and developing the products. Each business unit was also told to concentrate production in fewer larger facilities to try to build global brands wherever possible, thereby eliminating marketing differences between countries, and to accelerate the development and launching of new products. In 1999 P&G announced that, as a result of this initiative, it would close down another ten factories and lay off 15,000 employees, mostly in Europe, where there was still extensive duplication of assets. The annual cost savings were estimated to be about $800 million. P&G planned to use the savings to cut prices and increase marketing spending in an effort to gain market share and thus further lower costs through the attainment of scale economies.

This time the strategy seemed to work. In 2003 and then again in 2004, P&G reported strong growth in both sales and profits. Between 2002 and 2004 revenues surged 28 percent, from $40.2 billion to $51.4 billion, while profits increased an impressive 46 percent, from $4.35 billion to $6.34 billion. Significantly, P&G's global competitors, such as Unilever, Kimberley-Clark, and Colgate-Palmolive, were struggling in 2003 and 2004.[1]

Overview

Procter & Gamble has a long history as one of the world's most successful multinational companies. As described in the *Opening Case*, it was one of the first companies to expand internationally and for decades profited handsomely from this strategy. By the early 1990s, however, it found itself out of step with the rapid emergence of a global marketplace. To improve the company's profitability and profit growth, P&G had to change its strategy, moving from a strategic posture that granted considerable autonomy to operations in individual countries to one that recognized that markets were becoming more global. P&G is not alone in having to make this shift. Many other companies, large and small, have had to struggle with the same issue and have changed their strategy as a result.

This chapter begins with a discussion of ongoing changes in the global competitive environment and discusses models managers can use for analyzing competition in different national markets. Next, the chapter discusses the various ways in which international expansion can increase a company's profitability and profit growth. It also looks at the advantages and disadvantages of different strategies companies can pursue to gain a competitive advantage in the global marketplace. This is followed by a discussion of two related strategic issues: (1) how managers decide which foreign markets to enter, when to enter them, and on what scale and (2) what kind of vehicle or means a company should use to expand globally and enter a foreign country. Once a company has entered a foreign market, it becomes a **multinational company,** that is, a company that does business in two or more national markets. The vehicles that companies can employ to enter foreign markets and become multinationals include exporting, licensing, setting up a joint venture with a foreign company, and setting up a wholly owned subsidiary. The chapter closes with a discussion of the benefits and costs of entering into strategic alliances with other global companies.

By the time you have completed this chapter, you will have a good understanding of the various strategic issues that companies face when they decide to expand their operations abroad to achieve competitive advantage and superior profitability.

The Global and National Environments

Fifty years ago most national markets were isolated from each other by significant barriers to international trade and investment. In those days, managers could focus on analyzing just those national markets in which their company competed. They did not need to pay much attention to entry by global competitors, for there were few and entry was difficult. Nor did they need to pay much attention to entering foreign markets, since that was often prohibitively expensive. All of this has now changed. Barriers to international trade and investment have tumbled, huge global markets for goods and services have been created, and companies from different nations are entering each other's home markets on a hitherto unprecedented scale, increasing the intensity of competition. Rivalry can no longer be understood merely in terms of what happens within the boundaries of a nation; managers now need to consider how globalization is impacting the environment in which their company competes and what strategies their company should adopt to exploit the unfolding opportunities and counter competitive threats. In this section we look at the changes ushered in by falling barriers to international trade and investment, and we discuss a model for analyzing the competitive situation in different nations.

■ The Globalization of Production and Markets

The past half-century has seen a dramatic lowering of barriers to international trade and investment. For example, the average tariff rate on manufactured goods traded between advanced nations has fallen from around 40 percent to under 4 percent. Similarly, in nation after nation, regulations prohibiting foreign companies from entering domestic markets and establishing production facilities, or acquiring domestic companies, have been removed. As a result of these two developments, there has been a surge in both the volume of international trade and the value of foreign direct investment. The volume of world-merchandised trade has been growing faster than the world economy since 1950.[2] From 1970 to 2003, the volume of world-merchandised trade expanded twenty-fivefold, outstripping world production, which grew about 7.5 times in real terms. Moreover, between 1992 and 2003 the total flow of foreign direct investment from all countries increased about 279 percent, while world trade grew by some 69 percent and world output by 28 percent.[3] These two trends have led to the globalization of production and the globalization of markets.[4]

The globalization of production has been increasing as companies take advantage of lower barriers to international trade and investment to disperse important parts of their production processes around the globe. Doing so enables them to take advantage of national differences in the cost and quality of factors of production such as labor, energy, land, and capital, which allow them to lower their cost structures and boost profits. For example, the Boeing Company's commercial jet aircraft, the 777, uses 132,500 engineered parts that are produced around the world by 545 suppliers. Eight Japanese suppliers make parts of the fuselage, doors, and wings; a supplier in Singapore makes the doors for the nose landing gear; three suppliers in Italy manufacture wing flaps; and so on. Part of Boeing's rationale for outsourcing so much production to foreign suppliers is that these suppliers are the best in the world at performing their particular activity. Therefore, the result of having foreign suppliers build specific parts is a better final product and higher profitability for Boeing.[5]

As for the globalization of markets, it has been argued that the world's economic system is moving from one in which national markets are distinct entities, isolated from each other by trade barriers and barriers of distance, time, and culture, toward a system in which national markets are merging into one huge global marketplace. Increasingly, customers around the world demand and use the same basic product offerings. Consequently, in many industries, it is no longer meaningful to talk about the German market, the U.S. market, or the Japanese market; there is only the global market. The global acceptance of Coca-Cola, Citigroup credit cards, blue jeans, the Sony PlayStation, McDonald's hamburgers, the Nokia wireless phone, and Microsoft's Windows operating system are examples of this trend.[6]

The trend toward the globalization of production and markets has several important implications for competition within an industry. First, industry boundaries do not stop at national borders. Because many industries are becoming global in scope, actual and potential competitors exist not only in a company's home market but also in other national markets. Managers who analyze only their home market can be caught unprepared by the entry of efficient foreign competitors. The globalization of markets and production implies that companies around the globe are finding their home markets under attack from foreign competitors. For example, in Japan, Merrill Lynch and Citicorp are making inroads against Japanese financial service institutions. In the United States, Finland's Nokia has taken the lead from Motorola in the market for wireless phone handsets (see Strategy in Action 8.1). In the European Union, the once dominant Dutch company Philips has seen its market share in the customer electronics industry taken by Japan's JVC, Matsushita, and Sony.

Second, the shift from national to global markets has intensified competitive rivalry in industry after industry. National markets that once were consolidated oligopolies, dominated by three or four companies and subjected to relatively little foreign competition, have been transformed into segments of fragmented global industries in which a large number of companies battle each other for market share in country after country. This rivalry has threatened to drive down profitability and made it all the more critical for companies to maximize their efficiency, quality, customer responsiveness, and innovative ability. The painful restructuring and downsizing that has been going on at companies such as Motorola and Kodak is as much a response to the increased intensity of global competition as it is to anything else. However, not all global industries are fragmented. Many remain consolidated oligopolies, except that now they are consolidated global, rather than national, oligopolies. In the videogame industry, for example, three companies are battling for global dominance, Microsoft from the United States and Nintendo and Sony from Japan. In the market for wireless handsets, Nokia of Finland does global battle against Motorola of the United States and Samsung from South Korea.

Finally, although globalization has increased both the threat of entry and the intensity of rivalry within many formerly protected national markets, it has also created enormous opportunities for companies based in those markets. The steady decline in barriers to cross-border trade and investment has opened up many once protected markets to companies based outside them. Thus, for example, in recent years, western European, Japanese, and U.S. companies have accelerated their investments in the nations of eastern Europe, Latin America, and Southeast Asia as they try to take advantage of growth opportunities in those areas.

Strategy in Action   8.1

Finland's Nokia

The wireless phone market is one of the great growth stories of the last decade. Starting from a very low base in 1990, annual global sales of wireless phones surged to reach 440 million units in 2003. By the end of 2003, there were over 1.2 billion wireless subscribers worldwide, up from less than 10 million in 1990. Nokia is a dominant player in the market for mobile telephone sales. Nokia's roots are in Finland, not normally a country that comes to mind when one talks about leading-edge technology companies. In the 1980s, Nokia was a rambling Finnish conglomerate with activities that embraced tire manufacturing, paper production, consumer electronics, and telecommunications equipment. By 2004 it had transformed itself into a focused telecommunications equipment manufacturer with a global reach, sales of over $30 billion, earnings of more than $5 billion, and a 38 percent share of the global market for wireless phones. How has this former conglomerate emerged to take a global leadership position in wireless telecommunications equipment? Much of the answer lies in the history, geography, and political economy of Finland and its Nordic neighbors.

In 1981 the Nordic nations cooperated to create the world's first international wireless telephone network. They had good reason to become pioneers: it cost far too much to lay down a traditional wire line telephone service in those sparsely populated and inhospitably cold countries. The same features made telecommunications all the more valuable: people driving through the Arctic winter and owners of remote northern houses needed a telephone to summon help if things went wrong. As a result, Sweden, Norway, and Finland became the first nations in the world to take wireless telecommunications seriously. They found, for example, that although it cost up to $800 per subscriber to bring a traditional wire line service to remote locations, the same locations could be linked by wireless cellular for only $500 per person. As a consequence, 12 percent of people in Scandinavia owned cellular phones by 1994, compared with less than 6 percent in the United States, the world's second most developed market. This lead continued over the next decade. By the end of 2003, 85 percent of the population in Finland owned a wireless phone, compared with 55 percent in the United States.

Nokia, a long-time telecommunications equipment supplier, was well positioned to take advantage of this development from the start, but there were also other forces at work that helped Nokia develop its competitive edge. Unlike virtually every other developed nation, Finland has never had a national telephone monopoly. Instead, the country's telephone services have long been provided by about fifty or so autonomous local telephone companies whose elected boards set prices by referendum (which naturally means low prices). This army of independent and cost-conscious telephone service providers prevented Nokia from taking anything for granted in its home country. With typical Finnish pragmatism, its customers were willing to buy from the lowest-cost supplier, whether that was Nokia, Ericsson, Motorola, or some other company. This situation contrasted sharply with that prevailing in most developed nations until the late 1980s and early 1990s, where domestic telephone monopolies typically purchased equipment from a dominant local supplier or made it themselves. Nokia responded to this competitive pressure by doing everything possible to drive down its manufacturing costs while staying at the leading edge of wireless technology.

The consequences of these forces are clear. Nokia is now the leader in digital wireless technology, which is the wave of the future. Many now regard Finland as the lead market for wireless telephone services. If you want to see the future of wireless, you don't go to New York or San Francisco; you go to Helsinki, where Finns use their wireless handsets not just to talk to each other but also to browse the Web, execute e-commerce transactions, control household heating and lighting systems, or purchase Coke from a wireless-enabled vending machine. Nokia has gained this lead because Scandinavia started switching to digital technology five years before the rest of the world. Spurred on by its cost-conscious Finnish customers, Nokia now has the lowest cost structure of any cellular phone equipment manufacturer in the world, and thus is a more profitable enterprise than Motorola, its leading global rival. It cost Nokia an average of $114 to make and sell each phone in 2002, compared with about $131 a year earlier. Its closest rival, Motorola Inc. of Schaumburg, Illinois, spent an average of $139 to make and sell each phone.[a]

■ National Competitive Advantage

Despite the globalization of production and markets, many of the most successful companies in certain industries are still clustered in a small number of countries. For example, many of the world's most successful biotechnology and computer companies are based in the United States, and many of the most successful customer electronics companies are based in Japan and South Korea. Germany is the base for many successful chemical and engineering companies. These facts suggest that the nation-state within which a company is based may have an important bearing on the competitive position of that company in the global marketplace.

In a study of national competitive advantage, Michael Porter identified four attributes of a national or country-specific environment that have an important impact on the global competitiveness of companies located within that nation:[7]

■ *Factor endowments:* A nation's position in factors of production such as skilled labor or the infrastructure necessary to compete in a given industry
■ *Local demand conditions:* The nature of home demand for the industry's product or service
■ *Competitiveness of related and supporting industries:* The presence or absence in a nation of supplier industries and related industries that are internationally competitive
■ *Intensity of rivalry:* The conditions in the nation governing how companies are created, organized, and managed and the nature of domestic rivalry

Porter speaks of these four attributes as constituting the *diamond*, arguing that companies from a given nation are most likely to succeed in industries or strategic groups in which the four attributes are favorable (see Figure 8.1). He also argues that the diamond's attributes form a mutually reinforcing system in which the effect of one attribute is dependent on the state of others.

FIGURE 8.1

National Competitive Advantage

Source: Adapted from M. E. Porter, "The Competitive Advantage of Nations," *Harvard Business Review,* March–April 1990, page 77.

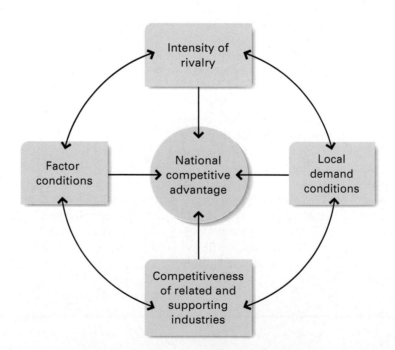

■ **Factor Endowments** **Factor endowments**—the cost and quality of factors of production—are a prime determinant of the competitive advantage that certain countries might have in certain industries. Factors of production include **basic factors**, such as land, labor, capital, and raw materials, and **advanced factors**, such as technological know-how, managerial sophistication, and physical infrastructure (roads, railways, and ports). The competitive advantage that the United States enjoys in biotechnology might be explained by the presence of certain advanced factors of production—for example, technological know-how—in combination with some basic factors, which might be a pool of relatively low-cost venture capital that can be used to fund risky start-ups in industries such as biotechnology.

■ **Local Demand Conditions** Home demand plays an important role in providing the impetus for "upgrading" competitive advantage. Companies are typically most sensitive to the needs of their closest customers. Thus, the characteristics of home demand are particularly important in shaping the attributes of domestically made products and creating pressures for innovation and quality. A nation's companies gain competitive advantage if their domestic customers are sophisticated and demanding and pressure local companies to meet high standards of product quality and produce innovative products. Japan's sophisticated and knowledgeable buyers of cameras helped stimulate the Japanese camera industry to improve product quality and introduce innovative models. A similar example can be found in the cellular phone equipment industry, where sophisticated and demanding local customers in Scandinavia helped push Nokia of Finland and Ericsson of Sweden to invest in cellular phone technology long before demand for cellular phones took off in other developed nations. As a result, Nokia and Ericsson, together with Motorola, are significant players in the global cellular telephone equipment industry. The case of Nokia is reviewed in more depth in Strategy in Action 8.1.

■ **Competitiveness of Related and Supporting Industries** The third broad attribute of national advantage in an industry is the presence of internationally competitive suppliers or related industries. The benefits of investments in advanced factors of production by related and supporting industries can spill over into an industry, thereby helping it achieve a strong competitive position internationally. Swedish strength in fabricated steel products (such as ball bearings and cutting tools) has drawn on strengths in Sweden's specialty steel industry. Switzerland's success in pharmaceuticals is closely related to its previous international success in the technologically related dye industry. One consequence of this process is that successful industries within a country tend to be grouped into clusters of related industries. Indeed, this was one of the most pervasive findings of Porter's study. One such cluster is the German textile and apparel sector, which includes high-quality cotton, wool, synthetic fibers, sewing machine needles, and a wide range of textile machinery.

■ **Intensity of Rivalry** The fourth broad attribute of national competitive advantage in Porter's model is the intensity of rivalry of firms within a nation. Porter makes two important points here. First, different nations are characterized by different management ideologies, which either help them or do not help them to build national competitive advantage. For example, Porter noted the predominance of engineers in top management at German and Japanese firms. He attributed this to these firms' emphasis on improving manufacturing processes and product design. In contrast, Porter noted a predominance of people with finance backgrounds leading many U.S. firms. He linked this to U.S. firms' lack of attention to improving manufacturing processes and product design. He argued that the dominance of finance led to an overemphasis on maximizing short-term financial returns. According to Porter, one consequence of these different management ideologies was a relative loss of U.S. competitiveness in those engineering-based industries where manufacturing processes and product design issues are all-important (such as the automobile industry).

Porter's second point is that there is a strong association between vigorous domestic rivalry and the creation and persistence of competitive advantage in an industry. Rivalry induces companies to look for ways to improve efficiency, which makes them better international competitors. Domestic rivalry creates pressures to innovate, improve quality, reduce costs, and invest in upgrading advanced factors. All this helps to create world-class competitors. The stimulating effects of strong domestic competition are clear in the story of the rise of Nokia of Finland in the market for wireless handsets and telephone equipment (see Strategy in Action 8.1).

■ **Using the Framework** The framework just described can help managers to identify where their most significant global competitors are likely to come from. For example, there is an emerging cluster of computer service and software companies in Bangalore, India, that includes two of the fastest-growing information technology companies in the world, Infosys and Wipro. These companies might soon emerge as aggressive competitors on the global stage. Indeed, there are signs that this is now happening, since both companies have recently opened up offices in the European Union and United States so they can better compete against the likes of IBM and EDS.

The framework can also be used to help managers decide where they might want to locate certain productive activities. Seeking to take advantage of U.S. expertise in biotechnology, many foreign companies have set up research facilities in San Diego, Boston, and Seattle, where U.S. biotechnology companies tend to be clustered. Similarly, in an attempt to take advantage of Japanese success in customer electronics, many U.S. electronics companies have set up research and production facilities in Japan, often in conjunction with Japanese partners.

Finally, the framework can help a company assess how tough it might be to enter certain national markets. If a nation has a competitive advantage in certain industries, it might be challenging for foreigners to enter those industries. For example, the highly competitive retailing industry in the United States has proved to be a very difficult one for foreign companies to enter. Successful foreign retailers such as Britain's Marks & Spencer and IKEA from Sweden have found it tough going in the United States, precisely because the U.S. retailing industry is the most competitive in the world.

Increasing Profitability and Profit Growth Through Global Expansion

Here we look at a number of ways in which expanding globally can enable companies to increase their profitability and grow their profits more rapidly. At the most basic level, global expansion increases the size of the market a company is addressing, thereby boosting profit growth. Moreover, as we shall see, global expansion offers opportunities for reducing the cost structure of the enterprise or adding value through differentiation, thereby potentially boosting profitability.

■ **Expanding the Market: Leveraging Products**

A company can increase its growth rate by taking goods or services developed at home and selling them internationally. Indeed, almost all multinationals started out doing just this. Procter & Gamble, for example, developed most of its best-selling products at home and then sold them around the world (Pampers and Ivory Soap being cases in point). Similarly, from its earliest days, Microsoft has always focused on selling its software around the world. Automobile companies like Ford, Volkswagen, and Toyota also grew by developing products at home and then selling them in international markets. The returns from such a strategy are likely to be greater if indigenous competitors in the nations a company enters lack comparable products. Thus Toyota has grown its profits by entering the large automobile markets of North America and Europe and by offering products that are differentiated from those offered by local rivals (Ford and GM) by their superior quality and reliability.

It is important to note that the success of many multinational companies is based not just on the goods or services that they sell in foreign nations, but also on the distinctive competencies (unique skills) that underlie the production and marketing of those goods or services. Thus Toyota's success is based on its distinctive competency in manufacturing automobiles, and expanding internationally can be seen as a way of generating greater returns from this competency. Similarly, Procter & Gamble's global success was based on more than its portfolio of consumer products; it was also based on the company's skills in mass-marketing consumer goods. P&G grew rapidly in international markets between 1950 and 1990 because it was one of the most skilled mass-marketing enterprises in the world and could "outmarket" indigenous competitors in the nations it entered. Global expansion was thus a way of generating higher returns from its competency in marketing.

Pushing this further, one could say that since distinctive competencies are in essence the most valuable aspects of a company's business model, the successful global expansion by manufacturing companies like Toyota and P&G was based on their ability to transfer aspects of their business model and apply it to foreign markets.

The same can be said of companies engaged in the service sectors of an economy, such as financial institutions, retailers, restaurant chains, and hotels. Expanding the market for their services often means replicating their business model in foreign nations (albeit with some changes to account for local differences, which we will discuss in more detail shortly). Starbucks, for example, is expanding rapidly outside of the United States by taking the basic business model it developed at home and using that as a blueprint for establishing international operations. As explained in the *Running Case*, Wal-Mart has done the same thing, establishing stores in nine other nations since 1992 following the blueprint it developed in the United States. Similarly, McDonald's is famous for its international expansion strategy, which has taken the company into more than 120 nations that collectively generate over half of the company's revenues.

■ **Realizing Cost Economies from Global Volume**

In addition to growing profits more rapidly, by expanding its sales volume through international expansion a company can realize cost savings from economies of scale, thereby boosting profitability. Such scale economies come from several sources. First, by spreading the fixed costs associated with developing a product and setting up production facilities over its global sales volume, a company can lower its average unit cost. Thus, Microsoft can garner significant scale economies by spreading the $1 billion it cost to develop Windows XP over global demand. Second, by serving a

Running Case

Wal-Mart's Global Expansion

In the early 1990s managers at Wal-Mart realized that the company's opportunities for growth in the United States were becoming more limited. By 1995 the company would be active in all fifty states, and management calculated that by the early 2000s domestic growth opportunities would be constrained because of market saturation. So the company decided to expand globally. Initially, the critics scoffed. Wal-Mart, they said, was too American a company. While its business model was well suited to America, it would not work in other countries where infrastructure was different, where consumer tastes and preferences varied, and where established retailers already dominated.

Unperturbed, in 1991 Wal-Mart started to expand internationally with the opening of its first stores in Mexico. The Mexican operation was established as a joint venture with Cifera, the largest local retailer. Initially, Wal-Mart made a number of missteps that seemed to prove the critics right. It had problems replicating its efficient distribution system in Mexico. Poor infrastructure, crowded roads, and a lack of leverage with local suppliers, many of whom could not or would not deliver directly to Wal-Mart's stores or distribution centers, resulted in stocking problems and raised costs and prices. Initially, prices at Wal-Mart in Mexico were some 20 percent above prices for comparable products in the company's U.S. stores, which limited Wal-Mart's ability to gain market share. There were also problems with merchandise selection. Many of the stores in Mexico carried items that were popular in the United States. These included ice skates, riding lawn mowers, leaf blowers, and fishing tackle. Not surprisingly, these items did not sell well in Mexico, so managers would slash prices to move inventory, only to find that the company's automated information systems would immediately order more inventory to replenish the depleted stock.

By the mid 1990s, however, Wal-Mart had learned from its early mistakes and had adapted its operations in Mexico to match the local environment. A partnership with a Mexican trucking company dramatically improved the distribution system, while more careful stocking practices meant that the Mexican stores sold merchandise that appealed more to local tastes and preferences. As Wal-Mart's presence grew, many of Wal-Mart's suppliers built factories close by its Mexican distribution centers so that they could better serve the company, which helped to further drive down inventory and logistics costs. Today, Mexico is a leading light in Wal-Mart's international operations. In 1998, Wal-Mart acquired a controlling interest in Cifera. By 2003, Wal-Mart was more than twice the size of its nearest rival in Mexico, with 623 stores and revenues of over $11 billion.

The Mexican experience proved to Wal-Mart that it could compete outside of the United States. It has subsequently expanded into nine other countries. In Canada, Britain, Germany, Japan, and South Korea, Wal-Mart entered by acquiring existing retailers and then transferring its information systems, logistics, and management expertise. In Puerto Rico, Brazil, Argentina, and China, Wal-Mart established its own stores. As a result of these moves, by 2003 the company had over 1,350 stores outside the United States, employed 330,000 associates, and generated international revenues of more than $46 billion.

In addition to greater growth, expanding internationally brought Wal-Mart two other major benefits. First, Wal-Mart has also been able to reap significant economies of scale from its global buying power. Many of Wal-Mart's key suppliers have long been international companies; for example, GE (appliances), Unilever (food products), and Procter & Gamble (personal care products) are all major Wal-Mart suppliers that have long had their own global operations. By building international reach, Wal-Mart has been able to use its enhanced size to demand deeper discounts from the local operations of its global suppliers, increasing the company's ability to lower prices to consumers, gain market share, and ultimately earn greater profits. Second, Wal-Mart has found that it is benefiting from the flow of ideas across the eleven countries in which it now competes. For example, a two-level store in New York State came about because of the success of multilevel stores in South Korea. Other ideas, such as wine departments in its stores in Argentina, have now been integrated into layouts worldwide.

Wal-Mart realized that if it didn't expand internationally, other global retailers would beat it to the punch. In fact, Wal-Mart does face significant global competition from Carrefour of France, Ahold of Holland, and Tesco from the United Kingdom. Carrefour, the world's second largest retailer, is perhaps the most global of the lot. This pioneer of the hypermarket concept now operates in twenty-six countries and generates more than 50 percent of its sales outside France. Compared to Carrefour, Wal-Mart is a laggard, with just 18.5 percent of its sales in 2003 generated from international operations. However, there is still room for significant global expansion because the global retailing market is still very fragmented. In 2003 the top twenty-five retailers controlled less than 20 percent of worldwide retail sales, although forecasts suggest the figure could reach 40 percent by 2009, with Latin America, Southeast Asia, and eastern Europe being the main battlegrounds.[b]

global market, a company can potentially utilize its production facilities more intensively, which leads to higher productivity, lower costs, and greater profitability. For example, if Intel sold microprocessors only in the United States, it might only be able to keep its factories open for one shift, five days a week. But by serving a global market from the same factories, it might be able to utilize those assets for two shifts, seven days a week. In other words, the capital invested in those factories is used more intensively if Intel sells to a global as opposed to a national market, which translates into higher capital productivity and a higher return on invested capital. Third, as global sales increase the size of the enterprise, so its bargaining power with suppliers increases, which may allow it to bargain down the cost of key inputs and boost profitability that way. Wal-Mart has been able to use its enormous sales volume as a lever to bargain down the price it pays suppliers for merchandise sold through its stores.

In addition to the cost savings that come from economies of scale, companies that sell to a global as opposed to local marketplace may be able to realize further cost savings from learning effects. We first discussed learning effects in Chapter 4, where we noted that employee productivity increases with cumulative increases in output over time (for example, it costs considerably less to build the one-hundredth aircraft off a Boeing assembly line than the tenth because employees learn how to perform their tasks more efficiently over time). By selling to a global market, a company may be able to increase its sales volume more rapidly, and thus the cumulative output from its plants, which in turn should result in quicker learning, higher employee productivity, and a cost advantage over competitors that are growing more slowly because they lack international markets.

■ **Realizing Location Economies** Earlier in this chapter we discussed how countries differ from each other along a number of dimensions, including differences in the cost and quality of factors of production. These differences imply that some locations are more suited than others for producing certain goods and services.[8] **Location economies** are the economic benefits that arise from performing a value creation activity in the optimal location for that activity, wherever in the world that might be (transportation costs and trade barriers permitting). Locating a value creation activity in the optimal location for that activity can have one of two effects: (1) it can lower the costs of value creation, helping the company achieve a low-cost position, or (2) it can enable a company to differentiate its product offering, which gives it the option of charging a premium price or keeping price low and using differentiation as a means of increasing sales volume. Thus, efforts to realize location economies are consistent with the business-level strategies of low cost and differentiation. In theory, a company that realizes location economies by dispersing each of its value creation activities to the optimal location for that activity should have a competitive advantage over a company that bases all of its value creation activities at a single location. It should be able to differentiate its product offering better and lower its cost structure more than its single-location competitor. In a world where competitive pressures are increasing, such a strategy may well become an imperative for survival.

For an example of how this works in an international business, consider Clear Vision, a manufacturer and distributor of eyewear. Started in the 1970s by David Glassman, the firm now generates annual gross revenues of more than $100 million. Not exactly small, but no corporate giant either, Clear Vision is a multinational firm with production facilities on three continents and customers around the world. Clear Vision began its move toward becoming a multinational in the early 1980s. The strong dollar at that time made U.S.-based manufacturing very expensive. Low-priced imports were taking an ever larger share of the U.S. eyewear market, and Clear Vision realized it could not survive unless it also began to import. Initially the firm bought from independent overseas manufacturers, primarily in Hong Kong. However, it became dissatisfied with these suppliers' product quality and delivery. As Clear Vision's volume of imports increased, Glassman decided that the best way to guarantee quality and delivery was to set up Clear Vision's own manufacturing operation overseas. Accordingly, Clear Vision found a Chinese partner, and together they opened a manufacturing facility in Hong Kong, with Clear Vision being the majority shareholder.

The choice of the Hong Kong location was influenced by its combination of low labor costs, a skilled work force, and tax breaks given by the Hong Kong government. The firm's objective at this point was to lower production costs by locating value creation activities at an appropriate location. After a few years, however, the increasing industrialization of Hong Kong and a growing labor shortage had pushed up wage rates to the extent that it was no longer a low-cost location. In response, Glassman and his Chinese partner moved part of their manufacturing to a plant in mainland China to take advantage of the lower wage rates there. Again, the goal was to lower production costs. The parts for eyewear frames manufactured at this plant are shipped to the Hong Kong factory for final assembly and then distributed to markets in North and South America. The Hong Kong factory now employs 80 people and the China plant between 300 and 400.

At the same time, Clear Vision was looking for opportunities to invest in foreign eyewear firms with reputations for fashionable design and high quality. Its objective was not to reduce production costs but to launch a line of high-quality, differentiated, "designer" eyewear. Clear Vision did not have the design capability in-house to support such a line, but Glassman knew that certain foreign manufacturers did. As a result, Clear Vision invested in factories in Japan, France, and Italy, holding a minority shareholding in each case. These factories now supply eyewear for Clear Vision's Status Eye division, which markets high-priced designer eyewear.[9]

■ **Some Caveats** Introducing transportation costs and trade barriers complicates this picture somewhat. New Zealand might have a comparative advantage for low-cost car assembly operations, but high transportation costs make it an uneconomical location from which to serve global markets. Factoring transportation costs and trade barriers into the cost equation helps explain why many U.S. companies have been shifting their production from Asia to Mexico. Mexico has three distinct advantages over many Asian countries as a location for value creation activities: low labor costs; Mexico's proximity to the large U.S. market, which reduces transportation costs; and the North American Free Trade Agreement (NAFTA), which has removed many trade barriers between Mexico, the United States, and Canada, increasing Mexico's attractiveness as a production site for the North American market. Thus, although the relative costs of value creation are important, transportation costs and trade barriers also must be considered in location decisions.

Another caveat concerns the importance of assessing political and economic risks when making location decisions. Even if a country looks very attractive as a production location when measured against cost or differentiation criteria, if its government is unstable or totalitarian, companies are usually well advised not to base production there. Similarly, if a particular national government appears to be pursuing inappropriate social or economic policies, this might be another reason for not basing production in that location, even if other factors look favorable.

Leveraging the Skills of Global Subsidiaries

Initially, many multinational companies develop the valuable competencies and skills that underpin their business model in their home nation and then expand internationally, primarily by selling products and services based on those competencies. Thus, Wal-Mart honed its retailing skills in the United States before transferring them to foreign locations. However, for more mature multinational enterprises that have already established a network of subsidiary operations in foreign markets, the development of valuable skills can just as well occur in foreign subsidiaries.[10] Skills can be created anywhere within a multinational's global network of operations, wherever people have the opportunity and incentive to try new ways of doing things. The creation of skills that help to lower the costs of production, or to enhance perceived value and support higher product pricing, is not the monopoly of the corporate center.

Leveraging the skills created within subsidiaries and applying them to other operations within the firm's global network may create value. For example, McDonald's increasingly is finding that its foreign franchisees are a source of valuable new ideas. Faced with slow growth in France, its local franchisees have begun to experiment not only with the menu but also with the layout and theme of restaurants. Gone are the ubiquitous Golden Arches; gone too are many of the utilitarian chairs and tables and other plastic features of the fast-food giant. Many McDonald's restaurants in France now have hardwood floors, exposed brick walls, and even armchairs. Half of the 930 or so outlets in France have been upgraded to a level that would make them unrecognizable to an American. The menu, too, has been changed to include premier sandwiches, such as chicken on focaccia bread, priced some 30 percent higher than the average hamburger. In France at least, the strategy seems to be working. Following the change, increases in same-store sales rose from 1 percent annually to 3.4 percent. Impressed with the impact, McDonald's executives are now considering adopting similar changes at other McDonald's restaurants in markets where same-store sales growth is sluggish, including the United States.[11]

For the managers of a multinational enterprise, this phenomenon creates important new challenges. First, they must have the humility to recognize that valuable skills can arise anywhere within the firm's global network, not just at the corporate center. Second, they must establish an incentive system that encourages local employees to acquire new competencies. This is not as easy as it sounds. Creating new competencies involves a degree of risk. Not all new skills add value. For every valuable idea created by a McDonald's subsidiary in a foreign country, there may be several failures. The management of the multinational must install incentives that encourage employees to take the necessary risks, and the company must reward people for successes and not sanction them unnecessarily for taking risks that did not pan out. Third, managers must have a process for identifying when valuable new skills have been created in a subsidiary, and finally, they need to act as facilitators, helping to transfer valuable skills within the firm.

Cost Pressures and Pressures for Local Responsiveness

Companies that compete in the global marketplace typically face two types of competitive pressures: *pressures for cost reductions* and *pressures to be locally responsive* (see Figure 8.2).[12] These competitive pressures place conflicting demands on a company. Responding to pressures for cost reductions requires that a company try to minimize its unit costs. To attain this goal, it may have to base its productive activities at the most favorable low-cost location, wherever in the world that might be. It may also have to offer a standardized product to the global marketplace in order to realize the cost savings that come from economies of scale and learning effects. On the other hand, responding to pressures to be locally responsive requires that a company differentiate its product offering and marketing strategy from country to country in an effort to accommodate the diverse demands arising from national differences in consumer tastes and preferences, business practices, distribution channels, competitive conditions, and government policies. Because differentiation across countries can involve significant duplication and a lack of product standardization, it may raise costs.

While some companies, such as Company A in Figure 8.2, face high pressures for cost reductions and low pressures for local responsiveness, and others, such as Company B, face low pressures for cost reductions and high pressures for local responsiveness, many companies are in the position of Company C. They face high pressures for *both* cost reductions and local responsiveness. Dealing with these conflicting and contradictory pressures is a difficult strategic challenge, primarily because being locally responsive tends to raise costs.

FIGURE 8.2

Pressures for Cost Reductions and Local Responsiveness

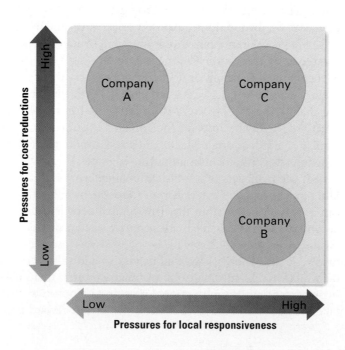

■ Pressures for Cost Reductions

In competitive global markets, international businesses often face pressures for cost reductions. To respond to these pressures, a firm must try to lower the costs of value creation. A manufacturer, for example, might mass-produce a standardized product at the optimal location in the world, wherever that might be, to realize economies of scale and location economies. Alternatively, it might outsource certain functions to low-cost foreign suppliers in an attempt to reduce costs. Thus, many computer companies have outsourced their telephone-based customer service functions to India, where qualified technicians who speak English can be hired for a lower wage rate than in the United States. In the same vein, a retailer like Wal-Mart might push its suppliers (who are manufacturers) to also lower their prices. (In fact, the pressure that Wal-Mart has placed on its suppliers to reduce prices has been cited as a major cause of the trend among North American manufacturers to shift production to China.)[13] A service business, such as a bank, might move some back-office functions, such as information processing, to developing nations where wage rates are lower.

Cost reduction pressures can be particularly intense in industries producing commodity-type products where meaningful differentiation on nonprice factors is difficult and price is the main competitive weapon. This tends to be the case for products that serve universal needs. Universal needs exist when the tastes and preferences of consumers in different nations are similar if not identical, such as for bulk chemicals, petroleum, steel, sugar, and the like. They also exist for many industrial and consumer products: for example, hand-held calculators, semiconductor chips, personal computers, and liquid crystal display screens. Pressures for cost reductions are also intense in industries where major competitors are based in low-cost locations, where there is persistent excess capacity, and where consumers are powerful and face low switching costs. Many commentators have argued that the liberalization of the world trade and investment environment in recent decades, by facilitating greater international competition, has generally increased cost pressures.[14]

■ Pressures for Local Responsiveness

Pressures for local responsiveness arise from differences in consumer tastes and preferences, infrastructure and traditional practices, distribution channels, and host government demands. Responding to pressures to be locally responsive requires that a company differentiate its products and marketing strategy from country to country to accommodate these factors, all of which tends to raise a company's cost structure.

■ Differences in Customer Tastes and Preferences

Strong pressures for local responsiveness emerge when customer tastes and preferences differ significantly between countries, as they may for historic or cultural reasons. In such cases, a multinational company's products and marketing message have to be customized to appeal to the tastes and preferences of local customers. The company is then typically pressured to delegate production and marketing responsibilities and functions to a company's overseas subsidiaries.

For example, the automobile industry in the 1980s and early 1990s moved toward the creation of "world cars." The idea was that global companies such as General Motors, Ford, and Toyota would be able to sell the same basic vehicle the world over, sourcing it from centralized production locations. If successful, the strategy would have enabled automobile companies to reap significant gains from global scale economies. However, this strategy frequently ran aground upon the hard rocks of consumer reality. Consumers in different automobile markets seem to have different tastes and preferences, and these require different types of vehicles. North American consumers show a strong demand for pickup trucks. This is particularly true in the South and West where many families have a pickup truck as a second or third car. But in European countries, pickup trucks are seen purely as utility vehicles and are purchased primarily by firms rather than individuals. As a consequence, the product mix and marketing message need to be tailored to take into account the different nature of demand in North America and Europe. Another example of the need to respond to national differences in tastes and preferences is given in Strategy in Action 8.2, which looks at the experience of MTV Networks in foreign markets.

Notwithstanding the experiences of companies such as MTV, some commentators have argued that customer demands for local customization are on the decline worldwide.[15] According to this argument, modern communications and transport technologies have created the conditions for a convergence of the tastes and preferences of customers from different nations. The result is the emergence of enormous global markets for standardized consumer products. The worldwide acceptance of McDonald's hamburgers, Coca-Cola, Gap clothes, Nokia cell phones, and Sony television sets, all of which are sold globally as standardized products, is often cited as evidence of the increasing homogeneity of the global marketplace.

Others, however, consider this argument to be extreme. For example, Christopher Bartlett and Sumantra Ghoshal have observed that in the consumer electronics industry, buyers reacted to an overdose of standardized global products by showing a renewed preference for products that are differentiated to local conditions.[16]

■ Differences in Infrastructure and Traditional Practices

Pressures for local responsiveness also arise from differences in infrastructure or traditional practices among countries, creating a need to customize products accordingly. To meet this need, companies may have to delegate manufacturing and production functions to foreign subsidiaries. For example, in North America, consumer electrical systems are based on 110 volts, whereas in some European countries 240-volt systems are standard. Thus, domestic electrical appliances have to be customized to take this difference in infrastructure into account. Traditional practices also often vary across nations. For example, in Britain, people drive on the left-hand side of the road, creating a demand for right-hand-drive cars, whereas in France (and the rest of Europe), people drive on the right-hand side of the road and therefore want left-hand-drive cars. Obviously, automobiles have to be customized to take this difference in traditional practices into account.

Although many of the country differences in infrastructure are rooted in history, some are quite recent. For example, in the wireless telecommunications industry, different technical standards are found in different parts of the world. A technical standard known as GSM is common in Europe, and an alternative standard, CDMA, is more common in the United States and parts of Asia. The significance of these different standards is that equipment designed for GSM will not work on a CDMA network, and vice versa. Thus, companies such as Nokia, Motorola, and Ericsson, which manufacture wireless handsets and infrastructure such as switches, need to customize their product offering according to the technical standard prevailing in a given country.

■ Differences in Distribution Channels

A company's marketing strategies may have to be responsive to differences in distribution channels among countries, which may necessitate delegating marketing functions to national subsidiaries. In the pharmaceutical industry, for example, the British and Japanese

Strategy in Action   8.2

MTV Goes Global, with a Local Accent

MTV Networks has become a symbol of globalization. Established in 1981, the U.S.-based music TV network has been expanding outside its North American base since 1987, when it opened MTV Europe. Now owned by media conglomerate Viacom, MTV Networks, which includes siblings Nickelodeon and VH1, the music station for the aging baby boomers, generates more than $1 billion in revenues outside the United States. Since 1987, MTV has become the most ubiquitous cable programmer in the world. By 2004 the network had seventy-two channels, or distinct feeds, that reached a combined total of 321 million households in 140 countries.

While the United States still leads in number of households, with 70 million, the most rapid growth is elsewhere, particularly in Asia, where nearly two-thirds of the region's 3 billion people are under thirty-five, the middle class is expanding quickly, and TV ownership is spreading rapidly. MTV Networks figures that every second of every day almost 2 million people are watching MTV around the world, the majority outside the United States.

Despite its international success, MTV's global expansion got off to a weak start. In 1987, it piped a single feed across Europe almost entirely composed of American programming with English-speaking veejays. Naively, the network's U.S. managers thought Europeans would flock to the American programming. But while viewers in Europe shared a common interest in a handful of global superstars, who at the time included Madonna and Michael Jackson, their tastes turned out to be surprisingly local. What was popular in Germany might not be popular in Great Britain. Many staples of the American music scene left Europeans cold, and MTV suffered as a result. Soon local copycat stations were springing up in Europe that focused on the music scene in individual countries. These stations took viewers and advertisers away from MTV. As explained by Tom Freston, chairman of MTV Networks, "We were going for the most shallow layer of what united viewers and brought them together. It didn't go over too well."

In 1995, MTV changed its strategy and broke Europe into regional feeds, of which there are now eight: one for the United Kingdom and Ireland; another for Germany, Austria, and Switzerland; one for Scandinavia; one for Italy; one for France; one for Spain; one for Holland; and a feed for other European nations, including Belgium and Greece. The network adopted the same localization strategy elsewhere in the world. For example, in Asia it has an English-Hindi channel for India, separate Mandarin feeds for China and Taiwan, a Korean feed for South Korea, a Bahasa-language feed for Indonesia, a Japanese feed for Japan, and so on. Digital and satellite technology have made the localization of programming cheaper and easier. MTV Networks can now beam half a dozen feeds off one satellite transponder.

While MTV Networks exercises creative control over these different feeds, and while all the channels have the same familiar frenetic look and feel of MTV in the United States, a significant share of the programming and content is now local. When MTV opens a local station now, it first asks expatriates from elsewhere in the world to do a "gene transfer" of company culture and operating principles—in other words, its business model. But once these are established, the network switches to local employees and the expatriates move on. The idea is to "get inside the heads" of the local population and produce programming that matches their tastes. Although as much as 60 percent of the programming still originates in the United States, with staples such as *The Real World* having equivalents in different countries, an increasing share of programming is local in conception. In Italy, *MTV Kitchen* combines cooking with a music countdown. *Erotica* airs in Brazil and features a panel of youngsters discussing sex. The Indian channel produces twenty-one homegrown shows hosted by local veejays who speak "Hinglish," a city-bred mix of Hindi and English. Hit shows include *MTV Cricket in Control*, appropriate for a land where cricket is a national obsession, *MTV Housefull*, which hones in on Hindi film stars (India has the biggest film industry outside of Hollywood), and *MTV Bakra*, which is modeled after *Candid Camera*.

This localization push has reaped big benefits for MTV, capturing viewers back from local imitators. In India, ratings increased by more than 700 percent between 1996, when the localization push began, and 2000. In turn, localization helps MTV to capture more of those all-important advertising revenues, even from other multinationals such as Coca-Cola, whose own advertising budgets are often locally determined. In Europe, MTV's advertising revenues increased by 50 percent between 1995 and 2000. While the total market for pan-European advertising is valued at just $200 million, the total market for local advertising across Europe is a much bigger pie, valued at $12 billion. MTV now gets 70 percent of its European advertising revenue from local spots, up from 15 percent in 1995. Similar trends are evident elsewhere in the world.[c]

distribution system is radically different from the U.S. system. British and Japanese doctors will not accept or respond favorably to a U.S.-style high-pressure sales force. Thus, pharmaceutical companies have to adopt different marketing practices in Britain and Japan compared with the United States—soft sell versus hard sell.

■ **Host Government Demands**   Finally, economic and political demands imposed by host country governments may require local responsiveness. For example, pharmaceutical companies are subject to local clinical testing, registration procedures, and pricing restrictions, all of which make it necessary that the manufacturing and marketing of a drug should meet local requirements. Moreover, because governments and government agencies control a significant proportion of the health care budget in most countries, they are in a powerful position to demand a high level of local responsiveness.

More generally, threats of protectionism, economic nationalism, and local content rules (which require that a certain percentage of a product should be manufactured locally) dictate that international businesses manufacture locally. As an example, consider Bombardier, the Canadian-based manufacturer of railcars, aircraft, jet boats, and snowmobiles. Bombardier has twelve railcar factories across Europe. Critics of the company argue that the resulting duplication of manufacturing facilities leads to high costs and helps explain why Bombardier makes lower profit margins on its railcar operations than on its other business lines. In reply, managers at Bombardier argue that in Europe, informal rules with regard to local content favor people who use local workers. To sell railcars in Germany, they claim, you must manufacture in Germany. The same goes for Belgium, Austria, and France. To try to address its cost structure in Europe, Bombardier has centralized its engineering and purchasing functions, but it has no plans to centralize manufacturing.[17]

Choosing a Global Strategy

Pressures for local responsiveness imply that it may not be possible for a firm to realize the full benefits from economies of scale and location economies. It may not be possible to serve the global marketplace from a single low-cost location, producing a globally standardized product, and marketing it worldwide to achieve economies of scale. In practice, the need to customize the product offering to local conditions may work against the implementation of such a strategy. For example, automobile firms have found that Japanese, American, and European consumers demand different kinds of cars, and this necessitates producing products that are customized for local markets. In response, firms like Honda, Ford, and Toyota are pursuing a strategy of establishing top-to-bottom design and production facilities in each of these regions so that they can better serve local demands. Although such customization brings benefits, it also limits the ability of a firm to realize significant scale economies and location economies.

In addition, pressures for local responsiveness imply that it may not be possible to leverage skills and products associated with a firm's distinctive competencies wholesale from one nation to another. Concessions often have to be made to local conditions. Despite being depicted as "poster boy" for the proliferation of standardized global products, even McDonald's has found that it has to customize its product offerings (its menu) in order to account for national differences in tastes and preferences.

Given the need to balance the cost and differentiation (value) sides of a company's business model, how do differences in the strength of pressures for cost reductions versus those for local responsiveness affect the choice of a company's strategy? Companies typically choose among four main strategic postures when competing

FIGURE 8.3

Four Basic Strategies

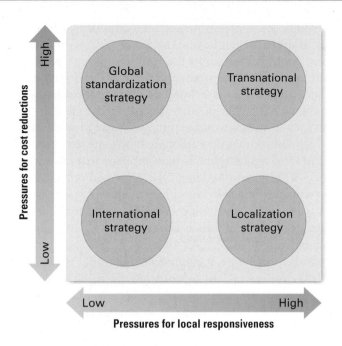

internationally: a global standardization strategy, a localization strategy, a transnational strategy, and an international strategy.[18] The appropriateness of each strategy varies with the extent of pressures for cost reductions and local responsiveness. Figure 8.3 illustrates the conditions under which each of these strategies is most appropriate.

Global Standardization Strategy

Companies that pursue a **global standardization strategy** focus on increasing profitability by reaping the cost reductions that come from economies of scale and location economies; that is, their business model is based on pursuing a low-cost strategy on a global scale. The production, marketing, and R&D activities of companies pursuing a global strategy are concentrated in a few favorable locations. These companies try not to customize their product offering and marketing strategy to local conditions because customization, which involves shorter production runs and the duplication of functions, can raise costs. Instead, they prefer to market a standardized product worldwide so that they can reap the maximum benefits from economies of scale. They also tend to use their cost advantage to support aggressive pricing in world markets.

This strategy makes most sense when there are strong pressures for cost reductions and demand for local responsiveness is minimal. Increasingly, these conditions prevail in many industrial goods industries, whose products often serve universal needs. In the semiconductor industry, for example, global standards have emerged, creating enormous demands for standardized global products. Accordingly, companies such as Intel, Texas Instruments, and Motorola all pursue a global strategy.

In many consumer goods markets, however, demands for local responsiveness remain high. In these markets the global standardization strategy is inappropriate.

Localization Strategy

A localization strategy focuses on increasing profitability by customizing the company's goods or services so that they provide a good match to tastes and preferences in different national markets. Localization is most appropriate when there are substantial differences across nations with regard to consumer tastes and preferences and where cost pressures are not too intense. By customizing the product offering to local demands, the company increases the value of that product in the local market. On the downside, because it involves some duplication of functions and smaller production runs, customization limits the ability of the company to capture the cost reductions associated with mass-producing a standardized product for global consumption. The strategy may make sense, however, if the added value associated with local customization supports higher pricing, which would enable the company to recoup its higher costs, or if it leads to substantially greater local demand, enabling the company to reduce costs through the attainment of some scale economies in the local market.

MTV is a good example of a company that has had to pursue a localization strategy (see Strategy in Action 8.2). If MTV had not localized its programming to match the demands of viewers in different nations, it would have lost market share to local competitors, its advertising revenues would have fallen, and its profitability would have declined. Thus, even though it raised costs, localization became a strategic imperative at MTV.

At the same time, it is important to realize that companies like MTV still have to keep a close eye on costs. Companies pursuing a localization strategy still need to be efficient and, whenever possible, capture some scale economies from their global reach. As noted earlier, many automobile companies have found that they have to customize some of their product offerings to local market demands—for example, by producing large pickup trucks for U.S. consumers and small fuel-efficient cars for Europeans and Japanese. At the same time, these companies try to get some scale economies from their global volume by using common vehicle platforms and components across many different models and by manufacturing those platforms and components at efficiently scaled factories that are optimally located. By designing their products in this way, these companies have been able to localize their product offering, yet simultaneously capture some scale economies.

■ Transnational Strategy

We have argued that a global standardization strategy makes most sense when cost pressures are intense and demands for local responsiveness limited. Conversely, a localization strategy makes most sense when demands for local responsiveness are high but cost pressures are moderate or low. What happens, however, when the company simultaneously faces both strong cost pressures and strong pressures for local responsiveness? How can managers balance out such competing and inconsistent demands? According to some researchers, the answer is by pursuing what has been called a transnational strategy.

Two of these researchers, Christopher Bartlett and Sumantra Ghoshal, argue that in today's global environment, competitive conditions are so intense that, to survive, companies must do all they can to respond to pressures for both cost reductions and local responsiveness. They must try to realize location economies and economies of scale from global volume, transfer distinctive competencies and skills within the company, and simultaneously pay attention to pressures for local responsiveness.[19] Moreover, Bartlett and Ghoshal note that, in the modern multinational enterprise, distinctive competencies and skills do not reside just in the home country but can develop in any of the company's worldwide operations. Thus, they maintain that the flow of skills and product offerings should not be all one way, from home company to foreign subsidiary. Rather, the flow should also be from foreign subsidiary to home country and from foreign subsidiary to foreign subsidiary. Transnational companies, in other words, must also focus on leveraging subsidiary skills.

In essence, companies that pursue a transnational strategy are trying to develop a business model that simultaneously achieves low costs, differentiates the product offering across geographic markets, and fosters a flow of skills between different subsidiaries in the company's global network of operations. As attractive as this may sound, the strategy is not an easy one to pursue because it places conflicting demands on the company. Differentiating the product to respond to local demands in different geographic markets raises costs, which runs counter to the goal of reducing costs. Companies like Ford and ABB (one of the world's largest engineering conglomerates) have tried to embrace a transnational strategy and have found it difficult to implement in practice.

Indeed, how best to implement a transnational strategy is one of the most complex questions that large global companies are grappling with today. It may be that few if any companies have perfected this strategic posture. But some clues to the right approach can be derived from a number of companies. Consider, for example, the case of Caterpillar. The need to compete with low-cost competitors such as Komatsu of Japan forced Caterpillar to look for greater cost economies. However, variations in construction practices and government regulations across countries meant that Caterpillar also had to be responsive to local demands. Therefore, Caterpillar confronted significant pressures for cost reductions *and* for local responsiveness.

To deal with cost pressures, Caterpillar redesigned its products to use many identical components and invested in a few large-scale component-manufacturing facilities, sited at favorable locations, to fill global demand and realize scale economies. At the same time, the company augments the centralized manufacturing of components with assembly plants in each of its major global markets. At these plants, Caterpillar adds local product features, tailoring the finished product to local needs. Thus, Caterpillar is able to realize many of the benefits of global manufacturing while reacting to pressures for local responsiveness by differentiating its product among national markets.[20] Caterpillar started to pursue this strategy in 1979, and by 1997 it had succeeded in doubling output per employee, significantly reducing its overall cost structure in the process. Meanwhile, Komatsu and Hitachi, which are still wedded to a Japan-centric global strategy, have seen their cost advantages evaporate and have been steadily losing market share to Caterpillar.

However, building an organization capable of supporting a transnational strategy is a complex and challenging task. Indeed, some would say it is too complex, because the strategy implementation problems of creating a viable organizational structure and control systems to manage this strategy are immense. We shall return to this issue in Chapter 13.

■ International Strategy

Sometimes it is possible to identify multinational companies that find themselves in the fortunate position of being confronted with low cost pressures and low pressures for local responsiveness. Typically these enterprises are selling a product that serves universal needs, but because they do not face significant competitors, they are not confronted with pressures to reduce their cost structure. Xerox found itself in this position in the 1960s after its invention and commercialization of the photocopier. The technology underlying the photocopier was protected by strong patents, so for several years Xerox did not face competitors—it had a monopoly. Since the product was highly valued in most developed nations, Xerox was able to sell the same basic product the world over and charge a relatively high price for it. At the same time, because it did not face direct competitors, the company did not have to deal with strong pressures to minimize its costs.

Historically, companies like Xerox have followed a similar developmental pattern as they build their international operations. They tend to centralize product development functions such as R&D at home. However, they also tend to establish manufacturing and marketing functions in each major country or geographic region in which they do business. Although they may undertake some local customization of product offering and marketing strategy, this tends to be rather limited in scope. Ultimately, in most international companies, the head office retains tight control over marketing and product strategy.

Other companies that have pursued this strategy include Procter & Gamble, which historically always developed innovative new products in Cincinnati and then transferred them wholesale to local markets. Another company that has followed a similar strategy is Microsoft. The bulk of Microsoft's product development work takes place in Redmond, Washington State, where the company is headquartered. Although some localization work is undertaken elsewhere, this is limited to producing foreign-language versions of popular Microsoft programs such as Office.

■ **Changes in Strategy over Time**

The Achilles heel of the international strategy is that, over time, competitors inevitably emerge, and if managers do not take proactive steps to reduce their cost structure, their company may be rapidly outflanked by efficient global competitors. This is exactly what happened to Xerox. Japanese companies such as Canon ultimately invented their way around Xerox's patents, produced their own photocopiers in very efficient manufacturing plants, priced them below Xerox's products, and rapidly took global market share from Xerox. Xerox's demise was not due to the emergence of competitors, for ultimately that was bound to occur, but rather to its failure to proactively reduce its cost structure in advance of the emergence of efficient global competitors. The message in this story is that an international strategy may not be viable in the long term, and to survive companies that are able to pursue it need to shift toward a global standardization strategy, or perhaps a transnational strategy, in advance of competitors (see Figure 8.4).

FIGURE 8.4

Changes over Time

The same can be said about a localization strategy. Localization may give a company a competitive edge, but if it is simultaneously facing aggressive competitors, the company will also have to reduce its cost structure, and the only way to do that may be to adopt more of a transnational strategy. Thus, as competition intensifies, international and localization strategies tend to become less viable, and managers need to orient their companies toward either a global standardization strategy or a transnational strategy.

Basic Entry Decisions

A company contemplating foreign expansion must make three basic decisions: which overseas markets to enter, when to enter those markets, and on what scale.

■ Which Overseas Markets to Enter

There are over two hundred nation-states in the world, and they do not all hold out the same profit potential for a company contemplating foreign expansion. The choice of foreign markets must be based on an assessment of their long-run profit potential. The attractiveness of a country as a potential market for international business depends on balancing the benefits, costs, and risks associated with doing business in that country. The long-run economic benefits of doing business in a country are a function of factors such as the size of a market (in terms of demographics), the existing wealth (purchasing power) of consumers in that market, and the likely future wealth of consumers. Some markets are very large when measured by numbers of consumers (such as China and India), but low living standards may imply limited purchasing power and therefore a relatively small market when measured in economic terms. The costs and risks associated with doing business in a foreign country are typically lower in economically advanced and politically stable democratic nations and greater in less developed and politically unstable nations.

By performing benefit-cost-risk calculations, a company can come up with a ranking of countries in terms of their attractiveness and long-run profit potential.[21] Obviously, preference is given to entering markets that rank highly. For an example, consider the case of the American financial services company Merrill Lynch, whose situation is profiled in Strategy in Action 8.3. During the past decade, Merrill Lynch greatly expanded its operations in the United Kingdom, Canada, and Japan. All three of these countries have a large pool of private savings and exhibit relatively low political and economic risks, so it makes sense that they would be attractive to Merrill Lynch. By offering its financial service products, such as mutual funds and investment advice, Merrill Lynch should be able to capture a large enough proportion of the private savings pool in each country to justify its investment in setting up business there. Of the three countries, Japan is probably the riskiest given the fragile state of its financial system, which is still suffering from a serious bad debt problem. However, the large size of the Japanese market and the fact that its government seems to be embarking on significant reform explain why Merrill has been attracted to this nation.

One other factor of importance is the value that a company's business model can create in a foreign market. This depends on the suitability of its business model to that market and the nature of indigenous competition.[22] Most important, if the company can offer a product that has not been widely available in that market and satisfies an unmet need, the value of that product to consumers is likely to be much greater than if the company simply offers the same type of product that indigenous competitors and other foreign entrants are already offering. Greater value translates into an ability to charge higher prices or build up unit sales volume more rapidly (or both). Again, on this count, Japan is clearly very attractive to Merrill Lynch.

Strategy in Action

8.3

Merrill Lynch in Japan

Merrill Lynch, the U.S.-based financial services institution, is an investment banking titan. It is the world's largest underwriter of debt and equity and the third largest adviser on mergers and acquisitions behind Morgan Stanley and Goldman Sachs. As one might expect, its investment banking operations have long had a global reach. The company has a dominant presence not only in New York but also in London and Tokyo. However, until recently, Merrill's international presence was limited to the investment banking side of its business. In contrast, its private client business, which offers banking, financial advice, and stockbrokerage services to individuals, has historically been concentrated in the United States. This is now changing rapidly. In 1995 Merrill purchased Smith New Court, the largest stockbrokerage firm in Britain, and in 1997 it acquired Mercury Asset Management, the U.K.'s leading manager of mutual funds. Then in 1998 Merrill acquired Midland Walwyn, Canada's last major independent stockbrokerage firm. The company's boldest moves, however, have probably been in Japan.

Merrill started to establish a private client business in Japan in the 1980s but met with limited success. At the time, it was the first foreign firm to enter Japan's private client investment market, and it had great difficulty in attracting employee talent and customers away from Japan's four big stockbrokerage firms, which traditionally had monopolized the Japanese market. Moreover, restrictive regulations made it almost impossible for Merrill to offer its Japanese private clients the range of services it offered clients in the United States. For example, foreign exchange regulations meant that it was very difficult for Merrill to sell non-Japanese stocks, bonds, and mutual funds to Japanese investors. In 1993, Merrill admitted defeat, closed down its six retail branches in Kobe and Kyoto, and withdrew from the private client market in Japan.

Over the next few years, however, things started to change. In the mid 1990s, Japan embarked on a wide-ranging deregulation of its financial services industry. Among other things, this led to the removal of many of the restrictions that had made it so difficult for Merrill to do business in Japan. For example, the relaxation of foreign exchange controls meant that by 1998 it was possible for Japanese citizens to purchase foreign stocks, bonds, and mutual funds. Meanwhile, Japan's four big stockbrokerage firms continued to struggle with serious financial problems, the result of the 1991 crash of that country's stock market. In November 1997, in what was a dramatic shock to many Japanese, one of these firms, Yamaichi Securities, declared that it was bankrupt: it had $2.2 billion in accumulated "hidden losses" and would shut its doors. Recognizing the country's financial system was strained and in need of fresh capital, know-how, and the stimulus of greater competition, the Japanese government signaled that it would adopt a much more relaxed attitude to foreign entry into its financial services industry. This attitude underlay Japan's wholehearted endorsement of a 1997 deal brokered by the World Trade Organization (WTO) to liberalize global financial services. Among other things, the WTO deal made it much easier for foreign firms to sell financial service products to Japanese investors.

By 1997, it had become clear to Merrill Lynch that the climate in Japan had changed significantly. The big attraction of the market was still the same: the financial assets owned by Japanese households are huge, amounting to a staggering 1,220 trillion yen in late 1997, with only 3 percent invested in mutual funds (most are invested in low-yielding bank accounts and government bonds). However, attitudes were changing, and it looked as if it would be much easier to do business in Japan.

Accordingly, in mid 1997, Merrill started to consider reentering the Japanese private client market. Initially, it considered a joint venture with Sanwa Bank to sell Merrill's mutual fund products to Japanese consumers through Sanwa's four hundred retail branches. The proposed alliance had the advantage of allowing Merrill to leverage Sanwa's existing distribution system rather than having to build a distribution system of its own from scratch. However, in the long run, the strategy would not have given Merrill the presence that it felt it needed to build a solid financial services business in Japan. Merrill's executives reasoned that it was important for them to make a major commitment to the Japanese market in order to establish its brand name as a premier provider of investment products and financial advice to individuals. This would enable the company to entrench itself as a major player before other foreign institutions entered the market—and before Japan's own stockbrokerages rose to the challenge. At the same time, given their prior experience in Japan, Merrill's executives were hesitant to go down this road because of the huge costs and risks.

The problem of how best to enter the Japanese market was solved by the bankruptcy of Yamaichi Securities. Suddenly Yamaichi's nationwide network of offices and 7,000 employees were up for grabs. In late December 1997, Merrill announced that it would hire some 2,000 of Yamaichi's employees and acquire up to fifty of Yamaichi's branch offices. The deal, enthusiastically endorsed by the Japanese government, significantly lowered Merrill's costs of establishing a retail network in Japan. Merrill's goal for the new subsidiary was to have $20 billion under management by 2000 and to break even by 2001.

The company got off to a quick start. In February 1998, Merrill Lynch launched its first mutual fund in Japan and saw the value of its assets swell to $1 billion by April. By mid 2002, it announced it had $12.9 billion under management in Japan. However, the collapse in global stock markets in 2001–2002 hit Merrill's Japanese unit hard. After losing $500 million in Japan on its investment, in January 2002 the company fired 75 percent of its Japanese work force and closed all but eight of its retail locations. Despite this costly downsizing, the company held on to almost all of the assets under management, continued to attract new accounts, and by mid 2002 was reportedly making a profit in Japan.[d]

■ Timing of Entry

Once a set of attractive national markets has been identified, it is important to consider the timing of entry: *early* (before other overseas companies) or *late* (after other international businesses have already established themselves in the market).

Several first-mover advantages are frequently associated with entering a market early.[23] One advantage is the ability to preempt rivals and capture demand by establishing a strong brand name. A second is the ability to build up demand, sales revenue, and market share in that country and ride down the experience curve ahead of future rivals. Both factors give the early entrant a cost advantage over later entrants, which may enable it to respond to later entry by cutting prices below those of later entrants and drive them out of the market. A third advantage is the ability of early entrants to create switching costs that tie customers into their products or services. Such switching costs make it difficult for later entrants to win business.

The case of Merrill Lynch illustrates these ideas. By entering the private client market in Japan early, Merrill hoped to establish a brand name that later entrants would find difficult to match. Moreover, by entering early with a valuable product offering, Merrill hoped to build up its sales volume rapidly, which will enable it to realize scale economies from establishing a network of Japanese branches. In addition, as Merrill trains its Japanese staff, their productivity should rise because of learning economies, which again translates into lower costs. Thus, Merrill should be able to ride down the experience curve and achieve a lower cost structure than later entrants.

Finally, Merrill's business model is based on establishing close relationships between its financial advisers (that is, stockbrokers) and private clients. Merrill's financial advisers are taught to get to know the needs of their clients and help manage their finances more effectively. Once these relationships are established, people rarely change. In other words, because of switching costs, they are unlikely to shift their business to later entrants. This effect is likely to be particularly strong in a country like Japan, where long-term relationships have traditionally been very important in business and social settings. For all of these reasons, Merrill Lynch may be able to capture first-mover advantages that will enable it to enjoy a strong competitive position in Japan for years to come.

There can also be first-mover disadvantages associated with entering a foreign market before other global companies.[24] These disadvantages are associated with *pioneering costs*, which an early entrant has to bear and which a later entrant can avoid. Pioneering costs arise when the business system in a foreign country is so different from that in a company's home market that a company has to devote considerable effort, time, and expense to learning the rules of the game. Pioneering costs also include the costs of business failure if the company, because of its ignorance of the overseas environment, makes major strategic mistakes. Thus, a global company that is one of the first to enter a national market has a certain liability.[25] Research evidence suggests that the probability of survival increases if an international business enters a national market *after* several other overseas companies have already done so.[26] The late entrant, it would appear, benefits by observing and learning from the mistakes made by early entrants.

Pioneering costs also include the costs of promoting and establishing a product offering, including the costs of educating customers. These costs can be particularly significant when the product being promoted is one that local customers are unfamiliar with. In many ways, Merrill Lynch will have to bear such pioneering costs in Japan. Most Japanese are not familiar with the type of investment products and services that it intends to sell, so Merrill will have to invest significant resources in customer education. In contrast, later entrants may be able to free-ride on an early entrant's investments in learning and customer education by watching how the early entrant proceeded in the market, avoiding costly mistakes made by the early entrant, and exploiting the market potential created by the early entrant's investments in customer education.

■ Scale of Entry and Strategic Commitments

The final issue that a company needs to consider when contemplating market entry is the scale of entry. Entering a market on a large scale involves the commitment of significant resources to that venture. Not all companies have the resources necessary to enter on a large scale, and even some large companies prefer to enter overseas markets on a small scale and then build their presence slowly over time as they become more familiar with the market. The original entry by Merrill Lynch into the private client market in Japan was on a small scale, involving only a handful of branches. In contrast, Merrill's reentry into the Japanese market in 1997 was on a significant scale.

The consequences of entering on a significant scale are associated with the value of the resulting strategic commitments.[27] A *strategic commitment* is a decision that has a long-term impact and is difficult to reverse. Deciding to enter a foreign market on a significant scale is a major strategic commitment. Strategic commitments, such as large-scale market entry, can have an important influence on the nature of competition in a market. For example, by entering Japan's private client business on a significant scale, Merrill has signaled its commitment to the market. This will have several effects. On the positive side, it will make it easier for Merrill to attract clients. The scale of entry gives potential clients reason for believing that Merrill will remain in the market for the long run. It may also give other overseas institutions considering entry into Japan's market pause for thought, since now they will have to compete not only against Japan's indigenous institutions but also against an aggressive and successful U.S. institution. On the negative side, the move may wake up Japan's financial institutions and elicit a vigorous competitive response from them. Moreover, by committing itself heavily to Japan, Merrill may have fewer resources available to support expansion in other desirable markets. In other words, Merrill's commitment to Japan limits its strategic flexibility.

As this example suggests, significant strategic commitments are neither unambiguously good nor bad. Rather, they tend to change the competitive playing field and unleash a number of changes, some of which may be desirable and some of which will not. It is therefore important for a company to think through the implications of large-scale entry into a market and act accordingly. Of particular relevance is trying to identify how actual and potential competitors might react to large-scale entry into a market. It is also important to bear in mind a connection between large-scale entry and first-mover advantages. Specifically, the large-scale entrant is more likely than the small-scale entrant to be able to capture first-mover advantages associated with demand preemption, scale economies, and switching costs.

Balanced against the value and risks of the commitments associated with large-scale entry are the benefits of entering on a small scale. Small-scale entry has the advantage of allowing a company to learn about a foreign market while simultaneously limiting the company's exposure to that market. In this sense, small-scale entry can be seen as a way of gathering more information about a foreign market before deciding whether to enter on a significant scale and how best to enter that market. In other words, by giving the company time to collect information, small-scale entry reduces the risks associated with a subsequent large-scale entry. On the other hand, the lack of commitment associated with small-scale entry may make it more difficult for the small-scale entrant to build market share and capture first-mover or early-mover advantages. The risk-averse company that enters a foreign market on a small scale may limit its potential losses, but it may also lose the chance to capture first-mover advantages.

The Choice of Entry Mode

The issue of when and how to enter a new national market raises the question of how to determine the best mode or vehicle for such entry. There are five main choices of entry mode: exporting, licensing, franchising, entering into a joint venture with a host country company, and setting up a wholly owned subsidiary in the host country. Each mode has its advantages and disadvantages, and managers must weigh these carefully when deciding which mode to use.[28]

■ Exporting

Most manufacturing companies begin their global expansion as exporters and only later switch to one of the other modes for serving a foreign market. Exporting has two distinct advantages: it avoids the costs of establishing manufacturing operations in the host country, which are often substantial, and it may be consistent with scale economies and location economies. By manufacturing the product in a centralized location and then exporting it to other national markets, the company may be able to realize substantial scale economies from its global sales volume. That is how Sony came to dominate the global television market, how Matsushita came to dominate the VCR market, and how many Japanese auto companies originally made inroads into the U.S. auto market.

There are also a number of drawbacks to exporting. First, exporting from the company's home base may not be appropriate if there are lower-cost locations for manufacturing the product abroad (that is, if the company can realize location economies by moving production elsewhere). Thus, particularly in the case of a company pursuing a global standardization or transnational strategy, it may pay to manufacture in a location where conditions are most favorable from a value creation perspective and then export from that location to the rest of the globe. This is not so much an argument against exporting as an argument against exporting from the company's home country. For example, many U.S. electronics companies have moved some of their manufacturing to Asia because low-cost but highly skilled labor is available there. They export from that location to the rest of the globe, including the United States.

Another drawback is that high transport costs can make exporting uneconomical, particularly in the case of bulk products. One way of getting around this problem is to manufacture bulk products on a regional basis, thereby realizing some economies from large-scale production while limiting transport costs. Many multinational chemical companies manufacture their products on a regional basis, serving several countries in a region from one facility.

Tariff barriers, too, can make exporting uneconomical, and a government's threat to impose tariff barriers can make the strategy very risky. Indeed, the implicit threat from the U.S. Congress to impose tariffs on Japanese cars imported into the United States led directly to the decision by many Japanese auto companies to set up manufacturing plants in the United States.

Finally, a common practice among companies that are just beginning to export also poses risks. A company may delegate marketing activities in each country in which it does business to a local agent, but there is no guarantee that the agent will act in the company's best interest. Often foreign agents also carry the products of competing companies and thus have divided loyalties. Consequently, they may not do as good a job as the company would if it managed marketing itself. One way to solve this problem is to set up a wholly owned subsidiary in the host country to handle local marketing. In this way, the company can reap the cost advantages that arise from manufacturing the product in a single location and exercise tight control over marketing strategy in the host country.

■ Licensing

International licensing is an arrangement whereby a foreign licensee buys the rights to produce a company's product in the licensee's country for a negotiated fee (normally, royalty payments on the number of units sold). The licensee then puts up most of the capital necessary to get the overseas operation going.[29] The advantage of licensing is that the company does not have to bear the development costs and risks associated with opening up a foreign market. Licensing therefore can be a very attractive option for companies that lack the capital to develop operations overseas. It can also be an attractive option for companies that are unwilling to commit substantial financial resources to an unfamiliar or politically volatile foreign market where political risks are particularly high.

Licensing has three serious drawbacks, however. First, it does not give a company the tight control over manufacturing, marketing, and strategic functions in foreign countries that it needs to have in order to realize scale economies and location economies—as companies pursuing both global standardization and transnational strategies try to do. Typically, each licensee sets up its own manufacturing operations. Hence, the company stands little chance of realizing scale economies and location economies by manufacturing its product in a centralized location. When these economies are likely to be important, licensing may not be the best way of expanding overseas.

Second, competing in a global marketplace may make it necessary for a company to coordinate strategic moves across countries so that the profits earned in one country can be used to support competitive attacks in another. Licensing, by its very nature, severely limits a company's ability to coordinate strategy in this way. A licensee is unlikely to let a multinational company take its profits (beyond those due in the form of royalty payments) and use them to support an entirely different licensee operating in another country.

A third problem with licensing is the risk associated with licensing technological know-how to foreign companies. For many multinational companies, technological know-how forms the basis of their competitive advantage, and they would want to maintain control over the use to which it is put. By licensing its technology, a company can quickly lose control over it. RCA, for instance, once licensed its color television technology to a number of Japanese companies. The Japanese companies quickly assimilated RCA's technology and then used it to enter the U.S. market. Now the Japanese have a bigger share of the U.S. market than the RCA brand does.

There are ways of reducing this risk. One way is by entering into a cross-licensing agreement with a foreign firm. Under a **cross-licensing agreement**, a firm might license some valuable intangible property to a foreign partner and, in addition to a royalty payment, also request that the foreign partner license some of its valuable know-how to the firm. Such agreements are reckoned to reduce the risks associated with licensing technological know-how, since the licensee realizes that if it violates the spirit of a licensing contract (by using the knowledge obtained to compete directly with the licensor), the licensor can do the same to it. Put differently, cross-licensing agreements enable firms to hold each other hostage, thereby reducing the probability that they will behave opportunistically toward each other.[30] Such cross-licensing agreements are increasingly common in high-technology industries. For example, the U.S. biotechnology firm Amgen has licensed one of its key drugs, Nuprogene, to Kirin, the Japanese pharmaceutical company. The license gives Kirin the right to sell Nuprogene in Japan. In return, Amgen receives a royalty payment, and through a licensing agreement it gains the right to sell certain of Kirin's products in the United States.

■ **Franchising**
In many respects, franchising is similar to licensing, although franchising tends to involve longer-term commitments than licensing. **Franchising** is basically a specialized form of licensing in which the franchiser not only sells intangible property to the franchisee (normally a trademark), but also insists that the franchisee agree to abide by strict rules as to how it does business. The franchiser will also often assist the franchisee to run the business on an ongoing basis. As with licensing, the franchiser typically receives a royalty payment, which amounts to some percentage of the franchisee revenues.

Whereas licensing is a strategy pursued primarily by manufacturing companies, franchising, which resembles it in some respects, is a strategy employed chiefly by service companies. McDonald's provides a good example of a firm that has grown by using a franchising strategy. McDonald's has set down strict rules as to how franchisees should operate a restaurant. These rules extend to control over the menu, cooking methods, staffing policies, and restaurant design and location. McDonald's also organizes the supply chain for its franchisees and provides management training and financial assistance.[31]

The advantages of franchising are similar to those of licensing. Specifically, the franchiser does not have to bear the development costs and risks of opening up a foreign market on its own, for the franchisee typically assumes those costs and risks. Thus, using a franchising strategy, a service company can build up a global presence quickly and at a low cost.

The disadvantages are less pronounced than in the case of licensing. Because franchising is a strategy used by service companies, a franchiser does not have to consider the need to coordinate manufacturing to achieve scale economies and location economies. Nevertheless, franchising may inhibit a company's ability to achieve global strategic coordination.

A more significant disadvantage of franchising is the lack of quality control. The foundation of franchising arrangements is the notion that the company's brand name conveys a message to consumers about the quality of the company's product. Thus, a traveler booking into a Hilton International hotel in Hong Kong can reasonably expect the same quality of room, food, and service as she would receive in New York; the Hilton brand name is a guarantee of the consistency of product quality. However, foreign franchisees may not be as concerned about quality as they should be, and poor quality may mean not only lost sales in the foreign market but also a decline in the company's worldwide reputation. For example, if the traveler has a bad experience at the Hilton in Hong Kong, she may never go to another Hilton hotel and may steer her colleagues away as well. The geographic distance separating it from its foreign franchisees and the sheer number of individual franchisees—tens of thousands in the case of McDonald's—can make it difficult for the franchiser to detect poor quality. Consequently, quality problems may persist.

To reduce this problem, a company can set up a subsidiary in each country or region in which it is expanding. The subsidiary, which might be wholly owned by the company or a joint venture with a foreign company, then assumes the rights and obligations to establish franchisees throughout that particular country or region. The combination of proximity and the limited number of independent franchisees that have to be monitored reduces the quality control problem. Besides, since the subsidiary is at least partly owned by the company, the company can place its own managers in the subsidiary to ensure the kind of quality monitoring it wants. This organizational arrangement has proved very popular in practice. It has been used by McDonald's, KFC, and Hilton Hotels Corp. to expand their international operations, to name just three examples.

■ Joint Ventures

Establishing a joint venture with a foreign company has long been a favored mode for entering a new market. One of the most famous long-term joint ventures is the Fuji-Xerox joint venture to produce photocopiers for the Japanese market. The most typical form of joint venture is a 50/50 joint venture, in which each party takes a 50 percent ownership stake and operating control is shared by a team of managers from both parent companies. Some companies have sought joint ventures in which they have a majority shareholding (for example, a 51 percent to 49 percent ownership split), which permits tighter control by the dominant partner.[32]

Joint ventures have a number of advantages. First, a company may feel that it can benefit from a local partner's knowledge of a host country's competitive conditions, culture, language, political systems, and business systems. Second, when the development costs and risks of opening up a foreign market are high, a company might gain by sharing these costs and risks with a local partner. Third, in some countries, political considerations make joint ventures the only feasible entry mode.[33] For example, historically many U.S. companies found it much easier to get permission to set up operations in Japan if they went in with a Japanese partner than if they tried to enter on their own. This is why Xerox originally teamed up with Fuji to sell photocopiers in Japan.

Despite these advantages, joint ventures can be difficult to establish and run because of two main drawbacks. First, as in the case of licensing, a company that enters into a joint venture risks losing control over its technology to its venture partner.

To minimize this risk, it can seek a majority ownership stake in the joint venture, and then as the dominant partner it would be able to exercise greater control over its technology. The trouble with this strategy is that it may be difficult to find a foreign partner willing to accept a minority ownership position.

The second disadvantage is that a joint venture does not give a company the tight control over its subsidiaries that it might need in order to realize scale economies or location economies—as both global standardization and transnational companies try to do—or to engage in coordinated global attacks against its global rivals. Consider the entry of Texas Instruments (TI) into the Japanese semiconductor market. When TI established semiconductor facilities in Japan, part of its objective was to limit Japanese manufacturers' market share and the amount of cash available to them to invade TI's global market. In other words, TI was engaging in global strategic coordination. To implement this strategy, TI's Japanese subsidiary had to be prepared to take instructions from the TI corporate headquarters regarding competitive strategy. The strategy also required that the Japanese subsidiary be run at a loss if necessary. Clearly, a Japanese joint venture partner would have been unlikely to accept such conditions since they would have meant a negative return on investment. Thus, in order to implement this strategy, TI set up a wholly owned subsidiary in Japan instead of entering this market through a joint venture.

Wholly Owned Subsidiaries

A **wholly owned subsidiary** is one in which the parent company owns 100 percent of the subsidiary's stock. To establish a wholly owned subsidiary in a foreign market, a company can either set up a completely new operation in that country or acquire an established host country company and use it to promote its products in the host market (as Merrill Lynch did when it acquired various assets of Yamaichi Securities; see Strategy in Action 8.3).

Setting up a wholly owned subsidiary offers three advantages. First, when a company's competitive advantage is based on its control of a technological competency, a wholly owned subsidiary will normally be the preferred entry mode, since it reduces the company's risk of losing this control. Consequently, many high-tech companies prefer wholly owned subsidiaries to joint ventures or licensing arrangements. Wholly owned subsidiaries tend to be the favored entry mode in the semiconductor, computer, electronics, and pharmaceutical industries. Second, a wholly owned subsidiary gives a company the kind of tight control over operations in different countries that it needs if it is going to engage in global strategic coordination—taking profits from one country to support competitive attacks in another.

Third, a wholly owned subsidiary may be the best choice if a company wants to realize location economies and the scale economies that flow from producing a standardized output from a single or limited number of manufacturing plants. When pressures on costs are intense, it may pay a company to configure its value chain in such a way that value added at each stage is maximized. Thus, a national subsidiary may specialize in manufacturing only part of the product line or certain components of the end product, exchanging parts and products with other subsidiaries in the company's global system. Establishing such a global production system requires a high degree of control over the operations of national affiliates. Different national operations have to be prepared to accept centrally determined decisions as to how they should produce, how much they should produce, and how their output should be priced for transfer between operations. A wholly owned subsidiary would have to comply with these mandates, whereas licensees or joint venture partners would most likely shun such a subservient role.

On the other hand, establishing a wholly owned subsidiary is generally the most costly method of serving a foreign market. The parent company must bear all the costs and risks of setting up overseas operations—in contrast to joint ventures, where the costs and risks are shared, or licensing, where the licensee bears most of the costs and risks. But the risks of learning to do business in a new culture diminish if the company acquires an established host country enterprise. Acquisitions, though, raise a whole set of additional problems, such as trying to marry divergent corporate cultures, and these problems may more than offset the benefits. (The problems associated with acquisitions are discussed in Chapter 10.)

■ **Choosing an Entry Strategy**

The advantages and disadvantages of the various entry modes are summarized in Table 8.1. Inevitably, there are tradeoffs in choosing one entry mode over another. For example, when considering entry into an unfamiliar country with a track record of nationalizing foreign-owned enterprises, a company might favor a joint venture with a local enterprise. Its rationale might be that the local partner will help it establish operations in an unfamiliar environment and speak out against nationalization should the possibility arise. But if the company's distinctive competency is based on proprietary technology, entering into a joint venture might mean risking loss of control over that technology to the joint venture partner, which would make this strategy unattractive. Despite such hazards, some generalizations can be offered about the optimal choice of entry mode.

TABLE 8.1

The Advantages and Disadvantages of Different Entry Modes

Entry Mode	Advantages	Disadvantages
Exporting	■ Ability to realize location- and scale-based economies	■ High transport costs ■ Trade barriers ■ Problems with local marketing agents
Licensing	■ Low development costs and risks	■ Inability to realize location- and scale-based economies ■ Inability to engage in global strategic coordination ■ Lack of control over technology
Franchising	■ Low development costs and risks	■ Inability to engage in global strategic coordination ■ Lack of control over quality
Joint ventures	■ Access to local partner's knowledge ■ Shared development costs and risks ■ Political dependency	■ Inability to engage in global strategic coordination ■ Inability to realize location- and scale-based economies ■ Lack of control over technology
Wholly owned subsidiaries	■ Protection of technology ■ Ability to engage in global strategic coordination ■ Ability to realize location- and scale-based economies	■ High costs and risks

■ **Distinctive Competencies and Entry Mode** When companies expand internationally to earn greater returns from their differentiated product offerings, entering markets where indigenous competitors lack comparable products, the companies are pursuing an international strategy. The optimal entry mode for such companies depends to some degree on the nature of their distinctive competency. In particular, we need to distinguish between companies with a distinctive competency in technological know-how and those with a distinctive competency in management know-how.

If a company's competitive advantage—its distinctive competency—derives from its control of proprietary *technological know-how*, licensing and joint venture arrangements should be avoided if possible to minimize the risk of losing control of that technology. Thus, if a high-tech company is considering setting up operations in a foreign country in order to profit from a distinctive competency in technological know-how, it should probably do so through a wholly owned subsidiary.

However, this rule should not be viewed as a hard and fast one. For instance, a licensing or joint venture arrangement might be structured in such a way as to reduce the risks that a company's technological know-how will be expropriated by licensees or joint venture partners. We consider this kind of arrangement in more detail later in the chapter when we discuss the issue of structuring strategic alliances. To take another exception to the rule, a company may perceive its technological advantage as being only transitory and expect rapid imitation of its core technology by competitors. In this situation, the company might want to license its technology as quickly as possible to foreign companies in order to gain global acceptance of its technology before imitation occurs.[34] Such a strategy has some advantages. By licensing its technology to competitors, the company may deter them from developing their own, possibly superior, technology. It also may be able to establish its technology as the dominant design in the industry (as Matsushita did with its VHS format for VCRs), ensuring a steady stream of royalty payments. Such situations apart, however, the attractions of licensing are probably outweighed by the risks of losing control of technology, and therefore licensing should be avoided.

The competitive advantage of many service companies, such as McDonald's or Hilton Hotels, is based on *management know-how*. For such companies, the risk of losing control of their management skills to franchisees or joint venture partners is not that great. The reason is that the valuable asset of such companies is their brand name, and brand names are generally well protected by international laws pertaining to trademarks. Given this fact, many of the issues that arise in the case of technological know-how do not arise in the case of management know-how. As a result, many service companies favor a combination of franchising and subsidiaries to control franchisees within a particular country or region. The subsidiary may be wholly owned or a joint venture. In most cases, however, service companies have found that entering into a joint venture with a local partner in order to set up a controlling subsidiary in a country or region works best because a joint venture is often politically more acceptable and brings a degree of local knowledge to the subsidiary.

■ **Pressures for Cost Reduction and Entry Mode** The greater the pressures for cost reductions are, the more likely it is that a company will want to pursue some combination of exporting and wholly owned subsidiaries. By manufacturing in the locations where factor conditions are optimal and then exporting to the rest of the world, a company may be able to realize substantial location economies and substantial scale economies. The company might then want to export the finished product to marketing subsidiaries based in various countries. Typically, these subsidiaries would be wholly owned and have the responsibility for overseeing distribution in a particular country. Setting up wholly owned marketing subsidiaries is preferable to a joint venture arrangement or using a foreign marketing agent because it gives the company the tight control over marketing that might be required to coordinate a globally dispersed value chain. In addition, tight control over a local operation enables the company to use the profits generated in one market to improve its competitive position in another market. Hence companies pursuing global or transnational strategies prefer to establish wholly owned subsidiaries.

Global Strategic Alliances

Global strategic alliances are cooperative agreements between companies from different countries that are actual or potential competitors. Strategic alliances run the range from formal joint ventures, in which two or more companies have an equity stake, to short-term contractual agreements, in which two companies may agree to cooperate on a particular problem (such as developing a new product).

Advantages of Strategic Alliances

Companies enter into strategic alliances with competitors to achieve a number of strategic objectives.[35] First, strategic alliances may be a way of *facilitating entry into a foreign market*. For example, Motorola initially found it very difficult to gain access to the Japanese cellular telephone market. In the mid 1980s, it complained loudly about formal and informal Japanese trade barriers. The turning point for Motorola came in 1987, when it formed its alliance with Toshiba to build microprocessors. As part of the deal, Toshiba provided Motorola with marketing help, including some of its best managers. This aided Motorola in the political game of winning government approval to enter the Japanese market and obtaining allocations of radio frequencies for its mobile communications systems. Since then, Motorola has played down the importance of Japan's informal trade barriers. Although privately the company still admits they exist, with Toshiba's help Motorola has become skilled at getting around them.[36]

Second, many companies enter into strategic alliances to share the *fixed costs and associated risks* that arise from the development of new products or processes. Motorola's alliance with Toshiba was partly motivated by a desire to share the high fixed costs associated with setting up an operation to manufacture microprocessors. The microprocessor business is so capital intensive (it cost Motorola and Toshiba close to $1 billion to set up their facility) that few companies can afford the costs and risks of going it alone. Similarly, an alliance between Boeing and a number of Japanese companies to build Boeing's latest commercial jetliner, the 787, was motivated by Boeing's desire to share the estimated $8 billion investment required to develop the aircraft.

Third, many alliances can be seen as a way of bringing together *complementary skills and assets* that neither company could easily develop on its own. In 2003, for example, Microsoft and Toshiba established an alliance aimed at developing embedded microprocessors (essentially tiny computers) that can perform a variety of entertainment functions in an automobile (such as run a back-seat DVD player or a wireless Internet connection). The processors will run a version of Microsoft's Windows CE operating system. Microsoft brings its software engineering skills to the alliance and Toshiba its skills in developing microprocessors.[37]

Finally, it may make sense to enter into an alliance if it helps the company *set technological standards for its industry* and if those standards benefit the company. For example, in 1999 Palm Computer, the leading maker of personal digital assistants (PDAs), entered into an alliance with Sony under which Sony agreed to license and use Palm's operating system in Sony PDAs. The motivation for the alliance was in part to help establish Palm's operating system as the industry standard for PDAs, as opposed to a rival Windows-based operating system from Microsoft.[38]

■ Disadvantages of Strategic Alliances

The various advantages can be very significant. Nevertheless, some commentators have criticized strategic alliances on the grounds that they give competitors a low-cost route to gain new technology and market access.[39] For example, a few years ago some commentators argued that many strategic alliances between U.S. and Japanese firms were part of an implicit Japanese strategy to keep higher-paying, higher-value-added jobs in Japan while gaining the project engineering and production process skills that underlie the competitive success of many U.S. companies.[40] They argued that Japanese success in the machine tool and semiconductor industries was built on U.S. technology acquired through strategic alliances. And they argued that U.S. managers were aiding the Japanese in achieving their goals by entering alliances that channel new inventions to Japan and provide a U.S. sales and distribution network for the resulting products. Although such deals may generate short-term profits, so the argument goes, in the long run the result is to "hollow out" U.S. firms, leaving them with no competitive advantage in the global marketplace.

These critics have a point: alliances do have risks. Unless it is careful, a company can give away more than it gets in return. Nevertheless, there are so many examples of apparently successful alliances between companies, including alliances between U.S. and Japanese companies, that this criticism seems extreme. It is difficult to see how the Motorola-Toshiba alliance or the long-standing alliance between Fuji Film and Xerox to manufacture photocopiers (Fuji-Xerox) fits their thesis. In all of these cases, both partners seemed to have gained from the alliance. Thus, we might ask: *Why do some alliances benefit the company, whereas in others, it can end up giving away technology and market access and get very little in return?* The next section provides an answer to this question.

Making Strategic Alliances Work

The failure rate for international strategic alliances is quite high. For example, one study of forty-nine international strategic alliances found that two-thirds run into serious managerial and financial troubles within two years of their formation, and that although many of these problems are ultimately solved, 33 percent are ultimately rated as failures by the parties involved.[41] The success of an alliance seems to be a function of three main factors: partner selection, alliance structure, and the manner in which the alliance is managed.

■ Partner Selection

One of the keys to making a strategic alliance work is to select the right kind of partner. A good partner has three principal characteristics. First, a good partner helps the company achieve strategic goals such as achieving market access, sharing the costs and risks of new-product development, or gaining access to critical core competencies. In other words, the partner must have capabilities that the company lacks and that it values. Second, a good partner shares the firm's vision for the purpose of the alliance. If two companies approach an alliance with radically different agendas, the chances are great that the relationship will not be harmonious and will end in divorce.

Third, a good partner is unlikely to try to exploit the alliance opportunistically for its own ends—that is, to expropriate the company's technological know-how while giving away little in return. In this respect, firms with reputations for fair play probably make the best partners. For example, IBM is involved in so many strategic alliances that it would not pay the company to trample over individual alliance partners (in early 2003 IBM reportedly had more than 150 major strategic alliances).[42] This would tarnish IBM's reputation of being a good ally and would make it more difficult for IBM to attract alliance partners. Because IBM attaches great importance to its alliances, it is unlikely to engage in the kind of opportunistic behavior that critics highlight. Similarly, their reputations make it less likely (but by no means impossible) that such Japanese firms as Sony, Toshiba, and Fuji, which have histories of alliances with non-Japanese firms, would opportunistically exploit an alliance partner.

To select a partner with these three characteristics, a company needs to conduct some comprehensive research on potential alliance candidates. To increase the probability of selecting a good partner, the company should collect as much pertinent publicly available information about potential allies as possible; collect data from informed third parties, including companies that have had alliances with the potential partners, investment bankers who have had dealings with them, and some of their former employees; and get to know potential partners as well as possible before committing to an alliance. This last step should include face-to-face meetings between senior managers (and perhaps middle-level managers) to ensure that the chemistry is right.

■ **Alliance Structure**

Having selected a partner, the alliance should be structured so that the company's risk of giving too much away to the partner is reduced to an acceptable level. Figure 8.5 depicts the four safeguards against opportunism by alliance partners that we discuss here. (**Opportunism** includes the "expropriation" of technology or markets.) First, alliances can be designed to make it difficult (if not impossible) to transfer technology not meant to be transferred. Specifically, the design, development, manufacture, and service of a product manufactured by an alliance can be structured so as to "wall off" sensitive technologies to prevent their leakage to the other participant. In the alliance between General Electric and Snecma to build commercial aircraft engines, for example, GE reduced the risk of "excess transfer" by walling off certain sections of the production process. The modularization effectively cut off the transfer of what GE regarded as key competitive technology while permitting Snecma access to final assembly. Similarly, in the alliance between Boeing and the Japanese to build the 767, Boeing walled off research, design, and marketing functions considered central to its competitive position, while allowing the Japanese to share in production technology. Boeing also walled off new technologies not required for 767 production.[43]

Second, contractual safeguards can be written into an alliance agreement to guard against the risk of opportunism by a partner. For example, TRW has three strategic alliances with large Japanese auto component suppliers to produce seat belts, engine valves, and steering gears for sale to Japanese-owned auto assembly plants in the

FIGURE 8.5

Structuring Alliances to Reduce Opportunism

United States. TRW has clauses in each of its alliance contracts that bar the Japanese firms from competing with TRW to supply U.S.-owned auto companies with component parts. By doing this, TRW protects itself against the possibility that the Japanese companies are entering into the alliances merely as a means of gaining access to the North American market to compete with TRW in its home market.

Third, both parties to an alliance can agree in advance to swap skills and technologies, thereby ensuring a chance for equitable gain. Cross-licensing agreements are one way to achieve this goal. For example, in the alliance between Motorola and Toshiba, Motorola has licensed some of its microprocessor technology to Toshiba, and in return Toshiba has licensed some of its memory chip technology to Motorola.

Fourth, the risk of opportunism by an alliance partner can be reduced if the firm extracts a significant credible commitment from its partner in advance. The long-term alliance between Xerox and Fuji to build photocopiers for the Asian market perhaps best illustrates this. Rather than enter into an informal agreement or some kind of licensing arrangement (which Fuji Photo initially wanted), Xerox insisted that Fuji invest in a 50/50 joint venture to serve Japan and East Asia. This venture constituted such a significant investment in people, equipment, and facilities that Fuji Photo was committed from the outset to making the alliance work in order to earn a return on its investment. By agreeing to the joint venture, Fuji essentially made a credible commitment to the alliance. Given this commitment, Xerox felt secure in transferring its photocopier technology to Fuji.[44]

■ Managing the Alliance

Once a partner has been selected and an appropriate alliance structure agreed on, the task facing the company is to maximize the benefits from the alliance. One important ingredient of success appears to be sensitivity to cultural differences. Many differences in management style are attributable to cultural differences, and managers need to make allowances for these in dealing with their partner. Beyond this, maximizing the benefits from an alliance seems to involve building trust between partners and learning from partners.[45]

Managing an alliance successfully requires building interpersonal relationships between the firms' managers, or what is sometimes referred to as *relational capital*.[46] This is one lesson that can be drawn from a successful strategic alliance between Ford and Mazda. Ford and Mazda set up a framework of meetings within which their managers not only discuss matters pertaining to the alliance but also have time to get to know each other better. The belief is that the resulting friendships help build trust and facilitate harmonious relations between the two firms. Personal relationships also foster an informal management network between the firms. This network can then be used to help solve problems arising in more formal contexts (such as in joint committee meetings between personnel from the two firms).

A major factor determining how much a company gains from an alliance is its ability to learn from alliance partners. Gary Hamel, Yves Doz, and C. K. Prahalad reached this conclusion after a five-year study of fifteen strategic alliances between major multinationals. They focused on a number of alliances between Japanese companies and Western (European or American) partners. In every case in which a Japanese company emerged from an alliance stronger than its Western partner, the Japanese company had made a greater effort to learn. Indeed, few Western companies seemed to want to learn from their Japanese partners. They tended to regard the alliance purely as a cost-sharing or risk-sharing device rather than as an opportunity to learn how a potential competitor does business.[47]

For an example of an alliance in which there was a clear learning asymmetry, consider the agreement between General Motors and Toyota Motor Corp. to build the Chevrolet Nova. This alliance was structured as a formal joint venture, New United Motor Manufacturing, in which both parties had a 50 percent equity stake. The venture owned an auto plant in Fremont, California. According to one of the Japanese managers, Toyota achieved most of its objectives from the alliance: "We learned about U.S. supply and transportation. And we got the confidence to manage U.S. workers." All that knowledge was then quickly transferred to Georgetown, Kentucky, where Toyota opened a plant of its own in 1988. By contrast, although General Motors got a new product, the Chevrolet Nova, some GM managers complained that their new knowledge was never put to good use inside GM. They say that they should have been kept together as a team to educate GM's engineers and workers about the Japanese system. Instead, they were dispersed to different GM subsidiaries.[48]

When entering an alliance, a company must take some measures to ensure that it learns from its alliance partner and then puts that knowledge to good use within its own organization. One suggested approach is to educate all operating employees about the partner's strengths and weaknesses and make clear to them how acquiring particular skills will bolster their company's competitive position. For such learning to be of value, the knowledge acquired from an alliance has to be diffused throughout the organization—as did not happen at GM. To spread this knowledge, the managers involved in an alliance should be used as a resource in familiarizing others within the company about the skills of an alliance partner.

Summary of Chapter

1. For some companies, international expansion represents a way of earning greater returns by transferring the skills and product offerings derived from their distinctive competencies to markets where indigenous competitors lack those skills. As barriers to international trade have fallen, industries have expanded beyond national boundaries and industry competition and opportunities have increased.

2. Because of national differences, it pays a company to base each value creation activity it performs at the location where factor conditions are most conducive to the performance of that activity. This strategy is known as focusing on the attainment of location economies.

3. By building sales volume more rapidly, international expansion can help a company gain a cost advantage through the realization of scale economies and learning effects.

4. The best strategy for a company to pursue may depend on the kind of pressures it must cope with: pressures for cost reductions or for local responsiveness. Pressures for cost reductions are greatest in industries producing commodity-type products, where price is the main competitive weapon. Pressures for local responsiveness arise from differences in consumer tastes and preferences, as well as from national infrastructure and traditional practices, distribution channels, and host government demands.

5. Companies pursuing an international strategy transfer the skills and products derived from distinctive competencies to foreign markets, while undertaking some limited local customization.

6. Companies pursuing a localization strategy customize their product offering, marketing strategy, and business strategy to national conditions.

7. Companies pursuing a global standardization strategy focus on reaping the cost reductions that come from scale economies and location economies.

8. Many industries are now so competitive that companies must adopt a transnational strategy. This involves a simultaneous focus on reducing costs, transferring skills and products, and being locally responsive. Implementing such a strategy may not be easy.

9. The most attractive foreign markets tend to be found in politically stable developed and developing nations that have free market systems.

10. Several advantages are associated with entering a national market early, before other international businesses have established themselves. These advantages

must be balanced against the pioneering costs that early entrants often have to bear, including the greater risk of business failure.

11. Large-scale entry into a national market constitutes a major strategic commitment that is likely to change the nature of competition in that market and limit the entrant's future strategic flexibility. The firm needs to think through the implications of such commitments before embarking on a large-scale entry. Although making major strategic commitments can yield many benefits, there are also risks associated with such a strategy.

12. There are five different ways of entering a foreign market: exporting, licensing, franchising, entering into a joint venture, and setting up a wholly owned subsidiary. The optimal choice among entry modes depends on the company's strategy.

13. Strategic alliances are cooperative agreements between actual or potential competitors. The advantages of alliances are that they facilitate entry into foreign markets, enable partners to share the fixed costs and risks associated with new products and processes, facilitate the transfer of complementary skills between companies, and help companies establish technical standards.

14. The drawbacks of a strategic alliance are that the company risks giving away technological know-how and market access to its alliance partner while getting very little in return.

15. The disadvantages associated with alliances can be reduced if the company selects partners carefully, paying close attention to reputation, and structures the alliance so as to avoid unintended transfers of know-how.

Discussion Questions

1. Plot the position of the following companies on Figure 8.3: Procter & Gamble, IBM, Coca-Cola, Dow Chemicals, Pfizer, and McDonald's. In each case, justify your answer.

2. Are the following global standardization industries or industries where localization is more important: bulk chemicals, pharmaceuticals, branded food products, moviemaking, television manufacture, personal computers, airline travel, and Internet online services such as AOL and MSN?

3. Discuss how the need for control over foreign operations varies with the strategy and distinctive competencies of a company. What are the implications of this relationship for the choice of entry mode?

4. Licensing proprietary technology to foreign competitors is the best way to give up a company's competitive advantage. Discuss.

5. What kind of companies stand to gain the most from entering into strategic alliances with potential competitors? Why?

Practicing Strategic Management

■ SMALL-GROUP EXERCISE
Developing a Global Strategy

Break into groups of three to five people, and discuss the following scenario. Appoint one group member as a spokesperson who will communicate your findings to the class. You work for a company in the soft drink industry that has developed a line of carbonated fruit-based drinks. You have already established a significant presence in your home market, and now you are planning the global strategy development of the company in the soft drink industry. You need to decide the following:

1. What overall strategy to pursue: a global standardization strategy, a localization strategy, an international strategy, or a transnational strategy

2. Which markets to enter first

3. What entry strategy to pursue (e.g., franchising, joint venture, wholly owned subsidiary)

4. What information do you need to make this kind of decision? On the basis of what you do know, what strategy would you recommend?

■ ARTICLE FILE 8

Find an example of a multinational company that in recent years has switched its strategy from a localization, international, or global standardization strategy to a transnational strategy. Identify why the company made the switch and any problems that the company may be encountering while it tries to change its strategic orientation.

■ STRATEGIC MANAGEMENT PROJECT
Module 8

This module requires you to identify how your company might profit from global expansion, the strategy that your company should pursue globally, and the entry mode that it might favor. With the information you have at your disposal, answer the questions regarding the following two situations:

Your company is already doing business in other countries.

1. Is your company creating value or lowering the costs of value creation by realizing location economies, transferring distinctive competencies abroad, or realizing cost economies from the economies of scale? If not, does it have the potential to?
2. How responsive is your company to differences among nations? Does it vary its product and marketing message from country to country? Should it?
3. What are the cost pressures and pressures for local responsiveness in the industry in which your company is based?
4. What strategy is your company pursuing to compete globally? In your opinion, is this the correct strategy, given cost pressures and pressures for local responsiveness?
5. What major foreign market does your company serve, and what mode has it used to enter this market? Why is your company active in these markets and not others? What are the advantages and disadvantages of using this mode? Might another mode be preferable?

Your company is not yet doing business in other countries.

1. What potential does your company have to add value to its products or lower the costs of value creation by expanding internationally?

2. On the international level, what are the cost pressures and pressures for local responsiveness in the industry in which your company is based? What implications do these pressures have for the strategy that your company might pursue if it chose to expand globally?
3. What foreign market might your company enter, and what entry mode should it use to enter this market? Justify your answer.

■ EXPLORING THE WEB
Visiting IBM

IBM stands for International Business Machines. Using the significant resources located at IBM's corporate website (**www.ibm.com**), including annual reports and company history, explain what the "International" means in IBM. Specifically, how many countries is IBM active in? How does IBM create value by expanding into foreign markets? What entry mode does IBM adopt in most markets? Can you find any exceptions to this? How would you characterize IBM's strategy for competing in the global marketplace? Is IBM pursuing a transnational, global standardization, international, or localization strategy?

General Task Search the Web for a company site where there is a good description of that company's international operations. On the basis of this information, try to establish how the company enters foreign markets and what overall strategy it is pursuing (global standardization, international, localization, transnational).

Closing Case

Planet Starbucks

Thirty years ago Starbucks was a single store in Seattle's Pike Place Market selling premium roasted coffee. Today it is a global roaster and retailer of coffee with more than 7,600 retail stores, some 2,000 of which are to be found in thirty-four countries outside the United States. Starbucks set out on its current course in the 1980s when the company's director of marketing, Howard Schultz, came back from a trip to Italy enchanted with the Italian coffeehouse experience. Schultz, who later became CEO, persuaded the

company's owners to experiment with the coffeehouse format—and the Starbucks experience was born. The basic business model was to sell the company's own premium roasted coffee, along with freshly brewed espresso-style coffee beverages, a variety of pastries, coffee accessories, teas, and other products, in a tastefully designed coffeehouse setting. The company also stressed providing superior customer service. Reasoning that motivated employees provide the best customer service, Starbucks executives devoted much attention to employee hiring and training programs and progressive compensation policies that gave even part-time employees stock option grants and medical benefits. The formula met with spectacular success in the United States, where Starbucks went from obscurity to one of the best-known brands in the country in a decade.

In 1995, with almost 700 stores across the United States, Starbucks began exploring foreign opportunities. The company established a joint venture with a local retailer, Sazaby Inc. Each company held a 50 percent stake in the venture, Starbucks Coffee of Japan. Starbucks initially invested $10 million in this venture, its first foreign direct investment. The Starbucks format was then licensed to the venture, which was charged with taking over responsibility for growing Starbucks' presence in Japan.

To make sure the Japanese operations replicated the North American "Starbucks experience," Starbucks transferred some employees to the Japanese operation. All Japanese store managers and employees were required to attend training classes similar to those given to U.S. employees. Stores also had to adhere to some basic design parameters established in the United States. In 2001, the company introduced a stock option plan for all Japanese employees, making it the first company in Japan to do so. Skeptics doubted that Starbucks would be able to replicate its North American success overseas, but by early 2004 Starbucks had more than 500 stores in Japan and the Japanese unit was predicted to make a healthy profit for the year.

After getting its feet wet in Japan, the company embarked on an aggressive foreign investment program. In 1998, it purchased Seattle Coffee, a British coffee chain with 60 retail stores, for $84 million. An American couple, originally from Seattle, had started Seattle Coffee with the intention of establishing a Starbucks-like chain in Britain. Also in the late 1990s, Starbucks opened stores throughout Asia, including Taiwan, China, Singapore, Thailand, South Korea, and Malaysia. By the end of 2002, with more than 1,200 stores in twenty-seven countries outside of North America, Starbucks was initiating aggressive expansion plans in continental Europe. The company's target was to open some 650 stores in six European countries, including the coffee cultures of France and Italy, by 2005.

As in Japan, much of Starbucks' international expansion has been undertaken with local joint venture partners, to whom the company licenses the Starbucks' format (the U.K. is an exception to this). In general, Starbucks only transfers small numbers of Americans to international markets, preferring foreign operations to be run by local managers who understand the market better. To cater to local tastes, Starbucks has introduced some novel products:

a green tea Frappuccino in Taiwan and Japan, for example, where it has rapidly become the largest-selling Frappuccino. Sometimes these local products have made it back into the United States: a strawberries and cream Frappuccino first sold in the United Kingdom was introduced into the United States in 2004. In some locations outside of the United States, such as China, Japan, and the United Kingdom, food is much more important in the product mix. Internationally, far more of what is ordered is consumed on the premises—about 85 percent—which requires more in-store seating and porcelain cups for those inclined to linger. In North America the pattern is exactly the opposite, with some 86 percent of items ordered to go, usually in paper cups. Real estate strategy has also been adjusted to cater to local conditions. In the United States, the strategy has been to find the best street corner locations in the best markets. This strategy did not work in the United Kingdom, where the best corners are on busy shopping streets where the rents are too high for even high-volume Starbucks stores.

Despite such local differences, however, the biggest surprise to Starbucks' management has been how well the basic Starbucks formula has succeeded in international markets. Lattes are becoming standard fare the world over, from noncoffee cultures such as China and tea cultures such as Japan, to the long established coffee cultures of western Europe. Starbucks is fast becoming one of the best-known global brands. In 2004, the magazine *Brandchannel* named Starbucks as one of the ten most impactful global brands for the third year in a row. Building on its international success, in April 2004 the company stated that it ultimately planned to have 10,000 stores in North America and some 15,000 in other counties, which would make Starbucks almost as globally ubiquitous as that other American restaurant icon, McDonald's.[49]

Case Discussion Questions

1. How has Starbucks' strategy of expanding overseas created value for the company's shareholders?

2. Using the global strategy framework outlined in this chapter, would you classify Starbucks as a localization, international, global standardization, or transnational enterprise? Do you think it has the right strategic posture?

3. Why do you think Starbucks has used joint ventures with local companies to enter many foreign markets?

4. Why do you think that Starbucks chose Japan as its first foreign market? Why did it pick Britain as its second? Why did the company wait until 2002 to open its first stores on the European mainland?

Chapter 9

Corporate-Level Strategy: Horizontal Integration, Vertical Integration, and Strategic Outsourcing

Opening Case

Read All About News Corp

Before television and the Internet, "Read all about it" was the cry of street vendors eager to persuade news-hungry customers to buy the most recent version of their newspaper. Now, TV channels like CNN and Web portals like Yahoo! and Google provide almost instantaneous news from around the world. "Read the latest" might also describe the growth of News Corporation Limited, or News Corp, the company headed by controversial CEO Rupert Murdoch, who every year for the last several decades has engineered some kind of acquisition or divestiture that has created one of the four largest and most powerful entertainment media companies in the world. What is the news about News Corp? What kinds of strategies did Murdoch use to create his media empire?

Rupert Murdoch was born into a newspaper family; his father owned and ran the *Adelaide News,* an Australian regional newspaper, and when his father died in 1952 Murdoch gained control of the paper. He quickly enlarged his customer base by acquiring more Australian newspapers. One of these had connections to a major British "pulp" newspaper, the *Mirror,* a paper similar to the *National Enquirer,* and Murdoch recognized he had an opportunity to copy the *Mirror*'s business model but make his paper even more sensational. His business model worked, and Murdoch established the *Sun* as a leading British tabloid.

Murdoch's growing reputation as an entrepreneur showed that he could create a much higher return from the assets he controlled (ROIC) than his competitors and enabled him to borrow increasing amounts of money from investors. With this money he bought well-known newspapers such as the *British Sunday Telegraph* and then his first U.S. newspaper, the *San Antonio Express.* Pursuing his sensational business model further, he launched the *National Star.* His growing profits and reputation allowed him to continue to borrow money, and in 1977 he bought the *New York Post.* Four years later, in 1981, he engineered a new coup when he bought the *Times* and *Sunday Times,* Britain's leading conservative publications—a far cry from the *Sun* tabloid.

Murdoch's strategy of horizontal integration through merger allowed him to create one of the world's biggest newspaper empires. However, he also realized that industries in the entertainment and media sector can be divided into those that provide media content or "software" (books, movies, and television programs) and those that provide the media channels or "hardware" necessary to bring software to customers (movie theaters, TV channels, TV cable, and satellite broadcasting). Murdoch decided that he could create the most profit by becoming involved in both the media software *and* hardware industries—that is, the entire value chain of the entertainment and media sector. This strategy of vertical integration gave him control over all the different industries, joined together like links in a chain that converted inputs such as stories into finished products like newspapers or books.

In the 1980s, Murdoch began purchasing global media companies in both the software and hardware stages of the entertainment sector. He also launched new ventures of his own. For example, sensing the potential of satellite broadcasting, in 1983 he launched Sky, the first satellite TV channel, in the United Kingdom. He also began a new strategy of horizontal integration by purchasing companies that owned television stations; for Metromedia, which owned seven stations that reached over 20 percent of U.S. households, he paid $1.5 billion. He scored another major coup in 1985 when he bought Twentieth Century Fox Movie Studios, a premium content provider. Now he had Fox's huge film library and its creative talents to make new films and TV programming.

In 1986, Murdoch decided to create the FOX Broadcasting Company and buy or create his own U.S. network of FOX affiliates that would show programming developed by his own FOX movie studios. After a slow start, the FOX network gained popularity with sensational shows like *The Simpsons*, which became FOX's first blockbuster program. Then in 1994 FOX purchased the sole rights to broadcast all NFL games for over $1 billion, thereby shutting out NBC and becoming the "fourth network." The FOX network has never looked back and, with Murdoch's sensational business model, was one of the first to create the "reality" programming that has proved so popular in the 2000s.

Realizing that he could create even more value by transmitting his growing media content over new channels, Murdoch also began to increase his company's presence in satellite broadcasting. In 1990, Murdoch merged his Sky satellite channel with British Satellite Broadcasting to form BSkyB, which has since become the leading satellite provider in the United Kingdom. Then, in 2003, News Corp announced it would buy DIRECTV, one of the two largest satellite TV providers, for $6.6 billion. At the same time, News Corp was also acquiring many other companies in both stages of the entertainment value chain to strengthen its competitive position in those industries.

By 2004, Murdoch's business model, based on strategies of horizontal and vertical integration, had created a global media empire. The company's profitability has ebbed and flowed because of the massive debt needed to fund Murdoch's acquisitions, debt that has frequently brought his company near to financial ruin. However, banks that understand the value of his assets, such as Citibank, have provided the money needed to service those debts. Meanwhile, New Corps's ROIC has been increasing. Indeed, in November 2004, it appeared that one of its largest investors, Liberty Media, sensing that News Corp's assets might be worth much more if they were combined with its own media assets or sold off to other companies, seemed ready to start a hostile takeover bid to gain control of News Corp's media empire.

Overview   Over the last decades Rupert Murdoch has acquired or started scores of companies in order to create a media empire, that is, a collection of businesses in different industries in the media sector. The overriding goal of managers is to maximize the value of a company for its shareholders, and theoretically Murdoch embarked on his quest because he believes that, by combining all these different businesses into one entity, he could increase their profitability. In other words, he believed that the value of the empire as a whole would be greater than the value of each part separately. Clearly, the scale of Murdoch's mission and vision for News Corp takes the issue of strategy formulation to a new level of complexity.

The News Corp story illustrates the use of corporate-level strategy to identify (1) which businesses and industries a company should compete in, (2) which value creation activities it should perform in those businesses, and (3) how it should enter or leave businesses or industries to maximize its long-run profitability. In formulating corporate-level strategy, managers must adopt a long-term perspective and consider how changes taking place in an industry and in its products, technology, customers, and competitors will affect their company's current business model and its future strategies. They then decide how to implement specific corporate-level strategies to redefine their company's business model so that it can achieve a competitive position in the changing industry environment by taking advantage of the opportunities and countering the threats. Thus the principal goal of corporate-level strategy is to enable a company to sustain or promote its competitive advantage and profitability in its present business and in any new businesses or industries that it enters.

This chapter is the first of two that deals with the role of corporate-level strategy in repositioning and redefining a company's business model. We discuss three corporate-level strategies—horizontal integration, vertical integration, and strategic outsourcing—that are primarily directed toward improving a company's competitive advantage and profitability in its present business or product market. Diversification, which entails entry into new kinds of markets or industries, is examined in the next chapter, along with guidelines for choosing the most profitable way to enter new markets or industries or to exit others. By the end of this and the next chapter, you will understand how the different levels of strategy contribute to the creation of a successful and profitable business or multibusiness model. You will also be able to differentiate between the types of corporate strategies managers use to maximize long-term company profitability.

Corporate-Level Strategy and the Multibusiness Model

The formulation of corporate-level strategies is the final part of the strategy formulation process. These strategies drive a company's business model over time and determine the kinds of business- and functional-level strategies that will maximize long-run profitability. The relationship between business-level strategy and functional-level strategy was discussed in Chapter 5. Strategic managers develop a business model and strategies that use their company's distinctive competencies to strive for a cost-leadership position and/or to differentiate its products. Chapter 8 described how global strategy is also an extension of these basic principles. Throughout this chapter and the next, we repeatedly stress that, to succeed, corporate-level strategies are also based on the choice of business-level strategies that increase profitability. To understand what this means, we must return to the concepts of profitability and the value chain introduced in Chapter 3.

To increase profitability, a corporate strategy should enable a company, or one or more of its business divisions or units, to perform one or more value-chain activities or functions (1) at a lower cost, and/or (2) in a way that allows for differentiation. A company can then choose the pricing option (lowest, average, or premium price) that allows it to maximize revenues and profitability. In addition, corporate-level strategy will boost profitability if it helps a company achieve a better competitive position, such as by reducing industry rivalry and lowering the threat of damaging price competition.

Thus, a company's corporate-level strategies should be chosen to promote the success of a company's business model and to allow it to achieve a sustainable competitive advantage at the business level. Competitive advantage leads to higher profitability.

Like News Corp, many companies choose to expand their business activities beyond one market or industry and enter others. When a company decides to expand in this way, it must construct its business model at two levels. First, it must develop a business model and strategies for each business unit or division in every industry in which it competes. Second, it must also develop a higher-level *multibusiness model* that justifies its entry into different businesses and industries. This model should explain how and why the company's current competencies and business strategies would increase its return on investment in the value chain of a new industry. For example, Dell used elements of its PC business model, such as direct selling over the Internet, to guide the business model developed for a new unit in the consumer electronics industry. News Corp used its expertise in sensational marketing that it learned from its involvement in the newspaper business and applied it to its FOX network to create reality TV programs and "racy" sitcoms.

A multibusiness model should also explain any other ways in which a company's involvement in more than one business or industry can increase its profitability. Dell, for example, might argue that its entry into computer consulting and the sale of printers and high-powered servers will enable it to offer its customers a complete line of computer products and services and thus better compete with HP or IBM. News Corp might argue that its entry into the satellite broadcasting industry will give it access to more viewers for its television programming, which will generate important advertising revenues. Much of what follows is a discussion of why some companies are better off staying within one industry while others may profit from entering other industries.

Horizontal Integration: Single-Industry Strategy

Managers use corporate-level strategy to identify which industries their company should compete in to maximize its long-run profitability. For many companies, profitable growth and expansion often entail competing successfully within a single market or industry. Examples of such companies include McDonald's, with its focus on the global fast-food restaurant business, and Wal-Mart, with its focus on global discount retailing.

Staying inside an industry allows a company to focus its total managerial, financial, technological, and functional resources and capabilities on competing successfully in one area. This is important in fast-growing and changing industries, where demands on a company's resources and capabilities are likely to be substantial but where the long-term profits from establishing a competitive advantage are also likely to be significant.

A second advantage of staying inside a single industry is that a company "sticks to the knitting," meaning that it stays focused on what it knows and does best. It does not make the mistake of entering new industries where its existing resources and capabilities add little value and/or where a whole new set of competitive industry forces—new competitors, suppliers, and customers—present unanticipated threats. Both Coca-Cola and Sears, like many other companies, have committed this strategic error. Coca-Cola once decided to expand into the movie business and acquired Columbia Pictures, and it also acquired a large wine-producing business. Sears, the clothing seller, once decided to become a one-stop shopping place and bought Allstate Insurance, Coldwell Banker (a real estate company), and Dean Witter (a financial services enterprise). Both companies found they not only lacked the competencies to compete successfully in their new industries but also that they had not foreseen the different kinds of competitive forces that existed in these industries. They concluded that entry into these new industries dissipated, rather than created, value and lowered their profitability, and they ultimately sold off their new businesses for a loss.

Even when a company stays inside one industry, sustaining a successful business model and strategies over time can be difficult because of changing conditions in the environment, such as advances in technology that allow new competitors into the market and blur the boundaries between different products or markets. A decade ago, when most telecommunications service companies were competing in the local and/or long-distance phone service market, the strategic issue was how to shape the company's line of phone service products to best meet customer demand and reduce industry rivalry. However, a new kind of product, wireless phone service, was emerging. At first it was so expensive that only business customers who really needed it could afford it. Within five years, however, wireless phone companies had developed a business model to lower the cost and price of wireless phone service, and many customers began to switch to the new product, a trend that has accelerated.

At the same time, the use of the Internet began to grow. At first it was not regarded as a substitute for wire line phone service, but today millions of people are using VOIP technology to make phone calls over the Internet, and companies that want to attract customers must now include services like digital messaging and wireless e-mail in their product line. Many of the leading phone companies did not sense how these changes in technology would affect industry competition and were late in changing their business models to add these new products and services. As a result, many have been swallowed up and acquired by companies like SBC, WorldCom, and Verizon, which did sense the emerging threats.

Thus, even inside one industry, it is all too easy for strategic managers to fail to see the "forest" (changing nature of the industry that results in new product/market opportunities) for the "trees" (focus on positioning current products). A focus on corporate-level strategy can help managers forecast future trends and position their company so it can compete successfully in a changing environment. Strategic managers must avoid becoming so immersed in positioning their company's *existing* product lines that they fail to consider new opportunities and threats. The task for corporate-level managers is to analyze how new emerging technologies might impact their business models, how and why these might change customer needs and customer groups in the future, and what kinds of new distinctive competencies will be needed to respond to these changes.

One corporate-level strategy that has been widely used to help managers better position their companies is horizontal integration. **Horizontal integration** is the process of acquiring or merging with industry competitors in an effort to achieve the competitive advantages that come with large scale and scope. An **acquisition** occurs when one company uses its capital resources, such as stock, debt, or cash, to purchase another company, and a **merger** is an agreement between equals to pool their operations and create a new entity. The *Opening Case* discusses how Rupert Murdoch made scores of acquisitions in the newspaper industry so that all his newspapers could take advantage of the stories written by News Corp journalists anywhere in the world, thus reducing costs.

Mergers and acquisitions have occurred in many industries. In the automobile industry, Chrysler merged with Daimler Benz to create DaimlerChrysler; in the aerospace industry, Boeing merged with McDonald Douglas to create the world's largest aerospace company; in the pharmaceutical industry, Pfizer acquired Warner-Lambert to become the largest pharmaceutical firm; in the financial services industry, Citicorp and Travelers merged to create Citigroup, the world's largest financial services company; and in the computer hardware industry, Compaq acquired Digital Equipment Corporation and then itself was acquired by Hewlett-Packard. The most recent wave of mergers and acquisitions peaked in 2000, when U.S. firms spent some $1.6 trillion on 11,000 mergers and acquisitions, up from $300 billion in 1991. Although not all of these acquisitions and mergers involved horizontal integration (some entailed vertical integration or diversification), the vast majority appear to have been horizontal.[1] Moreover, many of these mergers and acquisitions were cross-border affairs as companies raced to acquire foreign companies in the same industry. In 2000, companies from all nations spent around $1.1 trillion on 7,900 cross-border mergers and acquisitions, over 70 percent of them horizontal mergers and acquisitions.[2] In 2001, the number and value of both domestic and international mergers and acquisitions fell by 20 to 30 percent, although the figure remained high by historic standards.

The net result of this wave of mergers and acquisitions has been to increase the level of concentration in a wide range of industries. Consolidated oligopolies have been replacing more fragmented industry structures. For example, twenty years ago, cable television was dominated by a patchwork of thousands of small, family-owned businesses, but by 2002, three companies controlled nearly two-thirds of the market. In 1990, the three big publishers of college textbooks accounted for 35 percent of the market; by 2004, they accounted for over 65 percent. In the manufacture of basic DRAM semiconductor chips, because of mergers and acquisitions the four largest firms accounted for 83 percent of the global market in early 2002, up from 45 percent in 1995.[3] Why is this happening? An answer can be found by looking at the way horizontal integration can improve the competitive advantage and profitability of companies who choose to stay inside one industry.

■ **Benefits of Horizontal Integration**

In pursuing horizontal integration, managers have decided to invest their company's capital to purchase the assets of industry competitors as a way to increase the profitability of its business model. Profits and profitability increase when horizontal integration (1) lowers the cost structure, (2) increases product differentiation, (3) replicates the business model, (4) reduces rivalry within the industry, and (5) increases bargaining power over suppliers and buyers.

■ **Lower Cost Structure** Horizontal integration can lower a company's cost structure because it creates increasing *economies of scale*. Suppose there are five major competitors, each operating a manufacturing plant in some region of the United States, and none of these plants is operating at full capacity. If one competitor buys up another and shuts down that plant, it can operate its own plant at full capacity and so reduce its manufacturing costs. Achieving economies of scale is very important in industries that have a high fixed-cost structure. In such industries, large-scale production allows companies to spread their fixed costs over a large volume and in this way drive down average unit costs. In the telecommunications industry, for example, the fixed costs of building a fiber-optic or wireless network are very high, and to make such an investment pay off, a company needs a large volume of customers. Thus companies like SBC and Verizon acquired other telecommunications companies to get their customers. These new customers increased its utilization rate and thus reduced the costs of serving each customer. Similarly, mergers and acquisitions in the pharmaceutical industry have in part been driven by a desire to realize scale economies in sales and marketing. The fixed costs of building a nationwide pharmaceutical sales force are very high, and pharmaceutical companies need a good portfolio of products to effectively use that sales force. Pfizer acquired Warner-Lambert because its salespeople would then have more products to sell when they visited physicians and their productivity would therefore increase.

A company can also lower its cost structure when horizontal integration allows it to *reduce the duplication of resources* between two companies, such as by eliminating the need for two sets of corporate head offices, two separate sales forces, and so on. Thus, one way HP justified its strategy to acquire rival computer maker Compaq was that the acquisition would save the combined company $2.5 billion in annual expenses by eliminating redundant functions, as discussed in Strategy in Action 9.1.

Strategy in Action   9.1

Beating Dell: Why Hewlett-Packard Wanted to Acquire Compaq

In 2001, Hewlett-Packard (HP) shocked the business world when its CEO, Carly Fiorina, announced that rival computer maker Compaq had agreed to be acquired by HP. The announcement came at the end of a year in which slumping demand and strong competition from Dell had buffeted both companies. The merged company would have annual revenues of about $87.4 billion, putting it in the same league as IBM, and would be able to provide customers with a full range of computer products and services. With the exception of printers, where HP is the market leader, there was significant product overlap between HP and Compaq.

To justify the acquisition, Fiorina claimed that it would yield a number of benefits. First, there would be significant cost savings. Some $2.5 billion a year would be taken out of annual expenses by eliminating redundant administrative functions and cutting 15,000 employees. In addition, combining the PC businesses of HP and Compaq would enable HP to capture significant scale economies and compete more efficiently with Dell. The same would be true in the computer server and storage businesses, areas where Dell was gaining share. Critics, however, were quick to point out that Dell's competitive advantage was based on its cost-leadership business model, which was based on the efficient management of its supply chain—an area where both HP and Compaq lagged behind Dell. Although achieving economies of scale is desirable, would the merger allow the new HP to reduce its cost structure, such as by increasing its supply-chain efficiency? If the new

HP could not change its PC business model to match Dell's low costs, then the merger would not provide any real benefit.

In addition to the cost advantages of the merger, Fiorina argued that the acquisition would give HP a critical mass in the computer service and consultancy business, where it lagged behind leader IBM significantly. By being able to offer customers a total solution to their information technology needs, both hardware *and* services, Fiorina argued that HP could gain new market share among corporate customers, who would now buy its PCs as part of the total "computer package"; moreover, HP would be entering the higher-margin service business. Here too, however, critics were quick to perceive flaws. They argued that HP would still be a minnow in the service and consultancy area, with under 3 percent of market share.

In 2004, HP announced that it had achieved its cost savings target and that it was continuing to find ways to reduce the duplication of resources in the merged company. However, it also announced that Dell's entry into the printer business had hurt its profit margins and that the profit margins on the sales of its PCs were still well below those obtained by Dell. Thus HP has not been able to lower its cost structure to match Dell, while Dell has applied its cost-leadership model to a growing number of computer and electronic products and announced record profits. The result is that Dell's stock price has soared while HP's has sunk; it still has to find ways to realize the gains from its decision to pursue horizontal integration.[a]

Another example of using horizontal integration to reduce operating costs occurred in 2004 when Kmart and Sears announced that they were merging their companies to better position themselves to compete against Wal-Mart. They hope to share common purchasing and distribution facilities and combine their HRM functions to reduce costs. Some Kmart stores might be converted to Sears stores and vice versa, and in some areas the stores may be sold off to realize the value of the real estate. In addition, Kmart stores may carry some of Sears's well-known product lines, such as its appliances and Craftsman tools. This move would also result in differentiation advantages, which we discuss next.

■ **Increased Product Differentiation** Horizontal integration may also increase profitability when it increases product differentiation, for example, by allowing a company to combine the product lines of merged companies so that it can offer customers a wider range of products that can be bundled together. **Product bundling** involves offering customers the opportunity to buy a complete range of products at a single combined price. This increases the value of a company's product line because customers often obtain a price discount from buying a set of products and also become used to dealing with just one company and its representatives. A company may obtain a competitive advantage from increased product differentiation. A famous example of the value of product bundling is Microsoft Office, which is a bundle of different software programs, including a word processor, spreadsheet, and presentation program. In the early 1990s, Microsoft was number 2 or 3 in each of these product categories, behind companies such as WordPerfect (which led in the word processing category), Lotus (which had the best-selling spreadsheet), and Harvard Graphics (which had the best-selling presentation software). By offering all three programs in a single-price package, Microsoft presented consumers with a superior value proposition, and its product bundle quickly gained market share, ultimately accounting for more than 90 percent of all sales of word processors, spreadsheets, and presentation software.

A variation on the bundling theme is providing a "total solution." Becoming a total solution provider is an important rationale for horizontal integration in the computer sector, where companies have tried to increase the value of their offerings by providing all of the hardware and service needs of corporate customers. This was also one of the justifications for the HP-Compaq merger. Providing a total solution saves customers time and money (because they do not have to deal with several suppliers) and ensures that different parts of a customer's information technology system work seamlessly together. By increasing the value of the company's product line, the total solution provider gains market share, and developing this differentiated business model is one of the main reasons for IBM's current success in the computer industry.

Another way to increase product differentiation is through **cross-selling**, which involves a company taking advantage of or "leveraging" its established relationship with customers by acquiring additional product lines or categories that it can sell to them. This is a popular business-level strategy in the financial services industry and has been a major factor driving horizontal integration there. The concept behind cross-selling is that customers prefer to purchase all of their financial service products from a single provider—their checking account, mortgage loans, insurance policies, and investment services—in a sort of *financial services supermarket*. A major rationale for the creation of Citigroup from the merger of Citicorp and Travelers was to create a company that could sell insurance products directly to banking customers and banking services to insurance customers. Once again, product differentiation increases because customers prefer to do business with a single provider of such services and thus place a higher value on purchasing from a company that can provide such services.

▪ Replicating the Business Model

Given the ways in which horizontal integration can lead to both product differentiation and low-cost advantages, there is clearly great strategic value to finding ways to use horizontal integration to replicate a company's successful business model in new market segments within its industry. In the retail industry, for example, Wal-Mart took its low-cost/low-price discount retail business model to enter into the even lower-priced warehouse segment. It has also expanded the range of products it offers customers by entering the supermarket business and establishing a nationwide chain of Wal-Mart superstores that sell groceries and produce. It has replicated this business model globally by acquiring supermarket chains in several countries, such as the United Kingdom, Germany, and, most recently, Japan, where it can use its efficient global materials-management processes to pursue its cost-leadership strategy. In the United States, Wal-Mart launched an unsuccessful bid to acquire the Safeway supermarket chain to expand its presence in the supermarket segment. In the meantime, however, it is experimenting with new small-size supermarkets it calls "neighborhood markets" to expand its presence in the supermarket segment (see the *Running Case*)—perhaps until a new opportunity arises to acquire a national supermarket chain.

Running Case

Wal-Mart's New Chain of "Neighborhood Markets"

Wal-Mart has long recognized that its huge supercenters and discount stores do not serve the needs of customers who want a quick and convenient shopping experience, for example, when they want to pick up food for an evening meal. It has also recognized that places like neighborhood supermarkets, drugstores, and convenience stores are a very lucrative segment of the food retailing market and that customers spend billions of dollars shopping in these locations. So, in the late 1990s, Wal-Mart decided to explore the concept of opening a chain of what it calls "neighborhood markets." Each of these supermarkets is around 40,000 square feet, about a quarter of the size of a superstore, and stocks 20,000 to 30,000 items, as opposed to the over 100,000 items available in Wal-Mart's larger stores. According to the plan, the neighborhood markets would be positioned to compete directly with supermarkets like Kroger and Albertsons and would be open twenty-four hours a day. They would also have a pharmacy and film-processing unit to draw off trade from drugstores, since customers could shop for food while they waited for their prescriptions to be filled or their film to be developed. In addition, the stores would have a large health and beauty products section, which is a high-profit-margin business that encourages impulse buying.

To test whether its cost-leadership model would work at this small scale of operations, Wal-Mart opened stores slowly in good locations. Margins are small in the supermarket business, often between 1 and 2 percent, which is lower than Wal-Mart is accustomed to. To keep costs low, it located its new stores in areas where it has an efficient warehouse food preparation and delivery system. Its plan is to prepare items like bakery goods and meat and deli items in a central location and then ship them to supermarkets in prepackaged containers. Each neighborhood market store is also tied in by satellite to Wal-Mart's retail link network so that food service managers know what kind of food is selling and what is not. They can then adjust the food each store sells by changing the mix that is trucked fresh each day. In addition, because the stores have no butcher or baker, labor costs are reduced by 10 percent.

As a result of these measures, the sixty-plus U.S. stores that were opened by 2004 have been able to undercut the prices charged by supermarkets such as Publix, Winn-Dixie, Kroger, and Albertsons by 10 percent. A typical neighborhood market generates around $20 million a year in sales, has a staff of ninety, and obtains a 2.3 percent profit margin, which is significantly higher than average in the supermarket industry.

Wal-Mart has been opening stores in widely different locations, such as Manhattan, Dallas, Salt Lake City, Tampa, and Ogden, apparently to see if its business model for the new store will work in different kinds of urban settings. If it does, then it can roll out sixty to one hundred new stores each year and so build the neighborhood market chain in the way it has built its other chains. While Wal-Mart has been reticent to comment on how well its new chain is doing, perhaps for fear of alerting its competitors to the growing threat, there are reports that its new stores are even more profitable per square foot than its supercenters. If this is true, investing its capital to rapidly expand its chain will increase Wal-Mart's ROIC and further contribute to its growth and profitability. At the same time, the weaker of its rivals, such as Winn-Dixie and Albertsons, will find their revenues and profits falling, so a continuing shakeout in the supermarket industry is likely in the years ahead. Indeed, it is possible that growing competition from Wal-Mart may induce these companies to agree to be acquired by Wal-Mart.

■ **Reduced Industry Rivalry** Horizontal integration can help to reduce industry rivalry in two ways. First, acquiring or merging with a competitor helps to *eliminate excess capacity* in an industry, which, as we discuss in Chapter 6, often triggers price wars. By taking excess capacity out of an industry, horizontal integration creates a more benign environment in which prices might stabilize or even increase.

In addition, by reducing the number of players in an industry, horizontal integration often makes it easier to implement *tacit price coordination* between rivals, or coordination reached without communication (explicit communication to fix prices is illegal). In general, the larger the number of players in an industry, the more difficult it is to establish informal pricing agreements, such as price leadership by a dominant firm, that reduce the possibility that a price war will erupt. By increasing industry concentration and an oligopoly, horizontal integration can make it easier to establish tacit coordination among rivals.

Both of these motives also seem to have been behind the acquisition of Compaq by Hewlett-Packard in 2002. The PC industry was suffering from significant excess capacity and a serious price war, triggered by Dell's desire to gain market share. By acquiring Compaq, Hewlett-Packard hoped to be able to remove excess capacity in the industry, and by reducing the number of large players, the company hoped to be able to impose some pricing discipline. In fact, Dell continued to price aggressively throughout 2003, but in 2004 it increased the price of many of its PCs by 10 percent or more, signaling to HP that it should not start a new price war.

■ **Increased Bargaining Power** A final reason that some companies use horizontal integration is that it allows them to obtain bargaining power over suppliers or buyers and so increase their profitability at the expense of suppliers or buyers. By consolidating the industry through horizontal integration, a company becomes a much larger buyer of suppliers' products and uses this as leverage to bargain down the price it pays for its inputs, thereby lowering its cost structure. Similarly, by acquiring its competitors, a company gains control over a greater percentage of an industry's product or output. Other things being equal, it then has more power to raise prices and profits because customers have less choice of supplier and are more dependent on the company for their products.

When a company has greater ability to raise prices to buyers or bargain down the price paid for inputs, it has increased **market power**. For an example of how the process of consolidation through horizontal integration can play out, see Strategy in Action 9.2, which looks at the way in which health care providers in eastern Massachusetts have pursued horizontal integration to gain bargaining power, and hence market power, over insurance providers.

■ **Problems with Horizontal Integration** Although horizontal integration can clearly strengthen a company's business model in several ways, there are problems and limitations associated with this strategy. One problem concerns the numerous dangers associated with using mergers and acquisitions to pursue horizontal integration. We discuss these dangers in detail in Chapter 10, but for now the important issue is that a wealth of data suggests that the majority of mergers and acquisitions *do not* create value and that many actually *destroy* value.[4] For example, a recent study by KPMG, a large accounting and management consulting company, looked at seven hundred large acquisitions between 1996 and 1998 and found that although some 30 percent of these did increase the profitability of the acquiring company, 31 percent reduced profitability, and the remainder had little impact

Strategy in Action

Horizontal Integration in Health Care

9.2

In the United States, health maintenance organizations (HMOs) have become a powerful force in the health care sector. HMOs are health insurance companies that provide people with health care coverage, and often companies contract with HMOs on behalf of their employees for health insurance coverage. The HMOs then "supply" patients to health care providers. Thus, HMOs can be viewed as the suppliers of the critical input—patients— to health care providers. In turn, the revenues of health care providers are dependent on the number of patients who pass through their system. Clearly, it is in the interests of HMOs to bargain down the price they must pay health care providers for coverage, and to gain bargaining power HMOs have used horizontal integration to merge with each other until, today, they control a large volume of patients. However, to fight back, health care providers have also resorted to horizontal integration, and the battle is raging.

As an example of how this process plays out, consider how the relationship between HMOs and hospitals has evolved in eastern Massachusetts over the past decade. In the early 1990s, three big HMOs controlled 75 percent of the market for health insurance in eastern Massachusetts. In contrast, there were thirty-four separate hospital networks in the region. Thus, the insurance providers were consolidated, while the health care providers were fragmented, giving the insurance providers considerable bargaining power. The HMOs used their bargaining power to demand deep discounts from health care providers. If a hospital wouldn't offer discounts to an HMO, the HMO would threaten to remove it from its list of providers. Because losing all of those potential patients would severely damage the revenues that a hospital could earn, the hospitals had little choice but to comply with the request.

This began to change in 1994 when two of the most prestigious hospitals in the region, Massachusetts General and Brigham & Women's Hospital, merged with each other to form Partners HealthCare System. Since then, Partners has continued to pursue the strategy of acquiring other hospitals in order to gain power over HMOs. By 2002, it had seven hospitals and some 5,000 doctors in its system. Other regional hospitals pursued a similar strategy, and the number of independent hospital networks in the region fell from thirty-four in 1994 to twelve by 2002.

In 2000, Partners started to exercise its strengthened bargaining power by demanding that HMOs accept a fee increase for services offered by Partners hospitals. One of the biggest HMOs, Tufts, refused to accept the increase and informed nearly 200,000 of its 900,000 subscribers that they would no longer be able to use Partners hospitals or physicians affiliated with Partners. There was an enormous uproar from subscribers. So many employers threatened to pull out of the HMO and switch to another if the policy was not changed that Tufts quickly realized it had little choice but to accept the fee increase. Tufts went back to Partners and agreed to a 30 percent fee increase over three years. Thus, bargaining power in the system had shifted away from the HMOs and toward the hospital networks. However, the Massachusetts attorney general received so many complaints from employers about rising health care premiums that an investigation into market power and anticompetitive behavior among health care providers in eastern Massachusetts was started. Clearly, the battle is not over yet.[b]

on it.[5] The implication is that *implementing* a horizontal integration strategy is not an easy task for managers.

As we discuss in Chapter 10, mergers and acquisitions often fail to produce the anticipated gains, for a number of reasons: problems associated with merging very different company cultures, high management turnover in the acquired company when the acquisition was a hostile one, and a tendency of managers to overestimate the benefits to be had from a merger or acquisition and underestimate the problems involved in merging their operation. For example, much of the opposition to the merger between HP and Compaq was based on the belief that Carly Fiorina was glossing over the difficulties and costs associated with merging the operations of these two companies, especially since they had very different cultures.

Another problem with horizontal integration is that, when a company uses it to become a dominant industry competitor, an attempt to keep using the strategy to grow even larger brings a company into conflict with the Federal Trade Commission, the government agency responsible for enforcing antitrust law. Antitrust authorities are concerned about the potential for abuse of market power; they believe that more competition is generally better for consumers than less competition. They worry that large companies that dominate their industry may be in a position to abuse their market power and raise prices to consumers above the level that would exist in more competitive situations. They also believe that dominant companies can use their market power to crush potential competitors by, for example, cutting prices whenever new competitors enter a market and so forcing them out of business, and then raising prices again once the threat has been eliminated. Because of these concerns, any merger or acquisition that is perceived by the antitrust authorities as creating too much consolidation and the *potential* for future abuse of market power may be blocked. This happened when WorldCom tried to acquire Sprint because it realized it needed to have a strong presence in the wireless phone market. The Justice Department was concerned that the proposed acquisition would reduce the number of major long-distance providers in the United States from three to two and gives these companies too much market power. WorldCom was obliged to drop the acquisition bid.

Vertical Integration: Entering New Industries to Strengthen the "Core" Business Model

Many companies that use horizontal integration to strengthen their business model and improve their competitive position also use the corporate-level strategy of vertical integration for the same purpose. In pursuing vertical integration, however, a company is entering new industries to support the business model of its "core" industry, the one that is the primary source of its competitive advantage and profitability. At this point, therefore, a company has to formulate a multibusiness model that explains how entry into a new industry will enhance its long-term profitability. The multibusiness model justifying vertical integration is based on a company entering industries that *add value* to its core products because this increases product differentiation and/or lowers its cost structure.

A company pursuing a strategy of **vertical integration** expands its operations either backward into an industry that produces inputs for the company's products (*backward vertical integration*) or forward into an industry that uses, distributes, or sells the company's products (*forward vertical integration*). To enter an industry, it may establish its own operations and build the value chain needed to compete effectively in that industry, or it may acquire or merge with a company that is already in the industry. A steel company that supplies its iron ore needs from company-owned iron ore mines exemplifies backward integration. A PC maker that sells its PCs through company-owned retail outlets illustrates forward integration. For example, in 2001 Apple Computer entered the retail industry when it decided to set up a chain of Apple Stores to sell its computers and later iPods. IBM is a highly vertically integrated company; for example, it integrated backward into the disk drive industry to produce the disk drives that go into its computers and forward into the computer software and consulting services industries.

Figure 9.1 illustrates four *main* stages in a typical raw-materials-to-customer value-added chain. For a company based in the final assembly stage, backward integration means moving into component parts manufacturing and raw materials

FIGURE 9.1

Stages in the Raw-Materials-to-Customer Value-Added Chain

production. Forward integration means moving into distribution and sales (retail). At each stage in the chain, *value is added* to the product, meaning that a company at that stage takes the product produced in the previous stage and transforms it in some way so that it is worth more to a company at the next stage in the chain and, ultimately, to the customer. It is important to note that each stage of the value-added chain is a separate industry or industries in which many different companies may be competing. Moreover, within each industry, every company has a value chain composed of the value creation activities we discussed in Chapter 3: R&D, production, marketing, customer service, and so on. In other words, we can think of a value chain that runs *across* industries, and embedded within that are the value chains of companies *within* each industry.

As an example of the value-added concept, consider how companies in each industry involved in the production of a personal computer contribute to the final product (Figure 9.2). At the first stage in the chain are the raw materials companies that make specialty ceramics, chemicals, and metal, such as Kyocera of Japan, which manufactures the ceramic substrate for semiconductors. These companies sell their products to the makers of PC component products, such as Intel and Micron Technology, which transform the ceramics, chemicals, and metals they purchase into computer components such as microprocessors, disk drives, and memory chips. In the process, they *add value* to the raw materials they purchase. At the third stage, these components are then sold to companies that assemble PCs, such as Gateway, Apple, Dell, and HP, which take these components and transform them into PCs—that is, *add value* to the components they purchase. At stage 4 the finished PCs are then either

FIGURE 9.2

The Raw-Materials-to-Customer Value-Added Chain in the Personal Computer Industry

FIGURE 9.3

Full and Taper
Integration

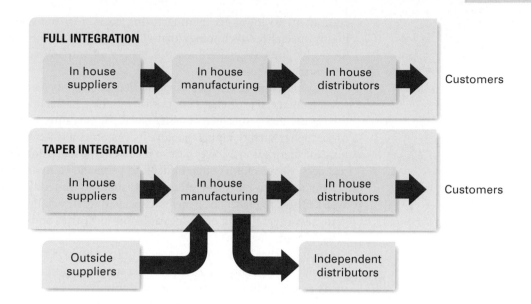

sold directly to the final customer, as Dell and Gateway do, or sold to companies such as OfficeMax and CompUSA that distribute and sell them to the final customer. Companies that distribute and sell PCs also *add value* to the product because they make it accessible to customers and provide customer service and support.

Thus companies in different industries add value at each stage in the raw-materials-to-customer chain. Viewed in this way, vertical integration presents companies with a choice about which industries in the raw-materials-to-customer chain to operate and compete in. This choice is determined by how much establishing operations at a stage in the value chain will increase product differentiation or lower costs, as we discuss below.

Finally, it is also important to distinguish between full integration and taper integration (see Figure 9.3).[6] A company achieves **full integration** when it produces *all* of a particular input needed for its processes or disposes of *all* of its completed products through its own operations. In **taper integration**, company buys from independent suppliers in addition to company-owned suppliers or disposes of its completed products through independent outlets in addition to company-owned outlets. The advantages of taper integration over full integration are discussed later in the chapter.

■ Increasing Profitability Through Vertical Integration

As noted earlier, a company pursues vertical integration to strengthen the business model of its original or core business and to improve its competitive position.[7] Vertical integration increases product differentiation, lowers costs, or reduces industry competition when it (1) facilitates investments in efficiency-enhancing specialized assets, (2) protects product quality, and (3) results in improved scheduling.

■ Facilitating Investments in Specialized Assets

A specialized asset is one that is designed to perform a specific task and whose value is significantly reduced in its next-best use.[8] The asset may be a piece of equipment that has a firm-specific use or the know-how or skills that a company or employees have acquired through training and experience. Companies invest in specialized assets because these assets allow them to lower their cost structure or to better differentiate their products, which facilitates premium pricing. A company might invest in specialized equipment to lower its manufacturing costs, for example, or it might invest in a highly specialized technology that allows it to develop better-quality products than its rivals. Thus, specialized assets can help a company achieve a competitive advantage at the business level.

Just as a company invests in specialized assets in its own industry to build competitive advantage, it is often necessary that suppliers invest in specialized assets to produce the inputs that a specific company needs. By investing in these assets, a supplier can make higher-quality inputs that give its customer a differentiation advantage, or it can now make inputs at a lower cost so it can charge its customer a lower price to keep its business. However, it is often difficult to persuade companies in adjacent stages of the raw-materials-to-customer value-added chain to undertake investments in specialized assets. Often, to realize the benefits associated with such investments, a company has to vertically integrate and enter into adjacent industries and make the investments itself. Why does this happen?

Imagine that Ford has developed a unique high-performance fuel injection system that will dramatically increase fuel efficiency and differentiate Ford's cars from those of its rivals, giving it a major competitive advantage. Ford has to decide whether to make the system in-house (vertical integration) or contract with an independent supplier to make the system. Manufacturing these new systems requires a substantial investment in specialized equipment that can be used only for this purpose. In other words, because of its unique design, the equipment cannot be used to manufacture any other type of fuel injection system for Ford or any other automaker. Thus this is an investment in specialized assets.

Consider this situation from the perspective of an independent supplier deciding whether or not to make this investment. The supplier might reason that once it has made the investment, it will become dependent on Ford for business because *Ford is the only possible customer for the fuel injection system made by this specialized equipment*. The supplier realizes that this puts Ford in a strong bargaining position and that Ford might use its power to demand lower prices for the fuel injection systems. Given the risks involved, the supplier declines to make the investment in specialized equipment.

Now consider Ford's position. Ford might reason that if it contracts out production of these systems to an independent supplier, it might become too dependent on that supplier for a vital input. Because specialized equipment is required to produce the fuel injection systems, Ford cannot switch its order to other suppliers. Ford realizes that this increases the bargaining power of the independent supplier and that the supplier might use its power to demand higher prices.

The situation of *mutual dependence* that would be created by the investment in specialized assets makes Ford hesitant to allow efficient suppliers to make the product, and makes suppliers hesitant to undertake such a risky investment. The problem is a lack of trust—neither Ford nor the supplier can trust the other to play fair in this situation. The lack of trust arises from the risk of **holdup**; that is, being taken advantage of by a trading partner after the investment in specialized assets has been made.[9] Because of this risk, Ford reasons that the only safe way to get the new fuel injection systems is to manufacture them itself.

To generalize from this example, if achieving a competitive advantage requires one company to make investments in specialized assets so it can trade with another, the risk of holdup may serve as a deterrent and the investment may not take place. Consequently, the potential for higher profitability from specialization will be lost. To prevent such loss, companies vertically integrate into adjacent stages in the value

Strategy in Action   9.3

Specialized Assets and Vertical Integration in the Aluminum Industry

The metal content and chemical composition of bauxite ore, used to produce aluminum, vary from deposit to deposit, so each type of ore requires a specialized refinery—that is, the refinery must be designed for a particular type of ore. Running one type of bauxite through a refinery designed for another type reportedly increases production costs by 20 percent to 100 percent. Thus, the value of an investment in a specialized aluminum refinery and the cost of the output produced by that refinery depend on receiving the right kind of bauxite ore.

Imagine that an aluminum company has to decide whether to invest in an aluminum refinery designed to refine a certain type of ore. Also assume that this ore is extracted by a company that owns a single bauxite mine. Using a different type of ore would raise production costs by 50 percent. Therefore, the value of the aluminum company's investment is dependent on the price it must pay the bauxite company for this bauxite. Recognizing this, once the aluminum company has made the investment in a new refinery, what is to stop the bauxite company from raising bauxite prices? Nothing. Once it has

made the investment, the aluminum company is locked into its relationship with its bauxite supplier. The bauxite supplier can increase prices because it knows that as long as the increase in the total production costs of the aluminum company is less than 50 percent, the aluminum company will continue to buy its ore. Thus, once the aluminum company has made the investment, the bauxite supplier can *hold up* the aluminum company.

How can the aluminum company reduce the risk of holdup? The answer is by purchasing the bauxite supplier. If the aluminum company can purchase the bauxite supplier's mine, it need no longer fear that bauxite prices will be increased after the investment in an aluminum refinery has been made. In other words, vertical integration, by eliminating the risk of holdup, makes the specialized investment worthwhile. In practice, it has been argued that these kinds of considerations have driven aluminum companies to pursue vertical integration to such a degree that, according to one study, 91 percent of the total volume of bauxite is transferred within vertically integrated aluminum companies.[c]

chain. Historically, the problems surrounding specific assets have driven automobile companies to vertically integrate backward into the production of component parts, steel companies to vertically integrate backward into the production of iron, computer companies to vertically integrate backward into chip production, and aluminum companies to vertically integrate backward into bauxite mining. The way specific asset issues have led to vertical integration in the aluminum industry is discussed in Strategy in Action 9.3.

■ **Enhancing Product Quality** By entering industries at other stages of the value-added chain, a company can often enhance the quality of the products in its core business, and so strengthen its differentiation advantage. For example, the ability to control the reliability and performance of components such as fuel injection systems may increase a company's competitive advantage in the luxury sedan market and enable it to charge a premium price. Conditions in the banana industry also illustrate the importance of vertical integration in maintaining product quality. Historically, a problem facing food companies that import bananas has been the variable quality of delivered bananas, which often arrive on the shelves of U.S. supermarkets too ripe or not ripe enough. To correct this problem, major U.S. food companies such as General Foods have integrated backward and now own banana plantations so they have control over the supply of bananas. As a result, they can now distribute and sell bananas of a standard quality at the optimal time to better satisfy customers. Knowing they can rely on the quality of these brands, customers are also willing to pay more for them. Thus, by vertically integrating backward into plantation ownership, banana companies have built customer confidence, which in turn has enabled them to charge a premium price for their product.

The same considerations can promote forward vertical integration. Ownership of retail outlets may be necessary if the required standards of after-sales service for complex products are to be maintained. For example, in the 1920s, Kodak owned retail outlets for distributing photographic equipment. The company felt that few established retail outlets had the skills necessary to sell and service its photographic equipment. By the 1930s, Kodak decided that it no longer needed to own its retail outlets because other retailers had begun to provide satisfactory distribution and service for Kodak products. It then withdrew from retailing.

■ **Improved Scheduling** Sometimes important strategic advantages can be obtained when vertical integration makes it quicker, easier, and more cost effective to plan, coordinate, and schedule the transfer of a product, such as raw materials or component parts, between adjacent stages of the value-added chain.[10] Such advantages can be crucial when a company wants to realize the benefits of just-in-time inventory systems. For example, in the 1920s, Ford profited from the tight coordination and scheduling that are possible with backward vertical integration. Ford integrated backward into steel foundries, iron ore shipping, and iron ore mining. Deliveries at Ford were coordinated to such an extent that iron ore unloaded at Ford's steel foundries on the Great Lakes was turned into engine blocks within twenty-four hours, which helped to lower Ford's cost structure.

Very often, the improved scheduling that vertical integration makes possible also enables a company to respond better to sudden changes in demand. For example, if demand drops, a company can quickly cut production of components, or when demand increases, a company can quickly increase production capacity to get its products into the marketplace faster.[11]

■ **Problems with Vertical Integration**

Vertical integration can often be used to strengthen a company's business model and increase profitability. However, the opposite can occur when vertical integration results in (1) an increasing cost structure, (2) disadvantages that arise when technology is changing fast, and (3) disadvantages that arise when demand is unpredictable. Sometimes these disadvantages are so great that vertical integration, rather than increasing profitability, may actually reduce it—in which case companies **vertically disintegrate** and exit industries adjacent in the industry value chain. For example, Ford, which was highly vertically integrated, sold all its companies involved in mining iron ore and making steel when more efficient and specialized steel producers emerged that were able to supply lower-priced steel.

■ **Increasing Cost Structure** Although vertical integration is often undertaken to lower a company's cost structure, it can raise costs if, over time, a company makes mistakes, such as continuing to purchase inputs from company-owned suppliers when low-cost independent suppliers that can supply the same inputs exist. During the early 1990s, for example, General Motors's (GM) company-owned suppliers made 68 percent of the component parts for its vehicles; this figure was higher than for any other major carmaker and made GM the highest-cost global carmaker. In 1992, it was paying $34.60 an hour in United Auto Workers wages and benefits to its employees at company-owned suppliers for work that rivals could get done by independent nonunionized suppliers at half these rates.[12] Thus, vertical integration can be a disadvantage when company-owned suppliers develop a higher cost structure than those of independent suppliers. Why would a company-owned supplier develop such a high cost structure?

One explanation is that company-owned or "in-house" suppliers know that they can always sell their components to the car-making divisions of their company—they have a "captive customer." When company-owned suppliers do not have to compete with independent suppliers for orders, they have much less *incentive* to look for new ways to reduce operating costs or increase quality. Indeed, in-house suppliers may simply pass on any cost increases to the car-making divisions in the form of higher **transfer prices**, the prices one division of a company charges other divisions for its products. Unlike independent suppliers, which constantly have to increase their efficiency to protect their competitive advantage, in-house suppliers face no such competition, and the resulting rising cost structure reduces a company's profitability.

The term *bureaucratic costs* refers to the costs of solving the transaction difficulties that arise from managerial inefficiencies and the need to manage the handoffs or exchanges between business units to promote increased differentiation or to lower a company's cost structure. Bureaucratic costs become a component of a company's cost structure because considerable managerial time and effort must be spent to reduce or eliminate managerial inefficiencies such as those that result when company-owned suppliers lose their incentive to increase efficiency.

This problem can be partially solved when a company pursues taper, rather than full, integration, because now in-house suppliers do have to compete with independent suppliers. In essence, independent suppliers provide a benchmark against which a company can measure the relative efficiency of its in-house suppliers, providing an incentive for company-owned suppliers to find ways to lower their cost structure.

■ **Technological Change** When technology is changing fast, vertical integration may lock a company into an old, inefficient technology and prevent it from changing to a new one that would strengthen its business model.[13] Consider a radio manufacturer that in the 1950s integrated backward and acquired a manufacturer of vacuum tubes to reduce costs. When transistors replaced vacuum tubes as a major component in radios in the 1960s, this company found itself locked into a technologically outdated business. However, if it had switched to transistors, the company would have had to write off its investment in vacuum tubes, and so managers were reluctant to adopt the new technology. Instead, they continued to use vacuum tubes in their radios while competitors that were not in the vacuum tube industry rapidly switched to the new technology. As a result, the company lost its competitive advantage, and its failing business model led to a rapid loss in market share. Thus, vertical integration can pose a serious disadvantage when it prevents a company from adopting new technology or changing its suppliers or distribution systems to match the requirements of changing technology.

■ **Demand Unpredictablility** Suppose the demand for a company's core product, such as cars or washing machines, is predictable and a company knows how many units it needs to make each month or year. Under these conditions vertical integration, by allowing the company to schedule and coordinate the flow of products along the value-added chain, may result in major cost savings. However, suppose the demand for cars or washing machines fluctuates wildly and is unpredictable. Now, if demand for cars suddenly plummets, the carmaker may find itself burdened with warehouses full of component parts it now no longer needs, and this is a major drain on profitability. Thus, vertical integration can be risky when demand is unpredictable because it is hard to manage the volume or flow of products along the value-added chain.

For example, an auto manufacturer might vertically integrate backward to acquire a supplier of fuel injection systems that can make exactly the number of systems the carmaker needs each month. However, if demand for cars now falls because gas prices soar, the carmaker finds itself locked into a business that is now inefficient because it is not producing at full capacity. Its cost structure then starts to rise. When demand is unpredictable, taper integration might be less risky than full integration because a company can keep its in-house suppliers running at full capacity and increase or reduce its orders from independent suppliers to match changing demand conditions.

■ The Limits of Vertical Integration

Thus, although there are many ways that vertical integration can strengthen a company's business model, it may weaken it (1) when bureaucratic costs increase because company-owned suppliers lack the incentive to reduce operating costs and (2) when changing technology or uncertain demand reduces a company's ability to change its business model to protect its competitive advantage. It is clear that strategic managers have to carefully assess the advantages and disadvantages of expanding the boundaries of their company by entering adjacent industries, either backward (upstream) or forward (downstream), in the value-added chain. Moreover, while the decision to enter a new industry to make crucial component parts might have been profitable in the past, it might make no economic sense today, when many low-cost global component parts suppliers exist that can compete for a company's business. The risks and returns on investing in vertical integration have to be continually evaluated, and companies should be as willing to vertically disintegrate as vertically integrate to strengthen their core business model. Finally, it is worth noting that taper integration rather than full vertical integration may decrease bureaucratic costs because it creates an incentive for in-house suppliers to reduce operating costs. There are other ways of achieving this, however, as we discuss next.

Alternatives to Vertical Integration: Cooperative Relationships

Is it possible to obtain the differentiation and cost advantages associated with vertical integration without having to bear the problems associated with this strategy? In other words, is there another corporate-level strategy that managers can use to obtain the advantages of vertical integration while allowing other companies to perform upstream and downstream activities? Today, many companies have found that they can realize many of the benefits associated with vertical integration by entering into long-term cooperative relationships with companies in industries along the value-added chain. **Strategic alliances** are long-term agreements between two or more companies to jointly develop new products that benefit all companies concerned; they were discussed in Chapter 8. The advantages of strategic alliances can be clarified by contrasting them with the benefits obtained if a company decides to enter into short-term contracts with other companies.

■ Short-Term Contracts and Competitive Bidding

Many companies use short-term contracts, which last for a year or less, to establish the price and conditions under which they will purchase raw materials or components from suppliers or sell their final products to distributors. A classic example is the carmaker that uses a *competitive bidding strategy* in which independent component suppliers compete to be the company that will be chosen to supply a particular part, made to agreed-upon specifications, at the lowest price. For example, GM typically solicits bids from global suppliers to produce a particular component and awards a one-year contract to the supplier submitting the lowest bid. At the end of the year, the contract is put out for competitive bid again. There is no guarantee that the company that wins the contract one year will hold on to it the next.

The advantage of this strategy for GM is that it forces suppliers to compete over price, which drives the cost of its inputs down. However, GM has no long-term commitment to individual suppliers, and it drives a hard bargain. For this reason, prospective suppliers will likely be unwilling to make the expensive investment in specialized assets that are needed to produce higher-quality or better-designed component parts. In addition, they will be reluctant to agree on tight scheduling, because that would allow GM to obtain the benefits from a just-in-time inventory system but would increase the suppliers' operating costs and so reduce their profitability. With no guarantee it will retain GM's business, the supplier may refuse to invest in specialized assets, and so to realize differentiation and cost gains GM will have to vertically integrate backward.

In other words, the strategy of short-term contracting and competitive bidding, *because it signals a company's lack of long-term commitment to its suppliers*, will make it difficult or impossible for that company to realize the gains associated with vertical integration. Of course, this is not a problem when there is minimal need for close cooperation and no need to invest in specialized assets to improve scheduling or product quality. In such cases, competitive bidding may be optimal. However, when this need is significant, a competitive bidding strategy can be a serious drawback.

Interestingly enough, in the past GM did place itself at a competitive disadvantage when it used a competitive bidding approach to negotiate with its suppliers. In 1992, the company instructed its parts suppliers to cut their prices by 10 percent, regardless of prior pricing agreements. In effect, GM tore up existing contracts and threatened to stop doing business with suppliers that did not agree to the price reduction. Although its action gave it a short-term benefit from lower costs, in the longer term the loss of trust and the hostility created between the company and its suppliers resulted in problems for GM. According to press reports, several suppliers claimed that they reduced the R&D spending necessary to design GM parts in the future, a form of specialized investment. They also indicated that they would first impart their new design knowledge to Chrysler (now DaimlerChrysler) and Ford, which both focused on forging cooperative long-term relationships with their suppliers.[14]

■ **Strategic Alliances and Long-Term Contracting**

As opposed to short-term contracts, strategic alliances are long-term cooperative relationships between two or more companies who agree to commit resources to develop new products. Typically, one company agrees to supply the other, and the other company agrees to continue purchasing from that supplier; both make a commitment to jointly seek ways to lower costs or increase input quality. A strategic alliance, by creating a stable long-term relationship, becomes a *substitute* for vertical integration; it allows both companies to share in the same kinds of benefits that result from vertical integration but avoids the problems linked with having to manage a company located in an adjacent industry in the value-added chain, such as lack of incentives or changing technology.

Consider the cooperative relationships, which often go back decades, that many Japanese carmakers have with their components suppliers (the *keiretsu* system), which exemplifies successful long-term contracting. Together, carmakers and suppliers work out ways to increase the value added—for example, by implementing just-in-time inventory systems or cooperating on component-parts designs to improve quality and lower assembly costs. As part of this process, the suppliers make substantial investments in specialized assets to better serve the needs of a particular carmaker. Any cost savings that result are shared by carmakers and suppliers. Thus, Japanese carmakers have been able to capture many of the benefits of vertical integration without having to enter and own companies in new industries. Similarly, the component suppliers also benefit because their business and profitability grow as the companies they supply grow.[15]

In contrast to their Japanese counterparts, U.S. carmakers have historically pursued vertical integration.[16] And, according to several studies, the result is that the ever increasing cost of managing scores or even hundreds of companies in different industries has put GM and Ford at a significant cost disadvantage relative to their Japanese competitors.[17] Moreover, even when U.S. auto companies decided not to integrate vertically, they tended to use their powerful position to pursue an aggressive competitive bidding strategy, playing off component suppliers against each other.[18] This mindset now seems to be changing. For details on how Daimler-Chrysler has attempted to build long-term cooperative relationships with suppliers, see Strategy in Action 9.4.

■ Building Long-Term Cooperative Relationships

The interesting question raised by the preceding section is, how does a company create a stable long-term strategic alliance with another company given the fear of holdup, and the possibility of being cheated, that arise when one company makes an investment in specialized assets to trade with another? How have companies like Toyota managed to develop such enduring relationships with their suppliers?

There are several steps companies can take to ensure the success of a long-term cooperative relationship and to lessen the chance that one company will renege on its agreement and try to cheat the other. One of those steps is for the company that makes the investment in specialized assets to demand a *hostage* from its partner. Another is to establish a *credible commitment* on both sides to build a trusting long-term relationship.[19]

■ **Hostage Taking** Hostage taking is essentially a means of guaranteeing that a partner will keep its side of the bargain. The cooperative relationship between Boeing and Northrop illustrates this type of situation. Northrop is a major subcontractor for Boeing's commercial airline division, providing many components for the 747 and 767 aircraft. To serve Boeing's special needs, Northrop has had to make substantial investments in specialized assets. In theory, because of the sunk costs associated with such investments, Northrop is dependent on Boeing, and Boeing is in a position to renege on previous agreements and use the threat to switch orders to other suppliers as a way of driving down prices. In practice, however, Boeing is highly unlikely to do this because it is a major supplier to Northrop's defense division and provides many parts for the Stealth bomber. Boeing also has had to make substantial investments in specialized assets to serve Northrop's needs. Thus, the companies are *mutually dependent*. Boeing is unlikely to renege on any pricing agreements with Northrop because it knows that Northrop could respond in kind. Each company holds a hostage—the specialized investment the other has made—as insurance against any attempt by the other company to renege on its prior pricing agreements.

■ **Credible Commitments** A credible commitment is a believable promise or pledge to support the development of a long-term relationship between companies.

Strategy in Action

9.4

DaimlerChrysler's U.S. *Keiretsu*

For most of its history, Chrysler (now DaimlerChrysler) managed suppliers through a competitive bidding process: suppliers were selected on the basis of their ability to supply components at the lowest possible cost to Chrysler. A supplier's track record on performance and quality was relatively unimportant in this process. Contracts were renegotiated every two years, with little or no commitment from Chrysler to continuing to do business with a particular supplier. As a result, the typical relationship between Chrysler and its suppliers was characterized by mutual distrust, suspicion, and a reluctance on the part of suppliers to invest too much in their relationship with Chrysler.

Since the early 1990s, Chrysler has systematically reorganized its dealings with suppliers in an attempt to build stable long-term relationships. The aim of this new approach has been to try to get suppliers to help Chrysler develop new products and improve its production processes. To encourage suppliers to cooperate and make investments specific to Chrysler's needs, the company has moved sharply away from its old adversarial approach. The average contract with suppliers has been lengthened from two years to over four and a half years. Furthermore, Chrysler has given 90 percent of its suppliers commitments that business will be extended for at least the life of a model, if not beyond. The company has also committed itself to sharing with suppliers the benefits of any process improvements they might suggest. The basic thinking behind offering suppliers such credible commitments is to align incentives between Chrysler and its suppliers to create a sense of "shared destiny" and encourage mutual cooperation to increase the size of the financial pie that they will share in the future.

By 1996 the fruits of this new approach were beginning to appear. By involving suppliers early on in product development and giving them greater responsibility for design and manufacturing, DaimlerChrysler was able to compress its product development cycle and substantially reduce the costs of the product development effort. DaimlerChrysler's U.S. division reduced the time it took to develop a new vehicle from 234 weeks during the mid-1980s to about 160 weeks by 1996. The total cost of developing a new vehicle also dropped by 20 to 40 percent, depending on the model. With development costs in the automobile industry running at between $1 and $2 billion, that translates into a huge financial saving. Many of these savings were the direct result of engineering improvements suggested by suppliers or of improved coordination between the company and suppliers in the design process. To facilitate this process, the number of resident engineers from suppliers who work side by side with DaimlerChrysler engineers in cross-company design teams increased from 30 in 1989 to more than 300 by 1996.

In 1990, Chrysler began implementing a program known internally as the supplier cost reduction effort (SCORE), which focuses on cooperation between DaimlerChrysler and suppliers to identify opportunities for process improvements. In its first two years of operation, SCORE generated 875 ideas from suppliers that were worth $170.8 million in annual savings to suppliers. In 1994, suppliers submitted 3,786 ideas that produced $504 million in annual savings. By December 1995, Chrysler had implemented 5,300 ideas that have generated more than $1.7 billion in annual savings. One supplier alone, Magna International, submitted 214 proposals; Chrysler adopted 129 of them for a total cost saving of $75.5 million. Many of the ideas themselves have a relatively small financial impact; for example, a Magna suggestion to change the type of decorative wood grain used on minivans saved $0.5 million per year. But the cumulative impact of thousands of such ideas has had a significant impact on DaimlerChrysler's bottom line.

DaimlerChrysler has continued to pursue this approach aggressively, so much so that in 2004 it announced that its long-term goal was for its suppliers to take over a much higher percentage of actual car production—which includes making the car body and assembling most of its major components. Chrysler believes that this will give suppliers greater motivation than its own car divisions to control quality and reduce costs. Thus it has a radical long-term business model: it wants to be a car designer and not a carmaker. The cars that come off the assembly line may have Chrysler's name on them, but it will have only designed them, not built them.[d]

To understand the concept of credibility in this context, consider the following relationship between General Electric and IBM. GE is one of the major suppliers of advanced semiconductor chips to IBM, and many of the chips are customized to IBM's requirements. To meet IBM's specific needs, GE has had to make substantial investments in specialized assets that have little other value. As a consequence, GE is dependent on IBM and faces a risk that IBM will take advantage of this dependence to demand lower prices. In theory, IBM could back up its demand by threatening to switch its business to another supplier. However, GE reduced this risk by having IBM enter into a contractual agreement that committed IBM to purchase chips from GE for a ten-year period. In addition, IBM agreed to share the costs of the specialized assets needed to develop the customized chips, thereby reducing GE's investment. Thus, by publicly committing itself to a long-term contract and putting some money into the chip development process, IBM essentially made a *credible commitment* to continue purchasing those chips from GE.

■ **Maintaining Market Discipline** Just as a company pursuing vertical integration faces the problem that its in-house suppliers might become lazy and inefficient, so a company that forms a strategic alliance with another to make its components runs the risk that the other company's costs will rise as it becomes progressively more lax or inefficient over time. This happens because the supplier knows it does not have to compete with other suppliers for the company's business. Consequently, a company seeking to form a long-term strategic alliance needs to possess some kind of power that it can use to discipline its partner should the need arise.

The company holds two strong cards over its supplier. First, even long-term contracts are periodically renegotiated, generally every four to five years, so the supplier knows that if it fails to live up to its commitments, the company may refuse to renew the contract. Second, some companies engaged in long-term relationships with suppliers use a **parallel sourcing policy**—that is, they enter into a long-term contract with *two* suppliers for the same part (as is the practice at Toyota, for example).[20] This arrangement gives the company a hedge against an uncooperative supplier because it knows that if it fails to comply with the agreement, the company can switch all its business to the other supplier. This threat rarely needs to be actualized because the mere fact that the company and its suppliers know that parallel sourcing is being used and that a supplier can be replaced at short notice injects an element of market discipline into their relationship.

The growing importance of just-in-time inventory systems as a way to reduce costs and enhance quality and so differentiation is increasing the pressure on companies to form strategic alliances in a wide range of industries. The number of strategic alliances formed each year, especially global strategic alliances, is increasing, and the popularity of vertical integration may be falling because so many low-cost global suppliers now exist in countries like Malaysia, Korea, and China.

Strategic Outsourcing

Vertical integration and strategic alliances are alternative ways of managing the value chain *across industries* to strengthen a company's core business model. However, just as low-cost suppliers of component parts exist, so today many *specialized companies* exist that can perform one of a company's *own value-chain activities* in a way that contributes to a company's differentiation advantage or that lowers its cost structure.

Strategic outsourcing is the decision to allow one or more of a company's value-chain activities or functions to be performed by independent specialist companies that focus all their skills and knowledge on just one kind of activity. The activity to be outsourced may encompass an entire function, such as the manufacturing function, or it may be just one kind of activity that a function performs. For example, many companies outsource the management of their pension systems while keeping other human resource activities within the company. When a company chooses to outsource a value-chain activity, it is choosing to focus on a *fewer* number of value-creation activities to strengthen its business model.

There has been a clear move among many companies to outsource activities that managers regard as being "noncore" or "nonstrategic," meaning they are not a source of a company's distinctive competencies and competitive advantage.[21] One survey found that some 54 percent of the companies polled had outsourced manufacturing processes or services in the past three years.[22] Another survey estimates that some 56 percent of all global product manufacturing is outsourced to manufacturing specialists.[23] Companies that outsource include Nike, which does not make its athletic shoes, and The Gap, which does not make its jeans and clothing; these products are made under contract at low-cost global locations. Similarly, many high-technology companies outsource much of their manufacturing activity to contract manufacturers that specialize in low-cost assembly. Cisco, which is in the router and switch business, does not actually manufacture routers and switches. Rather, they are made by contract manufacturers such as Flextronics and Jabil Circuit. What Cisco does is design the routers and switches, sell the routers and switches, and coordinate the supply chain to match demand for routers and switches with the supply of routers and switches (see Strategy in Action 9.5).

While manufacturing is probably the most popular form of strategic outsourcing, as we note earlier, many other kinds of noncore activities are also outsourced. Microsoft has long outsourced its entire customer technical support operation to an independent company, as does Dell. Both companies have extensive customer support operations in India that are staffed by skilled operatives who are paid a fraction of what their U.S. counterparts earn. BP Amoco outsourced almost all of its human resource function to Exult, a San Antonio company, in a five-year deal worth $600 million, and a few years later Exult won a ten-year $1.1 billion contract to handle HRM activities for all Bank of America's 150,000 employees. Similarly, in 2002, American Express outsourced its entire information technology function to IBM in a seven-year deal worth $4 billion.[24] The Gartner Group, a market research company, estimated that the information technology outsourcing market in North America was worth $101 billion in 2000 and would grow to $160 billion by 2005.[25]

Companies engage in strategic outsourcing to strengthen their business models and increase their profitability. The process of strategic outsourcing typically begins with strategic managers identifying the value-chain activities that form the basis of a company's competitive advantage; these are obviously kept within the company to protect them from competitors. Managers then systematically review the noncore functions to assess whether they can be performed more effectively and efficiently by independent companies that specialize in those activities. Because these companies specialize in a particular activity, they can perform it in ways that lower costs or improve differentiation. If managers decide there are differentiation or cost advantages, these activities are outsourced to those specialists.

Strategy in Action   9.5

Cisco's $2 Billion Blunder

During the late 1990s, Cisco Systems became famous for the way it focused on developing distinctive competencies in a few key value-chain activities while outsourcing the remainder to specialist companies. Cisco was known as the "hardware maker that didn't make hardware." While it dominated the market for Internet protocol (IP) routers and switches, critical components of IP networks, these products were actually made by several contract manufacturers. Cisco focused its energies on just three main activities: product innovation, marketing and selling (primarily through Cisco's website), and managing the supply chain. Cisco claimed that this speeded the development of new products and allowed it to avoid expensive investment in manufacturing facilities, which reduced its need for capital and boosted its return on invested capital. Moreover, Cisco boasted that, under its outsourcing strategy, it did not have to deal with the hassle and expense of holding inventory, which was the responsibility of the contract manufacturer that shipped the finished products directly to customers.

Cisco's supply chain was structured like a four-tier pyramid with Cisco at the pinnacle. The contract manufacturers responsible for final assembly of Cisco's products formed the second tier of the pyramid. These manufacturers were fed by a third tier that supplied components such as processor chips and optical gear. The third-tier companies drew on an even larger base of suppliers of commodity inputs. According to Cisco CEO John Chambers, the system was very responsive to shifts in demand, and Cisco could immediately transmit product orders it received through its website down the supply chain, which allowed contract manufacturers and component suppliers to optimize their production schedules in real time. This dramatically reduced the amount of inventory in the supply chain, which further reduced Cisco's capital requirements (since the company did not have to finance extensive inventories) and boosted the company's ROIC.

In May 2001, however, it became apparent that major problems had arisen with Cisco's vaunted outsourcing strategy. The company announced that it would take a $2.2 billion charge against earnings to write down the value of inventory in the supply chain that had been ordered but could not be used. The problem was that demand for routers and switches had collapsed, but Cisco's systems had not detected this until it was too late. How did this happen? Why did a system that has been praised for being responsive to shifts in demand fail to detect a major fall in demand?

There was a major flaw in the way in which Cisco managed its supply chain. During the boom years up to 2000, demand for routers and switches rocketed as almost every kind of company, from large established firms to new telecommunications companies and dot-coms, invested in IP networks. However, these customers had not been able to get Cisco's products quickly enough, so they had started to double- and triple-book orders for Cisco and its competitors products, knowing that they would ultimately make purchases from just one company. Cisco, however, did not detect this. As far as it knew, it couldn't produce products fast enough. Moreover, the problem was amplified as orders moved down the supply chain. Suppose Cisco ordered 10,000 units of a particular router. Each of the contract manufacturers would compete to fill the entire order, and to gain an edge they often tried to lock up supplies of scarce components. If three contract manufacturers were competing to build the same 10,000 routers, it would look like sudden demand for 30,000 routers, so component makers too would increase their output. The result was a huge surge in inventory that far outstripped underlying demand. When the telecommunications and dot-com bubble burst in early 2001, demand from these customers plunged and Cisco was left with a bloated supply chain full of inventory no longer needed.

To reduce the risk of this problem occurring again, Cisco reconfigured the way it manages its supply chain. It created a central Internet-based repository of information, known as eHub, that *all* participants in the supply chain can access. Now, if contract manufacturers get an order for 10,000 routers and all turn around and place orders for 10,000 chips each (for a total of 30,000) to try to tie up scarce components, the chip makers can access eHub and see that the true order is for just 10,000 routers, not 30,000, and plan accordingly.[e]

FIGURE 9.4

Strategic Outsourcing of Primary Value Creation Functions

One possible outcome of this process is illustrated in Figure 9.4, which shows the primary value-chain activities and boundaries of a company before and after it has pursued strategic outsourcing. In this example, the company decided to outsource its production and customer service functions, leaving just R&D and marketing and sales within the company.

Once outsourcing has been executed, the relationships between the company and its specialists are then often structured as long-term contractual relationships with rich information sharing between the company and the specialist organization to which it has contracted the activity. The term **virtual corporation** has been coined to describe companies that have pursued extensive strategic outsourcing.[26]

■ **Benefits of Outsourcing**

Strategic outsourcing has several advantages. It can help a company to (1) lower its cost structure, (2) better differentiate its products in the market,[27] and (3) focus on the distinctive competencies that are vital to its long-term competitive advantage and profitability.

■ **Reducing the Cost Structure** Outsourcing will reduce costs when the price that must be paid to a specialist company to perform a particular value-chain activity is less than what it would cost the company to perform that activity internally. Specialists are often able to perform an activity at a lower cost than the company because they are able to realize scale economies or other efficiencies not available to the company. For example, performing basic personnel activities, such as managing pay and benefit systems, requires a significant investment in developing a sophisticated information technology system. Purchasing this system represents a considerable fixed cost for one company. Moreover, the average cost of performing a personnel transaction can be driven down only if the IT system handles a large volume of transactions, and one company may not have the volume that allows this. By aggregating the demand from many different companies, a company that specializes in this activity, such as Exult and Paycheck, can obtain huge economies of scale that any one company could not hope to achieve by itself. Some of these cost savings are then passed on to client companies in the form of lower prices, which reduces their cost structure. A similar dynamic is at work in the contract manufacturing business. Once again, manufacturing specialists like Solectron, Flextronics, and Jabil Circuit make large capital investments to build efficient-scale manufacturing facilities, but then are able to spread those capital costs over a huge volume of outputs, thereby driving down unit costs so that they can make a product for less than the company can itself. In 2002, for example, IBM announced that it would no longer make PCs, although it would continue to design and sell them under the IBM brand name. Instead, it entered into an agreement with a contract manufacturer, Sanmina-SCI, to manufacture all of its PCs. As part of the agreement, IBM sold its PC manufacturing operations in the United States and Scotland to Sanmina for $200 million. IBM benefits from the lower prices it pays Sanmina for PCs because it can resell them under its own differentiated brand name, boosting its profitability.

In addition to the gains from scale economies, the greater acceleration in *cumulative* volume handled by specialists means that they are likely to obtain the cost savings associated with learning effects much more rapidly than a company that performs an activity just for itself (see Chapter 4 for a review of learning effects). For example, because a company like Flextronics is manufacturing similar products for several different companies, it is able to build up *cumulative* volume more rapidly, and it learns how to manage and operate the manufacturing process more efficiently than any of its clients could. This drives down the specialists' cost structure and allows them to charge client companies a lower price for a product than if they made it in-house.

The specialist may also be able to perform an activity at a lower cost than the company because it is based in a low-cost global location. Nike, for example, outsources the manufacture of its running shoe to companies based in China because of the much lower wage rates in China. The Chinese-based specialist can now assemble shoes, which is a very labor-intensive activity, at a much lower cost than if Nike performed the same activity itself in the United States. In theory, Nike could establish its own operations in China to manufacture running shoes. However, that would require a major capital investment and would limit its ability to switch production to an even lower-cost location later, say, Vietnam. So for Nike and most other consumer goods companies, the most efficient choice is to outsource manufacturing activity to both lower costs and give it the flexibility to switch to a more favorable location should labor costs change.

■ **Enhanced Differentiation** A company may also be able to differentiate its final products better by outsourcing certain noncore activities to specialists. For this to occur, the *quality* of the activity performed by specialists must be greater than if that same activity was performed by the company. On the reliability dimension of quality, for example, a specialist may be able to achieve a lower error rate in performing an activity, precisely because it focuses solely on that activity and has developed a strong distinctive competency in it. Again, this is one advantage claimed for contract manufacturers. Companies like Flextronics have adopted Six Sigma methodologies (see Chapter 4) and driven down the defect rate associated with manufacturing a product. This means they can provide more reliable products to their clients, which can now differentiate their products on the basis of their superior quality.

A company can also improve product differentiation by outsourcing to specialists when they stand out on the excellence dimension of quality. For example, the excellence of Dell's customer service, which is outsourced to an Indian specialist company, is a differentiating factor, and Dell stands at the top of customers' satisfaction ratings. Inside the United States, Dell also outsources its PC maintenance and repair function to specialist companies. A customer who has a problem with a product purchased from Dell can get excellent help over the phone. If it turns out that there is a defective part in the computer, a maintenance person will be dispatched to replace the part within twenty-four hours. The excellence of this service clearly differentiates Dell and helps to guarantee repeat purchases. In a similar way, carmakers often outsource specific kinds of vehicle component design activities, such as microchips or headlights, to specialists that have earned a reputation for design excellence in this particular activity.

■ **Focus on the Core Business** A final advantage of strategic outsourcing is that it allows managers to focus their energies and their company's resources on performing those core activities that have the most potential to create value and competitive advantage. In other words, companies can enhance their core competencies and so are able to push out the value frontier and create more value for their customers. Despite its mistakes, for example, Cisco remains the dominant competitor in the Internet router industry because it has focused on building its competencies in product design, marketing and sales, and supply-chain management. Companies that focus on the core activities essential for competitive advantage in their industry are better able to drive down the costs of performing those activities, and better differentiate their final products.

■ **Risks of Outsourcing**

Although outsourcing noncore activities has many benefits, there are also risks associated with it, risks such as holdup and the possible loss of important information when an activity is outsourced. Managers must assess these risks before they decide to outsource a particular activity, although, as we discuss below, these risks can be reduced when the appropriate steps are taken.

■ **Holdup** In the context of outsourcing, holdup refers to the risk that a company will become too dependent on the specialist provider of an outsourced activity and that the specialist will use this fact to raise prices beyond some previously agreed-on rate. As with strategic alliances, the risk of holdup can be reduced by outsourcing to several suppliers and pursuing a parallel sourcing policy, as Cisco does. Moreover, when an activity can be performed well by any one of several different providers, the threat that a contract will not be renewed in the future is normally sufficient to keep the chosen provider from exercising bargaining power over the company. For example, although IBM enters into long-term contracts to provide information technology services to a wide range of companies, it would be highly unlikely to try to raise prices after the contract has been signed because it knows full well that such an action would reduce its chance of getting the contract renewed in the future. Moreover, the fact that IBM has many strong competitors in the IT services business, such as EDS and Computer Sciences, gives it a very strong incentive to deliver significant value to its client and not to practice holdup.

■ **Loss of Information** A company that is not careful can lose important competitive information when it outsources an activity. For example, many computer hardware and software companies have outsourced their customer technical support function to specialists. Although this makes good sense from a cost and differentiation perspective, it may also mean that a critical point of contact with the customer, and a source of important feedback, is lost. Customer complaints can be a useful piece of information and a valuable input into future product design, but if those complaints are not clearly communicated to the company by the specialists performing the technical support activity, the company can lose that information. Again, this is not an argument against outsourcing. Rather, it is an argument for making sure that there is good communication flow between the outsourcing specialist and the company. At Dell, for example, a great deal of attention is paid to making sure that the specialist responsible for providing technical support and on-site maintenance collects and communicates all relevant data regarding product failures and other problems to Dell, so that Dell can design better products.

Summary of Chapter

1. A corporate strategy should enable a company, or one or more of its business units, to perform one or more of the value creation functions at a lower cost or in a way that allows for differentiation and a premium price.

2. Horizontal integration can be understood as a way of trying to increase the profitability of a company by (a) reducing costs, (b) increasing the value of the company's products through differentiation, (c) replicating the business model, (d) managing rivalry within the industry to reduce the risk of price warfare, and (e) increasing bargaining power over suppliers and buyers.

3. There are two drawbacks associated with horizontal integration: the numerous pitfalls associated with mergers and acquisitions and the fact that the strategy can bring a company into direct conflict with antitrust authorities.

4. Vertical integration can enable a company to achieve a competitive advantage by helping build barriers to entry, facilitating investments in specialized assets, protecting product quality, and helping to improve scheduling between adjacent stages in the value chain.

5. The disadvantages of vertical integration include increasing bureaucratic costs if a company's internal or in-house supplier becomes inefficient and a lack of flexibility when technology is changing fast or demand is uncertain.

6. Entering into a long-term contract can enable a company to realize many of the benefits associated with vertical integration without having to bear the same level of bureaucratic costs. However, to avoid the risks associated with becoming too dependent on its partner, it needs to seek a credible commitment from its partner or establish a mutual hostage-taking situation.

7. The strategic outsourcing of noncore value creation activities may allow a company to lower its costs, better differentiate its products, and make better use of scarce resources, while also enabling it to respond rapidly to changing market conditions. However, strategic outsourcing may have a detrimental effect if the company outsources important value creation activities or becomes too dependent on the key suppliers of those activities.

Discussion Questions

1. Why was it profitable for General Motors and Ford to integrate backward into component-parts manufacturing in the past, and why are both companies now trying to buy more of their parts from outside?

2. Under what conditions might horizontal integration be inconsistent with the goal of maximizing profitability?

3. What value creation activities should a company outsource to independent suppliers? What are the risks involved in outsourcing these activities?

4. What steps would you recommend that a company take in order to build long-term cooperative relationships with its suppliers that are mutually beneficial?

Practicing Strategic Management

■ SMALL-GROUP EXERCISE
Comparing Vertical Integration Strategies

Break up into small groups of three to five people, and discuss the following scenario. Appoint one group member as a spokesperson who will communicate your findings to the class when called on to do so by the instructor. Then read the following description of the activities of Seagate Technologies and Quantum Corporation, both of which manufacture computer disk drives. On the basis of this description, outline the pros and cons of a vertical integration strategy. Which strategy do you think makes most sense in the context of the computer disk drive industry?

Quantum Corporation and Seagate Technologies are major producers of disk drives for personal computers and workstations. The disk drive industry is characterized by sharp fluctuations in the level of demand, intense price competition, rapid technological change, and product life cycles of no more than twelve to eighteen months. In recent years, Quantum and Seagate have pursued very different vertical integration strategies.

Seagate is a vertically integrated manufacturer of disk drives, both designing and manufacturing the bulk of its own disk drives. Quantum specializes in design, while outsourcing most of its manufacturing to a number of independent suppliers, including, most importantly, Matsushita Kotobuki Electronics (MKE) of Japan. Quantum makes only its newest and most expensive products in-house. Once a new drive is perfected and ready for large-scale manufacturing, Quantum turns over manufacturing to MKE. MKE and Quantum have cemented their partnership over eight years. At each stage in designing a new product, Quantum's engineers send the newest drawings to a production team at MKE. MKE examines the drawings and is constantly proposing changes that make new disk drives easier to manufacture. When the product is ready for manufacture, eight to ten Quantum engineers travel to MKE's plant in Japan for at least a month to work on production ramp-up.

■ ARTICLE FILE 9

Find an example of a company whose horizontal or vertical integration strategy appears to have dissipated rather than created value. Identify why this has been the case and what the company should do to rectify the situation.

■ STRATEGIC MANAGEMENT PROJECT
Module 9

This module requires you to assess the horizontal and vertical integration strategy being pursued by your company. With the information you have at your disposal, answer the questions and perform the tasks listed:

1. Has your company ever pursued a horizontal integration strategy? What was the strategic reason for pursuing this strategy?
2. How vertically integrated is your company? If your company does have vertically integrated operations, is it pursuing a strategy of taper or full integration?
3. Assess the potential for your company to create value through vertical integration. In reaching your assessment, also consider the bureaucratic costs of managing vertical integration.
4. On the basis of your assessment in question 3, do you think your company should (a) outsource some operations that are currently performed in-house or (b) bring some operations in-house that are currently outsourced? Justify your recommendations.
5. Is your company involved in any long-term cooperative relationships with suppliers or buyers? If so, how are these relationships structured? Do you think that these relationships add value to the company? Why?
6. Is there any potential for your company to enter into (additional) long-term cooperative relationships with suppliers or buyers? If so, how might these relationships be structured?

■ EXPLORING THE WEB
Visiting Motorola

Visit Motorola's website (**www.motorola.com**), and review its various business activities. Using this information, answer the following questions:

1. To what extent is Motorola vertically integrated?
2. Does vertical integration help Motorola establish a competitive advantage, or does it put the company at a competitive disadvantage?

General Task Search the Web for an example of a company that has pursued a strategic outsourcing strategy. Describe that strategy, and assess whether the strategy has increased the profitability of the company.

Closing Case

The Rise of WorldCom

In 1983, WorldCom was a small reseller of long-distance telephone service. By 2001, the company had generated sales of $40 billion, making it the second largest provider of telecommunications services behind AT&T. WorldCom entered 2001 as the number 2 provider of long-distance phone service in the United States, with 19 percent of the market; the largest single carrier of Internet data in the country, with an estimated 37 percent of the market; and a dazzling array of strategic assets, including a 300,000-mile fiber-optic network that was global in its reach.

WorldCom was very much the creation of its swaggering cowboy CEO, Bernie Ebbers, whose strategy for growth was quite simple: acquire competitors. An apparently savvy dealmaker, over seventeen years Ebbers acquired some sixty other telecommunication service providers, capping off the spree with the acquisition of MCI Communications, which at the time was larger than WorldCom and the number 2 long-distance telephone company in the nation. Ebbers's deal making was financed by a combination of WorldCom stock and debt. As long as the stock continued to rise—and it increased by a staggering 7,000 percent during the 1990s—WorldCom could use its "currency" to buy other companies in the industry. In addition, WorldCom borrowed large amounts of money from the debt markets, some $30 billion by late 2001. The debt markets proved only too willing to lend to WorldCom given the company's glittering growth prospects.

Driving the buying spree were two strategic objectives that were central to WorldCom's business model: (1) the desire to reap scale economies in order to drive down costs and (2) the desire to capture and retain customers by bundling together telecommunications services, such as long-distance service and Internet access, and selling them under a single contract. Ebbers reasoned that the scale economies would come from assembling a nationwide and international network to transmit data and voice traffic. The costs of assembling such a network are primarily fixed and include the costs of laying fiber-optic networks and installing switches. Once the network has been built, the costs of sending additional traffic down the network are virtually zero. This gives the company with the largest volume of traffic a huge cost advantage, because it can spread the fixed costs of building and maintaining its network over a very large volume, driving down the average costs of serving each customer. In addition, Ebbers believed that customers would want only

one telecommunications service provider, and one bill, for all services they used, including long-distance and local phone service, Internet access, and wireless phone service. By assembling a company that could provide all of those services to consumers in a single bundle with a single bill, Ebbers believed that WorldCom would have a competitive advantage in the marketplace that would help it to increase volume more rapidly than rivals and thus better realize potential scale economies.

WorldCom grew through acquisition, as opposed to organically, because it was quicker to grow this way and cheaper to use a mix of WorldCom's high-flying stock and long-term debt to buy competitors than to build the network entirely on its own. Moreover, when WorldCom made an acquisition, it applied a fairly standard formula: cut the overhead, eliminate any duplication, and drive the traffic of the acquired customers through WorldCom's network to realize scale economies.

The strategy seemed to work well until 2000, when WorldCom made a bid to acquire Sprint for $115 billion. Sprint was the number 3 long-distance company in the United States with 8 percent of the market, operated the second largest data network in the country with 16 percent of the market, and was one of the largest providers of wireless service in the United States. The acquisition made perfect strategic sense. It would enable WorldCom to reap additional scale economies and bundle wireless service with its long-distance and Internet access service. Unfortunately for WorldCom, antitrust authorities in both the United States and the European Union thought that it would also give WorldCom substantial monopoly power, and both indicated that they would oppose the acquisition. The U.S. Justice Department claimed that the acquisition would create an unacceptable level of concentration in the long-distance phone business, with AT&T and WorldCom controlling 80 percent of the market after the acquisition. The Department of Justice also claimed that the acquisition would result in the monopolization of high-speed Internet data lines, creating a company that controlled 53 percent of Internet traffic and giving the expanded WorldCom the ability to discriminate against rivals and "irrevocably tip the market" toward a monopoly outcome.

In mid 2000, WorldCom announced that in the face of opposition from antitrust authorities, it would abandon the acquisition. This proved to be a turning point in the company's fortunes. During the next two years the company's stock plummeted from over $50 a share to under $1. A number of factors contributed to the implosion in the stock price. First, a price war erupted in the long-distance telephone service business. A combination of slowing growth and the entry of new competitors, particularly the Baby Bells that had been allowed by the 1996 Telecommunications Act to start offering long-distance telephone service, conspired to drive down prices for long-distance service. Second, in the data area, many of WorldCom's largest customers were other telecommunications providers, particularly new companies that had entered the market in the aftermath of the 1996 act. By mid 2001, many of these companies were in trouble. They had taken on too much debt to build out their own networks ahead of demand and now were unable to generate the cash flow to meet their debt obligations. As they crumbled into bankruptcy, WorldCom lost business that it had counted on to generate its own growth and service its debt commitments. It also started to lose the customers who had come with the acquisition of other carriers, such as MCI, and who complained that the quality of customer service had declined markedly under WorldCom.

The net result was that, by 2002, WorldCom was looking at declining revenues and steep losses, a far cry from the double-digit earnings growth it had been predicting eighteen months earlier. Suddenly the company was struggling to generate the cash flow required to service its debt commitments. Moreover, a May 2002 financial audit ordered by WorldCom's board of directors discovered that the company had understated expenses by $3 billion during 2001 and inflated its income by $1.4 billion in the quarter ending March 31, 2002. This revelation led to the resignation of several senior executives, including CEO Bernie Ebbers. The news of possible accounting fraud, taken together with WorldCom's sudden losses, led rating agencies to downgrade WorldCom's debt. This pushed up the interest rate on that debt, making it more expensive for WorldCom to serve. The company was now caught in a vice—on one side, due to unexpectedly poor business conditions its cash flow was plunging, and on the other, the price of serving its debt was surging. In July 2002, WorldCom bowed to the inevitable and declared bankruptcy. Bernie Ebbers's grand strategic vision lay in ruins.[28]

Case Discussion Questions

1. What was the rationale for WorldCom pursuing a strategy of horizontal integration?

2. Why did the strategy fail?

Chapter 10

Corporate-Level Strategy: Formulating and Implementing Related and Unrelated Diversification

Opening Case

United Technologies Has an "ACE in Its Pocket"

United Technologies Corporation (UTC), based in Hartford, Connecticut, is a *conglomerate*, a company that owns a wide variety of other companies that operate in different businesses and industries. Some of the companies in UTC's portfolio are more well known than UTC itself, such as Sikorsky Aircraft Corporation; Pratt & Whitney, the aircraft engine and component maker; Otis Elevator Company; Carrier air conditioning; and Chubb, the security and lock maker that UTC acquired in 2003. Today, investors frown upon companies like UTC that own and operate companies in widely different industries. There is a growing perception that managers can better manage a company's business model when the company operates as an independent or stand-alone entity. How can UTC justify holding all these companies together in a conglomerate? Why would this lead to a greater increase in their long-term profitability than if they operated as separate companies? In the last decade the boards of directors and CEOs of many conglomerates, such as Greyhound-Dial, ITT Industries, and Textron, have realized that by holding diverse companies together they were reducing, not increasing, the profitability of their companies. As a result, many conglomerates have been broken up and their companies spun off to allow them to operate as separate, independent entities.

UTC's CEO George David claims that he has created a unique and sophisticated multi-business model that adds value across UTC's diverse businesses. David joined Otis Elevator as an assistant to its CEO in 1975, but within one year Otis was acquired by UTC, during a decade when "bigger is better" ruled corporate America and mergers and acquisitions, of whatever kind, were seen as the best way to grow profits. UTC sent David to manage its South American operations and later gave him responsibility for its Japanese operations. Otis had formed an alliance with Matsushita to develop an elevator for the Japanese market, and the resulting "Elevonic 401," after being installed widely in Japanese buildings, proved to be a disaster. It broke down much more often than elevators made by other Japanese companies, and customers were concerned about its reliability and safety.

336

Matsushita was extremely embarrassed about the elevator's failure and assigned one of its leading total quality management (TQM) experts, Yuzuru Ito, to head a team of Otis engineers to find out why it performed so poorly. Under Ito's direction all the employees—managers, designers, and production workers—who had produced the elevator analyzed why the elevators were malfunctioning. This intensive study led to a total redesign of the elevator, and when their new and improved elevator was launched worldwide, it met with great success. Otis's share of the global elevator market increased dramatically, and one result was that David was named president of UTC in 1992. He was given the responsibility to cut costs across the entire corporation, including its important Pratt & Whitney division, and his success in reducing UTC's cost structure and increasing its ROIC led to his appointment as CEO in 1994.

Now responsible for all of UTC's diverse companies, David decided that the best way to increase UTC's profitability, which had been falling, was to find ways to improve efficiency and quality in all its constituent companies. He convinced Ito to move to Hartford and take responsibility for championing the kinds of improvements that had by now transformed the Otis division, and Ito began to develop UTC's TQM system, which is known as *Achieving Competitive Excellence,* or ACE.

ACE is a set of tasks and procedures that are used by employees from the shop floor to top managers to analyze all aspects of the way a product is made. The goal is to find ways to improve *quality and reliability,* to *lower the costs* of making the product, and especially to find ways to make the next generation of a particular product perform better—in other words, to encourage *technological innovation.* David makes every employee in every function and at every level take responsibility for achieving the incremental, step-by-step gains that can result in innovative and efficient products that enable a company to dominate its industry—to push back the value creation frontier.

David calls these techniques "process disciplines," and he has used them to increase the performance of all UTC companies. Through these techniques he has created the extra value for UTC that justifies it owning and operating such a diverse set of businesses. David's success can be seen in the performance that his company has achieved in the decade since he took control: he has quadrupled UTC's earnings per share, and in the first six months of 1994 profit grew by 25 percent to $1.4 billion, while sales increased by 26 percent to $18.3 billion. UTC has been in the top three performers of the companies that make up the Dow Jones industrial average for the last three years, and the company has consistently outperformed GE, another huge conglomerate, in its returns to investors.

David and his managers believe that the gains that can be achieved from UTC's process disciplines are never-ending because its own R&D—in which it invests over $2.5 billion a year—is constantly producing product innovations that can help all its businesses. Indeed, recognizing that its skills in creating process improvements are specific to manufacturing companies, UTC's strategy is to only acquire companies that make products that can benefit from the use of its ACE program—hence its Chubb acquisition. At the same time, David only invests in companies that have the potential to remain leading companies in their industries and so can charge above-average prices. His acquisitions strengthen the competencies of UTC's existing businesses. For example, he acquired a company called Sunderstrand, a leading aerospace and industrial systems company, and combined it with UTC's Hamilton aerospace division to create Hamilton Sunderstrand, which is now a major supplier to Boeing and makes products that command premium prices.

Overview George David utilizes ACE to increase the ROIC of UTC's companies or divisions, recognizing that UTC must own companies that are well positioned in their industries to maintain and grow their market share and protect their profit margins. David has developed a *multibusiness model* that (1) allows each company to pursue its own, industry-specific business model, (2) supplies each division with corporate support through its ACE performance-enhancing set of skills, and (3) uses the financial power of the UTC empire to make acquisitions and divestitures to allow companies to better position themselves vis-à-vis their competitors. As we discuss later, UTC is pursuing the corporate-level strategy of unrelated diversification to strengthen the business models of its individual companies and so increase their individual profitability—and thus the total profitability of the whole conglomerate.

In this chapter we continue our discussion of how companies can utilize their distinctive competencies, and the business models that are based on them, by formulating and implementing new corporate-level strategies to grow their profits and their free cash flow. Companies cannot stand still; they must continually search for ways to use their capital more efficiently and effectively. In a competitive environment, resources such as capital move to their most highly valued use, which means they are invested in companies that are expected to be the most profitable in the future. If a company's managers do not strive to build its distinctive competencies and competitive advantage, they will ultimately lose out to those companies that have found successful business models.

This chapter discusses the corporate-level strategy of diversification, which is a company's decision to enter one or more new industries to take advantage of its existing distinctive competencies and business model. We discuss two different types of diversification, related diversification and unrelated diversification, and we examine the different kinds of distinctive competencies and multibusiness models on which they are based. Then we look at three different methods or strategies companies can use to implement a diversification strategy: internal new ventures, acquisitions, and joint ventures. By the end of this chapter you will understand why some companies decide to diversify and enter new markets and industries and why they select a particular strategy to implement a diversification strategy in the most profitable way.

Expanding Beyond a Single Industry

The role of managers in corporate-level strategy is to identify which industries a company should compete in to maximize its long-run profitability. As we discuss in Chapter 9, for many companies, profitable growth and expansion often entail concentrating on a single market or industry. For example, McDonald's focuses on the global fast-food restaurant business and Wal-Mart on global discount retailing. Companies that stay inside one industry pursue horizontal integration and strategic outsourcing to strengthen their business models, expand their business, and increase their profitability. Even though vertical integration leads a company to enter industries at adjacent stages of the value chain, the intent is still to strengthen its core business model.

As a result of these strategies, a company's fortunes are tied closely to the profitability of its *original industry*—and this can be dangerous if that industry goes into decline. As an industry matures, the opportunities to grow profits often fall. Moreover, companies that concentrate on just one industry sometimes miss out on opportunities to increase their profitability by leveraging their distinctive competencies to make and sell products in *new industries*. There is compelling evidence to suggest that companies that rest on their laurels, do not engage in constant learning, and do not force themselves to stretch can lose out to agile new competitors that come along with superior business models.[1] For these reasons, many argue that companies must *leverage*, that is, find new ways to take advantage of their distinctive competencies and core business model in new markets and industries.

■ A Company as a Portfolio of Distinctive Competencies

Gary Hamel and C. K. Prahalad have developed a model that can help managers assess how and when they should expand beyond their current market or industry. According to these authors, a fruitful approach to identifying new product market opportunities is to think of a company not as a portfolio of products, but as a *portfolio of distinctive competencies*, and then consider how those competencies might be leveraged, that is, used to create more value and profit in new industries.[2]

Recall from Chapter 3 that a distinctive competency is a company-specific resource or capability that gives a company a competitive advantage. Hamel and Prahalad argue that when managers want to identify a profitable opportunity for diversification, they must first define and classify the company's *current* set of distinctive competencies. Then they can use a matrix like that illustrated in Figure 10.1 to establish an agenda for entering new markets or industries. This matrix distinguishes between existing competencies and new ones that would have to be developed to allow a company to compete in a new industry. It also distinguishes between the existing industries in which a company operates and new industries in which it might operate in the future. Each quadrant in the matrix has different strategic implications.

■ **Fill in the Blanks** The lower-left quadrant of Figure 10.1 represents the company's existing portfolio of competencies and products. In the 1900s, for example, Canon had distinctive competencies in precision mechanics, fine optics, and microelectronics and was active in two industries, cameras and photocopiers. It used its competencies in precision mechanics and fine optics to produce mechanical cameras. These two competencies plus an additional competency it had developed in microelectronics allowed it to produce photocopiers. The term *fill in the blanks* refers to the opportunity to improve a company's competitive position in its existing industries by sharing its current competencies between divisions. Canon, for example, realized that it could strengthen its camera business by giving it the microelectronics skills it had developed in its copier business. Then the camera division could make advanced cameras with electronic features such as auto-focusing.

■ **Premier Plus 10** The upper-left quadrant in Figure 10.1 is referred to as *premier plus 10*. The term is used to suggest another important question: What *new* distinctive competencies must be developed now to ensure that a company remains a *premier* provider of its existing products in *ten* years' time? To strengthen the business model of its copier business, Canon decided that it needed to build a new competency in electronic imaging (the ability to capture and store images in a digital format as opposed to the more traditional chemical-based photographic processes). By developing this new competency, Canon was able to protect its competitive advantage and make advanced products like laser copiers, color copiers, and digital cameras.

■ **White Spaces** The lower-right quadrant of Figure 10.1 is referred to as *white spaces* because the issue managers must address is how can it fill "white spaces," that is, opportunities to creatively redeploy or recombine its current distinctive competencies to produce new products in new industries. Canon was able to recombine its established competencies in precision mechanics and fine optics and its recently acquired competency in electronic imaging to produce fax machines and laser jet printers, thereby entering the fax and printer industries. In other words, it leveraged its distinctive competencies to take advantage of opportunities in other industries and create valuable new products.

■ **Mega-Opportunities** Opportunities represented by the upper-right quadrant of Figure 10.1 do not overlap with the company's current industries or its current competencies. Rather, they imply entry into new industries where the company currently has none of the competencies required to succeed. Nevertheless, a company may choose to pursue such opportunities if they are seen to be particularly attractive, significant, or relevant to its existing product market activities. For example, in 1979, Monsanto was primarily a manufacturer of chemicals, including fertilizers. However, the company saw enormous opportunities in the emerging biotechnology industry. Senior research scientists felt that it might be possible to produce genetically engineered crop seeds that would produce their own "organic" pesticides. In that year, the company embarked on a massive investment, which ultimately amounted to several hundred million dollars, to build a world-class competence in biotechnology. This investment was funded by cash flows generated from Monsanto's operations in the chemical industry. The investment paid off in the 1990s when Monsanto introduced a series of genetically engineered crop seeds that were resistant to many common pests. Roundup, a Monsanto herbicide that can be used to kill weeds but that will not kill its genetically engineered plants, became the industry leader.[3]

A focus on using or recombining existing competencies or building new competencies to enter new industries helps managers think strategically about how industry boundaries might change over time and how this will affect their current business models. By helping managers think about how to transfer and leverage competencies across industries, Prahalad and Hamel's model can help managers avoid the strategic mistake of entering new markets where their business model will fail to give them a competitive advantage, as many companies, such as Coca-Cola and Sears, discussed in the last chapter, have done.

Increasing Profitability Through Diversification

Diversification is the process of adding new businesses to the company that are distinct from its core industry. A multibusiness model then focuses on finding ways to use the company's distinctive competencies to increase the value of products in those new industries that it has entered. A **diversified company** is one that operates in two or more industries. In each industry a company enters, it establishes an operating division or business unit, which is essentially a self-contained company that makes and sells products for its particular market. To increase profitability, a diversification strategy should enable the company or one or more of its business units to perform one or more of the value-chain functions (1) at a lower cost, (2) in a way that allows for differentiation and gives the company pricing options, or (3) in a way that helps the company to manage industry rivalry better.

The managers of most companies first consider diversification when they are generating **free cash flow**, that is, cash *in excess* of that required to fund investments in the company's existing industry and to meet any debt commitments.[4] In other words, free cash flow is cash in excess of that which can be profitably reinvested in an existing business (*cash* is simply *capital* by another name). When a company is generating free cash flow, managers must decide whether to return that capital to shareholders in the form of higher dividend payouts or invest it in diversification. Technically, any free cash flow belongs to the company's owners—its shareholders. For diversification to make sense, the return on investing free cash flow to pursue diversification opportunities, that is, the return on invested capital (ROIC), *must* exceed the return that stockholders could get by investing that capital in a diversified portfolio of stocks and bonds. If this were not the case, it would be in the best interests of shareholders for the company to return any excess cash to them through higher dividends rather than pursue a diversification strategy. Thus, a diversification strategy is *not* consistent with maximizing returns to shareholders unless the multibusiness model managers use to justify entry into a new industry will significantly increase the value a company can create.

Six main justifications for pursuing a multibusiness model based on diversification can be identified. Diversification can increase company profitability when managers (1) transfer competencies between business units in different industries, (2) leverage competencies to create business units in new industries, (3) share resources between business units to realize economies of scope, (4) use product bundling, (5) use diversification to reduce rivalry in one or more industries, and (6) utilize *general* organizational competencies that increase the performance of all the company's business units.

■ Transferring Competencies Across Industries

Transferring competencies involves taking a distinctive competency developed in one industry and implanting it in an existing business unit in another industry. This business unit might be a company that the diversified company has acquired. Companies that base their diversification strategy on transferring competencies believe that they can use one or more of their distinctive competencies in a value-chain activity—for example, manufacturing, marketing, materials management, and R&D—to significantly strengthen the business model of the acquired company. For example, over time Philip Morris developed distinctive competencies in product development, consumer marketing, and brand positioning that had made it a leader in the tobacco industry. Sensing an opportunity, it acquired Miller Brewing, which at the time was a relatively small player in the brewing industry. Then, to create value in Miller, Philip Morris transferred some of its best marketing experts to Miller, where they applied the skills acquired at Philip Morris to turn around Miller's lackluster brewing business (see Figure 10.2). The result was the creation of Miller Light, the first light beer, and a marketing campaign that helped to push Miller from the number 6 to the number 2 company in the brewing industry in terms of market share.

Companies that base their diversification strategy on transferring competencies tend to acquire businesses *related* to their existing activities because of commonalities between one or more of their value-chain functions. A *commonality* is some kind of attribute shared by two or more business units that allows them to create more

FIGURE 10.2

Transfer of
Competencies at
Philip Morris

value when they operate together cohesively. For example, Miller Brewing was related to Philip Morris's tobacco business by marketing commonalities; both beer and tobacco are mass market consumer goods where brand positioning, advertising, and product development skills are important. In general, such competency transfers can increase profitability when they lower the cost structure of one or more of a diversified company's business units or enable one or more of its business units to better differentiate their products, which also gives that business unit pricing options.

For such a strategy to work, the competencies being transferred must involve value-chain activities that will become the source of a particular business unit's competitive advantage in the future. In other words, the distinctive competency being transferred must have real strategic value. However, all too often companies assume that *any* commonality between their value chains is sufficient for creating value. When they attempt to transfer competencies, they find the anticipated benefits are not forthcoming because the different business units did not share some important attribute in common. General Motors's acquisition of Hughes Aircraft, made simply because autos and auto manufacturing were "going electronic" and Hughes was an electronics company, demonstrates the folly of overestimating the commonalities among businesses. The acquisition failed to realize any of the anticipated gains for GM, whose competitive position did not improve, and GM subsequently sold off Hughes.

■ **Leveraging Competencies**

Leveraging competencies involves taking a distinctive competency developed by a business in one industry and using it to create a *new* business unit in a different industry. The central idea here is that the set of distinctive competencies that are the source of competitive advantage in one industry might also be applied to create a differentiation- or cost-based competitive advantage for a new business unit in a different industry. For example, Canon used its distinctive competencies in precision mechanics, fine optics, and electronic imaging to produce laser jet printers, which for Canon was a new business in a new industry. Its competitive advantage in laser printers came from the fact that its competencies enabled it to produce high-quality (differentiated) printers that could be manufactured at a low cost.

The difference between leveraging competencies and transferring competencies is that in the case of leveraging competencies an entirely *new* business is being created, whereas transferring competencies involves a transfer between *existing* businesses. Although the distinction may seem subtle, it is actually very important, because different managerial processes are involved. Companies that leverage competencies to establish new businesses tend to be technology-based enterprises that use their R&D competencies to create new business opportunities in diverse industries. In contrast, companies that transfer competencies typically enter new industries by acquiring established businesses. They then transfer competencies to the acquired businesses in order to enhance their profitability, as Philip Morris did with Miller Brewing.

A number of companies have based their diversification strategy on leveraging competencies and using them to create new businesses in different industries. Microsoft leveraged its skills in software development and marketing to create two new businesses, its online network MSN and the Xbox videogame business. Microsoft's managers believed that the company's diversification strategy was in the best interests of shareholders because the company's competencies would enable it to attain a competitive advantage in the videogame and online industries. In fact, they were wrong. In 2003, when Microsoft broke its profits down by business unit, it turned out that the software business was generating almost all the profit and most other business units were making a loss. Realizing that entry into new industries was not a way it could increase the value of the company for its shareholders, Microsoft decided it would give back over $30 billion, or half its $60 billion cash hoard, to shareholders in the form of a dividend in 2004. Microsoft still hopes its Xbox business will be a success in the future, however.

A company that is famous for its ability to leverage competencies to create *new* businesses in diverse industries is 3M, which among other things leveraged its skills in adhesives to create new business opportunities (see Strategy in Action 10.1). From a humble beginning as a manufacturer of sandpaper, 3M has become one of the most diversified corporations in the United States. Most of this diversification came about not through acquisitions but by internally venturing and creating new business units itself (a topic discussed later in the chapter).

■ Sharing Resources: Economies of Scope

When two or more business units in different industries share resources and capabilities, they may be able to realize economies of scope.[5] **Economies of scope** arise when one or more of a diversified company's business units are able to realize cost-saving or differentiation advantages because they can more effectively pool, share, and utilize expensive resources or capabilities, such as skilled people, equipment, manufacturing facilities, distribution channels, advertising campaigns, and R&D laboratories. If business units in different industries can share a common resource or function, they can collectively lower their cost structure.[6] For example, the costs of GE's consumer products advertising, sales, and service activities are spread over a wide range of products, such as small and large appliances, air conditioning, and furnaces, reducing unit costs. These cost reductions have two major sources.

First, companies that can share resources across business units have to invest proportionately less in the shared resource than companies that cannot share. For example, Procter & Gamble makes both disposable diapers and paper towels, paper-based products valued for their ability to absorb liquid without disintegrating. Because both products need the same attribute—absorbency—Procter & Gamble can share the R&D costs associated with producing an absorbent paper-based product across the two businesses. Similarly, because both products are sold to the same customer

Strategy in Action

10.1

Diversification at 3M: Leveraging Technology

3M is a 100-year-old industrial colossus that in 2004 generated over $16 billion in revenues and $1.4 billion in profits from a portfolio of more than 50,000 individual products ranging from sandpaper and sticky tape to medical devices, office supplies, and electronic components. The company has consistently created new businesses by leveraging its scientific knowledge to find new applications for its proprietary technology. Today, the company is composed of more than forty discrete business units grouped into six major sectors: transportation, health care, industrial, consumer and office, electronics and communications, and specialty materials. The company has consistently generated 30 percent of sales from products introduced within the prior five years and currently operates with the goal to produce 40 percent of sales revenues from products introduced within the previous four years.

The process of leveraging technology to create new businesses at 3M can be illustrated by the following quotation from William Coyne, head of R&D at 3M: "It began with sandpaper: mineral and glue on a substrate. After years as an abrasives company, it created a tape business. A researcher left off the mineral, and adapted the glue and substrate to create the first sticky tape. After creating many varieties of sticky tape—consumer, electrical, medical—researchers created the world's first audio and videotapes. In their search to create better tape backings, other researchers happened on multilayer films that, surprise, have remarkable light management qualities. This multiplayer film technology is being used in brightness enhancement films, which are incorporated in the displays of virtually all laptops and palm computers."

How does 3M do it? First, the company is a science-based enterprise with a strong tradition of innovation and risk taking. Risk taking is encouraged, and failure is not punished but seen as a natural part of the process of creating new products and business. Second, 3M's management is relentlessly focused on the company's customers and the problems they face. Many of 3M's products have come from helping customers to solve difficult problems. Third, managers set *stretch goals* that require the company to create new products and businesses at a rapid pace (such as the current goal that 40 percent of sales should come from products introduced within the last four years). Fourth, employees are given considerable autonomy to pursue their own ideas. An employee can spend 15 percent of his or her time working on a project of his or her own choosing without management approval. Many products have resulted from this autonomy, including the ubiquitous Post-it Notes. Fifth, while products belong to business units and it is business units that are responsible for generating profits, the technologies belong to every unit within the company. Anyone at 3M is free to try to develop new applications for a technology developed by its business units. Sixth, 3M has implemented an IT system that promotes the sharing of technological knowledge between business units so that new opportunities can be identified. Also, it hosts many in-house conferences where researchers from different business units are brought together to share the results of their work. Finally, 3M uses numerous mechanisms to recognize and reward those who develop new technologies, products, and businesses, including peer-nominated award programs, a corporate hall of fame, and of course, monetary rewards.[a]

group (supermarkets), it can use the same sales force to sell both products (see Figure 10.3). In contrast, competitors that make just paper towels or just disposable diapers cannot achieve the same economies and have to invest proportionately more in R&D and in maintaining a sales force. The net result is that, other things being equal, P&G will have lower expenses and earn a higher return on invested capital than companies that lack the ability to share resources.

Second, resource sharing across businesses may enable a company to use the shared resource more intensively, thereby realizing *economies of scale* (in other words, economies of scale are a source of economies of scope). For example, one of the motives behind the 1998 merger of Citicorp and Travelers to form Citigroup was that the

FIGURE 10.3

Sharing Resources at
Procter & Gamble

merger would allow Travelers to sell its insurance products and financial services through Citicorp's retail banking network. The merger allows the expanded group to better use an existing asset—its retail banking network—and thereby realize economies of scale. Because economies of scale lower the cost structure of one or more businesses, the net result is to increase the profitability of the diversified company.

Diversification to attain economies of scope is possible only when there are significant commonalities between one or more of the value-chain functions of a company's existing and new business units. Moreover, managers need to be aware that the costs of coordination necessary to achieve economies of scope within a company often outweigh the value that can be created by such a strategy.[7] Consequently, the strategy should be pursued only when sharing is likely to generate a *significant* competitive advantage in one or more of a company's business units.

■ **Using Product Bundling**

Increasingly, in their search for ways to differentiate their products, companies are entering into related industries in order to expand their product lines and so be able to satisfy customers' needs for a package of related products. This is currently happening in telecommunications, where customers are increasingly seeking a package price for wired phone service, wireless phone service, high-speed access to the Internet, VOIP phone service, television programming, online gaming, video on demand, or any combination of these services. To meet this need, many Baby Bell phone companies have been acquiring companies that provide one or more of these services, while cable companies such as Comcast Corporation have acquired or formed strategic alliances with companies that allow them to offer their customers phone service, and so on. In 2004, Microsoft announced an alliance with SBC whereby SBC would use its new software to allow it to provide television service and video on demand over DSL phone connections, as well as its other services. Similarly, EchoStar Communications Corp., the satellite broadcaster, formed an alliance with Verizon to offer its TV service with Verizon's phone service.

Just as companies like to reduce the number of their component suppliers, so the final customer wants to obtain the convenience, and reduced price, of bundled products. Another example of product bundling comes from the medical equipment industry, where the companies that used to produce different kinds of products, such as operating equipment, ultrasound devices, magnetic imaging, and x-ray equipment, have been merging to be able to offer hospitals a complete range of medical equipment. This development has been driven by hospitals because they want the convenience of dealing with a single supplier. In addition, because of the increased value of their orders, they also have increased bargaining power with the supplier.

■ **Managing Rivalry: Multipoint Competition**

Sometimes a company benefits by diversifying into an industry in order to hold a competitor in check that has either entered its industry or has the potential to do so. For example, if an aggressive company based in another industry enters a company's market and tries to gain market share by cutting prices, the company can respond in kind and diversify into the aggressor's home industry and also cut prices. In this way, the company sends a signal: "If you attack me, I'll respond in kind and make things tough for you." (This is an example of the strategy of tit-for-tat discussed in Chapter 6.) The hope is that such a move will cause the aggressor to pull back from its attack, thus moderating rivalry in the company's home industry and permitting higher prices and profits. Of course, for the tit-for-tat strategy to have its desired effect, the company would then need to pull back from its competitive attack in the aggressor's home market.

An example of diversification to keep a potential competitor in check occurred in the late 1990s when Microsoft awoke to the fact that Sony might emerge as a rival. Although Sony was in a different industry (consumer electronics as opposed to software), Microsoft realized that the Sony PlayStation was in essence nothing more than a specialized computer and, moreover, one that did not use a Microsoft operating system. Microsoft's fear was that Sony might use the PlayStation 2, which came equipped with web-browsing potential, as a "Trojan horse" to gain control of web browsing and computing from the living room, ultimately taking customers away from PCs with Microsoft operating systems. The desire to keep Sony's ambitions in check was another part of the rationale for Microsoft's diversification into the videogame industry with the launch of the Xbox.

Many diversified companies compete against each other in several different industries. Canon and Kodak compete against each other in photocopiers and digital cameras, for example. Similarly, Unilever and Procter & Gamble compete against each other in laundry detergents, personal care products, and packaged foods. When companies compete against each other in different industries, we refer to it as **multipoint competition.** Companies that are engaged in multipoint competition might be better able to manage rivalry by signaling that competitive attacks in one industry will be met by retaliatory attacks in another industry. If successful, such signaling might lead to *mutual forbearance,* and thus less intense rivalry and higher profit in each industry in which a company competes. It follows that the desire to manage rivalry better through multipoint competition might be a motive for diversification that increases profitability.

■ **Utilizing General Organizational Competencies**

By **general organizational competencies**, we mean competencies that transcend individual functions or business units and are found at the top or corporate level of the multibusiness company. Typically, these general competencies are the skills of a company's top managers and functional experts, such as George David and Yuzuru Ito of UTC. When these general competencies are present—and many times they are not—they help each business unit within a company perform at a higher level than it could if it operated as an independent company, thus increasing the profitability of the whole corporation.[8] We discuss three kinds of general organizational competencies that can result in superior performance: (1) entrepreneurial capabilities, (2) organizational design capabilities, and (3) strategic capabilities. These managerial skills are often not present because they are rare and difficult to develop and put into action.

■ **Entrepreneurial Capabilities** The example of 3M, profiled in Strategy in Action 10.1 above, provides many clues as to why entrepreneurial capabilities are important if the process of diversification is to increase profitability. A company may generate considerable excess cash flow, but to take advantage of it managers must identify new opportunities and act on them to create a stream of new and improved products in both existing and new industries. It appears that some companies are better able to stimulate their managers to act entrepreneurially than are others; examples are 3M, Hewlett-Packard, IBM, Canon, Sony, and Matsushita.[9]

These companies are able to promote entrepreneurship because they have an organization culture that stimulates managers to act entrepreneurially. The consequence is that these companies are able to create profitable new business units at a much higher rate than most other companies, which helps promote their diversification. We will highlight some of the systems required to generate profitable new businesses later in this chapter when we discuss internal new ventures. For now, note that the management systems of an entrepreneurial company must (1) encourage managers to take risks, (2) give them the time and resources to pursue novel ideas, (3) not punish managers when a new idea fails, but also (4) make sure the company does not waste resources pursuing too many risky ventures that have a low probability of generating a decent return on investment. Obviously, a difficult organizational balancing act is required here, for the company has to simultaneously encourage risk taking while limiting the amount of risk being undertaken.

Companies with entrepreneurial capabilities are able to achieve this balancing act. 3M's corporate goal of generating 40 percent of revenues from products introduced within the past four years focuses the organization on developing new products and businesses. The company's famous 15 percent rule, which has been copied by many companies, gives employees the time to pursue novel ideas. Its long-standing commitment to helping customers solve problems helps ensure that ideas for new businesses are customer focused. The company's celebration of employees who have created successful new businesses helps to reinforce the norm of entrepreneurship and risk taking. Similarly, there is a norm that failure should not be punished but viewed as a learning experience.

■ **Capabilities in Organizational Design** One of the main sources of entrepreneurial capabilities, as well as an important determinant of whether a company can obtain competencies at the functional level, is organizational design, a company's ability to create a structure, culture, and control systems that motivate and coordinate employees. The degree of autonomy the structure of an organization provides its managers, the kinds of norms and values present in its culture, and even the design of its headquarters buildings to encourage the free flow of ideas are important determinants of a diversified company's ability to reap the gains from its multibusiness model. Effective organizational structure and controls create incentives that encourage business unit (divisional) managers to maximize the efficiency and effectiveness of their units. Moreover, a good organizational design helps prevent the inertia that afflicts so many organizations, when employees become so absorbed in protecting their company's competitive position in existing markets that they lose sight of new or improved ways to do business or changing industry boundaries.

The last three chapters of this book take an in-depth look at these issues. To succeed in diversification, a company must have the structure and culture that enable it to rapidly change the way it motivates and coordinates its resources and capabilities. Companies that seem to be successful at managing their structures and cultures to further the diversification process share a number of features.[10] First, their different business units tend to be placed into self-contained divisions. Second, these business units tend to be managed by senior executives in a decentralized fashion. Rather than get involved in day-to-day operations, they set challenging financial goals for each unit, probe the managers of each unit about their strategies for attaining these goals, monitor their performance, and hold them accountable for that performance. Third, these internal monitoring and control mechanisms are linked with incentive pay systems that reward business unit managers who attain or surpass performance goals. Achieving these three things, and aligning a company's structure with its strategy, is a complex, never-ending task in a changing environment, and only top managers with superior organizational design skills can do it.

■ **Superior Strategic Capabilities** For diversification to increase profitability, a company's top managers must have superior strategic capabilities. Specifically, they must have certain intangible governance skills to manage different business units in a way that enables those units to perform better than they would if they were independent companies.[11] Simply put, the business of top management in the diversified company is to manage the managers of business units. This is not an easy thing to do well; governance skills are a rare and valuable capability. However, certain senior executives seem to have developed a skill for managing businesses and pushing the heads of business units to achieve superior performance. Examples include Jack Welch at General Electric, Bill Gates and Steve Ballmer at Microsoft, and George David of UTC, profiled in the *Opening Case*.

A flair for entrepreneurship is often found in top managers who have developed superior strategic capabilities or governance skills. As important, if not more so, is the ability to recognize ways to enhance the performance of individual managers, functions, and business units. Jack Welch, for example, was a master in improving the skills of his managers across the board in GE. He created organization-wide management development programs focusing on change management and created procedures to make middle managers question top management actions. At the functional and business levels, he instituted many of the techniques discussed in Chapter 4 to promote superior efficiency and quality, such as the Six Sigma quality improvement methodology, and he pushed hard to make sure that business unit managers used these techniques to improve the efficiency of their operations.

An especially important governance skill in the diversified company is the ability to diagnose the real source of performance problems in an underperforming business unit and take the appropriate steps to fix those problems, whether by pushing the top managers of the unit to take certain strategic actions or by replacing top managers with individuals better able to fix the problems. Top managers who have such governance skills tend to be very good at probing business unit managers for information and helping them think through strategic problems.

Related to this skill, an important way in which a diversified company can increase its profitability is by recognizing inefficient and poorly managed companies, acquiring them, and then restructuring them to improve their performance. The acquired company does not have to be in the same industry as the acquiring company for the strategy to work; thus, the strategy often leads to diversification. Improvements in the performance of the acquired company can come from a number of sources. First, the acquiring company usually replaces the top managers of the acquired company with a more aggressive management team. Second, the new managers of the acquired business are encouraged to sell off any unproductive assets, such as executive jets and elaborate corporate headquarters, and to reduce staffing levels. Third, the new management team is encouraged to intervene in the operations of the acquired business to seek out ways to improve the unit's efficiency, quality, innovativeness, and customer responsiveness. Fourth, to motivate the new management team and other employees of the acquired unit to undertake such actions, increases in their pay are typically linked to increases in the performance of the acquired unit. In addition, the acquiring company often establishes performance goals for the acquired company that cannot be met without significant improvements in operating efficiency. It also makes the new top managers aware that failure to achieve performance improvements consistent with these goals within a given amount of time will probably result in their being replaced.

Thus, the system of rewards and sanctions established by the acquiring company gives the new managers of the acquired unit strong incentives to look for ways to improve the performance of the unit under their charge. UTC has pursued the strategy of acquiring and restructuring underperforming companies with considerable success.

Two Types of Diversification

In the last section we discussed six principal ways in which companies can use diversification to implant their business models and strategies in other industries to increase their long-run profitability. It is possible to differentiate between two types of diversification based on their ability to realize these benefits: related diversification and unrelated diversification.[12]

■ Related Diversification

Related diversification is the strategy of establishing a business unit in a new industry that is *related* to a company's existing business units by some form of linkage or commonality between one or more components of each business unit's value chain. The goal is to obtain the benefits from transferring and leveraging distinctive competencies, sharing resources, and bundling products. These linkages are most commonly formed to take advantage of business models that have strong technological, manufacturing, marketing, and sales commonalities, meaning that the business model can be successfully "tweaked" to provide a competitive advantage in a new industry. Figure 10.4 provides some examples of the different kinds of linkages.

As an additional advantage, the related diversification process allows a company to use any general organizational competencies it possesses to increase overall business unit performance, such as by creating a culture that encourages entrepreneurship across units. The diversification of Philip Morris into the brewing industry with the acquisition of Miller Brewing is an example of related diversification because there are marketing and sales commonalities between the brewing and tobacco businesses: both are mass market consumer product businesses in which competitive success depends on brand-positioning skills and whose products can be sold and distributed together. 3M is another example of a company that has long pursued a strategy of related diversification. In 3M's case, the commonality is in the development of a set of core technologies, which are then shared among different kinds of business units. Improvements in technologies are also shared, and, as we discussed earlier, 3M

FIGURE 10.4

Commonalities Between the Value Chains of Three Business Units

has a general organizational competency in promoting cross-unit learning. Another example of related diversification is given in Strategy in Action 10.2, which looks at Intel's recent diversification into the communications chip business and the problems surrounding it.

■ Unrelated Diversification

The multibusiness model underlying **unrelated diversification** aims to enhance profits by implanting general organizational competencies in new business units, and perhaps to capture the benefits of multipoint competition. Companies pursuing a strategy of unrelated diversification have no intention of transferring or leveraging competencies between business units; their focus is on developing a multibusiness model that will strengthen the business model of each individual business unit.

UTC provides an excellent example of a company pursuing unrelated diversification. Its CEO George David uses all three kinds of general organizational competencies to improve the profitability of UTC's business units. First, UTC focuses only on basic manufacturing businesses where it can apply its ACE quality improvement tools. Then, it uses these ACE skills to encourage and build an entrepreneurial focus in its business units. Managers at all levels are charged with finding ways to increase innovation, and UTC spends $2.5 billion on R&D. Second, David makes acquisitions to strengthen an existing business unit's competitive position, such as when he combined Sunderstrand with Hamilton and combined their distinctive competencies. Then he practices good organizational design skills by restructuring the acquired company and streamlining its activities to reduce its cost structure; he also has a companywide incentive system in place to reward high-performing business units. Finally, from a strategic point of view, he only wants UTC to be in businesses that have pricing power and are not at the mercy of powerful buyers and suppliers, and he divests businesses that are in a weak competitive position. He also continually monitors the performance of UTC's business units through the ACE system and looks for ways to increase their performance.

Strategy in Action   10.2

Related Diversification at Intel

Although Intel has had a small presence in the communications chip business since the 1980s, the company focused most of its attention and resources on the booming business of making microprocessors for personal computers. According to managers at Intel, "feeding the processor monster" was a way to boost profitability, and the company invested all its substantial free cash flows into designing new generations of ever more powerful microprocessors and building the large-scale, and expensive, fabrication facilities necessary to manufacture them efficiently. The decision seemed logical: Intel had the dominant position in the microprocessor market, its primary customers (PC makers like Dell) were growing by leaps and bounds, and demand for its microprocessors was soaring. Indeed, if Intel had not made these investments to strengthen its core business model, it would have opened the door to competitors such as AMD.

This strategy of staying in a single business changed at a contentious strategy meeting of Intel's top executives in 1996. Intel's executives came away from that meeting with two important insights. First, the PC industry would approach market saturation in the early 2000s. This meant that the growth in demand for Intel's microprocessors would slow down. To maintain its profit growth, Intel needed to find a new "growth driver." Second, its executives decided that because of the growing use of the Internet, "communications was going to be the driver for everything in the future, that all computing was connected computing, and that connectivity had as important and strategic a role to play as the microprocessor did." Moreover, it was clear that demand for products of the communications industry such as communications network gear, which needed advanced communications chips, was accelerating rapidly.

Intel's executives decided that they could boost the company's ROIC by diverting some cash flow from new PC chip development and using Intel's competencies to build a new business model in the rapidly growing communications chip industry. This was a different industry: the production technology was different, the customers were different, and the competitors were different. Intel believed, however, that because the communications chip industry was related to the microprocessor industry, it could obtain a competitive advantage by transferring its leading-edge PC microprocessor technology, as well as its

manufacturing and marketing capabilities, to the communications chip industry.

Once the decision was made to enter the communications chip industry on a significant scale, Intel had to decide how best to execute the strategy. The company's managers decided that the only way they could get big enough fast enough to gain scale economies and establish a sustainable competitive advantage in this booming market was for the company to buy the required technology, fabrication facilities, and sales force. It could then improve the performance of the acquired businesses by transferring its competencies to them. So Intel went on an acquisition binge. Between January 1997 and June 2001, it made eighteen major acquisitions of companies in the communications chip industry for a combined total of $8 billion. As a result of these acquisitions, by mid 2001 Intel became the fourth largest global company in the communications chip industry, behind only Lucent, Motorola, and Texas Instruments, with revenues of $2.5 billion. Unfortunately, Intel and all these other companies were hard hit by the slump in global demand for telecommunications equipment in the early 2000s.

Then, to make matters worse, Intel's push into communications chips had launched it on the road to designing chips that were faster and faster because speed was seen as the most vital ingredient in communication. By 2003, however, it was clear that what customers wanted was chips that could support high bandwidth and could process vast amounts of information *simultaneously*. Both these capabilities are needed for high-quality music, movie viewing, and other multimedia applications such as video telephone conferencing. Intel lacked such a chip, but in the meantime Advanced Micro Devices (AMD), its major competitor, had perceived the need to develop it. Suddenly Intel found itself at a competitive disadvantage. In 2004, it announced plans to abandon its high-speed communications chips to focus on those that could support the bandwidth needed for sophisticated multimedia applications. Intel had made the mistake of not focusing on what PC users and digital content providers needed in next-generation chips. It was so concerned with the need to increase speed that it entered a new industry assuming there was a commonality based on speed, but it was not there. Intel should have focused on customer needs, not its own distinctive competencies.[b]

In sum, the multibusiness model in unrelated diversification is primarily based on using general organizational competencies to increase the profitability of each business unit in the diversified company. By contrast, the multibusiness model in related diversification is based on transferring and leveraging competencies, sharing resources, and bundling products. In addition, companies that pursue related diversification are far more likely to encounter each other in different industries than are those pursuing unrelated diversification. Thus, they are far more likely to use multipoint competition to manage industry rivalry.

Disadvantages and Limits of Diversification

As we have discussed, many companies, such as 3M, UTC, Intel, and GE, have reaped enormous advantages from pursuing a strategy of diversification and have consistently increased their profitability over time. Nevertheless, many companies that have pursued diversification have enjoyed far less success, and for some companies diversification has actually dissipated or reduced their profitability. As a result, over the last few decades many companies have *de-diversified* and sold off their constituent businesses to focus on their core business. Clearly, there must be important disadvantages associated with diversification that can make it a dangerous strategy to pursue over time. Three conditions can make diversification disadvantageous: changing industry- and firm-specific conditions, diversification for the wrong reasons, and the increasing bureaucratic costs of extensive diversification.

■ Changing Industry- and Firm-Specific Conditions

Diversification is a complex strategy to pursue, and top managers must have the entrepreneurial ability to sense profitable new opportunities and the ability to implement the strategies needed to make diversification pay off. Over time, however, a company's top management team changes: sometimes the most able executives join other companies and become their CEOs, and sometimes successful CEOs decide to retire or step down. When they leave, these managers often take their vision with them, and their successors may lack the skills or commitment needed to implement and manage diversification successfully over time. Thus, the multibusiness model loses its ability to create value, and, as we discuss below, the cost structure of the diversified company often starts to increase, swallowing up the gains the strategy produces.

Over time, too, the environment can change rapidly and in unpredictable ways. We discuss earlier how blurring industry boundaries can destroy the source of a company's competitive advantage. If this happens in its core business, then clearly benefits from transferring or leveraging distinctive competencies will disappear and a company will now be saddled with a collection of businesses that have all become poor performers in their respective industries. When the computer industry changed, for example, and PCs and servers became the dominant product, IBM was left with unprofitable operations in the mainframe hardware and software industries that almost led to its bankruptcy. Thus one major problem with diversification is that the future success of this strategy is hard to predict; therefore, if a company is to profit from it over time, managers should be as willing to divest businesses as they are to acquire them. Unfortunately, research suggests that managers do not behave in this way.

■ Diversification for the Wrong Reasons

As we have discussed, different multibusiness models justify a company pursuing either related or unrelated diversification. If a company pursues diversification, its managers must have a clear vision of how their entry into new industries will allow them to create more value. Over time, however, as the profitability of their diversification strategy falls for reasons just noted, managers, rather than divesting their businesses, often use false or mistaken justifications for keeping their collection of businesses together. There are many famous historical examples of this behavior.

For example, one justification for diversification that once was widely used was that diversification could be used to obtain the benefits of risk pooling. Many CEOs argued that diversification, particularly unrelated diversification into industries that have different business cycles so that their revenues rise and fall in different cycles, would allow them to create a more stable companywide income stream over time—one that avoids the sharp swings up and down that can make the value of a company's stock volatile and unpredictable. An example of risk pooling might be the diversification by U.S. Steel into the oil and gas industry in an attempt to offset the adverse effects of cyclical downturns in the steel industry. According to advocates of risk pooling, a more stable income stream reduces the risk of bankruptcy and is in the best interests of the company's stockholders.

This simple argument ignores two facts. First, stockholders can easily eliminate the risks inherent in holding an individual stock by diversifying their own portfolios, and they can do so at a much lower cost than the company can. Thus, far from being in the best interests of stockholders, attempts to pool risks through diversification represent an unproductive use of resources; instead, profits should be returned to shareholders in the form of increased dividends. Second, research on this topic suggests that corporate diversification is not an effective way to pool risks because the business cycles of different industries are *inherently difficult to predict* and a diversified company might just find that a general economic downturn hits all its industries simultaneously. If this happens, the company's profitability will plunge.[13]

When the core business is in trouble, another mistaken justification for diversification is that the new industries will rescue it. An example of a company that made this mistake is Kodak. In the 1980s, increased competition from low-cost Japanese competitors like Fuji, combined with the beginnings of the digital revolution, led its revenues and profits first to plateau and then to fall. Its managers should have done all they could to reduce its cost structure; instead they took its still huge free cash flow and spent tens of billions of dollars to enter new industries such as health care, biotechnology, and computer hardware in a desperate attempt to find ways to increase profitability.

This was a disaster, because every industry Kodak entered was populated by strong companies such as 3M, Canon, and Xerox, and Kodak's corporate managers lacked any general competencies to give their new business units a competitive advantage. Moreover, the more industries they entered, the greater the range of threats they encountered and the more time they had to spend dealing with these threats. As a result, they could spend much less time improving the performance of their core film business, which continued to decline. In reality, Kodak's diversification was just for growth itself, but *growth does not create value*; growth is just the byproduct, not the objective, of a diversification strategy. However, in desperation companies diversify for reasons of growth alone rather than to gain any well-thought-out strategic advantage.

A large number of academic studies suggest that *extensive* diversification tends to reduce rather than improve company profitability.[14] For example, in a study that looked at the diversification of thirty-three major U.S. corporations over thirty-five years, Michael Porter observed that the track record of corporate diversification has been poor.[15] Porter found that most of the companies had divested many more diversified acquisitions than they had kept. He and others have concluded that the corporate diversification strategies pursued by most companies can dissipate value instead of creating it.[16]

■ The Bureaucratic Costs of Diversification

A company diversifies to boost its profitability from higher product differentiation or a lower cost structure, but to achieve this it has to invest valuable resources. One reason that diversification often fails to boost profitability is that all too often the *bureaucratic costs* of diversification exceed the value created by the strategy. As we mentioned in the last chapter, **bureaucratic costs** are the costs associated with solving the transaction difficulties that arise between a company's business units, and between business units and corporate headquarters, as the company attempts to obtain the benefits from transferring, sharing, and leveraging competencies. They also include the costs of using general organizational competencies to solve managerial and functional inefficiencies. The level of bureaucratic costs in a diversified organization is a function of two factors: (1) the number of business units in a company's portfolio and (2) the extent to which coordination is required between these different business units to realize the benefits of diversification

■ Number of Businesses

The greater the number of business units in a company's portfolio, the more difficult it is for corporate managers to remain informed about the complexities of each business. Managers simply do not have the time to assess the business model of each unit. This problem began to occur at GE in the 1970s when its growth-hungry CEO Reg Jones acquired many new businesses. As Jones commented,

> I tried to review each plan [of each business unit] in great detail. This effort took untold hours and placed a tremendous burden on the corporate executive office. After a while I began to realize that no matter how hard we would work, we could not achieve the necessary in-depth understanding of the 40-odd business unit plans.[17]

The inability of top managers in extensively diversified companies to maintain a superior multibusiness model over time may lead them to base important resource allocation decisions on only the most superficial analysis of each business unit's competitive position. Thus, for example, a promising business unit may be starved of investment funds while other business units receive far more cash than they can profitably reinvest in their operations. Furthermore, because they are distant from the day-to-day operations of the business units, corporate managers may find that business unit managers try to hide information on poor performance to save their own jobs. For example, business unit managers might blame poor performance on difficult competitive conditions even when it is the result of their inability to craft a successful business model. One reason that ACE is so effective at UTC is that it is a standardized set of rules and procedures that can be applied easily across all its divisions so that George David and his top managers understand exactly what is happening throughout the company. But when inefficiencies such as the suboptimal allocation of capital within the company and a failure by corporate executives to successfully encourage and reward aggressive profit-seeking behavior by business unit managers become extensive, the time and effort top managers must devote to solve such problems cancel out the value created by diversification.

FIGURE 10.5

Coordination Among
Related Business
Units

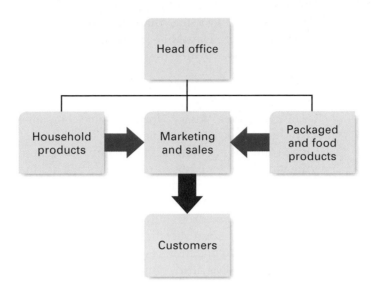

■ **Coordination Among Businesses** The coordination required to realize value from a diversification strategy based on transferring, sharing, or leveraging
competencies is a major source of bureaucratic costs. The bureaucratic mechanisms
needed to oversee and manage this coordination to reduce managerial inefficiencies,
such as cross-business-unit teams and management committees, are one source of
these costs. A second source is the costs associated with accurately measuring the performance, and therefore the unique profit contribution, of a business unit that is
transferring or sharing resources with another. Consider a company that has two
business units, one producing household products (such as liquid soap and laundry
detergent) and another producing packaged food products. The products of both
units are sold through supermarkets. To lower the costs of value creation, the parent
company decides to pool the marketing and sales functions of each business unit
using an organizational structure similar to that illustrated in Figure 10.5. The company is organized into three divisions: a household products division, a food products
division, and a marketing division.

    Although such an arrangement may result in substantial cost savings, it can also
give rise to substantial control problems and hence bureaucratic costs. For example,
if the performance of the household products business begins to slip, identifying
who is to be held accountable—managers in the household products division or
managers in the marketing division—may prove difficult. Indeed, each may blame
the other for poor performance. Although these kinds of problems can be resolved if
corporate management performs an in-depth audit of both divisions, the bureaucratic costs (managers' time and effort) involved in doing so may once again cancel
out any value achieved from diversification.

    In sum, diversification is the most complex and difficult strategy that a company
can pursue. Changing conditions both in the external environment and inside a
company can reduce the value creation advantages from pursuing this strategy, either
because they rob business units of their competitive advantage or because they increase the bureaucratic costs associated with pursuing this strategy, which then also
cancel out its advantages. Thus the existence of bureaucratic costs places a limit on the
amount of diversification that can profitably be pursued. It makes sense for a company

to diversify only as long as the value created by such a strategy exceeds the bureaucratic costs associated with expanding the boundaries of the organization to incorporate additional business activities.

Choosing a Strategy

■ Related Versus Unrelated Diversification

Because related diversification involves more sharing of competencies, one might say it can boost profitability in more ways than unrelated diversification and so is the better diversification strategy. However, some companies, such as UTC, can create as much or more value from pursuing unrelated diversification, so that approach must also have some substantial benefits. An unrelated company does *not* have to achieve coordination between business units, and so it has to cope only with the bureaucratic costs that arise from the number of businesses in its portfolio. In contrast, a related company has to achieve coordination *between* business units if it is to realize the gains that come from utilizing its distinctive competencies. Consequently, it has to cope with the bureaucratic costs that arise *both* from the number of business units in its portfolio *and* from coordination among business units. Thus, although it is true that related diversified companies can create value in more ways than unrelated companies, they also have to bear higher bureaucratic costs in order to do so. These higher costs may cancel out the higher benefits, making the strategy no more profitable than one of unrelated diversification.

How then does a company choose between these strategies? The choice depends on a comparison of the benefits of each strategy against the bureaucratic costs of pursuing it. It pays a company to pursue related diversification when (1) the company's competencies can be applied across a greater number of industries and (2) the company does have superior strategic capabilities that allow it to keep bureaucratic costs under close control—perhaps by encouraging entrepreneurship or by developing a value-creating organizational culture. Using the same logic, it pays a company to pursue unrelated diversification when (1) each business unit's functional competencies have few useful applications across industries but the company's top managers are skilled at raising the profitability of poorly run businesses; and (2) the company's managers have good organizational design skills to build distinctive competencies and keep bureaucratic costs in control and even to reduce them.

■ The Web of Corporate-Level Strategy

Finally, it is important to note that while some companies may choose to pursue a strategy of related or unrelated diversification, there is nothing that stops them from pursuing both of these strategies at the same time—*as well as all the other corporate-level strategies we have discussed*. The purpose of corporate-level strategy is to increase long-term profitability. A company should pursue any and all strategies as long as strategic managers have weighed the advantages and disadvantages of those strategies and arrived at a multibusiness model that justifies them. Figure 10.6 shows how Sony has entered into industries that have led it to pursue various strategies.

First, Sony's core business is its electronic consumer products business, which is well known for its generic distinctive competencies of innovation and marketing (it has one of the best-known brand names in the world). To protect the quality of its electronic products, Sony manufactures a high percentage of the component parts for its televisions, DVD players, and so on, and in this sense it has pursued a strategy of backward vertical integration. Sony also engages in forward vertical integration: after having acquired Columbia Pictures and MGM in 2004, it now operates in the movie industry and has opened several Sony stores in exclusive shopping malls. Sony also shared and leveraged its distinctive competencies by developing its own business

FIGURE 10.6

Sony's Web of Corporate-Level Strategy

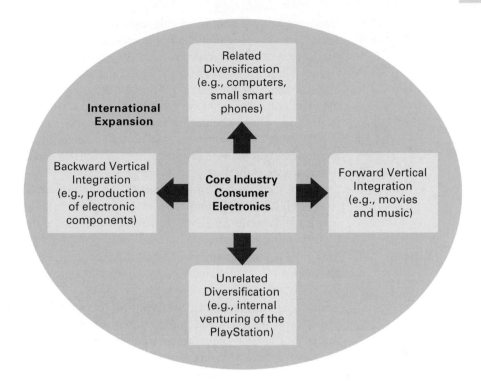

units that operate in the computer and smart phone industries, a strategy of related diversification. Finally, in deciding to enter the home videogame industry and developing its PlayStation to compete with Nintendo, it is also pursuing a strategy of unrelated diversification. Today this division contributes more to Sony's total profits than its core electronics business.

While Sony has had enormous success pursuing all these strategies in the past, in the last few years its profitability has fallen. Analysts claim that its multibusiness model, which led it to diversify extensively and focus on innovating high-quality products, led it to neglect its cost structure. They also claim that its strategy of giving each business unit great autonomy has led each unit to pursue its own goals at the expense of the company's "multibusiness model." Sony's escalating bureaucratic costs have been draining its profitability and slowing innovation, which has allowed competitors like Samsung to catch up and even overtake it in areas like cell phones and flat-screen LCDs. Sony has been responding to these problems: it has taken major steps to reduce bureaucratic costs, speed innovation, and lower its cost structure, including exiting industries like PDAs and videocassette recorders. The next few years will show whether the company has been able to better implement its corporate strategies to improve its profitability.

Entry Strategy: Internal New Ventures

Having discussed all the corporate-level strategies managers can use to formulate the multibusiness model, we can examine the three main strategies that can be used to implement it: internal new ventures, acquisitions, and joint ventures. In this section we look at pros and cons of using internal new ventures. In the following sections we look at acquisitions and joint ventures.

■ The Attractions of Internal New Venturing

Internal new venturing is typically used to implement corporate-level strategies when a company possesses one or more generic distinctive competencies in its core business model that can be leveraged or recombined to enter a new industry. As a rule, companies whose business model is based on using their technology to innovate new kinds of products for related markets or industries tend to favor internal new venturing as an entry strategy. Thus technology-based companies that pursue related diversification, like DuPont, which has created new markets with products such as cellophane, nylon, Freon, and Teflon, tend to use internal new venturing. 3M has a near-legendary knack for creating new products from internally generated ideas that enable it to dominate new markets (see Strategy in Action 10.1). Similarly, Hewlett-Packard moved into computers and peripherals through internal new venturing.

Even if it lacks the competencies required to compete in a new industry, a company may pursue an internal venturing strategy when it is entering a newly emerging or embryonic industry—one in which no company has yet developed the business model that gives it a dominant position in that industry. This was Monsanto's situation in 1979 when it contemplated entering the biotechnology field to produce herbicides and pest-resistant crop seeds. The biotechnology field was young at that time, and there were no incumbent companies focused on applying biotechnology to agricultural products. Accordingly, Monsanto established an internal new venture to enter the industry and develop the required competencies. Indeed, Monsanto's whole venturing strategy was built around creating a business model that would allow it to build competencies ahead of other potential competitors and so establish a strong competitive position in this newly emerging industry.

■ Pitfalls of New Ventures

Despite the popularity of the internal new-venture strategy, there is a high risk of failure. Research suggests that somewhere between 33 and 60 percent of all new products that reach the marketplace do not generate an adequate economic return,[18] and most of these products were the result of internal new ventures. Three reasons are often put forward to explain the relatively high failure rate of internal new ventures: (1) market entry on too small a scale, (2) poor commercialization of the new-venture product, and (3) poor corporate management of the venture process.[19]

■ Scale of Entry

Research suggests that large-scale entry into a new industry is often a critical precondition for the success of a new venture. This means that in the short run large-scale entry requires a substantial capital investment to develop the product—and thus the prospect of substantial losses. But, in the long run, which can be as long as five to twelve years, depending on the industry, such a large investment results in far greater returns than if a company enters on a small scale and limits its investment to reduce its potential losses.[20] Large-scale entrants can more rapidly realize scale economies, build brand loyalty, and gain access to distribution channels, all of which increase the probability of a new venture's success. In contrast, small-scale entrants may find themselves handicapped by high costs due to a lack of scale economies and a lack of market presence that limits their ability to build brand loyalty and gain access to distribution channels. These scale effects are particularly significant when a company is entering an established industry where incumbent companies do possess scale economies, brand loyalty, and access to distribution channels. Now, the new entrant has to make a major investment in order to succeed.

Figure 10.7 plots the relationship between scale of entry and profitability over time for successful small-scale and large-scale ventures. The figure shows that successful

FIGURE 10.7

Scale of Entry and
Profitability

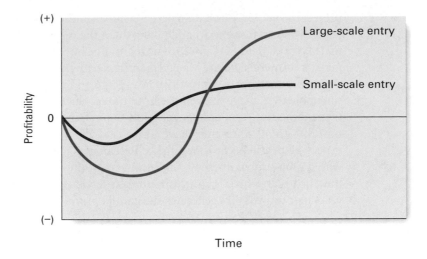

small-scale entry is associated with lower initial losses but that in the long run large-scale entry generates greater returns. However, because of the costs of large-scale entry and the huge potential losses if the venture fails, many companies make the mistake of choosing a small-scale entry strategy, which often means they fail to build the market share necessary for long-term success.

■ **Commercialization** Many internal new ventures are driven by the use of new or high technology to make better products, but to be commercially successful the products must be developed with customer requirements in mind. Many internal new ventures fail when a company ignores the needs of customers in a market and instead becomes blinded by the technological possibilities of a new product.[21] Thus, a new venture may fail because it is marketing a product based on a technology for which there is no demand, or because the company fails to commercialize or position the product correctly in the market.

For example, consider the desktop computer marketed by NeXT, the company started by the founder of Apple, Steven Jobs. The NeXT system failed to gain market share because the computer incorporated an array of expensive technologies that consumers simply did not want, such as optical disk drives and hi-fidelity sound. The optical disk drives, in particular, turned off customers because they made it tough to switch work from a PC with a floppy drive to a NeXT machine with an optical drive. In other words, NeXT failed because its founder was so dazzled by leading-edge technology that he ignored customer needs. However, Jobs redeemed himself when he successfully commercialized Apple's iPod, which dominated the MP3 player market in 2004.

■ **Poor Implementation** Managing the new-venture process raises difficult organization issues.[22] For example, one common mistake some companies make is to try to increase their chance of making a successful product by establishing many different internal new-venture projects at the same time. This "shotgun approach" of spreading the risks between projects places great demands on a company's cash flow and can result in the best ventures being starved of the cash they need to succeed.[23] Another common mistake is the failure of corporate managers to carefully develop upfront all the aspects of the business model that will be needed for the new-venture project to succeed—and to include scientists in the model-building process. Taking a team of research scientists and giving them the resources they need to do research in their favorite field may produce novel results, but these results may have little strategic or commercial value. Managers must clarify how and why the project will lead to a product that has a competitive advantage and establish strategic objectives and a timetable to manage the venture until the product reaches the market. Failure to anticipate the time and costs involved in the new-venture process constitutes a further mistake. Many companies have unrealistic expectations regarding the time frame, expecting profits to flow in quickly. Research suggests that some companies operate with a philosophy of killing new businesses if they do not turn a profit by the end of the third year, which is clearly an unrealistic view given that it can take five to twelve years before a venture generates substantial profits.

■ Guidelines for Successful Internal New Venturing

To avoid these pitfalls, a company should adopt a well-thought-out, structured approach to manage internal new venturing. New venturing begins with R&D, *exploratory research* to advance basic science and technology (the "R" in R&D), and *development research* to find and refine the commercial applications for a technology (the "D" in R&D). Companies with a strong track record of internal new venturing excel at both kinds of R&D: they help to advance basic science and then they find commercial applications for it.[24] To advance basic science, it is important for companies to (1) have strong links with universities, where much of the scientific knowledge that underlies new technologies is discovered, and (2) to make sure that significant research funds are under the control of researchers who can pursue "blue-sky" projects that might ultimately yield unexpected and commercially valuable technologies and products. For example, 3M has close links with several universities, including the University of Minnesota in its hometown, and funds basic research at those universities. And, as already mentioned, 3M's researchers spend 15 percent of their time on projects of their own choosing, many of which are basic research projects.

However, if the pursuit of basic research is all that a company does well, it will probably generate few successful commercial ventures. To translate good science into good products, it is critical that a major proportion of R&D funding be directed toward commercial ventures. Companies can take a number of steps to ensure that this happens. First, many companies place much of the funding for research in the hands of business unit managers who are responsible for narrowing down and then selecting the small number of research projects they believe have the best chance of a significant commercial payoff. Second, to make effective use of its R&D skills, a company's top managers must continually spell out the strategic objectives in its business model and communicate them clearly to scientists and engineers. Research must be in the pursuit of strategic goals.[25] For example, one of the biggest research projects at Microsoft has been language recognition software because a central objective of the company is to make computers easy to use. Researchers reason that if computers can understand spoken language, commands can be inputted by voice rather than through a keyboard, thus making computers easier to use and strengthening the Windows platform.

A company must also foster close links between R&D and marketing to increase the probability of a new product's commercial success, for this is the best way to ensure that research projects address the needs of the market. Also, a company should foster close links between R&D and manufacturing to ensure that it has the ability to make a proposed new product. Many companies successfully integrate the activities of different functions by creating cross-functional project teams to oversee the development of new products, from their inception to their market introduction. This approach can significantly reduce the time this process takes. For example, while R&D is working on the design, manufacturing is setting up facilities and is developing a campaign to show customers how much the new product will benefit them.

Finally, because large-scale entry often leads to greater long-term profits, a company can promote the success of internal new venturing by "thinking big." Well in advance, a company should construct efficient-scale manufacturing facilities and establish a large marketing program to develop a campaign for building a market presence and brand loyalty quickly. Corporate managers should not panic; they should accept that there will be initial losses and realize that, as long as market share is expanding, the product will eventually succeed.

Entry Strategy: Acquisitions

In Chapter 9 we explain that acquisitions are the main vehicle that companies use to implement a horizontal integration strategy, as well as vertical integration and diversification. In the *Opening Case,* we saw how UTC acquires new profitable businesses to pursue unrelated diversification. However, Chapter 9 also discusses how acquisitions may fail, and so it is necessary to understand both the benefits and risks associated with using acquisitions to implement a corporate-level strategy.

■ The Attractions of Acquisitions

Acquisitions are the principal strategy used to implement horizontal integration. With vertical integration or diversification, acquisitions are used when a company lacks the distinctive competencies to compete in an industry and therefore uses its capital to purchase an established company that has those competencies. A company is particularly likely to use acquisitions when it needs to move fast to establish a presence in an industry. Entering a new industry through internal venturing is a relatively slow process; acquisition is a much quicker way for a company to establish a significant market presence. A company can purchase a leading company with a strong competitive position in months rather than spend years building up a market leadership position through internal venturing. Thus, when speed is important, acquisition is the favored entry mode. Intel, for example, used acquisitions to build its communications chip business because it sensed that the market was developing very quickly and it would take too long to develop the required competencies internally (see Strategy in Action 10.2).

In addition, acquisitions are often perceived as somewhat less risky than internal new ventures, primarily because they involve less commercial uncertainty. Because of the risks associated with an internal new venture, it is difficult to predict its future profitability and cash flows. In contrast, when a company makes an acquisition it is acquiring a company with a reputation whose market share and profitability can be easily evaluated.

Finally, acquisitions are an attractive way to enter an industry that is protected by high barriers to entry. Recall from Chapter 2 that barriers to entry arise from factors associated with product differentiation (brand loyalty), absolute cost advantages, and economies of scale. When these barriers are substantial, a company may find it very difficult to enter an industry through internal new venturing because it will have to construct large-scale manufacturing facilities and invest in a massive advertising campaign to establish brand loyalty—difficult goals that require large capital expenditures. In contrast, if a company acquires an established company in the industry, it can circumvent most entry barriers because it has acquired a market leader that already has substantial scale economies and brand loyalty. In general, the greater the barriers to entry, the more likely it is that acquisitions will be the favored entry mode.

■ Acquisition Pitfalls

For these reasons, acquisitions have long been a popular vehicle for executing corporate-level strategies. However, despite this popularity, there is ample evidence that many acquisitions fail to add value for the acquiring company and, indeed, often end up dissipating value. For example, a study by Mercer Management Consulting looked at 150 acquisitions worth more than $500 million each that were undertaken between January 1990 and July 1995.[26] The Mercer study concluded that 50 percent of these acquisitions ended up eroding, or substantially eroding, shareholder value, and another 33 percent created only marginal returns. Only 17 percent of these acquisitions were judged to be successful. Similarly, a study by KPMG, an accounting and management consulting company, looked at 700 large acquisitions between 1996 and 1998 and found that although some 30 percent of these actually created value for the acquiring company, 31 percent destroyed value, and the remainder had little impact.[27]

More generally, a wealth of evidence from academic research suggests that many acquisitions fail to realize their anticipated benefits.[28] In a major study of the post-acquisition performance of acquired companies, David Ravenscraft and Mike Scherer concluded that the profitability and market shares of acquired companies often declined after acquisition.[29] They also noted that a smaller but substantial subset of acquired companies experienced traumatic difficulties that ultimately led to their being sold off by the acquiring company. This evidence suggests that many acquisitions destroy rather than create value.

Acquisitions may fail to create value for four reasons: (1) companies often experience difficulties when trying to integrate different organizational structures and cultures, (2) companies overestimate the potential economic benefits from an acquisition, (3) acquisitions tend to be very expensive, and (4) companies often do not adequately screen their acquisition targets.

■ Integrating the Acquired Company Once an acquisition has been made, the acquiring company has to integrate the acquired company and combine in with its own organizational structure and culture. Integration involves the adoption of common management and financial control systems, the joining together of operations from the acquired and the acquiring company, the establishment of bureaucratic mechanisms to share information and personnel, and the need to create a common culture. Experience has shown that many problems can occur as companies attempt to integrate their activities.

After an acquisition, many acquired companies experience high management turnover because their employees do not like the acquiring company's way of operating—its structure and culture.[30] Research suggests that the loss of management talent and expertise, to say nothing of the damage from constant tension between the businesses, can materially harm the performance of the acquired unit.[31] Strategy in Action 10.3 describes what happened at Boston Co. after it was acquired by Mellon Bank.

■ Overestimating Economic Benefits Even when companies find it easy to integrate their activities, they often overestimate the potential for creating value by joining together different businesses. They overestimate the competitive advantages that can be derived from the acquisition and so pay more for the target company than it is worth. Richard Roll has attributed this tendency to hubris on the part of top management. According to Roll, top managers typically overestimate their ability to create value from an acquisition, primarily because rising to the top of a corporation has given them an exaggerated sense of their own capabilities.[32] Coca-Cola's

Strategy in Action   10.3

Postacquisition Problems at Mellon Bank

In the search for a profitable way to expand his company's business, Frank Cahouet, the CEO of Philadelphia-based Mellon Bank, decided to reduce the large swings in Mellon's earnings because of changes in interest rates by diversifying into financial services to gain access to a steady flow of fee-based income from money management operations. As part of this strategy, he acquired Boston Co. for $1.45 billion. Boston is a high-profile money management company that manages investments for major institutional clients, such as state and corporate pension funds. Mellon followed up its Boston acquisition with the acquisition of mutual fund provider Dreyfus Corp., for $1.7 billion. As a result, almost half of Mellon's income was now generated from fee-based financial services.

Problems at Boston Co. began to surface soon after the Mellon acquisition. From the beginning there was a clash of corporate cultures. At Mellon, many managers arrived at their mundane offices by 7 A.M. and put in twelve-hour days for modest pay by banking industry standards. They were also accustomed to Frank Cahouet's management style, which emphasized cost containment and frugality. Boston Co. managers also put in twelve-hour days, but they expected considerable autonomy, flexible work schedules, high pay, ample perks, and large performance bonuses. In most years, the top twenty executives at Boston earned between $750,000 and $1 million each. Mellon executives who visited the Boston Co. unit were dumbstruck by its country club atmosphere and opulence. In its move to streamline Boston, Mellon insisted that Boston cut expenses and introduced new regulations for restricting travel, entertainment, and perks.

Things started to go wrong when the Wisconsin state pension fund complained to Mellon of lower returns on a portfolio run by Boston Co. Mellon was forced to liquidate the portfolio and take a $130 million charge against earnings; it also fired the responsible portfolio manager, claiming that this manager was making "unauthorized trades." At Boston Co., however, many managers saw Mellon's action

as violating the guarantees of operating autonomy that it had given Boston at the time of the acquisition. They blamed Mellon for prematurely liquidating a portfolio whose strategy, they claimed, Mellon executives had approved and that, moreover, could still prove a winner if interest rates fell (which they subsequently did).

Infuriated by Mellon's interference, seven of Boston Co.'s asset unit managers, including the unit's CEO, Desmond Heathwood, proposed a management buyout to Mellon. This unit was one of the gems in Boston's crown, with over $26 billion in assets under management. Heathwood had been openly disdainful of Mellon's bankers, believing that they were out of their league in the investment business. Mellon rejected the buyout proposal, and Heathwood promptly left to start his own investment management company. A few days later, Mellon asked employees at Boston to sign employment contracts that limited their ability to leave and work for Heathwood's competing business. Thirteen senior employees refused to sign and then quit to join Heathwood's new money management operation.

The defection of Heathwood and his colleagues was followed by a series of high-profile client defections. The Arizona State Retirement System, for example, pulled $1 billion out of Mellon and transferred it to Heathwood's firm, and the Fresno County Retirement System transferred $400 million in assets over to Heathwood. As one client stated, "We have a relationship with the Boston Co. that goes back over 30 years, and the people who worked on the account are the people who left—so we left too."

Reflecting on the episode, Frank Cahouet noted, "We've clearly been hurt. . . . But this episode is very manageable. We are not going to lose our momentum." Others were not so sure. In this incident, they saw yet another example of how difficult it can be to merge two divergent corporate cultures and how the management turnover that results from such attempts can deal a serious blow to any attempt to create value out of an acquisition.[c]

acquisition of a number of medium-sized wine-making companies illustrates this situation. Reasoning that a beverage is a beverage, Coca-Cola thought it would be able to use its distinctive competence in marketing to dominate the U.S. wine industry. But after buying three wine companies and enduring seven years of marginal profits, Coca-Cola finally conceded that wine and soft drinks are very different products, with different kinds of appeal, pricing systems, and distribution networks. It subsequently sold the wine operations to Joseph E. Seagram & Sons at a substantial loss when adjusted for inflation.[33]

■ **The Expense of Acquisitions** Perhaps the most important reason for the failure of acquisitions is that the acquisition of companies whose stock is publicly traded tends to be very expensive—and the expense of the acquisition cancels out the prospective value-creating gains from the acquisition described earlier. One reason is that the management of the target company is not likely to agree to an acquisition unless there is a substantial premium over its current market value. Another reason is that the stockholders of the acquired company are unlikely to sell their stock unless they are paid a significant premium over its current market value—and premiums tend to run *25 to 50 percent over a company's stock price prior to a takeover bid.* Therefore, the acquiring company must be able to increase the value of the acquired company after it has been integrated by at least the same amount to make the acquisition pay, a tall order. This is a major reason why acquisitions are frequently unprofitable for the acquiring company.

The problem for the acquiring company is that the stock price of the acquisition target gets bid up enormously during the acquisition process. This frequently occurs in the case of a contested bidding contest where two or more companies simultaneously bid to acquire the target company. In addition, when many acquisitions are happening in a particular sector or industry, the price of *potential* target companies gets bid up by investors who speculate that a bid for these companies will be made at some future point, which further increases the cost of making acquisitions. This happened in the telecommunications sector when, to make sure they could meet the needs of customers who were demanding leading-edge equipment, many large companies went on acquisition binges. JDS Uniphase, Cisco Systems, Nortel, Corning, and Lucent all raced each other to buy up smaller companies that were developing promising new telecommunications equipment. The result was that stock prices for these companies got bid up by investors. When the telecommunications boom turned to bust, the acquiring companies found that they had vastly overpaid for their acquisitions and had to take large accounting write-downs. In 2001, Nortel Networks wrote down $12.3 billion in goodwill on its balance sheet to reflect a reduction in the value of the assets it had acquired during the boom. Another telecom equipment supplier, Corning, wrote down $4.8 billion, and JDS Uniphase wrote down a staggering *$40 billion.*

■ **Inadequate Preacquisition Screening** Obviously, as these enormous losses suggest, many companies do a poor job of evaluating the value-creating potential of potential acquisitions. After researching acquisitions made by twenty different companies, a study by Philippe Haspeslagh and David Jemison came to the conclusion that one reason for acquisitions failure is management's inadequate attention to preacquisition screening.[34] They found that many companies decide to acquire other firms without thoroughly analyzing the potential benefits and costs. After the acquisition has been completed, many acquiring companies discover that, instead of buying a well-run business, they have purchased a troubled organization. Moreover, they often have to take on an enormous amount of debt to fund these acquisitions, and they frequently are unable to pay it once the weaknesses of the acquired company's business model become clear.

■ Guidelines for Successful Acquisition

To avoid pitfalls and make successful acquisitions, companies need to take a structured approach to purchasing companies based on four components: (1) target identification and preacquisition screening, (2) bidding strategy, (3) integration, and (4) learning from experience.[35]

■ Identification and Screening

Thorough preacquisition screening increases a company's knowledge about a potential takeover target and lessens the risk of purchasing a potential problem business—one with a weak business model. It also leads to a more realistic assessment of the problems involved in executing a particular acquisition so that a company can plan how to integrate the new business and blend the organizational structures and cultures. The screening process should begin with a detailed assessment of the strategic rationale for making the acquisition, an identification of the kind of company that would make an ideal acquisition candidate, and a thorough analysis of the strengths and weaknesses of its business model by comparing it to other possible acquisition targets.

Indeed, an acquiring company should scan a target population of potential acquisition candidates and evaluate each according to a detailed set of criteria, focusing on (1) its financial position, (2) its distinctive competencies and competitive advantage, (3) the changing industry boundaries, (4) its management capabilities, and (5) its corporate culture. Such an evaluation will help the company identify the strengths and weaknesses of each target and the potential economies of scale and scope between the acquiring and the acquired companies. It will also help it to recognize potential integration problems and the problems that might exist when it is necessary to integrate the corporate cultures of the acquiring and the acquired companies. In 2004, for example, Microsoft and SAP, the world's leading provider of enterprise resource planning software, sat down together to discuss a possible acquisition by Microsoft. Both companies decided that even though there was a strong strategic rationale for a merger—together they would dominate the global computing market for most large global companies—the problems of creating an organizational structure that could successfully integrate their hundreds of thousands of employees throughout the world and blend two very different cultures were insurmountable.

Once a company has reduced the list of potential acquisition candidates to the most favored one or two, it needs to contact expert third parties, such as investment bankers like Goldman Sachs and Merrill Lynch, that may be able to provide valuable insights about the attractiveness of the potential acquisition and that will also handle the many issues surrounding the acquisition, such as the process of establishing the bidding strategy for acquiring the company's stock.

■ Bidding Strategy

The objective of bidding strategy is to reduce the price that a company must pay for the target company. The most effective way a company can acquire another is to make a friendly takeover bid, which means the two companies work out an amicable way to merge the two companies that satisfies the needs of stockholders and top managers. A friendly takeover helps prevent speculators from bidding up stock prices. By contrast, in a hostile bid, such as the one between Oracle and PeopleSoft, the price of the target company often gets bid up by speculators who expect that the offer price will be raised by the acquirer or that another company, sometimes called a *white knight*, might come in with a counteroffer more favorable to the management of the target company.

Another essential element of a good bidding strategy is timing. For example, Hanson PLC, one of the most successful companies to pursue unrelated diversification, searched for essentially sound companies suffering from short-term problems due to cyclical industry factors or one underperforming division. Such companies are typically undervalued by the stock market and so can be acquired without the standard 25 to 50 percent stock premium. With good timing, a company can make a bargain purchase. UTC also seems to follow this practice: it buys essentially sound manufacturing companies that are underperforming their peers because of short-term problems and then uses its ACE business processes to build their distinctive competencies and so establish a competitive business model.

■ **Integration** Despite good screening and bidding, an acquisition will fail unless the acquiring company possesses the essential organizational design skills needed to integrate the acquired company into its operations and so quickly develop a viable multibusiness model. Integration should center on the source of the potential strategic advantages of the acquisition—for instance, opportunities to share marketing, manufacturing, logistics, R&D, financial, or management resources. Integration should also involve steps to eliminate any duplication of facilities or functions. In addition, any unwanted business units of the acquired company should be divested.

■ **Learning from Experience** Research suggests that although many acquisitions do fail to create value for the acquiring company, companies that acquire many companies over time—such as UTC—become expert in this process and so can generate significant value from their acquisitions.[36] One reason may be that they learn from their experience and develop a "playbook" of how to execute an acquisition most efficiently and effectively. Tyco, profiled in the *Closing Case*, has a playbook that includes not making hostile acquisitions, auditing the accounts of the target company in detail, acquiring companies that will help Tyco achieve critical mass in an industry, moving quickly to realize cost savings after an acquisition, promoting managers one or two layers down to lead the newly acquired entity, and introducing profit-based incentive pay systems in the acquired unit. UTC's playbook includes only buying manufacturing companies where it can apply its ACE skills, insisting that managers from the top down work hard to put these ACE principles into practice, evaluating and rewarding these managers on their ability to do so, and divesting companies that are developing a weak competitive position because of powerful buyers or some other competitive force. Nevertheless, experience alone does not guarantee success, and it is important for managers to always perform postacquisition audits and review what worked and what did not and how things might be improved next time.[37]

Entry Strategy: Joint Ventures

Joint ventures are not used as much as acquisitions and internal new ventures to establish business units in another industry. Rather, they are used to strengthen the business models of a company's existing divisions, such as when Sony formed an alliance with Samsung to work together to become dominant partners in the flat-screen LCD industry. However, suppose a company is contemplating a new internal venture to establish a business unit in an embryonic or growth industry. Such a move involves substantial risks and costs because the company must establish the set of value-chain activities needed to operate in that new market. In this situation a joint venture might be the right strategy because it allows a company to share the risks and costs associated with establishing the new business unit, especially when the companies share *complementary* skills or distinctive competencies. A joint venture with another company may increase the probability of success.

Consider the 50/50 equity joint venture between UTC and Dow Chemical to build plastic-based composite parts for the aerospace industry. UTC was already involved in the aerospace industry (it builds Sikorsky helicopters), and Dow Chemical had skills in the development and manufacture of plastic-based composites. The alliance called for UTC to contribute its advanced aerospace skills and Dow to contribute its skills in developing and manufacturing plastic-based composites. Through the venture, both companies would become involved in new activities and would be able to realize the benefits associated with related diversification without having to merge their activities into one company or bear the costs and risks of developing new products on their own. Thus both companies would enjoy the value-creating benefits of entering a new market without having to bear the increased bureaucratic costs.

Although in some situations joint ventures can benefit both companies, they have three main drawbacks. First, a joint venture allows companies to share the risks and costs of developing a new business, but it also requires that they share in the profits if it succeeds. Then, if one company's skills are more important, it will have to "give away" profits to the other party because of the 50/50 agreement. This can create conflict and sour the working relationship as time goes on. Second, the joint venture partners may have different business philosophies, time horizons, or investment preferences, and so once again substantial problems can arise. Conflicts over how to run the joint venture can tear it apart and result in business failure.

Third, a company that enters into a joint venture always runs the risk of giving critical know-how away to its partner, which might then take that know-how and use it to compete with the other partner in the future. For example, having gained access to Dow's expertise in plastic-based composites, UTC might have dissolved the alliance and produced these materials on its own. As discussed earlier, such a risk can be minimized if Dow gets a *credible commitment* from UTC, which is what it did. UTC had to invest in asset-specific investments to make the products the joint venture was formed to create.

In sum, when deciding whether to go it alone and internally venture a new business unit or cooperate with another company in a joint venture, strategic managers need to assess the pros and cons of the alternatives carefully. While joint ventures allow companies to share risks and returns in changing environments, how much the joint venture will benefit one company versus another is unclear. Today, as in the Sony example, joint ventures are probably most useful when companies need to cooperate to improve the quality or reduce the cost of components, such as LCD screens. They might both use the same screen in their final products, but ultimately the company that can design the product that customers want to buy will become the market leader.

Restructuring

Many companies expand into new markets and industries to increase profitability; however, sometimes they also need to exit markets and industries to achieve the same goal. **Restructuring**, the process of divesting businesses and exiting industries to focus on core distinctive competencies, has become an increasingly popular strategy.[38] Why are so many companies restructuring, and what are the strategies they use to exit markets and industries?

■ Why Restructure?

One main reason that diversified companies have restructured in recent years is that the stock market has valued their stock at a **diversification discount,** meaning that the stock of highly diversified companies is valued lower, relative to their earnings, than the stock of less diversified enterprises.[39] Investors see highly diversified companies as less attractive investments for four reasons. First, as we discuss earlier, investors often feel these companies do not have a multibusiness model that justifies their participation in many different industries; companies like UTC may be the exception rather than the norm. Second, the complexity of the consolidated financial statements of highly diversified enterprises does not provide good evidence of how the individual business units in the company are performing and thus whether the multibusiness model is succeeding for the reasons that the company claims. As a result, investors perceive the company as being riskier than companies that operate in one industry, whose competitive advantage and financial statements are more easily understood. In these cases restructuring can be an attempt to boost the returns to shareholders by splitting up the multibusiness company into separate and independent parts.

The third reason for the diversification discount is that many investors have learned from experience that managers often have a tendency to pursue too much diversification, or diversify for the wrong reasons: they may pursue growth for its own sake, rather than diversify for greater profitability.[40] Some top managers are empire builders: they cannot be trusted not to expand the scope of their company beyond that point where the additional value created by the diversification exceeds its bureaucratic costs. Restructuring is thus a response to declining financial performance.

A final factor leading to restructuring is that innovations in strategic management have diminished the advantages of vertical integration or diversification. For example, a few decades ago there was little understanding of how long-term cooperative relationships, or strategic alliances, between a company and its suppliers could be a viable alternative to vertical integration. Most companies considered only two alternatives for managing the supply chain: vertical integration or competitive bidding. As we discuss in Chapter 9, in many situations long-term cooperative relationships can create the most value, especially because they avoid the need to incur bureaucratic costs or dispense with market discipline. As this strategic innovation has spread throughout the business world, the relative advantages of vertical integration have declined.

Summary of Chapter

1. Managers often first consider diversification when their company is generating free cash flow, which are financial resources in excess of those necessary to maintain a competitive advantage in the company's original, or core, business.

2. A diversified company can create value by (a) transferring competencies among existing businesses, (b) leveraging competencies to create new businesses, (c) sharing resources to realize economies of scope, (d) using product bundling, (e) using diversification as a means of managing rivalry in one or more industries, and (f) exploiting general organizational competencies that enhance the performance of all business units within a diversified company. The bureaucratic costs of diversification are a function of the number of independent business units within the company and the extent of coordination between those business units.

3. Diversification motivated by a desire to pool risks or achieve greater growth is often associated with the dissipation of value.

4. There are three vehicles that companies use to enter new business areas: internal ventures, acquisition, and joint ventures.

5. Internal new venturing is typically employed as an entry strategy when a company has a set of valuable competencies in its existing businesses that can be leveraged or recombined to enter the new business area.

6. Many internal ventures fail because of entry on too small a scale, poor commercialization, and poor corporate management of the internal venture process. Guarding against failure involves a structured approach toward project selection and management, integration of R&D and marketing to improve commercialization of a venture idea, and entry on a significant scale.

7. Acquisitions are often favored as an entry strategy when the company lacks important competencies (resources and capabilities) required to compete in an area, but it can purchase an incumbent company that has those competencies and do so at a reasonable price. Acquisitions also tend to be favored when the barriers to entry into the target industry are high and the company is unwilling to accept the time frame, development costs, and risks of internal new venturing.

8. Many acquisitions fail because of poor postacquisition integration, overestimation of the value that can be created from an acquisition, the high cost of acquisition, and poor preacquisition screening. Guarding against acquisition failure requires structured screening, good bidding strategies, positive attempts to integrate the acquired company into the organization of the acquiring one, and learning from experience.

9. Joint ventures may be the preferred entry strategy when (a) the risks and costs associated with setting up a new business unit are more than the company is willing to assume on its own and (b) the company can increase the probability of successfully establishing a new business by teaming up with another company that has skills and assets complementing its own.

10. Restructuring is often a response to (a) an inadequate multibusiness model, (b) the complexity of consolidated financial statements, (c) excessive diversification due to top managers' empire building, and (c) innovations in the strategic management process that have reduced the advantages of vertical integration and diversification.

Discussion Questions

1. When is a company likely to choose related diversification and when unrelated diversification? Discuss with reference to an electronics manufacturer and an ocean shipping company.

2. Under what circumstances might it be best to enter a new business area by acquisition, and under what circumstances might internal new venturing be the preferred entry mode?

3. Imagine that IBM has decided to diversify into the cellular telecommunication provider business. What entry strategy would you recommend that the company pursue? Why?

4. Look at Honeywell's portfolio of businesses (described in Honeywell's 10-K statements, which can be accessed on the Web at **www.honeywell.com**). How many different industries is Honeywell involved in? Would you describe Honeywell as a related or unrelated diversification company? How do you think that Honeywell's diversification strategy increases profitability?

 # Practicing Strategic Management

■ SMALL-GROUP EXERCISE
Dun & Bradstreet

Break into small groups of three to five people, and discuss the following scenario. Appoint one group member as a spokesperson who will communicate your findings to the class. Then read the following news release from Dun & Bradstreet. On the basis of this information, identify the strategic rationale for the split and evaluate how the split might affect the performance of the three successor companies. If you were a stockholder in the old Dun & Bradstreet Corporation, would you approve of this split? Why?

Dun & Bradstreet CEO Robert E. Weissman today announced a sweeping strategy that will transform the 155-year-old business information giant into three publicly traded, global corporations. "This important action is designed to increase shareholder value by unlocking D&B's substantial underlying franchise strengths," said Weissman.

Building on preeminent Dun & Bradstreet businesses, the reorganization establishes three independent companies focused on high-growth information markets; financial information services; and consumer-product market research.

"Since the 1800s, D&B has grown by effectively managing a portfolio of businesses and gaining economies of scale," stated Weissman. "But the velocity of change in information markets has dramatically altered the rules of business survival. Today, market focus and speed are the primary drivers of competitive advantage. This plan is our blueprint for success in the 21st century," said Weissman.

The plan, approved today at a special meeting of D&B's board of directors, calls for D&B to create three separate companies by spinning off two of its businesses to shareholders. "D&B is the leader in business information," said Weissman. "By freeing our companies to tightly focus on our core vertical markets, we can more rapidly leverage this leadership position into emerging growth areas." The three new companies are:

- Cognizant Corporation, a new high-growth company, including IMS International, the leading global supplier of marketing information to the pharmaceutical and healthcare industries; Nielsen Media Research, the leader in audience measurement for electronic media; and Gartner Group, the premier provider of advisory services to high-tech users, vendors and suppliers, in which Cognizant will hold a majority interest.
- The Dun & Bradstreet Corporation, consisting of Dun & Bradstreet Information Services, the world's largest source of business-to-business marketing and commercial-credit information; Moody's Investors Service, a global leader in rating debt; and Reuben H. Donnelley, a premier provider of Yellow Pages marketing and publishing.
- A. C. Nielsen, the global leader in marketing information for the fast-moving consumer packaged goods industry.

"These three separate companies will tailor their strategies to the unique demands of their markets, determining investments, capital structures and policies that will strengthen their respective global capabilities. This plan also clarifies D&B from an investor's perspective by grouping the businesses into three logical investment categories, each with distinct risk/reward profiles," said Weissman.

The Dun & Bradstreet Corporation is the world's largest marketer of information, software and services for business decision-making, with worldwide revenue of $4.9 billion in 1994.

■ ARTICLE FILE 10

Find an example of a diversified company that made an acquisition that apparently failed to create any value. Identify and critically evaluate the rationale that top management used to justify the acquisition when it was made. Explain why the acquisition subsequently failed.

■ STRATEGIC MANAGEMENT PROJECT
Module 10

This module requires you to assess your company's use of acquisitions, internal new ventures, and joint ventures as strategies for entering a new business area or as attempts to restructure its portfolio of businesses.

A. Your company has entered a new industry during the past decade.
1. Pick one new industry that your company has entered during the past ten years.
2. Identify the rationale for entering this industry.
3. Identify the strategy used to enter this industry.
4. Evaluate the rationale for using this particular entry strategy. Do you think that this was the best entry strategy to use? Justify your answer.
5. Do you think that the addition of this business unit to the company has added or dissipated value? Again, justify your answer.

B. Your company has restructured its corporate portfolio during the past decade.
1. Identify the rationale for pursuing a restructuring strategy.
2. Pick one industry that your company has exited from during the past ten years.
3. Identify the strategy used to exit from this particular industry. Do you think that this was the best exit strategy to use? Justify your answer.
4. In general, do you think that exiting from this industry has been in the company's best interest?

■ EXPLORING THE WEB
Visiting General Electric

Visit the website of General Electric Company of the United States (**www.ge.com**). Using the information contained on that website, answer the following questions.
1. Review GE's portfolio of major businesses. Does this portfolio make sense from a value creation perspective? Why?
2. What (if any) changes would you make to GE's portfolio of businesses? Why would you make these changes?
3. What (if any) core competencies do you think are held in common by one or more of GE's major business units? Is there any evidence that GE creates new business units by leveraging its core competencies?

General Task By searching through information sources on the Web, find an example of a company that has recently restructured its portfolio of businesses. Identify and evaluate the strategic rationale behind this restructuring to determine whether it makes sense.

Closing Case

Tyco International

Tyco International has been one of the great growth stories of the past decade. Under the leadership of Dennis Kozlowski, who became CEO in 1992, Tyco's sales expanded from $3.1 billion in 1992 to $38 billion in 2001, when it earned some $5.12 billion in after-tax profits. Much of this growth was driven by acquisitions that took Tyco into a diverse range of businesses, including medical supplies, security equipment, electronic components, plastics, financial services, and telecommunications. Between 1996 and 2001, Tyco spent some $45 billion in cash (much of it raised from debt offerings) and stock to purchase more than one hundred companies. With the acquisitions fueling growth, Tyco's earnings expanded by 35 percent each year between 1996 and 2001.

Tyco's success has been attributed to the consistent application of a business model that comprises a number of elements. First, although the company is diversified, it seeks to attain a critical mass in the industries in which it competes. Through acquisitions, it has become one of the largest providers of security systems, basic medical supplies, and electronic components in the United States. Indeed, it sees itself as using acquisitions to consolidate fragmented industries and attain economies of scale, which give it a cost-based advantage over smaller rivals. Second, the company *never* makes hostile acquisitions, which would be too expensive and could result in bad feelings among the managers of an acquired company. Third, Tyco deliberately seeks out companies that make basic products that have a strong market franchise but have been underperforming relative to their peers in recent years. Tyco's management believes that this indicates there is substantial room for improvement. Once it identifies a potential target, Tyco approaches management to see if they are interested in backing a sale of the company. If they express interest in supporting an acquisition, Tyco sends in teams of independent auditors to carefully go through the books of the target and identify the potential for improving performance. If the target company has potential, Tyco makes a formal bid. As a precondition of the bid, the top managers of the target company normally agree to step down (with a substantial severance package). Tyco typically replaces them with up-and-coming managers two or three layers below.

Once an acquisition has been completed, Tyco sets to work improving the performance of the acquired unit. Typically excess capacity is shut down, corporate overhead slashed, unprofitable product lines sold off or discontinued, plants and sales forces merged with those of similar operations within Tyco to attain scale economies, and head count reduced. For example, in 1999, Tyco acquired AMP, the world's largest manufacturer of electronic components, for $12 billion in Tyco stock. Within months, Tyco had identified close to $1 billion in cost savings that could be implemented by 2002 by closing unprofitable plants and reducing the work force by 8,000. On average, Tyco finds cost savings in an acquisition that amount to about 11 percent of the target company's revenues.

In addition to taking excess costs out of a newly acquired company, Tyco gives the employees of the acquired unit incentives to boost profitability. No bonuses are paid to anyone at Tyco unless annual net income growth exceeds 10 percent. However, bonuses quickly ramp up for each increment above that minimum and are unlimited for senior managers. In the best years, senior managers receive bonuses that are multiples of their salaries, supervisors at the plant level can receive cash or stock options worth as much as 40 percent of their salary, and hourly factory workers receive two to three weeks of extra pay.

Tyco's corporate structure is also very lean. While he was CEO, Kozlowski ran operations on an arm's-length basis, and this approach is still used. There are only seventy employees at the head office, most of whom focus on tax and legal issues. Performance goals for the coming year are set by negotiation between top management and the management of operating units. Once targets are set, the policy is one of management by exception, with operating managers being given considerable autonomy so long as they hit or exceed their targets.

Despite Tyco's impressive track record, the stock price underperformed the general market during much of 1998–2001. The stock was given a "diversification discount" by investors, who were put off by the complexity of Tyco's financial accounts and the lack of transparency with regard to the profitability of individual operations. In 1999, Tyco was the target of criticism by analysts who accused the company of inappropriate accounting methods. However, a subsequent investigation by the Securities and Exchange Commission gave Tyco's accounting practices a clean bill of health. Despite this, the criticisms persisted, and in late 2001 the company came under renewed attack from critics who argued that it had systematically inflated its profitability to make its performance look better than it actually was. According to the critics, the management at several companies Tyco acquired all artificially depressed the profitability of their companies in the final months before the deals were completed. This was done by taking numerous charges, slowing sales, and pushing up expenses. Consequently, Tyco's operating results were "spring-loaded" for a quarter or two after the acquisition closed as sales and profit margins suddenly expanded. They also argued that the debt that Tyco had taken on to finance some of its acquisitions, which by early 2002 totaled some $23 billion, left the company excessively leveraged and potentially vulnerable should cash flow projections fall short.

Tyco dismissed the charges of accounting tricks and pointed out that it would generate over $4 billion in free cash flow during 2002, more than enough to cover all of its short-term debt commitments. Nevertheless, the attacks persisted, and the stock price slid to under $20 by May 2002. To try to halt the slide, Kozlowski floated a number of ideas, including splitting up the company into four independent units and selling off its plastics and financial services unit, then using the proceeds to pay down the company's debt. However, with none of these ideas seeming to help the stock price, Kozlowski ultimately stated that he would continue to run the company as a diversified entity and focus on generating cash flow to pay down the company's debt load. Tyco would sell off some of its acquired businesses,

but only if it could get a decent price for them, and it would use the proceeds to pay down debt. Whatever the ultimate outcome, it seems clear that after a decade of success, investors had turned sour on Tyco's business model, recognizing, belatedly perhaps, that Tyco's growth had been bought at the price of accumulating tremendous debt.

To complicate matters, in June 2002 Kozlowski resigned after being charged with tax evasion. He was replaced by John Fort, Tyco's CEO between 1982 and 1992. One of Fort's first actions was to complete a spinoff of CIT Group, Tyco's finance arm, for $4.6 billion, significantly less than the $11 billion Tyco had paid to acquire CIT in 2000. With this cash in hand, however, Tyco appeared to have enough funds to service its debt commitments, and since the company continued to generate positive cash flow, its survival seemed assured.[41]

Case Discussion Questions

1. What kind of corporate-level strategy is Tyco pursuing? What is Tyco's multibusiness model, and in what ways could it create value?
2. What are the dangers and disadvantages of this business model?
3. Collect some recent information on Tyco from sources like Yahoo! Finance. How successful has it been in pursuing its strategy?

Chapter 11

Corporate Performance, Governance, and Business Ethics

Opening Case

Nike: The Sweatshop Debate

Nike is in many ways the quintessential global corporation. Established in 1972 by former University of Oregon track star Phil Knight, Nike is now one of the leading marketers of athletic shoes and apparel in the world. By 2004 the company had more than $12 billion in annual revenues, had a return on invested capital of 17.5 percent, and sold its products in some 140 countries. Nike does not do any manufacturing. Rather, it designs and markets its products and contracts for their manufacture from a global network of 600 factories owned by subcontractors scattered around the globe that together employ some 550,000 people. This huge corporation has made founder Phil Knight into one of the richest people in America. Nike's marketing phrase, "Just Do It!" has become as recognizable in popular culture as its "swoosh" logo or the faces of its celebrity sponsors, such as Tiger Woods.

For all of its successes, the company has been dogged for more than a decade by repeated and persistent accusations that its products are made in "sweatshops" where workers, many of them children, slave away in hazardous conditions for wages that are below subsistence level. Nike's wealth, its detractors claim, has been built upon the backs of the world's poor. Many see Nike as a symbol of the evils of globalization: a rich Western corporation exploiting the world's poor to provide expensive shoes and apparel to the pampered consumers of the developed world. Nike's "Niketown" stores have become standard targets for antiglobalization protestors. Several nongovernmental organizations, such as San Francisco–based Global Exchange, a human rights organization dedicated to promoting environmental, political, and social justice around the world, have targeted Nike for repeated criticism and protests. News organizations such as CBS's *48 Hours*, hosted by Dan Rather, have run exposés on working conditions in foreign factories that supply Nike. And students on the campuses of several major U.S. universities with which Nike has lucrative sponsorship deals have protested against those deals, citing Nike's use of sweatshop labor.

Typical of the allegations were those detailed in the CBS news program *48 Hours* in 1996. The report painted a picture of young women at a Vietnamese subcontractor who worked six days a week, in poor working conditions with toxic materials, for only 20 cents an hour. The report also stated that a living wage in Vietnam was at least $3 a day, an income that could not be achieved without working substantial overtime. Nike was not breaking any laws, and nor were its subcontractors, but this report and others like it raised questions about the ethics of using "sweatshop labor" to make what were essentially fashion accessories. It may have been legal, it may have helped the company to increase its profitability, but was it ethical to use subcontractors who by Western standards clearly exploited their work force? Nike's critics thought not, and the company found itself the focus of a wave of demonstrations and consumer boycotts.

Adding fuel to the fire, in November 1997 Global Exchange obtained and leaked a confidential report by Ernst & Young of an audit that Nike had commissioned of a Vietnam factory owned by a Nike subcontractor. The factory had 9,200 workers and made 400,000 pairs of shoes a month. The Ernst & Young report painted a dismal picture of thousands of young women, most under age twenty-five, laboring ten and a half hours a day, six days a week, in excessive heat and noise and foul air, for slightly more than $10 a week. The report also found that workers with skin or breathing problems had not been transferred to departments free of chemicals. More than half the workers who dealt with dangerous chemicals did not wear protective masks or gloves. The report stated that in parts of the plant workers were exposed to carcinogens that exceeded local legal standards by 177 times and that 77 percent of the employees suffered from respiratory problems.

These exposés surrounding Nike's use of subcontractors forced the company to reexamine its policies. Realizing that its subcontracting policies were perceived as unethical, Nike's management took a number of steps. These included establishing a code of conduct for Nike subcontractors and setting up a scheme whereby all subcontractors would be monitored annually by independent auditors. Nike's code of conduct required that all employees at footwear factories be at least eighteen years old and that exposure to potentially toxic materials would not exceed the permissible exposure limits established by the U.S. Occupational Safety and Health Administration (OSHA) for workers in the United States. In short, Nike concluded that behaving ethically required going beyond the requirements of the law. It required the establishment and enforcement of rules that adhere to accepted moral principles of right and wrong.[1]

Overview

The Nike story detailed in the *Opening Case* is an important one because it illustrates what should be a cardinal principle of business: that the quest to maximize profitability should be constrained not just by the law but also by ethical obligations. In Chapter 1 we note that the goal of managers should be to pursue strategies that maximize long-run shareholder value, but we also note that managers *must* behave in an ethical and socially responsible manner when pursuing this goal.

In this chapter we take a close look at the governance mechanisms that shareholders put in place to make sure that managers are acting in their interests, that is, pursuing strategies that maximize shareholder value. But we also discuss how managers need to pay attention to other stakeholders as well, such as employees, suppliers, and customers. Balancing the needs of different stakeholder groups is in the long-run interests of the company's owners, its shareholders. Good governance mechanisms recognize this truth. In addition, we will spend some time discussing the ethical implications of strategic decisions, and we will discuss how managers can make sure that their strategic decisions are founded on strong ethical principles.

Stakeholders and Corporate Performance

A company's **stakeholders** are individuals or groups with an interest, claim, or stake in the company, in what it does, and in how well it performs.[2] They include stockholders, creditors, employees, customers, the communities in which the company does business, and the general public. Stakeholders can be divided into internal stakeholders and external stakeholders (see Figure 11.1). **Internal stakeholders** are stockholders and employees, including executive officers, other managers, and board members. **External stakeholders** are all other individuals and groups that have some claim on the company. Typically, this group comprises customers, suppliers, creditors (including banks and bondholders), governments, unions, local communities, and the general public.

All stakeholders are in an exchange relationship with the company. Each of the stakeholder groups listed in Figure 11.1 supplies the organization with important

FIGURE 11.1
Stakeholders and the
Enterprise

resources (or contributions), and in exchange each expects its interests to be satisfied (by inducements).[3] Stockholders provide the enterprise with risk capital and in exchange expect management to try to maximize the return on their investment. Creditors, and particularly bondholders, also provide the company with capital in the form of debt, and they expect to be repaid on time with interest. Employees provide labor and skills and in exchange expect commensurate income, job satisfaction, job security, and good working conditions. Customers provide a company with its revenues and in exchange want high-quality reliable products that represent value for money. Suppliers provide a company with inputs and in exchange seek revenues and dependable buyers. Governments provide a company with rules and regulations that govern business practice and maintain fair competition. In exchange they want companies that adhere to these rules. Unions help to provide a company with productive employees, and in exchange they want benefits for their members in proportion to their contributions to the company. Local communities provide companies with local infrastructure and in exchange want companies that are responsible citizens. The general public provides companies with national infrastructure and in exchange seeks some assurance that the quality of life will be improved as a result of the company's existence.

A company must take these claims into account when formulating its strategies, or else stakeholders may withdraw their support. For example, stockholders may sell their shares, bondholders may demand higher interest payments on new bonds, employees may leave their jobs, and customers may buy elsewhere. Suppliers may seek more dependable buyers. Unions may engage in disruptive labor disputes. Government may take civil or criminal action against the company and its top officers, imposing fines and in some cases jail terms. Communities may oppose the company's attempts to locate its facilities in their area, and the general public may form pressure groups, demanding action against companies that impair the quality of life. Any of these reactions can have a damaging impact on an enterprise. A detailed example is given in Strategy in Action 11.1, which looks at how Bill Agee, the former CEO of Morrison Knudsen, lost his job because the strategies he pursued failed to satisfy the interests of two important stakeholder groups: the company's employees and its stockholders.

■ **Stakeholder**
Impact Analysis

A company cannot always satisfy the claims of all stakeholders. The goals of different groups may conflict, and in practice few organizations have the resources to manage all stakeholders.[4] For example, union claims for higher wages can conflict with consumer demands for reasonable prices and stockholder demands for acceptable returns. Often the company must make choices. To do so, it must identify the most

Strategy in Action

Bill Agee at Morrison Knudsen

11.1

Bill Agee made his name as a whiz kid who became the chief financial officer of paper maker Boise Cascade during the 1970s while he was in his early thirties. He left Boise Cascade after the company was forced to write down its profits by $250 million because of earlier overstatements of the value of timberland sales. At the time, the write-downs were the largest in corporate history, but this did not stop Agee from being appointed CEO of defense contractor Bendix in 1976 when he was only thirty-eight years old. At Bendix, Agee became involved in a famous corporate soap opera that began when he promoted a young manager, Mary Cunningham, to a senior post over the heads of many other more experienced executives. At the time, many felt the promotion occurred because the two were romantically involved. Both denied this, but in 1982 Agee divorced his wife and married Cunningham, who by this time had left Bendix.

In 1988, Agee became CEO of Idaho-based Morrison Knudsen (MK), a seventy-five-year-old construction company that had made its name as the prime contractor on a number of large western construction projects, including the Hoover Dam and the Trans Alaska pipeline. By the time Agee joined the company, MK was perceived as a venerable institution that wasn't quite living up to its performance potential. Agee's strategy for improving performance was to sell off certain of MK's assets and invest the proceeds in the securities of other companies. At the same time, he pushed MK to pursue large construction projects aggressively and to develop its rail car manufacturing business. At one time, the rail car manufacturing business had been a major success story at MK, but it had fallen on hard times, unable to hold its own in the face of aggressive competition.

On the surface, MK appeared to be prospering under Agee's leadership. In 1993, MK earned $35.8 million, and Agee proclaimed it a "banner year" and a "watershed period" for the company's drive into railroad and mass transit industries. Underneath the surface, however, things were unraveling for Bill Agee. For one thing, 62 percent of MK's profits in 1993 came from Agee's financial plays in securities trading and capital gains on asset sales. Strip out these one-time gains, and it was clear that the operating performance of MK was poor. A prime reason seems to have been Agee's insistence that, in order to win new business,

MK should be the low bidder on large contracts. For instance, when MK bid on a contract to build eighty transit cars for the Bay Area Rapid Transit District (BART) in Oakland, California, Agee knocked down the bid to $142 million. According to one insider, the result was that "we were looking at a $14 million loss on the contract the day we won it." In the second quarter of 1994, MK announced a $40.5 million loss after taking a $59.4 million charge for underbidding various transit car contracts. Similarly, in the third quarter of 1994, MK took a $9.2 million charge against profits for underbidding on a $100 million contract to rebuild locomotives for Southern Pacific.

To compound matters, there had been significant employee opposition to Agee's leadership. An anonymous letter sent to MK's board in November 1994 by a group of MK executives calling themselves the MK Committee for Excellence leveled a large number of charges at Agee. They claimed that Agee irked subordinates immediately by removing the portrait of MK's founder from the headquarters and replacing it with a nearly life-sized portrait of himself and his wife, Mary Cunningham, paid for by the company. Agee further estranged insiders by quietly moving the CEO's office to his Pebble Beach estate in California and by scoffing at the company's engineering-oriented culture. Several old-hand MK engineering executives, who had top reputations in their field, were fired, usually after crossing swords with Agee over his policies.

There was also the matter of Agee's pay and perks. At $2.4 million, Agee's 1993 compensation was equal to 6.8 percent of MK's net income, more than any other CEO of a company with earnings in that range, according to a *Forbes* magazine list. According to insiders, MK paid $4 million a year for a corporate jet for Agee, equal to 13 percent of the company's general and administrative budget. The company also paid for landscaping services at Agee's Pebble Beach estate.

Things came to a head on February 1, 1995, when MK's board announced that the company would record a large loss for 1994. The board also announced that Agee would be stepping down as CEO, although initial indications were that he would stay on as chairman of the board. Preliminary figures suggested that MK would have to take a $179.6 million pretax charge in its 1994 fourth quarter, which would result in a net loss of $141 million for the quarter. At the same time, Standard & Poor's downgraded MK's long-term debt to junk bond rating, signaling that a significant risk of default existed.

The announcement gave rise to a blizzard of shareholder lawsuits and criticism, not only of Agee, but also of MK's board for acting so slowly. Many commentators wondered why it took a huge loss and an anonymous letter from MK employees to prod the board into action. Privately, several board members, most of whom were appointees and long-time friends of Agee, indicated that they were led astray by Agee, who repeatedly urged them not to worry about poor results. Still, many felt that the audit committee of the board of directors had not done a good job of vetting MK's financial accounts under Agee's

leadership. Stung by this criticism, the growing evidence of financial mismanagement under Agee's leadership, and the downgrade of MK's debt by Standard & Poor's, the board reversed its earlier position and decided to strip Agee of all posts at MK.

The shareholder lawsuits were settled in September 1995. Under the agreement, MK was to pay out $63 million in cash and stock to shareholders. The settlement also required the company to strengthen its board by adding seven new directors over the next two years. As part of the settlement, Agee agreed to relinquish rights to about $3 million in severance pay and to a cut in his MK pension from $303,000 a year for life to $99,750 a year for life.[a]

important stakeholders and give highest priority to pursuing strategies that satisfy their needs. Stakeholder impact analysis can provide such identification. Typically, stakeholder impact analysis follows these steps:

1. Identify stakeholders.

2. Identify stakeholders' interests and concerns.

3. As a result, identify what claims stakeholders are likely to make on the organization.

4. Identify the stakeholders who are most important from the organization's perspective.

5. Identify the resulting strategic challenges.[5]

Such an analysis enables a company to identify the stakeholders most critical to its survival and to make sure that the satisfaction of their needs is paramount. Most companies that have gone through this process quickly come to the conclusion that three stakeholder groups must be satisfied above all others if a company is to survive and prosper: customers, employees, and stockholders. Bill Agee, for example, lost his position because he failed to satisfy the demands of stockholders for a good return on their investment and the demands of employees for income, job satisfaction, job security, and good working conditions. More generally, companies that fail to satisfy the needs of their customers soon see their revenues fall and ultimately go out of business. Interestingly, Agee probably was satisfying the needs of customers because he was insisting on low prices; however, at the prices Agee was requiring, Morrison Knudsen could not possibly have been profitable.

■ The Unique Role of Stockholders

A company's stockholders are usually put in a different class from other stakeholder groups, and for good reason. Stockholders are legal owners and the providers of risk capital, a major source of the capital resources that allow a company to operate its business. The capital that stockholders provide to a company is seen as **risk capital** because there is no guarantee that stockholders will ever recoup their investment and or earn a decent return.

Recent history demonstrates all too clearly the nature of risk capital. Many investors who bought shares in companies that went public during the late 1990s and early 2000s through an initial public offering (IPO) subsequently saw the value of their holdings decline to zero, or something close to it. For example, in early 2000, Oniva.com, a provider of an online business-to-business marketplace aimed at small businesses, went public. On the first day of trading, the shares hit $25. They fell steadily afterward, and two years later, having lost 99 percent of their value, they were trading at $0.25, effectively wiping out the investment many made in the company. Of course, there are also some spectacular successes: investors who purchased shares of Dell, Microsoft, or Intel at their IPO have done extraordinarily well. But this is the nature of risk capital: the variance of returns is very high. To reward stockholders for providing the company with risk capital, management is obligated to pursue strategies that maximize the returns that stockholders get from their investment in the company's stock.

Over the past decade, maximizing returns to stockholders has taken on added importance as more and more employees have themselves become stockholders in the company for which they work through an employee stock ownership plan (ESOP). At Wal-Mart, for example, all employees who have served for more than one year are eligible for the company's ESOP. Under an ESOP, employees are given the opportunity to purchase stock in their company, sometimes at a discount to the market value of the stock. The company may also contribute to a certain proportion of the purchase price. By making employees stockholders, ESOPs tend to increase the already strong emphasis on maximizing returns to stockholders, for they now help to satisfy two key stakeholder groups: stockholders and employees.

■ Profitability, Profit Growth, and Stakeholder Claims

Because of the unique position assigned to stockholders, managers normally seek to pursue strategies that maximize the returns that stockholders receive from holding shares in the company. As we noted in Chapter 1, stockholders receive a return on their investment in a company's stock in two ways: from dividend payments and from capital appreciation in the market value of a share (that is, by increases in stock market prices). The best way for managers to generate the funds for future dividend payments and to keep the stock price appreciating is for them to pursue strategies that maximize the company's long-run profitability (as measured by the return on invested capital or ROIC) and grow the profits of the company over time.[6]

As we saw in Chapter 3, ROIC is an excellent measure of the profitability of a company. It tells managers how efficiently they are using the capital resources of the company (including the risk capital provided by stockholders) to generate profits. A company that is generating a positive ROIC is covering all of its ongoing expenses and has money left over, which is then added to shareholders' equity, thereby increasing the value of a company and thus the value of a share of stock in the company. The value of each share will increase further if a company can grow its profits over time, because then the profit that is attributable to every share (that is, the company's earning per share) will also grow. As we have seen in this book, to grow their profits companies must be doing one or more of the following: (a) participating in a market that is growing, (b) taking market share from competitors, (c) consolidating the industry through horizontal integration, and (d) developing new markets through international expansion, vertical integration, or diversification.

While managers should strive for profit growth if they are trying to maximize shareholder value, the relationship between profitability and profit growth is a complex one because attaining future profit growth may require investments that reduce the current rate of profitability. The task of managers is to find the right balance between profitability and profit growth.[7] Too much emphasis on current profitability at the expense of future profitability and profit growth can make an enterprise less attractive to shareholders. Too much emphasis on profit growth can reduce the profitability of the enterprise and have the same effect. In an uncertain world where the future is unknowable, finding the right balance between profitability and profit growth is certainly as much art as it is science, but it is something that managers must try to do.

In addition to maximizing returns to stockholders, boosting a company's profitability and profit growth rate is also consistent with satisfying the claims of several other key stakeholder groups. When a company is profitable and its profits are growing, it can pay higher salaries to productive employees and can also afford benefits such as health insurance coverage, all of which help to satisfy employees. In addition, companies with a high level of profitability and profit growth have no problem meeting their debt commitments, which provides creditors, including bondholders, with a measure of security. More profitable companies are also better able to undertake philanthropic investments, which can help to satisfy some of the claims that local communities and the general public place on a company. Pursuing strategies that maximize the long-run profitability and profit growth of the company is therefore generally consistent with satisfying the claims of various stakeholder groups.

There is an important cause-and-effect relationship here. It is pursuing strategies to maximize profitability and profit growth that helps a company to better satisfy the demands that several stakeholder groups place on it, not the other way around. The company that overpays its employees in the current period, for example, may have very happy employees for a short while, but such action will raise the company's cost structure and limit its ability to attain a competitive advantage in the marketplace, thereby depressing its long-run profitability and hurting its ability to award future pay increases. As far as employees are concerned, the way many companies deal with this situation is to make future pay increases contingent on improvements in labor productivity. If labor productivity goes up, labor costs as a percentage of revenues will fall, profitability will rise, and the company can afford to pay its employees more and offer greater benefits.

Of course, not all stakeholder groups want the company to maximize its long-run profitability and profit growth. Suppliers are more comfortable about selling goods and services to profitable companies because they can be assured that the company will have the funds to pay for those products. Similarly, customers may be more willing to purchase from profitable companies because they can be assured that those companies will be around in the long run to provide after-sales services and support. But neither suppliers nor customers want the company to maximize its profitability *at their expense*. Rather, they would like to capture some of these profits from the company in the form of higher prices for their goods and services (in the case of suppliers) or lower prices for the products they purchase from the company (in the case of customers). Thus, the company is in a bargaining relationship with some of its stakeholders, which was a phenomenon we discussed in Chapter 2.

Moreover, despite the argument that maximizing long-run profitability and profit growth is the best way to satisfy the claims of several key stakeholder groups, it should be noted that a company must do so within the limits set by the law and in a manner consistent with societal expectations. The unfettered pursuit of profit can lead to behaviors that are outlawed by government regulations, opposed by important public constituencies, or simply unethical. Governments have enacted a wide range of regulations to govern business behavior, including antitrust laws, environmental laws, and laws pertaining to health and safety in the workplace. It is incumbent on managers to make sure that the company is in compliance with these laws when pursuing strategies.

Unfortunately, there is plenty of evidence that managers can be tempted to cross the line between the legal and illegal in their pursuit of greater profitability and profit growth. For example, in mid 2003 the air force stripped Boeing of $1 billion in contracts to launch satellites when it was discovered that Boeing had obtained thousand of pages of proprietary information from rival Lockheed Martin. Boeing had used that information to prepare its winning bid for the satellite contract. This was followed by the revelation that Boeing's CFO, Mike Sears, had offered a government official, Darleen Druyun, a lucrative job at Boeing while Druyun was still involved in evaluating whether Boeing should be awarded a $17 billion contract to build tankers for the air force. Boeing won the contract against strong competition from Airbus, and Druyun was hired by Boeing. It was clear that the job offer may have had an impact on the air force decision. Boeing fired the CFO and Druyun, and shortly afterwards Boeing CEO Phil Condit resigned in a tacit acknowledgment that he bore responsibility for the ethics violations that had occurred at Boeing during his tenure as leader.[8] In another example, the chief executive of Archer Daniels Midland, one of the world's largest producers of agricultural products, was sent to jail after an FBI investigation revealed that the company had systematically tried to fix the price for lysine by colluding with other manufacturers in the global marketplace. In another case of price fixing, the seventy-six-year-old chairman of Sotheby's auction house was sentenced to a jail term and the former CEO to house arrest for fixing prices with rival auction house Christie's over a six-year period (see Strategy in Action 11.2).

Examples such as these beg the question of why managers would engage in such risky behavior. A body of academic work collectively known as agency theory

Strategy in Action   11.2

Price Fixing at Sotheby's and Christie's

Sotheby's and Christie's are the two largest fine art auction houses in the world. In the mid 1990s, the two companies controlled 90 percent of the fine art auction market, which at the time was worth some $4 billion a year. Traditionally, auction houses make their profit by the commission they charge on auction sales. In good times, these commissions can range as high as 10 percent on some items, but in the early 1990s, the auction business was in a slump, with the supply of art for auction drying up. With Sotheby's and Christie's desperate for works of art, sellers played the two houses off against each other, driving commissions down to 2 percent or even lower.

To try to control this situation, Sotheby's CEO, Dede Brooks, met with her opposite number at Christie's, Christopher Davidge, in a series of clandestine meetings held in car parking lots that began in 1993. Brooks claims that she was acting on behalf of her boss, Alfred Taubman, the chairman and controlling shareholder of Sotheby's. According to Brooks, Taubman had agreed with the chairman of Christie's, Anthony Tennant, to work together in the weak auction market and limit price competition. In their meetings, Brooks and Davidge agreed to a fixed and nonnegotiable commission structure. Based on a sliding scale, the commission structure would range from 10 percent on a $100,000 item to 2 percent on a $5 million item. In effect, Brooks and Davidge were agreeing to eliminate price competition between them, thereby guaranteeing both auction houses higher profits. The price-fixing agreement started in 1993 and continued unabated for six years until federal investigators uncovered the arrangement and brought charges against Sotheby's and Christie's.

With the deal out in the open, lawyers filed several class action lawsuits on behalf of sellers who had been defrauded by Sotheby's and Christie's. Ultimately, some 100,000 sellers signed on to the class action lawsuits, which the auction houses settled with a $512 million payment. The auction houses also pleaded guilty to

price fixing and paid $45 million in fines to U.S. antitrust authorities. As for the key players, the chairman of Christie's, as a British subject, was able to avoid prosecution in the United States (price fixing is not an offense for which someone can be extradited). Christie's CEO, Davidge, struck a deal with prosecutors and in return for amnesty handed over incriminating documents to the authorities. Brooks also cooperated with federal prosecutors and avoided jail (in April 2002 she was sentenced to three years' probation, six months' home detention, 1,000 hours of community service, and a $350,000 fine). Taubman, ultimately isolated by all his former co-conspirators, was sentenced to a year in jail and fined $7.5 million.[b]

provides an explanation for why managers might engage in behavior that is either illegal or, at the very least, not in the interest of the company's shareholders.

Agency Theory

Agency theory looks at the problems that can arise in a business relationship when one person delegates decision-making authority to another. It offers a way of understanding why managers do not always act in the best interests of stakeholders and why they might sometimes behave unethically, and perhaps also illegally.[9] Although agency theory was originally formulated to capture the relationship between management and stockholders, the basic principles have also been extended to cover the relationship with other key stakeholders, such as employees, as well as relationships between different layers of management within a corporation.[10] While the focus of attention in this section is on the relationship between senior management and stockholders, some of the same language can be applied to the relationship between other stakeholders and top managers and between top management and lower levels of management.

■ Principal-Agent Relationships

The basic propositions of agency theory are relatively straightforward. First, an **agency relationship** is held to arise whenever one party delegates decision-making authority or control over resources to another. The **principal** is the person delegating authority, and the **agent** is the person to whom authority is delegated. The relationship between stockholders and senior managers is the classic example of an agency relationship. Stockholders, who are the *principals,* provide the company with risk capital, but they delegate control over that capital to senior managers, and particularly the CEO, who as their *agent* is expected to use that capital in a manner that is consistent with the best interests of stockholders. As we have seen, this means using that capital to maximize the company's long-run profitability and profit growth rate.

The agency relationship continues on down within the company. For example, in the large, complex, multibusiness company, top managers cannot possibly make all important decisions, so they delegate some decision-making authority and control over capital resources to business unit (divisional) managers. Thus, just as senior managers such as the CEO are the *agents* of stockholders, business unit managers are the *agents* of the CEO (and in this context, the CEO is the *principal*). The CEO entrusts business unit managers to use the resources over which they have control in the most effective manner so that they maximize the performance of their units, which helps the CEO to make sure that he or she maximizes the performance of the entire company, thereby discharging agency obligation to stockholders. More generally, whenever managers delegate authority to managers below them in the hierarchy and give them the right to control resources, an agency relation is established.

■ **The Agency Problem**

While agency relationships often work well, problems may arise if agents and principals have different goals and if agents take actions that are not in the best interests of their principals. Agents may be able to do this because there is an **information asymmetry** between the principal and the agent: agents almost always have more information about the resources they are managing than the principal does. Unscrupulous agents can take advantage of any information asymmetry to mislead principals and maximize their own interests at the expense of principals.

In the case of stockholders, the information asymmetry arises because they delegate decision-making authority to the CEO, their agent, who by virtue of his or her position inside the company is likely to know far more than stockholders do about the company's operations. Indeed, there may be certain information about the company that the CEO is unwilling to share with stockholders because it would also help competitors. In such a case, withholding some information from stockholders may be in their best interests. More generally, the CEO, involved in the day-to-day running of the company, is bound to have an information advantage over stockholders, just as the CEO's subordinates may well have an information advantage over the CEO with regard to the resources under their control.

The information asymmetry between principals and agents is not necessarily a bad thing, but it can make it difficult for principals to measure how well an agent is performing, and thus hold the agent accountable for how well he or she is using the entrusted resources. There is a certain amount of performance ambiguity inherent in the relationship between a principal and agent: principals cannot know for sure if the agent is acting in his or her best interests. They cannot know for sure if the agent is using the resources to which he or she has been entrusted as effectively and efficiently as possible. To an extent, principals have to *trust* the agent to do the right thing.

Of course, this trust is not blind: principals do put mechanisms in place whose purpose is to monitor agents, evaluate their performance, and if necessary, take corrective action. As we shall see shortly, the board of directors is one such mechanism, for in part the board exists to monitor and evaluate senior managers on behalf of stockholders. Other mechanisms serve a similar purpose. In the United States, publicly owned companies must regularly file detailed financial statements with the Securities and Exchange Commission (SEC) that are in accordance with generally agreed-upon accounting principles (GAAP). This requirement exists to give stockholders consistent and detailed information about how well management is using the capital with which it has been entrusted. Similarly, internal control systems within a company are there to help the CEO make sure that subordinates are using the resources with which they have been entrusted as efficiently and effectively as possible.

Despite the existence of governance mechanisms and comprehensive measurement and control systems, a degree of information asymmetry will always remain between principals and agents, and there is always an element of trust involved in the relationship. Unfortunately, not all agents are worthy of this trust. A minority will deliberately mislead principals for personal gain, sometimes behaving unethically or breaking laws in the process. The interests of principals and agents are not always the same; they diverge, and some agents may take advantage of information asymmetries to maximize their own interests at the expense of principals and to engage in behaviors that the principals would never condone.

For example, some authors have argued that, like many other people, senior managers are motivated by desires for status, power, job security, and income.[11] By virtue of their position within the company, certain managers, such as the CEO, can use their authority and control over corporate funds to satisfy these desires at the cost of returns to stockholders. CEOs might use their position to invest corporate funds in various perks that enhance their status—executive jets, lavish offices, and expense-paid trips to exotic locations—rather than investing those funds in ways that increase stockholder returns. Economists have termed such behavior *on-the-job consumption*.[12] Bill Agee is an example of a CEO who appeared to engage in excessive on-the-job consumption (see Strategy in Action 11.1).

Besides engaging in on-the-job consumption, CEOs, along with other senior managers, might satisfy their desires for greater income by using their influence or control over the board of directors to get the compensation committee of the board to grant pay increases. Critics of U.S. industry claim that extraordinary pay has now become an endemic problem and that senior managers are enriching themselves at the expense of stockholders and other employees. They point out that CEO pay has been increasing far more rapidly than the pay of average workers, primarily because of very liberal stock option grants that enable a CEO to earn huge pay bonuses in a rising stock market, even if the company underperforms the market and competitors.[13] In 1950, when *Business Week* started its annual survey of CEO pay, the highest-paid executive was General Motors CEO Charles Wilson, whose $652,156 pay packet translates into $4.5 million in inflation-adjusted dollars in 2003. In contrast, the highest-paid executive in *Business Week*'s 2003 survey, Reuben Mark of Colgate-Palmolive, earned $141.1 million, primarily from exercising stock options.[14] In 1980, the average CEO in *Business Week*'s survey earned forty-two times what the average blue collar-worker earned. By 1990, this figure had increased to eighty-five times. Today, the average CEO in the survey earns more than two hundred times the pay of the average blue-collar worker.[15]

What rankles critics is the size of some CEO pay packages and their apparent lack of relationship to company performance.[16] In 1998, for example, Disney CEO Michael Eisner earned $575 million, mostly in the form of stock options, despite the fact that Disney did not do particularly well that year and the stock price fell 10 percent. A big gainer in 2001, Jozef Straus, earned $150 million from stock options in a year when the company he serves as CEO, JDS Uniphase, recorded a $50 billion loss related to the writing down of goodwill for companies acquired at premium prices during the booming 1990s. Critics feel that the size of these pay awards was out of all proportion to the achievement of the CEOs.[17] If so, this represents a clear example of the agency problem.

A further concern is that in trying to satisfy a desire for status, security, power, and income, a CEO might engage in *empire building*, buying many new businesses in an attempt to increase the size of the company through diversification.[18] Although such growth may depress the company's long-run profitability and thus stockholder returns, it increases the size of the empire under the CEO's control and, by extension, the CEO's status, power, security, and income (there is a strong relationship between company size and CEO pay). Instead of trying to maximize stockholder returns by

FIGURE 11.2

The Tradeoff Between Profitability and Revenue Growth Rates

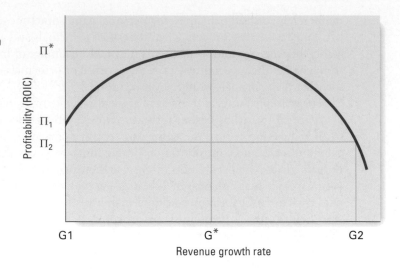

seeking the right balance between profitability and profit growth, some senior managers may trade long-run profitability for greater company growth by buying new businesses. Figure 11.2 graphs long-run profitability against the rate of growth in company revenues. A company that does not grow is probably missing out on some profitable opportunities.[19] A moderate revenue growth rate of G^* allows a company to maximize long-run profitability, generating a return of Π^*. Thus, a growth rate of $G1$ in Figure 11.2 is not consistent with maximizing profitability ($\Pi1 < \Pi^*$). By the same token, however, attaining growth in excess of G^* requires diversification into areas that the company knows little about. Consequently, it can be achieved only by sacrificing profitability; that is, past G^*, the investment required to finance further growth does not produce an adequate return and the company's profitability declines. Yet $G2$ may be the growth rate favored by an empire-building CEO, for it will increase his or her power, status, and income. At this growth rate, profitability is equal only to $\Pi2$. Because $\Pi^* > \Pi2$, a company growing at this rate is clearly not maximizing its long-run profitability or the wealth of its stockholders.

For an example of this kind of excessive growth, consider the case of Tyco International, profiled in the *Closing Case* in Chapter 10. Under the leadership of Dennis Kozlowski, who became CEO of the company in 1992, Tyco's revenues expanded from $3.1 billion in 1992 to $38 billion in 2001. Most of this growth was due to a series of acquisitions that took Tyco into a diverse range of unrelated businesses. Tyco financed the acquisitions by taking on significant debt commitments, which by 2002 exceeded $23 billion. As Tyco expanded, some questioned Tyco's ability to service its debt commitments and claimed that the company was engaging in "accounting tricks" to pad its books and make the company appear more profitable than it actually was. These criticisms, which were ignored for several years, were finally shown to have some validity in 2002 when Kozlowski was forced out by the board and subsequently charged with tax evasion by federal authorities. Among other charges, it has been claimed that Kozlowski treated Tyco as his personal treasury, drawing on company funds to purchase an expensive Manhattan apartment and a world-class art collection that he obviously thought were befitting of the CEO of a major corporation. Kozlowski even used company funds to help pay for an expensive birthday party for his wife that included toga-clad women, gladiators, chariots, and other over-the-top scenarios. Kozlowski was replaced by a company outsider, Edward Breen. In 2003 Tyco took a $1.5 billion charge against earnings for accounting errors made during the Kozlowski era (in other words, Tyco's profits had been overstated by $1.5 billion during Kozlowski's tenure). Breen also set about dismantling parts of the empire that Kozlowski had built, divesting several businesses.[20]

Just how serious agency problems could be was emphasized in the early 2000s when a series of scandals swept through the corporate world, many of which could be attributed to self-interest seeking by senior executives and a failure of corporate governance mechanisms to hold the largess of those executives in check. Between 2001 and 2004 accounting scandals unfolded at a number of major corporations, including Enron, WorldCom, Tyco, Computer Associates, HealthSouth, Adelphia Communications, Dynegy, Royal Dutch Shell, and most recently, the major Italian food company, Parmalat. At Enron, some $27 billion in debt was hidden from shareholders, employees, and regulators in special partnerships that were kept off the balance sheet. At Parmalat, managers apparently "invented" some $8 to $12 billion in assets to shore up the company's balance sheet, assets that never existed. In the case of Royal Dutch Shell, senior managers knowingly inflated the value of the company's oil reserves by one-fifth, which amounted to 4 billion barrels of oil that never existed, making the company appear much more valuable than it actually was. At the other companies, earnings were systematically overstated, often by hundreds of millions of dollars, or even billions of dollars in the case of Tyco (see above) and WorldCom, which understated its expenses by $3 billion in 2001. Strategy in Action 11.3 discusses accounting fraud at Computer Associates. In all of these cases, the prime motivation seems to have been an effort to present a more favorable view of corporate affairs to shareholders than was actually the case, thereby securing senior executives significantly higher pay packets.[21]

It is important to remember that the agency problem is not confined to the relationship between senior managers and stockholders. It can also bedevil the relationship between the CEO and subordinates and between them and their subordinates. Subordinates might use control over information to distort the true performance of their unit in order to enhance their pay, increase their job security, or make sure their unit gets more than its fair share of company resources.

Confronted with agency problems, the challenge for principals is to (1) shape the behavior of agents so that they act in accordance with the goals set by principals, (2) reduce the information asymmetry between agents and principals, and (3) develop mechanisms for removing agents who do not act in accordance with the goals of principals and mislead them. Principals try to deal with these challenges through a series of governance mechanisms.

Governance Mechanisms

Governance mechanisms are mechanisms that principals put in place to align incentives between principals and agents and to monitor and control agents. The purpose of governance mechanisms is to reduce the scope and frequency of the agency problem: to help ensure that agents act in a manner that is consistent with the best interests of their principals. In this section, the primary focus is on the governance mechanisms that exist to align the interests of senior managers (as agents) with their principals, stockholders. It should not be forgotten, however, that governance mechanisms also exist to align the interests of business unit managers with those of their superiors, and so on down within the organization.

Strategy in Action

Did Computer Associates Inflate Revenues to Enrich Managers?

11.3

Computer Associates is one of the world's largest software companies. During the 1990s, its stock price appreciated at a rapid rate, driven in large part by surging revenues and a commensurate rise in profits. Because its revenues were growing more rapidly than those of rivals during the late 1990s, investors assumed that the company was gaining market share and that high profitability would follow, so they bid up the price of the company's stock. The senior managers of Computer Associates were major beneficiaries of this process.

Under a generous incentive program given to the company's three top managers by the board of directors—Charles Wang, then CEO and chairman of the board; Sanjay Kumar, the chief operating officer; and Russell Artzt, the chief technology officer—if the stock price stayed above $53.13 for sixty days, they would receive a special incentive stock award amounting to some 20 million shares. In May 1998, Kumar announced that Computer Associates had "record" revenues and earnings for the quarter. The stock price surged over the $53.13 trigger and stayed there long enough for all three to receive the special incentive stock award, then valued at $1.1 billion.

In late July 1998, after all three had received the award, Kumar announced that the effect of Asian economic turmoil and the year 2000 bug "leads us to believe that our revenue and earnings growth will slow over the next few quarters." The stock price promptly fell from the high 50s to under $40 a share. What followed was a series of class action lawsuits, undertaken on behalf of stockholders, that claimed that management had misled stockholders to enrich themselves. As a result of the lawsuits, the three were compelled to give back some of their gains, and the size of the award was reduced to 4.5 million shares. Wang stepped down as CEO, although he retained his position as chairman of the board, and Kumar became the CEO.

This was not the end of matters, however, for Computer Associates had attracted the attention of both the Justice Department and the SEC, which launched a joint investigation into the company's accounting practices. By 2002, they were reportedly focusing on a little-noticed action the company had taken in May 2000 to reduce its revenues by 10 percent, or $1.76 billion, below what it had previously reported for the three fiscal years that ended March 2000. The downward revisions, detailed in the company's 10-K filings with the SEC, retroactively

took hundreds of millions of dollars away from the top line in the fourteen months preceding the May 1998 stock award to senior managers, including some $513 million for the year ending March 1998. According to the company, earnings were unaffected by the revision because the lost revenue was offset by a commensurate downward revision of expenses. The downward revision reportedly came at the urging of auditor KPMG, which replaced Ernst & Young as the company's accountant in June 1999.

The implication that some observers were drawing was that Computer Associates deliberately overstated its revenues in the period prior to May 1998 to enrich the three top managers. The losers in this process were stockholders who purchased shares at the inflated price and longer-term shareholders who saw the value of their holdings diluted by the stock awarded to Wang, Kumar, and Artzt. In a statement issued after a report of the ongoing investigation was published in the *Wall Street Journal*, Computer Associates stated that it changed how it classified revenue and expenses at the advice of its auditors. "We continue to believe CA has acted appropriately," the company said. "This change in presentation had no impact on reported earnings, earnings per share, or cash flows."

By 2004, it was clear that Computer Associates had been acting anything but appropriately. According to the SEC investigation, between 1998 and 2000 the company adopted a policy of backdating contracts to boost revenues. For example, in January 2000 Computer Associates negotiated a $300 million contract with a customer but backdated the contract so that the revenues appeared in 1999. Although initially this may have been done to help secure the $1.1 billion special stock award, by 2000 the practice represented an increasingly desperate attempt to meet financial projects that the company was routinely missing.

Under increasing pressure, in 2002 Charles Wang stepped down as chairman, and in 2004 Kumar was forced to resign as CEO by the board of Computer Associates, which had belatedly come to recognize that the company's financial statements were fraudulent. Matters culminated in September 2004 when Kumar was indicted by federal prosecutors on charges of obstruction of justice and securities fraud.[c]

Here we look at four main types of governance mechanisms for aligning stockholder and management interests: the board of directors, stock-based compensation, financial statements, and the takeover constraint. The section closes with a discussion of governance mechanisms within a company to align the interest of senior and lower-level managers.

■ **The Board of Directors**

The board of directors is the centerpiece of the corporate governance system in the United States and the United Kingdom. Board members are directly elected by stockholders, and under corporate law they represent the stockholders' interests in the company. Hence, the board can be held legally accountable for the company's actions. Its position at the apex of decision making within the company allows it to monitor corporate strategy decisions and ensure that they are consistent with stockholder interests. If the board's sense is that corporate strategies are not in the best interest of stockholders, it can apply sanctions, such as voting against management nominations to the board of directors or submitting its own nominees. In addition, the board has the legal authority to hire, fire, and compensate corporate employees, including, most importantly, the CEO.[22] The board is also responsible for making sure that audited financial statements of the company present a true picture of its financial situation. Thus, the board exists to reduce the information asymmetry between stockholders and managers and to monitor and control management actions on behalf of stockholders.

The typical board of directors is composed of a mix of inside and outside directors. *Inside directors* are senior employees of the company, such as the CEO. They are required on the board because they have valuable information about the company's activities. Without such information, the board cannot adequately perform its monitoring function. But because insiders are full-time employees of the company, their interests tend to be aligned with those of management. Hence, outside directors are needed to bring objectivity to the monitoring and evaluation processes. *Outside directors* are not full-time employees of the company. Many of them are full-time professional directors who hold positions on the boards of several companies. The need to maintain a reputation as competent outside directors gives them an incentive to perform their tasks as objectively and effectively as possible.[23]

There is little doubt that many boards perform their assigned functions admirably. For example, one factor that led to the dismissal of Morrison Knudsen's CEO, Bill Agee, was that his strategies lost the support of the board (see Strategy in Action 11.1). Similarly, when the board of Sotheby's discovered that the company had been engaged in price fixing with Christie's, board members moved quickly to oust both the CEO and the chairman of the company (see Strategy in Action 11.2). But not all boards perform as well as they should. The board of now bankrupt energy company Enron signed off on that company's audited financial statements, which were later shown to be grossly misleading.

Critics of the existing governance system charge that inside directors often dominate the outsiders on the board. Insiders can use their position within the management hierarchy to exercise control over what kind of company-specific information the board receives. Consequently, they can present information in a way that puts them in a favorable light. In addition, because insiders have intimate knowledge of the company's operations and because superior knowledge and control over information are sources of power, they may be better positioned than outsiders to influence boardroom decision making. The board may become the captive of insiders and merely rubber-stamp management decisions instead of guarding stockholder interests.

Some observers contend that many boards are dominated by the company CEO, particularly when the CEO is also the chairman of the board.[24] To support this view, they point out that both inside and outside directors are often the personal nominees of the CEO. The typical inside director is subordinate to the CEO in the company's hierarchy and therefore unlikely to criticize the boss. Because outside directors are frequently the CEO's nominees as well, they can hardly be expected to evaluate the CEO objectively. Thus, the loyalty of the board may be biased toward the CEO, not the stockholders. Moreover, a CEO who is also chairman of the board may be able to control the agenda of board discussions in such a manner as to deflect any criticisms of his or her leadership. This was a problem in the case of Bill Agee: he was both CEO and chairman of the board at Morrison Knudsen.

In the aftermath of a wave of corporate scandals that hit the corporate world in the early 2000s, there are clear signs that many corporate boards are moving away from merely rubber-stamping top management decisions and are beginning to play a much more active role in corporate governance. In part they have been prompted by new legislation, such as the 2002 Sarbanes-Oxley Act in the United States, which tightened rules governing corporate reporting and corporate governance. Also important has been a growing trend on the part of the courts to hold directors liable for corporate misstatements. Powerful institutional investors such as pension funds have also been more aggressive in exerting their power, often pushing for more outside representation on the board of directors and for a separation between the roles of chairman and CEO, with the chairman role going to an outsider. Partly as a result, over 50 percent of big companies had outside directors in the chairman's role by the early 2000s, up from less than half of that number in 1990. Separating the role of chairman and CEO limits the ability of corporate insiders, and particularly of the CEO, to exercise control over the board. It is notable that the removal of Robert Stempel as the CEO of General Motors in the late 1990s followed the appointment of an outside director, John Smale, as chairman of the GM board. Still, when all is said and done, it must be recognized that boards of directors do not work as well as they should in theory, and other mechanisms are need to align the interests of stockholders and managers.

■ Stock-Based Compensation

According to agency theory, one of the best ways to reduce the scope of the agency problem is for principals to establish incentives for agents to behave in their best interest through pay-for-performance systems. In the case of stockholders and top managers, stockholders can encourage top managers to pursue strategies that maximize a company's long-run profitability and profit growth, and thus the gains from holding its stock, by linking the pay of those managers to the performance of the stock price.

The most common pay-for-performance system has been to give managers stock options: the right to buy the company's shares at a predetermined (strike) price at some point in the future, usually within ten years of the grant date. Typically, the strike price is the price that the stock was trading at when the option was originally granted. The idea behind stock options is to motivate managers to adopt strategies that increase the share price of the company, for in doing so they will also increase the value of their own stock options.

Several academic studies suggest that stock-based compensation schemes for executives, such as stock options, can align management and stockholder interests. For instance, one study found that managers were more likely to consider the effects of their acquisition decisions on stockholder returns if they themselves were significant shareholders.[25] According to another study, managers who were significant stockholders were less likely to pursue strategies that would maximize the size of the company rather than its profitability.[26] More generally, it is difficult to argue with the proposition that the chance to get rich from exercising stock options is the primary reason for the fourteen-hour days and six-day workweeks that many employees of fast-growing companies put in.

Many top managers often earn huge bonuses from exercising stock options that were granted several years previously. While not denying that these options do motivate managers to improve company performance, critics claim that they are often too generous. A particular cause for concern is that stock options are often granted at such low strike prices that the CEO can hardly fail to make a significant amount of money by exercising them, even if the company underperforms the stock market by a significant margin.

Other critics, including the famous investor Warren Buffett, complain that huge stock option grants increase the outstanding number of shares in a company and therefore dilute the equity of stockholders; accordingly, they should be shown in company accounts as an expense against profits. Under current accounting regulations, stock options, unlike wages and salaries, were not expensed until 2005, when new accounting regulations came into force. Buffett has noted that when his investment company, Berkshire Hathaway, "acquires an option issuing company, we promptly substitute a cash compensation plan having an economic value equivalent to that of the previous option plan. The acquiree's true compensation cost is therefore brought out of the closet and charged, as it should be, against earnings."[27] Buffett's point is that stock options are accounted for incorrectly in company financial statements. Table 11.1 details the amount that reported profits would have been reduced during the 1996–2000 period for several high-profile companies if stock options had been accounted for as an expense and deducted from profits. As can be seen, the impact would have been to depress profits severely at some of these companies, and by extension, profitability.

In theory, stock options and other stock-based compensation methods are a good idea; in practice, they have been abused. To limit the abuse, Alan Greenspan, chairman of the U.S. Federal Reserve, has joined Warren Buffett in arguing that accounting

TABLE 11.1

How Options Skew the Bottom Line

Company	Reduction in Net Profit If Options Had Been Expensed
AOL Time Warner	75 percent
Viacom	66 percent
NVIDIA	40 percent
MedImmune	31 percent
Lucent	30 percent
Pharmacia	28 percent
Cisco Systems	26 percent
Boise Cascade	17 percent

Source: D. Henry and M. Conlin, "Too Much of a Good Incentive?" *Business Week,* March 4, 2002, pp. 38–39.

rules should be changed to treat options as an expense that must be charged against profits. Some companies have taken matters into their own hands even without a change in accounting rules. Microsoft, for example, stopped issuing options to employees in 2003, replacing them with smaller stock grants. Since 2002, Boeing has expensed options in its accounts. In an effort to align management and stockholder interests, the aerospace company has also gone an important step further by issuing what it calls "performance share" units that are convertible into common stock only if its stock appreciates at least 10 percent annually for five years. Similarly, Unilever has created a system in which stock options do not vest unless the company achieves total shareholder returns over a rolling three-year period that are above the median for the group of twenty peer companies, including Coca-Cola, Nestlé, and Procter & Gamble. What all of these companies are trying to do in their own way is to limit the free ride that many holders of stock options enjoyed during the boom of the 1990s, while continuing to maintain a focus on aligning management and stockholder interests through stock-based compensation schemes.[28]

■ Financial Statements and Auditors

Publicly trading companies in the United States are required to file quarterly and annual reports with the SEC that are prepared according to GAAP. The purpose of this requirement is to give consistent, detailed, and accurate information about how efficiently and effectively the agents of stockholders, the managers, are running the company. To make sure that managers do not misrepresent this financial information, the SEC also requires that the accounts be audited by an independent and accredited accounting firm. Similar regulations exist in most other developed nations. If the system works as intended, stockholders can have a lot of faith that the information contained in financial statements accurately reflects the state of affairs at a company. Among other things, such information can enable a stockholder to calculate the profitability (ROIC) of a company in which he or she invests and to compare its ROIC against that of competitors.

Unfortunately, in the United States at least, this system has not been working as intended. Although the vast majority of companies do file accurate information in their financial statements and although most auditors do a good job of reviewing that information, there is substantial evidence that a minority of companies have abused the system, aided in part by the compliance of auditors. This was clearly an issue at bankrupt energy trader Enron, where the CFO and others misrepresented the true financial state of the company to investors by creating off-balance-sheet partnerships that hid the true state of Enron's indebtedness from public view. Enron's auditor, Arthur Andersen, also apparently went along with this deception, in direct violation of its fiduciary duty. Arthur Anderson also had lucrative consulting contracts with Enron that it did not want to jeopardize by questioning the accuracy of the company's financial statements. The losers in this mutual deception were shareholders, who had to rely on inaccurate information to make their investment decisions.

There have been numerous examples in recent years of managers' gaming financial statements to present a distorted picture of their company's finances to investors. The typical motive has been to inflate the earnings or revenues of a company, thereby generating investor enthusiasm and propelling the stock price higher, which gives managers an opportunity to cash in stock option grants for huge personal gain, obviously at the expense of stockholders who have been mislead by the reports. Another alleged example of such behavior is given in Strategy in Action 11.3, which discusses how top managers at Computer Associates may have managed that company's financial statements to present a rosy picture and cash in very lucrative stock awards.

The gaming of financial statements by companies such as Enron and Computer Associates raises serious questions about the accuracy of the information contained in audited financial statements. In response, in 2002 the United States passed the Sarbanes-Oxley bill into law, which represents the biggest overhaul of accounting rules and corporate governance procedures since the 1930s. Among other things, Sarbanes-Oxley set up a new oversight board for accounting firms, required CEOs and CFOs to endorse their company's financial statements, and barred companies from hiring the same accounting firm for auditing and consulting services. However, many critics felt that this legislation did not go far enough and that it should have contained other elements, such as a requirement that stock options be treated as an expense. Some companies took matters into their own hands even before the 2005 change in accounting rules requiring stock options to be expensed.

The Takeover Constraint

Given the imperfections in corporate governance mechanisms, it is clear that the agency problem may still exist at some companies. However, stockholders still have some residual power, for they can always sell their shares. If they start doing so in large numbers, the price of the company's shares will decline. If the share price falls far enough, the company might be worth less on the stock market than the book value of its assets. At this point, it may become an attractive acquisition target and runs the risk of being purchased by another enterprise, against the wishes of the target company's management.

The risk of being acquired by another company is known as the **takeover constraint.** The takeover constraint limits the extent to which managers can pursue strategies and take actions that put their own interests above those of stockholders. If they ignore stockholder interests and the company is acquired, senior managers typically lose their independence and probably their jobs as well. So the threat of takeover can constrain management action and limit the worst excesses of the agency problem.

During the 1980s and early 1990s, the threat of takeover was often enforced by **corporate raiders**: individuals or corporations that buy up large blocks of shares in companies that they think are pursuing strategies inconsistent with maximizing stockholder wealth. Corporate raiders argue that if these underperforming companies pursued different strategies, they could create more wealth for stockholders. Raiders buy stock in a company either to take over the business and run it more efficiently, or to precipitate a change in the top management, replacing the existing team with one more likely to maximize stockholder returns. Raiders are motivated not by altruism but by gain. If they succeed in their takeover bid, they can institute strategies that create value for stockholders, including themselves. Even if a takeover bid fails, raiders can still earn millions, for their stockholdings will typically be bought out by the defending company for a hefty premium. Called **greenmail**, this source of gain stirred much controversy and debate about its benefits. While some claim that the threat posed by raiders has had a salutary effect on enterprise performance by pushing corporate management to run their companies better, others claim there is little evidence of this.[29]

Although the incidence of hostile takeover bids has fallen off significantly since the early 1990s, this should not be taken to imply that the takeover constraint is no longer operating. Unique circumstances exist in the early 2000s that have made it more difficult to execute hostile takeovers. The boom years of the 1990s left many corporations with excessive debt (corporate America entered the new century with record levels of debt on its balance sheets), which limits the ability of companies to finance acquisitions, particularly hostile acquisitions, which are often particularly expensive. In addition, the market valuations of many companies got so out of line with underlying fundamentals during the stock market bubble of the 1990s that even after a substantial fall in certain segments of the stock market, such as the technology sector, valuations are still high relative to historic norms, making the hostile acquisition of even poorly run and unprofitable companies expensive. However, takeovers tend to go in cycles, and it seems likely that once excesses are worked out of the stock market and worked off corporate balance sheets, the takeover constraint will begin to reassert itself. It should be remembered that the takeover constraint is the governance mechanism of last resort and is often invoked only when other governance mechanisms have failed.

■ Governance Mechanisms Inside a Company

So far this section has focused on the governance mechanisms designed to reduce the agency problem that potentially exists between stockholders and managers. Agency relationships also exist within a company, and the agency problem can thus arise *between* levels of management. In this section, we explore how the agency problem can be reduced within a company by using two complementary governance mechanisms to align the incentives and behavior of employees with those of upper-level management: strategic control systems and incentive systems.

■ Strategic Control Systems

Strategic control systems are the primary governance mechanisms established within a company to reduce the scope of the agency problem between levels of management. These systems are the formal target setting, measurement, and feedback systems that allow managers to evaluate whether a company is executing the strategies necessary to maximize its long-run profitability and, in particular, whether the company is achieving superior efficiency, quality, innovation, and customer responsiveness. They are discussed in more detail in subsequent chapters.

The purpose of strategic control systems is to (1) establish standards and targets against which performance can be measured, (2) create systems for measuring and monitoring performance on a regular basis, (3) compare actual performance against the established targets, and (4) evaluate results and take corrective action if necessary. In governance terms, their purpose is to make sure that lower-level managers, as the agents of top managers, are acting in a way that is consistent with top managers' goals, which should be to maximize the wealth of stockholders, subject to legal and ethical constraints.

One increasingly influential model that guides managers through the process of creating the right kind of strategic control systems to enhance organizational performance is the balanced scorecard model.[30] According to the **balanced scorecard model**, traditionally managers have primarily used financial measures of performance such as return on invested capital to measure and evaluate organizational performance. Financial information is extremely important, but it is not enough by itself. If managers are to obtain a true picture of organizational performance, financial information must be supplemented with performance measures that indicate how well an organization has been achieving the four building blocks of competitive advantage: efficiency, quality, innovation, and responsiveness to customers. This is so because financial results simply inform strategic managers about the results of decisions they have *already taken*; the other measures balance this picture of performance by informing managers about how accurately the organization has put in place the building blocks that drive *future performance*.[31]

One version of the way the balanced scorecard operates is presented in Figure 11.3. Based on an organization's mission and goals, strategic managers develop a set of

FIGURE 11.3

A Balanced Scorecard
Approach

strategies to build competitive advantage to achieve these goals. They then establish an organizational structure to use resources to obtain a competitive advantage.[32] To evaluate how well the strategy and structure are working, managers develop specific performance measures that assess how well the four building blocks of competitive advantage are being achieved:

- *Efficiency* can be measured by the level of production costs, the productivity of labor (such as the employee hours needed to make a product), the productivity of capital (such as revenues per dollar invested in property, plant, and equipment), and the cost of raw materials.

- *Quality* can be measured by the number of rejects, the number of defective products returned from customers, and the level of product reliability over time.

- *Innovation* can be measured by the number of new products introduced, the percentage of revenues generated from new products in a defined period, the time taken to develop the next generation of new products versus the competition, and the productivity of R&D (how much R&D spending is required to produce a successful product).

- *Responsiveness to customers* can be measured by the number of repeat customers, customer defection rates, level of on-time delivery to customers, and level of customer service.

As Kaplan and Norton, the developers of this approach, suggest, "Think of the balanced scorecard as the dials and indicators in an airplane cockpit. For the complex task of navigating and flying an airplane, pilots need detailed information about many aspects of the flight. They need information on fuel, air speed, altitude, learning, destination, and other indicators that summarize the current and predicted environment. Reliance on one instrument can be fatal. Similarly, the complexity of managing an organization today requires that managers be able to view performance in several areas simultaneously."[33]

The way in which managers' ability to build a competitive advantage translates into organizational performance is then measured using financial measures such as the return on invested capital, the return on sales, and the capital turnover ratio (see Chapter 3). Based on an evaluation of the complete set of measures in the balanced scorecard, strategic managers are in a good position to reevaluate the company's mission and goals and take corrective action to rectify problems, limit the agency problem, or exploit new opportunities by changing the organization's strategy and structure—which is the purpose of strategic control.

■ **Employee Incentives** Control systems alone may not be sufficient to align incentives between stockholders, senior management, and the rest of the organization. To help do this, positive incentive systems are often put into place to motivate employees to work toward goals that are central to maximizing long-run profitability. As already noted, employee stock ownership plans (ESOPs) are one form of positive incentive, as are stock option grants. In the 1990s, ESOPs and stock ownership grants were pushed down deep within many organizations. The logic behind such systems is straightforward: recognizing that the stock price, and therefore their own wealth, is dependent on the profitability of the company, employees will work toward maximizing profitability.

In addition to stock-based compensation systems, employee compensation can also be tied to goals that are linked to the attainment of superior efficiency, quality, innovation, and customer responsiveness. For example, the bonus pay of a manufacturing employee might depend on attaining quality and productivity targets, which if reached will lower the costs of the company, increase customer satisfaction, and boost profitability. Similarly, the bonus pay of a salesperson might be dependent on surpassing sales targets, and of an R&D employee on the success of new products he or she had a hand in developing.

Ethics and Strategy

The term **ethics** refers to accepted principles of right or wrong that govern the conduct of a person, the members of a profession, or the actions of an organization. **Business ethics** are the accepted principles of right or wrong governing the conduct of businesspeople. Ethical decisions are in accordance with those accepted principles, whereas unethical decisions violate accepted principles. This is not as straightforward as it sounds. Managers may be confronted with **ethical dilemmas**, which are situations where there is no agreement over exactly what the accepted principles of right and wrong are, or where none of the available alternatives seems ethically acceptable.

In our society many accepted principles of right and wrong are not only universally recognized but also codified into law. In the business arena there are laws governing product liability (*tort laws*), contracts and breaches of contract (*contract law*), the protection of intellectual property (*intellectual property law*), competitive behavior (*antitrust law*), and the selling of securities (*securities law*). Not only is it unethical to break these laws, it is illegal.

In this book we argue that the preeminent goal of managers in a business should be to pursue strategies that maximize the long-run profitability and profit growth of the enterprise, thereby boosting returns to stockholders. Strategies, of course, must be consistent with the laws that govern business behavior: managers must act legally while seeking to maximize the long-run profitability of the enterprise. Unfortunately, as we have already seen in this chapter, there are examples of managers breaking the law. Moreover, managers may take advantage of ambiguities and gray areas in the law, of which there are many in our common law system, to pursue actions that are at best legally suspect and, in any event, clearly unethical. It is important to realize, however, that behaving ethically goes beyond staying within the bounds of the law. There are many examples of strategies and actions that, while legal, do not seem to be ethical. As we saw in the *Opening Case* on Nike's use of "sweatshop" labor in developing nations, while Nike was not breaking any laws, and neither were its subcontractors, many considered it unethical to use subcontractors who by Western standards clearly exploited their work force.

In this section we take a closer look at the ethical issues that managers may confront when developing strategy and at the steps managers can take to ensure that strategic decisions are not only legal, but also ethical.

■ **Ethical Issues in Strategy**   The ethical issues that strategic managers confront cover a wide range of topics, but most are due to a potential conflict between the goals of the enterprise, or the goals of individual managers, and the fundamental rights of important stakeholders, including stockholders, customers, employees, suppliers, competitors, communities, and the general public. Stakeholders have basic rights that should be respected, and it is unethical to violate those rights.

Stockholders have the right to timely and accurate information about their investment (in accounting statements), and it is unethical to violate that right. Customers have the right to be fully informed about the products and services they purchase, including the right to information about how those products might cause harm to them or others, and it is unethical to restrict their access to such information. Employees have the right to safe working conditions, fair compensation for the work they perform, and just treatment by managers. Suppliers have the right to expect contracts to be respected, and the firm should not take advantage of a power disparity between itself and a supplier to opportunistically rewrite a contract. Competitors have the right to expect that the firm will abide by the rules of competition and not violate the basic principles of antitrust laws. Communities and the general public, including their political representatives in government, have the right to expect that a firm will not violate the basic expectations that society places on enterprises: for example, by dumping toxic pollutants into the environment or overcharging for work performed on government contracts.

Those who take the stakeholder view of business ethics often argue that it is in the enlightened self-interest of managers to behave in an ethical manner that recognizes and respects the fundamental rights of stakeholders, because doing so will ensure the support of stakeholders and thus ultimately benefit the firm and its managers. Others go beyond this instrumental approach to ethics to argue that, in many cases, acting ethically is simply the right thing to do. They argue that businesses need to recognize their *noblesse oblige* and give something back to the society that made their success possible. *Noblesse oblige* is a French term that refers to honorable and benevolent behavior that is considered the responsibility of people of high (noble) birth. In a business setting, it is taken to mean benevolent behavior that is the moral responsibility of successful enterprises.

Unethical behavior often arises in a corporate setting when managers decide to put the attainment of their own personal goals, or the goals of the enterprise, above the fundamental rights of one or more stakeholder groups (in other words, unethical behavior may arise from agency problems). The most common examples of such behavior involve self-dealing, information manipulation, anticompetitive behavior, opportunistic exploitation of other players in the value chain in which the firm is embedded (including suppliers, complement providers, and distributors), the maintenance of substandard working conditions, environmental degradation, and corruption.

Self-dealing occurs when managers find a way to feather their own nests with corporate monies, and we have already discussed several examples in this chapter (such as Tyco and Computer Associates). **Information manipulation** occurs when managers use their control over corporate data to distort or hide information in order to enhance their own financial situation or the competitive position of the firm. As we have seen, many of the recent accounting scandals involved the deliberate manipulation of financial information. Information manipulation can also occur with regard to nonfinancial data. This occurred when managers at the tobacco companies suppressed internal research that linked smoking to health problems, violating the rights of consumers to accurate information about the dangers of smoking. When evidence of this came to light, lawyers brought class action suits against the tobacco companies, claiming that they had intentionally caused harm to smokers: they had broken tort law by promoting a product that they knew did serious harm to consumers. In 1999, the tobacco companies settled a lawsuit brought by the states who sought to recover health care costs associated with tobacco-related illnesses; the total payout to the states was $260 billion.

Anticompetitive behavior covers a range of actions aimed at harming actual or potential competitors, most often by using monopoly power, and thereby enhancing the long-run prospects of the firm. For example, in the 1990s the Justice Department claimed that Microsoft used its monopoly in operating systems to force PC makers to bundle Microsoft's web browser, Internet Explorer, with Windows and to display Internet explorer prominently on the computer desktop (the screen you see when you start a personal computer). Microsoft reportedly told PC makers that it would not supply them with Windows unless they did this. Since the PC makers had to have Windows to sell their machines, this was a powerful threat. The alleged aim of the action, which is an example of "tie-in-sales," which is illegal under antitrust laws, was to drive a competing browser maker, Netscape, out of business. The courts ruled that Microsoft was indeed abusing its monopoly power in this case, and under a 2001 consent decree the company agreed to stop the practice.

Putting the legal issues aside, action such as that allegedly undertaken by managers at Microsoft is unethical on at least three counts; first, it violates the rights of end-users by unfairly limiting their choice; second, it violates the rights of downstream participants in the industry value chain, in this case PC makers, by forcing them to incorporate a particular product in their design; and third, it violates the rights of competitors to free and fair competition.

Opportunistic exploitation of other players in the value chain in which the firm is embedded is another example of unethical behavior. Exploitation of this kind typically occurs when the managers of a firm seek to unilaterally rewrite the terms of a contract with suppliers, buyers, or complement providers in a way that is more favorable to the firm, often using their power to force the revision through. For example, in the late 1990s Boeing entered into a $2 billion contract with Titanium Metals Corporation to buy certain amounts of titanium annually for ten years. In 2000, after Titanium Metals had already spent $100 million to expand its production capacity to fulfill the contract, Boeing demanded that the contract be renegotiated, asking for lower prices and an end to minimum purchase agreements. As a major purchaser of titanium, managers at Boeing probably thought they had the power to push this contract revision through, and the investment by Titanium meant that they would be unlikely to walk away from the deal. Titanium promptly sued Boeing for breach of contract. The dispute was settled out of court, and under a revised agreement Boeing agreed to pay monetary damages to Titanium Metals (reported to be in the $60 million range) and entered into an amended contract to purchase titanium. Irrespective of the legality of this action, it was arguably unethical because it violated the rights of suppliers to have buyers who deal with them in a fair and open way.

Substandard working conditions arise when managers underinvest in working conditions, or pay employees below-market rates, in order to reduce their costs of production. The most extreme examples of such behavior occur when a firm establishes operations in countries that lack the workplace regulations found in developed nations such as the United States. The example of Nike, which was given earlier, falls into this category. However, many companies have also been accused of maintaining substandard working conditions at home. As noted in the *Running Case*, in recent years Wal-Mart has been the target of numerous lawsuits alleging that, among other things, the company discriminates against female employees and requires employees to work overtime for no additional pay.

Environmental degradation occurs when the firm takes actions that directly or indirectly result in pollution or other forms of environmental harm. Environmental degradation can violate the rights of local communities and the general public for such things as clean air and water, land that is free from pollution by toxic chemicals, and properly managed forests (because forests absorb rainfall, improper deforestation results in land erosion and floods).

Finally, **corruption** can arise in a business context when managers pay bribes to gain access to lucrative business contracts. For example, it was alleged that Halliburton was part of a consortium that paid some $180 million in bribes to win a lucrative contract to build a natural gas plant in Nigeria. Corruption is clearly unethical because it violates a bundle of rights, including the right of competitors to a level playing field when bidding for contracts and, when government officials are involved, the right of citizens to expect that government officials act in the best interest of the local community or nation and not in response to corrupt payments that feather their own nests.

■ The Roots of Unethical Behavior

Why do some managers behave unethically? What motivates them to engage in actions that violate accepted principals of right and wrong, trample on the rights of one or more stakeholder groups, or simply break the law? While there is no simple answer to this question, a few generalizations can be made. First, it is important to recognize that business ethics are not divorced from *personal ethics*, which are the generally accepted principles of right and wrong governing the conduct of individuals. As individuals we are taught that it is wrong to lie and cheat and that it is right to behave with integrity and honor and to stand up for what we believe to be right and true. The personal ethical code that guides our behavior comes from a number of sources, including our parents, our schools, our religion, and the media. Our personal ethical code will exert a profound influence on the way we behave as businesspeople. An individual with a strong sense of personal ethics is less likely to behave in an unethical manner in a business setting; in particular, he or she is less likely to engage in self-dealing and more likely to behave with integrity.

Second, many studies of unethical behavior in a business setting have come to the conclusion that businesspeople sometimes do not realize that they are behaving unethically, primarily because they simply fail to ask the relevant question: Is this decision or action ethical? Instead, they apply a straightforward business calculus to what they perceive to be a business decision, forgetting that the decision may also have an important ethical dimension. The fault here lies in processes that do not incorporate ethical considerations into business decision making. This may have been the case at Nike when managers originally made subcontracting decisions (see the *Opening Case*). Those decisions were probably made on the basis of good economic logic. Subcontractors were probably chosen on the basis of business variables such as cost, delivery, and product quality, and key managers simply failed to ask, "How does this subcontractor treat its work force?" If they thought about the question at all, they probably reasoned that it was the subcontractor's concern, not theirs.

Running Case

Working Conditions at Wal-Mart

When Sam Walton founded Wal-Mart, one of his core values was that if you treated employees with respect, tied compensation to the performance of the enterprise, trusted them with important information and decisions, and provided ample opportunities for advancement, they would repay the company with dedication and hard work. For years the formula seemed to work. Employees were called "associates" to reflect their status within the company, even the lowest hourly employee was eligible to participate in profit sharing schemes and could use profit sharing bonuses to purchase company stock at a discount to its market value, and the company made a virtue of promoting from within (two-thirds of managers at Wal-Mart started as hourly employees). At the same time, Walton and his successors always demanded loyalty and hard work from employees. For example, managers were expected to move to a new store on very short notice, and base pay for hourly workers was very low. Still, as long as the upside was there, little grumbling was heard from employees.

In the last ten years, however, the relationship between the company and its employees has been strained by a succession of lawsuits claiming that Wal-Mart pressures hourly employees to work overtime without compensating them, systematically discriminates against women, and knowingly uses contractors who hire undocumented immigrant workers to clean its stores, paying them below minimum wage.

For example, a class action lawsuit in Washington State claims that Wal-Mart routinely (a) pressured hourly employees not to report all their time worked, (b) failed to keep true time records, sometimes shaving hours from employee logs, (c) failed to give employees full rest or meal breaks, (d) threatened to fire or demote employees who would not work off the clock, and (e) required workers to attend unpaid meetings and computer training sessions. Moreover, the suit claims that Wal-Mart has a strict "no overtime" policy, punishing employees who work more than forty hours a week, but that the company also gives employees more work than can be completed in a forty-hour week. The Washington suit is one of more than thirty suits that have been filed around the nation in recent years.

With regard to discrimination against women, complaints date back to 1996, when an assistant manager in a California store, Stephanie Odle, came across the W2 of a male assistant manager who worked in the same store. The W2 showed that he was paid $10,000 more than Odle. When she asked her boss to explain the disparity, she was told that her coworker had "a wife and kids to support." When Odle, who is a single mother, protested, she was asked to submit a personal household budget. She was then granted a $2,080 raise. She was subsequently fired, she claims for speaking up. In 1998 she filed a discrimination suit against the company. Others began to file suits around the same time, and by 2004 the legal action had evolved into a class action suit that covered 1.6 million current and former female employees at Wal-Mart. The suit claims that Wal-Mart did not pay female employees the same as their male counterparts and did not provide them with equal opportunities for promotion.

In the case of both undocumented overtime and discrimination, Wal-Mart admits to no wrongdoing. The company does recognize that, with some 1.4 million employees, some problems are bound to arise, but it claims that there is no systematic companywide effort to get hourly employees to work without pay or to discriminate against women. Indeed, the company claims that this could not be the case since hiring and promotion decisions are made at the store level.

For their part, critics charge that while the company may have no policies that promote undocumented overtime or discrimination, its hard-driving cost-containment culture has created an environment where abuses can thrive. Store managers, for example, are expected to meet challenging performance goals, and in an effort to do so they may be tempted to pressure subordinates to work additional hours without pay. Similarly, company policy requiring managers to move to new stores at short notice unfairly discriminates against women, who lack the flexibility to uproot their families and move them to another state at short notice.

While the lawsuits are still ongoing and may take years to resolve, Wal-Mart has taken steps to change its employment practices. For example, the company has created a director of diversity and a diversity compliance team, and it has restructured its pay scales to promote equal pay regardless of gender.[d]

Unfortunately, the climate in some businesses does not encourage people to think through the ethical consequences of business decisions. This brings us to the third cause of unethical behavior in businesses: an organizational culture that de-emphasizes business ethics and considers all decisions to be purely economic ones. A related fourth cause of unethical behavior may be pressure from top management to meet performance goals that are unrealistic and can only be attained by cutting corners or acting in an unethical manner. As explained in the *Running Case*, this may have been an issue at Wal-Mart, where the pressure to meet performance goals may have encouraged store managers to pressure their subordinates to work extra hours without pay.

An organizational culture can "legitimize" behavior that society would judge as unethical, particularly when this is mixed with a focus on unrealistic performance goals, such as maximizing short-term economic performance regardless of the costs. In such circumstances, there is a greater-than-average probability that managers will violate their own personal ethics and engage in behavior that is unethical. By the same token, an organization culture can do just the opposite and reinforce the need for ethical behavior. At Hewlett-Packard, for example, Bill Hewlett and David Packard, the company's founders, propagated a set of values known as "The HP Way." These values, which shape the way business is conducted both within and by the corporation, have an important ethical component. Among other things, they stress the need for confidence in and respect for people, open communication, and concern for the individual employee.

This brings us to a fifth root cause of unethical behavior: *unethical leadership*. Leaders help to establish the culture of an organization, and they set the example that others follow. Other employees in a business often take their cues from business leaders, and if those leaders do not behave in an ethical manner, employees might not either. It is not what leaders say that matters, but what they do. A good example is Ken Lay, the former CEO of the failed energy company Enron. While constantly referring to Enron's code of ethics in public statements, Lay simultaneously engaged in behavior that was ethically suspect. Among other things, he failed to discipline subordinates who had inflated earnings by engaging in corrupt energy trading schemes. Such behavior sent a very clear message to Enron's employees—unethical behavior would be tolerated if it boosted earnings.

■ Philosophical Approaches to Ethics

In this section we take a look at the philosophical underpinnings of business ethics, for ultimately it is a philosophy that can provide managers with a moral compass that will help them to navigate their way through difficult ethical issues. We will start with the approach suggested by the Nobel Prize–winning economist Milton Friedman.

■ The Friedman Doctrine

In 1970 Milton Friedman wrote an article that has since become a classic straw man that business ethics scholars outline only to then tear down. Friedman's basic position is that the only social responsibility of business is to increase profits, so long as the company stays within the rules of law. He explicitly rejects the idea that businesses should undertake social expenditures beyond those mandated by the law and required for the efficient running of a business. For example, his arguments suggest that improving working conditions beyond the level required by the law *and* necessary to maximize employee productivity will reduce profits and are therefore not appropriate. His belief is that a firm should maximize its profits, since that is the way to maximize the returns that accrue to the owners of the firm, its stockholders. If stockholders then wish to use the proceeds to make social investments, that is their right, according to Friedman, but managers of the firm should not make that decision for them.

Although Friedman is talking about social responsibility, rather than business ethics per se, most business ethics scholars equate social responsibility with ethical behavior, and thus believe Friedman is also arguing against business ethics. However, the assumption that Friedman is arguing against ethics is not quite true, for Friedman does state the following:

> There is one and only one social responsibility of business—to use its resources and engage in activities designed to increase its profits so long as it stays within the rules of the game, which is to say that it engages in open and free competition without deception or fraud.

In other words, Friedman does state that businesses should behave in an ethical manner, and not engage in deception and fraud.

Nevertheless, Friedman's arguments break down under closer examination. This is particularly true where the "rules of the game" are not well established, are ambiguous and open to different interpretations, or differ substantially from country to country. Consider again the case of sweatshop labor: using child labor may not be against the law in a developing nation, but it is still immoral to employee children because the practice conflicts with widely held views about what is the right thing to do. Similarly, there may be no rules against pollution in a developed nation, and spending money on pollution control may reduce the profit rate of the firm, but generalized notions of morality hold that it is still unethical to dump toxic pollutants into rivers or foul the air with gas releases. In addition to the local consequences of such pollution, which may have serious health effects for the surrounding population, there is also a global consequence because pollutants degrade those two global environments that we all have a stake in: the atmosphere and the oceans.

■ **Utilitarian and Kantian Ethics** Utilitarian and Kantian approaches to business ethics were developed in the eighteenth and nineteenth centuries. Utilitarian approaches to ethics hold that the moral worth of actions or practices is determined by their consequences. An action is judged to be desirable if it leads to the best possible balance of good consequences over bad consequences. Utilitarianism is committed to the maximization of good and the minimization of harm. It recognizes that actions have multiple consequences, some of which are good in a social sense, and some of which are harmful. As a philosophy for business ethics, it focuses attention on the need to carefully weigh all of the social benefits and costs of a business action and to only pursue those actions where the benefits outweigh the costs. The best decisions, from a utilitarian perspective, are those that produce the greatest good for the greatest number of people.

Many businesses have adopted specific tools, such as cost-benefit analysis and risk assessment, that are firmly rooted in a utilitarian philosophy. Managers often weigh the benefits and costs of a course of action before deciding whether to pursue it. An oil company considering drilling in the Alaskan wildlife preserve must weigh the economic benefits of increased oil production and the creation of jobs against the costs of environmental degradation in a fragile ecosystem.

For all of its appeal, however, the utilitarian philosophy has some serious drawbacks. One problem is measuring the benefits, costs, and risks of a course of action. In the case of an oil company considering drilling in Alaska, how does one measure the potential harm done to the fragile ecosystem of the region? In general, utilitarian philosophers recognize that benefits, costs, and risks often cannot be measured because of limited knowledge.

The second problem with utilitarianism is that the philosophy does not consider justice. The action that produces the greatest good for the greatest number of people may result in the unjustified treatment of a minority. Such action cannot be ethical, precisely because it is unjust. For example, suppose that in the interests of keeping down health insurance costs the government decides to screen people for the HIV virus and deny insurance coverage to those who are HIV positive. By reducing health costs, such action might produce significant benefits for a large number of people, but the action is unjust because it discriminates unfairly against a minority.

Kantian ethics are based on the philosophy of Immanuel Kant (1724–1804). Kant argued that people should be treated as ends and never purely as *means* to the ends of others. People are not instruments, like a machine. People have dignity and need to be respected as such. Employing people in sweatshops where they work long hours for low pay in poor work conditions is a violation of ethics according to Kantian philosophy because it treats people as mere cogs in a machine and not as conscious moral beings that have dignity. Although contemporary moral philosophers tend to view Kant's ethical philosophy as incomplete—for example, his system has no place for moral emotions or sentiments such as sympathy or caring—the notion that people should be respected and treated with dignity still resonates in the modern world.

■ **Rights Theories** Developed in the twentieth century, **rights theories** recognize that human beings have fundamental rights and privileges. Rights establish a minimum level of morally acceptable behavior. One well-known definition of a fundamental right construes it as something that takes precedence over or "trumps" a collective good. Thus we might say that the right to free speech is a fundamental right that takes precedence over all but the most compelling collective goals; for example, it overrides the interest of the state in civil harmony or moral consensus. Moral theorists argue that fundamental human rights form the basis for the *moral compass* managers should navigate by when making decisions that have an ethical component. In a business setting, stakeholder theory provides a useful way for managers to frame any discussion of rights. As noted earlier, stakeholders have basic rights that should be respected, and it is unethical to violate those rights.

It is important to note that along with *rights* come *obligations*. Because we have the right to free speech, we are also obligated to make sure that we respect the free speech of others. Within the framework of a theory of rights, certain people or institutions are obligated to provide benefits or services that secure the rights of others. Such obligations also fall upon more than one class of moral agent (a moral agent is any person or institution that is capable of moral action, such as a government or corporation).

For example, in the late 1980s, to escape the high costs of toxic waste disposal in the West, several firms shipped their waste in bulk to African nations, where it was disposed of at a much lower cost. In 1987 five European ships unloaded toxic waste containing dangerous poisons in Nigeria. Workers wearing thongs and shorts unloaded the barrels for $2.50 a day and placed them in a dirt lot in a residential area. They were not told about the contents of the barrels. Who bears the obligation for protecting the safety rights of workers and residents in a case like this? According to rights theorists, the obligation rests not on the shoulders of one moral agent but on the shoulders of all moral agents whose actions might harm, or contribute to the harm of, the workers and residents. Thus it was the obligation not just of the Nigerian government, but also of the multinational firms that shipped the toxic waste, to make sure that it did no harm to residents and workers. In this case, both the government and the multinationals obviously failed to recognize their basic obligation to protect the fundamental human rights of others.

■ **Justice Theories** Justice theories focus on the attainment of a just distribution of economic goods and services. A **just distribution** is one that is considered fair and equitable. The most famous theory of justice is attributed to philosopher John Rawls. Rawls argues that all economic goods and services should be distributed equally except when an unequal distribution would work to everyone's advantage.

According to Rawls, valid principles of justice are those to which all persons would agree with if they could freely and impartially consider the situation. Impartiality is guaranteed by a conceptual device that Rawls calls the *veil of ignorance*. Under the veil of ignorance, everyone is imagined to be ignorant of all of his or her particular characteristics, for example, his or her race, sex, intelligence, nationality, family background, and special talents. Rawls then asks, what system would people design under a veil of ignorance? His answer is that, under these conditions, people would unanimously agree on two fundamental principles of justice.

The first principle is that each person should be permitted the maximum amount of basic liberty compatible with a similar liberty for others. Roughly speaking, Rawls takes these liberties to be political liberty (the right to vote), freedom of speech and assembly, liberty of conscience and freedom of thought, the freedom and right to hold personal property, and freedom from arbitrary arrest and seizure. The second principle is that once equal basic liberty is ensured, inequality in basic social goods—such as income, wealth, and opportunities—is to be allowed *only* if it benefits everyone. Rawls believes that inequalities can be just as long as the system that produces them is to the advantage of everyone. More precisely, he formulates what he calls the *difference principle*, which is that inequalities are justified if they benefit the position of the least advantaged person. So, for example, the wide variations in income and wealth that we see in the United States can be considered "just" if the market-based system that produces this unequal distribution also benefits the least advantaged members of society.

In the context of business ethics, Rawls's theory creates an interesting perspective. Managers could ask themselves whether the policies they adopt would be considered "just" under Rawls's *veil of ignorance*. Is it "just," for example, to pay foreign workers less than workers in the firm's home country? Rawls's second principle would suggest that it is, as long as the inequality benefits the least advantaged members of the global society (which is what economic theory suggests). Alternatively, it is difficult to imagine that managers operating under a veil of ignorance would design a system where employees are paid subsistence wages to work long hours in sweatshop conditions and be exposed to toxic materials. Such working conditions are clearly unjust in Rawls's framework, and therefore it is unethical to adopt them. Similarly, operating under a veil of ignorance, most people would probably design a system that imparts protection from environmental degradation, preserves a free and fair playing field for competition, and prohibits self-dealing. Thus Rawls's veil of ignorance is a conceptual tool that helps define the moral compass managers can use to navigate through difficult ethical dilemmas.

■ **Behaving Ethically**

What then is the best way for managers to ensure that ethical considerations are taken into account? In many cases, there is no easy answer to this question, for many of the most vexing ethical problems involve very real dilemmas and suggest no obvious right course of action. Nevertheless, managers can and should do at least seven things to ensure that basic ethical principles are adhered to and that ethical issues are routinely considered when making business decisions. They can (1) favor hiring and promoting people with a well-grounded sense of personal ethics; (2) build an organizational culture that places a high value on ethical behavior; (3) make sure that leaders within the business not only articulate the rhetoric of ethical behavior but also act in a manner that is consistent with that rhetoric; (4) put decision-making processes in place that require people to consider the ethical dimension of business decisions; (5) use ethics officers; (6) put strong governance processes in place; and (7) act with moral courage.

■ **Hiring and Promotion**   It seems obvious that businesses should strive to hire people who have a strong sense of personal ethics and would not engage in unethical or illegal behavior. Similarly, you would rightly expect a business to not promote people, and perhaps fire people, whose behavior does not match generally accepted ethical standards. But doing so is actually very difficult. How do you know that someone has a poor sense of personal ethics? In our society, if someone lacks personal ethics, he or she may hide this fact to retain people's trust.

Is there anything that businesses can do to make sure that they do not hire people who turn out to have poor personal ethics, particularly given that people have an incentive to hide this from public view (indeed, unethical people may well lie about their nature)? Businesses can give potential employees psychological tests to try to discern their ethical predisposition, and they can check with prior employees regarding someone's reputation, such as by asking for letters of reference and talking to people who have worked with the prospective employee. The latter approach is certainly not uncommon and does indeed influence the hiring process. As for promoting people who have displayed poor ethics, that should not occur in a company where the organization culture values ethical behavior and where leaders act accordingly.

■ **Organization Culture and Leadership**   To foster ethical behavior, businesses need to build an organization culture that places a high value on ethical behavior. Three actions are particularly important. First, businesses must explicitly articulate values that place a strong emphasis on ethical behavior. Many companies now do this by drafting a **code of ethics**, a formal statement of the ethical priorities a business adheres to. Others have incorporated ethical statements into documents that articulate the values or mission of the business. For example, the food and consumer products giant Unilever has a code of ethics that includes the following points: "We will not use any form of forced, compulsory or child labor" and "No employee may offer, give or receive any gift or payment which is, or may be construed as being, a bribe. Any demand for, or offer of, a bribe must be rejected immediately and reported to management." Unilever's principles send a very clear message to managers and employees within the organization.

Having articulated values in a code of ethics or some other document, it is important that leaders in the business give life and meaning to those words by repeatedly emphasizing their importance *and then acting on them*. This means using every relevant opportunity to stress the importance of business ethics and making sure that key business decisions not only make good economic sense but also are ethical.

Many companies have gone a step further and hired independent firms to audit them and make sure that they are behaving in a manner consistent with their ethical code. Nike, for example, has in recent years hired independent auditors to make sure that its subcontractors are living up to Nike's code of conduct.

Finally, building an organization culture that places a high value on ethical behavior requires incentive and reward systems, including promotion systems, that reward people who engage in ethical behavior and sanction those who do not.

■ **Decision-Making Processes** In addition to establishing the right kind of ethical culture in an organization, businesspeople must be able to think through the ethical implications of decisions in a systematic way. To do this, they need a moral compass, and both rights theories and Rawls's theory of justice help to provide such a compass. Beyond these theories, some experts on ethics have proposed a straightforward practical guide, or ethical algorithm, to determine whether a decision is ethical. A decision is acceptable on ethical grounds if a businessperson can answer "yes" to each of these questions:

1. Does my decision fall within the accepted values or standards that typically apply in the organizational environment (as articulated in a code of ethics or some other corporate statement)?

2. Am I willing to see the decision communicated to all stakeholders affected by it— for example, by having it reported in newspapers or on television?

3. Would the people with whom I have a significant personal relationship, such as family members, friends, or even managers in other businesses, approve of the decision?

■ **Ethics Officers** To make sure that a business behaves in an ethical manner, a number of firms now have ethics officers. These individuals are responsible for making sure that all employees are trained to be ethically aware, that ethical considerations enter the business decision-making process, and that the company's code of ethics is adhered to. Ethics officers may also be responsible for auditing decisions to make sure that they are consistent with this code. In many businesses, ethics officers act as an internal ombudsperson with responsibility for handling confidential inquiries from employees, investigating complaints from employees or others, reporting findings, and making recommendations for change.

United Technologies, a large aerospace company with worldwide revenues of over $28 billion, has had a formal code of ethics since 1990. There are now some 160 "business practice officers" within United Technologies (this is the company's name for ethics officers) who are responsible for making sure that the code is adhered to. United Technologies also established an ombudsperson program in 1986 that lets employees inquire anonymously about ethics issues. The program has received some 56,000 inquiries since 1986, and 8,000 cases have been handled by an ombudsperson.

■ **Strong Corporate Governance** Strong corporate governance procedures are needed to make sure that managers adhere to ethical norms, in particular, that senior managers do not engage in self-dealing or information manipulation. The key to strong corporate governance procedures is an independent board of directors that is willing to hold top managers to account for self-dealing and is able to question the information provided to them by managers. If companies like Tyco, WorldCom, and Enron had had a strong board of directors, it is unlikely that they would have been racked by accounting scandals or that top managers would have been able to view the funds of these corporations as their own personal treasuries.

There are five cornerstones of strong governance. The first is a board of directors that is composed of a majority of outside directors who have no management responsibilities in the firm, are willing and able to hold top managers to account, and do not have business ties with important insiders. The outside directors should be individuals of high integrity whose reputation is based on their ability to act independently. The second cornerstone is a board where the positions of CEO and chairman are held by separate individuals and the chairman is an outside director. When the CEO is also chairman of the board of directors, he or she can control the agenda, thereby furthering his or her own personal agenda (which may include self-dealing) or limiting criticism against current corporate policies. The third cornerstone is a compensation committee formed by the board that is composed entirely of outside directors. It is the compensation committee that sets the level of pay for top managers, including stock option grants and the like. By making sure that the compensation committee is independent of managers, one reduces the scope of self-dealing. Fourth, the audit committee of the board, which reviews the financial statements of the firm, should also be composed of outsiders, thereby encouraging vigorous independent questioning of the firm's financial statements. Finally, the board should use outside auditors who are truly independent and do not have a conflict of interest. This was not the case in many recent accounting scandals, where the outside auditors were also consultants to the corporation and therefore less likely to ask hard questions of management for fear that doing so would jeopardize lucrative consulting contracts.

■ **Moral Courage** It is important to recognize that sometimes managers and others need significant *moral courage*. It is moral courage that enables managers to walk away from a decision that is profitable but unethical, that gives employees the strength to say no to superiors who instruct them to behave unethically, and that gives employees the integrity to go to the media and blow the whistle on persistent unethical behavior in a company. Moral courage does not come easily; there are well-known cases where individuals have lost their jobs because they blew the whistle on corporate behaviors.

Companies can strengthen the moral courage of employees by committing themselves to not take retribution on employees that exercise moral courage, say no to superiors, or otherwise complain about unethical actions. For example, Unilever's code of ethics includes the following:

> Any breaches of the Code must be reported in accordance with the procedures specified by the Joint Secretaries. The Board of Unilever will not criticize management for any loss of business resulting from adherence to these principles and other mandatory policies and instructions. The Board of Unilever expects employees to bring to their attention, or to that of senior management, any breach or suspected breach of these principles. Provision has been made for employees to be able to report in confidence and no employee will suffer as a consequence of doing so.

This statement gives "permission" to employees to exercise moral courage. Companies can also set up ethics hotlines that allow employees to anonymously register a complaint with a corporate ethics officer.

■ **Final Words** The steps discussed here can help to ensure that, when managers make business decisions, they are fully cognizant of the ethical implications and do not violate basic ethical prescripts. At the same time, not all ethical dilemmas have a clean and obvious solution—that is why they are dilemmas. At the end of the day, there are clearly things that a business should not do, and there are things that they should do, but there are also actions that present managers with true dilemmas. In these cases a premium is placed on the ability of managers to make sense out of complex, messy situations and to make balanced decisions that are as just as possible.

Summary of Chapter

1. Stakeholders are individuals or groups that have an interest, claim, or stake in the company, in what it does, and in how well it performs.

2. Stakeholders are in an exchange relationship with the company. They supply the organization with important resources (or contributions) and in exchange expect their interests to be satisfied (by inducements).

3. A company cannot always satisfy the claims of all stakeholders. The goals of different groups may conflict. The company must identify the most important stakeholders and give highest priority to pursuing strategies that satisfy their needs.

4. A company's stockholders are its legal owners and the providers of risk capital, a major source of the capital resources that allow a company to operate its business. As such, they have a unique role among stakeholder groups.

5. Maximizing long-run profitability and profit growth is the route to maximizing returns to stockholders, and it is also consistent with satisfying the claims of several other key stakeholder groups.

6. When pursuing strategies that maximize profitability, a company has the obligation to do so within the limits set by the law and in a manner consistent with societal expectations.

7. An agency relationship is held to arise whenever one party delegates decision-making authority or control over resources to another.

8. The essence of the agency problem is that the interests of principals and agents are not always the same, and some agents may take advantage of information asymmetries to maximize their own interests at the expense of principals.

9. A number of governance mechanisms serve to limit the agency problem between stockholders and managers. These include the board of directors, stock-based compensation schemes, financial statements and auditors, and the threat of a takeover.

10. The term **ethics** refers to accepted principles of right or wrong that govern the conduct of a person, the members of a profession, or the actions of an organization. **Business ethics** are the accepted principles of right or wrong governing the conduct of businesspeople, and an ethical strategy is one that does not violate these accepted principles.

11. Unethical behavior is rooted in poor personal ethics; the inability to recognize that ethical issues are at stake, as when there are psychological and geographical distances between a foreign subsidiary and the home office; failure to incorporate ethical issues into strategic and operational decision making; a dysfunctional culture; and failure of leaders to act in an ethical manner.

12. Philosophies underlying business ethics include the Friedman doctrine, utilitarianism, Kantian ethics, rights theories, and justice theories such as that proposed by Rawls.

13. To make sure that ethical issues are considered in business decisions, managers should (a) favor hiring and promoting people with a well-grounded sense of personal ethics; (b) build an organizational culture that places a high value on ethical behavior; (c) make sure that leaders within the business not only articulate the rhetoric of ethical behavior but also act in a manner that is consistent with that rhetoric; (d) put decision-making processes in place that require people to consider the ethical dimension of business decisions; (e) use ethics officers; (f) have strong corporate governance procedures; and (g) be morally courageous and encourage others to be the same.

Discussion Questions

1. How prevalent was the agency problem in corporate America during the late 1990s?

2. During the late 1990s there was a boom in initial public offerings of Internet companies (dot.com companies). The boom was supported by sky high valuations often assigned to Internet start-ups that had no revenues or earnings. The boom came to an abrupt end in 2001 when the NASDAQ stock market collapsed, losing almost 80% of its value. Who do you think benefited most from this boom: investors (stockholders) in those companies, managers, or investment bankers?

3. Why is maximizing return on invested capital consistent with maximizing returns to stockholders?

4. How might a company configure its strategy-making processes to reduce the probability that managers will pursue their own self-interest at the expense of stockholders?

5. Should stock options be treated as an expense? If they were, what impact would this have on a company?

6. Under what conditions is it ethically defensible to outsource production to producers in the developing world who have much lower labor costs when such actions involve laying off long-term employees in the firm's home country?

Practicing Strategic Management

■ SMALL-GROUP EXERCISE
Evaluating Stakeholder Claims

Break up into groups of three to five people, and appoint one group member as a spokesperson who will communicate your findings to the class when called on by the instructor. Discuss the following:

1. Identify the key stakeholders of your educational institution. What claims do they place on the institution?

2. Strategically, how is the institution responding to those claims? Do you think the institution is pursuing the correct strategies in view of those claims? What might it do differently, if anything?

3. Prioritize the stakeholders in order of their importance for the survival and health of the institution. Do the claims of different stakeholder groups conflict with each other? If claims conflict, whose should be tackled first?

■ ARTICLE FILE 11

Find an example of a company that ran into trouble because it failed to take into account the rights of one of its stakeholder groups when making an important strategic decision.

■ STRATEGIC MANAGEMENT PROJECT
Module 11

This module deals with the relationships your company has with its major stakeholder groups. With the information you have at your disposal, perform the tasks and answer the questions that follow:

1. Identify the main stakeholder groups in your company. What claims do they place on the company? How is the company trying to satisfy those claims?

2. Evaluate the performance of the CEO of your company from the perspective of (a) stockholders, (b) employees, (c) customers, and (d) suppliers. What does this evaluation tell you about the ability of the CEO and the priorities that he or she is committed to?

3. Try to establish whether the governance mechanisms that operate in your company do a good job of aligning the interests of top managers with those of stockholders.

4. Pick a major strategic decision made by your company in recent years, and try to think through the ethical implications of that decision. In light of your review, do you think that the company acted correctly?

■ EXPLORING THE WEB
Visiting Merck

Visit the website of Merck, the world's largest pharmaceutical company (**www.merck.com/overview/philosophy.html**), and read the mission statement posted there. Then answer the following questions:

1. Evaluate this mission statement in light of the material contained in this chapter. Does the mission statement clearly state what Merck's basic strategic goal is? Do the values listed provide a good guideline for managerial action at Merck? Do those values recognize stakeholder claims?

2. Read the section on Merck's corporate responsibility and code of conduct. How does Merck attempt to balance

the goals of providing stockholders with an adequate rate of return on their investment while at the same time developing medicines that benefit humanity and that can be acquired by people in need at an affordable price? Do you think that Merck does a good job of balancing these goals?

3. In late September 2004 Merck recalled one of its best drugs, Vioxx, after research showed that people who used Vioxx had an elevated risk of suffering a heart at-

tack. To what extent do you think Merck's values and code of conduct played a part in this decision? Do you think Merck pulled the drug from the market quickly enough? (You may want to take a look at press reports on this issue.)

General Task   Using the Web, find an example of a company where there was overt conflict between principals and agents over the future strategic direction of the organization.

Closing Case

The Collapse of Enron

In early December 2001, the Enron Corporation filed for Chapter 11 bankruptcy protection. Enron, which started off as a natural gas pipeline operator and independent power producer, had emerged during the late 1990s as the principal player in the rapidly expanding market for energy trading. At its height in 2000, the company had boasted revenues of $101 billion, a stock market capitalization of $63 billion, and a chairman, Kenneth Lay, who was a high-profile confidant of then president-elect George W. Bush. The company was leveraging its expertise in energy trading to other market opportunities, including trading in paper, metals, water, and telecommunication capacity (or broadband). Enron believed that it could exploit the power of the Internet to create online markets in almost anything. The media loved the company. In 2000, *Fortune* magazine voted Enron "the most innovative company of the year." The *Economist* wrote that Enron "has created what may be the most successful Internet venture of any company in any industry anywhere."

A few months after these words were written, Enron had ceased to exist as a functioning entity. On its last trading day, the stock stood at 61 cents per share, down from a high of $90 just a year earlier. Numbered among the stockholders who had seen their Enron holdings implode in value were many Enron employees, who had been obliged by company policies to hold Enron stock in their retirement accounts.

What made the collapse of Enron so disturbing was not just the size of the failure, but the manner in which the company unraveled. What brought Enron down so rapidly was an accumulation of more than $27 billion in

off-balance-sheet debt held by partnerships hidden from the view of most investors, employees, and regulators. These partnerships were set up to exploit Enron's forays into ever more exotic online trading ventures, such as water and bandwidth trading. The partnerships were controlled by Enron managers but not owned by Enron, so the debt did not appear on Enron's balance sheets and thus did not affect the company's credit rating and borrowing costs. The partnerships were financed with debt raised from institutional investors. Using the company's high-flying stock as collateral, Enron guaranteed that debt. It often transferred its own assets to the partnerships, registering the transfer as revenues.

The partnerships were the brainchild of Enron's chief financial officer, Andrew Fastow, who used them as a way of making Enron's balance sheet and earnings look stronger than they really were. Fastow also personally profited from the partnerships, many of which he controlled, reportedly making over $30 million from them. The partnership strategy, however, was very risky. If the aggressive investments the partnerships were making did not pan out, Enron, as the guarantor of partnership debt, would be on the hook. Moreover, if Enron's stock fell too far, guarantees backed by stock would have to be replaced by cash, which would require Enron to raise more debt.

The first cracks in Enron's facade started to appear in August 2001 when the CEO, Jeffrey Skilling, suddenly and unexpectedly resigned, citing "personal reasons." Skilling had sold some $17.5 million of Enron stock in the months before he quit. Chairman Kenneth Lay, himself the former

CEO, stepped back into the CEO position and reassured investors, who were spooked by Skilling's sudden departure. Then, in October 2001, Enron recorded a third-quarter loss of $618 million and announced that it was reducing shareholder equity by $1.2 billion, primarily because of losses accumulated at partnerships. Enron's stock, which had lost half its value since December 2000, suddenly plummeted. This created a death spiral in which Enron had to raise debt to guarantee debt accumulated at partnerships, a spiral that quickly led to bankruptcy.

When the existence of the partnerships was revealed, the financial community was stunned: there had been scarcely a reference to any of them in Enron's audited financial statements. By implication, investors were ignorant of the tremendous risks associated with the partnership strategy. It was difficult to escape the conclusion that Enron's management had deliberately played down the existence of the partnerships in order to mislead the financial markets about the true state of the company. Questions were also asked about Enron's auditor, Arthur Andersen. Why had it not drawn attention to the partnerships? Surely, as auditor, it must have known about them. Why had Andersen apparently agreed with the tactic of keeping these partnerships hidden from public view? Was it to protect a lucrative financial relationship with an important client? Enron paid Andersen some $52 million in 2000—$25 million for auditing services and $27 million for consulting services. The questions about Andersen's role became even sharper when it was revealed that the Andersen partner responsible for the Enron audit had instructed his staff to shred documents relating to the audit. Was Andersen trying to hide what it had known about the true financial state of the company?

The voices of critics grew louder when it was discovered that, in August 2001, a midlevel Enron official, Sherron Watkins, had sent a memo to Kenneth Lay outlining the risks associated with the partnership strategy. Watkins warned Lay that Enron could implode in a wave of accounting scandals. Lay apparently expressed concern but continued to present a bullish face to the outside world and appears to have done nothing to rein in the CFO, Fastow. Lay moved to replace Fastow only on October 24, two days after the Securities and Exchange Commission announced that it had started an investigation into Enron's accounting practices. Worse still, throughout 2001, Enron's senior managers continued to sell millions of dollars of their own holdings in Enron's stock, while many employees were limited or prohibited from selling the Enron stock they held in their retirement accounts. Did the managers know something that they kept hidden from their own employees?

A 2002 exposé of Enron by author Robert Bryce added interesting details to the Enron story. Bryce painted a picture of widespread self-dealing and fraud at Enron. According to Bryce, top managers systematically enriched themselves and their own families at shareholders' expense. Bryce tells how former Enron CEO Kenneth Lay made sure that his own family benefited handsomely from Enron. Much of Enron's corporate travel business was handled by a travel agency partly owned by Lay's sister. When an internal auditor recommended that the company could do better by using another travel agency, he soon found himself out of a job. In 1997 Enron acquired a company owed by Kenneth Lay's son, Mark Lay, which was trying to establish a business trading paper and pulp products. At the time Mark Lay and another company he controlled were targets of a federal criminal investigation of bankruptcy fraud and embezzlement. As part of the deal, Enron hired Mark Lay as an executive with a three-year contract that guaranteed him at least $1 million in pay over that period, plus options to purchase about 20,000 shares of Enron. Bryce also details how Lay's grown daughter used an Enron jet to transport her king-sized bed to France.

Bryce also discussed how Lay's successor as CEO at Enron, Jeff Skilling, put a performance evaluation system in place that weeded out 15 percent of underperformers every six months. According to Bryce, this created a pressure cooker culture with a myopic focus on short-run performance. Some executives and energy traders responded to that pressure by falsifying their performance, such as by inflating the value of trades, to make it look as if they were doing better than was actually the case.

In the aftermath of Enron's collapse, the U.S. Congress announced that it would investigate allegations of financial misdealing at the company. Called before a House Committee, Lay and Fastow took the Fifth, while Skilling claimed ignorance of the details of the partnership dealings. Was the law broken? It would seem so. By late 2004 several former Enron executives were in jail for fraud, including CFO Fastow, who was serving a ten-year jail sentence for fraud, while others, including Lay and Skilling, had been indicted by prosecutors and were scheduled to stand trial. For his part, Lay has acknowledged that there was wrongdoing at Enron, but he claims that he did not know about it. Lay has blamed Enron's troubles on Fastow, who he says "betrayed" his position of trust in the company.[34]

Case Discussion Questions

1. In whose best interests were Fastow, Lay, and Skilling acting? Do you think what happened at Enron is an example of the agency problem?

2. Do you think the Enron board exercised its fiduciary duty during the late 1990s? To what extent might the effectiveness of the board have been limited by the fact that Kenneth Lay, the former CEO, was chairman? What does this tell you about how boards can work?

3. How might the culture of the company under the leadership of Lay and Skilling have contributed to Enron's ethical problems?

4. Do you think Lay is himself a victim of an agency problem, as he seems to claim? Does he bear any responsibility, legal or otherwise, for the demise of Enron?

5. Did Arthur Andersen behave ethically? If not, why not?

Chapter 12

Implementing Strategy in Companies That Compete in a Single Industry

Opening Case

Nokia's New Product Structure

Nokia is the world's largest cellular or mobile phone maker in the world, with sales of over $40 billion in 2004. The company was a pioneer of cell phone technology, and throughout the 1990s its sales surged every year; however, business has not been as good in the 2000s. Like Motorola, another cell phone pioneer, Nokia's profits have fallen because it has run into tough competition from companies like Samsung, Sony, and hand-held makers like Palm that have been rushing to offer their customers new and improved varieties of hand-held devices or smart phones. In the *Opening Case* to Chapter 5, we saw how Samsung was the first company to realize that customers wanted a color screen so that they could play games on their phones, as well as one of the first to realize the potential of integrating digital cameras into phones. The market is growing for game-playing phones, Internet-connected phones, and smart phones that include functions such as an MP3 player, record-keeping software, and applications software for PowerPoint presentations and word processing. Also growing rapidly is the market for wireless technology that can securely link smart phones used in the field to the company's central databases and the PCs in employees' offices or homes, especially now that broadband communication is becoming the norm.

Analysts claim that Nokia was slow to sense these emerging trends partly because of its organizational structure and culture. Nokia's way of operating was to push down or decentralize decision making to lower levels where teams of employees were made responsible for developing innovative new cell phone software and hardware. Bureaucracy was kept to a minimum, and team members normally discussed product development in informal meetings. In addition, Nokia's culture was based on Finnish values and norms that emphasized democratic, shared, and informal work relationships rather than the use of formal authority.

This way of implementing strategy had led to superior innovation and a successful business model, but as Nokia grew bigger, problems emerged. While the cell phone market was changing rapidly, Nokia's team structure was still resulting in slow decision making. It was taking more and more time for Nokia to innovate new products and bring them to the market. Higher-level managers had to wait longer to find out what the teams below them were doing, and then top managers from all parts of the organization had to meet in "company committees" to decide which products should be given most funding and priority. Another problem was that Nokia's top managers, headquartered in Espoo, Finland, were remote from global customers, and its marketing and engineering managers were slow to pick up on developing wireless trends, such as customers' desire for digital cameras. In particular, they did not appreciate how fast the global market was fragmenting into customers in rich countries like Japan and the United States who wanted sophisticated, broadband-capable smart phones and were prepared to pay high prices for them, and customers in developing countries such as South America, China, and India who needed an inexpensive cell phone infrastructure and service, as well as inexpensive cell phones.[1]

In the early 2000s, when the company's sales started to fall as its Japanese competitors took the lead, Nokia's managers realized they needed to change the way the company operated to quicken Nokia's response to the changing marketplace. Nokia's CEO, Jorma Ollila, announced that in 2004 Nokia would split up its activities into four separate product divisions, each of which would focus on developing cell phone software and hardware for a particular market segment. Three of these were new divisions: (1) the *mobile phone* division, which would primarily design and sell low-cost/low-priced handsets primarily for voice calls; (2) the *multimedia* division, which would design and sell advanced smart phones with features such as gaming and picture taking and which would pursue differentiation and, hopefully, premium pricing; and (3) the *networks* division, which would sell the technology necessary to build mobile phone networks and create wireless infrastructure in regions and countries around the globe. Finally, Nokia announced it would greatly expand the

activities of its *enterprise solutions* division, which was responsible for developing hardware and software products for corporate customers in search of a wireless corporate intranet. Here, it was competing directly against companies like Microsoft, IBM, and Hewlett-Packard.

The plan is that each product division will be under the control of its own team of top executives and each team will build the business model necessary to compete successfully in its market segment.[2] By decentralizing control to each division, Nokia hopes to speed up team decision making, reasoning that managers will be in much closer contract with these teams and can intervene quickly as the need arises. Nokia hopes the new structure will allow it to innovate new models of cell phones at a faster rate and lower cost and so combat the threat from Samsung. In addition, to get closer to its customers, Nokia announced that it would expand its overseas operations—for example, by outsourcing more manufacturing to Asia and establishing more local sales offices. It would also create a U.S. headquarters for its new enterprise solutions division, and it hired a former HP executive, Mary McDowell, to head the division and spearhead its push into this large and profitable corporate networking market. Only time will tell if Nokia's new structure will be successful, but the company announced that many new products would be introduced in 2005 and beyond and that its sales were once again on the upward path.[3]

Overview

As the story of Nokia suggests, organizational structure and culture can have a direct bearing on a company's profits. This chapter examines how managers can best implement their strategies through their organization's structure and culture to achieve a competitive advantage and superior performance. A well-thought-out business model becomes profitable only if it can be implemented successfully. In practice, however, implementing strategy through structure and culture is a difficult, challenging, and never-ending task. Managers cannot just create an organizing framework for a company's value-chain activities and then assume it will keep working efficiently and effectively over time, just as they cannot select strategies and assume that these strategies will still work in the future when the competitive environment is changing.

We begin by discussing the main elements of organizational design and the way they work together to create an organizing framework that allows a company to implement its strategy. We also discuss how strategic managers can use structure, control, and culture to pursue functional-level strategies that create and build distinctive competencies. The analysis then moves to the industry level and the issues facing managers in a single industry. The next chapter takes up where this one leaves off and examines strategy implementation across industries and countries—that is, corporate and global strategy. By the end of this chapter and the next, you will understand why the fortunes of a company often rest on its managers' ability to design and manage its structure, control systems, and culture to best implement its business model.

Implementing Strategy Through Organizational Design

Strategy implementation involves the use of **organizational design,** the process of deciding how a company should create, use, and combine organizational structure, control systems, and culture to pursue a business model successfully. **Organizational structure** assigns employees to specific value creation tasks and roles and specifies how these tasks and roles are to be linked together in a way that increases efficiency, quality, innovation, and responsiveness to customers—the distinctive competencies that build competitive advantage. The purpose of organizational structure is to *coordinate and integrate* the efforts of employees at all levels—corporate, business, and functional—and across a company's functions and business units so that they work together in the way that will allow it to achieve the specific set of strategies in its business model.

Organizational structure does not by itself provide the set of incentives through which people can be *motivated* to make it work. Hence, there is a need for control systems. The purpose of a **control system** is to provide managers with (1) a set of incentives to motivate employees to work toward increasing efficiency, quality, innovation, and responsiveness to customers and (2) specific feedback on how well an organization and its members are performing and building competitive advantage so that managers can constantly take action to strengthen a company's business model. Structure provides an organization with a skeleton; control gives it the muscles, sinews, nerves, and sensations that allow managers to regulate and govern its activities.

Organizational culture, the third element of organizational design, is the specific collection of values, norms, beliefs, and attitudes that are shared by people and groups in an organization and that control the way they interact with each other and with stakeholders outside the organization.[4] Organizational culture is a company's "way of doing something": it describes the characteristic ways in which members of an organization "get the job done," such as the way Nokia uses teams to speed innovation. As we discuss in detail below, top managers, because they can influence which kinds of beliefs and values develop in an organization, are an important determinant of how organizational members will work toward achieving organizational goals.[5]

Figure 12.1 sums up the discussion so far. Organizational structure, control, and culture are the means by which an organization motivates and coordinates its members to work toward achieving the building blocks of competitive advantage.

FIGURE 12.1

Implementing Strategy Through Organizational Design

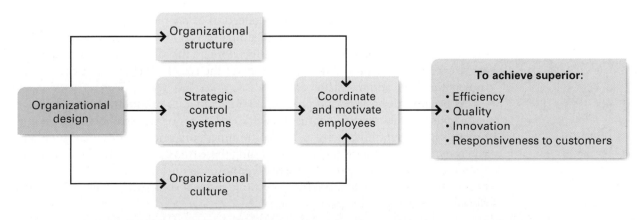

Top managers who wish to find out why it takes a long time for people to make decisions in a company, why there is a lack of cooperation between sales and manufacturing, or why product innovations are few and far between need to understand how the design of a company's structure and control system and the values and norms in its culture affect employee motivation and behavior. *Organizational structure, control, and culture shape people's behaviors, values, and attitudes and determine how they will implement an organization's business model and strategies.*[6] On the basis of such an analysis, top managers can devise a plan to restructure or change their company's structure, control systems, and culture to improve coordination and motivation. Effective organizational design allows a company to obtain a competitive advantage and achieve above-average profitability.

Building Blocks of Organizational Structure

After formulating a company's business model and strategies, managers must make designing an organizational structure their next priority. The value creation activities of organizational members are meaningless unless some type of structure is used to assign people to tasks and connect the activities of different people and functions.[7] Managers must make three basic choices:

1. How best to group tasks into functions and to group functions into business units or divisions to create distinctive competencies and pursue a particular strategy

2. How to allocate authority and responsibility to these functions and divisions

3. How to increase the level of coordination or integration between functions and divisions as a structure evolves and becomes more complex

We first discuss basic issues and then revisit them when considering appropriate choices of structure at different levels of strategy.

■ Grouping Tasks, Functions, and Divisions

Because, to a large degree, an organization's tasks are a function of its strategy, the dominant view is that companies choose a form of structure to match their organizational strategy. Perhaps the first person to address this issue formally was the Harvard business historian Alfred D. Chandler.[8] After studying the organizational problems experienced in large U.S. corporations such as DuPont and GM as they grew in the early decades of the twentieth century, Chandler reached two conclusions: (1) that, in principle, organizational structure follows the range and variety of tasks that the organization chooses to pursue; and (2) that U.S. companies' structures change as their strategy changes in a predictable way over time.[9] In general, this means that most companies first group people and tasks into functions, and then functions into divisions.[10]

As we discuss earlier, a *function* is a collection of people who work together and perform the same types of tasks or hold similar positions in an organization.[11] For example, the salespeople in a car dealership belong to the sales function. Together, car sales, car repair, car parts, and accounting are the set of functions that allow a car dealership to sell and maintain cars.

As organizations grow and produce a wider range of products, the amount and complexity of the *handoffs*, that is the work exchanges or transfers between people, functions, and subunits, increase. The communications and measurement problems and the managerial inefficiencies surrounding these transfers or handoffs are a major source of *bureaucratic costs*, the costs of monitoring and managing the exchanges necessary to add value to a product as it flows along a company's value chain to the final customer.[12]

We discuss why bureaucratic costs increase as companies pursue more complex strategies later in the chapter. For now, it is important to note that managers group tasks into functions and, when necessary, group functions into business units or divisions to reduce bureaucratic costs. For example, as Nokia started to produce a wide range of different mobile phones for different kinds of customers, it created separate product divisions. A *division* is a way of grouping functions to allow an organization to better produce and dispose of its goods and services to customers. In developing an organizational structure, managers must decide how to group an organization's activities by function and division in a way that achieves organizational goals effectively, such as happened at Nokia.[13]

Top managers can choose from among many kinds of structure to group their activities. The choice is made on the basis of the structure's ability to implement the company's business models and strategies successfully.

■ Allocating Authority and Responsibility

As organizations grow and produce a wider range of goods and services, the size and number of their functions and divisions increase. The number of handoffs or transfers between employees also increases, and to economize on bureaucratic costs and effectively coordinate the activities of people, functions, and divisions, managers must develop a clear and unambiguous **hierarchy of authority**, or chain of command, that defines each manager's relative authority, from the CEO down through the middle managers and first-line managers, to the nonmanagerial employees who actually make goods or provide services.[14] Every manager, at every level of the hierarchy, supervises one or more subordinates. The term **span of control** refers to the number of subordinates who report directly to a manager. When managers know exactly what their authority and responsibility are, information distortion problems that promote managerial inefficiencies are kept to a minimum, and handoffs or transfers can be negotiated and monitored to economize on bureaucratic costs. For example, managers are less likely to risk invading another manager's turf and thus can avoid the costly fights and conflicts that inevitably result from such encroachments.

■ Tall and Flat Organizations

Companies choose the number of hierarchical levels they need on the basis of their strategy and the functional tasks necessary to create distinctive competencies.[15] As an organization grows in size or complexity (measured by the number of its employees, functions, and divisions), its hierarchy of authority normally lengthens, making the organizational structure taller. A **tall structure** has many levels of authority relative to company size; a **flat structure** has fewer levels relative to company size (see Figure 12.2). As the hierarchy becomes taller, problems that make the organization's structure less flexible and slow managers' response to changes in the competitive environment may result. It is vital that managers understand how these problems arise so they know how to change a company's structure to respond to them.

First, communication problems may arise. When an organization has many levels in the hierarchy, it can take a long time for the decisions and orders of top managers to reach managers further down in the hierarchy, and it can take a long time for top managers to learn how well their decisions worked out. Feeling out of touch, top managers may want to verify that lower-level managers are following orders and may require written confirmation from them. Lower-level managers, who know they will be held strictly accountable for their actions, start devoting more time to the process of making decisions in order to improve their chances of being right. They might even try to avoid responsibility by making top managers decide what actions to take.

FIGURE 12.2

Tall and Flat Structures

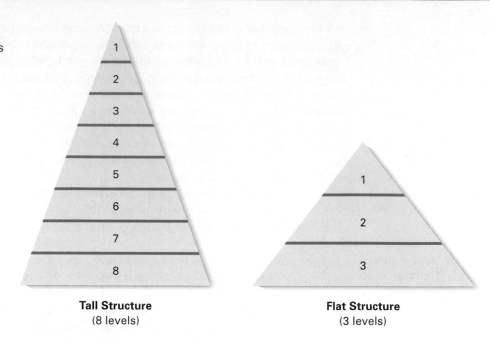

Tall Structure
(8 levels)

Flat Structure
(3 levels)

A second communication problem that can result is the distortion of commands and orders as they are transmitted up and down the hierarchy, which causes managers at different levels to interpret what is happening differently. Accidental distortion of orders and messages occurs when different managers interpret messages from their own narrow functional perspectives. Intentional distortion can occur because managers lower in the hierarchy decide to interpret information to increase their own personal advantage.

A third problem with tall hierarchies is that they usually indicate that an organization is employing *too many* managers, and managers are expensive. Managerial salaries, benefits, offices, and secretaries are a huge expense for organizations. Large companies such as IBM, General Motors, and Nokia pay their managers billions of dollars a year. In the 2000s, hundreds of thousands of middle managers were laid off as dot-coms collapsed and high-tech companies like Hewlett-Packard and Lucent attempted to reduce costs by restructuring and downsizing their work forces.

■ **The Minimum Chain of Command** To ward off the problems that result when an organization becomes too tall and employs too many managers, top managers need to ascertain whether they are employing the right number of top, middle, and first-line managers and see whether they can redesign their hierarchies to reduce the number of managers. Top managers might well follow a basic organizing principle: the **principle of the minimum chain of command**, which states that a company should choose the hierarchy with the *fewest* levels of authority necessary to use organizational resources efficiently and effectively.

Effective managers constantly scrutinize their hierarchies to see whether the number of levels can be reduced—for example, by eliminating one level and giving the responsibilities of managers at that level to managers above and empowering employees below. This practice has become increasingly common as companies battle with low-cost overseas competitors and search for ways to reduce costs. One manager who is constantly trying to empower employees and keep the hierarchy flat is Colleen C. Barrett, the number-two executive of Southwest Airlines.[16] Barrett, the highest-ranking woman in the airline industry, is well known for continually reaffirming Southwest's message that employees should feel free to go above and beyond their prescribed roles to provide better customer service. Her central message is that Southwest values and trusts its employees, who are empowered to take responsibility. Southwest employees are encouraged not to look to their superiors for guidance but rather to take responsibility to find ways to do the job better themselves. As a result, Southwest keeps the number of its middle managers to a minimum.

When companies become too tall and the chain of command too long, strategic managers tend to lose control over the hierarchy, which means that they lose control over their strategies. Disaster often follows because a tall organizational structure decreases, rather than promotes, motivation and coordination between employees and functions, and bureaucratic costs escalate as a result. One important way to overcome such problems, at least partially, and to lessen bureaucratic costs is to decentralize authority—that is, vest authority in the hierarchy's lower levels as well as at the top.

■ **Centralization or Decentralization?** Authority is centralized when managers at the upper levels of a company's hierarchy retain the authority to make the most important decisions. When authority is decentralized, it is delegated to divisions, functions, and employees at lower levels in the company. By delegating authority in this fashion, managers can economize on bureaucratic costs and avoid communication and coordination problems because information does not have to be constantly sent to the top of the organization for decisions to be made. There are three advantages to decentralization.

First, when top managers delegate operational decision-making responsibility to middle- and first-level managers, they reduce information overload and so are able to spend more time on positioning the company competitively and strengthening its business model. Second, when managers in the bottom layers of the company become responsible for implementing strategies to suit local conditions, their motivation and accountability increase. The result is that decentralization promotes flexibility and reduces bureaucratic costs because lower-level managers are authorized to make on-the-spot decisions; handoffs are not needed. The third advantage is that when lower-level employees are given the right to make important decisions, fewer managers are needed to oversee their activities and tell them what to do—a company can flatten its hierarchy. Strategy in Action 12.1 shows how Union Pacific experienced some of these advantages after it decentralized its operations.

If decentralization is so effective, why don't all companies decentralize decision making and avoid the problems of tall hierarchies? The answer is that centralization has its advantages too. Centralized decision making allows for easier coordination of the organizational activities needed to pursue a company's strategy. If managers at all levels can make their own decisions, overall planning becomes extremely difficult, and the company may lose control of its decision making.

Centralization also means that decisions fit broad organization objectives. When its branch operations were getting out of hand, for example, Merrill Lynch increased centralization by installing more information systems to give corporate managers greater control over branch activities. Similarly, Hewlett-Packard centralized R&D responsibility at the corporate level to provide a more directed corporate strategy.

Strategy in Action   12.1

Union Pacific Decentralizes to Increase Customer Responsiveness

Union Pacific, one of the biggest rail freight carriers in the United States, was experiencing a crisis in the late 1990s. The U.S. economic boom was causing a record increase in the amount of freight that the railroad had to transport, but at the same time, the railroad was experiencing record delays in moving the freight. Union Pacific's customers were irate and complaining bitterly about the problem, and the delays were costing the company millions of dollars in penalty payments—$150 million annually.

The problem stemmed from Union Pacific's very centralized management approach, devised in its attempt to cut costs. All scheduling and route planning were handled centrally at its headquarters office in an attempt to promote operating efficiency. The job of regional managers was largely to ensure the smooth flow of freight through their regions. Now, recognizing that efficiency had to be balanced by the need to be responsive to customers,

Union Pacific's CEO, Dick Davidson, announced a sweeping reorganization to the company's customers. Henceforth, regional managers were to be given the authority to make operational decisions at the level at which they were most important: field operations. Regional managers could now alter scheduling and routing to accommodate customer requests even if this raised costs. The goal of the organization was to "return to excellent performance by simplifying our processes and becoming easier to deal with." In making this decision, the company was following the lead of its competitors, most of which had already moved to decentralize their operations. Union Pacific has continued its decentralization approach in the 2000s. In its recent announcement that it was adding a new region, it stated that "the new four-region system will continue the effort to decentralize decision-making into the field, while fostering improved customer responsiveness, operational excellence, and personal accountability."[a]

Furthermore, in times of crisis, centralization of authority permits strong leadership because authority is focused on one person or group. This focus allows for speedy decision making and a concerted response by the whole organization. How to choose the right level of centralization for a particular strategy is discussed later.

■ **Integration and Integrating Mechanisms**   Much coordination takes place among people, functions, and divisions through the hierarchy of authority. Often, however, as a structure becomes complex, this is not enough, and top managers need to use various **integrating mechanisms** to increase communication and coordination among functions and divisions. The greater the complexity of an organization's structure, the greater is the need for coordination among people, functions, and divisions to make the organizational structure work efficiently.[17] We discuss three kinds of integrating mechanisms that illustrate the kinds of issues involved.[18] Once again, these mechanisms are employed to economize on the information distortion problems that commonly arise when managing the handoffs or transfers among the ideas and activities of different people, functions, and divisions.

■ **Direct Contact**   Direct contact among managers creates a context within which managers from different functions or divisions can work together to solve mutual problems. However, several problems are associated with establishing this contact. Managers from different functions may have different views about what must be done to achieve organizational goals. But if the managers have equal authority (as functional managers typically do), the only manager who can tell them what to do is the CEO. If functional managers cannot reach agreement, no mechanism exists to resolve the conflict apart from the authority of the boss. In fact, one sign of a poorly performing organizational structure is the number of problems sent up the hierarchy for top managers to solve. The need to solve everyday conflicts and solve handoff or transfer problems raises bureaucratic costs. To reduce such conflicts and solve transfer problems, top managers use more complex integrating mechanisms to increase coordination among functions and divisions.

■ **Liaison Roles** Managers can increase coordination among functions and divisions by establishing liaison roles. When the volume of contacts between two functions increases, one way to improve coordination is to give one manager in each function or division the responsibility for coordinating with the other. These managers may meet daily, weekly, monthly, or as needed to solve handoff issues and transfer problems. The responsibility for coordination is part of the liaison's full-time job, and usually an informal relationship forms between the people involved, greatly easing strains between functions. Furthermore, liaison roles provide a way of transmitting information across an organization, which is important in large organizations where employees may know no one outside their immediate function or division.

■ **Teams** When more than two functions or divisions share many common problems, direct contact and liaison roles may not provide sufficient coordination. In these cases, a more complex integrating mechanism, the **team**, may be appropriate. One manager from each relevant function or division is assigned to a team that meets to solve a specific mutual problem; members are responsible for reporting back to their subunits on the issues addressed and the solutions recommended. Teams are increasingly being used at all organizational levels.

Strategic Control Systems

Strategic managers choose the organizational strategies and structure they hope will allow the organization to use its resources most effectively to pursue its business model and create value and profit. Then they create **strategic control systems**, tools that allow them to monitor and evaluate whether, in fact, their strategy and structure are working as intended, how they could be improved, and how they should be changed if they are not working.

Strategic control is not just about monitoring how well an organization and its members are performing currently or about how well the firm is using its existing resources. It is also about how to create the incentives to keep employees motivated and focused on the important problems that may confront an organization in the future so that they work together to find solutions that can help an organization perform better over time.[19] To understand the vital importance of strategic control, consider how it helps managers to obtain superior efficiency, quality, innovation, and responsiveness to customers, the four basic building blocks of competitive advantage:

■ *Control and efficiency.* To determine how *efficiently* they are using organizational resources, managers must be able to measure accurately how many units of inputs (raw materials, human resources, and so on) are being used to produce a unit of output. They must also be able to measure the number of units of outputs (goods and services) they produce. A control system contains the measures or yardsticks that allow managers to assess how efficiently they are producing goods and services. Moreover, if managers experiment to find a more efficient way to produce goods and services, these measures tell managers how successful they have been. Without a control system in place, managers have no idea how well their organizations are performing and how they can make it perform better, something that is becoming increasingly important in today's highly competitive environment.[20]

■ *Control and quality.* Today, competition often revolves around increasing the *quality* of goods and services. In the car industry, for example, within each price range, cars compete against one another in terms of their features, design, and reliability. So whether a customer buys a Ford Taurus, a GM Cavalier, a Chrysler Intrepid, a Toyota Camry, or a Honda Accord depends significantly on the quality of each company's product. Strategic control is important in determining the quality of goods and services because it gives managers feedback on product quality. If managers consistently measure the number of customers' complaints and the number of new cars returned for repairs, they have a good indication of how much quality they have built into their product.

■ *Control and innovation.* Strategic control can help to raise the level of *innovation* in an organization. Successful innovation takes place when managers create an organizational setting in which employees feel empowered to be creative and authority is decentralized to employees so that they feel free to experiment and take risks, such as at Nokia. Deciding on the appropriate control systems to encourage risk taking is an important management challenge, and, as discussed later in the chapter, an organization's culture becomes important in this regard.

■ *Control and responsiveness to customers.* Finally, strategic managers can help make their organizations more *responsive to customers* if they develop a control system that allows them to evaluate how well employees with customer contact are performing their jobs. Monitoring employees' behavior can help managers find ways to help increase employees' performance level, perhaps by revealing areas in which skills training can help employees or by finding new procedures that allow employees to perform their jobs better. When employees know their behaviors are being monitored, they may have more incentive to be helpful and consistent in the way they act toward customers.

Strategic control systems are the formal target-setting, measurement, and feedback systems that allow strategic managers to evaluate whether a company is achieving superior efficiency, quality, innovation, and customer responsiveness and implementing its strategy successfully. An effective control system should have three characteristics. It should be *flexible* enough to allow managers to respond as necessary to unexpected events; it should provide *accurate information*, giving a true picture of organizational performance; and it should supply managers with the information in a *timely manner* because making decisions on the basis of outdated information is a recipe for failure.[21] As Figure 12.3 shows, designing an effective strategic control system requires four steps: establishing standards and targets, creating measuring and monitoring systems, comparing performance against targets, and evaluating the result.

■ **Levels of Strategic Control**

Strategic control systems are developed to measure performance at four levels in a company: corporate, divisional, functional, and individual. Managers at all levels must develop the most appropriate set of measures to evaluate corporate-, business-, and functional-level performance. As the balanced scorecard approach discussed in Chapter 11 suggests, these measures should be tied as closely as possibly to the goals of developing distinctive competencies in efficiency, quality, innovativeness, and

FIGURE 12.3

Steps in Designing
an Effective Control
System

responsiveness to customers. Care must be taken, however, to ensure that the standards used at each level do not cause problems at the other levels—for example, that a division's attempts to improve its performance does not conflict with corporate performance. Furthermore, controls at each level should provide the basis on which managers at lower levels design their control systems. Figure 12.4 illustrates these links.

FIGURE 12.4

Levels of Organizational Control

■ Types of Strategic Control Systems

In Chapter 11, the balanced scorecard approach was discussed as a way to ensure that managers complement the use of ROIC with other kinds of strategic controls to ensure they are pursuing strategies that maximize long-run profitability. Here we consider three more types of control systems: *personal control, output control*, and *behavior control.*

■ Personal Control

Personal control is the desire to shape and influence the behavior of a person in a *face-to-face interaction* in the pursuit of a company's goals. The most obvious kind of personal control is direct supervision from a manager further up in the hierarchy. The personal approach is useful because managers can question and probe subordinates about problems or new issues they are facing to get a better understanding of the situation, as well as to ensure that subordinates are performing their work effectively and not hiding any information that could cause problems down the line. Personal control also can come from a group of peers, such as occurs when people work in teams. Once again, personal control at the group level means that there is more possibility for learning to occur and competencies to develop, as well as greater opportunities to prevent free-riding or shirking.

■ Output Control

Output control is a system in which strategic managers estimate or forecast appropriate performance goals for each division, department, and employee and then measure actual performance relative to these goals. Often a company's reward system is linked to performance on these goals, so output control also provides an incentive structure for motivating employees at all levels in the organization. Goals keep managers informed about how well their strategies are creating a competitive advantage and building the distinctive competencies that lead to future success. Goals exist at all levels in an organization.

Divisional goals state corporate managers' expectations for each division concerning performance on such dimensions as efficiency, quality, innovation, and responsiveness to customers. Generally, corporate managers set challenging divisional goals to encourage divisional managers to create more effective strategies and structures in the future. At Nokia, for example, each product division now has a clear performance goal to achieve, and divisional managers are given considerable autonomy in formulating the strategies necessary to achieve their business model and to meet this goal. For example, the mobile phone division's managers must decide how best to pursue a cost-leadership model and the smart phone division's managers must decide how best to pursue a differentiation model.

Output control at the functional and individual levels is a continuation of control at the divisional level. Divisional managers set goals for functional managers that will allow the division to achieve its goals. As at the divisional level, functional goals are established to encourage the development of the generic competencies that provide the company with a competitive advantage, and functional performance is evaluated by how well a function develops a competency. In the sales function, for example, goals related to efficiency (such as cost of sales), quality (such as number of returns), and customer responsiveness (such as the time needed to respond to customer needs) can be established for the whole function.

Finally, functional managers establish goals that individual employees are expected to achieve to allow the function to achieve its goals. Sales personnel, for example, can be given specific goals (related to functional goals) that they are required to achieve. Functions and individuals are then evaluated on the basis of achieving or not achieving their goals, and in sales, compensation is commonly pegged to achievement.

The achievement of these goals is a sign that the company's strategy is working and meeting organizational objectives.

The inappropriate use of output control can promote conflict among divisions. In general, setting across-the-board output targets, such as ROIC targets, for divisions can lead to destructive results if divisions single-mindedly try to maximize divisional ROIC at the expense of corporate ROIC. Moreover, to reach output targets, divisions may start to distort the numbers and engage in strategic manipulation of the figures to make their divisions look good—which increases bureaucratic costs.[22]

■ **Behavior Control** **Behavior control** is control through the establishment of a comprehensive system of rules and procedures to direct the actions or behavior of divisions, functions, and individuals.[23] The intent of behavior controls is not to specify the g*oals* but to standardize the *way or means* of reaching them. Rules standardize behavior and make outcomes predictable. If employees follow the rules, then actions are performed and decisions handled the same way time and time again. The result is predictability and accuracy, the aim of all control systems. The main kinds of behavior controls are operating budgets, standardization, and rules and procedures.

Once managers at each level have been given a goal to achieve, they establish operating budgets that regulate how managers and workers are to attain those goals. An **operating budget** is a blueprint that states how managers intend to use organizational resources to achieve organizational goals most efficiently. Most commonly, managers at one level allocate to managers at a lower level a specific amount of resources to use to produce goods and services. Once they have been given a budget, these lower-level managers must decide how they will allocate certain amounts of money for different organizational activities. They are then evaluated on the basis of their ability to stay inside the budget and make the best use of it. For example, managers at GE's washing machine division might have a budget of $50 million to develop and sell a new line of washing machines; they have to decide how much money to allocate to R&D, engineering, sales, and so on so that the division generates the most revenue and hence makes the biggest profit. Most commonly, large companies treat each division as a stand-alone profit center, and corporate managers evaluate each division's performance by its relative contribution to corporate profitability, something discussed in detail in the next chapter.

Standardization refers to the degree to which a company specifies how decisions are to be made so that employees' behavior becomes predictable.[24] In practice, there are three things an organization can standardize: *inputs, conversion activities*, and *outputs*.

When managers standardize, they screen *inputs* according to preestablished criteria or standards that determine which inputs to allow into the organization. If employees are the input in question, for example, then one way of standardizing them is to specify which qualities and skills they must possess and then to select only applicants who possess them. If the inputs in question are raw materials or component parts, the same considerations apply. The Japanese are renowned for the high quality and precise tolerances they demand from component parts to minimize problems with the product at the manufacturing stage. Just-in-time inventory systems also help standardize the flow of inputs.

The aim of standardizing *conversion activities* is to program work activities so that they are done the same way time and time again. The goal is predictability. Behavior controls, such as rules and procedures, are among the chief means by which companies can standardize throughputs. Fast-food restaurants such as McDonald's and

Burger King standardize all aspects of their restaurant operations; the result is consistent fast food.

The goal of standardizing *outputs* is to specify what the performance characteristics of the final product or service should be—the dimensions or tolerances the product should conform to, for example. To ensure that their products are standardized, companies apply quality control and use various criteria to measure this standardization. One criterion might be the number of goods returned from customers or the number of customers' complaints. On production lines, periodic sampling of products can indicate whether they are meeting performance characteristics.

As with other kinds of controls, the use of behavior control is accompanied by potential pitfalls that must be managed if the organization is to avoid strategic problems. Top management must be careful to monitor and evaluate the usefulness of behavior controls over time. Rules constrain people and lead to standardized, predictable behavior. However, rules are always easier to establish than to get rid of, and over time the number of rules an organization uses tends to increase. As new developments lead to additional rules, often the old rules are not discarded, and the company becomes overly bureaucratized. Consequently, the organization and the people in it become inflexible and are slow to react to changing or unusual circumstances. Such inflexibility can reduce a company's competitive advantage by lowering the pace of innovation and reducing its responsiveness to customers.

■ Using Information Technology

Information technology is playing an increasing role in strategy implementation at all organizational levels. In fact, it is making it much easier for organizations to cost-effectively develop output and behavior controls that give strategic managers much more and much better information to monitor the many aspects of their strategies and to respond appropriately. IT, which provides a way of standardizing behavior through the use of a consistent, often cross-functional software platform, is a form of behavior control. IT is also a form of output control because when all employees or functions use the same software platform to provide up-to-date information on their activities, this codifies and standardizes organizational knowledge and makes it easier to monitor progress toward strategic objectives. IT is also a kind of integrating mechanism because it provides people at all levels in the hierarchy and across all functions with more of the information and knowledge they need to perform their roles effectively. For example, today functional-level employees are able to access information easily from other functions using cross-functional software systems that keep them all informed about changes in product design, engineering, manufacturing schedules, and marketing plans that will have an impact on their activities. In this sense, IT overlays the structure of tasks and roles that is normally regarded as the "real" organizational structure. The many ways in which IT affects strategy implementation is discussed in different sections of this and the next chapter. Strategy in Action 12.2 illustrates one way in which IT can help managers monitor and coordinate the effectiveness with which their strategies are being put into action.

■ Strategic Reward Systems

Organizations strive to control employees' behavior by linking reward systems to their control systems.[25] Based on the company's strategy (cost leadership or differentiation, for example), strategic managers must decide which behaviors to reward. They then create a control system to measure these behaviors and link the reward structure to them. Determining how to relate rewards to performance is a crucial strategic decision because it determines the incentive structure that affects the way managers and employees at all levels in the organization behave. As Chapter 11 points out, top managers

Strategy in Action   12.2

Control at Cypress Semiconductor

In the fast-moving semiconductor business, a premium is placed on organizational adaptability. At Cypress Semiconductor, CEO T. J. Rodgers was facing a problem: how to control his growing 1,500-employee organization without developing a bureaucratic management hierarchy. Rodgers believed that a tall hierarchy hinders the ability of an organization to adapt to changing conditions. He was committed to maintaining a flat and decentralized organizational structure with a minimum of management layers. At the same time, he needed to control his employees to ensure that they performed in a manner consistent with company goals. The solution that Rodgers adopted was to implement a computer-based information system through which he can manage what every employee and team is doing in the decentralized organization. Each employee maintains a list of ten to fifteen goals, such as "Meet with marketing for new product launch" or "Make sure to check with customer X." Noted next to each goal is when it was agreed on, when it is due to be finished, and whether it has been finished. All of this information is stored on a central computer. Rodgers claims that he can review the goals of all 1,500 employees in about four hours, and he does so each week. He can do this because he manages by exception, looking only for employees who are falling behind. He then calls them—not to scold but to ask whether there is anything he can do to help them get the job done. It takes only about half an hour each week for employees to review and update their lists. This system allows Rodgers to exercise control over his organization without resorting to the expensive layers of a management hierarchy.[b]

can be encouraged to work in shareholders' interests by being rewarded with stock options linked to a company's long-term performance. Furthermore, companies such as Kodak and GM require managers to buy company stock, and when managers become shareholders they are more motivated to pursue long-term rather than short-term goals. Similarly, in designing a pay system for salespeople, the choice is whether to motivate them through straight salary or salary plus a bonus based on how much they sell. Neiman Marcus, the luxury retailer, pays employees a straight salary because it wants to encourage high-quality service but discourage a hard-sell approach. Thus, there are no incentives based on quantity sold. On the other hand, the pay system for rewarding car salespeople encourages high-pressure selling; it typically contains a large bonus based on the number and price of cars sold.

Organizational Culture

The third element that goes into successful strategy implementation is managing *organizational culture*, the specific collection of values and norms shared by people and groups in an organization.[26] Organizational values are beliefs and ideas about what kinds of goals members of an organization *should* pursue and about the appropriate kinds or standards of behavior organizational members *should* use to achieve these goals. Bill Gates is famous for the set of organizational values that he emphasizes: entrepreneurship, ownership, creativity, honesty, frankness, and open communication. By stressing entrepreneurship and ownership, he strives to get his employees to feel that Microsoft is not one "big bureaucracy" but a collection of smaller and very adaptive companies run by their members. Gates emphasizes giving lower-level managers autonomy and encourages them to take risks—to act like entrepreneurs, not corporate bureaucrats.[27]

From organizational values develop organizational norms, guidelines, or expectations that *prescribe* appropriate kinds of behavior by employees in particular situations and control the behavior of organizational members toward one another. The norms of behavior for software programmers at Microsoft include working long hours and weekends, wearing whatever clothing is comfortable (but never a suit and tie), consuming junk food, and communicating with other employees by e-mail and the company's state-of-the-art intranet.

Organizational culture functions as a kind of control in that strategic managers can influence the kind of values and norms that develop in an organization—values and norms that specify appropriate and inappropriate behaviors and that shape and influence the way its members behave.[28] Strategic managers such as Gates deliberately cultivate values that tell their subordinates how they should perform their roles; in Microsoft and Nokia, innovation and creativity are stressed. These companies establish and support norms that tell employees they should be innovative and entrepreneurial and should experiment even if there is a significant chance of failure.

Other managers might cultivate values that tell employees they should always be conservative and cautious in their dealings with others, consult with their superiors before they make important decisions, and record their actions in writing so they can be held accountable for what happens. Managers of organizations such as chemical and oil companies, financial institutions, and insurance companies—any organization in which great caution is needed—may encourage a conservative, vigilant approach to making decisions.[29] In a bank or mutual fund, for example, the risk of losing investors' money makes a cautious approach to investing highly appropriate. Thus, we might expect that managers of different kinds of organizations will deliberately try to cultivate and develop the organizational values and norms that are best suited to their strategy and structure.

Organizational socialization is the term used to describe how people learn organizational culture. Through socialization, people internalize and learn the norms and values of the culture so that they *become* organizational members.[30] Control through culture is so powerful that once these values have been internalized, they become part of the individual's values, and the individual follows organizational values without thinking about them.[31] Often the values and norms of an organization's culture are transmitted to its members through the stories, myths, and language that people in the organization use, as well as by other means.

■ Culture and Strategic Leadership

Organizational culture is created by the strategic leadership provided by an organization's founder and top managers. The organization's founder is particularly important in determining culture because the founder imprints his or her values and management style on the organization. Walt Disney's conservative influence on the company he established continued until well after his death. Managers were afraid to experiment with new forms of entertainment because they were afraid "Walt Disney wouldn't like it." It took the installation of a new management team under Michael Eisner to turn around the company's fortunes and allow it to deal with the realities of the new entertainment industry.

The leadership style established by the founder is transmitted to the company's managers, and as the company grows, it typically attracts new managers and employees who share the same values. Moreover, members of the organization typically recruit and select only those who share their values. Thus, a company's culture becomes more and more distinct as its members become more similar. The virtue of these shared values and common culture is that it *increases integration and improves coordination among organizational members.* For example, the common language that typically emerges in an organization because people share the same beliefs and values facilitates cooperation among managers. Similarly, rules and procedures and direct supervision are less important when shared norms and values control behavior and motivate employees. When organizational members buy into cultural norms and values, they feel bonded to the organization and are more committed to finding new ways to help it succeed. Strategy in Action 12.3 profiles how Ray Kroc built a strong culture at McDonald's.

Strategic leadership also affects organizational culture through the way managers design organizational structure, that is, the way they delegate authority and divide up task relationships. Thus, the way an organization designs its structure affects the cultural norms and values that develop within the organization. Managers need to be aware of this fact when implementing their strategies. Nokia changed its structure to change its cultural values and norms. Its emphasis on innovation is no longer sufficient to give the company a competitive advantage; today it also needs to emphasize responsiveness to customers to succeed in the cell phone business.

Strategy in Action   12.3

How Ray Kroc Established McDonald's Culture

In the restaurant business, maintaining product quality is all-important because the quality of the food and the service varies with the chefs and waiters as they come and go. If a customer gets a bad meal, poor service, or dirty silverware, that customer may not come back, and other potential customers may stay away as negative comments travel by word of mouth. This was the problem that Ray Kroc, the man who pioneered McDonald's growth, faced when McDonald's franchises began to open by the thousands throughout the United States. Kroc solved his problem by developing a sophisticated control system that specified every detail of how each McDonald's restaurant was to be operated and managed. This control system also created a distinct organizational culture.

First, Kroc developed a comprehensive system of rules and procedures for franchise owners and employees to follow in running each restaurant. The most effective way to perform tasks, from cooking burgers to cleaning tables, was worked out in advance, written down in rule books, and then taught to each McDonald's manager and employee through a formal training process. Prospective franchise owners had to attend "Hamburger University," the company's training center in Chicago, where in an intensive, month-long program they learned all aspects of a McDonald's operation. They were then expected to train their work force and make sure that employees thoroughly understood operating procedures. Kroc's goal in establishing this system of rules and procedures was to build a common culture so that customers would always find the

same level of quality in food and service. If customers always get what they expect from a restaurant, the restaurant has developed superior customer responsiveness.

Kroc also developed the McDonald's franchise system to help the company control its structure as it grew. He believed that a manager who is also a franchise owner (and thus receives a large share of the profits) is more motivated to buy into a company's culture than a manager paid on a straight salary. Thus, the McDonald's reward and incentive system allowed it to keep control over its operating structure as it expanded. Moreover, McDonald's was very selective in selling to its franchisees; they had to be people with the skills and capabilities that Kroc believed McDonald's managers should have.

Within each restaurant, franchise owners were instructed to pay particular attention to training their employees and instilling in them McDonald's concepts of efficiency, quality, and customer service. Shared norms, values, and an organizational culture also helped McDonald's standardize employees' behavior so that customers would know how they would be treated in a McDonald's restaurant. Moreover, McDonald's includes customers in its culture: it asks customers to bus their own tables, and it also shows concern for customers' needs by building playgrounds, offering Happy Meals, and organizing birthday parties for children. In creating its family-oriented culture, McDonald's ensures future customer loyalty because satisfied children are likely to become loyal adult customers.

■ Traits of Strong and Adaptive Corporate Cultures

Few environments are stable for any prolonged period of time. If an organization is to survive, managers must take actions that enable it to adapt to environmental changes. If they do not take such action, they may find themselves faced with declining demand for their products.

Managers can try to create an **adaptive culture**, one that is innovative and that encourages and rewards middle - and lower-level managers for taking the initiative.[32] Managers in organizations with adaptive cultures are able to introduce changes in the way the organization operates, including changes in its strategy and structure that allow it to adapt to changes in the external environment. Organizations with adaptive cultures are more likely to survive in a changing environment and indeed should have higher performance than organizations with inert cultures.

Several scholars in the field have tried to uncover the common traits that strong and adaptive corporate cultures share and to find out whether there is a particular set of values that dominates adaptive cultures that is missing from weak or inert ones. An early but still influential attempt is T. J. Peters and R. H. Waterman's account of the values and norms characteristic of successful organizations and their cultures.[33] They argue that adaptive organizations show three common value sets. First, successful companies have values promoting a *bias for action*. The emphasis is on autonomy and entrepreneurship, and employees are encouraged to take risks—for example, to create new products—even though there is no assurance that these products will be winners. Managers are closely involved in the day-to-day operations of the company and do not simply make strategic decisions isolated in some ivory tower, and employees have a hands-on, value-driven approach.

The second set of values stems from the *nature of the organization's mission*. The company must stick with what it does best and develop a business model focused on its mission. A company can easily get sidetracked into pursuing activities outside its area of expertise just because they seem to promise a quick return. Management should cultivate values so that a company sticks to its knitting, which means strengthening its business model. A company must also establish close relationships with customers as a way of improving its competitive position. After all, who knows more about a company's performance than those who use its products or services? By emphasizing customer-oriented values, organizations are able to learn customers' needs and improve their ability to develop products and services that customers desire. All of these management values are strongly represented in companies such as McDonald's, Wal-Mart, and Toyota, which are sure of their mission and continually take steps to maintain it.

The third set of values bears on *how to operate the organization*. A company should try to establish an organizational design that will motivate employees to do their best. Inherent in this set of values is the belief that productivity is obtained through people and that respect for the individual is the primary means by which a company can create the right atmosphere for productive behavior. An emphasis on entrepreneurship and respect for the employee leads to the establishment of a structure that gives employees the latitude to make decisions and motivates them to succeed. Because a simple structure and a lean staff best fit this situation, the organization should be designed with only the number of managers and hierarchical levels that are necessary to get the job done. The organization should also be sufficiently decentralized to permit employees' participation but centralized enough for management to make sure that the company pursues its strategic mission and that cultural values are followed.

In summary, these three main sets of values are at the heart of an organization's culture, and management transmits and maintains them through strategic leadership.

Strategy implementation continues as managers build strategic control systems that help perpetuate a strong adaptive culture, further the development of distinctive competencies, and provide employees with the incentive to build a company's competitive advantage. Finally, organizational structure contributes to the implementation process by providing the framework of tasks and roles that reduces transaction difficulties and allows employees to think and behave in ways that enable a company to achieve superior performance. The *Running Case* describes the way in which the frugal Sam Walton (he used to drive a thirty-year-old pickup truck and lived in a very modest home) used all the kinds of control systems discussed here to implement Wal-Mart's cost-leadership business model.

Building Distinctive Competencies at the Functional Level

In this section we turn to the issue of creating specific kinds of structure, control systems, and culture to implement a company's business model. The first level of strategy to examine is the functional level because, as Chapters 3 and 4 discuss, a company's business model is implemented through the functional strategies managers adopt to develop the distinctive competencies that allow it to pursue a particular business model.[34] What is the best kind of structure to use to group people and tasks to build competencies? The answer for most companies is to group them by function and create a functional structure.

■ Functional Structure: Grouping by Function

In the quest to deliver a final product to the customer, two related value-chain management problems increase. First, the range of value-chain activities that must be performed expands, and it quickly becomes clear that a company lacks the expertise needed to perform them effectively. For example, in a new company it quickly becomes apparent that the services of a professional accountant, a production manager, or a marketing expert are needed to take control of specialized tasks as sales increase. Second, it also becomes clear that no one person can successfully perform more than one value-chain activity without becoming overloaded. The new company's founder, for instance, who may have been performing many value-chain activities, realizes that he or she can no longer simultaneously make and sell the product. As most entrepreneurs discover, they have to decide how to group new employees to perform the various value-chain activities most efficiently. Most choose the functional structure.

Functional structures group people on the basis of their common expertise and experience or because they use the same resources.[35] For example, engineers are grouped in a function because they perform the same tasks and use the same skills or equipment. Figure 12.5 shows a typical functional structure. Each of the rectangles

FIGURE 12.5

Functional Structure

Running Case

Sam Walton's Approach to Implementing Wal-Mart's Strategy

Wal-Mart, headquartered in Bentonville, Arkansas, is the largest retailer in the world, with sales of over $80 billion in 2004. Its success rests on the way that its founder, the late Sam Walton, decided to implement the company's business model. Walton wanted all his managers and workers to have a hands-on approach to their jobs and to be totally committed to Wal-Mart's main goal, which he defined as total customer satisfaction. To motivate his employees, Walton created a sophisticated control system and a culture that gave employees at all levels continuous feedback about their own and the company's performance.

First, Walton developed a financial control system that provided managers with day-to-day feedback about the performance of all aspects of the business. Through a sophisticated companywide satellite system, corporate managers at its Bentonville headquarters can evaluate the performance of each store, and even of each department in each store. Information about store profits and the rate of turnover of goods is provided to store managers daily, and store managers in turn communicate this information to Wal-Mart's 625,000 employees (who are called associates). Through such information sharing, Walton's method encourages all associates to learn the fundamentals of the retailing business so they can work to improve it.

If any store seems to be underperforming, managers and associates meet to probe the reasons and to find solutions to help raise performance. Wal-Mart's top managers routinely visit stores that are having problems to lend their expertise, and each month top managers use the company's aircraft to fly to various Wal-Mart stores so they can keep their fingers on the pulse of the business. It is also customary for Wal-Mart's top managers to spend their Saturdays meeting together to discuss the week's financial results and their implications for the future.

Walton insisted on linking performance to rewards. Each manager's individual performance, measured by his or her ability to meet specific goals or output targets, is reflected in pay raises and chances for promotion (promotion to bigger stores in the company's 3,000-store empire and even to corporate headquarters, because Wal-Mart routinely promotes from within the company rather than hires managers from other companies). Top managers receive large stock options linked to the company's performance targets and stock price, and even ordinary associates receive stock in the company. An associate who started with Walton in the 1970s would by now have accumulated more than $250,000 in stock because of the appreciation of Wal-Mart's stock over time.

Walton instituted an elaborate system of controls, such as rules and budgets, to shape employees' behavior. Each store performs the same activities in the same way, and all employees receive the same kind of training so they know how to behave toward customers. In this way, Wal-Mart is able to standardize its operations, which leads to major cost savings and allows managers to make storewide changes easily.

Finally, Walton was not content just to use output and behavior controls and monetary rewards to motivate his associates. To involve associates in the business and encourage them to develop work behaviors focused on providing quality customer service, he established strong cultural values and norms for his company. Some norms that associates are expected to follow include the *ten-foot attitude*, which developed when Walton, during his visits to the stores, encouraged associates to "promise that whenever you come within 10 feet of a customer you will look him in the eye, greet him, and ask him if you can help him"; the *sundown rule*, which states that employees should strive to answer customers' requests by sundown on the day they receive them; and the Wal-Mart cheer ("Give me a W, give me an A," and so on), which is used in all its stores.

The strong customer-oriented values that Walton created are exemplified in the stories its members tell one another about the company's concern for its customers. They include stories such as the one about Sheila, who risked her own safety when she jumped in front of a car to prevent a little boy from being struck; about Phyllis, who administered CPR to a customer who had suffered a heart attack in her store; and about Annette, who gave up the Power Ranger she had on layaway for her own son so a customer's son could have his birthday wish. The strong Wal-Mart culture also helps to control and motivate its employees and helps associates to achieve the stringent output and financial targets the company has set for itself.[c]

represents a different functional specialization—R&D, sales and marketing, manufacturing, and so on—and each function concentrates on its own specialized task.[36]

Functional structures have several advantages. First, if people who perform similar tasks are grouped together, they can learn from one another and become more specialized and productive at what they do. This can create capabilities and competencies in each function. Second, they can monitor each other to make sure that all are performing their tasks effectively and not shirking their responsibilities. As a result, the work process becomes more efficient, reducing manufacturing costs and increasing operational flexibility. A third important advantage of functional structures is that they give managers greater control of organizational activities. As already noted, many difficulties arise when the number of levels in the hierarchy increases. If people are grouped into different functions, each with their own managers, then *several different hierarchies are created*, and the company can avoid becoming too tall. There will be one hierarchy in manufacturing, for example, and another in accounting and finance. Managing the business is much easier when different groups specialize in different organizational tasks and are managed separately.

■ The Role of Strategic Control

An important element of strategic control is to design a system that sets ambitious goals and targets for all managers and employees and then develops performance measures that *stretch and encourage managers and employees* to excel in their quest to raise performance. A functional structure promotes this goal because it increases the ability of managers and employees to monitor and make constant improvements to operating procedures. The structure also encourages organizational learning because managers, working closely with subordinates, can mentor them and help develop their technical skills.

Grouping by function also makes it easier to apply output control. Measurement criteria can be developed to suit the needs of each function to encourage members to stretch themselves. Each function knows how well it is contributing to overall performance, and indeed the part it plays in reducing the cost of goods sold or the gross margin. Managers can look closely to see if they are following the principle of the minimum chain of command and whether they need several levels of middle managers. Perhaps, instead of using middle managers, they could practice **management by objectives**, a system in which employees are encouraged to help set their own goals so that managers, like Cypress's Rodgers, *manage by exception*, intervening only when they sense something is not going right. Given this increase in control, a functional structure also makes it possible to institute an effective strategic reward system in which pay can be closely linked to performance and managers can accurately assess the value of each person's contributions.

■ Developing Culture at the Functional Level

Often functional structures offer the easiest way for managers to build a strong, cohesive culture. We discussed earlier how both Ray Kroc and Sam Walton, both of whom first developed a functional structure to implement their cost-leadership business models, worked hard to create values and norms that were shared by the members of all a company's different functions. To see how structure, control, and culture help create distinctive competencies, we consider how they affect the way three functions—manufacturing, R&D, and sales—operate.

■ Manufacturing
In manufacturing, functional strategy usually centers on improving efficiency and quality. A company must create an organizational setting in

which managers can learn how to economize on costs and lower the cost structure. Many companies today follow the lead of Japanese companies such as Toyota and Honda, which developed strong capabilities in manufacturing by operating total quality management (TQM) and flexible manufacturing systems (see Chapter 4).

With TQM, the inputs and involvement of all employees in the decision-making process are necessary to improve production efficiency and quality. Thus, it becomes necessary to decentralize authority to motivate employees to improve the production process. In TQM, work teams are created, and workers are given the responsibility and authority to discover and implement improved work procedures. Managers assume the role of coach and facilitator, and team members jointly take on the supervisory burdens. Work teams are often given the responsibility to control and discipline their own members and even to decide who should work in their team. Frequently, work teams develop strong norms and values, and work group culture becomes an important means of control; this type of control matches the new decentralized team approach. Quality control circles are created to exchange information and suggestions about problems and work procedures. A bonus system or employee stock ownership plan (ESOP) is frequently established to motivate workers and to allow them to share in the increased value that TQM often produces.

Nevertheless, to move down the experience curve quickly, most companies still exercise tight control over work activities and create behavior and output controls that standardize the manufacturing process. For example, human inputs are standardized through the recruitment and training of skilled personnel, the work process is programmed, often by computers, and quality control is used to make sure that outputs are being produced correctly. In addition, managers use output controls such as operating budgets to continuously monitor costs and quality. The extensive use of output controls and the continuous measurement of efficiency and quality ensure that the work team's activities meet the goals set for the function by management. Efficiency and quality increase as new and improved work rules and procedures are developed to raise the level of standardization. The aim is to find the match between structure and control and a TQM approach so that manufacturing develops the distinctive competency that leads to superior efficiency and quality.

■ **R&D** The functional strategy for an R&D department is to develop distinctive competencies in innovation and quality as excellence that result in products that fit customers' needs. Consequently, the R&D department's structure, control, and culture should provide the coordination necessary for scientists and engineers to bring high-quality products quickly to market. Moreover, these systems should motivate R&D scientists to develop innovative products.

In practice, R&D departments typically have a flat, decentralized structure that gives their members the freedom and autonomy to experiment and be innovative. Scientists and engineers are also grouped into teams because their performance can typically be judged only over the long term (it may take several years for a project to be completed). Consequently, extensive supervision by managers and the use of behavior control are a waste of managerial time and effort.[37] By letting teams manage their own transfer and handoff issues rather than using managers and the hierarchy of authority to coordinate work activities, managers avoid the information distortion problems that cause bureaucratic costs. Strategic managers take advantage of scientists' ability to work jointly to solve problems and to enhance each other's performance. In small teams, too, the professional values and norms that highly trained employees bring to the situation promote coordination. A culture for innovation frequently emerges to control employees' behavior, as at Nokia, Intel, and Microsoft, where the race to be first energizes the R&D teams. To create an innovative culture and speed product development, Intel uses a team structure in its R&D function. Intel has many work teams that operate side by side to develop the next generation of chips. So, when it makes mistakes, as it has recently, it can act quickly to join each team's innovations together to make a state-of-the-art chip that does meet customer needs, such as for multimedia chips. At the same time, to sustain its leading-edge technology, the company creates healthy competition between teams to encourage its scientists and engineers to champion new product innovations that will allow Intel to control the technology of tomorrow.[38]

To spur teams to work effectively, the reward system should be linked to the performance of the team and company. If scientists, individually or in a team, do not share in the profits a company obtains from its new products, they may have little motivation to contribute wholeheartedly to the team. To prevent the departure of their key employees and encourage high motivation, companies such as Merck, Intel, and Microsoft give their researchers stock options, stock, and other rewards that are tied to their individual performance, their team performance, and the company's performance.

■ **Sales** Salespeople work directly with customers, and when they are dispersed in the field, these employees are especially difficult to monitor. The cost-effective way to monitor their behavior and encourage high responsiveness to customers is usually to develop sophisticated output and behavior controls. Output controls, such as specific sales goals or goals for increasing responsiveness to customers, can be easily established and monitored by sales managers. Then, these controls can be linked to a bonus reward system to motivate salespeople. Behavior controls, such as detailed reports that salespeople file describing their interactions with customers, can also be used to standardize salespeople's behavior and make it easier for supervisors to review their performance.[39]

Usually, few managers are needed to monitor salespeople's activities, and a sales director and regional sales managers can oversee even large sales forces because outputs and behavior controls are employed. Frequently, however, and especially when salespeople deal with complex products such as pharmaceutical drugs or even luxury clothing, it becomes important to develop shared employee values and norms about the importance of patient safety or high-quality customer service, and managers spend considerable time training and educating employees to create such norms.

Similar considerations apply to the other functions, such as accounting, finance, engineering, and human resource management. Managers must implement functional strategy through the combination of structure, control, and culture to allow each function to create the competencies that lead to superior efficiency, quality, innovation, and responsiveness to customers. Strategic managers must also develop the incentive systems that motivate and align employees' interests with those of their companies.

■ **Functional Structure and Bureaucratic Costs**

No matter how complex their strategies become, most companies always retain a functional orientation because of its many advantages. Whenever different functions work together, however, bureaucratic costs inevitably arise because of information distortions that lead to the communications and measurement problems discussed in Chapter 10. Often these problems arise from the transfers or handoffs across different functions that are necessary to deliver the final product to the customer.[40]

Indeed, it is the need to economize on the bureaucratic costs of solving such problems that leads managers to adopt new organizational arrangements that reduce the scope of information distortions. Most commonly, companies divide their activities according to a more complex plan to match their business model and strategy in a discriminating way. These more complex structures are discussed later in the chapter. First, we review five areas in which information distortions can arise—communications, measurement, customers, location, and strategy.

■ **Communication Problems** As separate functional hierarchies evolve, functions can grow more remote from one another, and it becomes increasingly difficult to communicate across functions and to coordinate their activities. This communication problem stems from *differences in goal orientations*: the various functions develop distinct outlooks or understandings of the strategic issues facing a company.[41] For example, often the pursuit of different competencies can lead to different time or goal orientations. Some functions, such as manufacturing, have a short time frame and concentrate on achieving short-run goals, such as reducing manufacturing costs. Others, such as R&D, have a long-term point of view; their product development goals may have a time horizon of several years. These factors may cause each function to develop a different view of the strategic issues facing the company. Manufacturing, for example, may see the strategic issue as the need to reduce costs, sales may see it as the need to increase customer responsiveness, and R&D may see it as the need to create new products. These communication and coordination problems between functions increase bureaucratic costs.

■ **Measurement Problems** Often a company's product range widens as it develops new competencies and enters new market segments, as happened to Nokia. When this happens, a company may find it difficult to gauge or measure the contribution of a product or a group of products to its overall profitability—as noted in Chapter 10. Consequently, the company may turn out some unprofitable products without realizing it and may also make poor decisions about resource allocation. This means that the company's measurement systems are not complex enough to serve its needs. Dell Computer's explosive growth in the early 1990s, for example, caused it to lose control of its inventory management systems; hence, it could not accurately project supply and demand for the components that go into its personal computers. Problems with its organizational structure plagued Dell, reducing efficiency and quality. As one manager commented, designing its structure to keep pace with its growth was like "building a high-performance car while going around the race track."[42] However, Dell succeeded and today enjoys a 10 to 20 percent cost advantage over competitors like Gateway and Hewlett-Packard.

■ **Customer Problems** As the range and quality of an organization's goods and services increase, often more, and different kinds of, customers are attracted to its products. Servicing the needs of more customer groups and tailoring products to suit new kinds of customers result in increasing handoff problems between functions. It becomes increasingly difficult to coordinate the activities of value-chain functions across the growing product range. Also, functions like production, marketing, and sales have little opportunity to differentiate products and increase value for customers by specializing in the needs of particular customer groups. Instead, they are responsible for servicing the complete product range. Thus, the ability to identify and satisfy customer needs may fall short in a functional structure.

■ **Location Problems** Location factors may hamper coordination and control. If a growing company begins producing or selling in many different regional areas, then a functional structure may not be able to provide the flexibility needed for managers to respond to the different customer needs or preferences in the various regions. A functional structure is simply not the right way to handle regional diversity.

■ **Strategic Problems** Sometimes the combined effect of all these factors is that long-term strategic considerations are ignored because managers are preoccupied with solving communication and coordination problems. As a result, a company may lose direction and fail to take advantage of new opportunities while bureaucratic costs escalate.

Experiencing one or more of these problems is a sign that bureaucratic costs are increasing and that managers must change and adapt their organization's structure, control systems, and culture to economize on bureaucratic costs, build new distinctive competencies, and strengthen its business model. These problems indicate that the company has outgrown its structure and that managers need to develop a more complex structure that can meet the needs of their competitive strategy. An alternative, however, is to reduce these problems by adopting the outsourcing option.

■ **The Outsourcing Option** Rather than move to a more complex, expensive structure, increasingly companies are turning to the outsourcing option (discussed in Chapter 9) and solving the organizational design problem by contracting with other companies to perform specific functional tasks. Obviously it does not make sense to outsource activities in which a company has a distinctive competency, because this would lessen its competitive advantage. But it does make sense to outsource and contract with companies to perform particular value-chain activities in which they specialize and therefore have a competitive advantage.

Thus, one way of avoiding the kinds of communication and measurement problems that arise when a company's product line becomes complex is to reduce the number of functional value-chain activities it performs. This allows a company to focus on those competencies that are at the heart of its competitive advantage and to economize on bureaucratic costs. Today, responsibility for activities such as a company's marketing, pension and health benefits, materials management, and information systems is being increasingly outsourced to companies that often specialize in the needs of a company in a particular industry. More outsourcing options, such as using a global network structure, are considered in Chapter 13.

Implementing Strategy in a Single Industry

Building capabilities in organizational design that allow a company to develop a competitive advantage starts at the functional level. However, to pursue its business model successfully, managers must find the right combination of structure, control, and culture that *links and combines* the competencies in a company's value-chain functions in a way that enhances its ability to differentiate products or lower the cost structure. Therefore, it is important to coordinate and integrate across functions and business units or divisions. In organizational design, there are two important issues that managers must take into consideration: one concerns the revenue side of the profit equation and the other the cost side, as Figure 12.6 illustrates.

First, effective organizational design improves the way in which people and groups choose the business-level strategies that lead to increasing differentiation, more value

FIGURE 12.6

How Organizational
Design Increases
Profitability

for customers, and the opportunity to charge a premium price. For example, capabilities in managing its structure and culture allow a company to more rapidly and effectively combine its distinctive competencies or transfer or leverage competencies across business units to create new and improved differentiated products.

Second, effective organizational design reduces the bureaucratic costs associated with solving the measurement and communications problems that derive from such things as transferring a product in progress between functions or a lack of cooperation between marketing and manufacturing or between business units. A poorly designed or inappropriate choice of structure or control system or a slow-moving bureaucratic culture (for example, a structure that is too centralized, an incentive system that causes functions to compete and not to cooperate, or a culture whose value and norms have little impact on employees) can cause the motivation, communication, measurement, and coordination problems that lead to high bureaucratic costs.

Effective organizational design often means moving to a more complex structure that economizes on bureaucratic costs. A more complex structure will cost more to operate because additional, experienced, and more highly paid managers will be needed, a more expensive IT system will be required, there may be a need for extra offices and buildings, and so on. However, these are simply costs of doing business, and a company will happily bear this extra expense provided its new structure leads to increased revenues from product differentiation and/or new ways to lower its *overall* cost structure by obtaining economies of scale or scope from its expanded operations.

In the following sections, we first examine the implementation and organizational design issues involved in pursuing a cost-leadership or differentiation business model. Then we describe different kinds of organizational structures that allow companies to pursue business models oriented at (1) managing a wide range of products; (2) being responsive to customers; (3) expanding nationally; (4) competing in a fast-changing high-tech environment; and (5) focusing on a narrow product line.

■ Implementing Cost Leadership

The aim of a company pursuing cost leadership is to become the lowest-cost producer in the industry, and this involves reducing costs across *all* functions in the organization, including R&D and sales and marketing.[43] If a company is pursuing a cost-leadership strategy, its R&D efforts probably focus on product and process development rather than on the more expensive product innovation, which carries no guarantee of success. In other words, the company stresses competencies that improve product characteristics or lower the cost of making existing products. Similarly, a company tries to decrease the cost of sales and marketing by offering a standard product to a mass market rather than different products aimed at different market segments, which is also more expensive.[44]

To implement cost leadership, a company chooses a combination of structure, control, and culture compatible with lowering its cost structure while preserving its ability to attract customers. In practice, the functional structure is the most suitable provided that care is taken to select integrating mechanisms that will reduce communication and measurement problems. For example, a TQM program can be effectively implemented when a functional structure is overlaid with cross-functional teams, for now team members can search for ways to improve operating rules and procedures that lower the cost structure or standardize and raise product quality.[45]

Cost leadership also requires that managers continuously monitor their structures and control systems to find ways to restructure or streamline them so that they operate more effectively. For example, managers need to be alert to ways to use IT to standardize operations and lower costs. To reduce costs further, cost leaders use the cheapest and easiest forms of control available: output controls. For each function, a cost leader adopts output controls that allow it to closely monitor and evaluate functional performance. In the manufacturing function, for example, the company imposes tight controls and stresses meeting budgets based on production, cost, or quality targets.[46] In R&D, too, the emphasis falls on the bottom line, and to demonstrate their contribution to cost savings, R&D teams focus on improving process technology. Cost leaders are likely to reward employees through generous incentive and bonus plans to encourage high performance. Often their culture is based on values that emphasize the bottom line, such as those of Wal-Mart, Dell, and McDonald's.

■ Implementing Differentiation

Effective strategy implementation can improve a company's ability to add value and to differentiate its products. To make its product unique in the eyes of the customer, for example, a differentiated company must design its structure, control, and culture around the *particular source* of its competitive advantage.[47] Specifically, differentiators need to design their structures around the source of their distinctive competencies, the differentiated qualities of their product, and the customer groups they serve. Commonly, in pursuing differentiation, a company starts to produce a wider range of products to serve more market segments, which means it has to customize its products for different groups of customers. These factors make it more difficult to standardize activities and usually increase the bureaucratic costs associated with managing the handoffs or transfers between functions. Integration becomes much more of a problem; communications, measurement, location, and strategic problems increasingly arise; and the demands on functional managers increase.

To respond to these problems, strategic managers develop more sophisticated control systems, increasingly make use of IT, and focus on developing cultural norms and values that overcome problems associated with differences in functional orientations and focus on cross-functional objectives. The control systems used to match the structure are geared to a company's distinctive competencies. For successful differentiation, it is important that the various functions do not pull in different directions; indeed, cooperation among the functions is vital for cross-functional integration. However, when functions work together, output controls become much harder to use. In general, it is much more difficult to measure the performance of people in different functions when they are engaged in cooperative efforts. Consequently, a differentiator must rely more on behavior controls and shared norms and values.

That is why companies pursuing differentiation often have a markedly different kind of culture from those pursuing cost leadership. Because human resources— good scientists, designers, or marketing people—are often the source of differentiation, these organizations have a culture based on professionalism or collegiality, one that emphasizes the distinctiveness of the human resource rather than the high pressure of the bottom line.[48] Hewlett-Packard, Motorola, and Coca-Cola, all of which emphasize some kind of distinctive competency, exemplify companies with professional cultures.

In practice, the implementation decisions that confront managers who must simultaneously strive for differentiation and a low cost structure are dealt with together as strategic managers move to implement new, more complex kinds of organizational structure. As a company's business model and strategies evolve, strategic managers usually start to *superimpose* a more complex divisional grouping of activities on its functional structure to better coordinate value-chain activities. This is especially true of those companies that are seeking to become *broad differentiators*, the companies that have the ability to both increase differentiation and lower their cost structures. These, the most profitable companies in their industry, have to be especially adept at organizational design, for this is a major source of a differentiation and cost advantage (see Figure 12.6). No matter what their business model, however, although more complex structures cost more to operate than a simple functional structure, managers are willing to bear this extra cost so long as the new structure makes better use of functional competencies, increases revenues, and lowers the overall cost structure.

■ Product Structure: Implementing a Wide Product Line

The structure that organizations most commonly adopt to solve the control problems that result from producing many different kinds of products for many different market segments is the *product structure*. The intent is to break up a company's growing product line into a number of smaller, more manageable subunits to reduce bureaucratic costs due to communication, measurement, and other problems. This was the problem facing Nokia in the *Opening Case*, and, as we discussed, Nokia moved to a product structure.

An organization that chooses a product structure first divides its overall product line into product groups or categories (see Figure 12.7). Each product group focuses on satisfying the needs of a particular customer group and is managed by its own team of managers. Second, to keep costs as low as possible, value-chain support functions such as basic R&D, marketing, materials, and finance are centralized at the top

FIGURE 12.7

Nokia's Product Structure

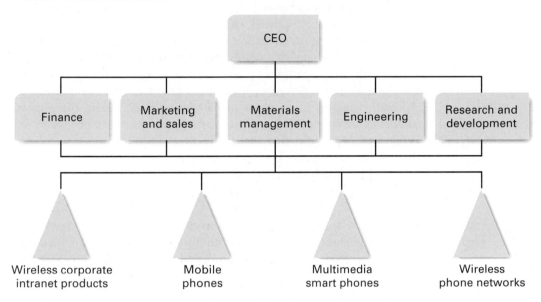

of the organization, and the different product groups share their services. Each support function, in turn, is divided into product-oriented teams of functional specialists who focus on the needs of one particular product group. This arrangement allows each team to specialize and become expert in managing the needs of its product group. However, because all of the R&D teams belong to the same centralized function, they can share knowledge and information with each other and so can build their competence over time.

Strategic control systems can now be developed to measure the performance of each product group separately from the others. Thus, the performance of each product group is easy to monitor and evaluate, and corporate managers at the center can move more quickly to intervene if necessary. Also, the strategic reward system can be more closely linked to the performance of each product group, although top managers can still decide to make rewards based on corporate performance an important part of the incentive system. Doing so will encourage the different product groups to share ideas and knowledge and promote the development of a corporate culture, as well as the product group culture that naturally develops inside each product group. A product structure is commonly used by food processors, furniture makers, personal and health products companies, and large electronics companies like Nokia.

■ **Market Structure: Increasing Responsiveness to Customer Groups**

Suppose the source of competitive advantage in an industry depends on the ability to meet the needs of distinct and important sets of customers or different customer groups. What is the best way of implementing strategy now? Many companies develop a **market structure** that is conceptually quite similar to the product structure except that the focus is on customer groups instead of product groups.

For a company pursuing a strategy based on increasing responsiveness to customers, it is vital that the nature and needs of each different customer group be identified. Then people and functions are grouped by customer or market segment, and a different set of managers becomes responsible for developing the products that each group of customers wants and tailoring or customizing products to the needs of each particular customer group. In other words, to promote superior responsiveness to customers, companies design a structure around their customers and a market structure is adopted. A typical market structure is shown in Figure 12.8.

A market structure brings customer group managers and employees closer to specific groups of customers. These people can then take their detailed knowledge and feed it back to the support functions, which are kept centralized to reduce costs. For example, information about changes in customers' preferences can be quickly fed back to R&D and product design so that a company can protect its competitive advantage by supplying a constant stream of improved products for its installed customer base. This is especially important when a company serves well-identified customer groups such as *Fortune 500* companies or small businesses.

■ Geographic Structure: Expanding Nationally

Suppose a company starts to expand nationally through internal expansion or by engaging in horizontal integration and merging with other companies to expand its geographical reach. A company pursuing this competitive approach frequently moves to a **geographic structure** in which geographic regions become the basis for the grouping of organizational activities (see Figure 12.9). A company may divide its manufacturing operations and establish manufacturing plants in different regions of the country, for example. This allows it to be responsive to the needs of regional customers and reduces transportation costs. Similarly, as a service organization such as a store chain or bank expands beyond one geographic area, it may begin to organize sales and marketing activities on a regional level to better serve the needs of customers in different regions.

A geographic structure provides more coordination and control than a functional structure because several regional hierarchies are created to take over the work, just as in a product structure several product group hierarchies are created. A company such as FedEx clearly needs to operate a geographic structure to fulfill its corporate goal: next-day delivery. Large merchandising organizations, such as Neiman Marcus, Dillard's Department Stores, and Wal-Mart, also moved to a geographic structure as they started building stores across the country. With this type of struc-

FIGURE 12.8

Market Structure

FIGURE 12.9

Geographic Structure

ture, different regional clothing needs (for example, sunwear in the South, down coats in the Midwest) can be handled as required. At the same time, because the information systems, purchasing, distribution, and marketing functions remain centralized, they can leverage their skills across all the regions. Thus, in using a geographic structure, a company can achieve economies of scale in buying, distributing, and selling and lower its cost structure while at the same time being more responsive (differentiated) to customer needs.

Neiman Marcus developed a geographic structure similar to the one shown in Figure 12.9 to manage its nationwide chain of stores. In each region, it established a team of regional buyers to respond to the needs of customers in each geographic area, for example, the western, central, eastern, and southern regions. The regional buyers then fed their information to the central buyers at corporate headquarters, who coordinated their demands to obtain purchasing economies and to ensure that Neiman Marcus's high-quality standards, on which its differentiation advantage depends, were maintained nationally.

■ **Matrix and Product-Team Structures: Competing in Fast-Changing, High-Tech Environments**

The communication and measurement problems that lead to bureaucratic costs escalate quickly when technology is rapidly changing and industry boundaries are blurring. Frequently, competitive success depends on fast mobilization of a company's skills and resources, and managers face complex strategy implementation issues. A new grouping of people and resources becomes necessary, often one that is based on fostering a company's distinctive competencies in R&D, and managers need to make structure, control, and culture choices around the R&D function. At the same time, they need to ensure that implementation will result in new products that meet customer needs and in a way that is cost-effective and will not result in high-priced products that are so expensive customers will not wish to buy them.

■ **Matrix Structure** To address these problems many companies choose a matrix structure.[49] In a **matrix structure**, value-chain activities are grouped in two ways (see Figure 12.10). First, activities are grouped vertically by *function*, so that there is a familiar differentiation of tasks into functions such as engineering, sales and marketing, and R&D. In addition, superimposed on this vertical pattern is a horizontal pattern based on grouping by *product or project* in which people and resources are grouped to meet ongoing product development needs. The resulting network of reporting relationships among projects and functions is designed to make R&D the focus of attention.

Matrix structures are flat and decentralized, and employees inside a matrix have two bosses: a *functional boss*, who is the head of a function, and a *product or project boss*, who is responsible for managing the individual projects. Employees work on a project team with specialists from other functions and report to the project boss on

FIGURE 12.10

Matrix Structure

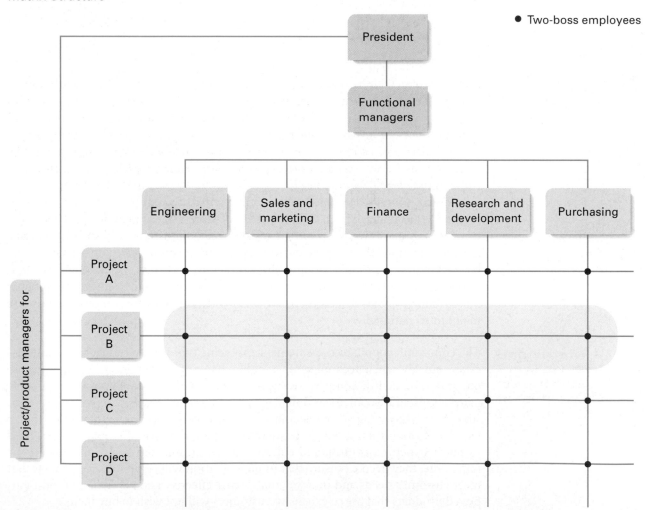

project matters and the functional boss on matters relating to functional issues. All employees who work in a project team are called **two-boss employees** and are responsible for managing coordination and communication among the functions and projects.

Implementing a matrix structure promotes innovation and speeds product development, for this type of structure permits intensive cross-functional integration. Integrating mechanisms such as teams help transfer knowledge among functions and are designed around the R&D function. Sales, marketing, and production targets are geared to R&D goals, marketing devises advertise programs that focus on technological possibilities, and salespeople are evaluated on their understanding of new-product characteristics and their ability to inform potential customers about them.

Matrix structures were first developed by companies in high-technology industries such as aerospace and electronics, for example, TRW and Hughes. These companies were developing radically new products in uncertain, competitive environments, and speed of product development was the crucial consideration. They needed a structure that could respond to this need, but the functional structure was too inflexible to allow the complex role and task interactions necessary to meet new-product development requirements. Moreover, employees in these companies tend to be highly qualified and professional and perform best in autonomous, flexible working conditions. The matrix structure provides such conditions.

This structure requires a minimum of direct hierarchical control by supervisors. Team members control their own behavior, and participation in project teams allows them to monitor other team members and learn from each other. Furthermore, as the project goes through its different phases, different specialists from various functions are required. For example, at the first stage, the services of R&D specialists may be called for, and then at the next stage, engineers and marketing specialists may be needed to make cost and marketing projections. As the demand for the type of specialist changes, team members can be moved to other projects that require their services. Thus, the matrix structure can make maximum use of employees' skills as existing projects are completed and new ones come into existence. The freedom given by the matrix not only provides the autonomy to motivate employees but also leaves top management free to concentrate on strategic issues, since they do not have to become involved in operating matters. On all these counts, the matrix is an excellent tool for creating the flexibility necessary for quick reactions to competitive conditions.

In terms of strategic control and culture, the development of norms and values based on innovation and product excellence is vital if a matrix structure is to work effectively.[50] The constant movement of employees around the matrix means that time and money are spent establishing new team relationships and getting the project off the ground. The two-boss employee's role, balancing as it does the interests of the project with the function, means that cooperation between people is problematic and conflict between different functions and between functions and projects is possible and must be managed. Furthermore, the changing composition of product teams, the ambiguity arising from having two bosses, and the greater difficulty of monitoring and evaluating the work of teams increase the problems of coordinating task activities. A strong and cohesive culture with unifying norms and values can mitigate these problems, as can a strategic reward system based on a group- and organizational-level reward system.

■ **Product-Team Structure** A major structural innovation in recent years has been the **product-team structure**. Its advantages are similar to those of a matrix structure, but it is much easier and far less costly to operate because of the way people are organized into permanent cross-functional teams, as Figure 12.11 illustrates. In the product-team structure, as in the matrix structure, tasks are divided along product or project lines. However, instead of being assigned only *temporarily* to different projects, as in the matrix structure, functional specialists become part of a *permanent* cross-functional team that focuses on the development of one particular range of products such as luxury cars or computer workstations. As a result, the problems associated with coordinating cross-functional transfers or handoffs are much lower than in a matrix structure, in which tasks and reporting relationships change rapidly. Moreover, cross-functional teams are formed at the beginning of the product development process so that any difficulties that arise can be ironed out early, before they lead to major redesign problems. When all functions have direct input from the beginning, design costs and subsequent manufacturing costs can be kept low. Moreover, the use of cross-functional teams speeds innovation and customer responsiveness because when authority is decentralized, team decisions can be made more quickly.

A product-team structure groups tasks by product, and each product group is managed by a cross-functional product team that has all the support services necessary to bring the product to market. This is why it is different from the product structure, where support functions remain centralized. The role of the product team is to protect and enhance a company's differentiation advantage and at the same time coordinate with manufacturing to lower costs.

■ **Focusing on a Narrow Product Line**

As Chapter 5 discusses, a focused company concentrates on developing a narrow range of products aimed at one or two market segments, which may be defined by type of customer or location. As a result, a focuser tends to have a higher cost structure than a cost leader or differentiator because output levels are lower, making it harder to obtain substantial scale economies. For this reason, a focused company

FIGURE 12.11
Product-Team Structure

must exercise cost control. On the other hand, some attribute of its product gives the focuser its distinctive competency—possibly its ability to provide customers with high-quality, personalized service. For both reasons, the structure and control system adopted by a focused company has to be inexpensive to operate but flexible enough to allow a distinctive competency to emerge.

A company using a focus strategy normally adopts a functional structure to meet these needs. This structure is appropriate because it is complex enough to manage the activities necessary to make and sell a narrow range of products for one or a few market segments. At the same time, the handoff problems are likely to be relatively easy to solve because a focuser remains small and specialized. Thus, a functional structure can provide all the integration necessary, provided that the focused firm has a strong, adaptive culture, which is vital to the development of some kind of distinctive competency.[51] Additionally, because such a company's competitive advantage is often based on personalized service, the flexibility of this kind of structure lets the company respond quickly to customers' needs and change its products in response to customers' requests. The way in which Lexmark reorganized itself to focus on the production of office printers, examined in Strategy in Action 12.4, illustrates many of the issues in implementing a focus strategy.

Strategy in Action   12.4

Restructuring at Lexmark

Lexmark, a printer and typewriter manufacturer, was one of IBM's many divisions, but IBM sold it after years of losses brought on by high operating costs and an inability to produce new printers that could compete with those made by Hewlett-Packard and Canon. Marvin Mann, an ex-IBM executive, was given the task of finding a way to restructure the company and turn it around. Mann realized at once that the company had to focus on producing a particular kind of printer to lower its out-of-control cost structure.

One of the biggest contributors to its high cost structure was Lexmark's structure and control system, so Mann decided to transform it. Then, he believed, he could begin to focus the company on producing a line of state-of-the-art laser and ink jet office printers. Like the rest of IBM at that time, Lexmark had developed a tall, centralized structure, and all important decision making was made by top managers. This slowed decision making and made it very difficult to communicate across functions because so many managers at different levels and in different functions had to approve new plans. Moving quickly to change this system, Mann streamlined the company's hierarchy, which meant terminating 50 percent of its managers. This action cut out three levels in the hierarchy. He then decentralized authority to the managers

of each of the company's four product lines and told them to develop their own plans and goals. In addition, to continue the process of decentralization, product managers were instructed to develop cross-functional teams comprising employees from all functions, with the goal of finding new and improved ways of organizing task activities to reduce costs. The teams were to use competitive benchmarking and evaluate their competitors' products in order to establish new performance standards to guide their activities. Finally, as an incentive for employees to work hard at increasing efficiency, innovation, and quality, Mann established a company stock ownership scheme to reward employees for their efforts.

Mann's strategy of restructuring Lexmark to focus on a narrow range of printers was successful. Within two years, the cost of launching new products went down by 50 percent and its new-product development cycle speeded up by 30 percent. Focusing on a narrow range of products also improved Lexmark's R&D competence. Lexmark is a technology leader in the laser and ink jet industry and makes the printers sold by Dell—showing that it is a focused cost leader in the printer market. Its stock has performed well as a result, and the company is enjoying considerable success against HP and Japanese competitors.

The message of the preceding sections is clear. Strategic managers must continually monitor the performance of their organization as measured by its ability to increase differentiation, lower costs, and increase profitability. When managers sense declining performance or sense ways to increase performance, they must move quickly to change the way people and activities are organized and controlled. Organizational design, the process of combining and harmonizing structure, control, and culture, is a demanding and difficult task but one that is crucial to promoting and sustaining competitive advantage.

Restructuring and Reengineering

To improve performance a single business company often employs restructuring and reengineering. **Restructuring** a company involves two steps: (1) streamlining the hierarchy of authority and reducing the number of levels in the hierarchy to a minimum, and then (2) reducing the number of employees to lower operating costs. When Jack Smith took over as head of General Motors, for example, GM had more than twenty-two levels in the hierarchy and more than 20,000 corporate managers. Describing his organization as a top-heavy bureaucracy, Smith quickly moved to slash costs and restructure the company. Today, GM has only twelve levels in the hierarchy and half as many corporate managers. In 2004, Kodak announced it would lay off 20 percent of its work force over a three-year period to reduce costs.

Restructuring and downsizing become necessary for many reasons.[52] Sometimes a change in the business environment occurs that could not have been foreseen; perhaps a shift in technology made the company's products obsolete, as happened to Kodak as the use of digital cameras exploded. Sometimes an organization has excess capacity because customers no longer want the goods and services it provides, perhaps because they are outdated or offer poor value for the money—as happened to Nokia when it was slow to catch up with changing customer needs. Sometimes organizations downsize because they have grown too tall and inflexible and bureaucratic costs have become much too high—as happened to IBM. Sometimes they restructure even when they are in a strong position simply to build and improve their competitive advantage and stay on top—which Dell and Microsoft frequently do.

All too often, however, companies are forced to downsize and lay off employees because they fail to monitor and control their basic business operations and have not made the incremental changes to their strategies and structures over time that allow them to adjust to changing conditions. Advances in management, such as the development of new models for organizing work activities, or advances in information technology offer strategic managers the opportunity to implement their strategies in more effective ways.

One way of helping a company operate more effectively is to use **reengineering**, which involves the "fundamental rethinking and radical redesign of business processes to achieve dramatic improvements in critical, contemporary measures of performance such as cost, quality, service, and speed."[53] As this definition suggests, strategic managers who use reengineering must completely rethink how they organize their value-chain activities. Instead of focusing on how a company's *functions* operate, strategic managers make business *processes* the focus of attention.

A **business process** is any activity that is vital to delivering goods and services to customers quickly or that promotes high quality or low costs (such as IT, materials management, or product development) and that is not the responsibility of any *one* function but *cuts across functions*. Because reengineering focuses on business processes and not on functions, a company that reengineers always has to adopt a different approach to organizing its activities. Companies that take up reengineering deliberately ignore the existing arrangement of tasks, roles, and work activities. They start the reengineering process with the customer (not the product or service) and ask, "How can we reorganize the way we do our work, our business processes, to provide the best quality and the lowest-cost goods and services to the customer?"

Frequently, when companies ask this question, they realize that there are more effective ways to organize their value-chain activities. For example, a business process that encompasses members of ten different functions working sequentially to provide goods and services might be performed by one person or a few people at a fraction of the cost. Often individual jobs become increasingly complex, and people are grouped into cross-functional teams as business processes are reengineered to reduce costs and increase quality.

Hallmark Cards, for example, reengineered its card design process with great success. Before the reengineering effort, artists, writers, and editors worked separately in different functions to produce all kinds of cards. After reengineering, these same artists, writers, and editors were put in cross-functional teams, each of which now works on a specific type of card, such as birthday, Christmas, or Mother's Day. The result is that the time it took to bring a new card to market dropped from years to months, and Hallmark's performance increased dramatically.

Reengineering and total quality management (TQM), discussed in Chapter 4, are highly interrelated and complementary. After reengineering has taken place and value-chain activities have been altered to speed the product to the final customer, TQM takes over, with its focus on how to continue to improve and refine the new process and find better ways of managing task and role relationships. Successful organizations examine both questions simultaneously and continuously attempt to identify new and better processes for meeting the goals of increased efficiency, quality, and customer responsiveness. Thus, they are always seeking to improve their visions of their desired future state.

Another example of reengineering is the change program that took place at IBM Credit, a wholly owned division of IBM that manages the financing and leasing of IBM computers, particularly mainframes, to IBM's customers. Before reengineering took place, when a financing request arrived at the division's headquarters in Old Greenwich, Connecticut, it went through a five-step approval process that involved the activities of five different functions. First, the IBM salesperson called the credit department, which logged the request and took details about the potential customer. Second, this information was taken to the credit-checking department, where a credit check on the potential customer was made. Third, when the credit check was complete, the request was taken to the contracts department, which wrote the contract. Fourth, from there it went to the pricing department, which determined the actual financial details of the loan, such as the interest rate and the term of the loan. Finally, the whole package of information was assembled by the dispatching department and delivered to the sales representative, who gave it to the customer.

This series of cross-functional activities took an average of seven days to complete, and sales representatives constantly complained that this delay resulted in a low level of customer responsiveness that reduced customer satisfaction. Also, potential customers were tempted to shop around for financing and even to look at competitors' machines. The delay in closing the deal caused uncertainty for all concerned.

The change process began when two senior IBM credit managers reviewed the finance approval process. They found that the time spent by different specialists in the different functions actually processing a loan application was only ninety minutes. The seven-day approval process was caused because of the delay in transmitting information and requests between departments. The managers also came to understand that the activities taking place in each department were not complex; each department had its own computer system containing its own work procedures, but the work done in each department was pretty routine.

Armed with this information, IBM managers realized that the approval process could be reengineered into one overarching process handled by one person with a computer system containing all the necessary information and work procedures to perform the five loan-processing activities. If the application were complex, a team of experts stood ready to help process it, but IBM found that after the reengineering effort a typical application could be done in four hours rather than the previous seven days. A sales representative could go back to the customer the same day to close the deal, and all the uncertainty surrounding the transaction was removed.

As reengineering consultants Hammer and Champy note, this dramatic performance increase was brought about by a radical change to the process as a whole. Change through reengineering requires managers to go back to the basics and pull apart each step in the work process to identify a better way to coordinate and integrate the activities necessary to provide customers with goods and services. As this example makes clear, the introduction of new IT is an integral aspect of reengineering. IT also allows a company to restructure its hierarchy because it provides more and better-quality information. IT today is an integral part of the strategy implementation process.

Summary of Chapter

1. Implementing a company's business model and strategies successfully depends on organizational design, the process of selecting the right combination of organizational structure, control systems, and culture. Companies need to monitor and oversee the organizational design process to achieve superior profitability.

2. Effective organizational design can increase profitability in two ways. First, it economizes on bureaucratic costs and helps a company lower its cost structure. Second, it enhances the ability of a company's value creation functions to achieve superior efficiency, quality, innovativeness, and customer responsiveness and to obtain the advantages of differentiation.

3. The main issues in designing organizational structure are how to group tasks, functions, and divisions; how to allocate authority and responsibility (whether to have a tall or flat organization, or to have a centralized or decentralized structure); and how to use integrating mechanisms to improve coordination between functions (such as direct contacts, liaison roles, and teams).

4. Strategic control provides the monitoring and incentive systems necessary to make an organizational structure work as intended and extends corporate governance down to all levels inside the company. The main kinds of strategic control systems are personal control, output control, and behavior control. Information technology is an aid to output and behavior control, and reward systems are linked to every control system.

5. Organizational culture is the set of values, norms, beliefs, and attitudes that help to energize and motivate employees and control their behavior. Culture is a way of doing something, and a company's founder and top managers help determine which kinds of values emerge in an organization.

6. At the functional level, each function requires a different combination of structure and control system to achieve its functional objectives.

7. To successfully implement a company's business model, structure, control, and culture must be combined in ways that increase the relationships among all functions to build distinctive competencies.

8. Cost leadership and differentiation each require a structure and control system that strengthens the business model that is the source of their competitive advantage. Managers have to use organizational design in a way that balances pressures to increase differentiation against pressures to lower the cost structure.

9. Other specialized kinds of structures include the product, market, geographic, matrix, and product-team structures. Each has a specialized use and is implemented as a company's strategy warrants.

10. Restructuring and reengineering are two ways of implementing a company's business model more effectively.

Discussion Questions

1. What is the relationship of organizational structure, control, and culture? Give some examples of when and under what conditions a mismatch between these components might arise.

2. What kind of structure best describes the way your (a) business school and (b) university operate? Why is the structure appropriate? Would another structure fit better?

3. When would a company choose a matrix structure? What are the problems associated with managing this structure, and why might a product-team structure be preferable?

4. For each of the structures discussed in the chapter, outline the most suitable control systems.

5. What kind of structure, controls, and culture would you be likely to find in (a) a small manufacturing company, (b) a chain store, (c) a high-tech company, and (d) a Big Four accounting firm?

Practicing Strategic Management

■ SMALL-GROUP EXERCISE
Deciding on an Organizational Structure

Break up into groups of three to five people, and discuss the following scenario. You are a group of managers of a major soft drink company that is going head-to-head with Coca-Cola to increase market share. Your business model is based on increasing your product range to offer a soft drink in every segment of the market to attract customers. Currently you have a functional structure. What you are trying to work out now is how best to implement your business model in order to launch your new products. Should you move to a more complex kind of product structure, and, if so, which one? Alternatively, should you establish new-venture divisions, and spin off each kind of new soft drink into its own company so that it can focus its resources on its market niche? Thinking strategically, debate the pros and cons of the possible organizational structures, and decide which structure you will implement.

■ ARTICLE FILE 12

Find an example of a company that competes in one industry and that has recently changed the way it implements its business model and strategies. What changes did it make? Why did it make these changes? What effect did these changes have on the behavior of people and functions?

■ STRATEGIC MANAGEMENT PROJECT
Module 12

This module asks you to identify how your company implements its business model and strategy. For this part of your project, you need to obtain information about your company's structure, control systems, and culture. This information may be hard to obtain unless you can interview managers directly. But you can make many inferences about the company's structure from the nature of its activities, and if you write to the company, it may provide you with an organizational chart and other information. Also, published information, such as compensation for top management, is available in the company's annual reports or 10-K reports. If your company is well known, magazines such as *Fortune* and *Business Week* frequently report on corporate culture or control issues. Nevertheless, you may be forced to make some bold assumptions to complete this part of the project.

1. How large is the company as measured by the number of its employees? How many levels in the hierarchy does it have from the top to the bottom? Based on these two measures and any other information you may have, would you say your company operates with a relatively tall or flat structure? Does your company have a centralized or decentralized approach to decision making?

2. What changes (if any) would you make to the way the company allocates authority and responsibility?

3. Draw an organizational chart showing the main way in which your company groups its activities. Based on this chart, decide what kind of structure (functional, product, or divisional) your company operates with.

4. Why did your company choose this structure? In what ways is it appropriate for its business model? In what ways is it not?

5. What kind of integration or integration mechanisms does your company use?

6. What are the main kinds of control systems your company is using? What kinds of behaviors is the organization trying to (a) shape and (b) motivate through the use of these control systems?

7. What role does the top management team play in creating the culture of your organization? Can you identify the characteristic norms and values that describe the way people behave in your organization? How does the design of the organization's structure affect its culture?

8. What are the sources of your company's distinctive competencies? Which functions are most important to it? How does your company design its structure, control, and culture to enhance its (a) efficiency, (b) quality, (c) innovativeness, and (d) responsiveness to customers?

9. How does it design its structure and control systems to strengthen its business model? For example, what steps does it take to further cross-functional integration? Does it have a functional, product, or matrix structure?

10. How does your company's culture support its business model? Can you determine any ways in which its top management team influences its culture?

11. Based on this analysis, would you say your company is coordinating and motivating its people and subunits effectively? Why or why not? What changes (if any) would you make to the way your company's structure operates? What use could it make of restructuring or reengineering?

■ EXPLORING THE WEB
Visiting Home Depot

Go to **www.homedepot.com**, and examine corporate information such as the company overview, history, and press releases. Based on this information, what kind of structure, control systems, and culture do you think Home Depot has in place to implement its business model and strategies?

General Task Search the Web for an example of a company that has been changing the way it implements its business model. What were its problems? How did it use structure, control, and culture to improve the way it operates?

Closing Case

Strategy Implementation at Dell Computer

Dell Computer was one of the fastest-growing companies of the 1990s, and its stock price increased at the rate of 100 percent a year, delighting its stockholders. Achieving this high return has been a constant challenge for Michael Dell, and one of his biggest battles has been to manage and change Dell's organizational structure, control systems, and culture as his company grows.

Dell was nineteen when, in 1984, he took $1,000 and spent it on the computer parts he assembled himself into PCs that he then sold over the phone. Increasing demand for his PCs meant that within a few weeks he needed to hire people to help him, and soon he found himself supervising three employees who worked together around a six-foot table to assemble computers while two more employees took orders over the phone.

By 1993, Dell employed 4,500 workers and was hiring over 100 new workers each week just to keep pace with the demand for the computers. When he found himself working eighteen-hour days managing the company, he realized that he could not lead the company single-handedly. The company's growth had to be managed, and he knew that he had to recruit and hire strategic managers who had experience in managing different functional areas, such as marketing, finance, and manufacturing. He recruited executives from IBM and Compaq and with their help created a functional structure, one in which employees are grouped by the common skills they have or tasks they perform, such as sales or manufacturing, to organize the value-chain activities necessary to deliver his PCs to customers. As a part of this organizing process, Dell's structure also became taller, with more levels in the management hierarchy, to ensure that he and his managers had sufficient control over the different activities of his growing business. Dell delegated authority to control Dell's functional value-chain activities to his managers, which gave him the time he needed to perform his entrepreneurial task of finding new opportunities for the company.

Dell's functional structure worked well, and under its new management team, the company's growth continued to soar. By 1993, the company had sales of over $2 billion, twice as much as in 1992. Moreover, Dell's new structure had given functional managers the control they needed to squeeze out costs, and Dell had become the lowest-cost PC maker. Analysts also reported that Dell had developed a lean organizational culture, meaning that employees had developed norms and values that emphasized the importance of working hard to help each other find innovative new ways of making products to keep costs low and increase their reliability. Indeed, with the fewest customer complaints, Dell rose to the top of the customer satisfaction rankings for PC makers; its employees became known for the excellent customer service they gave to PC buyers who were experiencing problems with setting up their computers.

However, Michael Dell realized that new and different kinds of problems were arising. Dell was now selling huge numbers of computers to different kinds of customers, for example, home, business, and educational customers and the different branches of government. Because customers now demanded computers with very different features or different amounts of computing power, the company's product line broadened rapidly. It started to become more difficult for employees to meet the needs of these different kinds of customers efficiently because each employee needed information about all product features or all of Dell's thousands of different sales offers across its product range.

In 1995, Dell moved to change his company to a market structure and created separate divisions, each geared to the needs of a different group of customers: a consumer division, a business division, and so on. In each division, teams of employees specialize in servicing the needs of one of these customer groups. This move to a more complex structure also allowed each division to

develop a unique subculture that suited its tasks, and employees were able to obtain in-depth knowledge about the needs of their market that helped them to respond better to their customers' needs. So successful was this change in structure and culture that by 1999 Dell's revenues were over $30 billion and its profits were in excess of $2.5 billion, a staggering increase from 1984.

Dell has continued to alter his company's structure to respond to changing customer needs and to the company's increase in distinctive competencies. For example, Dell realized he could leverage his company's strengths in materials management, manufacturing, and Internet sales over a wider range of computer hardware products. So he decided to begin assembling servers, workstations, and storage devices to compete with IBM, Sun, and Compaq. The increasing importance of the Internet led him to split the market divisions into thirty-five smaller subunits that focus on more specialized groups of customers, and they all conduct the majority of their business over the Internet. Today, for example, Dell can offer large and small companies and private buyers a complete range of computers, workstations, and storage devices that can be customized to their needs.

To help coordinate its growing activities, Dell is increasingly making use of its corporate intranet and using information technology (IT) to standardize activities across divisions so as to integrate across functions. Dell's hierarchy is shrinking as managers are increasingly delegating everyday decision making to employees who have access, through IT, to the information they need to provide excellent customer service. To help reduce costs, Dell has also outsourced some of its customer service activities. As a result of these moves, Dell's work force has become even more committed to sustaining its low-cost advantage, and its cost-conscious culture has become an important source of competitive advantage that is the envy of its competitors.[54]

Case Discussion Questions

1. How has Dell redesigned its structure over time to better implement its cost-leadership model?

2. What organizational design lessons could other companies learn from Dell's example?

Chapter 13

Implementing Strategy in Companies That Compete Across Industries and Countries

Opening Case

GM Searches for the Right Global Structure

In the past, GM, like the other major U.S. carmakers, decentralized control of its overseas car operations to the managers who controlled its global car divisions in countries such as the United Kingdom, Germany, Australia, and Sweden. Each of GM's global car divisions was responsible for designing cars that suited local customer tastes, and each global division had its own design, component parts, manufacturing, and sales functions. Today, GM has to rethink the way its global structure operates. Although it is the world's biggest carmaker in terms of volume of sales, it is one of the least profitable. GM currently only makes about 1 percent profit margin on the cars it sells in the United States, and it loses money on its sales overseas. The problem facing GM is to find ways to make its global structure operate more efficiently and effectively to implement its global business model.

The major reason for GM's low profit margins is its high cost structure, which is largely due to the way it has allowed its global divisions to operate autonomously in a decentralized fashion. Over time, this mode of operating led its divisions to become fiercely independent to protect their own interests, and this independence resulted in a massive duplication of functional activities. For example, when GM asked its Saab division to work on building a small car based on the Vectra platform developed by its German division as a way to share resources, Saab managers proceeded to give the car a whole new electrical system and engine mounting, expensive modifications that eroded all the potential cost savings from sharing resources.

To reduce its global cost structure, GM decided to place all authority over important car design and production decisions with top managers at its U.S. corporate headquarters. Now its top executives tell its global divisions what they must do to keep costs down, such as which global component suppliers to buy from. As an example of how this can reduce costs, in the past GM's global divisions bought 270 different kinds of radios from global suppliers, and if GM can achieve its goal of reducing this number to 50 by 2006, it will slash 40 percent off the cost of its global radio purchases.

Another goal of GM's policy of recentralizing control of decision making is to better coordinate the activities of its global engineering and design groups to speed the development of new car models. GM now tells its global divisions how they should work together and share their expertise to design cars that can be sold anywhere in the world. It currently takes GM about five years to design a new model, whereas it takes Toyota only three—a tremendous advantage. Now a global council in Detroit makes the key model development decisions. Although this activity involves a $7 billion yearly investment in new car design, it also prevents global car divisions from pursuing their own goals. In fact, after the Saab debacle GM basically took away all authority from Saab's engineering department and its engineers now work according to GM's master plan. Similarly, GM's Daewoo division in Korea decided it didn't want to use an existing GM SUV platform and modify it to fit the Korean market, but instead to create a new one from scratch. GM squashed the resistance and took the steps necessary to make its division toe the line. Although GM wants cars to be customized to the needs of each market, CEO Rich Waggoner says he wants "all these variations to be 'plug and play,'" meaning they do not involve costly redesigns that can adds hundreds of millions of dollars to the new car design budget.

Despite its cost problems, GM, like other U.S. carmakers, has been rapidly catching up with the quality of Japanese carmakers and has closed the gap substantially. So, on the differentiation side of the equation, it must facilitate communication between its global car divisions to take advantage of the enormous pool of talent that it has throughout the world. If it can use its new more centralized global product-group structure to design cars that better satisfy customer needs more quickly, it will be able to compete effectively against companies such as Toyota and Honda in the future.

Overview

The story of GM's efforts to develop a competitive global business model to compete effectively in car markets around the world suggests how complex strategic thinking can become at the corporate level. Companies have to continually examine how to improve the way they implement their business and multibusiness models to increase their long-run profitability and grow their profits. This chapter takes off where the last one ends and examines how to implement strategy when a company decides to enter and compete in new industries, or in new countries when it expands globally, and when it chooses strategies such as merger or outsourcing to strengthen its business model. The strategy implementation issue remains the same: how to use organizational design and combine organizational structure, control, and culture to allow a company to pursue its business model and strategies successfully. Once a company decides to compete across industries and countries, however, it confronts a new set of problems, some of them continuations of problems discussed in Chapter 12 and some of them a direct consequence of its decision to enter and compete in overseas markets and new industries. As a result, it has to make a new series of organizational design decisions to successful implement its new global and multibusiness model.

By the end of the chapter, you will appreciate the many complex issues and choices confronting managers of multibusiness and global companies and the reasons that strategy implementation is an integral part of achieving superior performance.

Managing Corporate Strategy Through the Multidivisional Structure

As Chapter 10 discusses, there are many ways in which corporate-level strategies such as vertical integration or diversification can be used to strengthen a company's business model to improve its competitive position. However, substantial implementation problems arise as well, many of them due to the increasing bureaucratic costs associated with managing a larger collection of companies that operate in different industries. These costs are especially high when a company is seeking to gain the differentiation and low-cost advantages of transferring, sharing, or leveraging its distinctive competencies across its business units in different industries. For companies pursuing a multibusiness model, the problems and costs of managing the handoffs or transfers between value-chain functions across industries to obtain these benefits rise sharply. It is the need to economize on these costs that propels strategic managers to search for improved ways of implementing the corporate-level strategies necessary to pursue a multibusiness model.

As a company begins to enter new industries and produce completely different kinds of products such as cars, fast food, and computers, the structures described in Chapter 12, such as the functional and product structures, are not up to the task. They cannot provide sufficient coordination between functions and motivation to employees that implementing a multibusiness model requires. As a result, the control problems that give rise to bureaucratic costs, such as those related to measurement, customers, location, or strategy, escalate. Experiencing these problems is a sign that the company has outgrown its structure. Strategic managers need to invest more resources to develop a more complex structure—one that can meet the needs of its multibusiness model and strategies. The answer for most large, complex companies is to move to a multidivisional structure, design a cross-industry control system, and fashion a corporate culture to reduce these problems and economize on bureaucratic costs.

The multidivisional structure possesses two main innovations over a functional or product structure that allow a company to grow and diversify while reducing the coordination and control problems inherent in entering and competing in new industries. First, in each industry in which a company operates, strategic managers organize its business units or companies in that industry into one or more *divisions*. Sometimes each division contains a full set of all the value-chain functions it needs to pursue its business model; in this case, it is called a *self-contained division*. For example, GE competes in over 150 different industries, and in each industry, all of its divisions are self-sufficient and perform all the value creation functions. Sometimes, however, divisions in *different* industries *share* value-chain functions to obtain cost savings and to benefit from leveraging competencies across divisions, as discussed in detail below. For example, PepsiCo has two major divisions in the soft drink and snack foods industries; each has its own R&D and manufacturing functions, but they share the marketing and distribution functions to lower operating costs and achieve the gains from differentiation.

Second, the office of *corporate headquarters staff* is created to monitor divisional activities and to exercise financial control over each of the divisions.[1] This staff contains the corporate-level managers who oversee the activities of divisional managers. Hence, the organizational hierarchy is taller in a multidivisional structure than in a product or functional structure. The role of the new level of corporate management is to develop strategic control systems that lower a company's overall cost structure, including finding ways to economize on the costs of controlling the handoffs and transfers between divisions. The extra cost of these corporate managers is more than justified if their actions can lower the cost structure of the operating divisions or increase divisions' ability to differentiate their product—both of which boost a company's return on invested capital (ROIC).

In the multidivisional structure, day-to-day operations of each division are the responsibility of divisional management; that is, divisional management has *operating responsibility*. The corporate headquarters, which includes top executives as well as their support staff, is responsible for overseeing the company's long-term multibusiness model and for providing guidance for interdivisional projects. These executives

FIGURE 13.1

Multidivisional Structure

Oil division
(functional structure)

Pharmaceuticals division
(product-team structure)

Plastics division
(matrix structure)

have *strategic responsibility*. Such a combination of self-contained divisions with a centralized corporate management provides the extra coordination and control necessary to manage entry into new industries.

Figure 13.1 illustrates a typical multidivisional structure found in a large chemical company such as DuPont. Although this company might easily have twenty different divisions, only three—the oil, pharmaceuticals, and plastics divisions—are represented here. Each division possesses some combination of the value-chain functions it needs to pursue its own business model. Each is also normally treated by the corporate center as a profit center, and strategic control measures such as ROIC are used to monitor and evaluate each division's performance.[2] The use of this kind of output control makes it easier for corporate managers to identify high-performing and underperforming divisions and to take corrective action as necessary.

Because they have been separated into subunits by industry, each division is also able to develop the structure and culture that best suit its particular business model, for example, a product, matrix, or market structure. As a result, implementing a multidivisional structure allows a multibusiness company to take into account the need for each separate division to adopt the structure and control systems necessary to implement its business model and strategies effectively.

Figure 13.1 shows that the oil division has a functional structure because it is pursuing cost leadership. The pharmaceuticals division has a product-team structure to encourage speedy development of new drugs, and the plastics division has a matrix structure to allow it to quickly develop new kinds of customized plastic products to suit the changing needs of its customers—these divisions are pursuing differentiation based on a distinctive competence in innovation. Sometimes the size of its operations alone is enough to compel a company to use a multidivisional structure.

For example, inside one industry, the car industry, GM operates the whole corporation through a multidivisional structure, and each of its main car brands—Cadillac, Buick, and so on—is organized as a separate division. In addition, as we discuss in the *Opening Case,* GM has an overseas division in each country abroad in which it assembles cars. A former GM CEO, Alfred Sloan, implemented its multidivisional structure in 1921, noting that GM "needs to find a principle for coordination without losing the advantages of decentralization."

Each of GM's different car brands was placed in a self-contained division with support services like sales, production, engineering, and finance. Each division became a profit center and was evaluated on its return on investment. Sloan was quite clear about the main advantage of linking decentralization to return on investment: it raised the visibility of each division's performance. And, Sloan observed, it (1) "increases the morale of the organization by placing each operation on its own foundation,…assuming its own responsibility and contributing its share to the final result"; (2) "develops statistics correctly reflecting…the true measure of efficiency"; and (3) "enables the corporation to direct the placing of additional capital where it will result in the greatest benefit to the corporation as a whole."[3]

Sloan recommended that exchanges or handoffs between divisions be set by a *transfer-pricing scheme* based on cost plus some predetermined rate of return. However, to avoid protecting a high-cost internal supplier, he also recommended a number of steps involving analysis of the operations of outside competitors to determine the fair price. Sloan established a strong, professional, centralized headquarters management staff to perform such calculations. Corporate management's primary role was to audit divisional performance and plan strategy for the total organization. Divisional managers were to be responsible for all product-related decisions.

As the *Opening Case* relates, fierce competition from efficient Japanese competitors resulted in GM reassessing the way its multidivisional structure was operating. The duplication of R&D and engineering between divisions at home and abroad, and the purchasing of components by each division independently, was costing the company billions of extra dollars. Globally, GM has reduced the number of cars in its product range and the number of different platforms used to make cars. It has also vertically disintegrated by spinning off high-cost internal suppliers and has recentralized the purchasing of component parts using the car industry's sophisticated B2B network, Covisint, to outsource more of its components. As GM's experience suggests, operating a multidivisional structure is a *continuing* challenge for managers. Because the multidivisional structure is so widely used, it is necessary to look closely at its advantages and disadvantages.

■ **Advantages of a Multidivisional Structure**

When managed effectively at both the corporate and the divisional levels, a multidivisional structure offers several advantages. Together, they can raise corporate profitability to a new peak because they allow a company to more effectively implement its multibusiness model and strategies at all levels.

■ **Enhanced Corporate Financial Control** The profitability of different business divisions is clearly visible in the multidivisional structure.[4] Because each division is its own profit center, financial controls can be applied to each business on the basis of profitability criteria such as ROIC. Typically, these controls cover establishing targets, monitoring performance on a regular basis, and selectively intervening when problems arise. Corporate headquarters is also in a better position to allocate corporate financial resources among competing divisions. The visibility of divisional performance means that corporate headquarters can identify the divisions in which investment of funds will yield the greatest long-term ROIC. In a sense, the corporate office is in a position to act as the investor or banker in an internal capital market, channeling funds to high-yield uses.

■ **Enhanced Strategic Control** The multidivisional structure frees corporate managers from business-level responsibilities. Corporate managers have the time and scope for contemplating wider strategic issues and for developing responses to environmental changes, such as quickly changing industry boundaries. The multidivisional structure also enables corporate headquarters to obtain the proper information to perform long-run strategic and scenario planning for the entire corporation, including decisions about which businesses to expand and which to exit from.

■ **Growth** The multidivisional structure lets the company overcome an organizational limit to its growth. Because information overload at the center is reduced, corporate managers can consider emerging opportunities for further growth and diversification. Communication problems are reduced because the same set of standardized accounting and financial output controls can be used for all divisions. Also, from a behavior control perspective, corporate managers are able to implement a policy of management by exception, which means that they intervene only when problems arise.

■ **Stronger Pursuit of Internal Efficiency** As a company grows, it often becomes difficult for managers to accurately assess the profit contribution of each functional activity because their activities are so interdependent. This means that it is often more difficult for top managers to evaluate how well their company is performing relative to others in its industry. As a result, inside one company considerable degrees of organizational slack—that is, the unproductive use of functional resources—can go undetected. For example, the head of the finance function might employ a larger staff than required for efficiency to reduce work pressures inside the department and to bring the manager higher status. In a multidivisional structure, however, corporate managers can compare the performance of one division against another in terms of its cost structure or the profit it generates. The corporate office is thus in a better position to identify the managerial inefficiencies that result in bureaucratic costs, and divisional managers can have no alibis for poor performance.

■ **Problems in Implementing a Multidivisional Structure**

Although research suggests that large companies that adopt a multidivisional structure outperform those that retain the functional structure, this structure has its disadvantages as well.[5] Good management can eliminate some of them, but others are inherent in the way the structure operates and require constant managerial attention, as GM's problems suggest.

■ **Establishing the Divisional-Corporate Authority Relationship**
The authority relationship between corporate headquarters and the divisions must be correctly established. The multidivisional structure introduces a new level in the hierarchy: the corporate level. The problem lies in deciding how much authority and control to delegate to the operating divisions and how much authority to retain at corporate headquarters to increase long-run profitability. This was the problem Sloan encountered when he implemented GM's multidivisional structure.[6] What Sloan found was that when headquarters retained too much power and authority, the operating divisions lacked sufficient autonomy to develop the business model and strategies that best met

their needs. On the other hand, when too much power was delegated to the divisions, they pursued divisional objectives, with little heed to the needs of the whole corporation. As a result, not all the potential gains from using this structure could be achieved.

Thus, the central issue in managing the multidivisional structure is how much authority should be *centralized* at corporate headquarters and how much should be *decentralized* to the divisions. This issue must be decided by each company in reference to the nature of its business- and corporate-level strategies. There are no easy answers, and as the environment changes or the company alters its multibusiness model strategies over time, the balance between corporate and divisional control will also change, as Strategy in Action 13.1 suggests.

Strategy in Action   13.1

Amoco, ARCO, and Burmah Castrol Become Part of BP

As with most other global oil companies, Amoco was engaged in three major activities: oil exploration, refining, and chemicals manufacturing. To manage these activities, it used a three-legged structure and created three independent operating *subsidiaries* to manage each of its three main activities. Each subsidiary had its own set of managers responsible for overseeing all the many different *divisions* inside each subsidiary; thus, there was an extra level of control: the subsidiary level. The managers of all three subsidiaries then reported to Amoco's corporate-level managers, who oversaw their activities and made the final decision on what each subsidiary should be doing. Because all important decision making at Amoco was centralized at the top, it often took a long time to make decisions because of the many managerial layers between Amoco's corporate managers and its divisional managers. The slow decision-making process hampered divisional managers' attempts to build a competitive advantage, but this situation was left unattended too during the prosperous oil industry of the 1980s.

By the 1990s, Amoco, like other global oil companies such as Exxon, British Petroleum, and Mobil, had experienced intense pressure to reduce costs because of flat gas prices. To try to boost profits, Amoco laid off more than one-quarter of its work force, but this did not work. Amoco's managers then took a close look at its structure to see whether there was a way to increase its performance.

Amoco's CEO, H. Laurence Fuller, decided that a massive reorganization of Amoco's structure was necessary. Fuller eliminated Amoco's three-legged structure completely and removed all the managers at the subsidiary level. The three subsidiaries were divided into seventeen independent divisions according to their industry, and Amoco changed to a multidivisional structure. Henceforth, strategic responsibilities were decentralized to the managers of each division, who were free to pursue the most effective business model. Each division was evaluated on the basis of its ability to reach certain ROIC targets set by corporate managers, but their own managers determined the way they achieved those targets.

By 1996, it was clear that Fuller's move to a multidivisional structure had worked. Managers were acting more entrepreneurially, and the company was operating more efficiently. However, in the late 1990s, oil industry companies began to consolidate further to make better use of their resources and lower their cost structure. Fuller agreed to merge Amoco with British Petroleum (BP).[7] Because many of both companies' divisions were competing in the same industries, their functional activities overlapped and duplicated one another, so BP developed a value creation grid and then merged Amoco's seventeen divisions with its own thirty-three divisions. In 2001, BP acquired ARCO for its extensive gas reserves and Burmah Castrol, the well-known fuel oil maker. Once again, it integrated these companies into its existing operations, and from these mergers it strengthened its differentiated position in its major sectors of oil, gas, chemicals, and downstream activities such as retailing. BP also announced that it expected to achieve $5.9 billion in cost savings from these moves. BP has continued to make new acquisitions or form joint ventures around the world to strengthen its position in many emerging markets. For example, it took a 20 percent stake in China's biggest gas refiner and gas station chain to leverage the use of its resources into this fast-growing market.[a]

■ **Distortion of Information** If corporate headquarters places too much emphasis on each division's individual profitability—for instance, by setting very high and stringent ROIC targets—divisional managers may choose to distort the information they supply top management and paint a rosy picture of it at the expense of future profitability. Bureaucratic costs now increase as divisions may attempt to make ROIC look better by cutting product development or new investments or marketing expenditures. Although such actions might boost short-run ROIC, they do so at the cost of cutting back on investments and expenditures necessary to maintain the long-term profitability of the company. The problem stems from too tight financial control. GM suffered from this problem in recent years as declining performance prompted divisional managers to try to make their divisions look good to corporate headquarters to secure greater funds for future investment. Managing the corporate-divisional interface requires coping with subtle power issues.

■ **Competition for Resources** The third problem of managing a multidivisional structure is that the divisions themselves may compete for resources and this rivalry can make it difficult or impossible to obtain the gains from transferring, sharing, or leveraging distinctive competencies across business units. For example, the amount of capital for investment that corporate managers have to distribute to the divisions is fixed. Generally, the divisions that can demonstrate the highest ROIC get the lion's share of the money. Because that large share strengthens them in the next time period, the strong divisions grow stronger. Consequently, divisions may actively compete for resources and thereby reduce interdivisional coordination. As a result, the potential gains from pursuing a multibusiness model will be lost.

■ **Transfer Pricing** Divisional competition may lead to battles over **transfer pricing,** that is, conflicts over establishing the fair or "competitive" price of a resource or skill developed in one division that is to be transferred and sold to other divisions that require it. As we discuss in Chapter 9, one of the origins of the problems of handoffs or transfers between divisions, and thus a major source of bureaucratic costs, is the problem of setting prices for resource transfers to obtain the benefits of the multibusiness models when pursuing a vertical integration or related diversification strategy.

Rivalry among divisions is common in the transfer pricing process because each supplying division has the incentive to set the highest price for its resources or skills to maximize its own revenues and profits. However, purchasing divisions view attempts to charge high prices as undermining their own profitability—hence the problem. Such competition can completely undermine the corporate culture and make a company a battleground. If such battles go unresolved, the benefits of the multibusiness model will not be achieved. Hence, there is a need for the sensitive design of incentive and control systems to make the multidivisional structure work.

■ **Short-Term R&D Focus** If corporate headquarters sets extremely high and rigid ROIC targets, there is a danger that the divisions will cut back on R&D expenditures to improve their financial performance. Although this inflates divisional performance in the short term, it undermines a division's ability to develop new products and leads to a fall in the stream of long-term profits. Hence, corporate headquarters personnel must carefully control their interactions with the divisions to ensure that both the short- and long-term goals of the business are being achieved.

■ **Duplication of Functional Resources** Because each division often possesses its own set of value-chain functions, multidivisional structures are expensive to run and manage. R&D is an especially costly activity, and so some companies centralize such functions at the corporate level to serve all divisions. The duplication of specialist services is not a problem if the cost and differentiation gains from having separate specialist functions are substantial, however. Corporate managers decide whether duplication is financially justified and, if so, which functions to centralize or decentralize to optimize short- and long-run profitability.

In sum, the advantages of divisional structures must be balanced against problems of implementing them, but an observant, professional management team that is aware of the issues involved can manage these problems. The increasing use of information technology is also making implementation easier. We discuss information technology after we describe the use of structure, control, and culture for different kinds of multibusiness models.

■ **Structure, Control, Culture, and Corporate-Level Strategy**

Once strategic managers select a multidivisional structure, they must then make choices about what kind of integrating mechanisms and control systems to use to make the structure work efficiently. Such choices depend on whether a company chooses to pursue a multibusiness model based on a strategy of unrelated diversification, vertical integration, or related diversification.

As discussed in Chapter 9, many possible differentiation and cost advantages derive from vertical integration. A company can coordinate resource-scheduling decisions among divisions operating in adjacent industries to reduce manufacturing costs and improve quality, for example.[8] This might mean locating a rolling mill next to a steel furnace to save the costs of reheating steel ingots and make it easier to control the quality of the final product.

The principal benefits from related diversification also come from transferring, sharing, or leveraging functional resources or skills across divisions, such as sharing distribution and sales networks to increase differentiation or lower the overall cost structure. With both strategies, the benefits to the company come from some *exchange of distinctive competencies* among divisions. To secure these benefits, the company must coordinate activities among divisions. Consequently, structure and control must be designed to handle the handoffs or transfers among divisions.

In the case of unrelated diversification, the multibusiness model is based on using general managerial capabilities in entrepreneurship, organizational design, or strategy—for example, through top managers' ability to create a culture that supports entrepreneurial behavior that leads to rapid product development; or from restructuring an underperforming company and establishing an efficient internal capital market that allows corporate managers to make superior capital allocation decisions than would be possible using the external capital market. With this strategy, there are no exchanges among divisions, each operates separately and independently, and the exchanges that need to be coordinated take place between divisions and corporate headquarters. Structure and control must therefore be designed to allow each division to operate independently while giving corporate managers easy ability to monitor and to intervene if necessary.

The choice of structure and control mechanisms depends on the degree to which a company using a multidivisional structure needs to control the handoffs and interactions among divisions. The more interdependent the divisions—that is, the more they depend on each other for skills, resources, and competencies—the greater are the

TABLE 13.1

Corporate Strategy and Structure and Control

Corporate Strategy	Appropriate Structure	Need for Integration	Type of Control		
			Financial Control	Behavior Control	Organizational Culture
Unrelated Diversification	Multidivisional	Low (no exchanges between divisions)	Great use (e.g., ROIC)	Some use (e.g., budgets)	Little use
Vertical Integration	Multidivisional	Medium (scheduling resource transfers)	Great use (e.g., ROIC, transfer pricing)	Great use (e.g., standardization, budgets)	Some use (e.g., shared norms and values)
Related Diversification	Multidivisional	High (achieving synergies between divisions by integrating roles)	Little use	Great use (e.g., rules, budgets)	Great use (e.g., norms, values, common language)

bureaucratic costs associated with obtaining the potential benefits from a particular strategy.[9] Table 13.1 indicates what forms of structure and control companies should adopt to economize on the bureaucratic costs associated with the three corporate strategies of unrelated diversification, vertical integration, and related diversification.[10] We examine these strategies in detail in the next sections.

■ **Unrelated Diversification** Because there are *no exchanges or linkages* among divisions, unrelated diversification is the easiest and cheapest strategy to manage; it is associated with the lowest level of bureaucratic costs. The main requirement of the structure and control system is that it allows corporate managers to evaluate divisional performance easily and accurately. Thus, companies use a multidivisional structure, and each division is evaluated by output controls such as return on invested capital. A company also applies sophisticated accounting controls to obtain information quickly from the divisions so that corporate managers can readily compare divisions on several dimensions. Textron and Dover are good examples of companies that use sophisticated computer networks and accounting controls to manage their structures, which allow them almost daily access to divisional performance.

Divisions usually have considerable autonomy *unless* they fail to reach their ROIC goals. Generally, corporate headquarters will not intervene in the operations of a division unless there are problems. If problems arise, corporate headquarters may step in to take corrective action, perhaps replacing managers or providing additional financial resources, depending on the reason for the problem. If they see no possibility of a turnaround, they may decide to divest the division. The multidivisional structure allows the unrelated company to operate its businesses as a portfolio of investments that can be bought and sold as business conditions change. Often managers in the various divisions do not know one another; they may not even know what other companies are in the corporate portfolio. Hence, the idea of a corporate culture is meaningless.

The use of financial controls to manage a company means that no integration among divisions is necessary. This is why the bureaucratic costs of managing an unrelated company are low. The biggest problem facing corporate personnel is determining capital allocations to the various divisions so that the overall profitability of the portfolio is maximized. They also have to oversee divisional managers and make sure that divisions are achieving ROIC targets.

Alco Standard, based in Valley Forge, Pennsylvania, demonstrates how to operate a successful strategy of unrelated diversification. Alco is one of the largest office supply companies in the United States, distributing office and paper supplies and materials through a nationwide network of wholly owned distribution companies. The policy of Alco's top management is that authority and control should be completely decentralized to the managers in each of the company's fifty divisions. Each division is left alone to make its own manufacturing or purchasing decisions even though some potential benefits, in the form of corporate-wide purchasing or marketing, are being lost. Top management pursues this nonintervention policy because it believes that the gains from allowing its managers to act as independent entrepreneurs exceed any potential cost savings that might result from coordinating interdivisional activities. It believes that a decentralized operating system allows a big company to act in a way that is similar to a small company, avoiding the problem of growing bureaucracy and organizational inertia.

At Alco, top management interprets its role as relieving the divisions of administrative chores, such as bookkeeping and accounting, and collecting market information on competitive pricing and products, which allows divisional managers to improve their business-level strategy. Centralizing these information activities reduces each division's cost structure and provides the standardization that lets top management make better decisions about resource allocation. Alco's division heads are regarded as partners in the corporate enterprise and are rewarded through stock options linked to the performance of their divisions. So far, Alco has been very successful with its decentralized operating structure and has achieved a compound growth rate of 19 percent a year.

■ **Vertical Integration** Vertical integration is a more expensive strategy to manage than unrelated diversification because *sequential resource flows* from one division to the next must be coordinated. Once again, the multidivisional structure economizes on the bureaucratic costs associated with achieving such coordination. This structure provides the centralized control necessary for the vertically integrated company to achieve benefits from the control of resource transfers. Corporate personnel assume the responsibility for devising financial output and behavior controls that solve the problems of transferring resources among divisions; for example, they are involved in solving transfer pricing problems. Also, complex rules and procedures are instituted that specify how exchanges are to be made to solve potential transaction problems. As previously noted, complex resource exchanges can lead to conflict among divisions, and corporate managers must try to minimize divisional conflicts.

Centralizing authority at corporate headquarters must be done with care in vertically related companies. It carries the risk of involving corporate managers in operating issues at the business level to the point at which the divisions lose their autonomy and motivation. These companies must strike the right balance of centralized control at corporate headquarters and decentralized control at the divisional level if they are to implement this strategy successfully.

Because their interests are at stake, divisions need to have input into scheduling and decisions regarding resource transfer. For example, the plastics division in a chemical company has a vital interest in the activities of the oil division, for the quality of the products it gets from the oil division determines the quality of its own products. Divisional integrating mechanisms can bring about direct coordination and information transfers among divisions.[11] To handle communication among divisions, a company sets up teams for that purpose; it can also use **integrating roles,** whereby an experienced senior manager assumes responsibility for managing complex transfers between two or more divisions. The use of integrating roles to coordinate divisions is common in high-tech and chemical companies, for example.

Thus, a strategy of vertical integration is managed through a combination of corporate and divisional controls. As a result, the organizational structure and control systems used for managing this strategy to economize on bureaucratic costs are more complex and more difficult to implement than those used for unrelated diversification. However, as long as the benefits that derive from vertical integration are realized, the extra expense in implementing this strategy can be justified.

■ **Related Diversification** In the case of related diversification, the gains from pursuing this multibusiness model derive from the transfer, sharing, or leveraging of R&D knowledge, industry information, customer bases, and so on across divisions. Also, with this structure, the high level of resource sharing and joint production by divisions makes it hard for corporate managers to measure the performance of each individual division.[12] Thus, bureaucratic costs are substantial. The multidivisional structure helps to economize on these costs because it provides some of the extra coordination and control that is required. However, if a related company is to obtain the potential benefits from using its competencies efficiently and effectively, it has to adopt more complicated forms of integration and control at the divisional level to make the structure work.

First, output control is difficult to use because divisions share resources, so it is not easy to measure the performance of an individual division. Therefore, a company needs to develop a corporate culture that stresses cooperation among divisions and corporate rather than purely divisional goals. Second, corporate managers must establish sophisticated integrating devices to ensure coordination among divisions. Integrating roles and even integrating teams of managers are often essential because they provide the context in which managers from different divisions can meet and develop a common vision of corporate goals. HP, for instance, created a high-level integrating team composed of scores of managers to coordinate the merger process with Compaq.[13]

An organization with a multidivisional structure must have the right mix of incentives and rewards for cooperation if it is to achieve gains from sharing skills and resources among divisions.[14] With unrelated diversification, divisions operate autonomously, and the company can quite easily reward managers on their division's individual performance. With related diversification, however, rewarding divisions is more difficult because they are engaged in so many shared activities, and strategic managers must be sensitive and alert to achieve equity in rewards among divisions. The aim always is to design structure and control systems so that they can maximize the benefits from pursuing the strategy while economizing on bureaucratic costs.

■ The Role of Information Technology

The expanding use of IT is increasing the advantages and reducing the problems associated with implementing a multibusiness model effectively. IT does this because it facilitates output control, behavior control, and integration between divisions and between divisions and corporate headquarters.

On the advantage side, IT provides a common software platform that can make it much less problematic for divisions to share information and knowledge and obtain the benefits from leveraging their competencies. IT also facilitates output and financial control, making it easier for corporate headquarters to monitor divisional performance and decide when to intervene selectively. It also helps corporate managers better use their strategic and implementation skills because they can react more quickly given that they possess higher-quality, more timely information from the use of a sophisticated cross-organizational IT infrastructure.

In a similar fashion, IT makes it easier to manage the problems that occur when implementing a multidivisional structure. Because it provides both corporate and divisional managers with more and better information, it makes it easier for corporate managers to decentralize control to divisional managers and yet react quickly if the need arises. IT can also make it more difficult to distort information and hide bad news because divisional managers must provide standardized information that can be compared across divisions. Finally, IT eases the transfer pricing problem because divisional managers have access to detailed up-to-date information about how much a certain resource or skill would cost to buy in the external marketplace. Thus, a fair transfer price is easier to determine. The way in which SAP's enterprise resources planning software helps to integrate the activities of divisions in a multidivisional structure is discussed in Strategy in Action 13.2.

Implementing Strategy Across Countries

Global strategy can play a crucial role in strengthening the business model of both single-business and multibusiness companies. Indeed, few large companies that have expanded into new industries have not already expanded globally and replicated their business model in new countries to grow their profits. Companies can use four basic strategies as they begin to market their products and establish production facilities abroad:

- A *localization strategy* is oriented toward local responsiveness, and a company decentralizes control to subsidiaries and divisions in each country in which it operates to produce and customize products to local markets.

- An *international strategy* is based on R&D and marketing being centralized at home and all the other value creation functions being decentralized to national units.

- A *global standardization strategy* is oriented toward cost reduction, with all the principal value creation functions centralized at the optimal global location.

- A *transnational strategy* is focused so that it can achieve local responsiveness and cost reduction. Some functions are centralized and others decentralized at the global location best suited to achieving these objectives.

The need to coordinate and integrate global value-chain activities increases as a company moves from a localization to an international to a global standardization and then to a transnational strategy. To obtain the benefits of pursuing a transnational strategy, a company must transfer its distinctive competencies to the global location where they can create the most value and establish a global network to coordinate its divisions at home and abroad. The objective of such coordination is to obtain the benefits from transferring or leveraging competencies across a company's

Strategy in Action

13.2

SAP's ERP Systems

SAP is the world's leading supplier of enterprise resources planning (ERP) software; it introduced the world's first ERP system in 1973. So great was the demand for its software that it had to train thousands of IT consultants from companies like IBM, HP, Accenture, and Cap Gemini to install and customize its software to meet the needs of companies around the globe. SAP's ERP system is popular because it manages functional activities at all stages of a company's value chain, as well as resource transfers between a company's different divisions.

First, SAP's software has modules specifically designed to manage each core functional activity. Each module contains the set of best practices that SAP's IT engineers have found works best to build competencies in efficiency, quality, innovation, and responsiveness to customers. Each function inputs its data into its functional module in the way specified by SAP. For example, sales inputs all the information about customer needs required by SAP's sales module, and materials management inputs information about the product specifications it requires from suppliers into SAP's materials-management module. Each SAP module functions as an *expert system* that can reason through the information that functional managers put into it. It then provides managers with real-time feedback about the current state of vital functional operations—and gives recommendations that allow managers to improve them. However, the magic of ERP does not stop there. SAP's ERP software then connects across functions inside each division. This means that managers in all functions of a division have access to other functions' expert systems, and SAP's software is designed to alert managers when their functional operations are affected by changes taking place in another function. *Thus, SAP's ERP allows managers across a division to better coordinate their activities*, which is a major source of competitive advantage.

Moreover, SAP software, running on corporate mainframe computers, takes the information from all the different expert systems in the divisions and creates a companywide ERP system that provides corporate managers with an overview of the operations of all a company's divisions. In essence, SAP's ERP system creates a sophisticated corporate-level expert system that can reason through the huge volume of information being provided by all its divisions and functions. The ERP system can then recognize and diagnose common issues and problems and recommend organization-wide solutions, such as by suggesting new ways to leverage, transfer, and share competencies and resources. Top managers, armed with the knowledge their ERP provides, can also use it to adjust their business model with the changing environment. The result, SAP claims, is that when a multidivisional company implements its corporatewide ERP software, it can achieve productivity gains of 30 to 50 percent, which amounts to billions of dollars of savings for large multinational companies like Nestlé and Exxon.

global business units. Thus, the bureaucratic costs associated with solving the communication and measurement problems that arise in managing handoffs or transfers across countries are much higher for companies pursuing a transnational strategy than for those pursuing the other strategies. The localization strategy does not require coordinating activities on a global level because value creation activities are handled locally, by country or world region. The international and global standardization strategies fit between the other two strategies: although products have to be sold and marketed globally, and hence global product transfers must be managed, there is less need to coordinate skill and resource transfers than for a transnational strategy.

The implication is that as companies change from a localization to an international, global standardization, or transnational strategy, they require a more complex structure, control system, and culture to coordinate the value creation activities associated with implementing that strategy. More complex structures economize on

TABLE 13.2

Global Strategy/Structure Relationships

	Localization Strategy	International Strategy	Global Standardization Strategy	Transnational Strategy
	Low ⟵——————————— Need for Coordination ——————————⟶ High			
	Low ⟵——————————— Bureaucratic Costs ——————————⟶ High			
Centralization of Authority	Decentralized to national unit	Core competencies centralized, others decentralized to national units	Centralized at optimal global location	Simultaneously centralized and decentralized
Horizontal Differentiation	Global-area structure	Global-division structure	Global product-group structure	Global-matrix structure, matrix-in-the-mind
Need for Complex Integrating Mechanisms	Low	Medium	High	Very high
Organizational Culture	Not important	Quite important	Important	Very important

bureaucratic costs. In general, the choice of structure and control systems for managing a global business is a function of three factors:

1. The decision on how to distribute and allocate responsibility and authority between managers at home and abroad so that effective control over a company's global operations is maintained

2. The selection of the organizational structure that groups divisions both at home and abroad in a way that allows the best use of resources and serves the needs of foreign customers most effectively

3. The selection of the right kinds of integration and control mechanisms and organizational culture to make the overall global structure function effectively

Table 13.2 summarizes the appropriate design choices for companies pursuing each of these strategies.

■ **Implementing a Localization Strategy**

When a company pursues a localization strategy, it generally operates with a global-area structure (see Figure 13.2). When using this structure, a company duplicates all value creation activities and establishes an overseas division in every country or world area in which it operates. Authority is decentralized to managers in each overseas division, who devise the appropriate strategy for responding to the needs of the local environment. Managers at global headquarters use market and output controls, such as ROIC, growth in market share, and operation costs, to evaluate the performance of overseas divisions. On the basis of such global comparisons, they can make decisions about capital allocation and orchestrate the transfer of new knowledge among divisions.

FIGURE 13.2

Global-Area Structure

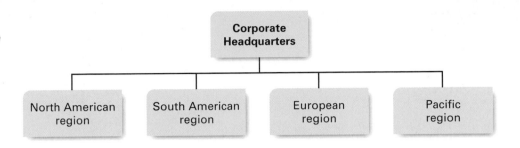

A company that makes and sells the same products in many different countries often groups its overseas divisions into world regions to simplify the coordination of products across countries. Europe might be one region, the Pacific Rim another, and the Middle East a third. Grouping allows the same set of output and behavior controls to be applied across all divisions inside a region. Thus, global companies can reduce communications and transfer problems because information can be transmitted more easily across countries with broadly similar cultures. For example, consumers' preferences regarding product design and marketing are likely to be more similar among countries in one world region than among countries in different world regions.

Because the overseas divisions themselves have little or no contact with others in different regions, no integrating mechanisms are needed. Nor does a global organizational culture develop because there are no transfers of skills or resources or transfer of personnel among managers from the various world regions. Historically, car companies such as DaimlerChrysler, GM, and Ford used global-area structures to manage their overseas operations. Ford of Europe, for example, had little or no contact with its U.S. parent; capital was the principal resource exchanged.

One problem with a global-area structure and a localization strategy is that the duplication of specialist activities across countries raises a company's overall cost structure. Moreover, the company is not taking advantage of opportunities to transfer, share, or leverage its competencies and capabilities on a global basis; for example, it cannot apply the low-cost manufacturing expertise that has developed in one world region in another. Thus, localization companies lose the many benefits of operating globally. As Chapter 8 discusses, the popularity of this strategic orientation has decreased.

■ **Implementing an International Strategy**

A company pursuing an international strategy adopts a different route to global expansion. Normally, the company shifts to this strategy when it decides to sell domestically made products in markets abroad. Until the 1990s, for example, companies such as Mercedes-Benz and Jaguar made no attempt to produce in a foreign market; instead, they distributed and sold their domestically produced cars internationally. Such companies usually just add a *foreign sales organization* to their existing structure and continue to use the same control system. If a company is using a functional structure, this department has to coordinate manufacturing, sales, and R&D activities with the needs of the foreign market. Efforts at customization are minimal. In overseas countries, a company usually establishes a subsidiary to handle local sales and distribution. For example, the Mercedes-Benz overseas subsidiaries allocate dealerships, organize supplies of spare parts, and, of course, sell cars. A system of behavior controls is then established to keep the home office informed of changes in sales, spare parts requirements, and so on.

FIGURE 13.3

Global Division
Structure

A company with many different products or businesses operating from a multidivisional structure has the challenging problem of coordinating the flow of different products across different countries. To manage these transfers, many companies create a *global division,* which they add to their existing divisional structure (see Figure 13.3).[15] Global operations are managed as a separate divisional business, with managers given the authority and responsibility for coordinating domestic product divisions with overseas markets. The global division also monitors and controls the overseas subsidiaries that market the products and decides how much authority to delegate to managers in these countries.

This arrangement of tasks and roles reduces the transaction of managing handoffs across countries and world regions. However, managers abroad are essentially under the control of managers in the global division, and if domestic and overseas managers compete for control of strategy making, conflict and lack of cooperation may result. Many companies such as IBM, Citibank, and DaimlerChrysler have experienced this problem. Very often, significant strategic control has been decentralized to overseas divisions. When cost pressures force corporate managers to reassess their strategy and they decide to intervene, this frequently provokes resistance, much of it due to differences in culture—not just corporate but also country differences.

■ **Implementing a Global Standardization Strategy**

When a company embarks on a global standardization strategy today, it locates its manufacturing and other value-chain activities at the global location that will allow it to increase efficiency, quality, and innovation. In doing so, it has to solve the problems of coordinating and integrating its global value-chain activities. It has to find a structure that lowers the bureaucratic costs associated with resource transfers between corporate headquarters and its overseas divisions and provides the centralized control that a global standardization strategy requires. The answer for many companies is a *global product-group structure* (see Figure 13.4).

In this structure, a product-group headquarters is created to coordinate the activities of its home and overseas operations. The managers at each product group's headquarters decide where to locate the different functions at the optimal global location for performing that activity. For example, Phillips has one product group responsible for global R&D, manufacturing, marketing, and sales of its light bulbs, another for

FIGURE 13.4

Global Product-Group
Structure

medical equipment, and so on. The headquarters of the medical division and its R&D is located in Bothell, Washington, manufacturing is done in Taiwan, and the products are sold by sales subsidiaries in each local market.

The product-group structure allows managers to decide how best to pursue a global standardization strategy—for example, to decide which value-chain activities, such as manufacturing or product design, should be performed in which country to increase efficiency. Increasingly, U.S. and Japanese companies are moving manufacturing to low-cost countries such as China but establishing product design centers in Europe or the United States to take advantage of foreign skills and capabilities to obtain the benefits from this strategy.

■ **Implementing
a Transnational
Strategy**

The main failing of the global product-group structure is that although it allows a company to achieve superior efficiency and quality, it is weak when it comes to responsiveness to customers because the focus is still on centralized control to reduce costs. Moreover, this structure makes it difficult for the *different product divisions* to trade information and knowledge and to obtain the benefits from transferring, sharing, and leveraging their competencies. Sometimes the potential gains from sharing product, marketing, or R&D knowledge between product groups are high, but so too are the bureaucratic costs associated with achieving these gains. Is there a structure that can simultaneously economize on these costs and provide the coordination necessary to obtain these benefits?

In the 1990s, many companies implemented a *global-matrix structure* to simultaneously lower their global cost structures *and* differentiate their activities through superior innovation and responsiveness to customers globally. Figure 13.5 shows such a structure that might be used by a company such as HP, SAP, or Nestlé. On the vertical axis, instead of functions, there are the company's product *groups*, which provide specialist services such as R&D, product design, and marketing information to its overseas divisions, which are often grouped by world region. These might be the petroleum, plastics, pharmaceuticals, or fertilizer product groups. On the horizontal axis are the company's *overseas divisions* in the various countries or world regions in which it operates. Managers at the regional or country level control local operations. Through a system of output and behavior controls, they then report to managers in product-group headquarters in the United States and ultimately to the CEO. Managers for world regions or countries are also responsible for working with U.S. product-group managers to develop the control and reward systems that will promote transfer, sharing, or leveraging of competencies.

FIGURE 13.5

Global-Matrix
Structure

● Individual operating companies

Implementing a matrix structure thus decentralizes control to overseas managers and provides them with considerable flexibility for managing local issues, but it can still give product-group and top corporate executives in the United States the centralized control they need to coordinate company activities on a global level. The matrix structure can allow knowledge and experience to be transferred among divisions in both product groups and geographic regions because it offers many opportunities for face-to-face contact between managers at home and abroad. The matrix also facilitates the transmission of a company's norms and values and, hence, the development of a global corporate culture. This is especially important for a company with far-flung global operations for which lines of communication are longer. Club Med, for instance, uses a matrix to standardize high-quality customer service across its global vacation villages. Nestlé's experience with the global-matrix structure is profiled in Strategy in Action 13.3.

Nestlé is not the only company to find the task of integrating and controlling a global-matrix structure a difficult task. Some, like ABB, Ford, and Motorola, have dismantled their matrix structures and moved to a simplified global product-group approach using IT to integrate across countries. If a matrix is chosen, however, other possible ways of making it work effectively include developing a strong cross-country organizational culture to facilitate communication and coordination among managers. For example, many companies are increasingly transferring managers between their domestic and overseas operations so they can implant the domestic culture in the new location and also learn by studying how their structure and systems work in the foreign country.

Toyota has made great efforts to understand how to manage car plants in overseas locations and how to transplant its culture into those plants. When it decided to enter and make cars in the United States, it first formed a joint venture with GM, and the companies combined their expertise in this car-making venture, which was known as NUMMI. Toyota was responsible for implanting its knowledge of lean production in this plant; all the workers were cross-trained and taught how to monitor and benchmark their own performance and how to work in quality teams to improve it.

Strategy in Action
Using IT to Make Nestlé's Global Structure Work

13.3

Nestlé, based in Vevey, Switzerland, is the world's biggest food company, with global sales in excess of $65 billion in 2004. The company has been pursuing an ambitious program of global expansion by acquiring many famous companies—for instance, Perrier, the French mineral water producer, and Rowntree, the British candy maker. In the United States, Nestlé bought the giant Carnation Company, Stouffer Foods, Contadina, Ralston Purina, and Dreyer's Grand Ice Cream.

Traditionally, Nestlé pursued a localization strategy and managed its operating companies through a global-area structure. In each country, each individual division (such as its Carnation division) was responsible for managing all aspects of its business-level strategy: in other words, companies were free to control their own product development and marketing and to manage all local operations. Nestlé's corporate executives decided acquisitions, expansions, and corporate resource decisions such as capital investment at the Vevey headquarters. Because all important decisions were made centrally, the size of the corporate staff increased dramatically. In the 1990s, Nestlé realized it had major problems.

Corporate managers had become remote from the difficulties experienced by the individual operating divisions or companies, and the centralized structure slowed decision making and made it difficult for Nestlé to respond quickly to the changing environment. Moreover, the company was forfeiting all the possible benefits from sharing and leveraging its distinctive competencies in food product development and marketing, both between divisions in a product group and between product groups and world regions. Because each product group operated separately, corporate executives could not integrate product-group activities around the world. To raise corporate performance, Nestlé's managers sought to find a new way of organizing its activities.

Its CEO at the time, Helmut Maucher, started restructuring Nestlé from the top down. He stripped away the power of corporate managers by decentralizing authority to the managers of seven global product groups that he created to oversee the company's major product lines (for example, coffee, milk, and candy). Each global product group was to integrate the activities of all the operating divisions in its group to transfer and leverage distinctive competencies to create value. After the change,

managers in the candy product group, for instance, began orchestrating the marketing and sale of Rowntree candy products such as After Eight Mints and Smarties throughout Europe and the United States, and sales climbed by 60 percent.

Maucher then grouped all divisions within a country or world region into one national or regional strategic business unit (SBU) and created a team of SBU managers to link, coordinate, and oversee their activities. When the different divisions started to share joint purchasing, marketing, and sales activities, major cost savings resulted. In the United States, the SBU management team reduced the number of sales officers nationwide from 115 to 22 and decreased the number of suppliers of packaging from 43 to 3.

Finally, Maucher decided to use a matrix structure to integrate the activities of the seven global-product groups with the operations of Nestlé's country-based SBUs. The goal of this matrix structure is to have the company pursue a transnational strategy that allows it to obtain the gains from both differentiation through global learning and cost reduction. For example, regional SBU managers now spend considerable time in Vevey with product-group executives discussing ways of exploiting and sharing the resources of the company on a global basis.

Although the new decentralized matrix structure improved Nestlé's ability to coordinate its structure, by 1998 it was clear that it still was not providing enough integration and coordination. Although more coordination was taking place between product groups *inside* a region such as the United States, little coordination was taking place across world regions. Nestlé's top managers searched for ways to improve integration on a global scale. Their conclusion was that more output and behavior control was needed so that different product groups and regional SBUs could learn from and understand what everyone else was doing—for example, what their product development plans were or how each product group handled its global supply chain.

Nestlé's solution was to sign a $300 million contract with SAP in 2002 to install and maintain a companywide ERP system to integrate across *all* its global operations. Top managers hoped this system would give them the information they needed to exert centralized control over operations, which the matrix structure apparently did not provide. In essence, Nestlé began to use SAP's value-chain management software as a *substitute* for the matrix structure. With this IT, they would no longer need to rely on divisional managers to transfer information but henceforth could obtain it from their ERP system. They would then be able to intervene at a global level as necessary.

Nestlé's "Globe Project" to create uniform business processes and computer systems around the world has led to major successes. Nestlé was able to shut down 15 percent of its global operating structure by 2005, which has saved billions of dollars and lowered its cost structure. At the

same time, it has been able to leverage the competencies of its product groups around the world by creating new kinds of food and candy products. However, its ROIC is still significantly lower than that of competitors like Hershey and Cadbury Schweppes because, some analysts claim, the company's global food empire is simply too big to manage—no global structure can make it operate profitably. What Nestlé should do is sell off many of its businesses, reduce the number of its product groups, exit countries where its profits are marginal, and in this way shrink until it can increase its ROIC and profits to match those of its competitors.[b]

Toyota then took all its learning from this venture and transferred it to its wholly owned car plant in Georgetown, Kentucky, where it turns out cars with as good a reliability record as those produced in its Japanese plants.

Every Toyota plant is under the control of Japanese managers, however, and managers from Toyota's Japanese headquarters are constantly monitoring its plant's performance and transferring and implanting Toyota's R&D innovations into its next car models. Toyota used a similar implementation strategy when it established car component and assembly operations in south Wales to serve the European Union market. Indeed, it chose south Wales and Virginia as locations for its plants because both regions have a strong local culture based on family and tradition that closely parallels Japan's culture. Toyota's managers felt that a similar local culture would enable them to better implement Toyota's highly efficient work processes and procedures.

As the example of Toyota suggests, forming global networks of managers who can move to and work in other countries so they can turn to each other for help is an important aspect of helping a company realize the benefits from its global operations. When managers can hold a "*matrix-in-the-mind*"—that is, learn to think about how they could transfer competencies around the company to create value—they can work to develop an information network that lets a company capitalize globally on the skills and capabilities of its employees.[16] To foster the development of the matrix-in-the-mind concept and promote cooperation, companies are increasingly making use of IT's integrating capability by using online teleconferencing, e-mail, and global intranets among the parts of their global operations. For example, Hitachi coordinates its nineteen Japanese laboratories by means of an online teleconferencing system. Both Microsoft and HP make extensive use of global intranets to integrate their activities, and Nestlé still hopes its Globe Project will accomplish the same goal.

Entry Mode and Implementation

As we discuss in Chapter 10, today many organizations are altering their business models and strategies and restructuring their organizations to find new ways to use their resources and capabilities to create value. This section focuses on the implementation issues that arise when companies use the three different modes of entry into new industries: internal new venturing, joint ventures, and mergers and acquisitions.

■ **Internal New Venturing**

Chapter 10 discusses how companies can enter new industries by using internal new venturing and by transferring and leveraging their existing resources to create the set of value-chain activities necessary to compete effectively in a new industry. How can managers create a setting in which employees are to be encouraged to act in ways that allow them to see how their functional competencies or products can be used in other industries? Specifically, how can structure, control, and culture be used to increase the success of the new-venturing process?

At the heart of the issue is that corporate managers must treat the internal new-venturing process as a form of entrepreneurship and the people who are to pioneer and lead new ventures as **intrapreneurs**, or inside or internal entrepreneurs. This means that organizational structure, control, and culture must be designed to encourage creativity and give new-venture managers autonomy and freedom to develop and champion new products. At the same time, corporate managers want to make sure that the investment in new markets will be profitable and that a fit does exist between the new industry and the old one so that benefits can in fact be leveraged.[17] As we discuss in Chapter 10, 3M is one company that carefully uses structure, control, and culture to create a formal organization-wide new-venturing process that is one of the best known for promoting product innovation. 3M's goal is that at least 30 percent of its growth in sales each year should be attributed to new products developed within the past five years. To achieve this challenging goal, 3M has developed an implementation formula to ensure that its employees are provided with the freedom and motivation to experiment and take risks.

On the structure side, 3M recognized early on the increasing importance of linking and coordinating the efforts of people in different functions to speed product development. As noted in the previous chapter, people in different functions tend to develop different subunit orientations and to focus their efforts on their own tasks to the exclusion of the needs of other functions. The danger of such tendencies is that each function will develop norms and values that suit its own needs but do little to promote organizational coordination and integration.

To avoid this problem, 3M established a system of cross-functional teams composed of members of product development, process development, marketing, manufacturing, packaging, and other functions to create organization-wide norms and values of innovation. So that all groups have a common focus, the teams work closely with customers; customers' needs become the platform on which the different functions can then apply their skills and capabilities.[18] For example, one of 3M's cross-functional teams worked closely with disposable diaper manufacturers to develop the right kind of sticky tape for their needs. To promote integration in the team and foster cooperative norms and values, each team is headed by a "product champion" who takes the responsibility for building cohesive team relationships and developing a team culture. In addition, one of 3M's senior managers becomes a "management sponsor" whose job is to help the team get resources and provide support when the going gets tough. After all, product development is a highly risky process; many projects do not succeed.

3M is also careful to use integrating mechanisms such as high-level product development committees to screen new ideas. Proven entrepreneurs and experienced managers from the other divisions and from R&D, marketing, sales, and manufacturing serve on this committee to screen the new ideas. New-product champions defend their products and projects before this committee to secure the resources for developing them. (Chapter 4 describes this development funnel.) On the control side,

3M copied HP and developed a companywide norm that researchers should use 15 percent of their time on their own projects, which helps create new products such as Post-it Notes. In addition, 3M is careful to establish career ladders for its scientists in order to gain their long-term commitment, and it rewards successful product innovators. For example, it established the "Golden Step" program that gives employees substantial monetary bonuses to honor and reward the launch of successful new products and to develop norms and values that support and reward the sharing of information among scientists and people in different functions.

3M's structure and control systems have created an atmosphere in which employees know it is better to take a chance and risk making a mistake than to do nothing at all. Managers understand that their job is to encourage creativity in their employees and teams and to foster a culture of innovation. However, the regular work of the organization goes on side by side with all this intrapreneurial activity.

The other main approach to internal new venturing has been championed by those who believe that the best way to encourage new-product development is to separate this effort from the rest of the organization. To provide new-venture managers with the autonomy to experiment and take risks, the company sets up a **new-venture division**, separate and independent from its other divisions, for the development of a new product. The logic behind this is that if a new-product team works from within a company's existing structure, its members will never have the freedom or autonomy to pursue radical new-product ideas. Away from the day-to-day scrutiny of top managers, new-venture managers will be able to pursue the creation of a new product and develop a new business model as though they were external entrepreneurs.

The new-venture division is controlled in a way that reinforces the entrepreneurial spirit. Thus, strict output controls are regarded as inappropriate because they can promote short-term thinking and inhibit risk taking. Instead, stock options are often used to reinforce a culture for entrepreneurship. Another issue with output controls is to keep top managers at bay. The thinking is that the up-front R&D costs of new venturing are high and its success uncertain. After spending millions of dollars, corporate managers might become concerned about the new-venture division's performance and might try to introduce tight output controls or strong budgets to increase accountability, measures that hurt the entrepreneurial culture.[19] Corporate managers may believe it is important to institute behavior and output controls that put some limits on freedom of action; otherwise, costly mistakes may be made and resources wasted on frivolous ideas.

Recently, there have been some indications that 3M's internal approach may be superior to the use of external new-venture divisions. It appears that many new-venture divisions have failed to get successful new products to market. And even if they do, usually the new-venture division eventually begins to operate like any other division, and a company's cost structure rises because of the duplication of value-chain activities.

Another issue is that scientists are often not the best people to develop successful business models because they lack formal training. Just as many medical doctors are earning MBAs today to understand the many strategic issues confronting their profession, so scientists need to be able to think strategically, and these skills may be lacking in a new-venture division.

HP illustrates many of these issues. Early in its history, HP used the new-venturing approach. As soon as a new self-supporting product was developed in one of HP's operating divisions, a new-venture division was spun off to develop and market the product. In this fashion, HP's goal was to keep its divisions small and entrepreneurial. Soon HP had over twenty-eight different divisions, each with its own value-chain functions. At first, the value these divisions created exceeded their operating costs, but then problems emerged because of changing technological conditions. Because they were operated separately, the divisions could not learn from each other, and because they all had separate R&D departments, sales forces, and so on, they began to compete for resources. For example, when one HP scientist pioneered what was to become biotechnology, the managers of other divisions could not see how it related to HP's existing activities and would not fund it. HP became saddled with high operating costs and missed-product opportunities. To solve the problem, it merged some divisions and brought their technologies and product lines together. It also sold off divisions to other companies to focus its activities and thus make it easier to transfer resources between its divisions.

■ **Joint Venturing**

Internal new venturing is one important way in which large, established companies can maintain their momentum and grow from within.[20] One alternative is for two companies to establish a joint venture and to collaborate on the development of a new business model to compete in a new market or industry. Often in joint venturing, two or more companies agree to pool specific resources and capabilities that they believe will create more value for both companies, and they appoint managers from both companies to oversee the new operation. In this case, no separate entity is set up. Sometimes companies do establish a separate company and agree to share ownership of the new company, often 50/50 ownership, but sometimes one company insists on having a 51 percent or more stake to give it the controlling interest. The companies then transfer to the new company whatever resources and capabilities they have agreed on to help it pursue the business model that will promote both companies' interests. From an implementation perspective, important issues concern the way the venture is structured and controlled and the problems that frequently emerge in managing differences between the cultures of companies in a joint venture.

Allocating authority and responsibility is the first major implementation issue companies have to decide on. Both companies need to be able to monitor the progress of the joint venture so that they can learn from what goes on and benefit from their investment in it. Some companies prefer to establish a new company and obtain a 51 percent ownership of it because then they can solve the problem of which company will have the ultimate authority and control over the new venture. As discussed in Chapter 8, a company also risks losing control of its core technology or competence when it enters into a strategic alliance. Because the future is unknown, it is unclear which company will benefit the most from whatever innovations the new company might develop.[21] A joint venture can also be dangerous not only because the partners may take their learning and then go it alone but also because the other party might be *acquired by a competitor*. For example, Compaq shared its technical knowledge with a company in the computer storage industry to promote joint product development, only to watch helplessly as that company was acquired by Sun Microsystems, which consequently obtained Compaq's knowledge.

The implementation issues are strongly dependent on whether the purpose of the joint venture is to share and develop technology, to jointly distribute and market products and brands, or to share access to customers. Sometimes companies can simply realize the joint benefits from collaboration without having to form a new company.

For example, in 2001, Nestlé and Coca-Cola announced a ten-year joint venture, to be called Beverage Partners Worldwide, through which Coca-Cola will distribute and sell Nestlé's Nestea iced tea, Nescafe, and other brands throughout the globe.[22] Similarly, Starbuck's Frappuccino is distributed by Pepsi. In this kind of joint venture, both companies can gain from sharing and pooling different competencies so that both realize value that would not otherwise be possible. In these cases, issues of ownership are less important, although the issue of allocating responsibility and monitoring performance remains.

Once the ownership issue has been settled, one company appoints the CEO, who is responsible for creating a cohesive top management team from the ranks of managers who have been transferred from the parent companies. The job of the top management team is to develop a successful business model. These managers then need to choose an organizational structure, such as the functional or product team, that will make the best use of the resources and skills transferred from the parent. The need to provide a framework that combines their activities and integrates across people and functions is of paramount importance. So is the need to build a new company culture that can unite the members of the hitherto different cultures. In essence, top managers need to solve all the implementation problems discussed in the previous chapter.

Because solving these issues is expensive and time-consuming, it is not surprising that if there is a lot at stake and the future possibilities are unknown, many companies decide that they would be better off by acquiring the other company and integrating it into their operations. This has been Microsoft's favored strategy in recent years as it enters new industries in the computer sector. Normally, it takes a 51 percent stake in an emerging company that gives it the right to buy out the company and integrate it into Microsoft should it have technology that proves vital to Microsoft's future interests. Then, Microsoft shares its resources and expertise with the new company to spur its research and development. If the stakes are less, however, and the future easier to forecast, as in the venture between Coca-Cola and Nestlé, then it makes sense to establish a new entity that can manage the transfers of complementary resources and skills between companies.

■ Mergers and Acquisitions

Mergers and acquisitions are the third, and most widely used, vehicle that companies can use to enter new industries or countries.[23] How to implement structure, control systems, and culture to manage a new acquisition is important because many acquisitions are unsuccessful. And one of the main reasons acquisitions perform poorly is that many companies do not anticipate the difficulties associated with merging or integrating new companies into their existing operations.[24]

At the level of structure, managers of both the acquiring and acquired companies have to confront the problem of how to establish new lines of authority and responsibility that will allow them to make the best use of both companies' competencies. The merger between HP and Compaq illustrates the issues (see the *Closing Case*). Before the merger the top management teams of both companies spent thousands of hours analyzing the range of both companies' activities and performing a value-chain analysis to determine how cost and differentiation advantages might be achieved. Based on this analysis, they merged all of both company's divisions into four main product groups.

Imagine the problems in deciding who would control which group and which operating division and to whom these managers would report! To counter fears that infighting would prevent the benefits of the merger from being realized, in press releases the companies' top executives were careful to announce that the process of merging divisions was going smoothly and that battles over responsibilities and control of resources were being resolved. One problem with a mishandled merger is that skilled managers who feel they have been demoted will leave the company, and if many do leave, this also may prevent its benefits from being realized.

Once the issue of lines of authority has been addressed, the merged companies must decide how to coordinate and streamline operations to reduce costs and leverage competencies. For large companies, the answer, as for HP, is the multidivisional structure, but important control issues have to be resolved. In general, the more similar or related are the acquired companies' products and markets (if a company has made a related acquisition, as in the HP case), the easier it is to integrate their operations. Providing the acquiring company has an efficient control system, it can be adapted to the new company to standardize the way its activities are monitored and measured. Or managers can work hard to combine the best elements of each company's control systems and cultures or introduce a new IT system.

If managers make unrelated acquisitions, however, and then try to interfere with a company's strategy in an industry they know little about or apply inappropriate structure and controls to manage the new business, then major strategy implementation problems can arise. For example, if managers try to integrate unrelated companies with related ones in the search for some elusive benefits, apply the wrong kinds of controls at the divisional level, or interfere in business-level strategy, corporate performance can suffer as bureaucratic costs skyrocket. These mistakes explain why related acquisitions are sometimes more successful than unrelated ones.[25]

Even in the case of related diversification, the business processes of each company frequently are different, and their computer systems may be incompatible, as in the Nestlé case. The issue facing the merged company is how to use output and behavior controls to standardize business processes and reduce the cost of handing off and transferring resources. While installing the SAP software, for example, managers in charge of the U.S. effort discovered that each of Nestlé's 150 different U.S. divisions was buying its own supply of the flavoring vanilla from the same set of suppliers. However, the divisions were not sharing information about how they were doing this, and vanilla suppliers, dealing with each Nestlé division separately, tried to charge each division as much as they could, with the result that each division paid a different price for the same input![26] How could this happen? Each division used a different code for its independent purchase, and managers at U.S. headquarters did not have the information to discover this. SAP's software provides such information.

Finally, even when acquiring a company in a closely related industry, managers must realize that each company has a unique culture, or way of doing things. Such idiosyncrasies must be understood in order to manage the merged company effectively. Indeed, such idiosyncrasies are likely to be especially important when companies from different countries merge. Over time, top managers can change the culture and alter the internal workings of the company, but this is a difficult implementation task. The differences between HP and Compaq are a case in point. HP has a research-oriented culture and prizes its technology and the people who create it. Compaq was a marketing-driven organization and prized a hands-on, value-driven approach. By 2004, after the departure of most top Compaq managers, it was clear that HP's culture would remain research oriented; however, the new HP has a very different culture than the old HP, which prided itself on a policy of no layoffs. To compete against Dell, HP was forced to lay off thousands of employees and shut down duplicate facilities.

Compaq's marketing skills have been a valuable addition, but unfortunately it did not acquire Dell's low-cost skills.

In sum, managers' capabilities in organizational design are vital to ensure the success of a merger or acquisition. Their ability to integrate and connect divisions to leverage competencies ultimately determines how well the new merged company will perform.[27] The path to merger and acquisition is fraught with dangers, which is why some companies claim that internal new venturing is the safest path and that it is best to grow organically from within. Yet with industry boundaries blurring and new global competitors emerging, companies often do not have the time or resources to go it alone. How to enter a new industry or country is a complex implementation issue that requires thorough strategic analysis.

Information Technology, the Internet, and Outsourcing

The many ways in which advances in IT impact strategy implementation is an important issue today. Evidence that managerial capabilities in managing IT can be a source of competitive advantage is growing; companies that do not adopt leading-edge information systems are likely to be at a competitive disadvantage. IT includes the many different varieties of computer software platforms and databases and the computer hardware on which they run, such as mainframes and servers. IT also encompasses a broad array of communication media and devices that link people, including voice-mail, e-mail, voice conferencing, videoconferencing, the Internet, groupware and corporate intranets, cell phones, fax machines, personal digital assistants (PDAs), smart phones, and so on.[28]

■ Information Technology and Strategy Implementation

At the level of organizational structure, control, and culture, IT has given strategic managers many new options in implementing their strategies. IT is instrumental in both shaping and integrating resources and capabilities—capabilities that can be difficult to imitate since they are often embedded in firm-specific IT skills. Wal-Mart, for example, legally protected what it regards as a core competency in IT by blocking the movement of some of its key programmers to dot-coms like amazon.com. A company's ability to pursue a cost-leadership or differentiation business model depends on its possession of distinctive competencies in efficiency, quality, innovation, and customer responsiveness, and IT has a major impact on these sources of competitive advantage.[29]

Information technology enables companies to integrate knowledge and expertise across functional groups so that they can deliver new differentiated goods and services to customers. The way in which Citibank implemented an organization-wide IT to increase responsiveness to customers is instructive. In 2000, Citibank set as its goal to be the premier global international financial company. After studying its business model, managers found that the main customer complaint was the amount of time customers had to wait for a response to their request, so it set out to solve this problem. Teams of managers examined the way Citibank's current IT worked and then redesigned it to empower employees and reduce the handoffs between people and functions. Employees were then given extensive training in operating the new IT system. Citibank has been able to document significant time and cost savings, as well as an increase in the level of personalized service it is able to offer its clients, which has led to a significant increase in the number of global customers.[30]

Indeed, IT has important effects on a company's ability to innovate. It improves the base of knowledge that employees draw on when they engage in problem solving and decision making and provides a mechanism for promoting collaboration and information sharing both inside and across functions and business units. However, knowledge or information availability alone will not lead to innovation; it is the ability to use knowledge creatively that is the key to promoting innovation and creating competitive advantage. One argument is that it is not the absolute level of knowledge a firm possesses that leads to competitive advantage, but the speed or velocity with which it is circulated in the firm.[31] IT transfers knowledge where it can add the highest value to the organization.

The project-based work characteristic of matrix structures provides a vivid example of this process. As a project progresses, the need for particular team members waxes and wanes. Some employees will be part of a project from beginning to end, and others will be asked to participate only at key times when their expertise is required. IT provides managers with the real-time capability to monitor project progress and needs and to allocate resources accordingly to increase the value added of each employee. Traditionally, product design has involved sequential processing across functions, with handoffs as each stage of the process is completed (see Chapter 4). This linear process is being replaced by parallel, concurrent engineering made possible through the application of IT that allows employees to work simultaneously with continual interaction through electronic communication. All of this can promote innovation.

IT has major effects on other aspects of a company's structure and control systems. The increasing use of IT has been associated with a flattening of the organizational hierarchy and a move toward greater decentralization and increased integration within organizations. By electronically providing managers with high-quality, timely, and relatively complete information, IT has reduced the need for a management hierarchy to coordinate organizational activities. E-mail systems and the development of organization-wide corporate intranets are breaking down the barriers that have traditionally separated departments, and the result has been improved performance.[32] To facilitate the use of IT and to make organizational structure work, however, a company must create a control and incentive structure to motivate people and subunits, as Strategy in Action 13.4 suggests.

Some companies are taking full advantage of IT's ability to help them integrate their activities to respond better to customer needs. These companies make the most cost-effective use of their employees' skills by using a virtual organizational structure. The **virtual organization** is composed of people who are linked by computers, faxes, computer-aided design systems, and video teleconferencing and who may rarely, if ever, see one another face to face. People come and go as their services are needed, much as in a matrix structure.

Accenture, the global management consulting company, is becoming just such a virtual organization. Consultants are connected by laptops to an organization's **knowledge management system**, its company-specific information system that systematizes the knowledge of its employees and provides them with access to other employees who have the expertise to solve the problems that they encounter as they perform their jobs. The consultants pool their knowledge in a massive internal database they can easily access through computer and the company's intranet. The company's 40,000 consultants often work from their homes, traveling to meet the company's clients throughout the world and only rarely stopping in at one of Accenture's branch offices to meet their superiors and colleagues. CEO George Shaheen says the company's headquarters are wherever he happens to be at the time. (He spends 80 percent of his time traveling.)[33]

Strategy in Action   13.4

Oracle's New Approach to Control

Oracle is the second largest independent software company after Microsoft. Like Bill Gates, Microsoft's chairman, Oracle's cofounder and chairman, Larry Ellison, recognized in 1999 that his company had a major problem: it was not using the software it had developed to control its own activities, even though its customers were! As a result, Oracle was having a difficult time understanding its customers' needs, and internally it was not experiencing the cost savings that could result from implementing its own database and financial control software. Ellison moved quickly to change Oracle's control systems so that they were Internet based.

One of the main advantages of Internet-based control software is that it permits the centralized management of a company's widespread operations. Corporate managers can easily compare and contrast the performance of different divisions spread throughout the globe in real time and can quickly identify problems and take corrective action. However, to his embarrassment, Ellison discovered that Oracle's financial and human resource information was located on over seventy different computing systems across the world. It took a lot of time and effort to track such basic things as the size of the company's work force and the sales of its leading products. As a result, it took a long time to take corrective action, and many opportunities were being missed.

Recognizing the irony of the situation, Ellison ordered his managers to change the way the company controlled—that is, monitored and evaluated—its activities and to implement its new Internet-based control systems as quickly as possible. His goal was to have all of Oracle's sales, cost, profit, and human resource information systems consolidated in two locations and to make this information available to managers throughout the company with one click of a mouse. In addition, he instructed managers to investigate which kinds of activities were being monitored and controlled by people and, wherever possible, to substitute Internet-based control. For example, previously Oracle had over three hundred people responsible for monitoring and managing such tasks as paper-based travel planning and expense report systems. These tasks were automated into software systems and put online, and employees were made responsible for filing their own reports. These three hundred people were then transferred into sales and consulting positions. The savings was over $1 billion a year.

By using Internet software-based control systems, Oracle's managers are also able to get closer to their customers. In 1999, Oracle gave all its salespeople new customer relationship management software and instructed them to enter into the system detailed information about customers' purchases, future plans, Web orders, and service requests. As a result, headquarters managers can now track sales orders easily, and if they see problems such as lost sales or multiple service requests, they can quickly contact customers to solve those problems. This speed builds better customer relations.

So amazed has Ellison been at the result of implementing Internet software systems that he has radically rethought Oracle's control systems. He now believes that because of the advances of modern computer information systems, Oracle's employees should be doing only one of three things: building its products, servicing its products, or selling its products. All other activities should be automated by developing new information control systems, and it should be the manager's job to use control only to facilitate one of these three front-line activities.

■ **Strategic Outsourcing and Network Structure**

Information technology has also affected a company's ability to pursue strategic outsourcing to strengthen its business model. As Chapter 9 discusses, the use of strategic outsourcing is increasing rapidly as organizations recognize the many opportunities it offers to promote differentiation, reduce costs, and increase flexibility. Recall that outsourcing occurs as companies use short- and long-term contracts, joint ventures, and strategic alliances to form relationships with other companies. IT increases the efficiency of such relationships. For example, it allows for the more efficient movement of raw materials and component parts between a company and its suppliers and distributors. It also promotes the transfer, sharing, and leveraging of competencies between companies, which can lead to design and engineering improvements that increase differentiation and lower costs.

As a consequence, there has been growing interest in electronic **business-to-business (B2B)** networks in which most or all of the companies in an industry (for example, carmakers) use the same software platform to link to each other and establish industry specifications and standards. Then these companies jointly list the quantity and specifications of the inputs they require and invite bids from the thousands of potential suppliers around the world. Since suppliers also use the same software platform, electronic bidding, auctions, and transactions are possible between buyers and sellers around the world. The idea is that high-volume standardized transactions can help drive down costs and raise quality at the industry level. The role Li & Fung plays in managing the global supply chain for companies in Southeast Asia is instructive in this regard, as Strategy in Action 13.5 shows.

Cross-company global electronic networks reduce the costs associated with finding and monitoring competing suppliers and make global strategic alliances and joint ventures more attractive than vertical integration. In addition, companies that use electronic networks not only reduce costs because they increase the pool of potential

Strategy in Action   13.5

Li & Fung's Global Supply-Chain Management

Finding the overseas suppliers that offer the lowest-priced and highest-quality products is an important task facing the managers of global organizations. These suppliers are located in thousands of cities in many countries around the world, so finding them is difficult. Often global companies use the services of foreign intermediaries or brokers, located near these suppliers, to find the one that best meets their input requirements. Li & Fung, now run by brothers Victor and William Fung, is one of these brokers that have helped hundreds of global companies to locate suitable foreign suppliers, especially suppliers in mainland China.

In the 2000s, managing global companies' supply chains became an even more complicated task because overseas suppliers were increasingly specializing in just one part of the task of producing a product in their search for ways to reduce costs. For example, in the past, a company such as Target might have negotiated with a supplier to manufacture 1 million units of a shirt at a certain cost per unit. But with specialization, Target might find it can reduce the costs of producing the shirt even further by splitting the operations involved in producing the shirt and having different suppliers, often in different countries, perform each operation. For example, to get the lowest cost per unit, Target might first negotiate with

a yarn manufacturer in Vietnam to make the yarn; then ship the yarn to a Chinese supplier to weave it into cloth; and then to several different factories in Malaysia and the Philippines to cut the cloth and sew the shirts. Another company might take responsibility for packaging and shipping the shirts to wherever in the world they are required. Since a company like Target has thousands of different clothing products under production and these change all the time, the problems of managing such a supply chain to get the full cost savings from global expansion are clear.

This is the opportunity that Li & Fung has capitalized on. Realizing that many global companies do not have the time or expertise to find such specialized low-price suppliers, they moved quickly to provide such a service. Li & Fung employs 3,600 agents who travel across thirty-seven countries to find new suppliers and inspect existing suppliers to find new ways to help their clients, global companies, get lower prices or higher-quality products. Global companies are happy to outsource their supply-chain management to Li & Fung because they realize significant cost savings. And although they pay a hefty fee to Li & Fung, they avoid the costs of employing their own agents. As the complexity of supply-chain management continues to increase, more and more companies like Li & Fung are appearing.

suppliers, but they also reduce the bargaining power of suppliers. Similarly, beyond using IT to link backward with suppliers, companies can use IT to link forward in the value chain to connect its operations with those of customers, something that reduces their costs and creates a disincentive for customers to seek other suppliers.

To implement outsourcing effectively, strategic managers must decide what organizational arrangements to adopt. Increasingly, a **network structure**—the set of strategic alliances that an organization creates with suppliers, manufacturers, and distributors to produce and market a product—is becoming the structure of choice to implement outsourcing. An example of a network structure is the series of strategic alliances that Japanese carmakers such as Toyota and Honda formed with their suppliers of inputs, such as car axles, gearboxes, and air-conditioning systems. Members of the network work together on a long-term basis to find new ways to reduce costs and increase the quality of their products. Moreover, developing a network structure allows an organization to avoid the high bureaucratic costs of operating a complex organizational structure. Finally, a network structure allows a company to form strategic alliances with foreign suppliers, which gives managers access to low-cost foreign sources of inputs. The way Nike uses a global network structure to produce and market its sports, casual, and dress shoes is instructive.

Nike, located in Beaverton, Oregon, is the largest and most profitable sports shoe manufacturer in the world. The key to Nike's success is the network structure that Philip Knight, its founder and CEO, created to allow his company to produce and market shoes. The most successful companies today simultaneously pursue a low-cost and a differentiation strategy. Knight realized this early on and created an organizational structure to allow his company to achieve this goal.

By far, the largest function at Nike's headquarters in Beaverton is the design function, staffed by talented designers who pioneer innovations in sports shoe design such as the air pump and Air Jordans that Nike introduced so successfully. Designers use computer-aided design (CAD) to design their shoes, and all new-product information, including manufacturing instructions, is stored electronically. When the designers have done their work, they relay the blueprints for the new products electronically to a network of suppliers and manufacturers throughout Southeast Asia with which Nike has formed strategic alliances. Instructions for the design of a new sole, for example, may be sent to a supplier in Taiwan, and instructions for the leather uppers to a supplier in Malaysia. These suppliers produce the shoe parts, which are then sent for final assembly to a manufacturer in China with which Nike has established an alliance. From China, these shoes are shipped to distributors throughout the world. Of the 99 million pairs of shoes Nike makes each year, 99 percent are made in Southeast Asia.

There are three main advantages to this network structure for Nike. First, Nike can lower its cost structure because wages in Southeast Asia are a fraction of what they are in the United States. Second, Nike is able to respond to changes in sports shoe fashion very quickly. Using its global computer system, it can, literally overnight, change the instructions it gives to each of its suppliers so that, within a few weeks, its foreign manufacturers are producing new kinds of shoes. Any alliance partners that fail to perform up to Nike's standards are replaced with new partners, so Nike has great control over its network structure. In fact, the company works closely with its suppliers to take advantage of any new developments in technology that can help it reduce costs and increase quality. Third, the ability to outsource all its manufacturing abroad allows Nike to keep its U.S. structure fluid and flexible. Nike uses a functional structure to organize its activities and decentralizes control of the design process to teams that are assigned to develop each of the new kinds of sports shoes for which Nike is known.

In conclusion, the implications of IT for strategy implementation are still evolving and will continue to do so as new software and hardware reshape a company's business model and its strategies. IT is changing the nature of value-chain activities both inside and between organizations, affecting all four building blocks of competitive advantage. For the multibusiness company as for the single-business company, the need to be alert to such changes to strengthen its position in its core business has become a vital matter, and the success of companies like Dell and Wal-Mart compared to the failure of others like Gateway and Kmart can be traced, in part, to their success in developing the IT capabilities that lead to sustained competitive advantage.

Summary of Chapter

1. A company uses organizational design to combine structure, control systems, and culture in ways that allow it to implement its multibusiness model successfully.

2. As a company grows and diversifies, it adopts a multidivisional structure. Although this structure costs more to operate than a functional or product structure, it economizes on the bureaucratic costs associated with operating through a functional structure and enables a company to handle its value creation activities more effectively.

3. As companies change their corporate strategies over time, they must change their structures because different strategies are managed in different ways. In particular, the move from unrelated diversification to vertical integration to related diversification increases the bureaucratic costs associated with managing a multibusiness model. Each requires a different combination on structure, control, and culture to economize on those costs.

4. As a company moves from a localization to an international, global standardization, and transnational strategy, it also needs to switch to a more complex structure that allows it to coordinate increasingly complex resource transfers. Similarly, it needs to adopt a more complex integration and control system that facilitates resource sharing and the leverage of competencies around the globe. When the gains are substantial, companies frequently adopt a global-matrix structure to share knowledge and expertise or to implement their control systems and culture.

5. To encourage internal new venturing, companies must design an internal venturing process that gives new-venture managers the autonomy they need to develop new products. Corporate managers need to provide the oversight that keeps new-venture managers motivated and on track.

6. The profitability of mergers and acquisitions depends on the structure and control systems that companies adopt to manage them and the way a company integrates them into its existing businesses.

7. IT is having increasingly important effects on the way multibusiness companies implement their strategies. Not only does IT help improve the efficiency with which the multidivisional structure operates, but it also allows for the better control of complex value-chain activities. The growth of outsourcing has also been promoted by IT, and some companies have developed network structures to coordinate their global value-chain activities.

Discussion Questions

1. When would a company decide to change from a functional to a multidivisional structure?

2. If a related company begins to buy unrelated businesses, in what ways should it change its structure or control mechanisms to manage the acquisitions?

3. What prompts a company to change from a global standardization to a transnational strategy, and what new implementation problems arise as it does so?

4. How would you design a structure and control system to encourage entrepreneurship in a large, established corporation?

5. What are the problems associated with implementing a strategy of related diversification through acquisitions?

Practicing Strategic Management

■ SMALL-GROUP EXERCISE
Deciding on an Organizational Structure (Continued)

Break into the same groups used for the Chapter 12 Small-Group Exercise. Reread the scenario in the Chapter 12 exercise, and recall your group's debate about the appropriate organizational structure for your soft drink company. Because it is your intention to compete with Coca-Cola for market share worldwide, there should also be a global dimension to your strategy, and you must consider what is the best structure globally as well as domestically. Debate the pros and cons of the types of global structures, and decide which is most appropriate and will best fit with your domestic structure.

■ ARTICLE FILE 13

Find an example of a company pursuing a multibusiness model that has changed its structure and control systems to manage its strategy better. What were the problems with the way it formerly implemented its strategy? What changes did it make to its structure and control systems? What effects does it expect these changes to have on performance?

■ STRATEGIC MANAGEMENT PROJECT
Module 13

Take the information you collected in the Chapter 12 Strategic Management Project on strategy implementation, and link it to the multibusiness model. You should collect information to determine if your company competes across industries or countries and also to see what role IT plays in allowing it to implement its business model. If your company does operate across countries or industries:

1. Does your company use a multidivisional structure? Why or why not? What crucial implementation problems must your company manage to implement its strategy effectively? For example, what kind of integration mechanisms does it employ?

2. What are your company's corporate-level strategies? How do they affect the way it uses organizational structure, control, and culture?

3. What kind of international strategy does your company pursue? How does it control its global activities? What kind of structure does it use? Why?

4. Can you suggest ways of altering the company's structure or control systems to strengthen its business model? Would this change increase or decrease bureaucratic costs?

5. Does your company have a particular entry mode that it has used to implement its strategy?

6. In what ways does your company use IT to coordinate its value-chain activities?

7. Assess how well you think your company has implemented its multibusiness (or business) model.

■ EXPLORING THE WEB
Visiting Sears

Go to **www.sears.com** and **www.kmart.com**, and locate information for investors. Study the information and press releases about the merger of these two companies. How has the merger strengthened the business model of the new company? What kinds of changes in structure, control systems, and culture have occurred as a result of the merger?

General Task   Search the Web for a multibusiness company that is in the process of modifying or changing the way it implements its business model and strategy. What changes is it making to its structure or control systems? Does IT have a role in the changes? What structure is it moving toward? Why is this structure more appropriate than the old one?

Closing Case

The New HP Gets Up to Speed

Between 2002 and 2004 Hewlett-Packard and Compaq moved steadily forward to combine their skills and resources to strengthen their competitive advantage. The new HP is a leading global multibusiness IT-infrastructure provider, selling a complete range of computer hardware, software and solutions, information services, and imaging and printing products. The task facing HP's managers was how to position the company to compete across industries against competitors like IBM, also a multibusiness IT-infrastructure provider, and Dell, the leader in the fiercely competitive PC industry.

The justification for the merger was that the new company would have cross-industry product lines that would allow it to reap the benefits of both cost savings and differentiation. Joining both companies' product lines would allow the new company to eliminate the duplication of costly functional activities and so achieve billions in cost savings. Combining joint operations would also allow both companies to transfer, share, and leverage competencies and achieve the value-creating benefits of increased product differentiation. Importantly, as a result of the merger HP will be able to use product bundling to provide customers with a *complete range* of totally compatible computing and IT products backed by a service group that will be able to provide software and expertise to customize these products to the needs of customers. As a result, HP claims its products will provide better flexibility, better interoperability, and the lowest cost of ownership of any company in the industry.

To achieve these benefits, the two companies' many business units have been integrated and reorganized into four major product divisions using a multidivisional structure: hardware, software, services, and imaging and printing. Each division is an independent profit center, and the divisions must work together to coordinate their new products and activities to make sure they are in keeping with its corporate strategy.

The task facing Carly Fiorina, HP's CEO, is to find ways to strengthen the company's multibusiness model and to forecast how changes in IT might shift industry boundaries and affect the company in the future. Formulating HP's global multibusiness strategy will also be one of her major concerns, for the complexity of HP's global operations is staggering. The need to customize products to the needs of different world regions and to work out where to make them to lower HP's cost structure and increase the appeal of its products are major questions confronting all of HP's top management.

Case Discussion Questions

1. What kind of multibusiness model is HP pursuing?

2. What kind of global strategy is most appropriate for the company in the future?

3. What kind of global structure will allow it to most effectively coordinate the production and sale of its products around the world?

Notes

Chapter 1

1. *Sources:* "How Big Can It Grow?" *Economist,* April 17, 2004, pp. 74–78; "Trial by Checkout," *Economist,* June 26, 2004, pp. 74–76; Wal-Mart 10-K, 2000; information at Wal-Mart's website (**www.walmartstores.com**); Robert Slater, *The Wal-Mart Triumph* (Portfolio Trade Books, 2004).

2. There are several different ratios for measuring profitability, such as return on invested capital, return on assets, and return on equity. Although these different measures are highly correlated with each other, finance theorists argue that the return on invested capital is the most accurate measure of profitability. See Tom Copeland, Tim Koller, and Jack Murrin, *Valuation: Measuring and Managing the Value of Companies* (New York: Wiley, 1996).

3. Trying to estimate the relative importance of industry effects and firm strategy on firm profitability has been one of the most important areas of research in the strategy literature during the past decade. See Y. E. Spanos and S. Lioukas, "An Examination of the Causal Logic of Rent Generation," *Strategic Management Journal* 22:10 (October 2001): 907–934; and R. P. Rumelt, "How Much Does Industry Matter?" *Strategic Management Journal* 12 (1991): 167–185. See also A. J. Mauri and M. P. Michaels, "Firm and Industry Effects Within Strategic Management: An Empirical Examination," *Strategic Management Journal* 19 (1998): 211–219.

4. This view is known as "agency theory." See M. C. Jensen and W. H. Meckling, "Theory of the Firm: Managerial Behavior, Agency Costs and Ownership Structure," *Journal of Financial Economics* 3 (1976): 305–360; and E. F. Fama, "Agency Problems and the Theory of the Firm," *Journal of Political Economy* 88 (1980): 375–390.

5. K. R. Andrews, *The Concept of Corporate Strategy* (Homewood, Ill.: Dow Jones Irwin, 1971); H. I. Ansoff, *Corporate Strategy* (New York: McGraw-Hill, 1965); C. W. Hofer and D. Schendel, *Strategy Formulation: Analytical Concepts* (St. Paul, Minn.: West, 1978). See also P. J. Brews and M. R. Hunt, "Learning to Plan and Planning to Learn," *Strategic Management Journal* 20 (1999): 889–913; and

R. W. Grant, "Planning in a Turbulent Environment," *Strategic Management Journal* 24 (2003): 491–517.

6. **www.kodak.com/US/en/corp/careers/why/ valuesmission.jhtml**.

7. **www.ford.com/en/company/about/overview.htm**.

8. These three questions were first proposed by P. F. Drucker, *Management—Tasks, Responsibilities, Practices* (New York: Harper & Row, 1974), pp. 74–94.

9. Derek F. Abell, *Defining the Business: The Starting Point of Strategic Planning* (Englewood Cliffs, N.J.: Prentice-Hall, 1980).

10. P. A. Kidwell and P. E. Ceruzzi, *Landmarks in Digital Computing* (Washington, D.C.: Smithsonian Institute, 1994).

11. See G. Hamel and C. K. Prahalad, "Strategic Intent," *Harvard Business Review* (May–June 1989): 64.

12. J. C. Collins and J. I. Porras, "Building Your Company's Vision," *Harvard Business Review* (September–October 1996): 65–77.

13. **www.nucor.com/**. Reprinted courtesy of Nucor.

14. See J. P. Kotter and J. L. Heskett, *Corporate Culture and Performance* (New York: Free Press, 1992). For similar work, see Collins and Porras, "Building Your Company's Vision."

15. E. Freeman, *Strategic Management: A Stakeholder Approach* (Boston: Pitman Press, 1984).

16. M. D. Richards, *Setting Strategic Goals and Objectives* (St. Paul, Minn.: West, 1986).

17. E. A. Locke, G. P. Latham, and M. Erez, "The Determinants of Goal Commitment," *Academy of Management Review* 13 (1988): 23–39.

18. R. E. Hoskisson, M. A. Hitt, and C. W. L. Hill, "Managerial Incentives and Investment in R&D in Large Multiproduct Firms," *Organization Science* 3 (1993): 325–341.

19. Robert H. Hayes and William J. Abernathy, "Managing Our Way to Economic Decline," *Harvard Business Review* (July–August 1980): 67–77.

20. Andrews, *Concept of Corporate Strategy;* Ansoff, *Corporate Strategy;* Hofer and Schendel, *Strategy Formulation.*

21. For details, see R. A. Burgelman, "Intraorganizational Ecology of Strategy Making and Organiza-

tional Adaptation: Theory and Field Research," *Organization Science* 2 (1991): 239–262; H. Mintzberg, "Patterns in Strategy Formulation," *Management Science* 24 (1978): 934–948; S. L. Hart, "An Integrative Framework for Strategy Making Processes," *Academy of Management Review* 17 (1992): 327–351; G. Hamel, "Strategy as Revolution," *Harvard Business Review* 74 (July–August 1996): 69–83; and R. W. Grant, "Planning in a Turbulent Environment," *Strategic Management Journal* 24 (2003): 491–517.

22. This is the premise of those who advocate that complexity and chaos theory should be applied to strategic management. See S. Brown and K. M. Eisenhardt, "The Art of Continuous Change: Linking Complexity Theory and Time Based Evolution in Relentlessly Shifting Organizations," *Administrative Science Quarterly* 29 (1997): 1–34; and R. Stacey and D. Parker, *Chaos, Management and Economics* (London: Institute for Economic Affairs, 1994). See also H. Courtney, J. Kirkland, and P. Viguerie, "Strategy Under Uncertainty," *Harvard Business Review* 75 (November–December 1997): 66–79.

23. Hart, "Integrative Framework"; Hamel, "Strategy as Revolution."

24. See Burgelman, "Intraorganizational Ecology," and Mintzberg, "Patterns in Strategy Formulation."

25. R. A. Burgelman and A. S. Grove, "Strategic Dissonance," *California Management Review* (Winter 1996): 8–28.

26. C. W. L. Hill and F. T. Rothaermel, "The Performance of Incumbent Firms in the Face of Radical Technological Innovation," *Academy of Management Review* 28 (2003): 257–274.

27. This story was related to the author by George Rathmann, who at one time was head of 3M's research activities.

28. Richard T. Pascale, "Perspectives on Strategy: The Real Story Behind Honda's Success," *California Management Review* 26 (1984): 47–72.

29. This viewpoint is strongly emphasized by Burgelman and Grove, "Strategic Dissonance."

30. C. C. Miller and L. B. Cardinal, "Strategic Planning and Firm Performance: A Synthesis of More than Two Decades of Research," *Academy of Management Journal* 37 (1994): 1649–1665. Also see P. R. Rogers, A. Miller, and W. Q. Judge, "Using Information Processing Theory to Understand Planning/Performance Relationships in the Context of Strategy," *Strategic Management Journal* 20 (1999): 567–577.

31. P. J. Brews and M. R. Hunt, "Learning to Plan and Planning to Learn," *Strategic Management Journal* (1999) 20: 889–913.

32. Courtney, Kirkland, and Viguerie, "Strategy Under Uncertainty."

33. P. J. H. Schoemaker, "Multiple Scenario Development: Its Conceptual and Behavioral Foundation," *Strategic Management Journal* 14 (1993): 193–213.

34. C. Kim and R. Mauborgne, "Procedural Justice, Strategic Decision Making, and the Knowledge Economy," *Strategic Management Journal* 19 (1998): 323–338; W. C. Kim and R. Mauborgne, "Fair Process: Managing in the Knowledge Economy," *Harvard Business Review* 75 (July–August 1997): 65–76.

35. G. Hamel and C. K. Prahalad, *Competing for the Future* (New York: Free Press, 1994).

36. See G. Hamel and C. K. Prahalad, "Strategic Intent," *Harvard Business Review* (May–June 1989): 64.

37. See C. R. Schwenk, "Cognitive Simplification Processes in Strategic Decision Making," *Strategic Management Journal* 5 (1984): 111–128; and K. M. Eisenhardt and M. Zbaracki, "Strategic Decision Making," *Strategic Management Journal* 13 (Special Issue, 1992): 17–37.

38. H. Simon, *Administrative Behavior* (New York: McGraw-Hill, 1957).

39. The original statement of this phenomenon was made by A. Tversky and D. Kahneman, "Judgment Under Uncertainty: Heuristics and Biases," *Science* 185 (1974): 1124–1131. See also D. Lovallo and D. Kahneman, "Delusions of Success: How Optimism Undermines Executives' Decisions," *Harvard Business Review* 81 (July 2003): 56–67; and J. S. Hammond, R. L. Keeny, and H. Raiffa, "The Hidden Traps in Decision Making," *Harvard Business Review* 76 (September–October 1998): 25–34.

40. Schwenk, "Cognitive Simplification Processes," pp. 111–128.

41. B. M. Staw, "The Escalation of Commitment to a Course of Action," *Academy of Management Review* 6 (1981): 577–587.

42. R. Roll, "The Hubris Hypotheses of Corporate Takeovers," *Journal of Business* 59 (1986): 197–216.

43. Irvin L. Janis, *Victims of Groupthink*, 2nd ed. (Boston: Houghton Mifflin, 1982). For an alternative view see S. R. Fuller and R. J. Aldag, "Organizational Tonypandy: Lessons from a Quarter Century of the Groupthink Phenomenon," *Organizational Behavior and Human Decision Processes* 73 (1998): 163–184.

44. See R. O. Mason, "A Dialectic Approach to Strategic Planning," *Management Science* 13 (1969): 403–414; R. A. Cosier and J. C. Aplin, "A Critical View of Dialectic Inquiry in Strategic Planning," *Strategic Management Journal* 1 (1980): 343–356; and I. I. Mintroff and R. O. Mason, "Structuring III—Structured Policy Issues: Further Explorations in a Methodology for Messy Problems," *Strategic Management Journal* 1 (1980): 331–342.

45. Mason, "A Dialectic Approach," pp. 403–414.

46. Lovallo and Kahneman, "Delusions of Success."

47. For a summary of research on strategic leadership, see D. C. Hambrick, "Putting Top Managers Back into the Picture," *Strategic Management Journal* 10 (Special Issue, 1989): 5–15. See also D. Goldman, "What Makes a Leader?" *Harvard Business Review* (November–December 1998): 92–105; H. Mintzberg, "Covert Leadership," *Harvard Business Review* (November–December 1998): 140–148; and R. S. Tedlow, "What Titans Can Teach Us," *Harvard Business Review* (December 2001): 70–79.

48. N. M. Tichy and D. O. Ulrich, "The Leadership Challenge: A Call for the Transformational Leader," *Sloan Management Review* (Fall 1984): 59–68; F. Westley and H. Mintzberg, "Visionary Leadership and Strategic Management," *Strategic Management Journal* 10 (Special Issue, 1989): 17–32.

49. E. Wrapp, "Good Managers Don't Make Policy Decisions," *Harvard Business Review* (September–October 1967): 91–99.

50. J. Pfeffer, *Managing with Power* (Boston: Harvard Business School Press, 1992).

51. D. Goldman, "What Makes a Leader?" *Harvard Business Review* (November–December 1998): 92–105.

52. *Sources*: Y. J. Dreazn, "Behind the Fiber Glut," *Wall Street Journal*, September 26, 2002, p. B1; R. Blumenstein, "Overbuilt Web: How the Fiber Barons Plunged the Nation into a Telecom Glut," *Wall Street Journal*, June 18, 2001, p. A1; D. K. Berman, "Level 3 Finds a Way to Fight Telecom Crash," *Wall Street Journal*, November 19, 2002, p. C1; Level 3 10-K Reports, 2002 and 2003.

53. *Sources*: C. Y. Baldwin, *Fundamental Enterprise Valuation: Return on Invested Capital*, Harvard Business School Note 9-801-125, July 3, 2004; T. Copeland et al., *Valuation: Measuring and Managing the Value of Companies* (New York: Wiley, 2000).

Chapter 2

1. *Sources:* Staff Reporter, "Pharm Exec 50," *Pharmaceutical Executive*, May 2004, pp. 61–68; J. A. DiMasi, R. W. Hansen, and H. G. Grabowski, "The Price of Innovation: New Estimates of Drug Development Costs," *Journal of Health Economics* 22 (March 2003): 151–170; Staff Reporter, "Where the Money Is: The Drug Industry," *Economist*, April 26, 2003, pp. 64–65; Value Line Investment Survey, various issues.

2. M. E. Porter, *Competitive Strategy* (New York: Free Press, 1980).

3. J. E. Bain, *Barriers to New Competition* (Cambridge, Mass.: Harvard University Press, 1956). For a review of the modern literature on barriers to entry, see R. J. Gilbert, "Mobility Barriers and the Value of Incumbency," in R. Schmalensee and R. D. Willig (eds.), *Handbook of Industrial Organization*, vol. 1 (Amsterdam: North-Holland, 1989). See also R. P. McAfee, H. M. Mialon, and M. A. Williams, "What Is a Barrier to Entry?" *American Economic Review* 94 (May 2004): 461–468.

4. A detailed discussion of switching costs and lock in can be found in C. Shapiro and H. R. Varian, *Information Rules: A Strategic Guide to the Network Economy* (Boston: Harvard Business School Press, 1999).

5. Most of this information on barriers to entry can be found in the industrial organization economics literature. See especially the following works: Bain, *Barriers to New Competition*; M. Mann, "Seller Concentration, Barriers to Entry and Rates of Return in 30 Industries," *Review of Economics and Statistics* 48 (1966): 296–307; W. S. Comanor and T. A. Wilson, "Advertising, Market Structure and Performance," *Review of Economics and Statistics* 49 (1967): 423–440; Gilbert, "Mobility Barriers"; and K. Cool, L.-H. Roller, and B. Leleux, "The Relative Impact of Actual and Potential Rivalry on Firm Profitability in the Pharmaceutical Industry," *Strategic Management Journal* 20 (1999): 1–14.

6. For a discussion of tacit agreements, see T. C. Schelling, *The Strategy of Conflict* (Cambridge, Mass.: Harvard University Press, 1960).

7. M. Busse, "Firm Financial Condition and Airline Price Wars," *Rand Journal of Economics* 33 (2002): 298–318.

8. For a review, see F. Karakaya, "Market Exit and Barriers to Exit: Theory and Practice," *Psychology and Marketing* 17 (2000): 651–668.

9. P. Ghemawat, *Commitment: The Dynamics of Strategy* (Boston: Harvard Business School Press, 1991).

10. A. S. Grove, *Only the Paranoid Survive* (New York: Doubleday, 1996).

11. In standard microeconomic theory, the concept used for assessing the strength of substitutes and complements is the cross elasticity of demand.

12. For details and further references, see Charles W. L. Hill, "Establishing a Standard: Competitive Strategy and Technology Standards in Winner Take All Industries," *Academy of Management Executive* 11 (1997): 7–25; and Shapiro and Varian, *Information Rules.*

13. The development of strategic group theory has been a strong theme in the strategy literature. Important contributions include the following: R. E. Caves and Michael E. Porter, "From Entry Barriers to Mobility Barriers," *Quarterly Journal of Economics* (May 1977): 241–262; K. R. Harrigan, "An Application of Clustering for Strategic Group Analysis," *Strategic Management Journal* 6 (1985): 55–73; K. J. Hatten and D. E. Schendel, "Heterogeneity Within an Industry: Firm Conduct in the U.S. Brewing Industry, 1952–71," *Journal of Industrial Economics* 26 (1977): 97–113; Michael E. Porter, "The Structure Within Industries and Companies' Performance," *Review of Economics and Statistics* 61 (1979): 214–227. See also K. Cool and D. Schendel, "Performance Differences Among Strategic Group Members," *Strategic Management Journal* 9 (1988): 207–233; A. Nair and S. Kotha, "Does Group Membership Matter? Evidence from the Japanese Steel Industry," *Strategic Management Journal* (2001): 221–235; and G. McNamara, D. L. Deephouse, and R. A. Luce, "Competitive Positioning Within and Across a Strategic Group Structure," Strategic *Management Journal* (2003): 161–180.

14. For details on the strategic group structure in the pharmaceutical industry, see K. Cool and I. Dierickx, "Rivalry, Strategic Groups, and Firm Profitability," *Strategic Management Journal* 14 (1993): 47–59.

15. Charles W. Hofer argued that life cycle considerations may be the most important contingency when formulating business strategy. See Hofer, "Towards a Contingency Theory of Business Strategy," *Academy of Management Journal* 18 (1975): 784–810. There is empirical evidence to support this view. See C. R. Anderson and C. P. Zeithaml, "Stages of the Product Life Cycle, Business Strategy, and Business Performance," *Academy of Management Journal* 27 (1984): 5–24; and D. C. Hambrick and D. Lei, "Towards an Empirical Prioritization of Contingency Variables for Business Strategy," *Academy of Management Journal* 28 (1985): 763–788. See also G. Miles, C. C. Snow, and M. P. Sharfman, "Industry Variety and Performance," *Strategic Management Journal* 14 (1993): 163–177; G. K. Deans, F. Kroeger, and S. Zeisel, "The Consolidation Curve," *Harvard Business Review* 80 (December 2002): 2–3.

16. The characteristics of declining industries have been summarized by K. R. Harrigan, "Strategy Formulation in Declining Industries," *Academy of Management Review* 5 (1980): 599–604. See also J. Anand and H. Singh, "Asset Redeployment, Acquisitions and Corporate Strategy in Declining Industries," *Strategic Management Journal* 18 (1997): 99–118.

17. This perspective is associated with the Austrian school of economics, which goes back to Schumpeter. For a summary of this school and its implications for strategy, see R. Jacobson, "The Austrian School of Strategy," *Academy of Management Review* 17 (1992): 782–807; and C. W. L. Hill and D. Deeds, "The Importance of Industry Structure for the Determination of Industry Profitability: A Neo-Austrian Approach," *Journal of Management Studies* 33 (1996): 429–451.

18. "A Tricky Business," *Economist*, June 30, 2001, pp. 55–56.

19. D. F. Barnett and R. W. Crandall, *Up from the Ashes* (Washington, D.C.: Brookings Institution, 1986).

20. M. E. Porter, *The Competitive Advantage of Nations* (New York: Free Press, 1990).

21. The term *punctuated equilibrium* is borrowed from evolutionary biology. For a detailed explanation of the concept, see M. L. Tushman, W. H. Newman, and E. Romanelli, "Convergence and Upheaval: Managing the Unsteady Pace of Organizational Evolution," *California Management Review* 29:1 (1985): 29–44; C. J. G. Gersick, "Revolutionary Change Theories: A Multilevel Exploration of the Punctuated Equilibrium Paradigm," *Academy of Management Review* 16 (1991): 10–36; and R. Adner and D. A. Levinthal, "The Emergence of Emerging Technologies," *California Management Review* 45 (Fall 2002): 50–65.

22. A. J. Slywotzky, *Value Migration: How to Think Several Moves Ahead of the Competition* (Boston: Harvard Business School Press, 1996).

23. R. D'Aveni, *Hypercompetition* (New York: Free Press, 1994).
24. G. McNamara, P. M. Vaaler, and C. Devers, "Same as It Ever Was: The Search for Evidence of Increasing Hypercompetition," *Strategic Management Journal* 24 (2003): 261–278.
25. Hill and Deeds, "Importance of Industry Structure."
26. R. P. Rumelt, "How Much Does Industry Matter?" *Strategic Management Journal* 12 (1991): 167–185. See also A. J. Mauri and M. P. Michaels, "Firm and Industry Effects Within Strategic Management: An Empirical Examination," *Strategic Management Journal* 19 (1998): 211–219.
27. See R. Schmalensee, "Inter-Industry Studies of Structure and Performance," in Schmalensee and Willig (eds.), *Handbook of Industrial Organization.* Similar results were found by A. N. McGahan and M. E. Porter, "How Much Does Industry Matter, Really?" *Strategic Management Journal* 18 (1997): 15–30.
28. For example, see K. Cool and D. Schendel, "Strategic Group Formation and Performance: The Case of the U.S. Pharmaceutical Industry, 1932–1992," *Management Science* (September 1987): 1102–1124.
29. See M. Gort and J. Klepper, "Time Paths in the Diffusion of Product Innovations," *Economic Journal* (September 1982): 630–653. Looking at the history of forty-six products, Gort and Klepper found that the length of time before other companies entered the markets created by a few inventive companies declined from an average of 14.4 years for products introduced before 1930 to 4.9 years for those introduced after 1949.
30. The phrase was originally coined by J. Schumpeter, *Capitalism, Socialism and Democracy* (London: Macmillan, 1950), p. 68.
31. M. E. Porter, "Strategy and the Internet," *Harvard Business Review* (March 2001): 62–79.
32. U.S. Dept. of Labor, Bureau of Labor Statistics.
33. *Economist, The Economist Book of Vital World Statistics* (New York: Random House, 1990).
34. For a detailed discussion of the importance of the structure of law as a factor explaining economic change and growth, see D. C. North, *Institutions, Institutional Change, and Economic Performance* (Cambridge: Cambridge University Press, 1990).
35. K. Fiewege, "Wall Street Hot on Airlines Despite 4th-Qtr Losses," Reuters Wire Report, January 15, 2002.
36. *Sources:* "Turbulent Skies: Low Cost Airlines," *Economist,* July 10, 2004, pp. 68–72; "Silver Linings, Darkening Clouds," *Economist,* March 27, 2004, pp. 90–92; W. Zellner and M. Arndt, "Big Airlines: Not Much Runway Left," *Business Week,* July 5, 2004, p. 50; S. McCartney, "Coast to Coast Fares Drop to New Low," *Wall Street Journal,* May 12, 2004, p. D4; H. W. Jenkins, "Let Failure Be an Option," *Wall Street Journal,* June 23, 2004, p. A17.

Chapter 3

1. *Sources:* D. Hunter, "How Dell Keeps from Stumbling," *Business Week,* May 14, 2001, pp. 38–40; "Enter the Eco-System: From Supply Chain to Network," *Economist,* November 11, 2000; "Dell's Direct Initiative," *Country Monitor,* June 7, 2000, p. 5; D. G. Jacobs, "Anatomy of a Supply Chain," *Transportation and Distribution,* June 2003, pp. 60–61; S. Scherreik, "How Efficient Is That Company," *Business Week,* December 23, 2003, pp. 94–95; *Dell Computer Corporation 10K,* January 2004; Staff Reporter, "Dell Is Market Leader on Strong Shipments," *Wall Street Journal,* April 16, 2004, p. A1.
2. M. Cusumano, *The Japanese Automobile Industry* (Cambridge, Mass.: Harvard University Press, 1989); S. Spear and H. K. Bowen, "Decoding the DNA of the Toyota Production System," *Harvard Business Review* (September–October 1999): 96–108.
3. The material in this section relies on the resource-based view of the company. For summaries of this perspective, see J. B. Barney, "Company Resources and Sustained Competitive Advantage," *Journal of Management* 17 (1991): 99–120; J. T. Mahoney and J. R. Pandian, "The Resource-Based View Within the Conversation of Strategic Management," *Strategic Management Journal* 13 (1992): 63–380; R. Amit and P. J. H. Schoemaker, "Strategic Assets and Organizational Rent," *Strategic Management Journal* 14 (1993): 33–46; M. A. Peteraf, "The Cornerstones of Competitive Advantage: A Resource-Based View," *Strategic Management Journal* 14 (1993): 179–191; B. Wernerfelt, "A Resource Based View of the Company," *Strategic Management Journal* 15 (1994): 171–180; and K. M. Eisenhardt and J. A. Martin, "Dynamic Capabilities: What Are They?" *Strategic Management Journal* 21 (2000): 1105–1121.

4. For a discussion of organizational capabilities, see R. R. Nelson and S. Winter, *An Evolutionary Theory of Economic Change* (Cambridge, Mass.: Belknap Press, 1982).

5. W. Chan Kim and R. Mauborgne, "Value Innovation: The Strategic Logic of High Growth," *Harvard Business Review* (January–February 1997): 102–115.

6. The concept of consumer surplus is an important one in economics. For a more detailed exposition, see D. Besanko, D. Dranove, and M. Shanley, *Economics of Strategy* (New York: Wiley, 1996).

7. However, $P = U$ only in the special case when the company has a perfect monopoly and it can charge each customer a unique price that reflects the utility of the product to that customer (i.e., where perfect price discrimination is possible). More generally, except in the limiting case of perfect price discrimination, even a monopolist will see most customers capture some of the utility of a product in the form of a consumer surplus.

8. This point is central to the work of Michael Porter. See M. E. Porter, *Competitive Advantage* (New York: Free Press, 1985). See also P. Ghemawat, *Commitment: The Dynamic of Strategy* (New York: Free Press, 1991), chap. 4.

9. L. Hawkins, "US Auto Makers Get Better Grades for Productivity," *Wall Street Journal,* June 11, 2004, p. A3.

10. Porter, *Competitive Advantage.*

11. Ibid.

12. This approach goes back to the pioneering work by K. Lancaster: *Consumer Demand, a New Approach* (New York: Columbia University Press 1971).

13. D. Garvin, "Competing on the Eight Dimensions of Quality," *Harvard Business Review* (November–December 1987): 101–119; P. Kotler, *Marketing Management* (Millennium ed.) (Upper Saddle River, N.J.: Prentice-Hall, 2000).

14. "Proton Bomb," *Economist,* May 8, 2004, p. 77.

15. C. K. Prahalad and M. S. Krishnan, "The New Meaning of Quality in the Information Age," *Harvard Business Review* (September–October 1999): 109–118.

16. See D. Garvin, "What Does Product Quality Really Mean," *Sloan Management Review* 26 (Fall 1984): 25–44; P. B. Crosby, *Quality Is Free* (New York: Mentor, 1980); and A. Gabor, *The Man Who Discovered Quality* (New York: Times Books, 1990).

17. M. Cusumano, *The Japanese Automobile Industry* (Cambridge, Mass.: Harvard University Press, 1989);

S. Spear and H. K. Bowen, "Decoding the DNA of the Toyota Production System," *Harvard Business Review* (September–October 1999): 96–108.

18. Kim and Mauborgne, "Value Innovation."

19. G. Stalk and T. M. Hout, *Competing Against Time* (New York: Free Press, 1990).

20. Ibid.

21. Tom Copeland, Tim Koller, and Jack Murrin, *Valuation: Measuring and Managing the Value of Companies* (New York: Wiley, 1996). See also S. F. Jablonsky and N. P. Barsky, *The Manager's Guide to Financial Statement Analysis* (New York: Wiley, 2001).

22. Copeland, Koller, and Murrin, *Valuation.*

23. This is done as follows. Signifying net profit by π, invested capital by K, and revenues by R, then ROIC $= \pi/K$. If we multiply through by revenues, R, this becomes $R \times (\pi/K) = (\pi \times R)/(K \times R)$, which can be rearranged as $\pi/R \times R/K$. π/R is the return on sales and R/K capital turnover.

24. Note that Figure 3.9 is a simplification and ignores some other important items that enter the calculation, such as depreciation/sales (a determinant of ROS) and other assets/sales (a determinant of capital turnover).

25. This is the nature of the competitive process. For more detail, see C. W. L. Hill and D. Deeds, "The Importance of Industry Structure for the Determination of Company Profitability: A Neo-Austrian Perspective," *Journal of Management Studies,* 33 (1996): 429–451.

26. As with resources and capabilities, so the concept of barriers to imitation is also grounded in the resource-based view of the company. For details, see R. Reed and R. J. DeFillippi, "Causal Ambiguity, Barriers to Imitation, and Sustainable Competitive Advantage," *Academy of Management Review* 15 (1990): 88–102.

27. E. Mansfield, "How Economists See R&D," *Harvard Business Review* (November–December 1981): 98–106.

28. S. L. Berman, J. Down, and C. W. L. Hill, "Tacit Knowledge as a Source of Competitive Advantage in the National Basketball Association," *Academy of Management Journal* (2002): 13–33.

29. P. Ghemawat, *Commitment: The Dynamic of Strategy* (New York: Free Press, 1991).

30. W. M. Cohen and D. A. Levinthal, "Absorptive Capacity: A New Perspective on Learning and Innovation," *Administrative Science Quarterly* 35 (1990): 128–152.

31. M. T. Hannah and J. Freeman, "Structural Inertia and Organizational Change," *American Sociological Review* 49 (1984): 149–164.

32. See "IBM Corporation," Harvard Business School Case #180-034.

33. Ghemawat, *Commitment.*

34. D. Miller, *The Icarus Paradox* (New York: Harper-Business, 1990).

35. P. M. Senge, *The Fifth Discipline: The Art and Practice of the Learning Organization* (New York: Doubleday, 1990).

36. D. Kearns, "Leadership Through Quality," *Academy of Management Executive* 4 (1990): 86–89.

37. The classic statement of this position was made by A. A. Alchain, "Uncertainty, Evolution, and Economic Theory," *Journal of Political Economy* 84 (1950): 488–500.

38. *Sources:* Google Form S1, filed with the SEC; "Spiders in the Web," *Economist,* May 15, 2004, pp. 14–16; "The Weakness of Google," *Economist,* May 1, 2004, pp. 67–68; B. Elgin, "Google's Success Is Spurring Competitors to Take Search Technology to the Next Level," *Business Week,* May 17, 2004, pp. 46–47.

Chapter 4

1. *Sources:* A. Latour and C. Nuzum, "Verizon Profit Soars Fivefold on Wireless Growth," *Wall Street Journal,* July 28, 2004, p. A3; S. Woolley, "Do You Fear Me Know?" *Forbes,* November 10, 2003, pp. 78–80; A. Z. Cuneo, "Call Verizon Victorious," *Advertising Age,* March 2004, pp. 3–5.

2. G. J. Miller, *Managerial Dilemmas: The Political Economy of Hierarchy* (Cambridge: Cambridge University Press, 1992).

3. H. Luft, J. Bunker, and A. Enthoven, "Should Operations Be Regionalized?" *New England Journal of Medicine* 301 (1979): 1364–1369.

4. S. Chambers and R. Johnston, "Experience Curves in Services," *International Journal of Operations and Production Management* 20 (2000): 842–860.

5. G. Hall and S. Howell, "The Experience Curve from an Economist's Perspective," *Strategic Management Journal* 6 (1985): 197–212; M. Lieberman, "The Learning Curve and Pricing in the Chemical Processing Industries," *RAND Journal of Economics* 15 (1984): 213–228; R. A. Thornton and P. Thompson, "Learning from Experience and Learning from Others," *American Economic Review* 91 (2001): 1350–1369.

6. Boston Consulting Group, *Perspectives on Experience* (Boston: Boston Consulting Group, 1972); Hall and Howell, "The Experience Curve," pp. 197–212; W. B. Hirschmann, "Profit from the Learning Curve," *Harvard Business Review* (January–February 1964): 125–139.

7. A. A. Alchian, "Reliability of Progress Curves in Airframe Production," *Econometrica* 31 (1963): 679–693.

8. M. Borrus, L. A. Tyson, and J. Zysman, "Creating Advantage: How Government Policies Create Trade in the Semi-Conductor Industry," in P. R. Krugman (ed.), *Strategic Trade Policy and the New International Economics* (Cambridge, Mass.: MIT Press, 1986); S. Ghoshal and C. A. Bartlett, "Matsushita Electrical Industrial (MEI) in 1987," Harvard Business School Case #388-144 (1988).

9. Abernathy and Wayne, "Limits of the Learning Curve," pp. 109–119.

10. D. F. Barnett and R. W. Crandall, *Up from the Ashes: The Rise of the Steel Minimill in the United States* (Washington, D.C.: Brookings Institution, 1986).

11. See P. Nemetz and L. Fry, "Flexible Manufacturing Organizations: Implications for Strategy Formulation," *Academy of Management Review* 13 (1988): 627–638; N. Greenwood, *Implementing Flexible Manufacturing Systems* (New York: Halstead Press, 1986); J. P. Womack, D. T. Jones, and D. Roos, *The Machine That Changed the World* (New York: Rawson Associates, 1990); and R. Parthasarthy and S. P. Seith, "The Impact of Flexible Automation on Business Strategy and Organizational Structure," *Academy of Management Review* 17 (1992): 86–111.

12. B. J. Pine, *Mass Customization: The New Frontier in Business Competition* (Boston: Harvard Business School Press, 1993); S. Kotha, "Mass Customization: Implementing the Emerging Paradigm for Competitive Advantage," *Strategic Management Journal* 16 (1995): 21–42; J. H. Gilmore and B. J. Pine II, "The Four Faces of Mass Customization," *Harvard Business Review* (January–February 1997): 91–101.

13. P. Waurzyniak, "Ford's Flexible Push," *Manufacturing Engineering,* September 2003.

14. F. F. Reichheld and W. E. Sasser, "Zero Defections: Quality Comes to Service," *Harvard Business Review* (September–October 1990): 105–111.

15. The example comes from ibid.

16. Ibid.

17. R. Narasimhan and J. R. Carter, "Organization, Communication and Coordination of International Sourcing," *International Marketing Review* 7 (1990): 6–20.

18. H. F. Busch, "Integrated Materials Management," *IJDP & MM* 18 (1990): 28–39.

19. G. Stalk and T. M. Hout, *Competing Against Time* (New York: Free Press, 1990).

20. See Peter Bamberger and Ilan Meshoulam, *Human Resource Strategy: Formulation, Implementation, and Impact* (Thousand Oaks, Calif.: Sage, 2000); P. M. Wright and S. Snell, "Towards a Unifying Framework for Exploring Fit and Flexibility in Human Resource Management," *Academy of Management Review* 23 (October 1998): 756–772.

21. A. Sorge and M. Warner, "Manpower Training, Manufacturing Organization, and Work Place Relations in Great Britain and West Germany," *British Journal of Industrial Relations* 18 (1980): 318–333; R. Jaikumar, "Postindustrial Manufacturing," *Harvard Business Review* (November–December 1986): 72–83.

22. J. Hoerr, "The Payoff from Teamwork," *Business Week*, July 10, 1989, pp. 56–62.

23. "The Trouble with Teams," *Economist*, January 14, 1995, p. 61.

24. T. C. Powell and A. Dent-Micallef, "Information Technology as Competitive Advantage: The Role of Human, Business, and Technology Resource," *Strategic Management Journal* 18 (1997): 375–405; B. Gates, *Business @ the Speed of Thought* (New York: Warner Books, 1999).

25. "Cisco@speed," *Economist*, June 26, 1999, p. 12; S. Tully, "How Cisco Mastered the Net," *Fortune*, August 17, 1997, pp. 207–210; C. Kano, "The Real King of the Internet," *Fortune*, September 7, 1998, pp. 82–93.

26. Gates, *Business @ the Speed of Thought.*

27. See the articles published in the special issue of the *Academy of Management Review on Total Quality Management* 19:3 (1994). The following article provides a good overview of many of the issues involved from an academic perspective: J. W. Dean and D. E. Bowen, "Management Theory and Total Quality," *Academy of Management Review* 19 (1994): 392–418. See also T. C. Powell, "Total Quality Management as Competitive Advantage," *Strategic Management Journal* 16 (1995): 15–37.

28. For general background information, see "How to Build Quality," *Economist*, September 23, 1989,

pp. 91–92; A. Gabor, *The Man Who Discovered Quality* (New York: Penguin, 1990); and P. B. Crosby, *Quality Is Free* (New York: Mentor, 1980).

29. W. E. Deming, "Improvement of Quality and Productivity Through Action by Management," *National Productivity Review* 1 (Winter 1981–1982): 12–22.

30. J. Bowles, "Is American Management Really Committed to Quality?" *Management Review* (April 1992): 42–46.

31. O. Port and G. Smith, "Quality," *Business Week*, November 30, 1992, pp. 66–75. See also "The Straining of Quality," *Economist*, January 14, 1995, pp. 55–56.

32. Bowles, "Is American Management Really Committed to Quality?" pp. 42–46; "The Straining of Quality," pp. 55–56.

33. Gabor, *The Man Who Discovered Quality.*

34. W. E. Deming, *Out of the Crisis* (Cambridge, Mass.: MIT Center for Advanced Engineering Study, 1986).

35. Deming, "Improvement of Quality and Productivity," pp. 12– 22.

36. A. Ries and J. Trout, *Positioning: The Battle for Your Mind* (New York: Warner Books, 1982).

37. R. G. Cooper, *Product Leadership* (Reading, Mass.: Perseus Books, 1999).

38. E. Mansfield, "How Economists See R&D," *Harvard Business Review* (November–December 1981): 98–106.

39. Ibid.

40. G. A. Stevens and J. Burley, "Piloting the Rocket of Radical Innovation," *Research Technology Management* 46 (2003): 16–26.

41. Ibid.; see also S. L. Brown and K. M. Eisenhardt, "Product Development: Past Research, Present Findings, and Future Directions," *Academy of Management Review* 20 (1995): 343–378; M. B. Lieberman and D. B. Montgomery, "First Mover Advantages," *Strategic Management Journal* 9 (Special Issue, Summer 1988): 41–58; D. J. Teece, "Profiting from Technological Innovation: Implications for Integration, Collaboration, Licensing and Public Policy," *Research Policy* 15 (1987): 285–305; and G. J. Tellis and P. N. Golder, "First to Market, First to Fail?" *Sloan Management Review* (Winter 1996): 65–75.

42. Stalk and Hout, *Competing Against Time.*

43. K. B. Clark and S. C. Wheelwright, *Managing New Product and Process Development* (New York: Free Press, 1993); M. A. Schilling and C. W. L. Hill,

"Managing the New Product Development Process," *Academy of Management Executive* 12:3 (August 1998): 67–81.

44. Clark and Wheelwright, *Managing New Product and Process Development*.

45. P. Sellers, "Getting Customers to Love You," *Fortune*, March 13, 1989, pp. 38–42.

46. O. Port, "Moving Past the Assembly Line," *Business Week* (Special Issue, Reinventing America, 1992): 177–180.

47. G. P. Pisano and S. C. Wheelwright, "The New Logic of High Tech R&D," *Harvard Business Review* (September–October 1995): 93–105.

48. K. B. Clark and T. Fujimoto, "The Power of Product Integrity," *Harvard Business Review* (November–December 1990): 107–118; Clark and Wheelwright, *Managing New Product and Process Development*; Brown and Eisenhardt, "Product Development"; Stalk and Hout, *Competing Against Time*.

49. C. Christensen, "Quantum Corporation-Business and Product Teams," Harvard Business School Case #9-692-023.

50. S. Caminiti, "A Mail Order Romance: Lands' End Courts Unseen Customers," *Fortune*, March 13, 1989, pp. 43–44.

51. Sellers, "Getting Customers to Love You."

52. Caminiti, "A Mail Order Romance," pp. 43–44.

53. Stalk and Hout, *Competing Against Time*.

54. *Sources:* D. Welch and K. Kerwin, "Detroit Tries It the Japanese Way," *Business Week*, January 26, 2004, p. 76; A. Taylor, "Detroit Buffs Up," *Fortune*, February 9, 2004, pp. 90–94; J. Muller, "The Little Car That Could," Forbes, December 8, 2003, p. 82; "The Year of the Car," *Economist*, January 3, 2004, p. 47.

Chapter 5

1. **www.samsung.com** (2004).

2. R. Foroohar and J. Lee, "Masters of the Digital Age," *Newsweek*, October 18, 2004, pp. E10–E13.

3. **www.samsung.com** (2004).

4. Derek F. Abell, *Defining the Business: The Starting Point of Strategic Planning* (Englewood Cliffs, N.J.: Prentice-Hall, 1980), p. 169.

5. R. Kotler, *Marketing Management*, 5th ed. (Englewood Cliffs, N.J.: Prentice-Hall, 1984); M. R. Darby and E. Karni, "Free Competition and the Optimal Amount of Fraud," *Journal of Law and Economics* 16 (1973): 67–86.

6. Abell, *Defining the Business*, p. 8.

7. Some of the theoretical underpinnings for this approach can be found in G. R. Jones and J. Butler, "Costs, Revenues, and Business Level Strategy," *Academy of Management Review* 13 (1988): 202–213; and C. W. L. Hill, "Differentiation Versus Low Cost or Differentiation and Low Cost: A Contingency Framework," *Academy of Management Review* 13 (1988): 401–412.

8. This section, and material on the business model, draw heavily on C. W. L. Hill and G. R. Jones, "The Dynamics of Business-Level Strategy" (unpublished paper, 2002).

9. Many authors have discussed cost leadership and differentiation as basic competitive approaches—for example, F. Scherer, *Industrial Market Structure and Economic Performance*, 10th ed. (Boston: Houghton Mifflin, 2000). The basic cost-leadership/differentiation dimension has received substantial empirical support; see, for example, D. C. Hambrick, "High Profit Strategies in Mature Capital Goods Industries: A Contingency Approach," *Academy of Management Journal* 26 (1983): 687–707.

10. Michael E. Porter, *Competitive Advantage: Creating and Sustaining Superior Performance* (New York: Free Press, 1985), p. 37.

11. Ibid., pp. 13–14.

12. **www.walmart.com** (2002).

13. D. Miller, "Configurations of Strategy and Structure: Towards a Synthesis," *Strategic Management Journal* 7 (1986): 217–231.

14. J. Guyon, "Can the Savoy Cut Costs and Be the Savoy?" *Wall Street Journal*, October 25, 1994, p. B1.

15. Michael E. Porter, *Competitive Strategy: Techniques for Analyzing Industries and Competitors* (New York: Free Press, 1980), p. 46.

16. Peter F. Drucker, *The Practice of Management* (New York: Harper, 1954).

17. Charles W. Hofer and D. Schendel, *Strategy Formulation: Analytical Concepts* (St. Paul, Minn.: West, 1978).

18. W. K. Hall, "Survival Strategies in a Hostile Environment," *Harvard Business Review* 58 (1980): 75–85; Hambrick, "High Profit Strategies," pp. 687–707.

19. J. Guyon, "Can the Savoy Cut Costs and Be the Savoy?" *Wall Street Journal*, October 25, 1994, p. B1.

20. The development of strategic-group theory has been a strong theme in the strategy literature. Important contributions include R. E. Caves and Michael Porter, "From Entry Barriers to Mobility

Barriers," *Quarterly Journal of Economics* (May 1977): 241–262; K. R. Harrigan, "An Application of Clustering for Strategic Group Analysis," *Strategic Management Journal* 6 (1985): 55–73; K. J. Hatten and D. E. Schendel, "Heterogeneity Within an Industry: Company Conduct in the U.S. Brewing Industry, 1952–1971," *Journal of Industrial Economics* 26, pp. 97–113; and Michael E. Porter, "The Structure Within Industries and Companies Performance," *Review of Economics and Statistics* 61 (1979): 214–227.

21. G. Hamel and C. K. Prahalad, *Competing for the Future* (Boston: Harvard Business School

22. *Sources:* www.E*trade.com (2004); www.E*trade.com, press releases (1999, 2001, 2004).

Chapter 6

1. www.nike.com (2004), press release.

2. "The New Nike," yahoo.com (2004), September 12.

3. www.nike.com (2004).

4. A. Wong, "Nike: Just Don't Do It," *Newsweek*, November 1, 2004, p. 84.

5. M. Porter, *Competitive Strategy: Techniques for Analyzing Industries and Competitors* (New York: Free Press, 1980), pp. 191–200.

6. S. A. Shane, "Hybrid Organizational Arrangements and Their Implications for Firm Growth and Survival: A Study of New Franchisors," *Academy of Management Journal* 1 (1996): 216–234.

7. Microsoft is often accused of not being an innovator, but the fact is that Gates and Allen wrote the first commercial software program for the first commercially available personal computer. Microsoft was the first mover in their industry. See P. Freiberger and M. Swaine, *Fire in the Valley* (New York: McGraw-Hill, 2000).

8. J. M. Utterback, *Mastering the Dynamics of Innovation* (Boston: Harvard Business School Press, 1994).

9. See Freiberger and Swaine, *Fire in the Valley.*

10. G. A. Moore, *Crossing the Chasm* (New York: HarperCollins, 1991).

11. Utterback, *Mastering the Dynamics of Innovation.*

12. Everett Rogers, *Diffusion of Innovations* (New York: Free Press, 1995).

13. Charles W. Hofer and D. Schendel, *Strategy Formulation: Analytical Concepts* (St. Paul, Minn.: West, 1978).

14. Ibid.

15. Ibid.

16. Ibid.

17. J. Brander and J. Eaton, "Product Line Rivalry," *American Economic Review* 74 (1985): 323–334.

18. Ibid.

19. Porter, *Competitive Strategy*, pp. 76–86.

20. O. Heil and T. S. Robertson, "Towards a Theory of Competitive Market Signaling: A Research Agenda," *Strategic Management Journal* 12 (1991): 403–418.

21. Robert Axelrod, *The Evolution of Cooperation* (New York: Basic Books, 1984).

22. F. Scherer, *Industrial Market Structure and Economic Performance*, 10th ed. (Boston: Houghton Mifflin, 2000), chap. 8.

23. The model differs from Ansoff's model for this reason.

24. H. Igor Ansoff, *Corporate Strategy* (London: Penguin Books, 1984), pp. 97–100.

25. Robert D. Buzzell, Bradley T. Gale, and Ralph G. M. Sultan, "Market Share—A Key to Profitability," *Harvard Business Review* (January–February 1975): 97–103; Robert Jacobson and David A. Aaker, "Is Market Share All That It's Cracked Up to Be?" *Journal of Marketing* 49 (1985): 11–22.

26. Ansoff, *Corporate Strategy*, pp. 98–99.

27. Figure copyright © Gareth R. Jones, 2004.

28. The next section draws heavily on Marvin B. Lieberman, "Strategies for Capacity Expansion," *Sloan Management Review* 8 (1987): 19–27; and Porter, *Competitive Strategy*, pp. 324–338.

29. For a basic introduction to game theory, see A. K. Dixit and B. J. Nalebuff, *Thinking Strategically* (London: W.W. Norton, 1991). See also A. M. Brandenburger and B. J. Nalebuff, "The Right Game: Using Game Theory to Shape Strategy," *Harvard Business Review* (July–August 1995): 59–71; and D. M. Kreps, *Game Theory and Economic Modeling* (Oxford: Oxford University Press, 1990).

30. www.zara.com (2004); www.gucci.com (2004); C. Vitzthum, "Just-in-Time-Fashion," *Wall Street Journal*, May 18, 2001, pp. B1, B4.

Chapter 7

1. *Sources:* D. Pringle, "Symbian Grabs Bigger Market Share," *Wall Street Journal*, August 3, 2004, p. B2; B. McDonough, "Microsoft Jostles for Mobile Market Position," Wireless.Newsfactor.com, February 19, 2002; A. Reinhardt, "Cell Phones:

Don't Count Linux Out," *Business Week*, September 6, 2003, p. 66.

2. Bureau of Economic Analysis, *Survey of United States Current Business*, 2001.

3. P. Woodall, "Survey: The New Economy: Untangling Economics," *Economist*, September 23, 2000, pp. S5–S7.

4. J. M. Utterback, *Mastering the Dynamics of Innovation* (Boston: Harvard Business School Press, 1994). C. Shapiro and H. R. Varian, *Information Rules: A Strategic Guide to the Network Economy* (Boston: Harvard Business School Press, 1999).

5. The layout is not universal, although it is widespread. The French, for example, use a different layout.

6. M. Craig, "Dueling DVD Recorder Formats," *Seattle Times*, January 9, 2002, p. C3.

7. For details, see Charles W. L. Hill, "Establishing a Standard: Competitive Strategy and Technology Standards in Winner Take All Industries," *Academy of Management Executive* 11 (1997): 7–25; Shapiro and Varian, *Information Rules;* B. Arthur, "Increasing Returns and the New World of Business," *Harvard Business Review* (July-August 1996): 100–109; G. Gowrisankaran and J. Stavins, "Network Externalities and Technology Adoption: Lessons from Electronic Payments," *Rand Journal of Economics* 35 (2004): 260–277; and V. Shankar and B. L. Bayus, "Network Effects and Competition: An Empirical Analysis of the Home Video Game Industry," *Strategic Management Journal* 24 (2003): 375–394.

8. See Shapiro and Varian, *Information Rules;* Hill, "Establishing a Standard"; and M. A. Shilling, "Technological Lockout: An Integrative Model of the Economic and Strategic Factors Driving Technology Success and Failure," *Academy of Management Review* 23:2 (1998): 267–285.

9. Microsoft does not disclose the per unit licensing fee that it gets from original equipment manufacturers.

10. P. M. Romer, "The Origins of Endogenous Growth," *Journal of Economic Perspectives* 8:1 (1994): 3–22.

11. Data from **www.btechnews.com**.

12. Shapiro and Varian, *Information Rules*.

13. International Federation of the Phonographic Industry, *Fighting Piracy*, 2003. Available from **www.ifpi.org**.

14. Business Software Alliance, *Seventh Annual BSA Global Software Piracy Study*, June 2003. Available from **www.bsa.org**.

15. Ibid.

16. N. Ridgeway, "Let Them Burn," *Forbes*, March 4, 2002, p. 88.

17. Much of this section is based on Charles W. L. Hill, Michael Heeley, and Jane Sakson, "Strategies for Profiting from Innovation," in *Advances in Global High Technology Management* (Greenwich, Conn.: JAI Press, 1993) 3: 79–95.

18. M. Lieberman and D. Montgomery, "First Mover Advantages," *Strategic Management Journal* 9 (Special Issue, Summer 1988): 41–58.

19. W. Boulding and M. Christen, "Sustainable Pioneering Advantage? Profit Implications of Market Entry Order?" *Marketing Science* 22 (2003): 371–386; C. Markides and P. Geroski, "Teaching Elephants to Dance and Other Silly Ideas," *Business Strategy Review* 13 (2003): 49–61.

20. J. Borzo, "Aging Gracefully," *Wall Street Journal*, October 15, 2001, p. R22.

21. The importance of complementary assets was first noted by D. J. Teece. See D. J. Teece, "Profiting from Technological Innovation," in D. J. Teece (ed.), *The Competitive Challenge* (New York: Harper & Row, 1986), pp. 26–54.

22. M. J. Chen and D. C. Hambrick, "Speed, Stealth, and Selective Attack: How Small Firms Differ from Large Firms in Competitive Behavior," *Academy of Management Journal* 38 (1995): 453–482.

23. E. Mansfield, M. Schwartz, and S. Wagner, "Imitation Costs and Patents: An Empirical Study," *Economic Journal* 91 (1981): 907–918.

24. E. Mansfield, "How Rapidly Does New Industrial Technology Leak Out?" *Journal of Industrial Economics* 34 (1985): 217–223.

25. This argument has been made in the game theory literature. See R. Caves, H. Cookell, and P. J. Killing, "The Imperfect Market for Technology Licenses," *Oxford Bulletin of Economics and Statistics* 45 (1983): 249–267; N. T. Gallini, "Deterrence by Market Sharing: A Strategic Incentive for Licensing," *American Economic Review* 74 (1984): 931–941; and C. Shapiro, "Patent Licensing and R&D Rivalry," *American Economic Review* 75 (1985): 25–30.

26. M. Christensen, *The Innovator's Dilemma* (Boston: Harvard Business School Press, 1997). R. N. Foster, *Innovation: The Attacker's Advantage* (New York: Summit Books, 1986).

27. Foster, *Innovation*.

28. Ray Kurzweil, *The Age of the Spiritual Machines* (New York: Penguin Books, 1999).

29. See Christensen, *The Innovator's Dilemma*; and C. M. Christensen and M. Overdorf, "Meeting the Challenge of Disruptive Change," *Harvard Business Review* (March–April 2000): 66–77.

30. Charles W. L. Hill and Frank T. Rothaermel, "The Performance of Incumbent Firms in the Face of Radical Technological Innovation," *Academy of Management Review* 28 (2003): 257–274.

31. *Sources:* S. Yoon, "The Mod Squad," *East Asian Economic Review*, November 7, 2002, pp. 34–36; R. Cunningham, "Controversy as Sony Loses Mod-Chip Verdict," *Managing Intellectual Property*, September 2002, pp. 15–18; A. Pham, "Video Game Losses Nearly $2 Billion," *Los Angeles Times*, February 18, 2002, p. C8; Andy Holloway, "License to Plunder," *Canadian Business*, November 10, 2003, p. 95.

Chapter 8

1. *Sources:* J. Neff, "P&G Outpacing Unilever in Five Year Battle," *Advertising Age*, November 3, 2003, pp. 1–3; G. Strauss, "Firm Restructuring into Truly Global Company," *USA Today*, September 10, 1999, p. B2; Procter & Gamble *10K Report, 2004*; M. Kolbasuk McGee, "P&G Jump-Starts Corporate Change," *Information Week*, November 1, 1999, pp. 30–34.

2. World Trade Organization, *International Trade Trends and Statistics, 2003* (Geneva: WTO, 2003). WTO press release, "World Trade for 2003: Prospects for 2004," April 4, 2004. Available at **www.wto.org**.

3. World Trade Organization, *International Trade Statistics, 2003* (Geneva: WTO, 2003), and United Nations, *World Investment Report, 2003*.

4. P. Dicken, *Global Shift* (New York: Guilford Press, 1992).

5. I. Metthee, "Playing a Large Part," *Seattle Post-Intelligencer*, April 9, 1994, p. 13.

6. T. Levitt, "The Globalization of Markets," *Harvard Business Review* (May–June 1983): 92–102.

7. M. E. Porter, *The Competitive Advantage of Nations* (New York: Free Press, 1990). See also R. Grant, "Porter's Competitive Advantage of Nations: An Assessment," *Strategic Management Journal* 7 (1991): 535–548.

8. Porter, *Competitive Advantage of Nations*.

9. Example is disguised. Comes from interviews by Charles Hill.

10. See J. Birkinshaw and N. Hood, "Multinational Subsidiary Evolution: Capability and Charter Change in Foreign Owned Subsidiary Companies," *Academy of Management Review* 23 (October 1998), pp. 773–795; A. K. Gupta and V. J. Govindarajan, "Knowledge Flows Within Multinational Corporations," *Strategic Management Journal* 21 (2000), pp. 473–496; V. J. Govindarajan and A. K. Gupta, *The Quest for Global Dominance* (San Francisco: Jossey-Bass, 2001); T. S. Frost, J. M. Birkinshaw, and P. C. Ensign, "Centers of Excellence in Multinational Corporations," *Strategic Management Journal* 23 (2002), pp. 997–1018; and U. Andersson, M. Forsgren, and U. Holm, "The Strategic Impact of External Networks," *Strategic Management Journal* 23 (2002), pp. 979–996.

11. S. Leung, "Armchairs, TVs and Espresso: Is It McDonald's?" *Wall Street Journal*, August 30, 2002, pp. A1, A6.

12. C. K. Prahalad and Yves L. Doz, *The Multinational Mission: Balancing Local Demands and Global Vision* (New York: Free Press, 1987). See also J. Birkinshaw, A. Morrison, and J. Hulland, "Structural and Competitive Determinants of a Global Integration Strategy," *Strategic Management Journal* 16 (1995): 637–655.

13. J. E. Garten, "Wal-Mart Gives Globalization a Bad Name," *Business Week*, March 8, 2004, p. 24.

14. Prahalad and Doz, *Multinational Mission*. Prahalad and Doz actually talk about local responsiveness rather than local customization.

15. Levitt, "Globalization of Markets."

16. C. A. Bartlett and S. Ghoshal, *Managing Across Borders* (Boston: Harvard Business School Press, 1989).

17. C. J. Chipello, "Local Presence Is Key to European Deals," *Wall Street Journal*, June 30, 1998, p. A15.

18. Bartlett and Ghoshal, *Managing Across Borders*.

19. Ibid.

20. T. Hout, M. E. Porter, and E. Rudden, "How Global Companies Win Out," *Harvard Business Review* (September–October 1982): 98–108.

21. See Charles W. L. Hill, *International Business: Competing in the Global Marketplace* (New York: McGraw-Hill, 2000).

22. This can be reconceptualized as the resource base of the entrant, relative to indigenous competitors. For work that focuses on this issue, see W. C. Bogenr, H. Thomas, and J. McGee, "A Longitudinal Study of the Competitive Positions and Entry Paths of European Firms in the U.S. Pharmaceutical

Market," *Strategic Management Journal* 17 (1996): 85–107; D. Collis, "A Resource Based Analysis of Global Competition," *Strategic Management Journal* 12 (1991): 49–68; and S. Tallman, "Strategic Management Models and Resource Based Strategies Among MNE's in a Host Market," *Strategic Management Journal* 12 (1991): 69–82.

23. For a discussion of first-mover advantages, see M. Liberman and D. Montgomery, "First Mover Advantages," *Strategic Management Journal* 9 (Special Issue, Summer 1988): 41–58.

24. J. M. Shaver, W. Mitchell, and B. Yeung, "The Effect of Own Company and Other Company Experience on Foreign Direct Investment Survival in the U.S., 1987–92," *Strategic Management Journal* 18 (1997): 811–824.

25. S. Zaheer and E. Mosakowski, "The Dynamics of the Liability of Foreignness: A Global Study of Survival in the Financial Services Industry," *Strategic Management Journal* 18 (1997): 439–464.

26. Shaver, Mitchell, and Yeung, "The Effect of Own Company and Other Company Experience."

27. P. Ghemawat, *Commitment: The Dynamics of Strategy* (New York: Free Press, 1991).

28. This section draws on several studies, including C. W. L. Hill, P. Hwang, and W. C. Kim, "An Eclectic Theory of the Choice of International Entry Mode," *Strategic Management Journal* 11 (1990): 117–128; C. W. L. Hill and W. C. Kim, "Searching for a Dynamic Theory of the Multinational Company: A Transaction Cost Model," *Strategic Management Journal* 9 (Special Issue on Strategy Content, 1988): 93–104; E. Anderson and H. Gatignon, "Modes of Foreign Entry: A Transaction Cost Analysis and Propositions," *Journal of International Business Studies* 17 (1986): 1–26; F. R. Root, *Entry Strategies for International Markets* (Lexington, Mass.: D. C. Heath, 1980); and A. Madhok, "Cost, Value and Foreign Market Entry: The Transaction and the Company," *Strategic Management Journal* 18 (1997): 39–61.

29. F. J. Contractor, "The Role of Licensing in International Strategy," *Columbia Journal of World Business* (Winter 1982): 73–83.

30. O. E. Williamson, *The Economic Institutions of Capitalism* (New York: Free Press, 1985).

31. Andrew E. Serwer, "McDonald's Conquers the World," *Fortune*, October 17, 1994, pp. 103–116.

32. B. Kogut, "Joint Ventures: Theoretical and Empirical Perspectives," *Strategic Management Journal* 9 (1988): 319–332.

33. D. G. Bradley, "Managing Against Expropriation," *Harvard Business Review* (July–August 1977): 78–90.

34. C. W. L. Hill, "Strategies for Exploiting Technological Innovations," *Organization Science* 3 (1992): 428–441.

35. See K. Ohmae, "The Global Logic of Strategic Alliances," *Harvard Business Review* (March–April 1989): 143–154; G. Hamel, Y. L. Doz, and C. K. Prahalad, "Collaborate with Your Competitors and Win!" *Harvard Business Review* (January–February 1989): 133–139; W. Burgers, C. W. L. Hill, and W. C. Kim, "Alliances in the Global Auto Industry," *Strategic Management Journal* 14 (1993): 419–432; and P. Kale, H. Singh, and H. Perlmutter, "Learning and Protection of Proprietary Assets in Strategic Alliances: Building Relational Capital," *Strategic Management Journal* 21 (2000): 217–237.

36. "Asia Beckons," *Economist*, May 30, 1992, pp. 63–64.

37. C. Souza, "Microsoft Teams with MIPS, Toshiba," *EBN*, February 10, 2003, p. 4.

38. M. Frankel, "Now Sony Is Giving Palm a Hand," *Business Week*, November 29, 2000, p. 50.

39. Kale, Singh, and Perlmutter, "Learning and Protection of Proprietary Assets."

40. R. B. Reich and E. D. Mankin, "Joint Ventures with Japan Give Away Our Future," *Harvard Business Review*, March–April 1986, pp. 78–90.

41. J. Bleeke and D. Ernst, "The Way to Win in Cross-Border Alliances," *Harvard Business Review* (November–December 1991): 127–135.

42. E. Booker and C. Krol, "IBM Finds Strength in Alliances," *B to B*, February 10, 2003, pp. 3, 27.

43. W. Roehl and J. F. Truitt, "Stormy Open Marriages Are Better," *Columbia Journal of World Business* (Summer 1987): 87–95.

44. K. McQuade and B. Gomes-Casseres, "Xerox and Fuji-Xerox," Harvard Business School Case #9–391–156.

45. See T. Khanna, R. Gulati, and N. Nohria, "The Dynamics of Learning Alliances: Competition, Cooperation, and Relative Scope," *Strategic Management Journal* 19 (1998), pp. 193–210; and Kale, Singh, and Perlmutter, "Learning and Protection of Proprietary Assets."

46. Kale, Singh, and Perlmutter, "Learning and Protection of Proprietary Assets."

47. Hamel, Doz, and Prahalad, "Collaborate with Your Competitors and Win!"

48. B. Wysocki, "Cross Border Alliances Become Favorite Way to Crack New Markets," *Wall Street Journal*, March 4, 1990, p. A1.

49. *Sources:* Starbucks 10-K, various years; C. McLean, "Starbucks Set to Invade Coffee-Loving Continent," *Seattle Times*, October 4, 2000, p. E1; J. Ordonez, "Starbucks to Start Major Expansion in Overseas Market," *Wall Street Journal*, October 27, 2000, p. B10; S. Homes and D. Bennett, "Planet Starbucks," *Business Week*, September 9, 2002, pp. 99–110; J. Batsell, "A Bean Counters Dream," *Seattle Times*, March 28, 2004, p. E1; Staff Reporter, "Boss Talk: It's a Grande Latte World," *Wall Street Journal*, December 15, 2003, p. B1.

Chapter 9

1. Y. J. Dreazen, G. Ip, and N. Kulish, "Why the Sudden Rise in the Urge to Merge and Create Oligopolies?" *Wall Street Journal*, February 25, 2002, p. A1; L. Kowalczyk, "A Matter of Style," *Boston Globe*, February 22, 2002, p. C1.

2. United Nations, *World Investment Report 2001* (New York: United Nations, November 2001).

3. Dreazen, Ip, and Kulish, "Why the Sudden Rise?"

4. For evidence on acquisitions and performance, see R. E. Caves, "Mergers, Takeovers, and Economic Efficiency," *International Journal of Industrial Organization* 7 (1989): 151–174; M. C. Jensen and R. S. Ruback, "The Market for Corporate Control: The Scientific Evidence," *Journal of Financial Economics* 11 (1983): 5–50; R. Roll, "Empirical Evidence on Takeover Activity and Shareholder Wealth," in J. C. Coffee, L. Lowenstein, and S. Rose (eds.), *Knights, Raiders and Targets* (Oxford: Oxford University Press, 1989); A. Schleifer and R. W. Vishny, "Takeovers in the 60s and 80s: Evidence and Implications," *Strategic Management Journal* 12 (Special Issue, Winter 1991): 51–60; and T. H. Brush, "Predicted Changes in Operational Synergy and Post Acquisition Performance of Acquired Businesses," *Strategic Management Journal* 17 (1996): 1–24.

5. "Few Takeovers Pay Off for Big Buyers," *Investors Business Daily*, May 25, 2001, p. 1.

6. K. R. Harrian, "Formulating Vertical Integration Strategies," *Academy of Management Review* 9 (1984): 638–652.

7. This is the essence of Chandler's argument. See Alfred D. Chandler, *Strategy and Structure* (Cambridge, Mass.: MIT Press, 1962). The same argument is also made by Jeffrey Pfeffer and Gerald R. Salancik, *The External Control of Organizations* (New York: Harper & Row, 1978). See also K. R. Harrigan, *Strategic Flexibility* (Lexington, Mass.: Lexington Books, 1985); K. R. Harrigan, "Vertical Integration and Corporate Strategy," *Academy of Management Journal* 28 (1985): 397–425; and F. M. Scherer, *Industrial Market Structure and Economic Performance* (Chicago: Rand McNally, 1981).

8. Oliver E. Williamson, *The Economic Institutions of Capitalism.* For recent empirical work that uses this framework, see L. Poppo and T. Zenger, "Testing Alternative Theories of the Firm: Transaction Cost, Knowledge Based, and Measurement Explanations for Make or Buy Decisions in Information Services," *Strategic Management Journal* 19 (1998): 853–878.

9. Williamson, *Economic Institutions of Capitalism.*

10. A. D. Chandler, *The Visible Hand* (Cambridge, Mass.: Harvard University Press, 1977).

11. Julia Pitta, "Score One for Vertical Integration," *Forbes,* January 18, 1993, pp. 88–89.

12. Joseph White and Neal Templin, "Harsh Regimen: A Swollen GM Finds It Hard to Stick with Its Crash Diet," *Wall Street Journal,* September 9, 1992, p. A1.

13. Harrigan, *Strategic Flexibility,* pp. 67–87. See also Allan Afuah, "Dynamic Boundaries of the Firm: Are Firms Better Off Being Vertically Integrated in the Face of a Technological Change?" *Academy of Management Journal* 44 (2001): 1121–1228.

14. Kevin Kelly, Zachary Schiller, and James Treece, "Cut Costs or Else," *Business Week,* March 22, 1993, pp. 28–29.

15. X. Martin, W. Mitchell, and A. Swaminathan, "Recreating and Extending Japanese Automobile Buyer-Supplier Links in North America," *Strategic Management Journal* 16 (1995): 589–619; C. W. L. Hill, "National Institutional Structures, Transaction Cost Economizing, and Competitive Advantage," *Organization Science* 6 (1995): 119–131.

16. Standard & Poor's Industry Survey, Autos—Auto Parts, June 24, 1993.

17. See James Womack, Daniel Jones, and Daniel Roos, *The Machine That Changed the World* (New York: Rawson Associates, 1990); and James Richardson, "Parallel Sourcing and Supplier Performance in the Japanese Automobile Industry," *Strategic Management Journal* 14 (1993): 339–350.

18. R. Mudambi and S. Helper, "The Close but Adversarial Model of Supplier Relations in the U.S. Auto Industry," *Strategic Management Journal* 19 (1998): 775–792.

19. Williamson, *Economic Institutions of Capitalism*. See also J. H. Dyer, "Effective Inter-Firm Collaboration: How Firms Minimize Transaction Costs and Maximize Transaction Value," *Strategic Management Journal* 18 (1997): 535–556.

20. Richardson, "Parallel Sourcing."

21. W. H. Davidow and M. S. Malone, *The Virtual Corporation* (New York: Harper & Row, 1992).

22. A. M. Porter, "Outsourcing Gains Popularity," *Purchasing*, March 11, 1999, pp. 22–24.

23. D. Garr, "Inside Outsourcing," *Fortune* 142:1 (2001): 85–92.

24. J. Krane, "American Express Hires IBM for $4 billion," *Columbian*, February 26, 2002, p. E2.

25. J. Vijayan, "The Outsourcing Boom," *Computerworld*, March 18, 2002, pp. 42–43.

26. Davidow and Malone, *The Virtual Corporation*.

27. Ibid; H. W. Chesbrough and D. J. Teece, "When Is Virtual Virtuous? Organizing for Innovation," *Harvard Business Review* (January–February 1996): 65–74; J. B. Quinn, "Strategic Outsourcing: Leveraging Knowledge Capabilities," *Sloan Management Review* (Summer 1999): 9–21.

28. *Sources:* S. N. Mehta, "Can Bernie Bounce Back?" *Fortune*, January 22, 2001; S. N. Mehta, "WorldCom's Bad Trip," *Fortune*, March 4, 2002; R. Blumenstein, J. R. Wilke, N. Harris, and D. Solomon, "Called Off?" *Wall Street Journal*, June 28, 2000, p. A1.

Chapter 10

1. G. Hamel and C. K. Prahalad, *Competing for the Future* (Boston: Harvard Business School Press, 1994).

2. Ibid.

3. D. Leonard Barton and G. Pisano, "Monsanto's March into Biotechnology," Harvard Business School Case #690-009 (1990). See Monsanto's homepage for details about its genetically engineered seed products (**http://www.monsanto.com**).

4. This resource-based view of diversification can be traced to Edith Penrose's seminal book, *The Theory of the Growth of the Firm* (Oxford: Oxford University Press, 1959).

5. D. J. Teece, "Economies of Scope and the Scope of the Enterprise," *Journal of Economic Behavior and Organization* 3 (1980): 223–247. For recent empirical work on this topic, see C. H. St. John and J. S. Harrison, "Manufacturing Based Relatedness, Synergy and Coordination," *Strategic Management Journal* 20 (1999): 129–145.

6. Teece, "Economies of Scope." For recent empirical work on this topic, see St. John and Harrison, "Manufacturing Based Relatedness, Synergy and Coordination."

7. For a detailed discussion, see C. W. L. Hill and R. E. Hoskisson, "Strategy and Structure in the Multiproduct Firm," *Academy of Management Review* 12 (1987): 331–341.

8. See, for example, G. R. Jones and C. W. L. Hill, "A Transaction Cost Analysis of Strategy Structure Choice," *Strategic Management Journal* (1988): 159–172; and Oliver E. Williamson, *Markets and Hierarchies, Analysis and Antitrust Implications* (New York: Free Press, 1975), pp. 132–175.

9. R. Buderi, *Engines of Tomorrow* (New York: Simon & Schuster, 2000).

10. C. W. L. Hill, "The Role of Headquarters in the Multidivisional Firm," in R. Rumelt, D. J. Teece, and D. Schendel (eds.), *Fundamental Issues in Strategy Research* (Cambridge, Mass.: Harvard Business School Press, 1994), pp. 297–321.

11. See, for example, Jones and Hill, "A Transaction Cost Analysis"; Williamson, *Markets and Hierarchies;* and Hill, "The Role of Headquarters in the Multidivisional Firm."

12. The distinction goes back to R. P. Rumelt, *Strategy, Structure and Economic Performance* (Cambridge, Mass.: Harvard Business School Press, 1974).

13. For evidence, see C. W. L. Hill, "Conglomerate Performance over the Economic Cycle," *Journal of Industrial Economics* 32 (1983): 197–212; and D. T. C. Mueller, "The Effects of Conglomerate Mergers," *Journal of Banking and Finance* 1 (1977): 315–347.

14. For reviews of the evidence, see V. Ramanujam and P. Varadarajan, "Research on Corporate Diversification: A Synthesis," *Strategic Management Journal* 10 (1989): 523–551; G. Dess, J. F. Hennart, C. W. L. Hill, and A. Gupta, "Research Issues in Strategic Management," *Journal of Management* 21 (1995): 357–392; and David C. Hyland and J. David Diltz, "Why Companies Diversify: An Empirical Examination," *Financial Management* 31 (Spring 2002): 51–81.

15. M. E. Porter, "From Competitive Advantage to Corporate Strategy," *Harvard Business Review* (May–June 1987): 43–59.

16. For reviews of the evidence, see Ramanujam and Varadarajan, "Research on Corporate Diversification"; Dess, Hennart, Hill, and Gupta, "Research Issues in Strategic Management"; and Hyland and Diltz, "Why Companies Diversify."

17. C. R. Christensen et al., *Business Policy Text and Cases* (Homewood, Ill.: Irwin, 1987), p. 778.

18. See Booz, Allen, and Hamilton, *New Products Management for the 1980's* (privately published, 1982); A. L. Page, "PDMA's New Product Development Practices Survey: Performance and Best Practices" (presented at the PDMA Fifteenth Annual International Conference, Boston, October 16, 1991); and E. Mansfield, "How Economists See R&D," *Harvard Business Review* (November–December 1981): 98–106.

19. See R. Biggadike, "The Risky Business of Diversification," *Harvard Business Review* (May–June 1979): 103–111; R. A. Burgelman, "A Process Model of Internal Corporate Venturing in the Diversified Major Firm," *Administrative Science Quarterly* 28 (1983): 223–244; and Z. Block and I. C. MacMillan, *Corporate Venturing* (Boston: Harvard Business School Press, 1993).

20. Biggadike, "The Risky Business of Diversification"; Block and Macmillan, *Corporate Venturing*.

21. Buderi, *Engines of Tomorrow*.

22. I. C. MacMillan and R. George, "Corporate Venturing: Challenges for Senior Managers," *Journal of Business Strategy* 5 (1985): 34–43.

23. See R. A. Burgelman, M. M. Maidique, and S. C. Wheelwright, *Strategic Management of Technology and Innovation* (Chicago: Irwin, 1996), pp. 493–507. Also see Buderi, *Engines of Tomorrow*.

24. Buderi, *Engines of Tomorrow*.

25. See Block and Macmillan, *Corporate Venturing*; and Burgelman, Maidique, and Wheelwright, *Strategic Management of Technology and Innovation*.

26. J. Warner, J. Templeman, and R. Horn, "The Case Against Mergers," *Business Week*, October 30, 1995, pp. 122–134.

27. "Few Takeovers Pay Off for Big Buyers," *Investors Business Daily*, May 25, 2001, p. 1.

28. For evidence on acquisitions and performance, see R. E. Caves, "Mergers, Takeovers, and Economic Efficiency," *International Journal of Industrial Organization* 7 (1989): 151–174; M. C. Jensen and R.

S. Ruback, "The Market for Corporate Control: The Scientific Evidence," *Journal of Financial Economics* 11 (1983): 5–50; R. Roll, "Empirical Evidence on Takeover Activity and Shareholder Wealth," in J. C. Coffee, L. Lowenstein, and S. Rose (eds.), *Knights, Raiders and Targets* (Oxford: Oxford University Press, 1989); A. Schleifer and R. W. Vishny, "Takeovers in the 60s and 80s: Evidence and Implications," *Strategic Management Journal* 12 (Special Issue, Winter 1991): 51–60; T. H. Brush, "Predicted Changes in Operational Synergy and Post Acquisition Performance of Acquired Businesses," *Strategic Management Journal* 17 (1996): 1–24; and T. Loughran and A. M. Vijh, "Do Long Term Shareholders Benefit from Corporate Acquisitions?" *Journal of Finance* 5 (1997): 1765–1787.

29. D. J. Ravenscraft and F. M. Scherer, *Mergers, Sell-offs, and Economic Efficiency* (Washington, D.C.: Brookings Institution, 1987).

30. See J. P. Walsh, "Top Management Turnover Following Mergers and Acquisitions," *Strategic Management Journal* 9 (1988): 173–183.

31. See A. A. Cannella and D. C. Hambrick, "Executive Departure and Acquisition Performance," *Strategic Management Journal* 14 (1993): 137–152.

32. R. Roll, "The Hubris Hypothesis of Corporate Takeovers," *Journal of Business* 59 (1986): 197–216.

33. "Coca-Cola: A Sobering Lesson from Its Journey into Wine," *Business Week*, June 3, 1985, pp. 96–98.

34. P. Haspeslagh and D. Jemison, *Managing Acquisitions* (New York: Free Press, 1991).

35. For views on this issue, see L. L. Fray, D. H. Gaylin, and J. W. Down, "Successful Acquisition Planning," *Journal of Business Strategy* 5 (1984): 46–55; C. W. L. Hill, "Profile of a Conglomerate Takeover: BTR and Thomas Tilling," *Journal of General Management* 10 (1984): 34–50; D. R. Willensky, "Making It Happen: How to Execute an Acquisition," *Business Horizons* (March–April 1985): 38–45; Haspeslagh and Jemison, *Managing Acquisitions*; and P. L. Anslinger and T. E. Copeland, "Growth Through Acquisition: A Fresh Look," *Harvard Business Review* (January–February 1996): 126–135.

36. M. L. A. Hayward, "When Do Firms Learn from Their Acquisition Experience? Evidence from 1990–1995," *Strategic Management Journal* 23 (2002): 21–39; K. G. Ahuja, "Technological Acquisitions and the Innovation Performance of Acquiring Firms: A Longitudinal Study," *Strategic*

Management Journal 23 (2001): 197–220; H. G. Barkema and F. Vermeulen, "International Expansion Through Startup or Acquisition," *Academy of Management Journal* 41 (1998): 7–26.

37. Hayward, "When Do Firms Learn from Their Acquisition Experience?"

38. For a review of the evidence and some contrary empirical evidence, see D. E. Hatfield, J. P. Liebskind, and T. C. Opler, "The Effects of Corporate Restructuring on Aggregate Industry Specialization," *Strategic Management Journal* 17 (1996): 55–72.

39. A. Lamont and C. Polk, "The Diversification Discount: Cash Flows Versus Returns," *Journal of Finance* 56 (October 2001): 1693–1721; R. Raju, H. Servaes, and L. Zingales, "The Cost of Diversity: The Diversification Discount and Inefficient Investment," *Journal of Finance* 55 (February 2000): 35–80.

40. For example, see Schleifer and Vishny, "Takeovers in the 60s and 80s."

41. *Sources:* J. R. Laing, "Tyco's Titan," *Barron's,* April 12, 1999, pp. 27–32; M. Maremont, "How Is Tyco Accounting for Cash Flow?" *Wall Street Journal,* March 5, 2002, p. C1; J. R. Laing, "Doubting Tyco," *Barron's,* January 28, 2002, pp. 19–20; Staff Reporter, "Tyco's Troubles," *Economist,* June 8th, 2002, p. 71.

Chapter 11

1. *Sources:* "Boycott Nike," CBS News *48 Hours,* October 17, 1996; D. Jones, "Critics Tie Sweatshop Sneakers to 'Air Jordan,'" *USA Today,* June 6, 1996, p. 1B; "Global Exchange Special Report: Nile Just Don't Do It," available at **http://www.globalexchange.org/education/ publications/newsltr6.97p2.html#nike;** S. Greenhouse, "Nike Shoeplant in Vietnam Is Called Unsafe for Workers," *New York Times,* November 8, 1997; V. Dobnik, "Chinese Workers Abused Making Nikes, Reeboks," *Seattle Times,* September 21, 1997, p. A4.

2. E. Freeman, *Strategic Management: A Stakeholder Approach* (Boston: Pitman Press, 1984).

3. C. W. L. Hill and T. M. Jones, "Stakeholder-Agency Theory," *Journal of Management Studies* 29 (1992): 131–154; J. G. March and H. A. Simon, *Organizations* (New York: Wiley, 1958).

4. Hill and Jones, "Stakeholder-Agency Theory."

5. I. C. Macmillan and P. E. Jones, *Strategy Formulation: Power and Politics* (St. Paul, Minn.: West, 1986).

6. Tom Copeland, Tim Koller, and Jack Murrin, *Valuation: Measuring and Managing the Value of Companies* (New York: Wiley, 1996).

7. R. S. Kaplan and D. P. Norton, *Strategy Maps* (Boston: Harvard Business School Press, 2004).

8. A. L. Velocci, D. A. Fulghum, and R. Wall, "Damage Control," *Aviation Week,* December 1, 2003, pp. 26–27.

9. M. C. Jensen and W. H. Meckling, "Theory of the Firm: Managerial Behavior, Agency Costs and Ownership Structure," *Journal of Financial Economics* 3 (1976): 305–360; E. F. Fama, "Agency Problems and the Theory of the Firm," *Journal of Political Economy* 88 (1980): 375–390.

10. Hill and Jones, "Stakeholder-Agency Theory."

11. For example, see R. Marris, *The Economic Theory of Managerial Capitalism* (London: Macmillan, 1964); and J. K. Galbraith, *The New Industrial State* (Boston: Houghton Mifflin, 1970).

12. Fama, "Agency Problems and the Theory of the Firm."

13. A. Rappaport, "New Thinking on How to Link Executive Pay with Performance," *Harvard Business Review* (March–April 1999): 91–105.

14. L. Lavelle, J. Hempel, and D. Brady, "Executive Pay," *Business Week,* April 19, 2004, pp. 106–112.

15. John Byrne et al., "How to Fix Corporate Governance," *Business Week,* May 6, 2002, pp. 69–78; Lavelle, Hempel, and Brady, "Executive Pay."

16. For academic studies that look at the determinants of CEO pay, see M. C. Jensen and K. J. Murphy, "Performance Pay and Top Management Incentives," *Journal of Political Economy* 98 (1990): 225–264; Charles W. L. Hill and Phillip Phan, "CEO Tenure as a Determinant of CEO Pay," *Academy of Management Journal* 34 (1991): 707–717; H. L. Tosi and L. R. Gomez-Mejia, "CEO Compensation Monitoring and Firm Performance," *Academy of Management Journal* 37 (1994): 1002–1016; and Joseph F. Porac, James B. Wade, and Timothy G. Pollock, "Industry Categories and the Politics of the Comparable Firm in CEO Compensation," *Administrative Science Quarterly* 44 (1999): 112–144.

17. Ellen Goodman, "CEO Pay Cap: Why Not Try It for Size?" *Houston Chronicle,* April 18, 1999, p. 6.

18. For recent research on this issue, see Peter J. Lane, A. A. Cannella, and M. H. Lubatkin, "Agency Problems as Antecedents to Unrelated Mergers and Diversification: Amihud and Lev Reconsidered," *Strategic Management Journal* 19 (1998): 555–578.

19. E. T. Penrose, *The Theory of the Growth of the Firm* (London: Macmillan, 1958).

20. "Money Well Spent: Corporate Parties," *Economist*, November 1, 2003, p. 79.

21. G. Edmondson and L. Cohn, "How Parmalat Went Sour," *Business Week*, January 12, 2004, pp. 46–50. "Another Enron? Royal Dutch Shell," *Economist*, March 13, 2004, p. 71.

22. O. E. Williamson, *The Economic Institutions of Capitalism* (New York: Free Press, 1985).

23. Fama, "Agency Problems and the Theory of the Firm."

24. S. Finkelstein and R. D'Aveni, "CEO Duality as a Double Edged Sword," *Academy of Management Journal* 37 (1994): 1079–1108; B. Ram Baliga and R. C. Moyer, "CEO Duality and Firm Performance," *Strategic Management Journal* 17 (1996): 41–53; M. L. Mace, *Directors: Myth and Reality* (Cambridge, Mass.: Harvard University Press, 1971); S. C. Vance, *Corporate Leadership: Boards of Directors and Strategy* (New York: McGraw-Hill, 1983).

25. W. G. Lewellen, C. Eoderer, and A. Rosenfeld, "Merger Decisions and Executive Stock Ownership in Acquiring Firms," *Journal of Accounting and Economics* 7 (1985): 209–231.

26. C. W. L. Hill and S. A. Snell, "External Control, Corporate Strategy, and Firm Performance," *Strategic Management Journal* 9 (1988): 577–590.

27. Quoted in G. Morgenson, "Stock Options Are Not a Free Lunch," *Forbes*, May 18, 1998, pp. 212–217.

28. D. Henry and M. Conlin, "Too Much of a Good Incentive?" *Business Week*, March 4, 2002, pp. 38–39.

29. J. P. Walsh and R. D. Kosnik, "Corporate Raiders and Their Disciplinary Role in the Market for Corporate Control," *Academy of Management Journal* 36 (1993): 671–700.

30. R. S. Kaplan and D. P. Norton, "The Balanced Scorecard—Measures That Drive Performance," *Harvard Business Review* (January–February 1992): 71–79; Kaplan and Norton, *Strategy Maps*.

31. R. S. Kaplan and D. P. Norton, "Using the Balanced Scorecard as a Strategic Management System," *Harvard Business Review* (January–February 1996): 75–85; Kaplan and Norton, *Strategy Maps*.

32. R. S. Kaplan and D. P. Norton, "Putting the Balanced Scorecard to Work," *Harvard Business Review* (September–October 1993): 134–147; Kaplan and Norton, *Strategy Maps*.

33. Kaplan and Norton, "The Balanced Scorecard," p. 72.

34. *Sources:* "Why Honesty Is the Best Policy," *Economist*, March 9, 2002; "The Amazing Disintegrating Firm—Enron," *Economist*, December 8, 2001; Wendy Zellner et al., "The Fall of Enron," *Business Week*, December 17, 2001, pp. 30–40; Ken Brown et al., "Paper Trail: Andersen Fires Partner It Says Led Shredding of Enron Documents," *Wall Street Journal*, January 16, 2002, p. A1; Johnathan Weil, "Justice Department Finds Building a Case Against Lay Tough," *Wall Street Journal*, August 26, 2002, p. A3; Robert Bryce, *Pipe Dreams: Greed, Ego, and the Death of Enron* (New York: Public Affairs, 2002); J. R. Emshwiller et al., "Lay Strikes Back as Indictment Cites Narrow Role in Enron Fraud," *Wall Street Journal*, July 9, 2004, p. A1.

Chapter 12

1. A. Reinhardt, "Can Nokia Capture Mobile Workers?" *Business Week*, February 9, 2004, p.80.

2. D. Pringle, "Nokia Unveils a Major Shake-Up," *Wall Street Journal*, September 29, 2003, p. B6.

3. **www.nokia.com** (2004, 2005).

4. L. Smircich, "Concepts of Culture and Organizational Analysis," *Administrative Science Quarterly* 28 (1983): 339–358.

5. G. R. Jones and J. M. George, "The Experience and Evolution of Trust: Implications for Cooperation and Teamwork," *Academy of Management Review* 3 (1998): 531–546.

6. Ibid.

7. J. R. Galbraith, *Designing Complex Organizations* (Reading, Mass.: Addison-Wesley, 1973).

8. Alfred D. Chandler, *Strategy and Structure* (Cambridge, Mass.: MIT Press, 1962).

9. The discussion draws heavily on ibid. and B. R. Scott, *Stages of Corporate Development* (Cambridge, Mass.: Intercollegiate Clearing House, Harvard Business School, 1971).

10. R. L. Daft, *Organizational Theory and Design*, 3rd ed. (St. Paul, Minn.: West, 1986), p. 215.

11. Child, *Organization*, pp. 52–70

12. G. R. Jones and J. Butler, "Costs, Revenues, and Business Level Strategy," *Academy of Management Review* 13 (1988): 202–213; G. R. Jones and C. W. L. Hill, "Transaction Cost Analysis of Strategy-Structure Choice," *Strategic Management Journal* 9 1988): 159–172.

13. G. R. Jones, *Organizational Theory: Text and Cases* (Englewood Cliffs, N.J.: Prentice-Hall, 2000).

14. P. Blau, "A Formal Theory of Differentiation in Organizations," *American Sociological Review* 35 (1970): 684–695.

15. G. R. Jones, "Organization-Client Transactions and Organizational Governance Structures," *Academy of Management Journal* 30 (1987): 197–218.

16. S. McCartney, "Airline Industry's Top-Ranked Woman Keeps Southwest's Small-Fry Spirit Alive," *Wall Street Journal,* November 30, 1995, p. B1; **www.southwest.com**, 2005.

17. P. R. Lawrence and J. Lorsch, *Organization and Environment* (Boston: Division of Research, Harvard Business School, 1967), pp. 50–55.

18. Galbraith, *Designing Complex Organizations,* chap. 1; J. R. Galbraith and R. K. Kazanjian, *Strategy Implementation: Structure System and Process,* 2nd ed. (St. Paul, Minn.: West, 1986), chap. 7.

19. R. Simmons, "Strategic Orientation and Top Management Attention to Control Systems," *Strategic Management Journal* 12 (1991): 49–62.

20. R. Simmons, "How New Top Managers Use Control Systems as Levers of Strategic Renewal," *Strategic Management Journal* 15 (1994): 169–189.

21. W. G. Ouchi, "The Transmission of Control Through Organizational Hierarchy," *Academy of Management Journal* 21 (1978): 173 192; and W. H. Newman, *Constructive Control* (Englewood Cliffs, N.J.: Prentice-Hall, 1975).

22. E. Flamholtz, "Organizational Control Systems as a Managerial Tool," *California Management Review* (Winter 1979): 50–58.

23. O. E. Williamson, *Markets and Hierarchies: Analysis and Antitrust Implications* (New York: Free Press, 1975); and W. G. Ouchi, "Markets, Bureaucracies, and Clans," *Administrative Science Quarterly* 25 (1980): 129–141.

24. H. Mintzberg, *The Structuring of Organizations* (Englewood Cliffs, N.J.: Prentice-Hall, 1979), pp. 5–9.

25. E. E. Lawler III, *Motivation in Work Organizations* (Monterey, Calif.: Brooks/Cole, 1973); and Galbraith and Kazanjian, *Strategy Implementation,* chap. 6.

26. Smircich, "Concepts of Culture and Organizational Analysis."

27. General Electric, Harvard Business School Case #9-385-315 (1984).

28. Ouchi, "Markets, Bureaucracies, and Clans," p. 130.

29. Jones, *Organizational Theory.*

30. J. Van Maanen and E. H. Schein, "Towards a Theory of Organizational Socialization," in B. M. Staw (ed.), *Research in Organizational Behavior* (Greenwich, Conn.: JAI Press, 1979), pp. 1, 209–264.

31. G. R. Jones, "Socialization Tactics, Self-Efficacy, and Newcomers' Adjustments to Organizations," *Academy of Management Journal* 29 (1986): 262–279.

32. J. P. Kotter and J. L. Heskett, *Corporate Culture and Performance.*

33. T. J. Peters and R. H. Waterman, *In Search of Excellence: Lessons from America's Best-Run Companies* (New York: Harper & Row, 1982).

34. G. Hamel and C. K. Prahalad, "Strategic Intent," *Harvard Business Review* (May–June 1989): 64.

35. Galbraith and Kazanjian, *Strategy Implementation;* Child, *Organization;* R. Duncan, "What Is the Right Organization Structure?" *Organizational Dynamics* (Winter 1979): 59–80.

36. J. Pettet, "Wal-Mart Yesterday and Today," *Discount Merchandiser* (December 1995): 66 67; M. Reid, "Stores of Value," *Economist,* March 4, 1995, pp. ss5–ss7; M. Troy, "The Culture Remains the Constant," *Discount Store News,* June 8, 1998, pp. 95–98; **www.walmart.com.id.**, p. 39.

37. W. G. Ouchi, "The Relationship Between Organizational Structure and Organizational Control," *Administrative Science Quarterly* 22 (1977): 95–113.

38. R. Bunderi, "Intel Researchers Aim to Think Big While Staying Close to Development," *Research-Technology Management* (March–April 1998): 3–4.

39. K. M. Eisenhardt, "Control: Organizational and Economic Approaches," *Management Science* 16 (1985): 134–148.

40. Williamson, *Markets and Hierarchies.*

41. Lawrence and Lorsch, *Organization and Environment.*

42. K. Pope, "Dell Refocuses on Groundwork to Cope with Rocketing Sales," *Wall Street Journal,* June 18, 1987, 7–32.

43. Michael E. Porter, *Competitive Strategy: Techniques for Analyzing Industries and Competitors* (New York: Free Press, 1980); D. Miller, "Configurations of Strategy and Structure," *Strategic Management Journal* 7 (1986): 233–249.

44. D. Miller and P. H. Freisen, *Organizations: A Quantum View* (Englewood Cliffs, N.J.: Prentice-Hall, 1984).

45. J. Woodward, *Industrial Organization: Theory and Practice* (London: Oxford University Press, 1965); Lawrence and Lorsch, *Organization and Environment.*

46. R. E. White, "Generic Business Strategies, Organizational Context and Performance: An Empirical Investigation," *Strategic Management Journal* 7 (1986): 217–231.

47. Porter, *Competitive Strategy*; Miller, "Configurations of Strategy and Structure."

48. E. Deal and A. A. Kennedy, *Corporate Cultures* (Reading, Mass.: Addison-Wesley, 1985); "Corporate Culture," *Business Week*, October 27, 1980, pp. 148–160.

49. S. M. Davis and R. R. Lawrence, *Matrix* (Reading, Mass.:Addison-Wesley, 1977); J. R. Galbraith, "Matrix Organization Designs: How to Combine Functional and Project Forms," *Business Horizons* 14 (1971): 29–40.

50. Duncan, "What Is the Right Organizational Structure?"; Davis and Lawrence, *Matrix*.

51. D. Miller, "Configurations of Strategy and Structure," in R. E. Miles and C. C. Snow (eds.), *Organizational Strategy, Structure, and Process* (New York: McGraw-Hill, 1978).

52. G. D. Bruton, J. K. Keels, and C. L. Shook, "Downsizing the Firm: Answering the Strategic Questions," *Academy of Management Executive* (May 1996): 38–45.

53. M. Hammer and J. Champy, *Reengineering the Corporation* (New York: HarperCollins, 1993).

54. *Sources:* G. McWilliams, "Dell Looks for Ways to Rekindle the Fire It Had as an Upstart," *Wall Street Journal*, August 31, 2000, pp. A.1, A.8; "Dell Hopes to Lead Firm out of Desert," *Houston Chronicle*, September, 3, 2000, p. 4D; www.dell.com (2004, 2005).

Chapter 13

1. Alfred D. Chandler, *Strategy and Structure* (Cambridge, Mass.: MIT Press, 1962); O. E. Williamson, *Markets and Hierarchies* (New York: Free Press, 1975); L. Wrigley, "Divisional Autonomy and Diversification" (Ph.D. diss., Harvard Business School, 1970).

2. R. P. Rumelt, *Strategy, Structure, and Economic Performance* (Boston: Division of Research, Harvard Business School, 1974); B. R. Scott, *Stages of Corporate Development* (Cambridge, Mass.: Intercollegiate Clearing House, Harvard Business School, 1971); Williamson, *Markets and Hierarchies.*

3. A. P. Sloan, *My Years at General Motors* (Garden City, N.Y.: Doubleday, 1946); A. Taylor III, "Can GM Remodel Itself?" *Fortune*, January 13, 1992, pp. 26–34; W. Hampton and J. Norman, "General Motors: What Went Wrong?" *Business Week*, March 16, 1987, pp. 102–110; www.gm.com (2002). The quotations are on pp. 46 and 50 in Sloan, *My Years at General Motors.*

4. The discussion draws on each of the sources cited in endnotes 20–27 and on G. R. Jones and C. W. L. Hill, "Transaction Cost Analysis of Strategy-Structure Choice," *Strategic Management Journal* 9 (1988): 159–172.

5. H. O. Armour and D. J. Teece, "Organizational Structure and Economic Performance: A Test of the Multidivisional Hypothesis," *Bell Journal of Economics* 9 (1978): 106–122.

6. Sloan, *My Years at General Motors.*

7. C. Soloman, "Amoco to Cut More Jobs and Radically Alter Its Structure," *Wall Street Journal*, July 22, 1995, p. B4; "Shell Reorganizes for Speed and Profit," *Oil and Gas Journal*, December 21, 1998, p. 31.

8. Jones and Hill, "Transaction Cost Analysis of Strategy-Structure Choice." *Strategic Management Journal* 9 (1988): 159–172.

9. Ibid.

10. R. A. D'Aveni and D. J. Ravenscraft, "Economies of Integration Versus Bureaucracy Costs: Does Vertical Integration Improve Performance?" *Academy of Management Journal* 5 (1994): 1167–1206.

11. P. R. Lawrence and J. Lorsch, *Organization and Environment* (Boston: Division of Research, Harvard Business School, 1967); J. R. Galbraith, *Designing Complex Organizations* (Reading, Mass.: Addison-Wesley, 1973); Michael Porter, *Competitive Advantage: Creating and Sustaining Superior Performance* (New York: Free Press, 1985).

12. P. R. Nayyar, "Performance Effects of Information Asymmetry and Economies of Scope in Diversified Service Firm," *Academy of Management Journal* 36 (1993): 28–57.

13. www.hp.com (2002).

14. L. R. Gomez-Mejia, "Structure and Process of Diversification, Compensation Strategy, and Performance," *Strategic Management Journal* 13 (1992): 381–397.

15. J. Stopford and L. Wells, *Managing the Multinational Enterprise* (London: Longman, 1972).

16. C. A. Bartlett and S. Ghoshal, *Managing Across Borders: The Transnational Solution* (Cambridge, Mass.: Harvard Business School, 1991).

17. R. A. Burgelman, "Managing the New Venture Division: Research Findings and the Implications for Strategic Management," *Strategic Management Journal* 6 (1985): 39–54.

18. G. Imperato, "3M Expert Tells How to Run Meetings That Really Work," *Fast Company,* May 23, 1999, p. 18.

19. Burgelman, "Managing the New Venture Division."

20. R. A. Burgelman, "Corporate Entrepreneurship and Strategic Management: Insights from a Process Study," *Management Science* 29 (1983): 1349–1364.

21. R. Jones, "Towards a Positive Interpretation of Transaction Cost Theory: The Central Role of Entrepreneurship and Trust," in M. Hitt, R. E. Freeman, and J. S. Harrison (eds.), *Handbook of Strategic Management* (London: Blackwell, 2001), pp. 208–228.

22. M. Prendergast, "Is Coke Turning into a Mickey Mouse Outfit?" *Wall Street Journal,* March 5, 2001, p. A.22.

23. M. S. Salter and W. A. Weinhold, *Diversification Through Acquisition* (New York: Free Press, 1979).

24. F. T. Paine and D. J. Power, "Merger Strategy: An Examination of Drucker's Five Rules for Successful Acquisitions," *Strategic Management Journal* 5 (1984): 99–110.

25. H. Singh and C. A. Montgomery, "Corporate Acquisitions and Economic Performance," unpublished manuscript, 1984.

26. B. Worthen, "Nestlé's ERP Odyssey," *CIO,* May 15, 2002, pp. 1–5.

27. G. D. Bruton, B. M. Oviatt, and M. A. White, "Performance of Acquisitions of Distressed Firms," *Academy of Management Journal* 4 (1994): 972–989.

28. T. Dewett and G. R. Jones, "The Role of Information Technology in the Organization: A Review, Model, and Assessment," *Journal of Management* 27 (2001): 313–346.

29. M. E. Porter, *Competitive Strategy* (New York: Free Press, 1980).

30. Rucker, 2000.

31. Hamel and Prahalad, "Strategic Intent."

32. Ibid.

33. "Andersen's Androids," *Economist,* May 4, 1996, p. 72.

34. Fulk and DeSanctis, 1995.

35. G. S. Capowski, "Designing a Corporate Identity," *Management Review* (June 1993): 37–38.

36. J. Marcia, "Just Doing It," *Distribution* (January 1995): 36–40.

37. *Sources:* M. Hays, "Compaq Maps Future," *Informationweek,* June 17, 1998, p. 14; A. Taylor III, "Compaq Looks Inside for Salvation," *Fortune,* August 16, pp. 124–128; **www.compaq.com**, press release (September 1999); **www.hp.com** (2002).

Box Source Notes

Chapter 1

a. *Sources:* Interviews by Charles Hill; R. J. Herbold, "Inside Microsoft: Balancing Creativity and Discipline," *Harvard Business Review* (January 2002), Vol 80, Number 1: 72–79.

b. *Source:* Interviews by Charles Hill.

c. *Source:* M. Dickson, "Back to the Future," *Financial Times,* May 30, 1994, p. 7. **www.3m.com/profile/looking/mcknight.jhtml.**

d. *Sources:* D. Priest and D. Linzer, "Panel Condemns Iraq Prewar Intelligence," *Washington Post,* July 10, 2004, p. A1; D. Jehl, "Senators Assail CIA Judgments of Iraq's Arms as Deeply Flawed," *New York Times,* July 10, 2004, p. A1; M. Isikoff, "The Dots Never Existed," *Newsweek,* July 19, 2004, pp. 36–40.

Chapter 2

a. *Sources:* A. Kaplan, "Cott Corporation," *Beverage World,* June 15, 2004, p. 32; J. Popp, "2004 Soft Drink Report," *Beverage Industry,* March 2004, Vol 95, Issue 3: pp. 13–18; L. Sparks, "From Coca-Colonization to Copy Catting: The Cott Corporation and Retailers Brand Soft Drinks in the UK and US," *Agribusiness,* March 1997, Vol 13, Issue 2: pp. 153–127; E. Cherney, "After Flat Sales, Cott Challenges Pepsi, Coca-Cola," *Wall Street Journal,* January 8, 2003, pp. B1, B8.

b. *Sources:* G. Morgenson, "Denial in Battle Creek," *Forbes,* October 7, 1996, p. 44; J. Muller, "Thinking out of the Cereal Box," *Business Week,* January 15, 2001, p. 54; A. Merrill, "General Mills Increases Prices," *Star Tribune,* June 5, 2001, p. 1D; S. Reyes, "Big G, Kellogg Attempt to Berry Each Other," *Brandweek,* October 7, 2002, p. 8.

c. *Sources:* "How Big Can it Grow—Wal-Mart," *Economist,* April 17, 2004, pp. 74–76; H. Gilman, "The Most Underrated CEO Ever," *Fortune,* April 5, 2004, pp. 242–247; K. Schaffner, "Psst! Want to Sell to Wal-Mart?" *Apparel Industry Magazine,* August 1996, pp. 18–20.

Chapter 3

a. *Sources:* R. Langreth, "High Anxiety: Rivals Threaten Prozac's Reign," *Wall Street Journal,* May 9, 1996, pp. B1–B2; G. Harris, "Drug Prices—Why They Keep Soaring," *Wall Street Journal,* April 18, 2002, p. A1; Pfizer 10-K report.

b. *Sources:* M. Troy, "Logistics Still the Corner Stone of Competitive Advantage," *DSN Retailing Today,* June 9, 2003, pp. 109–110; "How Big Can it Grow?" *Economist,* April 17, 2004, pp. 74–78; "Trial by Checkout," *Economist,* June 26, 2004, pp. 74–76; company 10-K reports.

c. *Sources:* M. Brelis, "Simple Strategy Makes Southwest a Model for Success," *Boston Globe,* November 5, 2000, p. F1; M. Trottman, "At Southwest, New CEO Sits in the Hot Seat," *Wall Street Journal,* July 19, 2004, p. B1; J. Helyar, "Southwest Finds Trouble in the Air," *Fortune,* August 9, 2004, p. 38; Southwest Airlines 10-K 2001.

d. *Sources:* D. Miller, *The Icarus Paradox* (New York: HarperBusiness, 1990); P. D. Llosa, "We Must Know What We Are Doing," *Fortune,* November 14, 1994, p. 68.

e. *Source:* Stephen Manes and Paul Andrews, *Gates* (New York: Simon & Schuster, 1993).

Chapter 4

a. *Sources:* G. Stalk and T. M. Hout, *Competing Against Time* (New York: Free Press, 1990); D. Miller, *The Icarus Paradox* (New York: HarperBusiness, 1990).

b. *Sources:* M. A. Cusumano, *The Japanese Automobile Industry* (Cambridge, Mass.: Harvard University Press, 1989); Ohno Taiichi, *Toyota Production System* (Cambridge, Mass.: Productivity Press, 1990); J. P. Womack, D. T. Jones, and D. Roos, *The Machine That Changed the World* (New York: Rawson Associates, 1990).

c. *Sources:* M. Prior, "Major Office Suppliers Hone Supply Chain Efficiencies," *DSN Retailing,* November 5, 2001, pp. 27–31; B. Albright, "Office

Depot Consolidates Supply Chain Operations," *Frontline Solutions,* March 2004, Volume 5, Issue 4: pp. 38–40.

d. *Sources:* Sam Walton, *Made in America* (Sam Walton, 1992); S. Maich, "Wal-Mart's Mid Life Crisis," *Maclean's,* August 23, 2004, p. 45; "The People Make It All Happen," *Chain Store Age,* October 1999, Vol 75, Issue 13: pp. 103–106; **www .walmartstores.com.**

e. *Sources:* C. H. Deutsch, "Six-Sigma Enlightenment," *New York Times,* December 7, 1998, p. 1; J. J. Barshay, "The Six-Sigma Story," *Star Tribune,* June 14, 1999, p. 1; D. D. Bak, "Rethinking Industrial Drives," *Electrical/Electronics Technology,* November 30, 1998, p. 58.

f. *Sources:* I. R. Lazarus and K. Butler, "The Promise of Six-Sigma," *Managed Healthcare Executive* (October 2001): 22–26; D. Scalise, "Six-Sigma, the Quest for Quality," *Hospitals and Health Networks* (December 2001): 41–44; S. F. Gale, "Building Frameworks for Six Sigma Success," *Workforce* (May 2003), Vol 82, Issue 5: 64–69.

Chapter 5

a. *Sources:* D. McGinn, "Is This Any Way to Run an Airline?" *Newsweek,* October 4, 2004, pp. E14–E19; E. Torbenson, "Budget Carriers Rule the European Skies," *Dallas Morning News,* September 22, 2004, p. D1; **www.ryanair.com** (2004).

b. *Sources:* **www.llbean.com** (2004); D. McGinn, "Swimming Upstream," *Newsweek,* October 1, 2004, pp. E10–E12.

c. *Source:* **www.toyotausa.com** (2004).

d. *Sources:* "The Holiday Inns Trip: A Breeze for Decades, Bumpy Ride in the 1980s," *Wall Street Journal,* February 11, 1987, p. 1; Holiday Inns, Annual Report (1985); U.S. Bureau of Labor Statistics, *U.S. Industrial Output* (Washington, D.C.: U.S. Government Printing Office, 1986); Mark Gleason and Alan Salomon, "Fallon's Challenge: Make Holiday Inn More 'In,'" *Advertising Age,* September 2, 1996, p. 14; Julie Miller, "Amenities Range from Snacks to Technology," *Hotel and Motel Management,* July 3, 1996, pp. 38–40; **www.sixcontinenthotels.com** (2005).

Chapter 6

a. *Sources:* **www.clearchannel.com** (2004); A. W. Mathews, "From a Distance: A Giant Chain Is Perfecting the Art of Seeing Local," *Wall Street Journal,* February 25, 2002, pp. A1, A4.

b. *Sources:* **www.AOLTimeWarner.com** (2002, 2004); Kara Swisher, *aol.com* (New York: Random House, 1998).

c. *Sources:* **www.toysrus.com** (2002, 2004); M. Maremont and G. Bowens, "Brawls in Toyland," *Business Week,* December 21, 1992, pp. 36–37; S. Eads, "The Toys 'R' Us Empire Strikes Back," *Business Week,* June 7, 1999, pp. 55–59; **amazon.com** (2002).

d. *Sources:* **www.cocacola.com** (2004); **www.pepsico.com** (2004).

e. *Sources:* P. Haynes, "Western Electric Redux," *Forbes,* January 26, 1998, pp. 46–47.

Chapter 7

a. *Sources:* E. Ramstad, "DVD Makers Battle over Tech Standard," *Wall Street Journal,* November 9, 2000, p. B6; B. Dudley, "Dueling DVD-Recorder Formats Make Playing Discs a Challenge," *Seattle Times,* January 9, 2002, p. C3; K. Hun, "Consumers Early Casualties of the DVD Recorder Wars," *Chicago Tribune,* March 28, 2004, p. 2; H. Bray, "Stage Is Set for Another Format Fight," *Boston Globe,* March 22, 2004, p. D4.

b. *Sources:* M. Snider, "Ray Dolby, Audio Inventor," *USA Today,* December 28, 2000, p. D3; D. Dritas, "Dealerscope Hall of Fame: Ray Dolby," *Dealerscope* (January 2002): 74–76; J. Pinkerton, "At Dolby Laboratories: A Clean Audio Pipe," *Dealerscope* (December 2000): 33–34; Company history archived at **www.dolby.com**; L. Himelstein, "Dolby Gets Ready to Make a Big Noise," *Business Week,* February 9, 2004, p. 78.

c. *Sources:* Interviews by Charles W. L. Hill; SonoSite 10-K for 2003.

d. *Source:* M. Christensen, *The Innovator's Dilemma* (Boston: Harvard Business School Press, 1997).

Chapter 8

a. *Sources:* "Lessons from the Frozen North," *Economist,* October 8, 1994, pp. 76–77; G. Edmondson, "Grabbing Markets from the Giants," *Business Week* (Special Issue: 21st Century Capitalism, 1995), p. 156; Q. Hardy, "Bypassing the Bells—A Wireless World," *Wall Street Journal,* September 21, 1998, p. R16; Q. Hardy and G. Naik, "Nokia Takes the Lead as Wireless Makers Sell 162.9 Million Phones in 1998," *Wall Street Journal,* February 8, 1999, p. A1; "A Finnish Fable," *Economist,* October

14, 2000; M. Newman, "The U.S. Starts to Catch Up," *Wall Street Journal,* September 23, 2002, p. R6; D. Pringle, "How Nokia Thrives by Breaking the Rules," *Wall Street Journal,* January 3, 2003, p. A7; and Nokia website at **www.nokia.com.**

b. *Sources:* A. Lillo, "Wal-Mart Says Global Going Good," *Home Textiles Today,* September 15, 2003, pp. 12–13; A. de Rocha and L. A. Dib, "The Entry of Wal-Mart into Brazil," *International Journal of Retail and Distribution Management* 30 (2002): 61–73; Anonymous, "Wal-Mart: Mexico's Biggest Retailer," *Chain Store Age,* June 2001, pp. 52–54; M. N. Hamilton, "Global Food Fight," *Washington Post,* November 19, 2000, p. H1; "Global Strategy—Why Tesco Will Beat Carrefour," *Retail Week,* April 6, 2001, p. 14; "Shopping All Over the World," *Economist,* June 19, 1999, pp. 59–61; M. Flagg, "In Asia, Going to the Grocery Increasingly Means Heading for a European Retail Chain," *Wall Street Journal,* April 24, 2001, p. A21; and Wal-Mart website.

c. *Sources:* M. Gunther, "MTV's Passage to India," *Fortune,* August 9, 2004, pp. 117–122; B. Pulley and A. Tanzer, "Sumner's Gemstone," *Forbes,* February 21, 2000, pp. 107–111; K. Hoffman, "Youth TV's Old Hand Prepares for the Digital Challenge," *Financial Times,* February 18, 2000, p. 8; presentation by Sumner M. Redstone, chairman and CEO, Viacom Inc., delivered to Salomon Smith Barney 11th Annual Global Entertainment Media, Telecommunications Conference, Scottsdale, AZ, January 8, 2001, archived at **www.viacom.com**; Viacom 10-K Statement, 2003.

d. *Sources:* "Japan's Big Bang. Enter Merrill," *Economist,* January 3, 1998, p. 72; J. P. Donlon, "Merrill Cinch," *Chief Executive* (March 1998): 28–32; D. Holley, "Merrill Lynch to Open 31 Offices Throughout Japan," *Los Angeles Times,* February 13, 1998, p. D1; A. Rowley, "Merrill Thunders into Japan," *Banker* (March 1998): 6; Staff Reporter, "Hard Times: Foreign Brokers in Japan," *Economist,* February 23, 2002, pp. 78–79; and Merrill Lynch's website, **www.ml.com.**

Chapter 9

a. *Sources:* **www.hp.com** (2004); **www.dell.com** (2004); P. Burrows and A. Park, "Compaq and HP: What's an Investor to Do?" *Business Week,* March 18, 2002, pp. 62–64; "Carly v Walter," *Economist,* January 26, 2002; "Sheltering from the Storm," *Economist,* September 8, 2001.

b. *Sources:* Y. J. Dreazen, G. Ip, and N. Kulish, "Why the Sudden Rise in the Urge to Merge and Create Oligopolies?" *Wall Street Journal,* February 25, 2002, p. A1; L. Kowalczyk, "A Matter of Style," *Boston Globe,* February 22, 2002, p. C1.

c. *Source:* J-F. Hennart, "Upstream Vertical Integration in the Aluminum and Tin Industries," *Journal of Economic Behavior and Organization* 9 (1988): 281–299.

d. *Source:* J. H. Dyer, "How Chrysler Created an American Keiretsu," *Harvard Business Review* (July–August 1996): 42–56.

e. *Sources:* S. N. Mehta, "Cisco Fractures Its Own Fairy Tale," *Fortune,* May 14, 2001, pp. 104–112; P. Kaihla, "Inside Cisco's $2 Billion Blunder," *Business 2.0* (March 2002), available at **www.business2.com.**

Chapter 10

a. *Sources:* W. E. Coyne, "How 3M Innovates for Long-Term Growth," *Research Technology Management* (March–April 2001): 21–24; 3M's 2004 10-K form.

b. *Source:* R. Arensman, "Intel's Second Try," *Electronic Business* (March 2001): 62–70; Intel 10-K Report, 2001.

c. *Sources:* M. Murray and J. Rebelled, "Mellon Bank Corp: One Big Unhappy Family," *Wall Street Journal,* April 28, 1995, pp. B1, B4; K. Holland, "A Bank Eat Bank World—with Indigestion," *Business Week,* October 30, 1995, p. 130.

Chapter 11

a. *Sources:* J. E. Rigdon and J. S. Lubin, "Why Morrison Board Fired Agee," *Wall Street Journal,* February 13, 1995, p. B1; C. McCoy, "Worst Five and One Year Performer: Morrison Knudson," *Wall Street Journal,* February 29, 1996, p. R2; "Morrison Knudson Settles Most Shareholder Lawsuits," *Wall Street Journal,* September 21, 1995, p. B8; J. E. Rigdon, "William Agee to Leave Morrison Knudson," *Wall Street Journal,* February 2, 1995, p. B1.

b. *Sources:* S. Tully, "A House Divided," *Fortune,* December 18, 2000, pp. 264–275; J. Chaffin, "Sotheby's Ex CEO Spared Jail Sentence," *Financial Times,* April 30, 2002, p. 10; T. Thorncroft, "A Courtroom Battle of the Vanities," *Financial Times,* November 3, 2001, p. 3.

c. *Sources:* J. Guidera, "Probe of Computer Associates Centers on Firm's Revenues," *Wall Street Journal,* May 20, 2002,
pp. A3, 15; Ronna Abramson, "Computer Associates Probe Focus on 1998, 1999 Revenue," *The Street.Com,* May 20, 2002; C. Forelle, M. Maremont, and G. Fields, "U.S. Indicts Sanjay Kumar for Fraud, Lies," *Wall Street Journal,* September 23, 2004, p. A1.

d. *Sources:* S. Holt, "Wal-Mart Workers Suit Wins Class Action Status," *Seattle Times,* October 9, 2004, pp. E1, E4; C. Daniels, "Women v Wal-Mart," *Fortune,* July 21, 2003, pp. 79–82; C. R. Gentry, "Off the Clock," *Chain Store Age,* February 2003, pp. 33–36; M. Grimm, "Wal-Mart Uber Alles," *American Demographic,* October 2003, pp. 38–42.

Chapter 12

a. **www.unionpacific.com** (2005). 95, p. B.1.

b. **www.cypress.com,** press release, 1998; B. Dumaine, "The Bureaucracy Busters," *Fortune,* June 17, 1991, p. 46, pp. 5–9.

c. J. Pettet, "Wal-Mart Yesterday and Today," *Discount Merchandiser* (December 1995): 66–67; M. Reed, "Stories of Value" *Economist,* March 4, 1995, pp. ss5–ss7; M. Troy, "The Culture Remains the Constant," *Discount Store News,* June 8, 1998, pp. 95–98; **www.walmart.com.**

Chapter 13

a. *Source:* **www.bp.com** (2004).

b. *Sources:* A. Edgecliffe-Johnson, "Nestlé and Pillsbury Forge Ice Cream Alliance in U.S.," *Financial Times,* August 20, 1999, p. 2; B. Worthen, "Nestlé's ERP Odyssey," *CIO,* May 15, 2002, pp. 1–5.

c. *Source:* M. Moeller, "Oracle: Practicing What It Preaches," *Business Week,* August 16, 1999, pp. 1–5.

d. *Source:* "Business Link in the Global Chain," *Economist,* June 2, 2001, pp. 62–63.

Appendix:
Analyzing a Case Study and
Writing a Case Study Analysis

Case study analysis is an integral part of a course in strategic management. The purpose of a case study is to provide students with experience of the strategic management problems that actual organizations face. A case study presents an account of what happened to a business or industry over a number of years. It chronicles the events that managers had to deal with, such as changes in the competitive environment, and charts the managers' response, which usually involved changing the business- or corporate-level strategy. The cases in this book cover a wide range of issues and problems that managers have had to confront. Some cases are about finding the right business-level strategy to compete in changing conditions. Some are about companies that grew by acquisition, with little concern for the rationale behind their growth, and how growth by acquisition affected their future profitability. Each case is different because each organization is different. The underlying thread in all cases, however, is the use of strategic management techniques to solve business problems.

Cases prove valuable in a strategic management course for several reasons. First, cases provide you, the student, with experience of organizational problems that you probably have not had the opportunity to experience firsthand. In a relatively short period of time, you will have the chance to appreciate and analyze the problems faced by many different companies and to understand how managers tried to deal with them.

Second, cases illustrate the theory and content of strategic management. The meaning and implications of this information are made clearer when they are applied to case studies. The theory and concepts help reveal what is going on in the companies studied and allow you to evaluate the solutions that specific companies adopted to deal with their problems. Consequently, when you analyze cases, you will be like a detective who, with a set of conceptual tools, probes what happened and what or who was responsible and then marshals the evidence that provides the solution. Top managers enjoy the thrill of testing their problem-solving abilities in the real world. It is important to remember that no one knows what the right answer is. All that managers can do is to make the best guess. In fact, managers say repeatedly that they are happy if they are right only half the time in solving strategic problems. Strategic management is an uncertain game, and using cases to see how theory can be put into practice is one way of improving your skills of diagnostic investigation.

Third, case studies provide you with the opportunity to participate in class and to gain experience in presenting your ideas to others. Instructors may sometimes call on students as a group to identify what is going on in a case, and through classroom discussion the issues in and solutions to the case problem will reveal themselves. In such a situation, you will have to organize your views and conclusions so that you can present them to the class. Your classmates may have analyzed the issues differently from you, and they will want you to argue your points before they will accept your conclusions, so be prepared for debate. This mode of discussion is an example of the dialectical approach to decision making. This is how decisions are made in the actual business world.

Instructors also may assign an individual, but more commonly a group, to analyze the case before the whole class. The individual or group probably will be responsible for a thirty- to forty-minute presentation of the case to the class. That presentation must cover the issues posed, the problems facing the company, and a series of recommendations for resolving the problems. The discussion then will be thrown open to the class, and you will have to defend your ideas. Through such discussions and presentations, you will experience how to convey your ideas effectively to others. Remember that a great deal of managers' time is spent in these kinds of situations: presenting their ideas and engaging in discussion with other managers who have their own views about what is going on. Thus, you will experience in the classroom the actual process of strategic management, and this will serve you well in your future career.

If you work in groups to analyze case studies, you also will learn about the group process involved in working as a team. When people work in groups, it is often difficult to schedule time and allocate responsibility for the case analysis. There are always group members who shirk their responsibilities and group members who are so sure of their own ideas that they try to dominate the group's analysis. Most of the strategic management takes place in groups, however, and it is best if you learn about these problems now.

Analyzing a Case Study

The purpose of the case study is to let you apply the concepts of strategic management when you analyze the issues facing a specific company. To analyze a case study, therefore, you must examine closely the issues confronting the company. Most often you will need to read the case several times—once to grasp the overall picture of what is happening to the company and then several times more to discover and grasp the specific problems.

Generally, detailed analysis of a case study should include eight areas:

1. The history, development, and growth of the company over time

2. The identification of the company's internal strengths and weaknesses

3. The nature of the external environment surrounding the company

4. A SWOT analysis

5. The kind of corporate-level strategy that the company is pursuing

6. The nature of the company's business-level strategy

7. The company's structure and control systems and how they match its strategy

8. Recommendations

To analyze a case, you need to apply the concepts taught in this course to each of these areas. To help you further, we next offer a summary of the steps you can take to analyze the case material for each of the eight points we just noted:

1. *Analyze the company's history, development, and growth.* A convenient way to investigate how a company's past strategy and structure affect it in the present is to chart the critical incidents in its history—that is, the events that were the most unusual or the most essential for its development into the company it is today. Some of the events have to do with its founding, its initial products, how it makes new-product market decisions, and how it developed and chose functional competencies to pursue. Its entry into new businesses and shifts in its main lines of business are also important milestones to consider.

2. *Identify the company's internal strengths and weaknesses.* Once the historical profile is completed, you can begin the SWOT analysis. Use all the incidents you have charted to develop an account of the company's strengths and weaknesses as they have emerged historically. Examine each of the value creation functions of the company, and identify the functions in which the company is currently strong and currently weak. Some companies might be weak in marketing; some might be strong in research and development. Make lists of these strengths and weaknesses. The SWOT Checklist (Table 1) gives examples of what might go in these lists.

3. *Analyze the external environment.* To identify environmental opportunities and threats, apply all the concepts on industry and macroenvironments to analyze the environment the company is confronting. Of particular importance at the industry level are Porter's five forces model and the stage of the life cycle model. Which factors in the macroenvironment will appear salient depends on the specific company being analyzed. Use each factor in turn (for instance, demographic factors) to see whether it is relevant for the company in question.

    Having done this analysis, you will have generated both an analysis of the company's environment and a list of opportunities and threats. The SWOT Checklist table also lists some common environmental opportunities and threats that you may look for, but the list you generate will be specific to your company.

4. *Evaluate the SWOT analysis.* Having identified the company's external opportunities and threats as well as its internal strengths and weaknesses, consider what your findings mean. You need to balance strengths and weaknesses against opportunities and threats. Is the company in an overall strong competitive position? Can it continue to pursue its current business- or corporate-level strategy profitably? What can the company do to turn weaknesses into strengths and threats into opportunities? Can it develop new functional, business, or corporate strategies to accomplish this change? *Never merely generate the SWOT analysis and then put it aside.* Because it provides a succinct summary of the company's condition, a good SWOT analysis is the key to all the analyses that follow.

5. *Analyze corporate-level strategy.* To analyze corporate-level strategy, you first need to define the company's mission and goals. Sometimes the mission and goals are stated explicitly in the case; at other times, you will have to infer them from available information. The information you need to collect to find out the company's corporate strategy includes such factors as its lines of business and the nature of its subsidiaries and acquisitions. It is important to analyze the relationship among the company's businesses. Do they trade or exchange resources? Are there gains to be achieved from synergy? Alternatively, is the company just running a portfolio of investments? This analysis should enable you to define the corporate strategy that the company is pursuing (for example, related or unrelated diversification, or a

TABLE 1

A SWOT Checklist

Potential internal strengths	Potential internal weaknesses
Many product lines?	Obsolete, narrow product lines?
Broad market coverage?	Rising manufacturing costs?
Manufacturing competence?	Decline in R&D innovations?
Good marketing skills?	Poor marketing plan?
Good materials management systems?	Poor material management systems?
R&D skills and leadership?	Loss of customer good will?
Information system competencies?	Inadequate human resources?
Human resource competencies?	Inadequate information systems?
Brand name reputation?	Loss of brand name capital?
Portfolio management skills?	Growth without direction?
Cost of differentiation advantage?	Bad portfolio management?
New-venture management expertise?	Loss of corporate direction?
Appropriate management style?	Infighting among divisions?
Appropriate organizational structure?	Loss of corporate control?
Appropriate control systems?	Inappropriate organizational
Ability to manage strategic change?	structure and control systems?
Well-developed corporate strategy?	High conflict and politics?
Good financial management?	Poor financial management?
Others?	Others?
Potential environmental opportunities	Potential environmental threats
Expand core business(es)?	Attacks on core business(es)?
Exploit new market segments?	Increases in domestic competition?
Widen product range?	Increase in foreign competition?
Extend cost or differentiation advantage?	Change in consumer tastes?
Diversify into new growth businesses?	Fall in barriers to entry?
Expand into foreign markets?	Rise in new or substitute products?
Apply R&D skills in new areas?	Increase in industry rivalry?
Enter new related businesses?	New forms of industry competition?
Vertically integrate forward?	Potential for takeover?
Vertically integrate backward?	Existence of corporate raiders?
Enlarge corporate portfolio?	Increase in regional competition?
Overcome barriers to entry?	Changes in demographic factors?
Reduce rivalry among competitors?	Changes in economic factors?
Make profitable new acquisitions?	Downturn in economy?
Apply brand name capital in new areas?	Rising labor costs?
Seek fast market growth?	Slower market growth?
Others?	Others?

combination of both) and to conclude whether the company operates in just one core business. Then, using your SWOT analysis, debate the merits of this strategy. Is it appropriate given the environment the company is in? Could a change in corporate strategy provide the company with new opportunities or transform a weakness into a strength? For example, should the company diversify from its core business into new businesses?

Other issues should be considered as well. How and why has the company's strategy changed over time? What is the claimed rationale for any changes? Often, it is a good idea to analyze the company's businesses or products to assess its situation and identify which divisions contribute the most to or detract from its competitive advantage. It is also useful to explore how the company has built its portfolio over time. Did it acquire new businesses, or did it internally venture its own? All of these factors provide clues about the company and indicate ways of improving its future performance.

6. *Analyze business-level strategy.* Once you know the company's corporate-level strategy and have done the SWOT analysis, the next step is to identify the company's business-level strategy. If the company is a single-business company, its business-level strategy is identical to its corporate-level strategy. If the company is in many businesses, each business will have its own business-level strategy. You will need to identify the company's generic competitive strategy—differentiation, low cost, or focus—and its investment strategy, given its relative competitive position and the stage of the life cycle. The company also may market different products using different business-level strategies. For example, it may offer a low-cost product range and a line of differentiated products. Be sure to give a full account of a company's business-level strategy to show how it competes.

Identifying the functional strategies that a company pursues to build competitive advantage through superior efficiency, quality, innovation, and customer responsiveness and to achieve its business-level strategy is very important. The SWOT analysis will have provided you with information on the company's functional competencies. You should investigate its production, marketing, or research and development strategy further to gain a picture of where the company is going. For example, pursuing a low-cost or a differentiation strategy successfully requires very different sets of competencies. Has the company developed the right ones? If it has, how can it exploit them further? Can it pursue both a low-cost and a differentiation strategy simultaneously?

The SWOT analysis is especially important at this point if the industry analysis, particularly Porter's model, has revealed threats to the company from the environment. Can the company deal with these threats? How should it change its business-level strategy to counter them? To evaluate the potential of a company's business-level strategy, you must first perform a thorough SWOT analysis that captures the essence of its problems.

Once you complete this analysis, you will have a full picture of the way the company is operating and be in a position to evaluate the potential of its strategy. Thus, you will be able to make recommendations concerning the pattern of its future actions. However, first you need to consider strategy implementation, or the way the company tries to achieve its strategy.

7. *Analyze structure and control systems.* The aim of this analysis is to identify what structure and control systems the company is using to implement its strategy and to evaluate whether that structure is the appropriate one for the company. Different corporate and business strategies require different structures. You need to determine the *degree of fit between the company's strategy and structure.* For example, does the company have the right level of vertical differentiation (e.g., does it have the appropriate number of levels in the hierarchy or decentralized control?) or horizontal differentiation (does it use a functional structure when it should be using a product structure?)? Similarly, is the company using the right integration or control systems to manage its operations? Are managers being appropriately rewarded? Are the right rewards in place for encouraging cooperation among divisions? These are all issues to consider.

In some cases, there will be little information on these issues, whereas in others there will be a lot. In analyzing each case, you should gear the analysis toward its most salient issues. For example, organizational conflict, power, and politics will be important issues for some companies. Try to analyze why problems in these areas are occurring. Do they occur because of bad strategy formulation or because of bad strategy implementation?

Organizational change is an issue in many cases because the companies are attempting to alter their strategies or structures to solve strategic problems. Thus, as part of the analysis, you might suggest an action plan that the company in question could use to achieve its goals. For example, you might list in a logical sequence the steps the company would need to follow to alter its business-level strategy from differentiation to focus.

8. *Make recommendations.* The quality of your recommendations is a direct result of the thoroughness with which you prepared the case analysis. Recommendations are directed at solving whatever strategic problem the company is facing and increasing its future profitability. Your recommendations should be in line with your analysis; that is, they should follow logically from the previous discussion. For example, your recommendation generally will center on the specific ways of changing functional, business, and corporate strategies and organizational structure and control to improve business performance. The set of recommendations will be specific to each case, and so it is difficult to discuss these recommendations here. Such recommendations might include an increase in spending on specific research and development projects, the divesting of certain businesses, a change from a strategy of unrelated to related diversification, an increase in the level of integration among divisions by using task forces and teams, or a move to a different kind of structure to implement a new business-level strategy. Make sure your recommendations are mutually consistent and written in the form of an action plan. The plan might contain a timetable that sequences the actions for changing the company's strategy and a description of how changes at the corporate level will necessitate changes at the business level and subsequently at the functional level.

After following all these stages, you will have performed a thorough analysis of the case and will be in a position to join in class discussion or present your ideas to the class, depending on the format used by your professor. Remember that you must tailor your analysis to suit the specific issue discussed in your case. In some cases, you might completely omit one of the steps in the analysis because it is not relevant to the situation you are considering. You must be sensitive to the needs of the case and not apply the framework we have discussed in this section blindly. The framework is meant only as a guide, not as an outline.

Writing a Case Study Analysis

Often, as part of your course requirements, you will need to present a written case analysis. This may be an individual or a group report. Whatever the situation, there are certain guidelines to follow in writing a case analysis that will improve the evaluation your work will receive from your instructor. Before we discuss these guidelines and before you use them, make sure that they do not conflict with any directions your instructor has given you.

The structure of your written report is critical. Generally, if you follow the steps for analysis discussed in the previous section, *you already will have a good structure for your written discussion.* All reports begin with an *introduction* to the case. In it, outline briefly what the company does, how it developed historically, what problems it is experiencing, and how you are going to approach the issues in the case write-up. Do this sequentially by writing, for example, "First, we discuss the environment of Company X. . . . Third, we discuss Company X's business-level strategy. . . . Last, we provide recommendations for turning around Company X's business."

In the second part of the case write-up, the *strategic analysis* section, do the SWOT analysis, analyze and discuss the nature and problems of the company's business-level and corporate strategies, and then analyze its structure and control systems. Make sure you use plenty of headings and subheadings to structure your analysis. For example, have separate sections on any important conceptual tool you use. Thus, you might have a section on Porter's five forces model as part of your analysis of the environment. You might offer a separate section on portfolio techniques when analyzing a company's corporate strategy. Tailor the sections and subsections to the specific issues of importance in the case.

In the third part of the case write-up, present your *solutions and recommendations.* Be comprehensive, and make sure they are in line with the previous analysis so that the recommendations fit together and move logically from one to the next. The recommendations section is very revealing because your instructor will have a good idea of how much work you put into the case from the quality of your recommendations.

Following this framework will provide a good structure for most written reports, though it must be shaped to fit the individual case being considered. Some cases are about excellent companies experiencing no problems. In such instances, it is hard to write recommendations. Instead, you can focus on analyzing why the company is doing so well, using that analysis to structure the discussion. Following are some minor suggestions that can help make a good analysis even better:

1. Do not repeat in summary form large pieces of factual information from the case. The instructor has read the case and knows what is going on. Rather, use the information in the case to illustrate your statements, defend your arguments, or make salient points. Beyond the brief introduction to the company, you must avoid being *descriptive*; instead, you must be *analytical.*

2. Make sure the sections and subsections of your discussion flow logically and smoothly from one to the next. That is, try to build on what has gone before so that the analysis of the case study moves toward a climax. This is particularly important for group analysis, because there is a tendency for people in a group to split up the work and say, "I'll do the beginning, you take the middle, and I'll do the end." The result is a choppy, stilted analysis; the parts do not flow from one to the next, and it is obvious to the instructor that no real group work has been done.

3. Avoid grammatical and spelling errors. They make your work look sloppy.

4. In some instances, cases dealing with well-known companies end in 1998 or 1999 because no later information was available when the case was written. If possible, do a search for more information on what has happened to the company in subsequent years.

   Many libraries now have comprehensive web-based electronic data search facilities that offer such sources as *ABI/Inform, The Wall Street Journal Index,* the *F&S Index,* and the *Nexis-Lexis* databases. These enable you to identify any article that has been written in the business press on the company of your choice within the past few years. A number of nonelectronic data sources are also useful. For example, *F&S Predicasts* publishes an annual list of articles relating to major companies that appeared in the national and international business press. *S&P Industry Surveys* is a great source for basic industry data, and *Value Line Ratings and Reports* can contain good summaries of a firm's financial position and future prospects. You will also want to collect full financial information on the company. Again, this can be accessed from web-based electronic databases such as the Edgar database, which archives all forms that publicly quoted companies have to file with the Securities and Exchange Commission (SEC; e.g., 10-K filings can be accessed from the SEC's Edgar database). Most SEC forms for public companies can now be accessed from Internet-based financial sites, such as Yahoo's finance site (**http://finance.yahoo.com/**).

5. Sometimes instructors hand out questions for each case to help you in your analysis. Use these as a guide for writing the case analysis. They often illuminate the important issues that have to be covered in the discussion.

If you follow the guidelines in this section, you should be able to write a thorough and effective evaluation.

The Role of Financial Analysis in Case Study Analysis

An important aspect of analyzing a case study and writing a case study analysis is the role and use of financial information. A careful analysis of the company's financial condition immensely improves a case write-up. After all, financial data represent the concrete results of the company's strategy and structure. Although analyzing financial statements can be quite complex, a general idea of a company's financial position can be determined through the use of ratio analysis. Financial performance ratios can be calculated from the balance sheet and income statement. These ratios can be classified into five subgroups: profit ratios, liquidity ratios, activity ratios, leverage ratios, and shareholder-return ratios. These ratios should be compared with the industry average or the company's prior years of performance. It should be noted, however, that deviation from the average is not necessarily bad; it simply warrants further investigation. For example, young companies will have purchased assets at a different price and will likely have a different capital structure than older companies do. In addition to ratio analysis, a company's cash flow position is of critical importance and should be assessed. Cash flow shows how much actual cash a company possesses.

■ Profit Ratios

Profit ratios measure the efficiency with which the company uses its resources. The more efficient the company, the greater is its profitability. It is useful to compare a company's profitability against that of its major competitors in its industry to determine whether the company is operating more or less efficiently than its rivals. In addition, the change in a company's profit ratios over time tells whether its performance is improving or declining.

A number of different profit ratios can be used, and each of them measures a different aspect of a company's performance. Here, we look at the most commonly used profit ratios.

■ Return on Invested Capital

This ratio measures the profit earned on the capital invested in the company. It is defined as follows:

$$\text{Return on invested capital (ROIC)} = \frac{\text{Net profit}}{\text{Invested capital}}$$

Net profit is calculated by subtracting the total costs of operating the company away from its total revenues (total revenues − total costs). Total costs are the (1) costs of goods sold, (2) sales, general, and administrative expenses, (3) R&D expenses, and

(4) other expenses. Net profit can be calculated before or after taxes, although many financial analysts prefer the before-tax figure. Invested capital is the amount that is invested in the operations of a company—that is, in property, plant, equipment, inventories, and other assets. Invested capital comes from two main sources: interest-bearing debt and shareholders' equity. Interest-bearing debt is money the company borrows from banks and from those who purchase its bonds. Shareholders' equity is the money raised from selling shares to the public, *plus* earnings that have been retained by the company in prior years and are available to fund current investments. ROIC measures the effectiveness with which a company is using the capital funds that it has available for investment. As such, it is recognized to be an excellent measure of the value a company is creating.[1] Remember that a company's ROIC can be decomposed into its constituent parts.

■ **Return on Total Assets (ROA)** This ratio measures the profit earned on the employment of assets. It is defined as follows:

$$\text{Return on total assests} = \frac{\text{Net profit}}{\text{Total assets}}$$

■ **Return on Stockholders' Equity (ROE)** This ratio measures the percentage of profit earned on common stockholders' investment in the company. It is defined as follows:

$$\text{Return on stockholders' equity} = \frac{\text{Net profit}}{\text{Stockholders' equity}}$$

If a company has no debt, this will be the same as ROIC.

■ **Liquidity Ratios** A company's liquidity is a measure of its ability to meet short-term obligations. An asset is deemed liquid if it can be readily converted into cash. Liquid assets are current assets such as cash, marketable securities, accounts receivable, and so on. Two liquidity ratios are commonly used.

■ **Current Ratio** The current ratio measures the extent to which the claims of short-term creditors are covered by assets that can be quickly converted into cash. Most companies should have a ratio of at least 1, because failure to meet these commitments can lead to bankruptcy. The ratio is defined as follows:

$$\text{Current ratio} = \frac{\text{Current assets}}{\text{Current liabilities}}$$

■ **Quick Ratio** The quick ratio measures a company's ability to pay off the claims of short-term creditors without relying on selling its inventories. This is a valuable measure since in practice the sale of inventories is often difficult. It is defined as follows:

$$\text{Quick ratio} = \frac{\text{Current assets} - \text{inventory}}{\text{Current liabilities}}$$

[1] Tom Copeland, Tim Koller, and Jack Murrin, *Valuation: Measuring and Managing the Value of Companies* (New York: Wiley, 1996).

Activity Ratios

Activity ratios indicate how effectively a company is managing its assets. Two ratios are particularly useful.

Inventory Turnover

This measures the number of times inventory is turned over. It is useful in determining whether a firm is carrying excess stock in inventory. It is defined as follows:

$$\text{Inventory turnover} = \frac{\text{Cost of goods sold}}{\text{Inventory}}$$

Cost of goods sold is a better measure of turnover than sales because it is the cost of the inventory items. Inventory is taken at the balance sheet date. Some companies choose to compute an average inventory, beginning inventory, and ending inventory, but for simplicity, use the inventory at the balance sheet date.

Days Sales Outstanding (DSO) or Average Collection Period

This ratio is the average time a company has to wait to receive its cash after making a sale. It measures how effective the company's credit, billing, and collection procedures are. It is defined as follows:

$$\text{DSO} = \frac{\text{Accounts receivable}}{\text{Total sales}/360}$$

Accounts receivable is divided by average daily sales. The use of 360 is the standard number of days for most financial analysis.

Leverage Ratios

A company is said to be highly leveraged if it uses more debt than equity, including stock and retained earnings. The balance between debt and equity is called the *capital structure.* The optimal capital structure is determined by the individual company. Debt has a lower cost because creditors take less risk; they know they will get their interest and principal. However, debt can be risky to the firm because if enough profit is not made to cover the interest and principal payments, bankruptcy can result. Three leverage ratios are commonly used.

Debt-to-Assets Ratio

The debt-to-assets ratio is the most direct measure of the extent to which borrowed funds have been used to finance a company's investments. It is defined as follows:

$$\text{Debt-to-assets ratio} = \frac{\text{Total debt}}{\text{Total assets}}$$

Total debt is the sum of a company's current liabilities and its long-term debt, and total assets are the sum of fixed assets and current assets.

Debt-to-Equity Ratio

The debt-to-equity ratio indicates the balance between debt and equity in a company's capital structure. This is perhaps the most widely used measure of a company's leverage. It is defined as follows:

$$\text{Debt-to-equity ratio} = \frac{\text{Total debt}}{\text{Total equity}}$$

Times-Covered Ratio

The times-covered ratio measures the extent to which a company's gross profit covers its annual interest payments. If this ratio declines to less than 1, the company is unable to meet its interest costs and is technically insolvent. The ratio is defined as follows:

$$\text{Times-covered ratio} = \frac{\text{Profit before interest and tax}}{\text{Total interest charges}}$$

■ Shareholder-Return Ratios   Shareholder-return ratios measure the return that shareholders earn from holding stock in the company. Given the goal of maximizing stockholders' wealth, providing shareholders with an adequate rate of return is a primary objective of most companies. As with profit ratios, it can be helpful to compare a company's shareholder returns against those of similar companies as a yardstick for determining how well the company is satisfying the demands of this particularly important group of organizational constituents. Four ratios are commonly used.

■ Total Shareholder Returns   Total shareholder returns measure the returns earned by time $t + 1$ on an investment in a company's stock made at time t. (Time t is the time at which the initial investment is made.) Total shareholder returns include both dividend payments and appreciation in the value of the stock (adjusted for stock splits) and are defined as follows:

$$\text{Total shareholder returns} = \frac{\begin{array}{c}\text{Stock price } (t+1) - \text{stock price } (t) \\ + \text{ sum of annual dividends per share}\end{array}}{\text{Stock price } (t)}$$

If a shareholder invests \$2 at time t and at time $t + 1$ the share is worth \$3, while the sum of annual dividends for the period t to $t + 1$ has amounted to \$0.20, total shareholder returns are equal to $(3 - 2 + 0.2)/2 = 0.6$, which is a 60 percent return on an initial investment of \$2 made at time t.

■ Price-Earnings Ratio   The price-earnings ratio measures the amount investors are willing to pay per dollar of profit. It is defined as follows:

$$\text{Price-earnings ratio} = \frac{\text{Market price per share}}{\text{Earnings per share}}$$

■ Market-to-Book Value   Market-to-book value measures a company's expected future growth prospects. It is defined as follows:

$$\text{Market-to-book value} = \frac{\text{Market price per share}}{\text{Earnings per share}}$$

■ Dividend Yield   The dividend yield measures the return to shareholders received in the form of dividends. It is defined as follows:

$$\text{Dividend yield} = \frac{\text{Dividend per share}}{\text{Market price per share}}$$

Market price per share can be calculated for the first of the year, in which case the dividend yield refers to the return on an investment made at the beginning of the year. Alternatively, the average share price over the year may be used. A company must decide how much of its profits to pay to stockholders and how much to reinvest in the company. Companies with strong growth prospects should have a lower dividend payout ratio than mature companies. The rationale is that shareholders can invest the money elsewhere if the company is not growing. The optimal ratio depends on the individual firm, but the key decider is whether the company can produce better returns than the investor can earn elsewhere.

■ Cash Flow

Cash flow position is cash received minus cash distributed. The net cash flow can be taken from a company's statement of cash flows. Cash flow is important for what it reveals about a company's financing needs. A strong positive cash flow enables a company to fund future investments without having to borrow money from bankers or investors. This is desirable because the company avoids paying out interest or dividends. A weak or negative cash flow means that a company has to turn to external sources to fund future investments. Generally, companies in strong-growth industries often find themselves in a poor cash flow position (because their investment needs are substantial), whereas successful companies based in mature industries generally find themselves in a strong cash flow position.

A company's internally generated cash flow is calculated by adding back its depreciation provision to profits after interest, taxes, and dividend payments. If this figure is insufficient to cover proposed new investments, the company has little choice but to borrow funds to make up the shortfall or to curtail investments. If this figure exceeds proposed new investments, the company can use the excess to build up its liquidity (that is, through investments in financial assets) or repay existing loans ahead of schedule.

Conclusion

When evaluating a case, it is important to be *systematic*. Analyze the case in a logical fashion, beginning with the identification of operating and financial strengths and weaknesses and environmental opportunities and threats. Move on to assess the value of a company's current strategies only when you are fully conversant with the SWOT analysis of the company. Ask yourself whether the company's current strategies make sense given its SWOT analysis. If they do not, what changes need to be made? What are your recommendations? Above all, link any strategic recommendations you may make to the SWOT analysis. State explicitly how the strategies you identify take advantage of the company's strengths to exploit environmental opportunities, how they rectify the company's weaknesses, and how they counter environmental threats. Also, do not forget to outline what needs to be done to implement your recommendations.

Index

Aaker, David A., 496
ABB, 283, 470
Abell, Derek F., 487, 495
Abernathy, William J., 487, 493
ABI/Inform, 37
Abramson, Ronna, 511
Absolute cost advantage, 48
Absorptive capacity, 100
Accenture, 479
Accounting scandals, 385, 386
Accounting terms, 95
ACE, 337, 350, 354, 366
Acquisition, 308, 361–366
Acrobat Reader, 246
Adaptive culture, 428
Adelphia Communications, 385
Adobe, 253
Adobe Acrobat, 246
Advanced factors, 269
Advanced Micro Devices (AMD), 56, 351
Afuah, Allan, 500
Agee, Bill, 376–377
Agency problem, 382–385
Agency relationships, 381
Agency theory, 381–385
Agent, 381
Aggressive marketing, 240
Aging of the population, 69
Ahuja, K. G., 502
Airbus Industrie, 72
Air express industry, 215–217
Airline industry, 8, 63, 70, 73–74, 209
AirTran, 73
Albright, B., 508
Alchain, A. A., 493
Alco Standard, 462
Aldag, R. J., 488
Allard, Jay, 22
Allied Signal, 129
Allocating authority and responsibility, 415–418
Aluminum industry, 319
Amazon.com, 126, 134, 172, 178, 191
AMD, 56, 351
American Airlines, 73
American Express, 101, 327
America Online (AOL), 198
Ameritrade, 257
Amgen, 99, 291
Amit, R., 491
Amoco, 458
AMP, 371
Anand, J., 490
Anderson, C. R., 490, 499
Andersson, U., 498
Andreesen, Mark, 22
Andrews, K. R., 487
Andrews, Paul, 508
Anheuser-Busch, 191
Anslinger, P. L., 502
Anticompetitive behavior, 396
Antitrust law, 394
AOL, 198
AOL Time Warner, 108, 197, 389
Aplin, J. C., 489
Apple Computer, 44, 75, 101, 136, 200, 244–245, 248, 315
Apple Newton, 136, 137, 249
Apple Stores, 315
Applied Materials, 147
Applied research, 137–138
Archer Daniels Midland, 380
ARCO, 458

Arensman, W. E., 510
Armani, 227
Arm & Hammer, 156
Armour, H. O., 506
Arndt, M., 491
Arthur Andersen, 390
Articulation of business model, 33
Artzt, Russell, 386
AstraZeneca, 42
Athletic shoe market, 153
ATL, 244
AT&T, 251
Attributes associated with product offering, 134
AT&T Wireless, 109
Audit committee, 405
Auditors, 390
Auto component supply industry, 54–55
Automobile industry, 69, 82, 100, 147–148, 277
Autonomous action, 21
Average utility value per unit, 80
Axelrod, Robert, 496

B2B networks, 481
Babies "R" Us, 208
Baby Bell phone companies, 345
Baby boomers, 69
BackRub, 108
Backward vertical integration, 315
Bain, J. E., 489
Bak, D. D., 509
Balanced scorecard, 392, 393
Baldwin, C. Y., 489
Baliga, B. Ram, 504
Ballmer, Steve, 14, 348
Bally's, 189
Bamberger, Peter, 494
Banana industry, 319
Banking industry, 83–84
Bankruptcy regulations, 53
Bar-coding scanners, 87
Bargaining power of buyers, 54–55
Barkema, H. G., 503
Barnes & Noble, 65, 190
Barnett, D. F., 490, 493
Barney, J. B., 491
Barrett, Colleen C., 417
Barriers to entry, 47
Barriers to imitation, 98–99, 251
Barshay, J. J., 509
Barsky, N. P., 492
Bartlett, Christopher A., 282, 493, 498, 506
Barton, D. Leonard, 501
Basic/applied research, 137–138
Basic factors, 269
Basic research, 360
Batsell, J., 500
Bay of Pigs, 29
Bayus, B. L., 497
Bean, Leon Leonwood, 170
Bechtolsheim, Andy, 108
Behavior control, 423–424
Benchmarking, 104
Ben & Jerry's, 171
Berkshire Hathaway, 389
Berman, D. K., 489
Berman, S. L., 492
Besanko, D., 492
Best Buy, 190
Best industrial practice, 104
Betamax, 235–236, 241
Bethlehem Steel, 64
Beverage Partners Worldwide, 476

Bezos, Jeff, 194–195
Bias, 28–29
Bias for action, 428
BIC, 156
Bidding strategy, 365–366
Biggadike, R., 502
Birkinshaw, J., 498
Black belts, 130
Blau, P., 505
Bleeke, J., 499
Block, Z., 502
Blockbuster Video, 189, 191
Blue-sky projects, 360
Blumenstein, J. R., 489
Blumenstein, R., 501
BMW, 152, 153, 167, 176, 177, 180
Board of directors, 387–388, 405
Boeing, 72, 248, 265, 296, 298, 324, 380, 390, 396
Boeing 747, 254
Boeing 777, 265
Bogenr, W. C., 498
Boise Cascade, 389
Bombardier, 280
Bondholders, 375
Bonus pay, 125, 394
Booker, E., 499
Book-selling industry, 65
Borders, 190
Borrus, M., 493
Borzo, J., 497
Boston Co., 363
Boulding, W., 497
Bowen, D. E., 494
Bowen, H. K., 491
Bowens, G., 509
Bowles, J., 494
BP, 458
BP Amoco, 327
Bradley, D. G., 499
Brady, D., 503
Brandenburger, A. M., 496
Brander, J., 496
Brand loyalty, 48
Bray, H., 509
Breakfast cereal industry, 52
Breen, Edward, 385
Brelis, M., 508
Brews, P. J., 487, 488
Bribery, 397
Brin, Sergey, 107–108
British Petroleum (BP), 458
Broad differentiation, 173–179
Brooks, Dede, 380–381
Brooks Brothers, 172
Brown, Ken, 504
Brown, S. L., 488, 494
Brush, T. H., 500, 502
Bruton, G. D., 506, 507
Bryce, Robert, 409, 504
Buderi, R., 501, 502
Buffett, Warren, 389
Builders, 103
Building blocks of competitive advantage, 86–93
Bunderi, R., 505
Bundling, 311
Bunker, J., 493
Bureaucratic costs, 321, 354–356, 414, 433–435
Burgelman, Robert A., 21, 487, 502, 507
Burger King, 189, 424
Burgers, W., 499
Burley, J., 494
Burmah Castrol, 458

Burrows, P., 510
Busch, H. F., 494
Bush, George W., 70
Business ethics, 394–406
    board of directors, 405
    code of ethics, 403
    corporate governance, 404–405
    decision-making processes, 404
    defined, 394
    ethics officers, 404
    Friedman doctrine, 399–400
    hiring, 403
    justice theories, 402
    Kantian ethics, 401
    moral courage, 405
    organizational culture, 403–404
    promotion, 403
    rights theories, 401–402
    roots of unethical behavior, 397–398
    unethical behavior, 395–397
    utilitarianism, 400–401
    Wal-Mart, 398
Business-level manager, 10
Business-level strategy, 19, 149–228
    broad differentiation, 173–179
    capacity control, 212–214
    chaining, 189–190
    competitive positioning, 158–159. See also
        Competitive positioning
    cost leadership, 160–164
    crossing the chasm, 195–197
    customer groups, 153–156
    customer groups and market demand, 194–197
    customer needs, 151
    declining industries, 221–225
    deterring entry of potential rivals, 205–207
    differentiation, 166–169
    distinctive competencies, 156–158
    divestment strategy, 225
    embryonic industries, 191–201
    embryonic strategies, 202
    excess capacity, 207, 213
    focused cost leadership, 164–166
    focused differentiation, 169–172
    fragmental industries, 188–189
    franchising, 190–191
    game theory, 214–221
    generic strategies, 159–172
    growth industries, 191–201
    growth strategies, 202–203
    harvest strategy, 225
    horizontal merger, 191
    leadership strategy, 223–224
    manage industry rivalry, 207–210
    market growth rate, 198–201
    marketing penetration, 210–211
    market segmentation, 154–156
    maturity industries, 204–221
    niche strategy, 224–225
    nonprice competition, 210–214
    price-cutting, 206–207
    price leadership, 209–210
    price signaling, 207–209
    product development, 211–212
    product differentiation, 152–153
    product proliferation, 205–206, 212
    shakeout strategies, 203
    strategic-group analysis, 179–181
Business model, 6–7, 92, 93, 150.
        See also Business-level strategy
Business practice officers, 404
Business process, 446
Business-to-business (B2B) networks, 481
Business unit, 10
Busse, M., 489
Butler, J., 495, 504
Butler, K., 509
Buyers, 54–55

Buying power of suppliers, 55–56
Buzzell, Robert D., 496
Byrne, John, 503

Cadbury Schweppes, 44
Cahouet, Frank, 363
Caminiti, S., 495
Cannella, A. A., 502, 503
Canon, 27, 253, 339, 340, 342, 346, 347
Capabilities, 78, 102
Capability of competitors, 100
Capable competitors, 251
Capacity control, 212–214
Capacity utilization, 119
Capital productivity, 88
Capital turnover, 94, 95
Capowski, G. S., 507
Captive customer, 321
Cardinal, L. B., 488
Carrefour, 263, 272–273
Carter, J. R., 494
Caterpillar, 27, 84, 99, 144–145, 257, 283
Caves, R. E., 490, 495, 497, 500, 502
CD, 240–241
CDMA, 109–110, 278
Cell phone, 199, 229–230
Cellular telephone industry, 61
Century 21 Real Estate, 190
CEO, 9
CEO pay, 383
Ceruzzi, P. E., 487
Chaffin, J., 510
Chaining, 189–190
Chain of command, 416–417
Chambers, John, 328
Chambers, S., 493
Champy, James, 448, 506
Chandler, Alfred D., 414, 500, 504, 506
Chanel, 227
Change, 64
Changing industry conditions, 55
Chaparral Steel, 64
Chasm, 197
Chen, M. J., 497
Cheney, Dick, 31
Cherney, E., 508
Chesbrough, H. W., 501
Chevrolet Nova, 300
Chief executive officer (CEO), 9, 382–385, 388
Chipello, C. J., 498
Christen, M., 498
Christensen, C. R., 502
Christensen, Clayton M., 256–259, 495, 498
Christensen, M., 497, 509
Christie's, 380–381
Chrysler, 99, 100, 103, 178
Churchill, Winston, 32
Churn rates, 109, 119–121
Cifera, 272
Cingular, 109
Cisco Systems, 125–126, 135, 172, 248, 258, 327,
        328, 331, 364, 389
CIT Group, 372
Citibank, 468, 478
Citicorp, 266
Citicorp-Travelers merger, 311, 344–345
Citigroup, 311, 344–345
Clark, K. B., 494
Clear Channel Communications, 191, 192
Clear Vision, 274
Club Med, 470
Coca-Cola, 44–46, 49, 70, 99, 220–221, 251, 279,
        307, 363–364, 390, 476
Code of ethics, 403
Coffee, J. C., 500, 502
Cognitive bias, 28
COGS, 95

COGS/sales, 94–96
Cohen, W. M., 492
Cohn, L., 504
Colgate-Palmolive, 264
Collins, J. C., 487
Collis, D., 499
Color TV, 116
Comcast Corporation, 48, 345
Commercialization, 136–137, 359
Commitment, 33
Compact disk (CD), 240–241
Company infrastructure, 86, 126
Company-owned suppliers, 321
Compaq Computer, 101, 104, 141, 310, 475
Comparative cost economics, 242–243
Compatibility, 200
Compensation committee, 405
Competitive advantage, 6
    building blocks, 86–93
    defined, 77
    distinctive competencies, 77–79
    durability, 98–101
    profitability, 79–82, 94–98
    sustainable, 77, 101–105
    value creation, 79–82
    value creation cycle, 93
Competitive bidding, 322–323
Competitive chasm, 197
Competitive positioning
    business-level strategy, 158–159
    dynamics of, 172, 173
    failure, 181–183
    generic strategies, 159–172
    strategic groups, 179–181
    superior performance, 173–179
Complacency, 116
Complementary assets, 250–251
Complementors, 57
Complements, 239
Complexity, 200
CompuServe, 198
Computer Associates, 18, 386
Computer Sciences, 331
Computer sector, 44–45
Concorde, 254
Condit, Phil, 380
Conlin, M., 504
Consolidated industry, 50–51
Consolidated oligopolies, 309
Consumer surplus, 80
Continental Airlines, 73
Continuous improvement, 103
Contract law, 394
Contractor, F. J., 499
Control Data, 253
Control systems. See Strategic control systems
Cookell, H., 497
Cool, K., 489, 491
Cooper, Robert, 135
Cooper, Robert G., 494
Cooperating with competitors, 240–241
Cooperation between functions, 132–133
Coordination strategy, 214
Copeland, T. E., 502
Copeland, Tom, 487, 489, 492, 503
Corning, 364
Corporate governance, 404–405. See also
        Governance mechanisms
Corporate headquarters staff, 454
Corporate-level managers, 9–10
Corporate-level strategy, 19, 304–372
    acquisition, 361–366
    choosing a strategy, 356–357
    competitive bidding, 322–323
    diversification. See Diversification
    Hamel-Prahalad matrix, 338–340
    horizontal integration, 307–315.
        See also Horizontal integration

internal new ventures, 357–361
joint venture, 366–367
long-term cooperative relationships, 323–326
multibusiness model, 306–307
multidivisional structure, 460–464
outsourcing, 326–332. *See also* Strategic outsourcing
restructuring, 367–368
short-term contracting, 323
strategic alliance, 323–326
vertical integration, 315–322. *See also* Vertical integration
Corporate managers, 422
Corporate raiders, 391
Corporate scandals, 385, 386
Corruption, 397
Cosier, R. A., 489
Cost-benefit analysis, 400
Costco, 1, 172
Cost economies (global volume), 271–273
Cost leadership, 160–164, 437
Cost of goods sold (COGS), 95
Costs, 82
Cost structure, 83, 116
Cost structure of firms, 53
Cott Corporation, 49
Courtney, H., 488
Coyne, William E., 344, 510
Craftsmen, 103
Craig, M., 497
Crandall, R. W., 490, 493
Credible commitment, 324, 326
Creditors, 375
Crestor, 42
Crosby, P. B., 492, 494
Cross-company global electronic networks, 481
Cross-docking, 87
Cross-functional integration, 139–140
Cross-functional product development teams, 140
Crossing the chasm, 195–197, 249
Cross-licensing agreement, 291, 299
Cross-selling, 311
Crowe, Jim, 38, 39
CT scanners, 250–252
Cunningham, Mary, 376
Cunningham, R., 498
Currency exchange rates, 68
Curve Ball, 31
Customer churn, 109, 119–121
Customer complaints, 332
Customer defection rates, 119–121
Customer demand, 199
Customer focus, 131, 142–143
Customer groups, 153–156
Customer groups and market demand, 194–197
Customer needs, 144–145, 151
Customer-oriented mission statement, 15
Customer response time, 92
Customers, 375
Customer service, 84
Customer switching costs, 48
Customer tastes/preferences, 277–278
Customization, 144
Cusumano, M. A., 491, 508
Cycle time, 137
Cypress Semiconductor, 425

Daft, R. L., 504
Daimler Benz, 180
DaimlerChrysler, 55, 147–148, 176, 308, 325, 467, 468
Daniels, C., 511
Darby, M. R., 495
Dasani, 44
D'Aveni, Richard A., 65, 66, 491, 504, 506
David, George, 336–337, 346, 348, 354
Davidge, Christopher, 380–381

Davidow, W. H., 501
Davidson, Dick, 418
Davis, S. M., 506
Days Inn, 182
Deal, E., 506
Dean, J. W., 494
Deans, G. K., 490
DEC, 101, 103, 104, 253
Decentralized planning, 26–27
Decision making, 28–32
Decision-making processes, 404
Decision trees, 215, 216
Declining industries, 63, 221–225
Deeds, D., 492, 491
Deephouse, D. L., 490
Deere & Company, 104
Defection rates, 119–121
Defects, 131
DeFillippi, R. J., 492
Deflation, 68
DeHavilland, 248
Delegation, 34
Dell, Michael, 450–451
Dell Computer, 3, 5, 41, 44, 64, 75–76, 101, 122, 133, 162, 167, 172, 178, 207, 310, 327, 331, 332, 434, 446, 450–451, 483
Delouvrier, Christian, 171
Delta Airlines, 73
Demand, 81
Demand unpredictability, 321–322
Deming, W. Edwards, 127, 128, 131, 132, 494
Demographic forces, 69
Dent-Micallef, A., 494
de Rocha, A., 510
Dess, G., 501, 502
Deterring entry of potential rivals, 205–207
Deutsch, C. H., 509
Development funnel, 138
Development research, 360
Devers, C., 491
Devil's advocacy, 30, 32
Dewett, T., 507
Dialectic inquiry, 30–31, 32
Dib, L. A., 510
Dicken, P., 498
Dickson, M., 508
Dick's Sporting Goods, 170
Dierickx, I., 490
Difference principle, 402
Differentiation, 82, 133, 152, 166–169, 437–438
Digital Equipment Corporation (DEC), 101, 103, 104, 253
Digitalization, 244, 245
Digital television broadcasts (DTV), 234
Dillard's, 172, 191, 227, 228, 440
Diltz, J. David, 501, 502
DiMasi, J. A., 489
Dior, 227
Direct contact, 418
Direct selling to customer, 179
Discount retailers, 59
Diseconomies of scale, 112–113
Disney Company, 79, 426
Disruptive technology, 256–260
Distinctive competencies, 77–79, 86, 93, 156–158, 162, 201–202, 295
Distinctive products, 152
Diversification, 336–372
   bureaucratic costs, 354–356
   defined, 340
   disadvantages/limits, 352–356
   economies of scope, 343–345
   entrepreneurial capabilities, 347
   general organizational competencies, 346–347
   leveraging competencies, 342–343
   managing rivalry, 346
   multipoint competition, 346

organizational design, 347
product bundling, 345–346
related, 349–350, 351, 356, 463
sharing resources, 343–345
strategic capabilities, 348–349
transferring competencies across industries, 341–342
unrelated, 350, 352, 356, 461–462
Diversification discount, 367
Diversified company, 340
Divestment strategy, 225
Division, 415, 454. *See also* Multidivisional structure
Divisional-corporate authority relationship, 457–458
Divisional goals, 422
Divisional managers, 422
Division of labor, 112
Dixit, A. K., 496
Dobnik, V., 503
Dolby, 237–238, 241
Dolby, Ray, 237
Dollar-to-yen exchange rate, 68
Dominant design, 231
Dominant strategy, 217
Domino's Pizza, 143
Donlon, J. P., 510
Dover, 461
Dow Chemical, 367
Down, J. W., 492, 502
Doz, Yves L., 299, 498, 499
Dranove, D., 492
Dreazen, Y. J., 489, 499, 510
Drew, Richard, 23
Dreyfus Corp., 363
Dritas, D., 509
Drucker, Peter F., 487, 495
Druyun, Darleen, 380
DTV, 234
Ducasse, Alaine, 171
Dudley, B., 509
Dumaine, B., 511
Duncan, R., 505
DuPont, 135, 358, 455
DuPont formula, 94
Durability of competitive advantage, 98–101
DVD Forum, 233
DVD recorders, 233
DVD technology, 232–233
Dyer, J. H., 501, 510
Dyment, Roy, 143
Dynamic industry environment, 100
Dynegy, 385

Eads, S., 509
Early adopters, 194–197
Early majority, 195–197
Ease of manufacture, 132
Easy CD Creator, 247
Easy Writer, 240
Eaton, J., 496
eBay, 67, 191
Ebbers, Bernie, 334, 335
EchoStar Communications, 345
Economic decline, 66
Economic growth, 66
Economies of scale, 47–48, 111–113, 309
Economies of scope, 343–345
Edgecliffe-Johnson, A., 511
Edmondson, G., 504, 509
EDS, 331
Efficiency, 86–88, 111–127
   customer defection rates, 119–121
   economies of scale, 111–113
   experience curve, 114–117
   flexible manufacturing, 117–119
   human resource strategy, 123–125

Efficiency (*continued*)
   information systems, 125–126
   infrastructure, 126
   learning effects, 113–114
   marketing, 119–121
   materials management, 121
   measure of, 111
   R&D, 123
   supply-chain management, 121–122
Eisenhardt, K. M., 488, 491, 494, 505
Eisner, Michael, 79, 383, 426
Elgin, B., 493
Eli Lilly, 58, 85
Ellison, Larry, 480
Embryonic industries, 60–61, 191–201
Embryonic strategies, 202
Emergent strategies, 24
EMI, 250–252
Emotional intelligence, 34–35
Empathy, 34
Empire building, 383–384
Employee incentives, 394
Employee productivity, 88
Employees, 375
Employee stock ownership plans (ESOPs),
   388–390, 394
Employee training, 124
Empowerment, 34, 125
Emshwiller, J. R., 504
Enbrel, 99, 250
Endnotes, 487–511
Enron, 18, 70, 385, 390, 408–409
Ensign, P. C., 498
Enterprise resources planning (ERP) software,
   465
Enterprise valuation, 40–41
Enthoven, A., 493
Entrepreneurial capabilities, 347
Entry barriers, 47
Entry-deterring strategies, 205–207
Environmental degradation, 397
Eoderer, C., 504
Equal pay for equal work, 69
Erez, M., 487
Ericsson, 229, 269, 278
Ernst, D., 499
ERP system, 465
Escalating commitment, 28
ESOPs, 388–390, 394
Essex House, 171
Ethical dilemma, 394
Ethics, 394. *See also* Business ethics
Ethics codes, 403
Ethics officers, 404
E*TRADE, 186, 257
Everyday conflicts, 419
Excavators, 257
Excellence, 133–135
Excess capacity, 207, 213
Exchange rates, 68
Executive compensation, 383
Exit barriers, 53, 63
Experience curve, 114–117
Exploitation, 396
Exploratory research, 360
Exporting, 289–290
Express Mail, 92, 144
Express mail and parcel delivery industry,
   53–54
External analysis, 18–19, 42–74
   industry life cycle analysis, 60–63, 63–64
   limitations, 63–66
   macroenvironment, 66–70
   Porter's five forces model, 46–57. *See also*
      Porter's five forces model
   strategic groups, 57–60
External stakeholders, 374, 375
Exult, 330

Factor endowments, 269
Failure, 101–105, 135–136, 181–183
Fama, E. F., 487, 503, 504
Fashion industry, 227–228
Fast-food chains, 213
Fastow, Andrew, 408–409
Federal Communications Commission (FCC),
   234
Federal Express, 53–54, 167, 215–217
Federal Trade Commission (FTC), 315
Feedback loop, 20
Feigenbaum, A. V., 127
Fields, G., 511
Fiewege, K., 491
15 percent rule, 347
Fill in the blanks, 339
Filo, David, 108
Financial services industry, 311
Financial statements, 390
Finkelstein, S., 504
Fiorina, Carly, 310, 485
First mover, 247
First-mover advantages, 247–252
First-mover disadvantages, 249–250
Fit model of strategy making, 27, 28
Five forces model, 46–57
Fixed capital, 95
Fixed costs, 53, 111
Flagg, M., 510
Flamholtz, E., 505
Flatscreen LCD industry, 366
Flat structure, 416
Flexible machine cells, 118–119
Flexible manufacturing, 117–119, 176–177
Flexible manufacturing cells, 176
Flextronics, 327, 330
Florida Power & Light, 104, 131
Focused cost leadership, 164–166
Focused differentiation, 169–172
Focus strategy, 444–445
Foley's, 172
Food retail industry, 190
Ford, Henry, 193
Ford, Thomas, 228
Ford Motor Company, 13, 16, 55, 98, 99, 100, 112,
   119, 147–148, 156, 176, 178, 180,
   217–220, 271, 277, 280, 283, 299, 318,
   320, 324, 467, 470
Forelle, C., 511
Forest Labs, 58, 59
Format wars, 231, 235–238
Foroohar, R., 495
Forsgren, M., 498
Fort, John, 372
Forward vertical integration, 315
Foster, Richard N., 253–256, 497
Four Seasons, 143
FOX Broadcasting Company, 305
Fragmented industries, 50, 51, 188–189
France Telecom, 249–250
Franchising, 190–191, 291–292
Frankel, M., 499
Fray, L. L., 502
Fred Meyer, 59
Free cash flow, 341
Freeman, E., 487, 503
Freeman, J., 493
Freeman, R. E., 507
Freiberger, P., 496
Freisen, P. H., 505
Friedman, Milton, 399–400
Friedman doctrine, 399–400
Friendly takeover, 365
Frost, T. S., 498
Fry, L., 493
F&S Index, 37
F&S Predicasts, 37

FTC, 315
Fuji, 253, 298
Fujimoto, T., 495
Fuji-Xerox joint venture, 292, 297, 298
Fulghum, D. A., 503
Fuller, H. Laurence, 458
Fuller, S. R., 488
Full integration, 317
Function, 414
Functional boss, 442
Functional-level managers, 10–11
Functional-level strategy, 19, 109–148
   defined, 110
   efficiency, 111–127. *See also* Efficiency
   innovation, 135–142. *See also* Innovation
   quality, 127–135. *See also* Quality
   responsiveness to customers, 142–145
Functional managers, 8–9, 422
Functional structure, 429–435
   advantages, 431
   bureaucratic costs, 433–435
   defined, 429
   manufacturing, 431–432
   outsourcing, 435
   R&D, 432–433
   sales, 433
   strategic control, 431
Fundamental human rights, 401
Fung, Victor and William, 481

g, 40
Gabor, A., 494
Galbraith, J. K., 503, 505
Galbraith, J. R., 504, 505, 506
Gale, Bradley T., 496
Gale, F., 509
Gallini, N. T., 497
Gallo, 204
Game theory, 214–221
Gaming of financial statements, 390–391
Gander Mountain, 170
Gap, Inc., 59, 327
Garr, D., 501
Garten, J. E., 498
Gartner Group, 327
Garvin, D., 492
Gates, Bill, 14, 21, 32–33, 38, 105, 243, 348, 425, 496
Gateway, 3, 44, 75, 76, 483
Gatignon, H., 499
Gaylin, D. H., 502
GE Medical Systems, 250–252
General Electric (GE), 10, 26, 69, 103, 125, 129, 251,
   272, 298, 326, 343, 370, 423
General Foods, 319
General managers, 8–9
General Mills, 52
General Motors (GM), 17, 27, 55, 82, 84, 98, 100,
   101, 137, 147–148, 178, 180, 217–220,
   277, 300, 320, 323, 324, 342, 416, 425,
   446, 452–453, 456, 467
General organizational competencies, 346–347
Generic business-level strategies, 159–172
Generic competitive strategy, 160
Generic distinctive competencies, 86
Generic drug strategic group, 58
Gentry, C. R., 511
Genuity, 38, 39
Geographic structure, 440–441
George, J. M., 504
George, R., 502
Geroski, P., 497
Gersick, C. J. G., 490
Ghemawat, Pankaj, 100, 102, 490, 492, 493, 499
Ghoshal, Sumantra, 282, 493, 498, 506
Gilbert, R. J., 489
Gillette, 166, 211, 240
Gilman, H., 508

Gilmore, J. H., 493
Glassman, David, 274
Gleason, Mark, 509
Global-area structure, 466, 467
Global Crossing, 38, 39, 50
Global division structure, 468
Global electronic networks, 481
Global environment, 263–303
    basic entry decisions, 285–289
    caveats, 274–275
    cost economies (global volume), 271–273
    customer tastes/preferences, 277–278
    distinctive competencies, 295
    distribution channels, 278–280
    entry mode, 289–296, 472–478
    expanding the market, 271
    exporting, 289–290
    franchising, 291–292
    globalization of markets, 266
    globalization of production, 265–266
    global standardization strategy, 281, 468–469
    host government demands, 280
    infrastructure differences, 278
    internal new venture, 473–475
    international strategy, 283–284, 467–468
    joint venture, 292–293, 475–476
    leveraging skills of global subsidiaries,
        275–276
    licensing, 290–291
    localization strategy, 281–282, 466–467
    location economies, 273–274
    mergers and acquisitions, 476–478
    national competitive advantage, 268–270
    political risk, 275
    pressures for cost reductions, 277, 295–296
    pressures for local responsiveness, 277–280
    scale of entry, 288–289
    strategic alliance, 296–300
    strategic commitments, 288–289
    strategy changes over time, 284–285
    strategy implementation, 464–472
    timing of entry, 287–288
    trade barriers, 274–275
    transnational strategy, 282–283, 469–472
    transportation costs, 274–275
    which markets to enter, 285
    wholly owned subsidiary, 293–294
Global Exchange, 373
Global expansion, 271
Global forces, 68
Global intranets, 472
Globalization of markets, 266
Globalization of production, 265–266
Global-matrix structure, 469, 470
Global product-group structure, 468, 469
Global standardization strategy, 281, 464, 468–469
Global strategic alliances, 296–300
Global strategy, 19
GM. See General Motors (GM).
Goals, 17–18, 132, 422
Going it alone, 252
Golder, P. N., 494
Goldman, Daniel, 34–35, 489
Goldman Sachs, 365
Gomes-Casseres, B., 499
Gomez-Mejia, L. R., 503, 506
Goodman, Ellen, 503
Google, 107–108, 172
Gort, M., 491
Governance mechanisms, 385
    auditors, 390
    board of directors, 387–388
    defined, 385
    employee incentives, 394
    financial statements, 390
    stock-based compensation, 388–390
    strategic control systems, 392–394
    takeover constraint, 391–392

Governance skill, 348
Government regulation, 48–49
Governments, 375
Govindarajan, V. J., 498
Gowrisankaran, G., 497
Grabowski, H. G., 489
Graffit, 249
Grant, R., 498
Grant, R. W., 487
Greenhouse, S., 503
Greenmail, 391
Greenspan, Alan, 389
Grimm, M., 511
Grouping tasks, functions, divisions, 414–415
Groupthink, 29–31
Grove, Andrew S., 21, 57, 488, 490
Growth industries, 61, 191–201
Growth strategies, 202–203
GSM, 278
Gucci, 227, 228
Guerrilla marketing, 187, 210
Guidera, J., 511
Gulati, R., 499
Gulf & Western, 103
Gunther, M., 510
Gupta, A. K., 498, 501, 502
Guyon, J., 495

Hall, G., 493
Hall, W. K., 495
Halliburton, 397
Hallmark Cards, 447
Hambrick, D. C., 489, 490, 495, 497, 502
Hamburger University, 427
Hamel, Gary, 27, 28, 299, 338–340, 487, 488, 496,
    499, 501, 505, 507
Hamel-Prahalad matrix, 338–340
Hamilton, M. N., 510
Hamilton Sundstrand, 337
Hammer, Michael, 448, 506
Hammond, J. S., 488
Hampton, W., 506
Handoffs, 414
Hannah, M. T., 493
Hansen, R. W., 489
Hanson PLC, 365
Hardy, Q., 509
Harrigan, K. R., 490, 496, 500
Harris, G., 508
Harris, N., 501
Harrison, J. S., 501, 507
Hart, S. L., 488
Harvest strategy, 203, 225
Haspeslagh, Philippe, 364, 502
Hatten, K. J., 490, 496
Hatfield, D. E., 503
Hawkins, L., 492
Hayes, Robert H., 487
Haynes, R., 509
Hays, M., 507
Hayward, M. L. A., 502
Headquarters staff, 454
Health care industry, 314
Health consciousness, 70
Health maintenance organization (HMO), 314
HealthSouth, 385
Heathwood, Desmond, 363
Hee, Lee Kun, 149, 150
Heeley, Michael, 497
Heil, O., 493
Helper, S., 501
Helyar, J., 508
Hempel, J., 503
Hennart, J-F., 501, 502, 510
Henry, D., 504
Herbold, Bob, 14
Herbold, R. J., 508

Heskett, J. L., 487, 505
Heuristics, 28
Hewlett-Packard (HP), 17, 44, 75, 76, 122, 138, 240,
    253, 259, 310, 347, 358, 416, 417, 469,
    472, 474–475, 485
Hierarchy of authority, 415
High-tech industries, 229–262
    aggressive marketing, 240
    barriers to imitation, 251
    capable competitors, 251
    complementary assets, 250–251
    complements, 239
    cooperating with competitors, 240–241
    costs, 242–244
    defined, 230
    digitalization, 245
    disruptive technology, 256–260
    first-mover advantages, 247–252
    first-mover disadvantages, 249–250
    format wars, 231, 235–238
    going it alone, 252
    innovation strategies, 252
    intellectual property, 244–247
    joint venture, 252
    killer applications, 239–240
    licensing, 241, 252
    natural limits of technology, 253–256
    network effects, 235–238
    paradigm shifts, 253–260
    piracy, 246
    positive feedback loops, 236–238
    S-curve, 254
    standards, 231–238
    strategic alliance, 252
    strategic significance, 243–244
Hill, Charles W. L., 487, 490, 491, 494–509
Hilton Hotels, 292, 295
Himelstein, L., 509
Hinglish, 279
Hiring, 123, 403
Hirschmann, W. B., 493
Hitachi, 283, 472
Hitt, M. A., 487, 507
HMO, 314
Hoerr, J., 494
Hofer, Charles W., 487, 490, 495, 496
Hoffman, K., 510
Hold-and-maintain strategy, 204
Holdup, 318, 331, 332
Holiday Inn, 182
Holland, K., 510
Holley, D., 510
Holloway, Andy, 498
Hollywood Video, 189
Holm, U., 498
Holt, S., 511
Home demand, 269
Home Depot, 6, 190, 450
Honda, 24–25, 84, 144, 166, 176, 211–212, 280, 482
Hood, N., 498
Horizontal integration, 307–315
    bargaining power, 313
    benefits, 309–313
    cost structure, 309–310
    defined, 308
    industry rivalry, 313
    mergers and acquisitions, 308–309
    problems with, 313–315
    product differentiation, 310–311
    replicating business model, 311–312
Horizontal merger, 191
Horn, R., 502
Hoskisson, R. E., 487, 501
Hostage taking, 324
Host government demands, 280
Hostile takeover, 391
Hostile takeover bid, 365
Hotel industry, 213

Hotmail, 201
Hout, T. M., 492, 494, 498, 508
Howell, S., 493
HP. *See* Hewlett-Packard (HP).
HP-Compaq merger, 309–315, 476–478, 485
HTML, 234
Hubris, 362
Hubris hypothesis, 29
Hughes Aircraft, 342, 443
Hulland, J., 498
Human resources, 86
Human resource strategy, 123–125
Hun, K., 509
Hunt, M. R., 487, 488
Hunter, D., 491
Hwang, P., 499
Hydraulic systems, 257
Hyland, David C., 501, 502
Hypercompetitive, 65
Hypertext markup language (HTML), 234

Iacocca, Lee, 99
IBM, 16, 101, 102, 105, 141, 183, 240, 253, 297, 302,
        315, 326, 330, 331, 347, 352, 416, 446,
        468
IBM Credit, 447–448
Icarus, 102–103
Icarus paradox, 103
"I Have a Dream" speech (King), 32
IKEA, 270
Illusion of control, 29
Imitating capabilities, 99
Imitating resources, 98–99
Immelt, Jeffrey, 10
Immunex, 99, 250
Imperato, G., 507
Implementing strategy. *See* Strategy implementation
Incentive pay, 125
Incremental innovation, 136
Industry, 44–46
Industry boundaries, 46
Industry competitive structure, 50–51
Industry demand, 52–53
Industry differences in performance, 7
Industry dynamism, 100–101
Industry forum, 234
Industry life cycle, 60
Industry life cycle analysis, 60–63, 63–64
Industry shakehout, 61–62
Industry standard, 231–235
Inertia, 102, 104–105
Inflation, 68
Information asymmetry, 382
Information manipulation, 395
Information systems, 86, 125–126
Information technology (IT), 424, 464, 478–483
Infosys, 270
Infrastructure, 126
In-house suppliers, 321
Initial public offering (IPO), 378
Ink jet printer, 259
Innovation, 64, 91–92, 135–142
        basic/applied research, 137–138
        commercialization, 136–137
        cross-functional integration, 139–140
        failure rate, 135–136
        partly parallel development process, 140–141
        positioning strategy, 137
        product development teams, 140
        project selection and management, 138–139
        slow to market, 137
        technological myopia, 137
        uncertainty, 136
Innovation strategies, 252
Innovators, 194–197
Inputs, 86
Inside directors, 387

Intangible resources, 77
Integrating mechanisms, 418–419
Integrating roles, 463
Intel, 5, 55, 116, 135, 141, 235, 351
Intellectual property, 244–247
Intellectual property law, 394
Intended strategies, 24
Interest rates, 66–67
Internal analysis, 75–108
        building blocks of competitive advantage,
            86–93
        competitive advantage. *See* Competitive
            advantage
        differentiation, 82
        distinctive competencies, 77–79, 86
        durability of competitive advantage,
            98–101
        efficiency, 86–88
        failure, 101–105
        innovation, 91–92
        quality, 89–91
        responsiveness to customers, 92
        value chain, 83–86
        value creation, 79–82
Internal new ventures, 357–361, 473–475
Internal stakeholders, 374, 375
International expansion, 271. *See also* Global
        environment
International licensing, 290–291
International strategy, 283–284, 464, 467–468
Internet, 69, 179, 191
Internet-based retailers, 126
Intrapreneur, 473
Inventory turnover, 87
Invested capital, 94, 95
Investment strategy, 201
Ip, G., 499
IPO, 378
Isikoff, M., 508
IT, 424, 464, 478–483
Ito, Yuzuru, 346
ITT, 103
Iverson, Ken, 33
Ivory tower planning, 26

J. C. Bamford, 257
J. I. Case, 257
Jabil Circuit, 327, 330
Jablonsky, S. F., 492
Jacobs, D. G., 491
Jacobson, R., 490
Jacobson, Robert, 496
Jaeger, 227
Jaguar, 177, 178, 467
Jaikumar, R., 494
James, LeBron, 187
Janis, Irvin L., 29, 488
JDS Uniphase, 364, 383
Jehl, D., 508
Jemison, David, 364, 502
Jenkins, H. W., 491
Jensen, M. C., 487, 500, 502, 503
JetBlue, 73
JIT inventory systems, 121, 131
Jobs, Steve, 136, 137, 359
John Deere, 257
Johnson & Johnson, 107, 250
Johnston, R., 493
Joint venture, 252, 292–293, 366–367, 475–476
Jones, D., 500
Jones, Daniel T., 493, 500, 508
Jones, G. R., 495, 501, 503–506
Jones, P. E., 503
Jones, R., 507
Jones, Reg, 354
Jones, T. M., 503
Jordan, Michael, 187

Joseph E. Seagram & Sons, 364
JPMorgan, 4
Judge, W. Q., 488
Juran, Joseph, 127
Just distribution, 402
Justice theories, 402
Just-in-time (JIT) inventory system, 121, 131
JVC, 241

Kahneman, Daniel, 31–32, 488
Kaihla, P., 510
Kale, P., 499
Kano, C., 494
Kant, Immanuel, 401
Kantian ethics, 401
Kaplan, A., 508
Kaplan, Robert S., 393, 503, 504
Karakaya, F., 489
Karni, E., 495
Kazanjian, R. K., 505
Kearns, D., 493
Keels, J. K., 506
Keeny, R. L., 488
Keiretsu, 323
Kelleher, Herb, 33, 183
Kellogg, 52
Kelly, Kevin, 500
Kennedy, A. A., 506
Kennedy, John F., 29, 32
Kerwin, K., 495
KFC, 292
Khanna, T., 499
Kidwell, P. A., 487
Kids "R" Us, 208
Killer applications, 239–240
Killing, P. J., 497
Kim, W. Chan, 27, 488, 492, 499
Kimberley-Clark, 264
King, Martin Luther, Jr., 32
Kirin, 291
Kirkland, J., 488
Klepper, J., 491
KLH, 237
Kloss, Henry, 237
Kmart, 1, 3, 6, 56, 59, 87, 172, 208, 310, 483
Knight, Phil, 187, 373, 482
Knowledge management system, 479
Know thy customer, 143
Know thy rival, 217
Kodak, 13, 253, 261, 266, 320, 346, 353, 425, 446
Kogut, B., 499
Koller, Tim, 487, 492, 503
Komatsu, 27, 283
Kosnik, R. D., 504
Kotha, S., 490, 493
Kotler, P., 492
Kotler, R., 495
Kotter, J. P., 487, 505
Kowalczyk, L., 500, 510
Kozlowski, Dennis, 366, 371–372, 384–385
Kraft, 52
Krane, J., 501
Kreps, D. M., 496
Krishnan, M. S., 492
Krispy Kreme Doughnuts, 183
Kroc, Ray, 33, 427
Kroeger, F., 490
Krol, C., 499
Krugman, P. R., 493
Kulish, N., 500, 510
Kumar, Sanjay, 386
Kurzweil, Ray, 497

Laggards, 195–197
Laing, J. R., 503
Lamont, A., 503

Lancaster, K., 492
Lands' End, 143
Landsend.com, 170
Lane, Peter J., 503
Langreth, R., 508
Late majority, 195–197
Latham, G. P., 487
Latour, A., 493
Laura Ashley, 227
Lavelle, L., 503
Lawler, E. E., III, 505
Law of diminishing returns, 242
Lawrence, P. R., 505, 506
Lay, Kenneth, 399, 408–409
Lay, Mark, 409
Lazarus, I. R., 509
Leadership, 32–35, 426–427. *See also* Strategic
    leadership
Leadership strategy, 223–224
Lean production, 77, 91, 117
Learning effects, 113–114
Learning organization, 103–104
Lee, J., 495
Lee Kun Hee, 149, 150
Lei, D., 490
Leleux, B., 489
Lenovo, 44
Leung, S., 498
Level 3 Communications, 38–39, 50
Levinthal, D. A., 490, 492
Levitt, T., 498
Lewellen, W. G., 504
Lexmark, 445
Lexus, 90–91, 152–153
Liaison roles, 419
Liberman, M., 499
Liberty Media, 305
Licensing, 241, 252, 290–291
Lieberman, M., 493, 497
Lieberman, M. B., 494
Lieberman, Marvin B., 496
Liebskind, J. P., 503
Li & Fung, 481
Lik-Sang, 262
Lillo, A., 510
Linzer, D., 508
Lioukas, S., 487
Lipitor, 42
L.L. Bean, 104, 131, 170
Llosa, P. D., 508
Local communities, 375
Local demand, 269
Localization strategy, 281–282, 464, 466–467
Location economies, 273–274
Locke, E. A., 487
Locked out, 236
Logistics, 85, 121
Long-term cooperative relationships, 323–326
Long-term goals, 18
Look forward and reason back, 215
Lorsch, J., 505, 506
Loughran, T., 502
Lovallo, D., 488
Lowenstein, L., 500, 502
Lowe's, 6
LTV, 64
Lubatkin, M. H., 503
Lubin, J. S., 510
Luce, R. A., 490
Lucent Technologies, 364, 389, 416
Luck, 105
Luft, H., 493
Luxury carmakers, 152–153

Mace, M. L., 504
MacMillan, I. C., 502
Macroeconomic forces, 66–68

Macroenvironment, 66–70
    demographic forces, 69
    global forces, 68
    macroeconomic forces, 66–68
    political and legal forces, 70
    social forces, 70
    technological forces, 68–69
Macy's, 227
Madhok, A., 499
Mahoney, J. T., 491
Maich, S., 509
Maidique, M. M., 502
Malone, M. S., 501
Manage industry rivalry, 207–210
Management by exception, 431
Management by objectives, 431
Management know-how, 295
Manes, Stephen, 508
Mankin, E. D., 499
Mann, Marvin, 445, 489
Mansfield, E., 492, 494, 497
Manufacturing, 431–432
March, J. G., 503
Marcia, J., 507
Maremont, M., 503, 509, 511
Mark, Reuben, 383
Market concentration, 203
Market demand, 235
Market discipline, 326
Market growth rate, 198–201
Marketing function, 84
Marketing penetration, 210–211
Marketing strategy, 119
Market power, 313
Market segmentation, 154–156
Market segments, 45
Market share, 201–202
Market structure, 439–440
Markides, C., 497
Marks & Spencer, 99, 270
Marris, R., 503
Martin, J. A., 491
Martin, X., 500
Masking tape, 23
Mason, R. O., 489
Mass customization, 118
Mass market, 193
Materials management, 85–86, 121
Mathews, A. W., 509
Matrix-in-the-mind, 472
Matrix structure, 442–443
Matsushita, 229, 235–236, 241, 347
Mature industries, 62
Maturity industries, 204–221
Mauborgne, Renee, 27, 488, 492
Maucher, Helmut, 471
Mauri, A. J., 487, 491
Maximizing shareholder value, 4
Maytag, 167
Mazda, 299
McAfee, R. P., 489
McCartney, S., 491, 505
McCormick, Chris, 170
McCoy, C., 510
McDonald's, 166, 189, 190, 206, 271, 275, 280, 291,
    292, 295, 307, 338, 423, 427, 428
McDonough, B., 496
McDowell, Mary, 412
McGahan, A. N., 491
McGee, J., 498
McGee, Kolbasuk M., 498
McGinn, D., 509
McKnight, William, 23
McLean, C., 500
McNamara, G., 491
McQuade, K., 499
McWilliams, G., 506
Mechanical excavators, 257

Meckling, W. H., 487, 503
MedImmune, 389
Mega-opportunities, 339, 340
Mehta, S. N., 501, 510
Mellon Bank, 363
Mercedes-Benz, 152, 153, 167, 168, 467
Merck, 42, 58, 407
Mercury Asset Management, 286
Merger, 308
Mergers and acquisitions, 308–309, 476–478
Merrill, A., 508
Merrill Lynch, 257, 266, 285–288, 365, 417
Meshoulam, Ilan, 494
Metromedia, 305
Metthee, I., 498
Mexico, 274–275
MFS Communications, 38
Mialon, H. M., 489
Michaels, M. P., 487, 491
Microsoft, 5, 14, 22, 41, 105, 108, 111–112, 229–230,
    235, 236, 241–242, 243, 251, 253, 262,
    271, 284, 296, 327, 343, 345, 346, 365,
    390, 446, 472, 476
Microsoft antitrust action, 396
Microsoft antitrust investigation, 243–244
Microsoft Office, 311
Microwave.com, 135
Midas International, 189
Midas Muffler, 189
Midland Walvyn, 286
Miles, G., 490
Miller, C. C., 488
Miller, D., 495, 505, 508
Miller, Danny, 102–103, 493
Miller, G. J., 493
Miller, Julie, 509
Miller Brewing Company, 70, 341–342, 349
Minimum chain of command, 416–417
Minitel, 249
Mintroff, I. I., 489
Mintzberg, Henry, 24, 25, 488, 489, 505
Minute Maid, 44
Mission, 13–16
Mission statement, 13–18
Mitchell, W., 499, 500
Mobility barriers, 59–60
Model T, 112
Moeller, M., 511
Monaghan, Tom, 143
Monopoly, 51
Monsanto, 340, 358
Montgomery, C. A., 507
Montgomery, D. B., 494, 499, 499
Moore, Geoffrey, 199–201
Moral compass, 401
Moral courage, 405
Morgan, J. P., 105
Morgenson, G., 504, 508
Morrison, A., 498
Morrison Knudsen, 376–377
Mosaic, 22
Mosakowski, E., 499
Motel 6, 182
Motivation, 34
Motley Fool, 69
Motorola, 46, 116, 129, 266, 267, 278, 296, 333, 470
Motorola-Toshiba alliance, 296, 297, 299
Mount Carmel Health, 133
Moyer, R. C., 504
MS-DOS, 105
MSN, 343
MTV, 278, 279, 282
MTV Bakra, 279
MTV Cricket in Control, 279
MTV Housefull, 279
MTV Kitchen, 279
Mudambi, R., 501
Mueller, D. T. C., 501

Mueller, R. P., 496
Muller, J., 495, 508
Multibusiness model, 306–307. *See also* Diversification
Multidivisional company, 9
Multidivisional structure, 453–464
  advantages, 456–457
  competition for resources, 459
  corporate-level strategy, 460–464
  distortion of information, 459
  divisional-corporate authority relationship, 457–458
  financial control, 456–457
  functional resources, 460
  information technology (IT), 464
  problems with, 457–460
  R&D focus, 459
  related diversification, 463
  strategic control, 457
  transfer pricing, 459
  unrelated diversification, 461–462
  vertical integration, 462–463
Multinational company, 264. *See also* Global environment
Multipoint competition, 346
Murdoch, Rupert, 304–305
Murphy, K. J., 503
Murray, M., 510
Murrin, Jack, 487, 492, 503
Music industry, 243, 247
Mutual forbearance, 346
Mylan Labs, 58

NAFTA, 273–274
Naik, G., 509
Nair, A., 490
Nalebuff, B. J., 496
Narasimhan, R., 494
Narrow product line, 444–445
National competitive advantage, 268–270
Natural limits of technology, 253–256
Naval, 224
Nayyar, P. R., 506
Neff, J., 498
Neighborhood markets, 312
Neiman Marcus, 167, 172, 227, 425, 441
Nelson, R. R., 492
Nemetz, P., 493
Nestlé, 390, 469, 470, 471–472, 476, 477
Net profit, 94, 95
Netscape, 22
Netscape Navigator, 22
Network airlines, 73–74
Network effects, 235–238
Network structure, 482
Newman, M., 510
Newman, W. H., 490, 505
New product development, 135–137. *See also* Innovation
News Corp., 304–305
News industry, 69
Newton, 136, 137, 239
New-venture division, 474
New-venture projects, 357–361
Nexis-Lexis, 37
NeXT, 137, 359
Niche, 172
Niche strategy, 224–225
Nike, 156, 187–188, 200, 210–211, 212, 327, 330, 373–374, 397, 404, 482–483
Nintendo, 262
Nohria, N., 499
Nokia, 16, 46, 135, 150, 229, 266, 267, 269, 278, 411–412, 416, 422, 439, 446
Nonprice competition, 210–214
Nonprofit sector, 7–8

NOPLAT, 40–41
Nordstrom, 59, 90, 93, 159, 167, 172, 227
Norman, J., 506
Nortel Networks, 364
North American Free Trade Agreement (NAFTA), 273–274
Northrop, 324
Northwest Airlines, 73
Norton, David P., 393, 503, 504
Nucor Steel, 3, 16, 33, 64, 78, 112–113, 123, 125, 165
NUMMI, 470
Nuprogene, 291
Nuzum, C., 493
NVIDIA, 389

Observability, 200
Obsolete technology, 249
O'Dell, Michael, 38
Odle, Stephanie, 398
Odlyzko, Andrew, 38, 39
Office Depot, 6, 122
Office Max, 122
Office superstores, 122
Ohmae, K., 499
O'Leary, Michael, 163
Oligopoly, 51
Ollila, Jorma, 412
Olson, Ken, 104
Online discount stockbrokers, 257
On-the-job consumption, 383
Operating budget, 423
Opinion leaders, 201
Opler, T. C., 503
Opportunism, 298
Opportunistic exploitation, 396
Opportunities, 43. *See also* External analysis
Oracle, 365, 480
Ordonez, J., 500
Organizational capabilities, 102
Organizational commitment to quality, 129–130
Organizational control, 419–425. *See also* Strategic control systems
Organizational culture, 399, 403–404, 425–429
Organizational design, 347, 413, 436
Organizational socialization, 426
Organizational structure, 414–419
Organizational values, 16–17, 425
Ouchi, W. G., 505
Output control, 422–423
Outputs, 86
Outside directors, 387, 405
Outside view, 31
Outsourcing, 326–332, 435. *See also* Strategic outsourcing
Overcapacity, 213
Overseas divisions, 469
Overture Services, 108
Oviatt, B. M., 507

Page, A. L., 502
Page, Larry, 107–108
Paine, F. T., 507
Palm, 46, 239, 248, 249
Palm Computer, 296–297
PalmPilot, 239, 249
PalmSource, 229–230
Pandian, J. R., 491
Paradigm shifts, 253–260
Parallel sourcing policy, 326
Park, A., 510
Parker, D., 488
Parmalat, 385
Parthasarthy, R., 493
Partly parallel development process, 140–141

Partners HealthCare System, 314
Pascale, Richard T., 24, 488
Patent, 251
Patent races, 59
Patents, 99
Paycheck, 330
Pay for performance, 125
Payoff matrix, 217–218, 220
PDA, 239
PDF formatted documents, 246
Penrose, Edith T., 501, 504
Pentium, 56
People Express, 182–183
PeopleSoft, 365
Pepsi challenge, 220, 221
PepsiCo, 17, 44–46, 49, 70, 220–221, 454
Perennial gale of creative destruction, 68
Performance share units, 390
Perlmutter, H., 499
Perrier, 84
Personal computer, 231–232
Personal computer industry, 44, 45, 55–56, 100, 316
Personal control, 422
Personal digital assistant (PDA), 239
Personal ethics, 397
Peteraf, M. A., 491
Peters, T. J., 428, 505
Pettet, J., 505, 511
Pfeffer, Jeffery, 34, 489
Pfizer, 42, 43, 58, 85, 135
P&G. *See* Procter & Gamble (P&G).
Pham, A., 498
Phan, Phillip, 503
Pharmaceutical industry, 8, 42–43, 58, 59
Pharmacia, 389
Philanthropic investments, 379
Philip Morris, 70, 223, 341–342, 349
Philips, 241, 266
Phillips, 468–469
Phone companies, 308
Pine, B. J., II, 493
Pinkerton, J., 509
Pioneering costs, 288
Pioneers, 103
Piracy, 246
Piracy (videogame market), 262
Pisano, G. P., 495, 501
Pitta, Julia, 500
Playbook, 366
PlayStation, 200, 239, 240
PlayStation 2, 262
Polaroid, 77–78
Political and legal forces, 70
Politically astute manager, 34
Political risk, 275
Polk, C., 503
Pollock, Timothy G., 503
Poor commercialization, 136
Pope, K., 505
Poppo, L., 500
Porac, Joseph F., 503
Porras, J. I., 487
Porsche, 156, 169, 177, 178, 180
Port, O., 494
Porter, A. M., 496
Porter, Michael E., 46, 64, 268–270, 353–354, 489–492, 495–498, 502, 505, 506
Porter's five forces model, 46–57
  bargaining power of buyers, 54–55
  buying power of suppliers, 55–56
  complementors, 57
  risk of entry by potential competitors, 46–50
  rivalry among established companies, 50–54
  substitute products, 57
Positioning strategy, 137
Positive feedback loops, 236–238
Potential competitors, 46–50

Powell, Colin, 31
Powell, T. C., 494
Power, 34
Power, D. J., 507
PPE, 95
PPE/sales ratio, 96–98
Prahalad, C. K., 27, 28, 299, 338–340, 487, 488, 492, 496–501, 505, 507
Preacquisition screening, 365
Preemptive strategy, 214
Premier plus 10, 339–340
Prendergast, M., 507
Pressplay, 247
Price, 80
Price-cutting, 206–207
Price deflation, 68
Price fixing (Sotheby's & Christie's), 380–381
Price inflation, 68
Price leadership, 209–210
Price signaling, 207–209
Price war, 51, 52
Pricing options, 80–82
Priest, D., 508
Primary activities, 83–84
Principal, 381
Principal-agent relationships, 381–382
Pringle, D., 496, 504, 510
Prior, M., 508
Prior hypothesis bias, 28
Prior strategic commitments, 102
Prisoner's dilemma, 218–219
Procedural justice, 27
Process innovation, 91, 123
Procter & Gamble (P&G), 54, 56, 103, 104, 211, 263–264, 271, 272, 284, 343–344, 345, 346, 390
Prodigy, 197, 198
Product boss, 442
Product bundling, 311, 345–346
Product development, 211–212
Product development teams, 140
Product differentiation, 152–153, 210, 310–311
Product excellence, 133–135
Product failures, 136
Product group structure, 468–469
Product innovation, 91
Production, 84
Productivity, 88
Product line, 438–439, 444–445
Product-oriented business definition, 13
Product proliferation, 205–206, 212
Product quality, 89–91, 319–320
Product structure, 438–439
Product-team structure, 443, 444
Profitability, 5, 79–82, 94–98
Profitable growth, 5
Profit growth, 5
Project boss, 442
Project management, 138
Project selection and management, 138–139
Promotion, 403
Property, plant, and equipment (PPE), 95
Proprietary drug strategic group, 58
Proton, 91
Prozac, 43, 85
Public domain, 234
Publicly trading companies, 382, 390
Publishing industry, 8
Pulley, B., 510
Punctuated equilibrium, 64–65

Q-DOS, 105
Quality, 89–91
    cooperation between functions, 132–133
    defects, 131
    ease of manufacture, 132

excellence, 133–135
focus on customer, 131
goals, 132
incentives, 132
measuring, 131–132
organizational commitment, 129–130
reliability, 127–129
Six Sigma, 127, 129–133
suppliers, 132
TQM, 127–128
Quality as excellence, 90
Quality as reliability, 90
Quality circles, 132
Quality control circles, 432
Quality gap, 131
Quality leaders, 130
Quantum Corporation, 140
Quantum innovation, 136
Quinn, J. B., 501
QWERTY format, 231
Qwest Communications, 38

Raiffa, H., 488
Raju, R., 503
Ramanujam, V., 501, 502
Ramstad, E., 509
Rappaport, A., 503
Rathmann, George, 488
Ravenscraft, David J., 362, 502, 506
Rawls, John, 402
Raw-materials-to-customer value-added chain, 315, 316
Razor-and-razor-blades strategy, 240
RCA, 291
R&D, 83–84, 123, 137–138, 360–361
R&D department, 432–433
R&D/sales, 94
Realized strategy, 24
Real Networks, 235
Real World, The, 279
Reasoning by analogy, 29
Rebelled, J., 510
Redstone, M., 510
Reed, R., 492
Reengineering, 446–448
Reference class, 31
Reich, R. B., 499
Reichheld, F. F., 493
Reid, M., 505
Reinhardt, A., 497, 504
Related diversification, 349–350, 351, 356, 463
Relational capital, 299
Relative advantage, 199
Reliability, 127–129
Reliable products, 91
Renault, 180
Representativeness, 29
Research and development (R&D), 83–84, 123, 137–138, 360–361
Research and development (R&D) department, 432–433
Reservation price, 80
Reshaping, 64
Resources, 72–78
Response team, 144–145
Responsiveness to customers, 92, 142–145, 439–440
Restaurant business, 171
Restructuring, 367–368, 445, 446
Retail industry, 59, 172
Return on invested capital (ROIC), 5, 40–41, 94–95, 378
Return on sales, 94, 95
Reward systems, 383, 424–425. See also Stock options

Reyes, S., 508
RFID tags, 87
Richards, M. D., 487
Richardson, James, 500
Richardson Electronics, 224
Ridgeway, N., 497
Ries, A., 494
Rigdon, J. E., 510, 510
Rights theories, 401–402
Risk of entry by potential competitors, 46–50
Risk pooling, 353
Rivalry, 50–54
Robertson, T. S., 496
Rock-paper-scissors, 215
Rodgers, T. J., 425
Roehl, W., 499
Rogers, P. R., 488
ROIC, 5, 40–41, 94–95, 378
Rolex watch, 89, 167
Roll, R., 502
Roll, Richard, 29, 362, 488, 500
Roller, L.-H., 489
Rolls-Royce, 152, 156
Romanelli, E., 490
Romer, P. M., 497
Roos, Daniel, 493, 500, 508
Root, F. R., 499
Rose, S., 500, 502
Rosenfeld, A., 504
Rothaermel, Frank T., 488, 498
Roundup, 340
Rowley, A., 510
Roxio, 247
Royal Dutch Shell, 26, 385
Ruback, R. S., 500, 502
Rudden, E., 498
Rumelt, Richard P., 66, 487, 491, 501, 506
Ryanair, 163, 165

Saks Fifth Avenue, 227
Sakson, Jane, 497
Salancik, Gerald R., 500
Sales, 84
Sales, general, and administrative expenses (SG&A), 95
Salespeople, 103, 433
Salomon, Alan, 509
Salter, M. S., 507
Samsung, 149–150, 366
Sanmina-SCI, 330
Sanwa Bank, 286
SAP, 365, 465, 469
Sarbanes-Oxley Act, 388, 391
Sasser, W. E., 493
Savoy Hotel, 168
SBC, 345
Scale diseconomies, 112–113
Scale economies, 47–48, 111–113
Scalise, D., 509
Scenario planning, 26
Schein, E. H., 505
Schelling, T. C., 489
Schendel, D. E., 487, 491, 495, 494, 496, 501
Scherer, F., 495, 496
Scherer, F. M., 500, 502
Scherer, Mike, 362
Schiller, Zachary, 500
Schleifer, A., 500, 502
Schmalensee, R., 491
Schoemaker, P. J. H., 488, 491
Schultz, Howard, 302
Schumpeter, J., 491
Schwartz, M., 497
Schwenk, C. R., 488
Scope economies, 343–345
SCORE, 325

Scotch Guard, 22
Scott, B. R., 504, 506
Scott, Walter, Jr., 38
S-curve, 254
Sears, 101, 172, 307, 310, 484
Sears, Mike, 380
Seattle Coffee, 303
Seattle Computer, 105
SEC, 382, 390
Sector, 44
Securities and Exchange Commission (SEC),
        382, 390
Securities law, 394
Sega, 3
Seiko, 166
Seith, S. P., 493
Selectron, 76
Self-awareness, 34
Self-contained division, 454
Self-dealing, 395
Self-managing teams, 125, 132
Self-regulation, 34
Self-service supermarket business model, 6
Sellers, P., 495
Semiconductor chips, 254
Senge, P. M., 493
Sequential move games, 215
Sequential process, 141
Serendipitous discoveries/events, 22–24
Servaes, H., 503
Service function, 84
Serwer, Andrew E., 499
Sexual harassment, 69
SG&A, 95
SG&A/sales, 94–97
Shaheen, George, 479
Shakeout stage, 61
Shakeout strategies, 203
Shane, S. A., 496
Shankar, V., 497
Shanley, M., 492
Shapiro, C., 489, 497, 497
Share-building strategy, 202
Shareholder value, 4
Share-increasing strategy, 203
Sharfman, M. P., 490
Shaver, J. M., 499
Shilling, M. A., 497
Shook, C. L., 506
Short-term contracting, 323
Short-term profitability goals, 18
Shotgun approach to new-venture projects, 359
Siemens, 229
Simmons, R., 505
Simon, H., 488
Simon, H. A., 503
Simultaneous move games, 215
Singh, H., 490, 499, 507
Sinofsky, Steve, 22
Six Sigma, 127, 129–133
Skilling, Jeffrey, 408–409
SKU, 56
Sloan, A. P., 506
Slow innovators, 137
Slywotzky, A. J., 490
Smale, John, 388
Smart phone, 229
Smircich, L., 504, 505
Smith, G., 494
Smith Corona, 15
Snecma, 298
Snell, S., 494
Snell, S. A., 504
Snider, M., 509
Snow, C. C., 490
Social forces, 70
Socialization, 426

Social skills, 34
Soft drink industry, 44, 49
Software industry, 8
Solectron, 330
Soloman, C., 506
Solomon, D., 501
SonoSite, 244
Sony, 3, 135, 150, 168, 229, 235–236, 239, 241, 253,
        262, 296, 298, 346, 347, 356–357, 366
Sony stores, 356
Sorge, A., 494
Sotheby's, 380–381
Southwest Airlines, 3, 89, 123, 165, 183, 417
Souza, C., 499
Span of control, 415
Spanos, Y. E., 487
Sparks, L., 508
Spear, S., 491
Spears, Britney, 221
Specialization, 112
Specialized assets, 317–319
S&P Industry Surveys, 37
Sports-utility vehicle, 156
St. John, C. H., 501
Stacey, R., 488
Stakeholder, 17, 374–381
    defined, 374
    external, 374, 375
    impact analysis, 375–377
    internal, 374, 375
    profitability, 378–381
    role, 377
Stakeholder impact analysis, 375–377
Stalk, G., 492, 494, 508
Standardization, 423–424
Standards, 231–238
Staples, 6, 91–92, 122
Starbucks, 271, 302–303
Statistical analysis of variation, 131
Stavins, J., 497
Staw, B. M., 488
Steel industry, 8, 63, 65, 116–117
Stempel, Robert, 388
Stevens, G. A., 494
Stock-based compensation, 388–390
Stockbrokerage industry, 65
Stockbrokers, 257
Stockholders, 375
Stock keeping unit (SKU), 56
Stock options, 388–390, 394
Stopford, J., 506
Strategic alliance, 252, 260, 296–300, 323–326
Strategic capabilities, 348–349
Strategic commitments, 100, 288–289
Strategic control systems, 392–394, 419–425
    behavior control, 423–424
    defined, 420
    importance, 419–420
    information technology (IT), 424
    levels of control, 420–421
    output control, 422–423
    personal control, 422
    reward systems, 424–425
Strategic decision making, 28–32
Strategic fit, 27, 28
Strategic-group analysis, 179–181
Strategic groups, 57–60
Strategic intent, 27–28, 181
Strategic leadership, 32–35, 426–427
    articulation of business model, 33
    being well-informed, 33–34
    commitment, 33
    delegation, 34
    emotional intelligence, 34–35
    empowerment, 34
    power, 34
    vision, eloquence, consistency, 32–33

Strategic managers, 8–11
Strategic outsourcing, 326–332
    benefits, 329–331
    cost structure, 329–330
    defined, 327
    differentiation, 330–331
    focus on core business, 331
    holdup, 332
    IT, 480–483
    loss of information, 332
    risks, 331–332
Strategic significance, 243–244
Strategy, 3
Strategy as emergent process, 20–25
    autonomous action, 21
    intended/emergent strategies, 24–25
    serendipitous discoveries/events, 22–24
    unpredictable world, 21
Strategy formulation, 3, 12
Strategy implementation, 3, 12, 20, 435–445
    cost leadership, 437
    differentiation, 437–438
    focus strategy, 444–445
    geographic structure, 440–441
    internal new venture, 473–475
    IT, 478–479
    joint venture, 475–476
    market structure, 439–440
    matrix structure, 442–443
    mergers and acquisitions, 476–478
    product structure, 438–439
    product-team structure, 443, 444
Strategy-making process, 11–20
    external analysis, 18–19
    feedback loop, 20
    mission statement, 13–18
    steps in process, 11
    strategy implementation, 20
    SWOT analysis, 19–20
Straus, Jozef, 383
Strengths. *See* High-tech industries; Internal
        analysis
Strong and adaptive culture, 428
Strong business leaders, 32–33
Substandard working conditions, 396
Substitute products, 57
Substitutes, 44
Sultan, Ralph G. M., 496
Sunderstrand, 337
Sundown rule, 430
Superior performance, 4–5
Supermarket, 190
Suppliers, 55–56, 132, 375
Supply-chain management, 121–122
Support activities, 85–86
Sustainable competitive advantage, 77, 101–105
Sustained competitive advantage, 6
SUV market segment, 156
Swaine, M., 496
Swaminathan, A., 500
Swisher, Kara, 509
Switching costs, 48, 236, 238, 248
SWOT analysis, 19–20
Symbian, 229
Systematic errors, 28

Taco Bell, 166
Takayama, Masayoshi, 171
Takeover constraint, 391–392
Tallman, S., 499
Tall structure, 415–416
Tangible resources, 77
Tanzer, A., 510
Taper integration, 317
Target, 1, 59, 87, 88, 96–97, 172, 189, 208
Tariff, 290

Taubman, Alfred, 380–381
Taylor, A., III, 506, 507
TCP/IP, 232, 234
Team, 419
Technical standards, 231–238
Technological change, 116
Technological forces, 68–69
Technological know-how, 99, 291, 295
Technological myopia, 137
Technological paradigm shifts, 253–260
Technology, 230. See also High-tech industries
Technology S-curve, 254
Techsonic Industries, 139
Tedlow, R. S., 489
Teece, D. J., 494, 497, 501, 506
Telecommunications equipment industry, 46
Telecommunications industry, 50
Telefunken, 241
Telephone service, 48
Tellis, G. J., 494
Templeman, J., 502
Templin, Neal, 500
Ten-foot attitude, 430
Tesco, 263, 272
Texas Instruments (TI), 76, 103, 116, 293
Textron, 461
Thatcher, Margaret, 32
The Gap, 59, 327
TheStreet.com, 69
Thomas, H., 498
Thompson, P., 493
Thorncroft, T., 510
Thornton, R. A., 493
Threats, 43. See also External analysis
3M, 22–23, 37, 135, 138, 207, 251, 343, 344, 347,
    349, 358, 360, 473–474
360 Networks, 38, 39, 50
TI, 76, 103, 116, 293
Tichy, N. M., 489
Tide, 211
Tie-in-sales, 396
Time Warner, 48
Titanium Metals, 396
Tit-for-tat strategy, 207
T-Mobile, 109
Tobacco industry, 70
Torbenson, E., 509
Tort law, 394
Toshiba, 296, 298
Tosi, H. L., 503
Total quality management (TQM), 90, 127–128,
    432
Total solution, 311
Toyota, 27, 77, 82, 84, 90, 91, 100, 103, 113, 118,
    152–153, 166, 175–178, 211–212, 271,
    277, 280, 300, 326, 428, 470, 472, 482
Toyota's lean production system, 118
Toys "R" Us, 6, 64, 208
TQM, 90, 127–128, 432
Trade barriers, 274–275
Training employees, 124
Transfer prices, 321
Transfer pricing, 459
Transnational strategy, 282–283, 464, 469–472
Transportation costs, 274–275
Treece, James, 500
Trottman, M., 508
Trout, J., 494
Troy, M., 505, 508, 511
Truitt, J. F., 499
TRW, 298–299, 443
Tufts, 314
Tully, S., 510
Tushman, M. L., 490
Tversky, A., 488
Twentieth Century Fox Movie Studios, 305
Two-boss employees, 442

Tyco International, 18, 371–372, 384–385
Tyson, L. A., 493

Ulrich, D. O., 489
Ultrasound, 244
Underwood, 15
Unethical behavior, 395–397
Unethical leadership, 399
Unfreezing, 64
Unilever, 54, 264, 272, 346, 390, 403, 405
Union Pacific, 418
Unions, 375
Uniqueness, 92
United Airlines, 3, 73
United Parcel Service (UPS), 53–54, 215–217
United States Steel Industry Association, 70
United Technologies Corporation (UTC), 336–337,
    349, 350, 354, 366, 367, 404
Universal Serial Bus (USB), 232
University-style research facilities, 138
Unrelated diversification, 350, 352, 356, 461,
    462
UPS, 53–54, 215–217
U.S. Steel, 353
US Airways, 3, 73
USB, 232
US Steel, 64
USX, 64
UTC, 336–337, 349, 350, 354, 366, 367
Utilitarianism, 400–401
Utility, 79–80
Utterback, J. M., 496
UUNet, 38

Vaaler, P. M., 491
Vacuum tube business, 224
Valuation of a company, 40–41
Value chain, 83–86, 93
Value creation, 79–82
Value creation cycle, 93
Value creation frontier, 159, 160, 164, 177
Value Line Ratings and Reports, 37
Values, 16–17
Vance, S. C., 504
Van Maanen, J., 505
Varadarajan, P., 501, 502
Varian, H. R., 489, 497
VCR, 235–236
Veil of ignorance, 402
Velocci, A. L., 503
Verizon Wireless, 109–110, 345
Vermeulen, F., 503
Vertical integration, 315–322, 462–463
    backward, 315
    benefits, 317–320
    cost structure, 320–321
    defined, 315
    demand unpredictability, 321–322
    forward, 315
    full integration, 317
    limits of, 322
    problems with, 320–322
    product quality, 319–320
    scheduling, 320
    specialized assets, 317–319
    taper integration, 317
    technological change, 321
VHS technology, 235–236, 241
Viacom, 389
Viagra, 242
Vickery second price auction, 108
Videocassette recorder (VCR), 235–236
Videogame industry, 240, 262, 266
Viguerie, P., 488
Vijayan, J., 501

Vijh, A., 502
Viral model of infection, 200–201
Virtual corporation, 329
Virtual organization, 479
Vishny, R. W., 500, 502
VisiCalc, 240
Vision, 16
Visionary leaders, 32
Voice tracking, 192
Volkswagen, 271
Volvo, 134, 152

Wade, James B., 503
Wagner, S., 497
Wall, R., 503
Wall Street Journal Index, 37
Wal-Mart, 1–7, 17, 33, 41, 49, 56, 59, 64, 85–86, 87,
    88, 90, 91, 93, 96–98, 121, 124, 156, 157,
    161, 162, 172, 189, 208, 214, 263,
    271–273, 275, 277, 307, 311–312, 338,
    398, 428, 430, 440, 478, 483
Walsh, J. P., 502, 504
Walt Disney Company, 79, 426
Walton, Sam, 1, 2, 32, 33, 56, 124, 398, 430,
    509
Wang, Charles, 386
Wang Computers, 253
Wang Labs, 103
Warner, J., 502
Warner, M., 494
Waterman, R. H., 428, 505
Watkins, Sherron, 409
Watson Pharmaceuticals, 58
Waurzyniak, P., 493
Weaknesses. See Internal analysis
Weapons of mass destruction (WMDs), 30–31
Web-based information systems, 126
Weil, Jonathan, 504
Weinhold, W. A., 507
Welch, D., 495
Welch, Jack, 32, 33, 129, 348
Well-informed, 33–34
Wells, L., 506
Wernerfelt, B., 491
Western Union, 23
Westley, F., 489
Wheelwright, S. C., 494, 502
Whirlpool Corporation, 69
White, Joseph, 500
White, M. A., 507
White, R. E., 505
White knight, 365
White spaces, 339, 340
Wholly owned subsidiary, 293–294
Wide product line, 438–439
Wilke, J. R., 501
Willensky, D. R., 502
Williams, M. A., 489
Williams, Serena, 187
Williamson, Oliver E., 500, 501, 504, 505
Willig, R. D., 489
Wilson, Charles, 383
Wilson, Kemmons, 182
Wilson, T. A., 489
Windows XP, 242
Wintel, 231–232, 238
Wintel standard, 235
Winter, S., 492
Wipro, 270
Wireless phones, 46
WMDs, 30–31
Womack, James P., 493, 500, 508
Wong, A., 496
Woodall, P., 497
Woods, Tiger, 187, 373
Woodward, J., 505

Woolley, S., 493
Working capital, 95
Working capital/sales, 96, 97
Work-in-progress, 119
World cars, 277
WorldCom, 18, 38, 39, 50, 315, 334–335, 385
Worthen, B., 511
Wrapp, Edward, 34, 489
Wright, P. M., 494
Wrigley, L., 506
Wysocki, B., 500

Xbox, 240, 262, 343
Xerox, 27, 104, 129, 132, 248, 251, 283, 284
XO Communications, 38, 39

Yahoo!, 108
Yamaha, 144
Yamaichi Securities, 287
Yeung, B., 499
Yoon, S., 498
YUHGFD layout, 231

Zaheer, S., 499
Zara, 227–228
Zeisel, S., 490
Zeithaml, C. P., 490
Zellner, Wendy, 491, 504
Zenger, T., 500
Zingales, L., 503
Zocor, 42
Zoloft, 85
Zysman, J., 493